The Trombone

Also available in the series

The Flute
Ardal Powell

Timpani and Percussion
Jeremy Montagu

The Oboe
Geoffrey Burgess and Bruce Haynes

THE YALE MUSICAL INSTRUMENT SERIES

The Trombone

Trevor Herbert

Yale University Press

New Haven and London

Copyright © 2006 Trevor Herbert

For information about this and other Yale University Press publications please contact:
U.S. Office: sales.press@yale.edu   yalebooks.com
Europe Office: sales@yaleup.co.uk   www.yaleup.co.uk
ISBN 978–0–300–10095–2

Library of Congress Control Number 2005930979

A catalogue record for this book is available from the British Library

Typeset in Columbus by Northern Phototypesetting Co. Ltd., Bolton, Lancs
Printed in Great Britaiin by T.J. International Ltd, Padstow

10 9 8 7 6 5 4 3 2

For Helen

Contents

Illustrations, Music Examples and Tables

Illustrations

Music examples

Tables

Acknowledgements

During the preparation of this book I have been the recipient of tremendous generosity from institutions, agencies and individuals. I have at various times received funding from the UK's Arts and Humanities Research Board, the British Academy and the Arts Faculty Research Committee at the Open University. Numerous institutions have kindly helped me by verifying or correcting information I sent to them, and many provided information of which I was ignorant. In this respect I am keen to acknowledge the help I received from museums which hold early trombones and are mentioned in Appendix 1, and music conservatoires which are mentioned in Table 1 (Chapter 7).

No researcher can get very far without the help of 'information services specialists', who used to be (and in some places mercifully still are) called librarians, and to these I would add archivists and museum curators. I wish to record my gratitude to the staff of the very many libraries, archives and collections I have visited, but especially those at the British Library; the National Library of Wales; Boosey & Hawkes archives; the Moravian Archives at Bethlehem, Pa.; the New York Public Library; Yale University Library; the Royal College of Music; the Guildhall School of Music and Drama; the UK and US Heritage Centres of the Salvation Army; the National Archives, London; the National Music Museum, Vermillion, SD; the Accademia Filarmonica, Verona; the Hogan Jazz Archive at Tulane University, New Orleans; the Institute of Jazz Studies at Rutgers University, Newark, NJ; and particularly the library of my own university, the Open University of the United Kingdom.

The musical examples were set by Bill Strang at the Music Department of the Open University. He advised me on matters of musical detail, including inconsistencies between sources with which I had provided him and the original scores. I am extremely grateful for his advice. Line drawings were produced with care and expertise in the Design Studio of the Open University by Andrew Whitehead.

Annette Musker prepared the index with an efficiency and precision on which I have come to rely. Paulène Fallows did the initial copy-editing, and brought to my attention many matters of detail that would otherwise have gone unnoticed. I am also keen to acknowledge the support I have received from staff at Yale University Press. There must be many from that organisation who have made important contributions to the production of this book whose identity is unknown to me, but to whom I am nevertheless grateful. My primary points of contact have been with Stephen Kent and Malcolm Gerratt, and I count myself lucky to have been dealing with such sympathetic and knowledgeable people.

A number of players have helped me – sometimes without knowing it – so I thank the many whom I have collared in bars, coffee rooms and restaurants to talk about their work. In particular, I would like to thank Peter Harvey, Peter Eklund, James Lincoln Collier, Dave Taylor, Joseph Alessi, Bruce Eidem, Dave Chandler and Roger Argente. To these I should add the large number of expert colleagues whose friendship I have taken advantage of outrageously. In particular, I am grateful to Donald Burrows, Keith Polk, Stewart Carter, Jeff Nussbaum, Herbert Heyde and Arnold Myers.

I particularly acknowledge a significant debt of gratitude to Howard Weiner, himself a consummate authority on the trombone, who read my manuscript, noticed errors and provided me with advice and information that I have found invaluable.

Finally, Dr Helen Barlow, Research Fellow at the Open University, to whom this book is dedicated: I have benefited enormously from her wisdom, clarity of thought and instinct for detail.

While I am pleased to acknowledge all the above and many others who are too numerous to mention, I should make it clear that I have not accepted all the advice I have been offered, and consequently the fault for any errors or shortcomings that remain in this book should be laid squarely at my door.

Author's note

Illustrations

Music illustrations are numbered sequentially within each chapter as Example 2.1, Example 2.2, and so on; all other illustrations (irrespective of type) are numbered sequentially through the book as Illustration 1, Illustration 2, and so on. Some musical extracts are listed as 'Illustrations' rather than 'Examples'. This is because musical 'Illustrations' (usually for reasons of copyright) are photographs of a page of score, while 'Examples' have been reset for the purposes of the book.

Note names and the harmonic series

The American Standard System is used to describe note pitches. In this system, middle C is called C_4, and A_4 = A440 Hz. The octave C0 includes the lowest pitches that are audible to the human ear, and C_9 to B_9 the highest notes known to have been written in western music. It goes without saying that this compass contains the tessitura of even the most virtuoso trombonists.

C_1 B_1 C_2 B_2 C_3 B_3 C_4 B_4 C_5 B_5 C_6 D_6 E_6 F_6 etc.

Example 1.1.

It is sometimes necessary for me to refer to partials of the harmonic series. In such instances, and irrespective of which harmonic series is being referred to, I call the first partial (the fundamental) H1 and subsequent partials H2, H3 and so on.

Instrument names and other terms

The names of some brass instruments invented in the nineteenth century were not standardized. I have done my best to avoid ambiguities. Similarly, some of the terms used to describe trombone techniques (for example, glissando/smear) and components of the instrument (for example, stays/braces, trigger/plug, water key/spit key) are understood differently in different countries. I have tried to minimize the potential for confusion, but I doubt whether I have dealt with all eventualities. The explanations given in Chapters 1 and 2, however, together with the associated diagrams, should keep such problems to a minimum.

A more substantial difficulty concerns the words that denote the main subject of this book. The trombone has had several names in its history, and these have been spelled in a variety of ways. The most common name in modern times is 'trombone' (which has always been the name used in Italy), though *Posaune* is ubiquitous in German-speaking countries (and again, always has been). A thornier problem arises in respect of the 'sackbut'. In modern times the word has been used for any trombone that is appropriate for performances of 'early music', an equally vague term (these are issues which I take up in Chapter 14). But strictly, words like 'sackbut' had a very limited use in the history of music, both chronologically and geographically (see Chapter 3). So throughout this book I use 'trombone', irrespective of the time and place with which I am dealing. The exceptions are where I am quoting, or where the use of different nomenclatures in close proximity would run the risk of making my meaning less than clear.

Bibliographical and other citations

All sources and media are cited using conventional procedures, though for references to *The New Grove Dictionary of Music and Musicians*, second edition (London: Macmillan, 2001), I have used the shortened title *New Grove 2*. The British Library, London, is designated by the abbreviation GB-LbL (from the library sigla devised by RISM, the Répertoire International des Sources Musicales). In the case of archival sources, some collections may be extremely well ordered without their items being minutely catalogued. This is particularly so in respect, for example, of company records, where the quantity and diversity of documentation present archivists with a huge challenge. I have always cited collections, but for these reasons I have not always been able to provide shelf marks.

Sound recordings

References to sound recordings are, wherever possible, to easily available CD remasterings. These usually give details of the original recordings, but they always provide sufficient information for original details of recordings to be determined through the major discographical reference tools (such as the Lord Jazz Index) and online catalogues such as those of the British Library Sound Archive and the recorded sound archive of the Library of Congress.

Quotations in translation

A large proportion of quotations are in translation. To prevent the book becoming unwieldy I have not given the text in the original language unless I have judged it important to do so – for example, because there is an element of ambiguity that may not be caught in the translation. Wherever possible, I have provided a note identifying the source of the original text and/or its translation.

Introduction

The trombone and its histories

The trombone was in existence and was called by that name during the fifteenth century. During the Renaissance it was ubiquitous in secular and sacred life in most regions of Europe. By the seventeenth century it was in the Americas, and in the nineteenth it was carried to most other continents of the world. But the most important journey that it has made is through many and multifaceted cultures: cultures that have been defined by time and place, but more importantly by people and the social, economic and aesthetic determinants that have fashioned the worlds in which they lived. It has passed through the sound worlds of all the periods of western art music, military music, vaudeville, jazz, Latino music, rock and roll, and countless hybrids.

The trombone, in other words, has not just one history but several. The main influences on these histories have been the designers and makers, the players and the composers who have written for the instrument. To these we might add the people who have listened to it. I hesitate to use the word 'audiences' because it conjures a particular meaning in modern times; perhaps it is sufficient to say that the attitudes of listeners have also shaped its progress. Gauging the relative strength of these influences is a tricky business, and one with which anybody who writes about the relationship of musical instruments to other strands of the historical process – repertoires, performance techniques, styles and so on – has to wrestle. The resolution of the question usually conditions the shape and content of the resultant narrative. I should therefore nail my colours to the mast on the first page of this book, and say that while I am convinced that any musical instrument's history can be properly understood only after close engagement with each of these main historical influences, for me it is the players who are the most important in this group. Though makers and composers have at various times been prominent in fashioning the instrument's idiom, it is the players who have put the culture into the trombone. It is they who, in all epochs, have given it a voice and positioned it in its soundscapes and cultural contexts. This judgement is shaped in roughly equal proportion by my experience as a player and my experience as an academic. My instincts as a player tell me it is true because I have always believed that the trombone is primarily what its players make of it, but the academic in me prompts a somewhat more rational analysis, if for no other reason than that histories are never as simple and uncluttered as our instincts would have them be.

This book, then, is an attempt to explain how the trombone has been understood at different times and in different places. Principal among my objectives has been to understand the preoccupations of its players – their musical values, the repertoires they played, the way they played, and any processes, events or other factors that impinged on the way in which they made their living. I have been particularly interested in patterns of continuity and change. Equally, I have been keen to explore the possibility that the story of trombone playing has not been linear: that several different (often contradictory) practices have prevailed simultaneously. I have found abundant evidence for such coexistences, and this is one of the factors that has influenced the shape of this book. The other factor has been my desire to examine periods in the trombone's history with certain key themes in mind.

Themes in the history of the trombone

Below I provide what I hope to be an unambiguous disclaimer about my status as an organologist. I stress this because organologists – those who take musical instruments as their primary focus of inquiry – have made significant and lasting contributions to the history of the trombone. My approach has been to engage with a wider range of sources and issues than the instrument itself, but it is obvious that its physical properties and its design and manufacture constitute a central theme in the story of the trombone. However, I have been less concerned with the fine detail of instruments than with the way that design, production and distribution have played a part in the wider story of the instrument's use. For example, there was a huge increase in the production of trombones (both slide and valve instruments) in the nineteenth century. This came about as changed modes of production and distribution both caused and responded to the sudden existence of a new market – a popular market made up of amateur players. To do this process justice would fill a volume in its own right, so I have cut my cloth accordingly, using only what I judge to be the superstructure of what happened in this period, to inform a more detailed examination of the ramifications of change.

The next theme is people, by which I mean trombone players: their identities, the ways in which they learned and conducted their trade, how they coped with what was expected of them, and the extent to which they shaped their own working lives. This theme is probably the dominant one in the book, because all others tend to converge on it. It is a particularly complex business because, like others who have written about a 'historical group', I have often encountered the dangers of generalization and oversimplification. To counteract this I have tried, when examining sources from different periods and cultures of trombone playing, to distinguish between the exceptional and the routine. This distinction applies in two ways: first to the routine practices of trombone playing, and secondly to the trombone players themselves. For example, we have good historical authority for judging what renaissance trombone players did in the great ceremonies and festivals that occurred in the period, but we know considerably less about what their ordinary routines were – the routines that rendered it sensible for cities and aristocrats to employ so many of them on monthly or annual salaries. Then there is the question of the lives that players led. In the centuries of the instrument's existence, a relatively small handful of players have left a mark on history that is recorded by more than their name and their paltry wage scribbled in a list of payments. These exceptional players fit readily into the story, but they do not entirely shape it – rather, it is the journeymen trombone players who have always been at the core of the trombonist's world. There is not enough space here to do their contribution justice, but these forgotten legions have nonetheless significantly shaped my narrative, prompting me to consider, for example, the profound changes of taste that transformed their way of life in the late seventeenth century, when, in so many places, the trombone slipped so decisively out of fashion, and again in the late 1920s, when the introduction of talking movies sent them to the dole cues in their thousands.

Such matters should not be seen merely as details of socio-historical context, because they impinge on another theme that has interested me: the repertoire of trombonists. The relationship of cultural and social trends to repertoire is not contextual but causal. Put somewhat differently, the repertoires of trombonists, and the practices that have had to be developed to enable these repertoires to be played, have been responsive to much broader aesthetic currents. The word 'repertoire' is one that I use somewhat uncomfortably here, because a significant proportion of the music that trombonists played was not codified: it was not written but existed only as performed music that was retained in the imaginations and memories of its players. Such traditions and processes account for much of the music played by trombonists up to at least the middle of the sixteenth century, and similar procedures were used in jazz and in the precursors of jazz and other popular idioms that stretch back to the nineteenth century. Of course, written repertoire exists too, and we think we know about most of it, but significant questions remain about the way that music was performed before the advent of sound recordings. Modern conceptions of older repertoire are laden with assumptions that owe nothing to any age other than the one in which we live. If there is a single generalization that can be applied to pre-twentieth-century performance values, it is that, before the onset of the process that we now call globalization, the trombone was understood and played in quite different ways in different parts of the world. Sound recordings from the first half of the twentieth century reveal these differences and confirm what we understand from documentary sources from much earlier periods.

It will be obvious that in dealing with these themes I have found it necessary to consult a wide body of evidence: surviving instruments, didactic treatises, published and unpublished documents, repertoire, paintings, photographs, sound recordings, and, in modern times, the spoken testimonies of players. The evidence taken together is considerable, but as I explain in the book, some daunting questions remain unanswered, and many parts of my narrative involve an element of what I may call informed speculation. This is not a dictionary; rather, it is a book which utilizes sources to construct a story. I do not belong to the school of positivists who hold firm to the idea that objective and definitive histories can be constructed by assembling enough information to effectively create a working model of the past. If I possessed any ambitions of that sort when I started working on this book, I soon recognized them as hopeless. As I am reminded elsewhere in this book, the past is dead and gone: history is what historians make of it. The reality is that when writing the history of a musical instrument, as with any other subject, we have to accept certain limitations.

Organology

I feel the need to say something in this introduction about organology, because it is a sector of scholarship from which I have drawn a great deal, but to which I have contributed very little. There are some good histories of instruments that do not mention a single player or indeed the repertoire that players have performed. This approach is neither flawed nor impoverished, for we learn much about instruments by seeing them stripped of such trappings. The authors of some of the formal classification systems for musical instruments bent over backwards to devise culturally neutral methods, and some of these have stood us in good stead. The benefits of this approach as far as the trombone is concerned can be understood by reference to three related factors. First, it focuses on instruments as acoustic devices which can be described and analysed objectively. The products of this approach are evident in the work of acousticians and organologists who explain why and how key components of trombone design cause instruments to sound, look and feel they way they do. Secondly, by looking at the development of instruments without recourse to cultural determinants, it is possible to imagine the problems that musical instrument designers have from time to time confronted, why they were perceived as problems, how their solutions were arrived at and what the musical consequences of the solutions were. Thirdly, and perhaps most importantly, organologists and instrument historians, along with curators (often one and the same group of people), are the primary custodians of the material history of musical instruments. It is an approach to history that is not short on complexities or subtleties. It is probably not an exaggeration to say that without organologists the history of instruments would hardly exist, and it is only in comparatively recent times that this branch of endeavour has been given the credit it so richly deserves (the word 'organology' was not afforded an entry in *Grove's Dictionary* until 1980, when the *New Grove Dictionary of Music and Musicians* was published). So why am I reluctant to see myself as an organologist, and why should this book be read with this reservation in mind?

The written legacy of organologists is considerable. It all started with Canon Francis Galpin, who (as I recount in Chapter 14) put trombone scholarship on the right track after it had spent most of the previous half-century in a wilderness of confusion. Latterly our understanding of the organology of the trombone has benefited from the many scholars who have published in journals devoted to musical instruments. Prominent among these are the *Galpin Society Journal*, the *Journal of the American Musical Instrument Society*, *Brass and Woodwind Quarterly* and the *Historic Brass Society Journal*. To these can be added monographs such as Anthony Baines's *Brass Instruments* (1976), which has acted as a starting point for anyone who has wished to grasp the wider picture of how brass instruments have developed, and the immensely detailed and authoritative *Musikinstrumenten-Museum der Karl-Marx-Universität, Katalog Band 3: Trompeten, Posaunen, Tuben* (1980) and *Das Ventilblasinstrument* (1987), both by Herbert Heyde. I mention this body of work because anyone who looks in this book for any advancement on the organological information it contains will search in vain. I have drawn fully on the work of those who have followed this path, but the fact is that my interests have a somewhat different flavour. I have described instruments, but I have added little to what is already known, and I have certainly not tried to be comprehensive in my coverage of the many manifestations of the trombone that have existed.

Structure and content

It follows from what I have already said that the format I have adopted for this book is both thematic and chronological. By this I mean that, though the historical aspects of the book are arranged logically, a number of chapters deal with the same or similar periods, but from different thematic perspectives. In fact very few chapters are confined to the periods that are hinted at in their titles. For example, the period between about 1400 and 1700 is dealt with in three different chapters in which the time-spans overlap. The first of these (Chapter 3) focuses on the origins of the instrument that became known as the trombone, the next deals with performers and the cultures within which they worked, and the next concentrates on repertoire and the way it was probably played. These three chapters are preceded by two mapping chapters: the first describing the instrument and the way it has changed in history, the second the way it is played and how key aspects of performance techniques have altered. It goes without saying that these two chapters provide a somewhat prosaic background for what follows, but not *too* prosaic I hope, because the mundane aspects of the instrument and the way it has been played became something of a talking point for me when I was writing this book. I found myself having probing discussions with friends and colleagues about minutiae that would send me scurrying back to the sources. Who first wrote a muted passage for trombone? Where was the first glissando notated? Did Teagarden really play trills or were they grace notes? When was the bass trombone introduced into dance bands? Who was the last professional player to remain loyal to the G trombone? The book, I regret to say, is scattered with cautionary disclaimers about such matters.

The sixth chapter, 'Decline, survival and rehabilitation', recounts the story of the trombone's fall from grace and its re-emergence in the 1760s. The remaining chapters continue to deal with themes, even though they also fit into what will be seen as a rational chronological sequence. Their ordering reflects three broad trends that I see as being the main sources of influence on the trombone's idiom for the last two centuries. The first of these trends is the advent of what I refer to as the conservatoire tradition, in which institutional instruction and the literature it inspired created new types of orthodox approaches to playing art music. As a result, this tradition defined and codified correct ways of playing and set standards which could be explained in terms of virtuosity and artistry. This was not a single standard because there were soon many conservatoires, but the principle of institutional instruction and its associated notions of elitism became common and have lasted. The second trend is the invention of popular music as a mass consumer commodity, enfranchising amateurs and igniting new forms of music that called for new playing styles – ultimately leading to the advent of jazz, which imposed a huge influence on the way the trombone was played in many forms of music. Jazz is the classic example of a new performance style, flourishing, giving birth to its own musical heroes and reinventing notions of virtuosity, while coexisting with an elite tradition that stretches back centuries. The most powerful manifestation of that tradition as far as the trombone is concerned is the orchestra: the opera orchestra and the symphony orchestra. I have dealt with this topic at some length but in a somewhat unorthodox manner: Chapter 8 deals with the development and reception of orchestral trombone playing, particularly in the nineteenth century, while Chapter 12, 'Orchestral trombone playing in the age of sound recordings', allows me to deal with the subject of performance style mainly (but not exclusively) using the evidence provided by recordings. These chapters are contextualized by Chapter 9, which deals with nineteenth-century inventions (valves, keyed instruments and so on) that either directly or indirectly affected the trombone.

A short chapter on 'The Moravians and other popular religions' (Chapter 11) is included for two reasons: first because the topics contained in it could not be comfortably included in other chapters, and secondly because it covers an interesting part of the trombone's story that is probably unknown to many. The main theme is the use of the trombone in Moravian communities in the USA, where it has had a special function and significance. But I have also discussed other forms of popular religion in which trombones or brass instruments more generally have been significant. The final chapter deals with two topics relevant to modern times, and their very juxtaposition serves to justify the use of the word 'postmodernism' in its title. The two themes are what I might loosely call the avant garde and the retrospection of the early music or period performance movement.

Presentation

The book is illustrated with pictures, drawings and other visual matter that is either directly related to textual comment or complementary to it. The same can be said for musical examples: some are there to explain what can not be properly explained by words alone, others give substance to more general comments about the way the instrument has been written for. One feature of the book that deserves particular explanation is my use of tables. I have always favoured tables because they allow the display of dense data without impeding the flow of narrative. Basically, I have used tables for two purposes: first, to convey important information about such things as repertoire, orchestral forces and certain types of literature such as method books; secondly, to summarize information which is either the result of original and new research, or is so vast in its scope that only such a summary could be conceived as being practicable. There are lots of tables in this book, some so long as to make it necessary for them to be included as appendices, and despite their advantages they contain inherent dangers. The major danger is that tables give the appearance of objectivity and neutrality. This is not the case. The very act of selection of data for a table involves either choice or something more random. I stress that every table I have written is intended to be indicative – to convey an impression rather than to be comprehensive.

Who am I writing for?

Before I started writing this book I sat in a chair and asked myself who I was writing it for. I had no desire to write the type of book that has already been written by others, neither did I want to write a book that would be read only by trombone players and organologists. I have felt it incumbent upon me to write a book that could have been written only as a result of rigorous research into primary and secondary sources, but equally I have held on to the slender hope that others will find something in these pages to interest them. So this is a book about phases in the history of music told from the perspective of one musical instrument and its players. The mode of address is fashioned by my work at the Open University, which teaches students through the written word, and where I have many mentors from whom to draw inspiration. This is far from the last word on the trombone, but I hope that it adds something, not just to the sum of knowledge, but to the way that such knowledge might be used.

Trevor Herbert
The Open University

Chapter 1

The instrument: its parts and their development

Continuity and tradition

The slide trombone is one of the truly great inventions in the history of music. Like so many of the most imaginative ideas, it is based on a concept of elegant simplicity – one that has needed little fundamental adjustment since the fifteenth century. The trombone slide enabled renaissance players (the first to use the instrument) to rise above the limitations experienced by ceremonial trumpeters, whose instruments were restricted by fixed tube lengths: it allowed them to obtain the full range of notes (theoretically the chromatic range) within their compass. But leaving aside this important practical advantage, the trombone was soon recognized to be an extraordinarily versatile instrument with a distinctive idiomatic character. This versatility and distinctiveness have sustained its popularity over the centuries of its existence.

The distinctive status of the slide trombone in music history may be best illustrated by its resilient survival in the light of the success of valve trombones in the nineteenth century. By the second half of the century, valve trombones were being produced and marketed with tremendous success by most of the leading brass instrument manufacturers in Europe and the USA. Indeed, there may well have been considerably more valve trombone players in the nineteenth century than players of the slide instrument. Valve trombones could be manufactured in large quantities relatively easily, and they had apparent advantages over the traditional trombone: they are played with the same technique as any other valve instrument, and valves help players make light work of fast, florid figurations. But through that century of dramatic technological and cultural change, when innovation was a value celebrated in its own right, the slide trombone never really slipped into the shadows: it always prevailed as the authentic voice of the instrument, not just in art music, but increasingly in the new and abundant forms of popular music-making too.

While slide trombone design and manufacturing processes have changed since the fifteenth century, the overall history of the instrument is characterized more by continuity than change. There have, however, been significant design modifications, most of them coming after about 1800. It is possible to think of these developments as falling into two very broad categories. In the first can be placed those aimed at making the instrument more efficient: for example, the introduction of tuning slides in the very late eighteenth century, and the water key and slide touch springs in the nineteenth century. In the second category are developments that came about in response to musical, cultural and even socio-economic trends. These developments are especially interesting because they usually signal a close, even causal, relationship between the instrument and the characters who influence it most: players, makers, composers and 'audiences'. It is to such developments that we can attribute, for example, the demand for smaller and larger instruments to satisfy the desire of composers to write in the outer extremes of the pitch register, and the twentieth-century preference for instruments with wide bore and bell sizes that were appropriate for large orchestras performing in spacious modern concert halls.

Another, perhaps less obvious, influence on the design and manufacture of trombones has been the modes of production and distribution. Developments were often responsive to market forces. For example, in the nineteenth century an entirely new species of trombone player emerged, and in unprecedented numbers: the working-class amateur. Trombone manufacturing moved from small-scale, individual craft workshops to somewhat larger (sometimes very large) factories which had many of the features of modern mass production and distribution. For the first time, trombone makers conceived of their clients as falling into large homogeneous sectors. Thus, for example, the idea of a routine distinction between 'cheap' and 'superior' instruments appeared. This trend continued, as manufacturers sought to address particular market sectors with instruments that suited consumers' pockets as well as their particular musical needs and preferences. The chain of events that prompted so many different preferences and requirements to appear will be dealt with in later chapters; here, it is necessary simply to restate the point at which I started: though it would be wrong to take the idea of continuity too literally, most of the changes to the design of the trombone have been variations on a relatively simple theme. It is the simplicity of the basic design of the trombone that has enabled it to endure and to provide players of such diverse periods and styles with opportunities for musical expression.

It was not only the valve trombone that might have posed a threat to the slide instrument, for while technical developments occurred that served the needs of players by helping them respond to aesthetic trends, several ideas were introduced in the nineteenth century that had little to do with musical values and offered no real musical advantages. Brass instruments seem to have been a special subject of interest for ambitious nineteenth-century inventors with fertile imaginations and boundless optimism. We can now reflect on the key moments of the trombone's design history from the perspective of hindsight, but in the white heat of the nineteenth-century technological revolution, the passion for innovation – any innovation – often obscured practical sense and inflicted a form of acute intellectual blindness. The patent offices of the great European cities hold abundant evidence of this phenomenon. It is well illustrated by the case of Mr T. G. Ghislin, a British inventor with remarkably original ideas and persistent optimism. In October 1860, the London Patents Office issued Mr Ghislin with provisional protection (GB 1860: 2661) for his idea of using a particular type of seaweed called *eiklonia buccinalis* to enhance the aesthetic appearance of trombones and other brass instruments. Ghislin believed that this seaweed, when suitably treated with chemicals, could be used for 'covering and ornamenting' instruments. We can only assume that Ghislin himself had second thoughts about the commercial and artistic value of his venture, for it was soon declared 'void for want of final specification'. But his belief that marine vegetation held potential for the future improvement of brass instruments was not exhausted – far from it. Within a year he had registered a patent to protect his idea that the most common forms of seaweed could be 'boiled in oil' and used to make brass instrument mouthpieces (GB 1861: 2482). To my knowledge, none of Ghislin's seaweed mouthpieces have survived, and one wonders if any were ever produced; but he held no monopoly on eccentric ideas. Contemporary with him were Dunbar and Harper, who invented a performer's aid in which negative and positive metals were 'conjoined' with an insulator so as to 'obtain an electric current in the mouth' when a player was performing (GB 1880: 4515). Then there was J. Engelhard's device of 1913 (GB 1913: 18,442) which was to be 'inserted between the lips, gums and teeth to facilitate the production of high and low notes'. Hopeless as these ideas were, they were no more so than the application submitted from the Adolphe Sax factory, proposing a device to provide trombones and other brass instruments 'with an inner double jacket for the reception of tar or other antiseptic liquid . . . so that the air inhaled by the performer is impregnated with the vapour of these substances' (GB 1865: 112). We can but ponder on the long-term welfare of any hapless trombonist who may have played the prototype of this invention: needless to say, it did not make it to mass production.

The stories of Ghislin, Dunbar and Harper, Engelhard and many others like them make an important point (albeit a somewhat exaggerated one) about the resilience that the trombone displayed to all but the most legitimate changes as it made its journey through time. Hundreds of improvements to brass instruments were proposed in the nineteenth and early twentieth centuries. Those that received patent protection are matters of record, but there were probably many more ideas which were never registered. Of the improvements to the trombone that were formally logged, only a tiny handful ever made an impression on the development of the instrument or had a morsel of commercial success. Dozens of instruments and amendments to instruments were produced, surviving specimens of which work perfectly well, and they can be seen in museum exhibition cases across the world; but they had no historical impact. Often the factor that intervened between success and failure was mere luck or even fashion. For example, on 1 October 1904, Grinstead and Stuart applied for patent protection at the London Patent Office for two inventions (neither of which may have been absolutely original). One was for a type of long-distance water key (GB 1904: 21,124), which enabled a trombone player to evacuate moisture when the instrument was in its normal playing position; this was done by means of a spring-activated valve at the base of the slide, operated by a finger hook mounted at the point where the moving slide is held. It was a perfectly valid, practical and intelligent device that was popular in some European countries (where it was independently patented), and is sometimes seen on museum instruments. It never really caught on to the extent that it warranted – perhaps because it would have involved makers in an extra and somewhat fussy stage of manufacture, and also perhaps because players simply didn't need such a facility – though it was used on some German models. But Grinstead and Stuart's other idea was for a disarmingly simple mechanism: a 'locking device for a slide trombone' comprising a rotatable collar that would secure the slide in closed position when it was not in use (GB 1904:

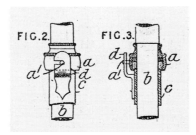

Illustration 1. C. Grinstead and E. E. Stuart's patent for the trombone slide lock (GB 1904: 21,125)

21,125). (Ill. 1) This was a version of the slide lock, now a standard device on trombones.[1]

A Victorian speculator might well have invested in the future of the long-distance water key rather than the slide lock, but the future of musical technology in the nineteenth century was hard to predict. The stock books of nineteenth-century brass instrument makers are replete with information about sales of species of brass instruments that were to fall out of use, but many served a useful purpose in their brief lives. A vast number were produced, bought, played and listened to, but relatively few survived the turn of the century, except as museum pieces. Four important factors seem to have ensured the slide trombone's endurance, comparatively unchanged, in a period when so much about the future of brass instruments was uncertain. First, even in the nineteenth century the slide instrument was recognized as having unique and inimitable musical qualities. Secondly, the cultural place of the trombone was being seen in a new light, mainly because of its exploitation by virtuoso player–teachers, especially those active in France and Germany, and a little later in America. Through them, a new, modern tradition of virtuoso slide trombone playing became established before (but only just before) valve instruments were widely available. Thirdly, many of the greatest Romantic composers were peculiarly conservative and possessed of a particular type of musical historicism: not all composers valued change above continuity – rather, they looked to the past for inspiration and cultural reference. A case in point can be found in the orchestral works of Brahms, almost all of whose brass writing exploited instruments and idioms that were flourishing by the later eighteenth century.[2] He was not alone in cherishing the capacity of trombones to summon those dark images that others as distant as Mozart and Monteverdi had exploited. Put somewhat differently, the slide trombone had acquired a capacity for cultural meaning and metaphorical communication that assured its status. Finally, whereas valve and slide trombones almost always appeared side by side in instrument catalogues of the period, they were regarded as essentially *different* instruments with distinctive and separate qualities; this distinction is also explicit in nineteenth- and early twentieth-century orchestration treatises. The valve trombone was used in symphony orchestras as well as bands, but the utility of valve instruments was best suited to the latter, and one senses a belief on the part of nineteenth-century composers and writers about instruments that a distinction needed to be made between the sound of the trombone in the military band and in the orchestra.

The naming of parts

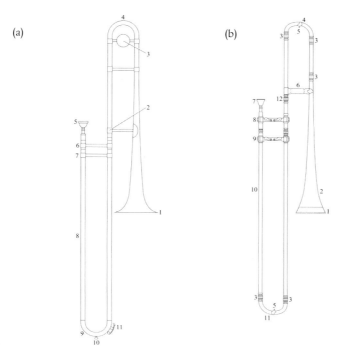

Illustration 2. Parts of the modern and baroque slide trombones
Parts of the modern slide trombone (a)
  1 Bell
  2 Joint of the bell section and the slide section
  3 Counterbalance weight
  4 Tuning slide (on the bell bow)
  5 Mouthpiece
  6 Slide stay – stays are sometimes called braces (on the static inner slide)
  7 Slide stay (on the moveable outer slide)
  8 Slide
  9 Slide bow
 10 Slide rest
 11 Water key

Parts of the baroque trombone (b)
  1 Bell garland
  2 Bell
  3 Ferrules (holding parts of the instrument together)
  4 Bell bow
  5 Rings (present on many early instruments, but it is uncertain what their purpose was)
  6 Bell stay
  7 Mouthpiece
  8 Slide stay (on the static inner slide)
  9 Slide stay (on the moveable outer slide)
 10 Slide
 11 Slide bow
 12 Joint of the bell section and the slide section.

Given that continuity has played a greater part than change in the history of the design of the trombone, what follows is a brief summary of the component parts of the instrument, with some notes about the ways in which they have been adapted or revised at various points in history. The rest of this chapter should be read in conjunction with the information provided in Illustration 2. At one level this section has a purely pragmatic objective: it will acquaint any reader who needs such acquaintance with the components of the trombone and how they have developed – it really is about the 'naming of parts' (to borrow the title of Henry Reed's poem). But even in this pragmatic description there is also room for a narrative, because every lasting change that has been introduced to a particular part of the instrument bears testimony to a perceived need for such change, and to players' willingness to accommodate it. For as I have already hinted, the trombone bears evidence, at every point of its development since the fifteenth century, of the influence of makers, players and composers.

A modern slide trombone is usually detached into three parts: the mouthpiece, the slide section and the bell section. These three sections have always existed, though a case can be made to show that very early instruments broke down into yet more parts because joints were held by inertia and wax sealings rather than by soldering. Furthermore, these early instruments had add-on parts, such as 'crooks' that were used to change the pitch of the instrument. Trombones made before 1800 had a less exaggerated terminal flare and generally smaller proportions than most modern instruments. Illustration 3 shows, for the purpose of broad comparison, three instruments: a faithful reproduction of an early seventeenth-century instrument made by the Egger company of Basel, Switzerland; a narrow-bore 'peashooter' trombone made by Boosey c.1938, typical of the kind that was popular from about 1850 to 1950; and a Conn model 8H trombone, one of the most popular models of the second half of the twentieth century.

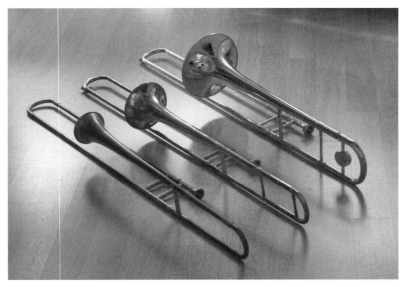

Illustration 3. Tenor trombones, all in B flat. From right to left, Conn 8H, c. 1980; Besson Imperial, c. 1938; reproduction by Egger (c. 1975) after Sebastian Hainlein, Nuremberg (1632).

The images provide a reasonable generalization (though it really is a generalization) of some of the main changes to tenor slide trombones in the last five hundred years (ignoring, for the time being, the introduction of thumb valves, which are discussed in Chapter 9). It can be seen that the Conn instrument has strikingly larger proportions than the other two, even though all three share an identical nominal pitch (B flat). But it is equally obvious that the geometry of the three instruments is fundamentally similar.

Each instrument is made preponderantly of cylindrical tubing which becomes conical at a point in the bell section. The mouthpiece fits into the slide section and is held there by its own inertia. The bell section and the slide section are also held together by the tightness of the fit, but most modern instruments also have a screw fitting at the junction of the bell and the slide sections to give additional stability. The

Illustration 4. A nineteenth-century buccin player. (With thanks to Howard Weiner.)

rods or bars that hold the instrument together are called stays, and the slide has to
have a minimum of two such stays, because there must be at least one on the
stationary section and one on the moving part of the slide. Modern instruments often
have a counterweight on the bell section to help the player balance the instrument.
The bells of these three instruments all point forwards, but some instruments
produced in the nineteenth century for military band use had backward-pointing
bells. Instruments with forward-pointing bells styled as the head of a serpent or
dragon were also introduced in the nineteenth century. (Ill. 4) Several of these
instruments, called buccins, survive in instrument collections; Berlioz scored for one
in the 'Resurrexit' of his *Messe solennelle* (1824).

The mouthpiece

The purpose of the mouthpiece (Ill. 5) is to provide an interface between the player
and the instrument. The buzzing of the lips within the mouthpiece initiates changes
in pressure that cause the instrument to sound. The size, shape and proportions of a
mouthpiece have a real effect on the acoustical process, but a mouthpiece can not be
evaluated in purely objective terms: players also choose a particular mouthpiece for
reasons that are subjective and personal. Much has been written about mouthpieces,
and many manufacturers have uttered exaggerated claims about their products. Since
the nineteenth century, novel ideas have been marketed, including mouthpieces with
a concave and India rubber rim or with a shock-absorbing shank, and complex
devices that purport to aid flexibility and accuracy. The practice of leading players
designing or endorsing mouthpieces also has a long history. The American virtuosi
Arthur Pryor and Frederick Innes both endorsed Conn mouthpieces. One of the most
successful ranges of mouthpieces has been designed by the British trombone player
Denis Wick. Joseph Alessi of the New York Philharmonic has also designed an
impressive range in collaboration with Greg Black. New instruments are always
supplied with a mouthpiece, but it is a commonly accepted and mysterious fact that
these new mouthpieces lie permanently idle – further testimony, perhaps, to the
idiosyncratic relationship of players with their mouthpieces.

The earliest mouthpiece that survives apparently with the instrument for which it
was made is by the Nuremberg maker Anton Schnitzer the Elder, and is in the
collection of the Palais Lascaris, Nice (cat. 2.1.1.1). The date on the bell garland of the
instrument is 1581.[3] Another, slightly earlier instrument by the same maker, with a
contemporaneous mouthpiece (but not definitely made at the same time as the
instrument) is owned by the Accademia Filarmonica, Verona (13.301). The garland of
this instrument is marked 'Anton Schnitzer Padre, Norimberga 1579'; the mouthpiece
is inscribed 'Nvremberg'. The two mouthpieces have broad similarities: they both
have flat narrow rims, shallow cups and sharp apertures relative to mouthpieces made
in modern times, but it is difficult to draw broad conclusions about early mouthpieces
on the basis of such limited evidence. We might well speculate that mouthpieces were
made or altered for players locally, and that their shape and proportions varied.
Documentary illustrations of early trombones shed only a dim light. Praetorius shows
instruments with mouthpieces in the *Theatrum instrumentorum* (1620) appended to

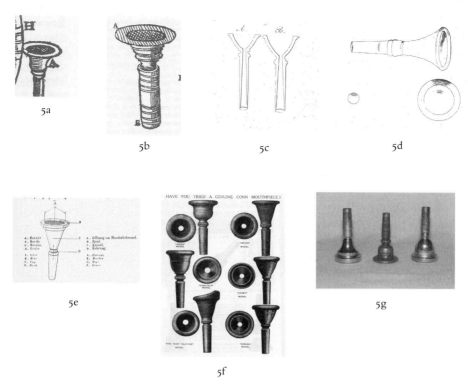

Illustration 5. Evidence of the vast variety of mouthpieces that have been used: 5a Trombone mouthpiece from Marin Mersenne's *Harmonie universelle* (1636); 5b Trumpet mouthpiece from the same source; 5c Tenor and bass trombone mouthpiece illustration in Andreas Nemetz's *Neueste Posaun-Schule* (1827); 5d Antoine Dieppo's *Méthode complète pour le trombone* (1837); 5e André Lafosse's *Méthode complète pour le trombone* (1921); 5f Conn 'New Wonder Model' catalogue (c. 1928); 5g Three twentieth-century mouthpieces – (from the left) Dennis Wick model 4AL (c. 1982); Conn Pryor model (c. 1910); Vincent Bach model 6½ AL (c. 1975).

Volume II of *Syntagma musicum* (1619), and makes it clear that the mouthpiece is detachable from the rest of the instrument, but says little more. Mersenne's illustration of a trombone with a mouthpiece fitted (1636) also provides only limited information, and it is probable that both writers were concerned more with capturing the idea that these instruments had mouthpieces than with conveying their detail. But in one respect Mersenne's drawing may be unwittingly revealing. He also illustrates a trumpet mouthpiece, and shows it to have a quite different profile from his trombone mouthpiece. Furthermore, Mersenne's drawing shows a pattern that broadly matches surviving specimens. His trombone mouthpiece seems to have a deeper cup and a rim that is narrower and more rounded than his trumpet mouthpiece. This is scant evidence, but it is consistent with what we would expect from the essentially different musical functions of the two instruments: trumpets had a more declamatory role than trombones at this time and needed to exploit much higher partials. Mersenne's trombone mouthpiece seems to accommodate players who play in lower registers with a more sonorous timbre. It is possible to conclude that, by the seventeenth century, the different idiomatic characters of the trombone and the trumpet were reflected in the way that mouthpieces were designed.

Most surviving early mouthpieces are made of metal, usually brass; but ivory was favoured too. The London music retailer Clementi, Collard & Collard was advertising trombone mouthpieces made from brass or ivory in its catalogue in the opening years of the nineteenth century,[4] and the Edinburgh music retailer John Glen was stocking a good proportion of his mouthpieces in ivory in the 1840s.[5] It is difficult to ascertain when trombone mouthpieces started to be manufactured from ivory, but ivory was used for cornett mouthpieces at least by the seventeenth century. Several modern manufacturers produce mouthpieces made of materials other than brass. A company set up by the French trumpeter Maurice Benterfa has successfully marketed mouthpieces with wooden screw cups made from ebony, kingwood and cocowood. In the USA, Jaztec has produced mouthpieces made of hard minerals such as coral and cobalt. But brass or plated brass mouthpieces have been the most widely used.

It is understandable that changes to the design and proportion of mouthpieces have occurred as a response to changes in instrument design more generally. Larger instruments require bigger mouthpieces – the shank (the part of the mouthpiece that fits into the mouthpiece receiver) needs to be wider to fit into the larger bore aperture, and there is a commensurate change in the cup diameter and depth. Smaller mouthpieces give support to playing in the higher register, while larger, deeper mouthpieces are used on bass instruments.

The slide

The movable U-shaped outer slide fits snugly over two stationary inner slides. (Ill. 6) On modern instruments, both slides are of nickel or are nickel-plated. On most instruments, bore size is identical on both the mouthpiece and the bell side of the slide, but not always; for example, in the 1930s George Case patented a slide on which the slide arm nearer the bell was wider than the outward arm. (This may not have been the first such instrument, and it certainly was not the last for several modern instruments are advertised with such slides.) Non-metal slides, such as the proposal for a graphite slide by Del Giudice in 1988 (US 1989: 4,860,62), have not been widely adopted. During the nineteenth century, slide 'stockings' (expansions to the lower ends of both inner slides) were introduced to help the slide glide smoothly. (Ill. 7) This was an important development because it decreased the amount of friction between the inner and outer slides.

Cream or oil is used to lubricate the slide: modern players apply a small amount of lubricant to the inner slides, then a frequent fine spray of water, to achieve an easy action. Slide lubricants started to be advertised in the early twentieth century. It is easy to imagine that before commercial products became available, players used any number of lubricants made from vegetable or animal oil, but there is little information about them. Ivor Ingram, who made a living as a trombone player in silent movies in the years immediately following the First World War, claimed to have used a potentially lethal home-made substance which he concocted from heated paraffin, candle wax and eau de cologne.[6] Early in the twentieth century, the American

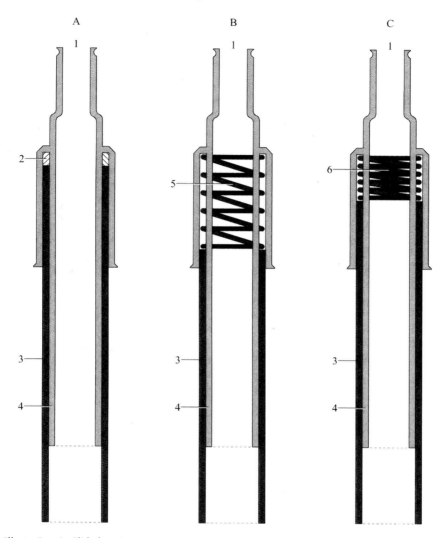

Illustration 6. Slide housings
Diagram A shows a slide butting against an unyielding cork stopper. Diagrams B and C show the effect of touch springs inserted inside the slide housing – diagram B with slide drawn in to meet the touch springs, diagram C with the slide drawn in further to sharpen the pitch.
1 Mouthpiece receiver (some modern instruments also have a mouthpipe that is not shown here)
2 Cork butt/stopper
3 Moveable outer slide
4 Static inner slide
5 Touch springs uncompressed
6 Touch springs compressed

trombone player Henry Fillmore was one of the first to attempt the mass-marketing of slide lubricant, but it almost bankrupted him. Pond's Cold Cream – a cosmetic product – was widely favoured by British and American players in the twentieth century, but proprietary products with brand names such as 'Superslick' and 'Trombotine' now dominate the market.

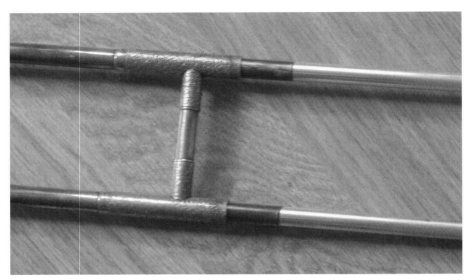

Illustration 7. The bottom of the inner slide (on the right) fitting into the outer slide (on the left). The darker section of the inner slide is the expanded section known as the stocking.

Several inventors have introduced changes to slide mechanisms. Many, such as F. A. Buescher's 1927 device (GB 1927: 276,566), in which ball bearings were inserted between the inner and outer slides, achieved no commercial success. However, in 1937 Reginald Birdsall Olds patented a radical design that met with some success: a slide with a fluted rather than a circular bore (US 1937: 472,510). These slides, and the instruments on which they were used, were well made and were adopted by some leading players. Olds's intention was originally to design a tube profile that would enable the stationary part of the slide to retain its lubrication more efficiently, but he also realized that the profile itself made for an easier slide action. The drawback seems to have come from the precision of the design. The slightest dent or abrasion caused the slide to malfunction badly, and such damage was difficult to repair.

Slide stockings and a general improvement in precision engineering probably contributed most to the smooth action of slides, but the other really significant development to the slide section of the instrument came with the introduction of touch springs. Touch springs are inserted within the two inner slide housings, so that when the slide is brought to its closed position it does not butt directly against an unyielding stopper, but rather against the freely expanded springs. This minimizes any jarring when the slide hits the home position abruptly, and it also solves a significant intonational problem in that it allows a player to fine-tune notes in the closed position. When the touch spring mechanism was patented in Britain in May 1897 by J. H. Guilmartin and the Besson Company, it specifically addressed the problem of achieving correct intonation on just one note – A flat, the seventh harmonic of the closed position on an instrument nominally pitched in B flat: 'The invention consists of an improvement in slide trombones, the slide . . . being caused to abut, when in the home position, against a spring . . ., so that by a slight extra pressure the length of the tube may be still further shortened. The upper A flat can thus be truly played.' (GB 1897: 10,896)

The water key

The water key was introduced in the nineteenth century to provide an easy means for players to evacuate the moisture accumulated by the condensation of breath inside the instrument. Previously, players would release moisture by detaching the slide and inverting it, a skill that modern players of faithfully copied period instruments have had to learn. There is some uncertainty about the inventor of the water key. There are several contestants, each of whom produced a different design. J. R. Cotter of County Cork, Ireland, patented a hibernicon with a sprung water key in 1823, and in 1830 Leopold Uhlmann patented a water key for a valve trombone in Vienna. But the first device for dealing with accumulated moisture seems to have been designed specifically for the trombone by Johann Friedheim (Ill. 8), who published the following announcement in his *Trente-six Exercices pour le trombone en si ♭* (Paris, 1821):

Notice

When one plays a piece of a certain length on the trombone, the water produced by the humid warmth of the breath collects in the bottom of the slide and produces a beating sound which especially makes the high notes disagreeable to the ear. To avoid this beating sound one must remove the slide in order to empty it. During this time, many measures elapse in which one does not play and the effect that the composer wanted to produce is spoiled, all the more so since this almost always affects fundamental notes of the chord, which are the responsibility of this instrument.

I have found a means of avoiding this inconvenience by adapting to the trombone a reservoir into which the water flows and from which it is then very easy to remove. The reservoir opens when necessary, and it takes at least half an hour of playing to fill it. This reservoir can be adapted to all trombones at little cost; it does not make the instrument more difficult to play, and the sound is not altered in any way.

It is at Halary, maker of instruments, Rue Mazarin No. 37, Paris, that I recommend to have them fitted, as it is together with him that I developed [these reservoirs]. He knows better than anybody else their inner construction.[7]

Illustration 8. Friedheim's reservoir (1821). (With thanks to Howard Weiner.)

Water keys that are operated by a single spring are usually placed off-centre on the bell side of the slide bow. In 1845 the same Jean-Louis Halary patented a 'Siphon' water key for the trombone. Siphon water keys were fitted to many nineteenth-century French instruments, but they also appear as special orders in the stock books of the English branch of the Besson company in the later nineteenth century. Both the spring and the siphon water keys are practicable, but the former has been more popular.

Tuning devices

Early trombonists were able to adjust the overall intonation of their instruments by adding lengths of tubing to them. Three devices seem to have been most commonly used: circular 'crooks' placed between the bell and slide sections; short, straight 'bits' between the mouthpiece and the slide; and also various substitutions for the bell bow. Trombone crooks are mentioned in the business letters of Georg Neuschel, the Nuremberg instrument maker, in 1541.[8] Praetorius and Mersenne illustrate such items, and several survive in instrument collections. The variety of shapes used suggests that while these devices were common, they were made individually and probably locally as expedient solutions to particular musical problems, as well as being supplied with a new instrument: surviving early crooks and bits often have decorative features that do not match the decorations of the instruments they apparently supplement.

Clearly the longer tuning insertions that were used on early trombones provided a means for altering the standing pitch of the instrument by a significant interval; players would have adjusted the finer nuances of intonation on the main slide or embouchure. Praetorius referred to this when he wrote that 'a skilled trombone player is able to modify the pitch . . . by means of the embouchure and mouthpiece without making use of crooks'.[9] The existence of a common pitch standard, together with improvements in the manufacture of instruments (including the introduction of touch springs and thumb valve attachments), now render additional crooks and similar devices unnecessary, except for period instrument performers.

The fine-tuning of the nominal pitch is achieved by use of a tuning slide which is usually a telescopic slide placed at the bell bow. Other tuning slides have been invented to achieve the same effect, including telescopic slides positioned on the main slide itself, such as the one fitted on the Case model trombone made by Boosey and Co. in the late nineteenth century. But the bell bow tuning slide is by far the most popular. The inventor credited with the introduction of the tuning slide is the Parisian manufacturer François Riedloker.[10] There are tuning slides on early Riedloker instruments (see, for example, the instrument dated c.1810 in the collection of the University of Edinburgh, Acc. No. 3534), but while these are the earliest surviving instruments with such a device, it is not entirely certain that the invention should be attributed to Riedloker. André Braun's *Gamme et méthode pour les trombonnes*, published between about 1793 and 1797, some years before Riedloker commenced business, contains a clear illustration and explanation of a tuning slide.[11]

Bore and bell sizes

The bore of the cylindrical portion of a trombone, together with the size and shape of the bell, are important in determining timbre. It has already been pointed out that instruments used before about 1800 were universally smaller than they are today, in terms of both bore and bell size. Few, if any, early instruments survive in their original condition as playing models, so the best insight we have into the practical effect of such instruments comes from the experiments of period instrument players. A wider variety of instrument designs were introduced in the nineteenth century, some of which survive in excellent condition. Indeed, if we take into account the fact that some nineteenth-century instruments continued to be used well into the twentieth century, we can also call on the evidence of sound recordings. The adjectives used to describe sounds are inherently inadequate, but as a broad generalization it is reasonable to say that instruments with narrower-bore profiles and small bells encourage a sound that is small, sweet, well focused and centred. Instruments with wider-bore profiles and larger bells with a proportional terminal flare generate a wider, more sonorous and euphonious timbre. These descriptors can be of some help when considering why, at different times in history, there has been a preference for instruments of different sizes. But it is important to stress that the proportions of an instrument – particularly its bore diameter – are not the sole factor to influence the sound players make. A fundamental factor is the musical culture in which they work and the way that they imagine the sound they wish to produce. This complex but fascinating subject is dealt with later in this book.

The sheet metal from which early instruments were made was relatively thin. The process of hammering and burnishing the bell produced further thinning, so the end of the bell needed to be secured by a garland. The best makers of reproduction instruments copy original designs faithfully, and mimic the original production methods. The resulting instruments are entirely convincing when played with other historic or historical instruments (such as viols) or with voices. They encourage an intimate sound when played quietly, but at the other end of the dynamic range the sound is penetrating and brassy. The subjective feel of these instruments is that they naturally match a smaller, more intimate sound world than that of (for example) the symphony orchestra.

Though there was a considerable variety of nineteenth-century slide trombone designs, a broad summary is possible. In the 1830s, a trombone of strikingly large proportions was produced by Sattler in Leipzig. This instrument, which influenced other makers in German-speaking countries, was designed in response to a perceived need for a tenor–bass instrument. The larger instrument became popular in Germany where it was used particularly in military bands, but did not entirely displace narrower-bore instruments. In France, England and some other countries, instruments continued to have relatively narrow bores and small bells. Indeed, instruments made by such firms as Besson, Distin, Higham, Hawkes and Boosey (the last two later amalgamated as Boosey & Hawkes) displayed the proportions that became known as the 'peashooter'. Such instruments prevailed until after the middle of the twentieth century in British orchestras and military and brass bands. Outside Germany, the trend towards larger-bore instruments developed further in the USA. Quite early in the twentieth century, C. G. Conn's catalogues show an intention simultaneously to serve several different needs and tastes. Thus there was a 'German Model', an 'Italian Model' and eventually a 'Symphony Model'.

Medium-bore tenor and bass trombones were used in jazz and dance bands in the 1930s and 40s on both sides of the Atlantic. 'Medium bore', 'wide bore' and 'narrow bore' were terms used in instrument makers' catalogues, especially those of American manufacturers. Wide-bore instruments were used in American orchestras by the 1940s. These American models started to be introduced into European orchestras in the very early 1950s. A feature of the large-bore instrument often cited by professional trombone players is that it provides a fairly consistent timbre across the entire pitch range and at all dynamic levels. This is less true of narrow-bore instruments, which tend to produce a harder, more brassy sound at high dynamic levels.

The members of orthodox British competitive brass bands are worth mentioning as a special case, because here the loyalty to traditional narrow-bore instruments lasted somewhat longer. Until the mid-1960s, trombonists in British brass and Salvation Army bands played on narrow-bore instruments, though from the late 1950s some British-made medium-bore instruments with exaggerated bell flares (such as the Besson Stratford and the new Boosey & Hawkes Imperial models) gained some popularity. At this time, all bands of this type played at a pitch standard equal to A = 452.5, almost a semitone higher than the standard A = 440. In 1965, Boosey & Hawkes and the Salvation Army's musical instrument making factory colluded in a decision to abandon the manufacture of sharp-pitch instruments. Attempts to modify the old sharp-pitch instruments by adding further lengths to the tuning slides proved unsuccessful. Soon the *British Bandsman*, the primary brass band periodical, was carrying advertisements from Barratts of Manchester, an agent for the Conn company, bringing to the attention of players the opportunity to move not only to a lower pitch, but also to a wider-bore instrument. (Ill. 9) These seductive advertisements were successful not just for the Conn company, but also for other American and some Japanese makers. Thus, the last large-scale usage of the narrow-bore trombone died quickly and without ceremony, another casualty being the British traditional bass trombone in G, which was all but standard in brass bands up to that time.

Slide and bell stays

The function of stays is to stabilize the tube lengths and provide a means by which the player can hold the instrument. The stays on early instruments were flat with hinged, often detachable, clasps that gripped the tube lengths. These stays, and particularly the clasps, frequently had elaborate decorations. Round stays were introduced in the seventeenth century. The slide stays at this time were often telescopic rather than rigid, so that they could expand and facilitate an easy slide action. A further elaboration required on older bass trombones was the 'handle' or 'lever'. This device, fitted to the movable outer slide stay, gave access to the distant positions which were out of reach for all but a very long-armed player. It was first illustrated by Praetorius in 1620, but it continued to be a feature of bass trombones prior to the wholesale adoption of thumb valve instruments in the later twentieth century. The configuration of slide stays affects the way the trombone is held in the playing position. Nineteenth-century trombone method books show players to be using a grip that is more or less the same as the standard modern grip, but renaissance and baroque images reveal more variety.[12]

Illustration 9. Advertisement from the *British Bandsman* (November 1964), exhorting players to consider changing to wider-bore instruments as they moved from a pitch of A=452.5 to A=440. (With thanks to Arnold Myers).

Mutes

Mutes are placed into or over the bell of the instrument to change the timbre of the sound. The most basic form of muting is the hand-over-the-bell, which may well have been the first muting technique employed by jazz players. Early trumpet mutes had the additional consequence of altering the pitch of an instrument. This is not the case with modern trombone mutes, but it may have occurred in the muting of pre-classical instruments. The change in timbre occurs because the mute reduces the radiating area at the bell end of the instrument where the air escapes, causing higher harmonics to dominate the sound. Muting also diminishes volume, but from the musical point of view the function of mutes is less to do with subduing volume than with the alteration of timbre – no mute alters the volume without altering timbre. There is some evidence that trombone muting was practised in the baroque period and then became obsolete until the nineteenth century. Different shapes or designs of mute produce different timbres, and in the twentieth century composers became increasingly specific when designating the use of mutes in brass instrument lines.

A selection of mute designs is shown in Illustration 10. They can be broadly categorised in two groups:[13] *passive* mutes such as the straight mute and the cup mute, which are inserted into the bell and condition the sound when the instrument is played in the normal way; and *active* mutes, which require the player to adopt a particular playing technique when using them. Into the latter category one can put the Harmon or 'wow-wow' mute, which works by the player covering and uncovering the central aperture with the hand; and the plunger mute, which is manipulated over the bell, often as the player inflects notes with growls or flutter-tonguing. Some players, such as 'Tricky Sam' Nanton, a member of Duke Ellington's band in the 1930s, developed a technique for using two mutes simultaneously: a straight trumpet mute inserted deep into the bell, over which he manipulated a trombone plunger mute.

Little is known about muting on trombones before the nineteenth century. An instruction in the score of Monteverdi's *Orfeo* (1607) says that if trumpets are to be

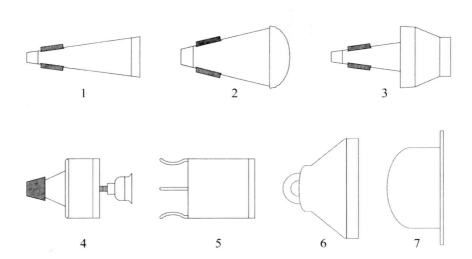

Illustration 10. Some trombone mutes
1 Straight fibre mute – secured to the inside of the bell by corks
2 Straight metal mute, similar to the fibre mute apart from its material
3 Cup mute
4 Harmon or 'wow-wow' mute – the effect is produced by the player covering and uncovering
   the protruding section
5 Bucket mute – clips onto the bell of the instrument
6 Plunger – originally, literally a sink plunger
7 High hat mute – favoured by dance band brass players

muted in the toccata, the parts need to be transposed up a tone. An illustration in Mersenne's *Harmonie universelle* shows a mute to be part of the trumpeter's equipment. Though its details are difficult to make out, the mute shown by Mersenne appears to be made of wood and is hollow. The fact that Mersenne shows the mute with the trumpet and not the trombone may suggest that only trumpeters used such devices at this time (at least as far as he knew). It seems likely that trumpet muting was not free of symbolic associations. The records of Masonic funerals from the late sixteenth century – telling as they do of ritual and ceremony – contain references to trumpeters playing both 'open' and 'closed' or 'covered'.[14]

Dietrich Buxtehude called for muted trombones in a number of works. His *Castrum doloris* (1705), the text of which survives though the music is now lost, contains the direction 'Die Posaunen und Trompeten mit Sourdinen / auch übrige Instrumenta allesampt gedämpffet' ('The trombones and trumpets with mutes, also all the other instruments muted'). He also calls for them in *Auf! Stimmt die Saiten* (1672), and in the 'Amen' of *Ihr lieben Christen freut euch nun* (1680?). Keith Polk suggests a yet earlier case of a slide instrument being muted. It is found in a Frankfurt document dated 1467, which gives a description of a festival in which instrumentalists and singers performed together. The writer refers to 'einer gedempten drompten'. Polk properly points out that in this context *drompten* should be taken to mean a slide trumpet; but it is more open to question whether *gedempten* – literally 'dampened' – should be taken to mean that a mute was used, though alternative explanations do not spring easily to mind.[15]

There is no evidence that trombone muting was practised as an unwritten convention in art music before the nineteenth century, and it seems unlikely that such a practice could have been common without some trace of it surviving. Similarly, the use of muted trombones in orchestral music is rare before the late nineteenth century. A passage in Wagner's *Götterdämmerung* (1876) may be the earliest example of a mute specification for trombone in orchestras. However, according to Rimsky-Korsakov, who may have been writing as early as 1872, 'mutes are applied indiscriminatingly to all brass instruments'.[16] An entry in Berlioz's *La Mort d'Orphée* (1827) has a uniform marking for all the brass 'mettez la sourdine', followed by 'sans sourdines' several bars later, but one wonders whether this really means what it appears to mean, for Berlioz says nothing about trombone mutes in his *Treatise on Instrumentation*. Indeed Richard Strauss, in his 1904–5 edition of that work, noted, 'Trombone mutes have been introduced recently with success. They are similar to the mutes of horns and are – similarly to the trumpet mutes – easy to handle. In forte they give the trombones a rattling sound, in pp a tremendously gruesome, fantastic and gloomy one.'[17]

Interesting evidence also comes from inventions patented in the nineteenth century. For example, in August 1887, L. Stradling applied for patent protection for his complex brass instrument mute (GB 1887: 14,401). This device was inserted into the bell, and the wide end was fitted with aerated rotatable plates, which could be adjusted to achieve the desired timbre. Stradling's invention appears to be the first British mute patent, but it was an application for an improvement rather than an entirely new device. It must surely have been the case that players were using mutes earlier in the nineteenth century, especially in popular music. Somewhat surprisingly however, it appears that they were not commonly used in brass band music. In a fairly wide scrutiny of surviving nineteenth-century brass band music before about 1870, I have found few muted passages, even though these types of repertoire often contain novelty pieces in which the use of mutes would have been especially appropriate.

By the early twentieth century the practice of muting was commonplace. Twentieth-century art music composers have used mutes extensively, but it is to jazz and other forms of popular idiom that credit should be given for the development of mutes and the playing techniques associated with them. The question of the introduction of muting is addressed further in later chapters.

Alto, soprano and bass trombones

The alto trombone was in use in the seventeenth century and perhaps earlier, but there are no surviving sixteenth-century examples, nor is there incontrovertible documentary evidence for the existence of the instrument before the seventeenth century. Praetorius shows an alto trombone which he actually calls an 'alto or discant', but says it sounds less well in the higher register than a tenor instrument played by a player with a good embouchure. In the eighteenth century the alto instrument was used for the upper voice in the trombone section, but there is scope to question whether this practice was as standard or frequent as is assumed today. The instrument has never been entirely out of use, but it had a revival in the second half of the twentieth century when tenor trombone players, now playing large-bored instruments, used the alto trombone to get a lighter sound for music of the classical period. Many players also found these instruments to be easier and 'safer' to play in the high register. Alto instruments are most frequently pitched in E flat or D.[18]

Soprano (or discant) trombones are much less important in the history of the trombone than other sizes of the instrument. The earliest surviving soprano trombone is believed to be the example made by Christian Kofahl, which is dated 1677.[19] Three of J. S. Bach's cantatas have soprano trombone parts, but there is little evidence of the instrument being widely used. This may be because of the extent to which the cornett became established as the soprano voice in ensemble with trombones. One of the few domains in which they have been used regularly and continuously is Moravian music (see Chapter 11). Trombone ensembles in Moravian communities in the USA have always used a discant trombone, usually in B flat an octave above the tenor trombone, for the top line of trombone choirs, a tradition that has continued to modern times; several instrument collections hold soprano trombones made in the nineteenth century.

Just one bass trombone from the sixteenth century survives: that made by Pierre Colbert of Reims, which is dated 1593 (now in the Gemeentemuseum in The Hague, MUZ-1952x0159). In the second volume of *Syntagma musicum* Praetorius shows three bass instruments pitched a fourth, a fifth and an octave below the tenor, which at that time was pitched in A. Praetorius mentioned that the lowest instruments had a wider bore size than the tenor, and claimed that, at the time of his writing, the contrabass trombone or *Octav-Posaune* had been in use for many years in chapels. However, the idea that the contrabass trombone was indeed used in the sixteenth century rests on very slim evidence. The town records of Dresden mention one that was kept as a rarity. Similarly, the Nuremberg documents contain a reference to a short, double-slide trombone (probably a contrabass) that was provided by Anton Schnitzer and apparently promptly returned because it was unsatisfactory.[20] In modern times, Praetorius's representation of and references to a contrabass instrument have been invoked to justify the doubling of the lowest part at an octave, in music that contains several trombones. For example, a processional written by Alessandro Striggio for the famous Bavarian wedding of 1568 could imply such a practice. Such experiments, however, have done little to enhance the idea that the instrument was widely used in the sixteenth century.

The most popular sizes of bass instrument even into the twentieth century were those in F and G. The F instrument was used in central European and German bands until the end of the nineteenth century. The G trombone was ubiquitous, but was largely confined to British orchestras, brass bands and military bands from the second decade of the nineteenth century to the mid-twentieth century. Though some British professional players were faithful to the species even into the early 1960s, by the 1950s it had largely given way to the several denominations of B flat instruments with added thumb valves which lower the pitch by a fourth or a fifth.[21]

The thumb valve (called the trigger or plug in some countries) was first introduced by Christian Friedrich Sattler in Leipzig in 1839. He applied it to a wide-bore instrument. Sattler called his invention a 'Quartventil' (fourth down valve). This provided an instrument that could traverse a wide tessitura from pedal notes to high tenor pitches without gaps in the lower register. It was this instrument and this function, rather than a replacement for the bass trombone in F, that Sattler aimed to provide. By the late twentieth century the thumb-valve B flat and F instrument became the most commonly used. These pitches are made as bass instruments and as tenor-bass instruments, the two being distinguished by the wider bore and bell size of the former. Bass trombones have also been built with two valves – F and D, or F and E flat – to afford yet deeper pitch possibilities for passages in the canonical repertoire where this is required. More is said about trombones with one or more valves in Chapter 9.

Chapter 2

Trombone technique

In the second half of the twentieth century, radical new ways of playing the trombone were introduced. Leaving aside John Cage's *Solo for Sliding Trombone* (1957–8), Luciano Berio's *Sequenza V* (1966) for solo trombone may be the most iconoclastic work written for the instrument up to that time. It is not simply that it was technically challenging, but also that it called for entirely new techniques, some of which stood in apparent contradiction to traditional notions of how the instrument should be played. Berio's reconfiguring of the trombone idiom brought together and developed some existing approaches – for example, it is easy to recognize some elements as being drawn from the idiosyncratic techniques of jazz trombonists; but *Sequenza V*, probably because it was such a coherent work, seemed to usher in a new type of writing for the instrument. It brought into sharp focus the full realization that the traditional orthodoxies of trombone technique were to be observed only by those composers who wished to do so, for from that time the sound palette of the instrument was decisively expanded, as was its expressive capacity. The so-called 'advanced techniques' of the post-war avant garde gained a new legitimacy that was to be developed in diverse ways. In contradiction of traditional practice, for instance, Vinko Globokar's *Res/As/Ex/Ins-pirer* (1973) required notes to be sounded through inhalation as well as blowing (Berio had called for a similar technique). The writing of multiphonics in several trombone solos posed the instrument as having a harmonic rather than just a melodic idiom. Added to this there have been radical incursions into the instrument's conventional physical configuration. For example, James Fulkerson's *Force Fields and Spaces* (1980–1) requires the substitution of the trombone mouthpiece for a saxophone mouthpiece.

Advanced techniques are dealt with specifically in Chapter 14, as are the works of a number of the composers mentioned above, and throughout this book more general themes concerning performance technique and practice are explored, but it is worth considering at this stage what the terms of reference and parameters of trombone technique actually are and what they have been at various points in history, for radicalism can only be measured against the common practices of a prevailing era. Advanced techniques, along with the techniques used by period instrumentalists and jazz musicians, are implicitly gauged against reference points in an orthodox performance tradition. For example, the jazz musician Miff Mole has been seen as the first jazz trombone player to have 'fully mastered the instrument'.[1] Evidently there is some cultural baggage here, but in fairness the writer's meaning is neither unclear nor unreasonable. He makes a point that is easy to grasp and is probably true: Mole's technique was sophisticated. Like other great jazz players he appeared to be limited only by the wealth of his ideas rather than his technical facility, and he certainly displayed unprecedented technical breadth. However, there is no sure evidence that earlier New Orleans jazz trombonists played as they did because their techniques were limited; all the evidence points to the fact that their approach to playing was moulded by the mode of expression that they had made for themselves.

The language of prevailing convention is always used to describe and demarcate the unorthodox, the unknown and the largely supposed, and this phenomenon applies strongly to our understanding of performance history. The temptation to use the values of our own time in respect of sound, articulation and style when we imagine performances of renaissance music is especially compelling. In this respect, our understanding of the trombone labours under the same challenges and afflictions as does any other subject of historical investigation. But as far as trombone technique is concerned, the reference point for what I have already termed 'orthodox technique' is the 'conservatoire tradition'. The development of this tradition is discussed in Chapter 7, but it has a number of key ingredients that are worth enumerating here. In the first place, it is based on a set of values that probably did not exist and was not codified until the nineteenth century, when didactic treatises started to be produced in abundance as a consequence of new processes in musical education. There are earlier theoretical works that deal with the trombone, but none provide systematic advice on how to learn to play the instrument. To put it somewhat differently, these earlier works provide a reflection on the way the instrument is played, rather than a programmatic system for learning. Secondly, all these didactic works are based on the legacy of a particular tonal era, in which the chromatic range of the instrument is used to exploit the major/minor key system and its attendant (largely Romantic) formal structures – indeed, most didactic treatises teach the rudiments of music in parallel with playing technique, and scales and arpeggios are usually unveiled early in the didactic method. Thirdly, and for understandable reasons, as far as repertoire is concerned, the conservatoire tradition has always favoured the prevailing canon. Oddly, this does not mean that it has always been exclusively biased towards elite art music, because military music, opera and the diverse, largely unclassifiable works that make up the trombone solo repertoire are all reflected in didactic methods. Fourthly, and perhaps most importantly, the conservatoire tradition is underpinned by a common assumption that there is a single *correct* way of playing. Until very recent times, the conservatoire tradition eschewed radicalism in favour of prevailing and largely conservative values, and very few conservatoires taught popular styles. This does not mean that the conservatoire tradition has been stagnant; indeed, the opposite is true. Trombone style and performance technique have developed in response to repertoire and other aesthetic factors. The most recent cultural force, globalization, has not undermined the conservatoire tradition; rather, it has probably reinforced it. But it is worth stressing that, as jazz trombonists achieve easy musical coherence without always observing such orthodoxies, it is possible that modern conventions provide fewer clues than we sometimes assume about how trombones were played in the distant past.

All this is but a preface to a chapter in which I describe some basics about how trombone players make their instrument work. My point of reference is indeed derived from the conservatoire tradition, but it is a point of reference that I touch upon rather than cling to. In subsequent chapters, I explore the possibility that performance techniques have always been multifaceted and determined by idiosyncratic geographical, historical and stylistic determinants.

Producing sound

The area of the player's lips upon which the mouthpiece rests – the part that joins the player to the instrument – is called the embouchure. The embouchure is not a precise part of the human anatomy because different players have distinctly different embouchures. Since the nineteenth century, tuition manuals have advocated an optimum position for the embouchure – usually in the centre of the lips, with the rim of the mouthpiece covering the upper and lower lips in about equal proportion. But a player's embouchure is idiosyncratic and personal; some fine players have had

Illustration 11. Embouchures and playing postures: 11a Antoine Dieppo, *Méthode complète pour le trombone* (1837); 11b right and wrong ways to play, from a Couesnon catalogue, c. 1900; 11c Tommy Dorsey; 11d the jazz trombonist 'Big Chief' Russell Moore.

highly unorthodox embouchures. Similarly, the angle at which the instrument is held has an effect on the embouchure position. Here too there is abundant advice about the optimum position, but many excellent players have had unconventional ways of holding the instrument against the lips. (Ill. 11)

Sound is produced when the player's lips, formed into an embouchure, vibrate in the mouthpiece so as to excite an air pressure wave inside the sounding length of the instrument. When the trombone slide is in a fixed position – say, fully closed – the player can produce the series of partials known as the harmonic series simply by adjusting the embouchure and diaphragm. This feature – the capacity to play a harmonic series on a fixed length of tubing – is common to all properly formed brass instruments, including natural trumpets and horns. The pitch of the series depends on the length of tubing that is being blown through. For example, a sounding length of 9 ft will produce the partials of the B flat harmonic series (the nominal pitch of modern tenor trombones); a sounding length of 7 ft will produce an E flat harmonic series (the nominal pitch of most modern alto trombones). The lowest note of any harmonic series (H1) is the *fundamental*. The fundamentals that can, in practice, be obtained on trombones are called *pedal notes*. There are no traces of pedal notes in written repertoire before the nineteenth century, but the pedal A (A_I – the fundamental of the highest harmonic series on early tenor trombones) is shown in illustrations of trombone slide positions in Daniel Speer's *Grund-richtiger . . . Unterricht der musicalischen Kunst* (1697) and Joseph F. B. C. Majer's *Museum musicum* (1732).

The trombone slide provides a means of changing the sounding length that a player blows through. Extending the slide by about 10–12 cm (the exact distance between slide shifts varies from instrument to instrument) increases the overall length of tubing sufficiently to obtain a harmonic series a semitone lower than the one above it. The trombone slide is long enough for a player to obtain seven adjacent harmonic series, each a semitone apart. The point at which the slide has to be placed to obtain any one of these series is called a 'position' (the word 'shift' is also used). The slide is also used to fine-tune the intonation of individual notes. Fine-tuning can also be achieved when a player adjusts the embouchure in a process known as 'lipping'.

Slide positions and pitch

When the slide of a modern tenor trombone in B flat is fully withdrawn, it is said to be in its 'closed' or 'first' position, and produces a B flat harmonic series. With the slide extended by about 10–12 cm to the second position, an A harmonic series can be played. A further 10–12-cm extension to the third position facilitates an A flat harmonic series, and so on. When the slide is at its most extended position – the seventh position – the instrument is long enough to provide the E harmonic series. It can be seen from Example 2.1 that several notes appear in the harmonic series of more than one position. Teaching methods written since the early nineteenth century state or imply that the notes of scales should mainly be played on what may be called 'primary' positions. The primary positions are almost always those nearest the mouthpiece; positions for the same note that are further down the slide are called 'alternative' positions.[2] But proficient players call on the full range of positions

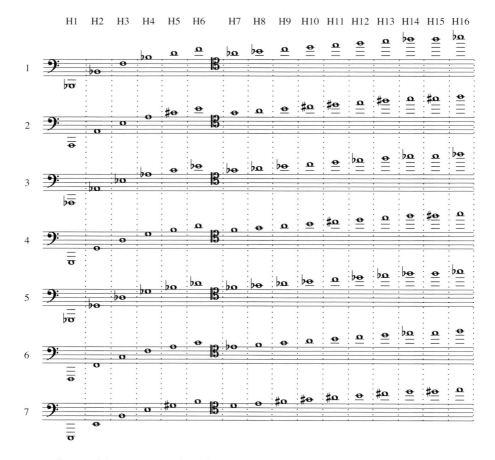

Example 2.1. Slide positions on the B flat trombone. The vertical axis on the left shows slide positions, the horizontal axis on top the partials of the harmonic series. The lower Hɪ partials would be too low for a tenor trombone, and the highest partials would be out of the range of all but the very finest high-note players. It is important to stress that not all partials of a series are in tune with the slide in a static position. Players adjust the slide to obtain good intonation. The positions given for extremely high notes are particularly approximate.

(primary and alternative) to achieve smooth phrasing or to play particularly rapid figurations. Important in this respect is the playing of slurs. A player can slur across different notes in a variety of ways. For example, a slur across two adjacent notes on the same harmonic series is clean and instantaneous; the player senses a slight break as one note gives way to another. Slurs across some other pairs of notes are achieved by moving the slide quickly and effecting a light articulation, a nuance which players call 'soft-tonguing'. Without the soft articulation and with a slide movement that is too slow, the effect would be that of a portamento or even a glissando. Gunther Schuller has named Jack Teagarden as one of the first players to use alternative positions.[3] It is certainly true that Teagarden chose his positions carefully to achieve smooth phrasing, and this was also the case in the ballad style used by Tommy Dorsey. But this technique is frequently encountered in nineteenth-century method books, and it is hard to believe that it was not used even earlier.

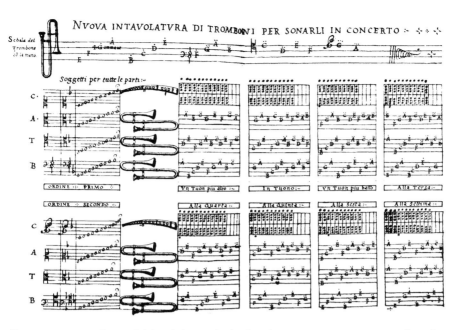

Illustration 12. Virgiliano, *Il dolcimelo* (c. 1600): the first diagrammatic representation of trombone positions, showing four diatonic positions.

Since the start of the nineteenth century, trombone players have learned to play by reference to the seven positions. This system is based on an understanding of the instrument as being essentially chromatic: each note in the chromatic spectrum has an equal status because it occurs in one or other of the major and minor keys. The first source in which trombone technique is explained in such terms is André Braun's *Gamme et méthode pour les trombonnes*, published in Paris between about 1793 and 1797.[4] (Ill. 13) The seven-position system is similarly explained (with indebtedness to Braun) in Volume 3 of Joseph Fröhlich's *Vollständige theoretisch-pracktische Musikschule*, published in Bonn around 1811. All subsequent didactic works describe the trombone in these terms.

Before the later eighteenth century, players recognized not seven but four positions. The evidence for this is found in many practical writings in which trombone playing is explained and illustrated. The earliest such source is Aurelio Virgiliano's unpublished and incomplete manuscript *Il dolcimelo*, which was compiled in northern Italy by about 1600. We know little of Virgiliano,[5] but his manuscript, unfinished though it is, reveals a sound understanding of several instruments of the period and their performance capabilities. He includes a chart showing the notes that were obtainable on each of the four positions. (Ill. 12) If we grant a measure of latitude to Virgiliano's precision as a draughtsman, the diagram makes complete sense. Furthermore, his scheme of four positions is consistent with what is found in later writings, particularly those of Daniel Speer (1697), Joseph Majer (1732) and Johann Philipp Eisel (1738).[6] It therefore follows that the scheme first described by Virgiliano was widely understood and was in place for centuries. It reveals two crucial facts about early trombonists and the way they learned and played before the eighteenth century: first, that for the most commonly used size – the tenor – players recognised four *diatonic* positions; and secondly, that its nominal pitch was A. Most writers signify three positions for the alto and bass instrument. Early players saw chromatic notes as variants of natural notes, which were therefore played at intermediate points between the natural positions. Majer addresses this point explicitly, saying that chromatic notes have to be played by drawing the slide in from the natural position for sharpened notes (*Semitonia majora*) and extending it for flattened notes (*Semitonia minora*). Eisel goes so far as to include two position charts for the bass trombone: one giving the natural notes, the other the chromatic notes.

The same writers also shed light on the pitches of other sizes of trombones. Usually just three positions are indicated for the alto trombone and *Quart* trombone. But Praetorius also shows one intermediate position for the bass trombone. It seems certain that the tenor instrument was pitched in A, even though many surviving early instruments appear to be in B flat by modern standards. Anthony Baines suggested that early German tenor trombones were pitched in A, but in a very sharp A; because these instruments had no tuning slides, it was necessary for them to be 'built with a considerable sharp tolerance'.[7] Without such an accommodation, players would not have been able to adjust to a sharp fixed pitch – for example, the pitch of a sharp organ. So if the instrument was built slightly sharp, the slide would not be entirely drawn in for the first position with normal intonation, but extended a little. This is exactly what early writers meant when they referred to the need for the slide to be extended by two *Querfinger* (the breadth of two fingers), about a quarter-tone, to obtain the true A in first position. Praetorius, in *Syntagma musicum* II (1619), seems to explain this precisely when he says that he knows of 'no better instrument for ascertaining the proper pitch than a trombone, especially those that were made in Nuremberg and are still made there; for if the slide is drawn out the width of two fingers from the end, it produces correctly and exactly, in the true choir pitch, the tenor "a"'.[8] Praetorius provides slide positions only for the *Quart-Posaune* – the bass trombone, pitched a fourth below the tenor – but he does give information about the sizes of instruments that he knew and their nominal pitches:

Alto	(*Alt oder Discant Posaun*)	D or E
Tenor	(*Gemeine rechte Posaun*)	A
Bass	(*Quart-Posaun oder Quint-Posaun*)	E and D
Contrabass	(*Octav-Posaun*)	A (an octave lower than the tenor)

The labelling of the tenor instrument as *Gemeine* (common or ordinary) indicates that this size of instrument had the widest utility, and this indeed seems to have been the case for the entire period of the instrument's existence.

With the exception of Virgiliano, all the evidence concerning pitch is found in German sources, and since there was no international standard we cannot be entirely certain that it applied universally. But German instruments seem to have been used throughout Europe before the eighteenth century. Furthermore, Howard Weiner – a professional trombone player as well as a scholar – has played several surviving instruments, and found that the idea of an instrument pitched in A makes perfect sense if the sharper pitch prevalent in the renaissance and baroque periods is taken into account.[9]

As has already been stated, the earliest writer to indicate that the pitch of tenor instruments had changed, and that players found it convenient to think in terms of seven positions, was André Braun, who was working in Paris in the closing decades of the eighteenth century. Manuscripts bound with the Bibliothèque Nationale copy of Louis-Joseph Francoeur's *Diapason général de tous les instruments à vent* (1772) contain a chart showing trombone positions. This chart unambiguously shows the nominal pitch for both the tenor and bass trombones to be B flat. Francoeur acknowledges Braun and two other figures at the Paris Opéra – the copyist Lefèvre, and a Mr Louis, who played contrabass and trombone – as his sources for this information.[10] So it appears that the move away from the four-position system can be traced back to the last quarter of the eighteenth century – but does the shift to a new nominal pitch date from a yet earlier period?

Stewart Carter has examined four strands of evidence relevant to the pitch of early trombones: surviving instruments, didactic and theoretical sources, evidence about pitch standards, and repertoire that includes labelled trombone parts.[11] The last group of sources is in many ways the most interesting and certainly the most important in practical terms. Carter found that the repertoire dating from before the eighteenth century is consistent with tenor trombones having A as their nominal pitch. This seems to continue into the eighteenth century, but a noticeable change occurs a little before 1710. Examining compositions written for the Viennese court that include

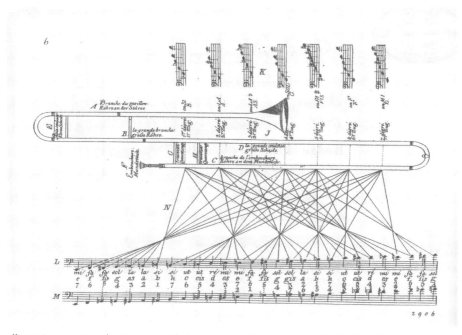

Illustration 13. Braun's *Gamme et méthode pour les trombonnes* (c. 1793–7): the first diagrammatic representation of the trombone with seven chromatic positions; also the first evidence for the slide bow tuning slide.

trombone obbligatos, Carter observed a shift from sharp to flat keys – a change coinciding with and probably caused by a sharpening of the Viennese pitch standard that effectively turned A trombones into B flat trombones without their undergoing any physical adjustment. He makes it clear that there is no reason to assume that Viennese practices were followed swiftly and universally: this of course was a period when the use of the trombone was confined to only a few centres, Vienna being something of an oasis, and a fairly self-contained one at that, as far as trombone playing was concerned. Indeed, he mentions a manuscript discovered at the Moravian Church at Zeist in the Netherlands, probably dating from before 1784, which appears to show loyalty to the older method of four diatonic positions commencing from A. The sources are not entirely consistent here. For example, a shift from A to B flat is not consistent with the information found in the writings of either Majer or Eisel. However, two points should be stressed. First, some of these writings may reflect their writer's indebtedness to earlier sources rather than an accurate observation of current practices (some of Majer's observations are taken directly from Speer, for example). Secondly, change did not occur overnight and practices were not standardized quickly. The *Cammerton/Cornett-ton* dichotomy, which was done away with in Vienna when the pitch standard changed, prevailed in Germany where it provided the somewhat confused point of reference for the remaining *Stadtpfeifer* trombonists.[12] This dichotomy also persisted as late as 1783 in Salzburg, where the surviving parts for the trombones and organ in Mozart's C minor Mass K427 (which were in *Cornett-ton*) are transposed down a whole tone to match the rest of the orchestra, which was obviously in *Cammerton*.[13]

By the final quarter of the eighteenth century there was a wide understanding of the tenor instrument as being in B flat and the alto in E flat, but as I say elsewhere in this book, a question arises about the frequency with which the small alto instrument was actually used. Solo works for trombone in the second half of the century are more often than not in flat keys. The opening of the famous 'Tuba mirum' trombone solo in Mozart's Requiem is little more than a decorated arpeggio on B flat, and this may well be seen as confirmation of the tonal focus that composers recognized for the instrument. This nominal pitch was to be consolidated in the nineteenth century, but tenor trombones in C were also briefly popular in England.

Glissando

The trombone is the only wind instrument that can achieve a true and wide glissando. True glissandos can be achieved only between two notes that share the same partial. Example 2.2 shows the glissandos that can be played from seventh to first position (or vice versa).

A passage for trombones in unison in Schoenberg's *Pelleas und Melisande* (1902–3) may be the first use of glissando in mainstream, orchestral music. (Ex. 2.3) It is marked:

Das „glissando" wird auf der Posaune folgendermaßen ausgeführt: der Ton [shows an octave in notation] wird als Grundton (beziehungsweise Oktave) des 6. Zuges

Example 2.2. The illustration shows the true glissandos that can be played on the B flat trombone. The first of each pair of notes shows the note obtainable in the most extended (seventh) position, and the note to which it is joined shows the note obtained in the closed (first) position above it. True glissandos are possible between any two notes within these intervals and in either direction.

mit den Lippen fixiert und dann das Rohr durch alle Züge zusammengeschoben, doch so, daß die chromatischen, sowie die dazwischenliegenden ¼-, ⅛- und kleinsten Intervalle deutlich hörbar sind, wie beim glissando der Streich-Instrumente.

[The 'glissando' is executed on the trombone in the following manner: the note – the fundamental note (or the octave) in sixth position – is held by the lips and then the slide is pulled inward through all the positions in such a way that the chromatic [intervals], as well as the ¼, ⅛ and the smallest intervals between them, are clearly heard, as in the glissando on string instruments.][14]

Schoenberg obviously thought it necessary to provide such explanatory detail, and at about the same time, musicians as experienced as Widor and Richard Strauss regarded trombone glissando as a recent invention.[15] But it is certain that glissando was used much earlier in popular music, probably as an *ad libitum* effect in show and circus bands. The glissando solo, also known as the slur solo, became something of a genre in the early twentieth century, when the trombone player Henry Fillmore (who composed and published many pieces based on the trombone glissando) claimed to have been inspired by the effects he had to employ as a circus musician. Glissando

Example 2.3. Arnold Schoenberg, *Pelleas und Melisande* (1902–3), bars 283–6
A very early example of glissando being notated in an orchestral score – so early, indeed, that the composer found it necessary to explain the technique in a footnote.

was also used extensively in jazz and was a characteristic of the early style known as 'tailgate'. Tailgate players used glissando not just decoratively but structurally, to emphasize cadence points, and they often enhanced the effect further with timbre changes such as growls.

'Harmonic' or 'inverted' glissandos have been used most prominently in modern music. This effect is obtained when a player moves quickly between a low note in a high position (such as first position) to a high note in an extended position, crossing several harmonic series in the process. A 'false' glissando is illustrated in Example 2.4.

Example 2.4. Alban Berg, *Wozzeck* (1917–22), Act 1, bar 269
This is not an isolated incidence of a composer writing a glissando that is theoretically impossible – the players have to simulate or fake a glissando effect.

Range

Before the twentieth century, works seldom required a tenor trombone to play higher than B flat (H8), but there are many twentieth-century pieces that require much higher notes. Classical and much Romantic orchestral writing has trombone parts that follow the vocal ranges for the alto, tenor and bass voices, and this undoubtedly owes something to the practice of trombones doubling vocal lines in sacred music. Extremely low parts are occasionally allocated to the contrabass trombone, which has existed since at least the seventeenth century, when Praetorius referred to it as the *Octav-Posaun*.

A distinction must be made between the actual range of instruments (the range that players can theoretically achieve), and the tessitura (the range that is most commonly used). The range that is theoretically possible for any size of instrument is dependent on the ability of an individual player; this is especially the case in respect of the upper range. The best evidence for the prevailing tessitura of trombones at any point in history is the repertoire. Only a tiny amount of repertoire with dedicated trombone parts exists from before the seventeenth century, but we know that trombones were ubiquitous in European music-making from the late fifteenth century, and if we assume that dance music and vocal music of the time is indicative of what trombonists played, we can also assume that the outer reaches of the range were not explored. That being said, several references exist to notable sixteenth-century players who were celebrated because they could play fast divisions and in a very high range (see Chapter 4).

Seventeenth-century solo and ensemble repertoire shows relatively few demands beyond the vocal ranges, and the same can be said in respect of the eighteenth century – even though the idiom of the instrument was otherwise changing. Wider extremities were explored in the nineteenth century. For example, Berlioz wrote pedal B flats for trombones in *Grande symphonie funèbre et triomphale* (1840). But generalizations about range in this period are problematic, because the ranges given in didactic treatises are at variance with what is known about playing standards. For example, notes kept with an autograph copy of symphonies by the English composer Samuel Wesley, probably written around 1802, show the effective ranges for the alto, tenor and bass instruments as being restricted to little more than an octave and a half,[16] and various commentators such as Berlioz, remarking upon the quality of trombone playing in the nineteenth century, testify to the variability of standards (see Chapter 8).

In the twentieth century, orchestral composers began to be much more ambitious in their writing for trombones, and jazz trombonists also led the way in developing techniques for playing very high notes accurately. A contributory factor in the development of higher-register playing among orchestral players came from the convention of players performing alto trombone parts, either from necessity or for convenience, on tenor trombones. In recent years, conductors as well as players have shown a preference for the alto trombone in appropriate contexts, for its sonic qualities rather than the assistance it affords for accurate playing.

Modern players are taught to achieve competence in the high register by using the diaphragm to increase the air pressure in support of the embouchure, but earlier players may have used somewhat different techniques. 'To obtain the high notes', the great nineteenth-century Parisian virtuoso Antoine Dieppo advised, the player should 'draw the lips a little closer together . . . [and p]ress the mouthpiece more strongly against the mouth.'[17] Similarly, in his *Méthode générale d'enseignement* (c. 1874), Boscher states: 'The higher one wishes to go, the more he is required to press the mouthpiece against the upper lip and to narrow the aperture between the lips.'[18] But later nineteenth-century writers such as Tilliard and Delisse are specific in cautioning against using too much lip pressure, and stress the importance of mastering the technique of abdominal breathing.[19]

Articulations

Notes are usually articulated with the tongue. A wide range of nuances is possible – many more, perhaps, than are in common use. The usual method of articulating notes that are not in very rapid succession is single-tonguing, and players employ levels of intensity of tonguing appropriate to the music that is being performed. Good players can play very rapid passages by single-tonguing, but techniques known as double-tonguing and triple-tonguing are also used routinely. These techniques are not new; double-tongued articulations were described in some detail by the cornett player and theorist Girolamo Dalla Casa in the preface to his manual on divisions, *Il vero modo di diminuir* (1584). The technique he described is close to that which would be employed on a trombone. The three species of tonguing require the production of notes through the articulation of syllables similar to da, da, da (single), tu-cu, tu-cu (double), and tu-tu-cu, tu-tu-cu (triple). Double- and triple-tonguing is almost always used to play very fast passages, and the double or triple articulations can be joined to play fast quadruplets and other figures. Dalla Casa saw these articulations as ways of achieving perfection of rhythm in decorative passages, and was at pains to distinguish between the degrees of hardness that were necessary for tasteful playing by adopting subtle variations to the spelling of his syllables (de-re, de-re, de-re and ler-re, ler-re, ler-re). Dalla Casa's advice was aimed at cornett players and others who employed divisions and other ornaments, but his writings, together with other treatises that deal with ornamentation, apply directly to the practices of the best renaissance trombonists.

Similarly helpful is the information found in the earliest didactic literature for the trumpet, but here a measure of caution is needed, because while the idioms of trombonists and trumpeters overlapped somewhat, they were also in many respects distinct. The earliest such work is *Tutta l'arte della trombetta* (1614) by Cesare Bendinelli, a Veronese trumpeter who was leader of the trumpet ensemble of the Duke of Bavaria. Bendinelli claimed to have devised a new set of syllables for military calls, which he outlines in his treatise, but in his Preface he makes it clear that several methods of articulating were used in his time: 'one can not write everything down, since there are diverse [people] who tongue differently'.[20] Relevant information is also found in Girolamo Fantini's *Modo per Imparare a sonare di Tromba* (1638). Like other authors, Fantini provides articulation syllables, but he stresses that the correct way to articulate a note is with 'the pointed tongue since blowing with the breath [alone] does not give a good effect'.[21] (Ill. 14)

Illustration 14. Articulations from Fantini's *Modo per Imparare a sonare di Tromba. . .* (1638). (With thanks to Edward H. Tarr.)

Vibrato

The main techniques for producing vibrato on the trombone are embouchure or lip vibrato and slide vibrato. Slide vibrato is thought of as a product of the jazz era, but as with so many stylistic techniques, one suspects that it may have been employed improvisationally by players in popular idioms somewhat earlier. The extent to which vibrato was used by renaissance players is something of a mystery, but while there is evidence that singers and other instrumentalists employed vibrato from the sixteenth century, it is equally clear that it was used not as a component of a player's basic tone, but rather as an expressive effect.

Trombonists in British brass bands have been steadfastly loyal to embouchure vibrato as part of their basic tone, and Russian and central European orchestral players also favoured vibrato, if recordings are anything to go by. Nineteenth-century method books say little about vibrato, but Gabriel Parès addresses it in his *Méthode complète de trombone à coulisse* (1895): 'to obtain this oscillation of sound . . . [one uses] a slight movement of the right hand: but one must be careful not to misuse this approach, which could become a great flaw'.[22] The misuse of vibrato is a consistent feature of writings on performance at this time. Vibrato was seen as a decoration, a device to employ tastefully for particular sorts of expression, rather than as a permanent constituent of tone colour. Oddly enough, the great American player Arthur Pryor had a habitual vibrato, and even more oddly – given his celebrity – it was seldom imitated. Pryor's detractors referred to his 'nanny goat' tone, and while this description may be unfair, the vibrato can be heard clearly on his recordings.[23]

The origin of slide vibrato is far from clear. By 1920 the French trombonist André Lafosse was reluctantly acknowledging it as a legitimate technique while castigating it as 'vulgar' (see Chapter 7), but in the 1930s, jazz and especially dance band players perfected sophisticated versions of the slide vibrato that were often highly personalized. For example, so-called 'terminal vibrato' – the application of vibrato towards the end of a long note – was one of the characteristics of Jack Teagarden's playing. Ravel specified the use of vibrato in the trombone solo in *L'Enfant et les sortilèges* (1920–5) (see Chapter 14). According to Michel Laplace, Ravel invited the dance band trombonist Léo Arnaud-Vauchant to his house in Montfort-l'Amaury, and asked him to play the solo. Arnaud-Vauchant was similarly asked to play the solo in *Bolero* (1927), which Ravel also wanted played in the dance band style.[24] In the years following the Second World War, French orchestras played with an extremely pronounced vibrato. A good example is captured on the recording of Rimsky-Korsakov's *Sheherazade* made by the Paris Conservatoire Orchestra with Ansermet in June 1948.[25]

Trills and other decorations

Trills can be performed effortlessly on the valve trombone, but they present more of a challenge for slide trombonists. Trill effects are obtained most easily between notes that are separated by a narrow interval (such as a second or third) and are either in the same or an adjacent harmonic series. Trombone trills are most convincing above the first octave and a half of the tenor instrument's range. Berlioz believed trills to be 'practicable on the trombone, but only on the notes of the top octave. They should be avoided on the bass trombone.'[26] The majority of method books and orchestration manuals since the nineteenth century have given attention to the performance of trills, but there are relatively few examples of trills in orchestral music (except by avant-garde composers), if one ignores those found in certain works by Verdi which were written with valve trombones in mind.

The authors of didactic methods – particularly those emanating from France – are similarly concerned with the teaching of decorations. One suspects that the persistence of this theme in French didactic writings owes more to tradition, and to ambition for respectability, than to practical utility. The fact is that the post-classical repertoire for solo trombone in which free decoration is appropriate or even possible is extremely limited. The exception, of course, is jazz, and it is easy to recognize elements in the long-line solo playing of some players – particularly Jack Teagarden – as formulaic decorations (a subject that is dealt with in Chapter 13), but the jazz player who really made trills a feature of his technique was Trummy Young.

The question of embellishment in pre-baroque music is more complex and interesting. Most trombone players in the sixteenth and seventeenth centuries also played instruments other than the trombone. All played in ensembles in which it would have been unthinkable for decoration to be absent: the point at issue was when embellishment should be omitted rather than inserted. There is no evidence that trombone players avoided embellishment, and, as I discuss in Chapter 5, certain sources that contain a stated or implied suitability for trombones are obviously intended to be embellished.[27]

Chapter 3

The origins of the trombone

The trombone evolved from the trumpet. Its immediate precursor was an instrument that has come to be called the renaissance slide trumpet: it had a single telescopic slide that was capable of playing the notes of about four adjacent harmonic series. The next stage was the development of the characteristic double 'U'-shaped slide. This instrument was effectively a trombone, and by the mid-fifteenth century it had most of the fundamental features that we find on modern trombones. People are often surprised that such a sophisticated piece of engineering existed on a musical instrument at such an early date, but the full impact of this instrument is yet more impressive when measured against the limitations of other instruments of that time. It was theoretically possible for every note in semitone steps between the highest and the lowest points of a wide melodic compass to be played. By adjusting the slide and the embouchure, a skilful player could amend the overall pitch of the instrument or adjust the intonation of particular notes. The slide provided a remarkable facility in this regard: as is the case with competent singers, adept and musically gifted trombone players need only to think in tune to be able to play in tune.

The instrument was quickly adopted and integrated into the major cultural centres of Europe. Within a short time, trombone players were among the most celebrated musical practitioners: their skills were prized in the cities, courts and cathedrals of western civilization, and they flourished in the sound world of the Renaissance. Not only did early instruments have a wide dynamic range compared to other instruments of the time, but players had more than one timbre at their disposal. Modern reproductions of early instruments can be blown loudly, so that they sound brassy, like a trumpet in its most declamatory mode, or quietly, so that they blend with other instruments or voices of a soft and restrained tone. A bewilderingly wide range of articulations was available: the instrument could imitate the articulations of most other ensemble instruments. Contemporary sources even suggest that trombonists could articulate in a manner that was sympathetic to the enunciation of words in vocal music. This feature was particularly prized in the sixteenth and seventeenth centuries, and morsels of evidence suggest that it was noticed even earlier.[1]

Of course, the musical practices and conventions of the fifteenth century neither recognized nor required all of the early trombone's theoretical capabilities. We read nothing in early sources that suggests that glissandos or more stylized vocalizations were used, even though they could theoretically have been employed. A more routine piece of modern musical culture that was foreign to renaissance players was chromaticism. The tonal and harmonic framework that underpinned music-making of this era was diatonic. Musicians of the time thought diatonically – though even the term 'diatonic' owes more to our own times than to the Renaissance: trombonists, like other musicians (singers in particular), conceived of tonal relationships in a modal framework, within which consonance was achieved through instinctive or conventional adjustments of pitch, in the process which we now refer to as *musica ficta*. Evidence for such a practice is found in explanations of trombone slide positions that exist from the late sixteenth century (see Chapter 2).

The most absorbing and sometimes puzzling questions about the trombone at this time concern the manner and the contexts in which it was played. Key sources that would cast a really vivid light on the idiom of renaissance players are wanting. No instruments survive from before the second half of the sixteenth century, and only a handful of notated music dated earlier than the seventeenth century is labelled with one of the many words meaning trombone; but neither of these factors should surprise or trouble us. It is true that the absence of instruments from the fifteenth century limits our objective knowledge significantly, but few instruments of any type have survived from this period. The fact that labelled parts for trombones do not exist from the fifteenth century or for much of the sixteenth century is even less surprising. Not only was the convention of labelling unusual until centuries later, but it is virtually certain that early trumpet and trombone players did not play from written music, or learn in a system in which notated music was central. Even if players could read music, they appear not to have depended on this skill to conduct their day-to-day professional business. This factor demonstrates rather than detracts from the accomplishments of early players. Their mode of musicianship was sophisticated and demanding precisely because it belonged to a world in which musical instincts, the skills of improvisation and the ability to memorize from aural stimuli were routine. All evidence shows that musical literacy was less important than it was to become in the later sixteenth century, and that fifteenth-century wind instrumentalists did not require it in the same way as it appears that singers and keyboard players did. The world in which the first trombone players practised their art was driven primarily by imperatives defined by the *function* of the music they performed, and the taste, accuracy and panache with which they performed it. In the Renaissance, the main roles of trombone players were in the performance of dance music, in sacred and secular ritual, and eventually in more intricate forms of small and large ensemble.

Sources and hypotheses

There is sufficient documentary evidence from the sixteenth century to make it clear that the trombone was ubiquitous, and to enable us to chart the patterns of activity with which professional players engaged. It is even possible confidently to make links between the instrument and areas of repertoire – even with some specific works. But before about 1500, in the absence of surviving instruments and a discernible written repertoire that takes us directly and unambiguously to trombone players, the sources are significantly thinner. However, even though we have to construct hypotheses for this period, it would be a mistake to confuse hypothesis with mere speculation. A quantity of source information survives: pictures and other visual representations, documents of diverse kinds, and even some musical texts offering clear signals about how and where trombonists performed. Inevitably, scholars have argued long and hard about how the fragments fit together, but many of the broad features of the story of the early trombone are the subject of wide, if not universal, consensus. So while we must recognize the difference between facts and assumptions in the history of the trombone, it is equally important to acknowledge that all histories worth the name require an imaginative use of sources. After all, the idea that an abundance of sources could allow us literally to create a comprehensive log of past events is too absurd to contemplate.[2]

One further issue is worthy of emphasis. It is tempting to see the earliest chapter of the trombone's history as a period of primitivism. This view is perhaps especially seductive when the scarcity of sources gives rise to so much uncertainty. But to adopt a negative view of the skills of early practitioners is both to do them an injustice and to encourage a historical distortion for which there are no grounds. The instruments and players of this period were part of a well-established and thriving musical culture; there are signs that trombonists were prominent and respected. So when we think about the progress of the trombone's idiom, we should understand it in the terms in which it unfolded, rather than merely from the perspective of the time in which we live. There is every possibility that this first period of the trombone's history is one of the most vibrant. In order for it to be seen in an appropriate context, it is necessary first to consider the world of the trumpet player in the Middle Ages.

Early trumpets

Trumpets existed in the most ancient civilizations, and have been used in many cultures as instruments of declamation and signal. They have also been important as signifiers of power and formal authority by aristocratic courts and religious and civic rulers. For this reason, even by the Middle Ages, trumpeters had acquired a distinctive status, and there is abundant evidence that they enjoyed special privileges and favours. They were also emissaries who were close to the centres of power and were entrusted with messages of the highest import. From an early date, the education of trumpeters was based on apprenticeship, and the art of trumpeting was a closely guarded and privileged secret. Privileges and their protection were eventually formalized through the creation of guilds, fraternities and licensing systems. These devices existed ostensibly to protect standards, but they also preserved the status and benefits of trumpeting within a relatively small number of dynasties in each musical centre.

Medieval trumpets were instruments with fixed sounding lengths, and before about 1300 most were made in a straight shape which could easily be fitted with banners and flags for ceremonials. Such instruments are depicted in contemporary pictures, many of which are symbolic or allegorical, showing angels and cherubs who play in attendance on higher deities. Of course, such portrayals, particularly those with a sacred narrative, are consistent with the actual use of trumpets for the signification of authority. But how accurately do they represent the instruments of the time? There are good grounds for believing that, though often conventional, some are nevertheless based on realistic depiction. Three factors can be offered in support of this claim. In the first place, the instruments often contain details (such as garlands and integral mouthpieces) that are not strictly necessary to convey symbolism alone. Secondly, the instruments are often held in a manner indicative of an entirely practical posture for playing. And thirdly, there is the more obvious point that it would make little sense to produce a symbolic or narrative image that lacked adequate information to make the meaning easily comprehensible. This does not mean, however, that these representations can always be taken at face value, for the iconography of early instruments offers substantial interpretative challenges. This note of caution is necessary, because it will soon become apparent that the reading of early images plays a critical part in our understanding of the early history of the trombone.

Our knowledge of the melodic nature of trumpet calls in the medieval period is extremely limited. Trumpets with a fixed tube length (what we now call 'natural trumpets') could only have been used to sound the notes emanating from that length, for there is no evidence of lipping or other techniques for obtaining non-harmonic tones. But one wonders about the region of the harmonic series that was commonly exploited by early trumpeters. Some have put forward the view that trumpeters in the late thirteenth and early fourteenth centuries used the first four harmonics (H1–H4), the lowest notes on a trumpet irrespective of its nominal pitch. This view has been extrapolated from a reading of *De musica* (c. 1300) by the medieval Parisian theorist Johannes de Grocheio, and it has gained currency with a number of writers.[3] The idea is tenable, but unlikely. Grocheio writes authoritatively and informatively about music in Paris and its environs around the year 1300, but he mentions trumpets only rarely, and says nothing directly about their performance compass. The fact is that the lowest (fundamental) partial of medieval trumpets would have been difficult to produce for purely acoustical reasons.[4] But Edward Tarr has made the interesting observation that depictions of very early trumpets sometimes show large integral mouthpieces which are consistent with the idea that trumpeters played in the lower partials.[5] (Ill. 15)

Further evidence exists for the playing tessitura of trumpets in the late fourteenth century. Here too the sources call for an imaginative interpretation. This evidence

Illustration 15. Lucca della Robbia, *Cantoria* (1431–8), detail (upper left panel) showing a trumpet apparently with a large integral mouthpiece. (Florence, Museo dell'Opera del Duomo.)

concerns lines in polyphonic vocal compositions where trumpet calls appear to be imitated or parodied. Such lines have come to be known as *trumpetum* parts. Prominent among such compositions are *rondeaux* and other songs by Machaut, but such writing is also found in the works of other composers. We cannot say for certain whether these lines genuinely allude to trumpet music; there is little contextual evidence for such a connection. But their apparently formulaic nature is suggestive. However, similar musical passages found a half-century later are often labelled with words such as *tuba* and *trompett*, surely banishing any lingering doubt that the allusion is intended. These and the earlier *trumpetum* lines may have been vocalized, but it is at least equally likely that these parts were played on a trumpet of some sort. An early fifteenth-century example is *Tuba gallicalis* (Gallic trumpet), the title of which, together with the restriction to harmonic series notes, leaves little to the imagination.[6] Taken together, such parts provide a loose basis for an important deduction. The play is upon the lower partials of the harmonic series – usually between H2 and H6. Thus it is possible to characterize the early trumpet as an instrument which was heard most often in its lower register. This in turn opens the possibility that the development from such trumpets to a slide instrument was a transition between two tenor rather than treble instruments.

From the fourteenth century, both the geometry and scale of trumpets begin to change, in, it would seem, a fairly uniform way. Keith Polk,[7] on the basis of a comparison of a wide range of mainly German iconographical sources, has dated the main developments as follows. Up to about 1375, trumpets continued to be made in the form of a single straight span. This basic design was ubiquitous, and there seems to be little doubt that it had been prevalent for several centuries. From about 1375, depictions of trumpets often show them to be formed into an 'S' shape. The technology for bending tubes was already in place at that time,[8] even though there is some doubt about how long such techniques had been refined.[9]

Why did the change occur, and why is it important? One reason is that a trumpet with an 'S'-shaped configuration would have been easier to hold than a straight instrument, particularly if a player was performing more complex musical tasks. It is worth considering that this development may reflect a significant step in the musical status of players. The new design did not lead to a more decorative instrument, one that ensured a more striking presence in ceremonials; the fact that the straight trumpet prevailed as the instrument of high ceremony, even after the 'S'-shaped instrument was introduced, suggests the opposite. It seems that the change in design was aimed at a practical improvement, one that almost certainly led to, or was caused by, an enhanced musical utility for the trumpet. So it is likely that this development came at the behest of players, rather than patrons or craftsmen producing instruments in isolation from players.

The second change came around 1400, when the 'S'-shaped trumpet was developed further by the introduction of a new type of instrument, in which the tube was folded twice to provide the raw prototype for the natural 'field trumpets' that were to be widely used in future centuries. It is important to emphasize again that while these three different designs – the straight, the 'S'-shaped and the folded trumpet – appeared sequentially, they coexisted by the mid-fifteenth century, and there were variants of each design. But for our purpose here, the folded and the 'S'-

shaped instruments are most important. It was to these types of instrument that a single telescopic slide was added early in the fifteenth century, to provide what has retrospectively been called the 'slide trumpet': the embryonic trombone. It has to be said that there is no conclusive evidence to link the slide trumpet with the trombone, but the circumstantial evidence is overwhelming.

The significance of the trumpet in the development of the trombone is not merely a matter of a transition resulting in the coexistence of one traditional and one essentially new species of trumpet. What happened at this time also required a change in attitudes among players, so that one group acquired new skills: skills which must have seemed distinctly quirky at the time. We should keep in mind two issues concerning this transition. The first is that, while the trombone emerged as a variant of the trumpet, the traditional instrument and its musical character continued without interruption, and trumpeters retained their professional processes and their social status. This was precisely because the traditional role of the trumpet as signifier made it more than a musical instrument. But the new slide instrument provided the Renaissance with a brass sonority that was not wedded to or inhibited by the heraldic tradition in which it had originated: its function was primarily musical rather than declamatory. Secondly, because trumpets were ubiquitous in the main cultural centres of Europe, there were existing locations for the new slide instruments to be taught and learned almost as soon as they were invented. This is important, because it gives some clues about how the first generation of Europe's slide instrument players emerged. Trombonists and trumpeters soon came to be seen as distinct groups. For example, by the middle of the fifteenth century, trombonists or 'sackbut' players received different levels of pay, and were cited separately in administrative documents. We do not know when exactly the transition took place – certainly by the middle decades of the fifteenth century – but when it did, it was swift and permanent.

The renaissance slide trumpet

The adjective 'renaissance' is needed here, because the nomenclature 'slide trumpet' is used at least three times in other contexts to denote entirely different instruments in later periods.[10] The renaissance instrument has been the subject of controversy. The idea of a slide trumpet is based on the assumption that, early in the fifteenth century, a single, movable, telescopic slide was placed at a point between the mouthpiece receiver and the rest of the sounding length of a folded or 'S'-shaped trumpet. Such a slide would have allowed a player to adjust the sounding length, so as to provide access on a single instrument to the partials of more than one harmonic series. In fact, such a slide, if it were to be long enough to take advantage of the full reach of a man's arm, would provide between three and four adjacent harmonic series, each successive series being separated by a semitone.

No single piece of evidence provides conclusive proof of the existence of the slide trumpet. Not only are there no surviving instruments, neither are there contemporary descriptions of it. The evidence for its existence is found largely in iconographical sources, but the evidential value of these images rests on whether or not the viewer believes that the artist was attempting to depict part of the instrument in motion.

16a

16b

16c

Illustration 16. Three details from Geertgen tot St Jans, *The Glorification of Mary* (c. 1490–5). Three different species of trumpet shown in the same painting: 16a straight, 16b folded – perhaps a slide trumpet, 16c a different pattern of folded trumpet. (Boijmans van Beuningen Museum, Rotterdam, Netherlands.)

Nomenclatures – the words that may denote the instrument – are not clear either; at least, not without considerable contextualization, and the term 'slide trumpet' never occurs in contemporary sources before the end of the fifteenth century. But words that denoted musical instruments remain particularly valuable; indeed, they may even provide the most convincing thread. Some, even though their use is not always entirely clear, seem to be applied in order to distinguish between one type of trumpet and another; thus it is important to bring an understanding of fifteenth-century trumpeting to the history of the trombone. What is certain is that in the fifteenth century the trumpet was not a single instrument but a family of instruments. A good illustration of this is found in a work by the Netherlandish painter Geertgen tot Sint Jans, dating from c. 1490–5 and depicting *The Glorification of Mary* (Rotterdam, Boijmans van Beuningen Museum). Here, three quite different trumpets are seen in the hands of angel musicians. (Ill. 16) It was from one offshoot of this family of instruments that the modern trombone emerged.

Debates about the slide trumpet have centred on the interpretation of a body of evidence that has been widely known for some time – no striking new discoveries have emerged in recent years. The most vigorous debate was initiated by Peter Downey,[11] who put forward a well-argued case for the radical and perfectly tenable idea that the slide trumpet never existed: that the evidence is inconclusive, and can be accounted for by a variety of alternatives. Downey's case rested upon a consistently pessimistic reading of the main strands of evidence that had been put forward for the existence of the instrument. Other scholars noted for their work in this field responded by marshalling the positive evidence.[12] Downey's polemic forced the most detailed debate about this subject, but it did not succeed in changing the consensus view. His was an alternative rather than a better reading of the available evidence.

The slide trumpet and the trombone

What is the positive evidence for the slide trumpet, and why is it important to the history of the trombone? The iconographical evidence is based on a number of fifteenth-century representations of trumpeters playing 'S'-shaped or folded instruments in which the players seem to be manipulating a slide. The left hand of the player appears to be consistently static, holding the instrument near the mouthpiece against the lips, while the right hand supports the main body of the instrument. Importantly, a comparison of different pictures suggests that the right hand is not static, but that it is extending or contracting the instrument along a slide. The right hand is not always in the same position: sometimes it is extended, and in other pictures it is nearer the mouthpiece. Some have even read into such depictions the idea that a movable slide contributes to the narrative element of a picture. Anthony Baines, for example, suggests that in an image from the late fifteenth-century *Mittelalterliches Hausbuch* (Ill. 17a), a player is shown pushing a slide out mischievously to frighten a dog.[13] In fact, a more convincing depiction of such an incident occurs in another illustration from the *Hausbuch* (Ill. 17b).[14]

A more interesting and consistent feature of such representations is the context in which the players of such instruments appear. Leaving aside certain allegorical images, the players of these instruments are usually shown with other wind players – particularly double-reed instrument players – forming a loud instrument band of the

(a)

(b)

Illustration 17. *Mittelalterliches Hausbuch* (late 15th century), two details from different pages, both showing trumpets. In *Brass Instruments* (1976), Baines speculated that the player in 17a might be pushing out the slide to tease the dog, but such an incident seems better illustrated by 17b.

alta type – the kind that would play for dances and secular feasts. (Ill. 18) Indeed, so consistent is the content of these representations, and so diverse are their regional origins, that it seems likely that they indicate common practices and conventions. As such, they point not just to the usual musical role of the slide trumpet and the instrumental groups with which it was most closely associated, but also to the characteristic repertoire it was used to perform. It seems that the development of the slide mechanism was in parallel with, and probably prompted by, the development of the wind band. Around 1400 there are many references to types of trumpets being incorporated with wind instruments in ensemble. These references clearly point to the embryonic *alta* band, and are found in Italy, France, the Low Countries and Germany. In French-language sources (for example, those relating to the Burgundian court) the players of this instrument were often designated as minstrel trumpeters; the significance of this designation is explained below.[15]

Illustration 18. Detail of a round dance with *alta* band, attributed to Taddeo Crivelli, from the Bible of Borso d'Este, MSS Lat 422 = V.G. 12 vi, f.280v, Biblioteca Estense, Modena, Italy. (By permission of the Ministero per i Beni e le Attività Culturali, Italy)

Pictures of fifteenth-century dance bands never show the performers to be playing from written music. This is consistent with the widely held view that fifteenth-century dance band players performed without reference to written texts. However, this does not mean that their performances were entirely improvised. There was undoubtedly an element of improvisation, but players rehearsed and performed in the context of a shared understanding of musical conventions and other social and cultural rules that related to their musical duties. Our understanding of dance band repertoire is based on transcriptions and arrangements of dance music that were compiled somewhat later in the century. Most of the written sources are keyboard arrangements that appear to be based on wind instrument music,[16] but one Italian source – the writings of an itinerant Venetian musician known as Zorzi Trombetta (of whom more is said in Chapter 5) – seems to be an attempt by a wind player to write down what was actually played.

The dances played by *alta* bands had features that seem to have been consistent and to have prevailed in both northern and southern musical centres. The dances were based on the polyphonic decoration of a relatively small number of *cantus firmus* melodies derived from popular songs. The melody was played as sustained notes in the tenor, each note synchronizing with stages in the choreography of the dance. A more florid decorative treble line was played on a treble shawm, with a contratenor filling in between the other two lines – much less static than the tenor, but somewhat less florid than the treble.

Neither the *cantus firmus* tenor of such pieces nor a reasonably interesting contratenor line could have been provided by a trumpet with access to just one harmonic series. Certainly the tenors of the most popular *cantus firmus* tunes such as *La Spagna* and *Filles à marrier* would have been inaccessible to a fixed-length instrument, but it also seems unlikely that the contratenor could have been accommodated on such a limited instrument. So what type of instrument was a slide trumpet, and what would its melodic capacity have been?

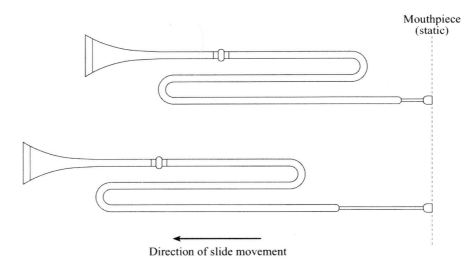

Illustration 19. Drawing of a hypothetical slide trumpet. (With thanks to Murray Campbell.)

To imagine the slide trumpet, one has to visualize (for example) an 'S'-shaped instrument similar to the one depicted in Illustration 19. The left hand grips the instrument at a point slightly beyond the mouthpiece, while the right hand grips another part of the instrument in a manner that enables the player to pull and push the instrument towards and away from him as it glides upon the single telescopic slide. The melodic capability of this instrument would depend on the proportion of the total sounding length of the instrument taken up by the slide section with the slide closed.

This would, in turn, be conditioned by another entirely practical factor: the length of the player's arm. The 'positions'[17] on a single-slide instrument would have been about 120–30 mm apart – twice the distance needed to alter the pitch of a trombone by a semitone. It therefore takes only a minor calculation to deduce that it would require a player of freakish proportions to manipulate the slide beyond the distance necessary to obtain about four adjacent semitones.

Anthony Baines has put forward a hypothesis for how such an instrument would work.[18] As Murray Campbell and Clive Greated have pointed out, it is dangerous to make assumptions about pitch changes on slide instruments purely on the basis of fractional changes to the length of tube, because an increase of the ratio of cylindrical tubing to flare on such an instrument will also have the effect of lowering the instrument's pitch by a factor depending upon the instrument's bore profile.[19] But Baines's hypothesis provides a helpful illustration of how such an instrument might have worked. I deal here with just one of Baines's models: the one based on the idea of an 'S'-shaped trumpet with a single telescopic slide – a type similar to that shown in Illustration 19.

Baines established proportions by taking points of reference from several pictures. He divided the main body of the instrument into three parts and ascribed to each a hypothetical length:

1. Bell section 64 cm
2. Middle section 38 cm
3. Slide section 63 cm (the mouthpiece – with inner slide – fits into this section)

To these measurements he added an extra 25 cm for the two bows, and a further 8 cm for the static area of tube near the mouthpiece where the player's left hand grips the instrument. He also accommodated the need for an 'over-run' of the inner and outer slide with an additional 5-cm portion of tube, but of course, this over-run would not contribute to the overall sounding length of the instrument.

Such an instrument would have a sounding length of about 190 cm, consistent with a nominal pitch (in modern terms) between low F and E. The single slide on such an instrument could be extended by some 50 cm. A 50 cm movable slide length would produce an extension equal to the distance required for the lowering of the overall pitch of the instrument by two tones. Thus the instrument could produce four adjacent harmonic series. This assumes that the instrument was held at the upper end of the slide section, but for reasons of balance it is likelier that it was held more in the middle of the instrument. This would have limited the distance to which the instrument could be extended. But notwithstanding such considerations, if the instrument were in F (for example), it could obtain all or some of the notes in the series of F, E, E flat and D. The slide expansion for such a range could reasonably be handled by a player of average height and proportions.

We do not know what the pitch of these instruments was, neither do we know their exact design or proportions; but taking the iconographical evidence and Baines's entirely sensible extrapolations into account, it seems certain that these instruments were played in the lower range – probably equating to the modern tenor register. Such an instrument could be played using the notes of up to four adjacent harmonic series. It could easily adjust to the intonation of other instruments and obtain notes required by the conventions of *musica ficta*. Furthermore, modern experiments with instruments based on hypotheses such as the one given above have shown that they were entirely practicable. Cumbersome and limited they may seem if compared to trombones, but in their heyday they were played day in and day out by specialists who probably exercised skills the level and manner of which were lost in the sixteenth century.

Nomenclatures

Nomenclatures play an important part in determining the origins of the trombone and its precursors, but some profound and long-lasting mistakes have been made because words in ancient documents have been misinterpreted. A catalogue of errors commenced in the sixteenth century when translators of the Bible made a fundamental mistake in dealing with passages referring to musical instruments, and the repercussions have not entirely subsided in modern times. (A discussion of the biblical text appears later in this chapter.)

Two basic facts need to be kept in mind when dealing with documents that mention brass instruments such as the trumpet. First, nomenclature was not standardized within countries, let alone across the continent, so while particular words may have been used in several places, each could have had a strictly local meaning. Secondly, in the vast majority of cases, words used to denote musical instruments were committed to paper by administrators who knew little or nothing about the subjects that they were describing. For the most part, they merely used words expediently, words they were familiar with, to record concepts that may have been familiar or new to them. Some writers were scribes engaged in what were purely bureaucratic and largely objective tasks; others were the authors of descriptive accounts of contemporary events, whose records were subjective and sometimes even speculative. None of them thought for a moment that, centuries hence, their words would be minutely examined by scholars seeking to understand things that may have lain well beyond the scribes' comprehension and to which they may have attached little significance.

Many words were used before the late fifteenth century to mean trumpet, and some of these same words came to signify what we now understand as the trombone. Writers summoned these words easily and frequently, often with little or no intention of providing an exact description of a particular instrument. Thus, words that derive from the Italian *tromba* (*trompette*, *trombone*, and so on, as well as words such as *drompten* used in the Low Countries), and those that originate in the Latin *busine* (*Posaune*, *bason*, and so on), constitute a perilous basis for making precise judgements about musical instruments unless they are verified by sound and substantial contextual support.

It has long been my view that, of the many terms that could have meant a slide instrument in the fifteenth century, only two can be relied upon with a fair degree of certainty consistently to signify a slide instrument. The first such term is *trompette des ménestrels* (as with all such terms, there are variants of the spelling), which is first found in Burgundian manuscripts in the fifteenth century, but subsequently appears in sources from other regions of continental Europe. The second is the group of words from which the now ubiquitous 'sackbut' is a descendant. This word has Spanish/Portuguese roots, and was used to the exclusion of others in those countries, and in France and England, until the eighteenth century. This group – the sackbut-type words – are the only ones that carry clues about the slide instrument mechanism within their etymological meaning.

The 'sackbut' group (shagbutt, saquabote, *sacabushe*, and so on) are especially important, because from the time they were introduced in the fifteenth century they appear always to have described a brass instrument with a slide. In 1906 Francis Galpin examined an allusion to the 'sackbut' in the Book of Daniel: 'when all the people heard the sound of the cornet, flute, harp, sackbut, psaltery, and all kinds of musick, all the people, the nations and the languages, fell down and worshipped'.[20] He showed that the use of 'sackbut' in this context was based on a faulty translation from the Vulgate edition of the Bible. The Geneva translation (1560) initiated the error, which was perpetuated in the Authorised Version of 1611 and the Revised Version of 1885. A considerable proportion of nineteenth-century brass instrument scholarship suffered from the legacy of this error, which has its root in a chronic misreading of the word *sambuca*, now known to mean a type of Greco-Roman angle harp (*sambukē*).

Galpin's explanation of the origin of 'sackbut' has been widely accepted by etymologists. He identified two elements, both of which have concordances in Spanish, Portuguese and French, but probably with the Spanish at their root. The first element, 'sac', is probably taken from the Spanish *sacar*, meaning to draw, in the sense of pulling. The second, 'bu', is equally probably derived from *bucha*, a corruption of the Latin *boxus*, in both cases meaning a tube or pipe. In the fifteenth century, the Spanish word *sacabuche* meant a 'draw pipe' or pump. Others have offered alternative possibilities,[21] and indeed Galpin put forward alternative explanations, notably one in which the French *saquier* (to pull) and *boter* (to push) are employed; but as he points out, the Spanish etymological strain has a much longer and more convincing contextual history.

The Spanish and other similar French and Portuguese derivations – and many were in use in France, Spain, Portugal and England from the fifteenth century – seem undeniably to imply the physical action of drawing as one does with a pump or indeed a slide.[22] Thus they are fundamentally different from words in the *trombone* and *Posaune* groups, in that they seem not only to denote the instrument, but also to describe the distinctive way it was played.

The term *trompette des ménestrels* does not have the same inherently descriptive quality, but it too is particularly important to the history of the trombone in the fifteenth century. This importance has full weight only when one takes into account the words that are often used alongside it. When the term *trompette des ménestrels* appears, it seems always to denote, even to emphasize, a deliberate distinction: a difference between one type of trumpet and another. Thus instruments and players called 'trumpet' (*trompette, trompetti,* and so on), and particularly *trompettes de guerre* (war trumpets), are distinguished from *trompettes des ménestrels* (minstrels' trumpets). (*Trompette de guerre* did not denote an instrument with an exclusively military function, but more broadly a trumpet of fixed sounding length that was used for court and civic ceremonials.) The distinction also seems to be made into the sixteenth century in Scotland, where the terms 'draucht trumpet' (drawn trumpet) and 'weir trumpet' (war trumpet) are used side by side. Both instruments are mentioned in a description of the marriage celebrations of Mary of Guise and James I of Scotland in 1538, where 'the king ressawit [received] the quen in his palice to the denner quhair [where] there was great mirth schallmes draught trumpattis and weir trumpattis witht playing'.[23]

The earliest reference to a 'ménestrel de trompette' is found in a document dated 1386, but here one is hesitant to afford it too much significance, since it is no more than a passing reference and seems early for a slide trumpet. But Burgundian court records from the second decade of the fifteenth century list a player called Hennequin van Pictre, who is employed to play both the *trompette des ménestrels* and the *trompette de guerre*. From about this time the distinction between the two types of instrument seems to be routine. From 1422 a *trompette des ménestrels* is listed in the retinue of Philip the Good.[24] These players and others like them later in the fifteenth century were employed specifically to play with the shawms in the *alta capella*; indeed, the shawm players were often referred to as 'les ménestrels' or 'les hauts ménestrels'. It goes without saying that this grouping is exactly consistent with the depictions of dance bands in pictures of the period. Furthermore, this differentiation between *trompettes des ménestrels* and other forms of trumpet is consistent throughout the century: it signifies a distinction between both the instruments and their players.

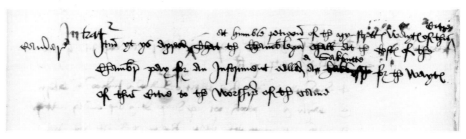

Illustration 20. The first purchase of a trombone for the City of London Waits in 1526. The scribe's unfamiliarity with the word 'sackbutte' may account for the fact that it took two attempts to write it: 'And yt ys agreed [insertion in the same hand: at humble petition of the wayts of this citie] that Mr Chamberleyne shall at the coste of the [city] pay for an instrument called a sackbutte for the wayts of this citie. . .'. GB Lgc R7. f.137. (The Corporation of London Records Office.)

It is important to stress that 'sackbut' and *trompette des ménestrels* are not the only words that meant trombone or slide trumpet in the fifteenth century. In some instances a word like *trombone* or *Posaune* in a fifteenth-century manuscript really means what it appears to mean. For example, Keith Polk has suggested that by 1400 the German *pusain* or *busain* – the antecedent of the modern *Posaune* – was seldom applied to a trumpet, and that by about 1450 it was routinely used to describe a slide instrument.[25] But while the position in the sixteenth century is clearer, in the fifteenth century a considerable degree of caution is required: words like *trombone* and *Posaune* can not be guaranteed to carry a consistently different meaning from words that mean trumpet.

Trombone is an augmentation of the Italian word *tromba* (trumpet). The word, or rather a version of it, first appears in 1439 in the records of the Este court,[26] where a performer called 'trumbonus' is listed among the trumpet players. It would be wrong to conclude too much from this, because nothing suggests that this man played a different instrument from those who are listed alongside his name; many musicians of this time seem to have been given musical nicknames, and this could be such a case. However, the word is found in Florentine documents in 1443[27] and in Sienese documents in 1459. The next interesting citation occurs in 1459, when shawms and a 'trombone' played a *saltarello* in a Florentine festival ('In questo tempo i pifferi e'l trombone / cominciaro a sonare un saltarello').[28] This may be a reference to a trombone, but it could equally have been a trumpet, with or (less likely) without a slide. By this time, 'trombone' is referred to routinely and conspicuously as a constituent of the shawm band. This obviously implies a slide instrument, but there is no ambiguity in a reference in *De inventione et usu musicae* (c. 1487) by the theorist Tinctoris, which does not simply draw the 'trombone' and 'sackbut' words together to convey a common meaning, but also alludes to the continuity of the instrument's function within the dance band: 'However, for the lowest contratenor parts, and often for any contratenor part, to the shawm players one adds brass players who play very harmoniously upon the kind of horn which is called *trompone* in Italy, *sacqueboute* in France.'[29]

The earliest musical source that unambiguously calls for a trombone does not appear until 1539, when music written for one of the famous sixteenth-century Medici weddings (the so-called 1539 Florentine Intermedii) shows parts labelled for *tromboni*.[30] Iconographical and documentary evidence provides clear proof that trombones were in use more than half a century earlier than this, but the Florentine source finally removes all doubt that by that time, and probably some time earlier, *trombone* was the preferred Italian word for the double-slide instrument.

The German *Posaune* is a corruption of *buzine*, a word ascribed in many places to the medieval straight trumpet, and having its origins in Latin (a root that also accounts for the *buccina*). One very early use of the *Posaune* strain has caused much excitement, and has been utilized to support the possibility that *trumpetum* lines and later parts that imitate trumpet calls in untexted fifteenth-century music were actually played by instruments – possibly slide instruments. The passage in question is found in the account of a procession at the Council of Constance in 1415. It focuses on the arrival of the English delegation, which was led by Richard Beauchamp, Earl of Warwick, and also included the Bishops of Salisbury, Bath and Wells, Coventry, Lichfield, Norwich, Hereford and St Davids, as well as the Abbot of Westminster and the Prior of Worcester. The whole English retinue was said to have numbered '800 horse'.[31] It had distinguished itself by its ceremonial at Cologne *en route*, and when it arrived at Constance, seven instrumentalists were in attendance: four shawms and three 'prusenen'.

The main description of the events at Constance is provided by Ulrich von Richental, and this is supplemented by a number of contemporary or near-contemporary sources. Richental's account was written some years later (probably c. 1425), but he is taken to have been an eyewitness and is regarded as reliable. However, his original manuscript no longer exists; it is now known to us through seven copies, none of them identical.[32] Nonetheless, his description of the English delegation's arrival is especially interesting, and stops only marginally short of being truly revealing: 'Die prusoner prusonettend überainander mit dry stymmen, als man sunst gewonlich singet.' (The trumpets played together in three parts, in the way that one normally sings).[33] It is easy to see why this source is welcomed so warmly by those keen to prove an early birth for the trombone, but the issue rests on the meaning of 'prusoner', and also on what Richental intended to convey by the phrase 'in the way that one normally sings'. It has been suggested that the 'prusoner' were actually trombonists,[34] but while the term may well signify slide instrument players, it surely does not indicate double-slide trombones at such an early date. Clearly, it is a variant of words that belong to the *busine/Posaune* strain, but such terms were used freely in fifteenth-century Germany to signify various species of trumpet. Writers such as Richental were not expected to apply discerning specialist knowledge. The statement 'as one normally sings' could indeed be loaded with accurate meaning about slide instruments, but it is equally possible that it is not, and that this form of words merely confers a compliment about the quality of the performance.

No evidence has come to light about the identity of the players. It is unlikely that they were in the employ of Richard Beauchamp. His household records name just one trumpet player, John Aleyn, who is actually listed among the Duke's valets.[35] The graphic *Pageants of Richard Beauchamp, Earl of Warwick*,[36] compiled in about 1490, shows trumpets in four of the 53 outline 'pageant' drawings,[37] but all are straight trumpets.

The clarion and the claret

This group of words is worth mentioning here for the sake of completeness. 'Clarion' occurs in English and French sources from early in the fourteenth century to refer to a type of trumpet. By the early fifteenth century, such words refer to instruments of fixed pitch that are short and play in the higher register. An instrument labelled 'Clareta' is given in Virdung.[38] The identical drawing is given in Agricola,[39] but he labels it wrongly. This 'clareta' should not be confused with another type of trumpet, unhelpfully called the 'claret' trumpet, which was a straight instrument with a detachable mouth pipe, and for which Smithers has identified a convincing iconographical source.[40] The fact that the high instrument is specifically suggested by these words lends modest support to the view that trumpets (and slide trumpets) played in the lower range. This in turn adds credibility to the notion that the slide trumpet, essentially a tenor instrument, provided the prototype for the trombone.

The early trombone

The earliest entirely convincing representation of a trombone in its modern form is found in a fresco by Filippino Lippi in the church of S. Maria sopra Minerva, Rome, depicting *The Assumption of the Virgin*. (Ill. 21) It has been dated 1488–93. However, two other paintings have also been cited as proof positive of the instrument's existence earlier in the fifteenth century: *The Coronation of the Blessed Virgin Mary* (c. 1485) by the Master of the Lyversberger Passion[41] (Munich, Alte Pinakothek); and a famous Florentine decorative painting known as the *Adimari Wedding Cassone*, possibly by Giovanni di Ser Giovanni, and dating from the mid-fifteenth century (Galleria Accademia, Florence). Timothy McGee has strongly disputed the accepted interpretations of this latter source, contending that the panel does not belong to a *cassone* (a wedding chest), and that it shows neither the Adimari wedding nor a trombone.[42] In each of these three pictures, the instrument is depicted with the bow of the bell section extending alongside or behind the player's head, in a configuration suggestive of a trombone. But the *Coronation* and *Adimari* paintings are deceptive. It is more likely that both instruments are slide trumpets, and that each image shows a player grasping the static part of the instrument with the left hand, while the rest of the instrument is moved backwards and forwards on a single telescopic slide. Only the fresco by Lippi seems incontrovertibly to show a double-slide instrument. Crucially, he depicts an instrument with stays – between the two lengths of the bell section, and between the two slide arms, for the player to hold in order to operate the slide as a modern player would. Stays are not shown in either of the other two images.

Lippi's fresco provides evidence of the existence of a double-slide instrument in the second half of the fifteenth century, but an important point needs emphasis here. Other images that are actually later in date clearly depict slide trumpets, and this supports the idea that slide trumpets remained common for most of the fifteenth century and indeed for some time beyond. A number of images, such as Holbein's drawing (c. 1540) of a trumpeter playing in a gallery in the English court (British Museum, London), and even a memorial plaque (c. 1587) in Exeter Cathedral to the precocious sixteen-year-old cathedral organist, Matthew Godwin, could be cited as evidence of slide trumpets, but they are not especially convincing. Like other

Illustration 21. The earliest known illustration of a trombone, dating from 1488–93, detail of a fresco of the *Assumption of the Virgin*, by Filippino Lippi, in the Church of S Maria sopra Minerva (Cappella Carafa), Rome. (By permission of the Ministero dell' Interno, Fondo Edifici di Culto, Rome.)

sixteenth-century stylized images, they do not seem to accord with what else we know about instruments in this period. However, two pictures, both depicting sixteenth-century civic ensembles, are worthy of mention. One shows an *alta* band, probably Spanish. Both are civic bands playing shawms, cornett and a brass instrument. The other (see Ill. 22 in Chapter 4) depicts four Graz *Stadtpfeifer*, and comes from Leonhard Flexel's *Festschießen in Graz* (1568). The brass instrument has features that are common to both the trombone and the trumpet, but match the expected specifications of neither. One of these images has been used to support a hypothesis that, in the sixteenth century, trombones were made as a set of interchangeable modules, so that a single collection of yards, bows and ferrules could be configured with a bell flare and a mouthpiece, so as to assemble a trombone, a trumpet *or* a slide trumpet.[43] The hypothesis is largely based on an experiment conducted on a well-made reproduction of a sixteenth-century instrument. The idea is tenable in theory, inasmuch as it is reasonable to assume that a workshop making trumpets and trombones would utilize a similarly or identically bored tubing for both types of instrument. Also, it is true that early trombones were cylindrical up to the commencement of the terminal flare of the bell, and that their joints were not soldered: each part of the instrument was held together by inertia (aided perhaps by a wax sealing) or loose-fitting clasps. But the hypothesis is unsupported by any other compelling historical evidence. Indeed, it is hard to see why a trombone player would want to convert his double-slide instrument to a less versatile single-slide instrument, and it seems improbable that there would be any need to convert a trombone into a trumpet. On the other hand, these images are convincing, and terminologies that clearly refer to a slide instrument continue to appear long after such words as 'sackbut' were common – as in the description quoted above of the marriage celebrations of Mary of Guise and James I of Scotland in 1538.

It seems likely that the single-slide instrument did indeed survive well into the sixteenth century. The most likely explanation for this is probably the simplest: that the instrument survived for as long as its playing tradition lasted. The picture of the Graz musicians shows a small-town civic group, where it is likely that the tradition of slide trumpet playing lasted longer, and stretched well beyond a single generation. Furthermore, the documentary and iconographical evidence shows just a single brass player with double-reed instruments and sometimes a cornett, implying that in such places the sound, if not the repertoire, of the *alta* tradition was also maintained. This suggests that the single- and double-slide instruments followed the pattern that occurs when virtually all innovations appear: the new and the older instruments coexist, along with their associated practices, until one or the other gains popular preference. Furthermore, while common sense points decisively to the conclusion that whoever designed the trombone did so as a development of the (single-)slide trumpet, there is in fact no conclusive evidence that proves such a progression.

Our knowledge of the first half-century of the history of the trombone is limited. It seems likely that the instrument existed by about 1440, and that players of the *trombone*, sackbut or *Posaune* were being appointed to musical institutions across Europe. But some nagging questions persist for which no entirely convincing answers have emerged. For what repertoire and musical practices was this instrument used, and was it used in the same way as, or differently from, the slide trumpet? How exactly did the instrument become a common feature of European music-making so quickly that, by about 1480, itinerant performers were able to negotiate for places in major musical institutions on the basis of their specific skill as trombone players? And perhaps most fundamentally, where was the double slide invented, and who was responsible for its design?

Craftsmen makers

The entry on the trombone in the first edition of *Grove's Dictionary of Music and Musicians* contains a statement that a trombone was discovered at the excavations of Pompeii in 1738. The author, William H. Stone MD, maintained that his circumstantial evidence for this assertion was considerable, quoting a source (which he claimed he could verify) that 'the King of Naples . . . gave this instrument to King George III of England who was present at the digging'. It is perhaps not surprising that there is no trace of this instrument at any of the Royal Households, and that even when Stone was compiling his article, the librarian of Windsor Castle denied 'all knowledge of it'.[44] This is a particularly frustrating business because the story – untrue though it clearly is – was probably based on something interesting. We know that trumpets existed in the ancient world, that they were sophisticated and that their functions were important. What we do not know enough about is *how* sophisticated they were, and quite how intricate were the manufacturing techniques. However, there is no doubt that sophisticated schools of brass instrument making were in operation in Europe by the fifteenth century – the century when the trombone evolved.[45] The main centres were located where there was easy access to the principal raw materials, and where there was a tradition of metal craftsmanship. In the late thirteenth century, brass making was particularly developed in the north of Europe. The towns of Aachen, Liège and especially Dinant were associated with the manufacture of a wide range of fine metal implements. By the mid-fifteenth century, brass instrument manufacture was under way in Nuremberg, a city that also had a high reputation for metal crafts. There were other places where brass instruments were made, but it was the Nuremberg makers who produced the largest quantities and set the highest standards for the next two centuries. If one is of a mind to speculate where the double slide was invented, Nuremberg seems a strong possibility: the evidence is conjectural but compelling. The town was established by the eleventh century, and was an important trading centre on a primary route to eastern and southern Europe. By the fifteenth century a robust system of civic government was in place. Even the authority of the church did not surpass that of the town council. Because there was no court authority, the civic council ambitiously promoted the town as a centre of trade, craftsmanship and manufacture. It became a thriving commercial centre that enjoyed a high reputation for the quality of its industry, and it was also a civilized and rounded community with a strong intellectual life.

Town musicians can first be identified in Nuremburg in 1219, and from 1363 payments to *Stadtpfeifer* are listed in the records of the town authorities.[46] We do not know the exact date when brass instrument production began there, but by the mid-fifteenth century the Neuschel family – one of the great dynasties of brass instrument making – had commenced its business in the town. The earliest information we have concerning the manufacture of trombones (though it does not appear until some time later) relates to those instruments that bear the names of members of this family. The first reference is to Hans Neuschel the Elder, who was granted master's rights as a coppersmith in 1479. It is possible that he was not the first generation of his family to conduct this or an analogous business in the town. In 1482 he was receiving fees for the repair of brass instruments, but by 1487, with an otherwise unknown maker called Hans Keymer, he was a supplier of *Ziehstücke*, a word almost certainly meaning trombone slides.[47]

The skills of all brass instrument making were derived from the trumpet maker's art. Indeed, it has been pointed out that the proportions and size of component parts of seventeenth-century Nuremberg trumpets and trombones are often so similar that the fittings of some instruments are interchangeable.[48] There is no reason to believe that this was not the case in the fifteenth century. While the making of fine, efficient trombone slides may have been a new and specialized craft within the art of trumpet making, a skilled trumpet maker did not need fundamentally new skills to make a trombone or slide trumpet. The bells and bows of such instruments may have been all but identical with those on trumpets. Branches were made by burnishing cold strips of metal over a solid hard-metal rod, then sealing the joint (to the extent that a seal was needed) with one of a variety of solders that were available. All that was needed for the manufacture of a telescopic slide was for the internal and external slide branches to be fashioned on rods of slightly different diameter. A host of available lubricants could have been used to achieve a smooth action. Furthermore, the stays that secured the various parts of the slide were held together by clamps rather than by unyielding solder. This would also have helped to make the slide freely mobile because the position of the stays could have been adjusted slightly to accommodate the best fit of the sides. We know little about mouthpieces from this period, but given that all evidence suggests that trumpeters played in what was a relatively low tessitura, it is possible that this too was a component that was initially similar or even common to trumpets and trombones. However, as I explain in Chapter 1, the evidence from seventeenth-century sources shows that the mouthpieces of the two instruments had somewhat different profiles by then.

One writer has suggested, with perhaps a little too much confidence, that 'In 1427 Hanns Franck fashioned the first German trumpet and trombone',[49] but no evidence is presented to support this claim. That the trombone was invented in Nuremberg is little more than speculation, but one factor offers support for such an idea – or at least for the prospect that the instrument originated in Germany – and that is that from the time that we are able to distinguish the trombone from other instruments, most of the players are German. Keith Polk has pointed out that trombone players with German names were active not just in Germany and the Low Countries in the second half of the fifteenth century, but also in Italian courts and civic bands.[50] Furthermore, when players of the 'Sakbussheys and shalmeys' (sackbuts and shawms) appeared at the English court, they too had German names. The instruments are first mentioned from 1495, but in documents written in 1501 their players are named as Hans Nagel and Hans Broen. Little is known about Broen, but we know a great deal about Nagel.

He had made his way to England from Leipzig via Augsburg, and was one of the most expert, well-travelled and in some respects notorious trombone players of his era. Nagel was one of the first trombone-playing celebrities of Europe, and an example of a new species of brass musician. More about him and his generation of players will be found in Chapter 4.

We struggle to understand the general patterns of manufacture and distribution of brass instruments before the late sixteenth century. There are frequent references to instruments being bought, paid for or received, but somewhat fewer that indicate exactly where these instruments came from. For example, Mark Anthony Petala, a Venetian trombonist who entered service in the English court, received a payment of more than £22 in August 1531 ('paied to m'ke Anthony a venician by the kinges comanndement: £22.10s.0d'). This was an enormous amount – almost a year's wages. We might surmise that it was for travel to Venice and perhaps the purchase of instruments.[51] But while instrument making in Venice was undoubtedly buoyant, it seems certain that Nuremberg maintained a pre-eminent status as a centre for brass instrument making for the whole of the sixteenth century and beyond. Nuremberg makers supplied instruments to courts and cities far and wide. A business letter from Jörg Neuschel, one of the great master brass instrument makers of Nuremberg, to an aristocrat addressed as 'Durchleuchtigster, Hochgeborner Furst Allergnedigster her', mentions that he has recently supplied the King of Poland, Duke Ottheinrich the Elector of the Rhine, and the King of England. However, notwithstanding the obvious importance of the major Nuremberg makers, a note of caution should be sounded. Herbert Heyde has pointed out that where there was regulatory control of instrument manufacture, the mandates often gave rights to *supply* musical instruments. Thus the maker's mark on the bell of an instrument could legitimately be inscribed by the manufacturer or by the retailer or dealer. There were undoubtedly many small workshops in Nuremberg producing brass instruments, and we must ask why the surviving instruments carry such a limited range of makers' names.[52]

While it is clear that the skills of instrument making were not confined to Germany, of the instruments that survive from before 1600, probably only two were made outside Nuremberg. One of these is a bass made in 1593 in Reims by Pierre Colbert (The Hague, Gemeentemuseum, MUZ-1952x0159). The Accademia Filarmonica in Verona possesses a tenor instrument (13.302) which bears no maker's mark or date. However, it has been suggested that it was probably made in Venice around 1560.[53] Trumpets made in other European cities also survive from this period, such as those made by Jacob Steiger of Basel and dated 1578. However, the patterns of distribution are probably not revealed properly by surviving sources, and certainly not by surviving instruments. Many makers of surviving seventeenth-century instruments were well established in the sixteenth century. Furthermore, there are manufacturers who left a trace of their existence, but for whom no instruments survive – as is the case with the London sackbut makers mentioned below.

While established workshops such as those of Schnitzer and Neuschel set standards and were probably the main suppliers of trombones to the major courts, it seems probable that instruments (perhaps less prestigious commissions – for town bands, for example) were produced by metal workers who exercised their craft in other, related trades. This was certainly true in other spheres of instrument making; for example, many viol makers were also makers of fine furniture and wooden implements.[54] It also seems that more prestigious instruments might be sent out to craftsmen who were not primarily instrument makers. The Siena civic records show that in July 1470 the town's chamberlain sent a silver trombone to Francesco di Antonio, because it 'lacked certain things'. Di Antonio was a goldsmith, and his services were again called on in December 1487, when he was required to provide a new silver trombone and seven silver trumpets.[55] Here we find an example of trombones being made not by a master instrument maker, but by a goldsmith. The first commission to Di Antonio was for him to reconfigure the town's silver trombone according to a design retained by the chamberlain. He may never have made a trombone before, but it is highly likely that goldsmiths were accustomed to making trumpets, and that the skills of the goldsmith could be turned to the purpose of making trombones if they were provided with appropriate templates. As it happens, the subsequent haggling between the town and the tradesman was not about the quality of the instrument, but rather, as one might expect, about its weight (that is, the precious metal content).

Some evidence concerning trombone and trumpet making in London in the late sixteenth century attests to a similar phenomenon. The case in point concerns Simon Brewer, an immigrant goldsmith who is listed among London aliens (immigrants) in 1582 as having been born in Brabant and being 'one of the Dutche churche', and George Langdale, who started receiving half-wages as a royal trumpeter in 1577, and progressed to be a fully waged court musician two years later. This Langdale was almost certainly the same man to whom Brewer refers as George Langdall, and who was indentured as a goldsmith in London, obtaining freedom of the goldsmiths, company in 1567.[56] In 1583 he received a privileged licence for the manufacture of sackbuts, and claimed to be the first English maker of the instruments. His claim had substance, for the licence states that he 'to his greate paines and charges hath byn the first deviser and maker within this our Realme of England of sackbutts and Trumpetts not hereto fore made'.[57] The letters patent grant him a twenty-year privilege for the exclusive manufacture of these instruments. The granting of this very licence prompted Brewer to petition the principal secretary to the Queen, '[p]itifullye complaininge' that he (Brewer) 'hath nothinge to lyve uppon nor aine othere trade but onlie to make Trumpetts and Sackbutts to mayntayne himselfe his wife and nyne poore children'. He was able to 'make and amende trompetts and sackbutts . . . bettr & cheaper than those of the said Langdalls making'.[58]

Brewer's petition is of course an objection to an effective monopoly, but from it we can also gather that trombones were being made in London by this time, and that at least some of the makers came from abroad. It also provides an insight into the precarious lives of immigrant families at this time, living like Brewer under the threat that 'his wife and children shall be enforced to begg and utterlie perish'. But what is also apparent is that the trade of trombone maker was practised within the related profession of the goldsmith. Indeed, Maurice Byrne has identified a line of goldsmiths who were trumpet makers in the sixteenth and seventeenth centuries.[59] There is no reason to assume that such practices were not widespread.

Another recurrent pattern that one notices in the fifteenth and sixteenth centuries is that makers are also players, or they are members of families in which there are both players and makers. Hans Neuschel the younger (d. 1533) was a trombone player to Emperor Maximilian I, and Hans Schnitzer, a member of another great Nuremberg family of the sixteenth century, was also a trombonist. The aforementioned Jacob Steiger was a town trumpeter in Basel, and many more examples could be similarly cited.

Chapter 4

Players and cultures in the later Renaissance

Cities, states and the geography of music

The focus of secular power and influence in Europe in the late fifteenth and the sixteenth centuries did not reside solely in nation states, as has tended to be the case since the nineteenth century, but also in urban centres. Such towns as Venice, Antwerp and Bruges existed as administrative and cultural entities that had acquired importance because of their economic strength and the fortunate coincidence of their geography. Such locations were either actually or effectively autonomous, and governed by councils usually made up of patricians. For the sake of convenience, I refer in this chapter to such countries as 'Germany' and 'Italy', and freely employ their adjectives, but while those terms are not entirely meaningless when applied to the political geography of the sixteenth century, they can be misleading: Italy and Germany were fragmented into many smaller states, and the political map of central and eastern Europe looked very different from its modern form. England was politically separate from Scotland, which stretched beyond its northern border, and Wales and Ireland were mere territories (and not very significant ones at that) of the English crown. Perhaps more so than in any other place, the cultural focus of England was the court. It was highly centralized on the monarch's various residences around London, though provincial cathedrals and civic authorities also employed musicians.

Such matters are important to us because the orbits and networks in which trombone players moved were fundamentally influenced by the infrastructure of European patronage. For them, centres of power were centres of employment – the places where the money was, and where the composers and 'audiences' were to be found. The loyalties of players were usually negotiable: even by the fifteenth century, trombonists moved from place to place in search of better employment and (presumably) higher wages. If we remember how large the world must have appeared in the sixteenth century, and how long and perilous journeys across Europe often were, it is impressive that there were such strong networks of trombone players, who appear to have held a shared understanding about so many things that affected their work.

Musical centres and internationalism

From the late fifteenth century to the last quarter of the seventeenth century,

Illustration 22. *Stadtpfeifer* of Graz (1568) – one of several illustrations from the sixteenth century that appear to show the continued use of a single-slide trumpet. Handschrift 10.116. (Österreichische Nationalbibliothek, Vienna.)

trombonists were employed in virtually all European centres with a modestly thriving music culture, and the best players were celebrated and sought after. Professional players had three principal sources of employment: aristocratic courts, civic authorities and the church. It was usual for a player to have a regular source of wages from one (usually secular) employer and also to engage in freelance work. For example, court and town band players often supplemented the music at cathedrals, and also played for processions and theatrical events. In England there appear to have been no detailed contracts, but many players in court or town bands elsewhere had a wide range of duties specified in their contracts. In Genoa in 1590, for example, the band was contracted to play daily in the public square, as well as for meals, processions, entertainments and other public celebrations.[1]

Most town bands – *Pfeifer* or *Stadtpfeifer* in Germany, *pifferi* in Italy and 'waits' in England – could trace their origins back much further than the sixteenth century, and their routines were embedded in wider patterns of urban life. Town bands were usually employed and controlled by local authorities; it is therefore the records of governing bodies or elders that provide the information about their activities. In most places it was the council that authorized the employment of individual players. Councils also specified their duties, regulated them and in many cases purchased their instruments. Usually there was just one official civic band. In Italy, however, arrangements seem to have been more fluid. At the end of the sixteenth century there were six different *pifferi* groups operating in Venice, in addition to the substantial musical establishment sustained by the Doge and the ecclesiastical foundations.[2]

The role of musicians in aristocratic court establishments was, by nature, dependent on the ambitions and tastes of the presiding authority. It therefore follows that musicians' duties were susceptible to patterns that were somewhat less than standardized and predictable. As the sixteenth century progressed, however, trombone players began increasingly to show loyalty to a single employer, such loyalty being rewarded by higher wages, New Year's gifts and even modest pensions. Church and court were often thinly separated institutions as far as the employment of instrumentalists was concerned, but from the later sixteenth century, trombone players were incorporated in church or cathedral statutes, just as organ players were. This meant that they were employed as part of the ecclesiastical establishment and were in receipt of regular wages – a move that usually signalled an allocation of weekly or even daily duties. But while the presence of trombonists in places of worship usually signified cultural opulence, the use of participating instrumentalists in acts of worship was determined primarily by religious politics rather than mere aesthetic taste.

From the fifteenth to the eighteenth centuries, church, court and town as institutions were the basis for a Europe-wide network of musical centres. Even domestic music-making mirrored the tastes, fashions and practices of whatever was the central focus of administrative or political authority. It therefore stands to reason that the predilections of these centres influenced – even determined – the economic as well as the artistic parameters of the musical world. Such practicalities were prominent in determining the careers of trombone players, who must have been keenly aware of the status of music in different towns through the reports of travellers; so much music-making, after all, took place in public. By the same token, the reputations of individual players were widely appreciated. Music was not merely an entertainment, a pleasant diversion from ordinary life. It was, in the orbits of authoritative institutions, a political and diplomatic device that conveyed and emphasized a sense of power, style and influence, with the European nobility constantly trying to outdo each other for opulence and ostentation. Cities and courts signified their status with an array of interlinked cultural gestures within which music was a vital ingredient. To the extent of its pecuniary means (and sometimes beyond it), each city or court tailored the quality and sophistication of its cultural life to match the perception it had of itself: its security, its ambition and the weight of its authority. It should therefore come as no surprise that from the earliest days of the trombone's existence, the best performers were keenly sought after. As Frank D'Accone has commented, the very best of them 'came and went as they pleased'.[3]

Many players lived and died in the city of their birth, but others moved apparently effortlessly from country to country in pursuit of highly successful and ambitious international careers. Thus, several musical institutions had both cosmopolitan and distinctively local proclivities and traditions. From the late fifteenth century, some centres seemed to have been forming or re-forming their instrumental music. There was an expansion of instrumental music in European courts, and this expansion took place as the trombone was becoming widely known and appreciated for its musical versatility. There were both musical and non-musical reasons for the reconfiguration of instrumental groupings. From this time, instrumental ensemble music became more popular, and signs can be seen of instrumental forms shaking off their dependence on vocal and dance music. As a consequence, town and court bands acquired increasing importance in musical life. In Venice from the late fifteenth century and through the sixteenth century, civic authority was underlined by elaborate processions in which trombones were usually present. They are seen with rebecs in a painting of 1496 by Gentile Bellini, *Procession in 1444 Carrying a Relic of the True Cross*,[4] showing such a ceremony taking place in Piazza San Marco. This pattern of elaborate ritual became a routine way of focusing the population on spheres of authority. Similarly, musical elaboration was developed as a way for cities and courts to assert status at moments of change through the acquisition of cultural symbols. In France the reign of Francis I (1515–47) signalled a renewed vigour in cultural life, and in England the accession of the House of Tudor in 1485 similarly marked the start of a conspicuous development of court music. Many of the additional players who took advantage of these new or reinvigorated establishments were foreigners, with players from the Low Countries, Italy, Germany and France being especially mobile.

From the second half of the sixteenth century, most musical establishments became ever more consolidated and players often stayed in one town for the greater part of their careers. But between the mid-fifteenth and sixteenth centuries, many trombonists seemed to have worked in more than one country. Germans were in Italy; Germans, Italians and Burgundians were in England; and many players moved across the boundaries of states within Germany and Italy. The traffic did not stop in the second half of the century but became a little slower, with Italians, who were always in demand, finding their way to Germany and Scandinavia. This type of internationalism and networking can be traced back considerably further. Even in the fourteenth century, international colloquia referred to as 'minstrel schools' were held annually, usually in France or the Low Countries. The minstrel schools had much in common with modern symposia. Trumpeters and other minstrels from throughout Europe gathered to demonstrate and share their professional skills and preoccupations. The events were held in Lent – specifically around the fourth Sunday of the Lenten season (*miquaresme*), when fasting and religious observance caused a lull in the more extravagant musical activities of courts and cities, making it possible for musicians to travel from their usual place of work. Indeed, many minstrels received support from their employers to travel, so that they would return familiar with the latest repertoire and other musical developments.[5]

Rob Wegman has identified the existence of minstrel schools extending over a period of 135 years from the second decade of the fourteenth century to 1447, when they appear to have stopped abruptly. They were held in cities rather than courts, and this suggests that the hosts were usually civic authorities – probably musicians' guilds or confraternities. The exact nature of the proceedings is uncertain, but it is easy to speculate that they included such rituals as feasts, communal worship, musical performances and even musical contests. However, the most important outcome was the sharing of knowledge about repertoire and musical performance. It seems inevitable that discussions about conditions of employment and remuneration figured in the discourse, as did talk about performers, new instruments and working practices. The performance of secular song was prominent, and new repertoire was both launched and acquired. Trumpeters seem to have been prominent in these gatherings, and it is hard to believe that the embryonic trombone, as it evolved from its origins within the trumpet family, did not figure significantly in the discourse.

The cultural impact of slide instruments

One can only wonder how the development of slide instruments was received among traditionalists in the mid- and late fifteenth century. How did minstrels and trumpeters view the arrival of slide instruments as they assembled for annual gatherings in such centres as Bruges, Brussels, Cambrai, Ypres and Savoy? There must have been a point when trumpeters became categorized according to the two specialisms that were becoming increasingly distinct. On the one hand, there was the well-established tradition of heraldic trumpeting, conjoined as it was to quasi-musical, symbolic and ceremonial functions. This type of trumpeter enjoyed a very high status at court and often had additional duties that were effectively those of an emissary. On the other hand there were 'slide trumpeters', *trompettes des ménestrels*, 'draught trumpeters', or whatever else they were called, who played not with other trumpeters – or at least, not solely with trumpeters – but with shawmists. Slide trumpeters performed on an instrument that required new techniques and was used for essentially musical rather than ritualistic and symbolic purposes: they were dance band players, and their musical terms of reference were necessarily different from those taught within the traditional confines of trumpeters' education.

The changes ushered in by this development must have been the subject of debate and controversy, and probably led to a reconfiguration of many an institution's musical forces. There is evidence that some town trumpet players became slide trumpeters and then trombonists. Frank D'Accone's comprehensive study of musical life in Siena provides ample evidence of this. D'Accone makes the point that as trumpeters moved to the trombone (in very few cases doubling on the two instruments) they also acquired new skills in improvisatory counterpoint.[6] But there is no doubt that the heraldic trumpet tradition remained robust. Trumpet fraternities did not diminish in size or status, and corps of trumpeters grew in proportion to the general expansion of music in courts and cities. Indeed there is evidence of increased opportunities for trumpeters at this time in the retinues of lesser noblemen.[7] By the late fifteenth century, the distinction between the two instruments – and the two types of player – was widely known and accepted, and the instrument that we now call the trombone was a familiar part of the musical landscape. From the second half of the fifteenth century, such words as *trombone*, *Posaune* and sackbut proliferate in documents that record transactions with instrumentalists. By this time – with just a few minor provisos, discussed below – these words can be taken to mean 'trombone'.

A little later, pictorial representations of the instrument are largely consistent with what we now understand to be the trombone. Furthermore there is plenty of documentary evidence to show that players were employed in large numbers across the continent. Players are seen to be arriving and leaving, and soon there is evidence of the employment tribulations that were to figure in the stories of musicians for the next couple of hundred years. In 1449 a trombone player in Siena called Maestro Ians was acrimoniously dismissed. The Concistoro of Siena decreed that 'Maestro Ians, who plays the trombone, [shall] no longer serve at the Palace because he [has] behaved dishonourably'.[8] This may be the same trombone player who was appointed in 1446, and he may have been the first civic trombonist. By about this time trombones had also been appointed to civic bands in Florence (1444), Ferrara (1456), Naples, (1450), Bologna (1469) and Mantua (1469).[9] At this time the Italian town bands almost always list three *pifferi* and one trombone, but they were not standardized; the Ferrarese and Venetian groups, for example, had two *pifferi* and two trombones, and the Mantuan group four *pifferi* and one trombone. A fresco in Siena Cathedral (Ill. 23) shows a group consisting of two *pifferi* and one trombone. The word *pifferi* was used to describe both the band as a collective group and the shawms that made up the majority.[10]

It seems certain that the instruments referred to as *tromboni* at this time really were trombones, because the types of event in which they are recorded as performing suggest that they were involved in more varied and sophisticated functions, with repertoires that were invariably polyphonic. In 1487, for instance, trombone players played at the baptismal ceremony of the son of Isabella and Ferdinand of Spain. And

Illustration 23. Detail of Pinturicchio's *The Coronation of Pius III* (1504), a fresco on the arch above the entrance to the Libreria Piccolomini, Siena Cathedral. (Opera della Metropolitana di Siena)

at around the same time there were trombonists in France, the Low Countries, Germany, eastern Europe and Scandinavia. In 1495 the thirteen players who received payments at the English court were six trumpeters, three 'stringmynstrels' and four 'shakebushes'. The trombonists were paid more than the string players and marginally less than the longer-established trumpet group, and this may have been because the trombonists were foreigners who had to be sweetened with high wages. In 1503 the sackbut players in the English band had been reduced to two, and payment accounts again reveal them both to be foreigners. Indeed the English trombone group, one of the largest in Europe, did not employ a single native-born musician until the 1550s, when 'sagbut' players with British credentials and British names such as John Peacock and Richard Welshe appear in the wages books.

The immigrant players in the English court band came from Venice, from the Burgundian court and from town bands in the Low Countries, where they had already made names for themselves. As a general rule it seems that players in town bands seem to have been no more or less itinerant than those who belonged to the music establishments of courts – except in so far as there appear to have been more civic than court players in circulation, because of the greater number of employment opportunities. But the trend for trombone players to be itinerant continued until the second half of the century.

Education and careers

Given that trombonists were so mobile, the question arises as to how adequate stability and continuity were maintained to foster the education of new generations of players. Virtually every detailed study of the careers of instrumentalists in the Renaissance reveals the same story. Skills were passed between male members of a family, from father to son, and sometimes to the males of the extended family through marriage: the daughters of musicians often married musicians who worked with their fathers. The education of professional trombonists was based on apprenticeship. It provided players with a thorough and rounded education that went beyond the immediate practicalities of performing on just one instrument.[11]

Dynasties of musicians spanned the century. However, this does not mean that the personnel of trombone corps within musical establishments was static. The opposite is true, for while established players often remained in a court or town band, many, having received their training in one place, moved elsewhere or became peripatetic for a large part of their careers. The Schubingers of Augsburg are a case in point. They were one of the leading families of musicians in southern Germany in the early sixteenth century. Ulrich, the father (1425–1491/2), and his four sons Michel (1450–c. 1520), Augustin (c. 1460–1532), Ulrich (c. 1465–c.1535) and Anthon (c. 1470–after 1511), all worked in Augsburg, but the sons, having completed their training, moved on. Two of the sons, Augustin and Ulrich, were trombone players. Augustin, the most celebrated of the family, worked at Brandenburg and Florence before settling at the Habsburg court. Ulrich moved from Augsburg to Mantua, then to the service of the Bishop of Salzburg.[12] Another example can be found in the English court, where there was a regular traffic of trombone players from the Low

Countries and Venice, with the name of Bassano appearing in the court lists for decades. Some players stayed and became key members of the Tudor court, but others moved on and settled elsewhere in Europe.

Brass players were not regarded as a lower social order among musicians. Indeed, they were generally better paid and more highly esteemed than others. In Siena, trombonists were paid more than trumpeters and singers, and exceptional players were paid a premium: the trombone player Santi di Pavolo, for example, was paid more than twice as much as the highest-paid singer.[13] In England in 1529 the 'sagbut' players earned significantly more than anyone else in the court band, except for the leader Philip van Wilder, who, in addition to playing and organizing the music, was also responsible for repairing and tuning instruments. The highest-paid trombone players (John van Wincle, Nicholas Forcivall and John van Herten) received 55 shillings a month, compared to the highest-paid lutenist (other than van Wilder), who earned 40 shillings a month – exactly the same wages as those of the six subordinate trombone players. Others in the band earned much less and were employed more tenuously on a daily basis.[14]

The skills of trombone playing were found mainly among professionals, and in the first part of the sixteenth century few amateurs attempted to master the secrets of the trumpet and trombone players' art. The training seems to have been extensive, and even the best players were required to perform on more than one instrument. There are several instances of instrumentalists who were trained as trumpeters or trombonists developing their careers in wider and more exalted musical spheres, Tylman Susato being one example. Susato was a member of the Antwerp town band where, in addition to his primary duties as a trombonist, he also played trumpet, crumhorn, recorders and flutes. He appears to have been trained as an instrumentalist at the same time as he was trained as a calligrapher. His composing, and more particularly his publishing business, eventually took him away from playing (though he had actually been dismissed, along with most of the Antwerp band, for an indiscretion at the procession for the Emperor Charles V in 1549). He probably died in Sweden, where he had been engaged in diplomatic and emissary duties.

Another composer who is likely to have started his career as a trombone player is Bartolomeo Tromboncino, one of the greatest composers of *frottole*. His father was a *piffero* in Verona, and the son may well have received his musical education in the town band. There is no direct evidence of this, but his father was known as 'Bernardino Piffero', so one wonders why the son would use the name Tromboncino if he were not a trombonist. This Tromboncino has been confused with the great Florentine trombonist Bartolomeo di Luigi. It is difficult to see how the confusion could have arisen, for several reasons, but if proof were needed that they were not one and the same person, one need only glance at descriptions of the two men's personalities. The trombone player is described as a modest, sweet and gentle man, a characterization that could not have been applied to the composer, who seems to have been an entirely unpopular and thoroughly intemperate character with proven homicidal tendencies.[15]

Trombone players did not need to move into composing or publishing to have a fulfilling and rewarding career, for the life of a trombonist was far from empty. The trombone player in the Antwerp band prior to Susato was Hans Nagel. Nagel was undoubtedly an expert player, and one of the most sought after of his time. His father was probably the Hans Nagel who was working as a *Stadtpfeifer* in Leipzig with his two sons from about 1478 to 1483.[16] The younger Hans is one of the first trombonists to be named in English court records. Along with Hans Broen he received fees as one of the 'joueurs de sacqubutes du roy d'Angleterre' in 1501, for playing before the King of Austria.[17] In 1503 he travelled to Brussels, where he is again described as one of the King of England's sackbut players. But by 1506 he was in the retinue of Archduke Philip the Fair, from where he went to the court of Margaret of Austria, and then to the town band of Mechelen, before settling in Antwerp in 1519, where he remained until his death. Nagel's celebrity was not confined to his skill as a musician. In the 1520s he acted as agent for the supply of Flemish trombone players (John and Henry van Arten, John and Lewes van Wincle and Nicholas Forcivall) to the English court. He also acted as an agent in another and somewhat darker sense. Dutch and English documents make it abundantly clear that he was a spy – probably a double agent. He was a central figure in a complex series of intrigues relating to Richard de la Pole, a pretender to the English throne who lived in exile at various locations in continental Europe.[18]

Nagel may not have been typical of early sixteenth-century trombone players, but neither was he entirely unusual. We know from documents relating to his spying activities that he was highly literate, and it appears that he was sufficiently adept in more than one language to be able to communicate effectively with high-ranking officials at various courts. Indeed, the fact that he did communicate at such a level is consistent with the idea that trombonists were treated as professionals rather than functionaries. He played more than one instrument (he was also an accomplished shawm player), and felt permanently bound to no single employer. Nagel, like so many other trombone players of the Renaissance, had a sense of his own worth. Other trombone players saw themselves in similar terms. Hans Schnitzer, a member of the instrument-making family, was similarly resolute in determining his own destiny. The family was based in Nuremberg, where he received his training before he moved to join the *Stadtpfeifer* group at Prague. He declined invitations to join the prestigious town band at Munich in order to become senior *Stadtpfeifer* in his home town, where he also undoubtedly played a part in the development of the family business.

Italian trombone players also acquired high reputations and were much sought after. It was to Venice that the French court looked for trombone players in the early sixteenth century, and it was also from there that members of the great Bassano family were recruited for the English court. Italian trombone players had started to work in England between 1521 and 1525 when the names Salvatore, Pelegryn and Antonia appear on the payment lists, taking the full complement of 'sagbut' players to nine. The Bassano family originates in the town of that name in the foothills of the Italian alps. Though it has never been entirely proved, there is circumstantial evidence that the family were Jews who disguised their identity. In all, seventeen members of the Bassano family served as musicians to the English king between about 1531, when Antonio Bassano the trombone player first arrived, and the late seventeenth century. Seven of them were trombone players. In addition to being distinguished performers many were instrument makers, but there is no evidence that they made brass instruments.

Opportunities for good players were especially plentiful, and some individuals achieved star status. One Italian writer, Cosimo Bartoli, extolled the merits of the Florentine trombone player Lorenzo da Lucca, who had in his playing 'a certain lightness, with a manner so pleasing as to make me dumbstruck, beyond which he even handles both a viola and lute with marvellous grace' ('una certa grazia, et una leggiadria, con modo tanto piacevole, che mi fa restare stupido').[19] Bartoli also cited the aforementioned Bartolomeo di Luigi.[20] Bartolomeo and da Lucca must have been formidable general musicians as well as trombone players, and they appear to have been highly respected: in 1543 the two were appointed to judge applicants for the post of organist at the Florentine baptistery – surely a signifier of the esteem in which they were held.

The quality of instrumental music in Italy was extremely high, its style was widely imitated and Italian players were especially valued. A letter from the Elector Augustus of Saxony to the Danish King laments that he has no Italian trumpeters, but 'only Germans who have learnt the Italian style'.[21] There is little doubt that this preference is reflected in the frequency with which Italian names are encountered outside Italy in the sixteenth century. But though Italy clearly had a deep tradition of trombone playing, this does not mean that it had a monopoly of great players. Virtuoso trombonists must have existed in considerable numbers across Europe throughout the sixteenth and seventeenth centuries. Praetorius mentioned the famed master Phileno of Munich, who could play in a very high register 'without any difficulty'. This was Fileno Cornazzani, who is elsewhere described as Lassus's 'bester Zinckhplaser' (best cornett player), trombonist, organist, and composer.[22] Praetorius also said that he had heard a player in Dresden (who had since moved to Poland) named Erhardus Borussus, who could play as high as a cornett and as low as a bass trombone.[23]

Amateurs and women players

While the trombone was primarily a professional instrument in the sixteenth century, and the skills of playing it were guarded, there is evidence that trombone playing was not unknown outside the confines of the music profession. Sir Thomas Elyot's pseudo-medical tract *The Castel of Helth* (1534) recommends that: 'The entrayles which be underneathe the myddreffe, be exercysed by blowynge, eyther by constraynte, or playenge on the Shaulmes, or Sackbottes, or other lyke instrumentes whyche doo requyre moche wynde.'[24] We do not know whether his advice was heeded, or indeed whether it was given after fair observation of professional players in action. It is certainly a rare example of the trombone being mentioned in a published source that is not primarily about music.

In 1587, John Howes, 'Renter and Gatherer of Legacies' at Christ's Hospital (an English school), judged it convenient that

the children should learne to singe, to play uppon all sorts of instruments, as to sounde the trumpette, the cornett, the recorder or flute to play uppon the shagbolts, shalmes & all other instruments that are to be played upon either with winde or finger, bycause nature yeilds her severall gifts and there is an aptnes of conceavinge every child apt to learne the one or the other.[25]

The wisdom of Howes's view seems to have been called into question less than two years later, however, when the governing body ordered: 'Henceforth none of the children in this Hospital shall be apprenticed to any musyssionar other than such as be blinde, lame, and not able to be put to other service.'[26] One can only ponder on what had passed to prompt such a bewildering change of policy.

A further English source, now known as 'The Custom Book of St Omer' and compiled in St Omer, France, around 1609, gives instruction concerning the education of boys at that time. It distinguishes between categories of instruments, and refers to the sackbut and cornett which 'require more lung-power' ('Alia etiam pneumatica plus laterum et spiritus postulant, v.g. Tuba ductilis (vulgo Sacbottum) et Tuba cornea (vulgo Cornett)').[27] Other examples of the trombone figuring in the general education of sons of the gentry (as opposed to the education of boys destined to be professional musicians) are few and far between. All professional trombone players before the nineteenth century were men. There is however a sprinkling of evidence that shows that female amateurs played the trombone. That they were not professionals is not especially surprising, given the view generally shared at the time that people of any rank or refinement did not mimic the activities of craftsmen and others whose services were paid for. This view is expressed succinctly and lucidly in Robert Pearson's translation of della Casa's *Galateo* (1576), where the playing of the cornett by people of rank was discouraged, 'if they not be of that base condition and calling, that they must make it a gaine & an art to live upon'.[28] In a similar vein, Castiglione's *Il libro del cortegiano* (*The Book of the Courtier*, 1528) directs the courtier to restrict himself to string instruments and singing, citing classical sources in support of his view that the very act of blowing a wind instrument has 'something repulsive about it', because it disfigures the face.[29]

Thus, while music-making was a widely practised domestic activity (especially by women), in the homes of the nobility and gentry it was primarily confined to singing, and the playing of softer instruments such as lute, virginal and viol. Given that so many publications of the time espoused such clear ideologies of class and gender, it is surprising that the trombone should have attracted the attention of women at all, but in fact, a number of instances of women trombone players are found in sixteenth- and seventeenth-century sources. A German embroidered tablecloth clearly shows a woman trombonist among a group of other women and men playing musical instruments. (Ill. 24) But the most significant examples are found in the context of certain kinds of institutional life. In Ferrara, for example, the nuns of San Vito were especially famous for their cornett and trombone playing. The Council of Trent explicitly forbade the performance of polyphony in convents, but this edict was clearly not observed at San Vito, and one wonders about the extent to which musical practices thrived in convents elsewhere in the Catholic world, especially in cloistered communities. Ellen Koskoff has pointed out that more than half of the compositions by women published in Italy between 1566 and 1700 were written by nuns,[30] so it seems probable that the nuns of San Vito were not unique. And prominent among other institutions where trombone playing by amateurs and women was heard were

(a)   (b)

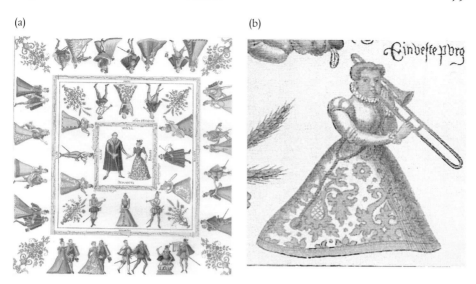

Illustration 24. 24a Nineteenth-century coloured engraving of a tablecloth made c. 1562–8, with silk, gold and silver embroidery (160 x 180 cm). Depicted in the middle are Count Poppo of Henneberg and his wife Sophie of Brunswick. The music framing the pair in the middle is a setting by Martin Agricola of Luther's 'Ein feste Burg'. Amongst the musicians is a woman trombone player. 24b Detail of the woman trombone player.

the Italian conservatoires of the sixteenth and seventeenth centuries. 'Conservatoire' should not be understood here as meaning the modern didactic institutions, but rather homes for orphaned children, in which music figured prominently in the academic and social curricula. In 1669 the Mendicanti conservatoire in Venice possessed two chamber organs, a spinet, three harpsichords, seven bowed instruments, two theorboes, three trombones and a bassoon.[31]

One enticing fragment of information found in an English source suggests that interest in the trombone was found in the highest circles. In January 1570, Edmund Dowring, a court administrator acting as executor of the will of John Tamworth, who had been a groom to Queen Elizabeth I's private chamber, drew up a list of monies paid out of the Queen's treasury by Tamworth in the period 1559–70. These items were accounted for discretely because they were for the Queen's personal use and paid for at her expense. The items listed include commodities of a personal nature such as clothing, bedding and other 'necessaries', among which is 'One greate sackbut provided for the Queens use'.[32] (Ill. 25) Whether this one sentence gives substance to the possibility that the Virgin Queen had toyed with some amateur trombone playing – even *bass* trombone playing – can be debated, and should probably be seen as unlikely, but it is hard to deny the possibility. The expenditure genuinely seems to be private rather than for the more general expenses incurred by the court. There is no ambiguity about the provenance of the source, and the text is entirely comprehensible. Two other musical items are mentioned in the inventory: a sum for the purchase of lute strings by Thomas Kytchefeld, 'one of the gromes of the privye Chambre, for her ma's. use', and under 'Wages and diettes' a sum of £15, to 'Marke Anthony, musicon, for pencon'. 'Sackbut' does have another meaning in the

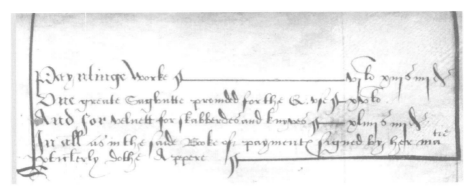

Illustration 25. Necessaries.
. . . One great sackbut provided for the Queens use. £15.0.0.2
GB Lbl Harl Roll AA23. (By permission of the British Library, London.)

English language: it is usually expressed 'sack-butt' and means a container of wine, literally a butt of sack. But the *Oxford English Dictionary* cites no use of this meaning prior to 1600. If there is a reluctance to take this source at face value, it may be because of modern cultural perceptions. On the other hand there could be another explanation: that this peculiar entry merely reflects an accounting expediency.[33]

Acculturation in colonies

Perhaps the most interesting example of the trombone being used by an entirely new constituency of players is found outside Europe. Colonized Latin America had a far richer musical life in the sixteenth and seventeenth centuries than is generally acknowledged. In January 1688 the Mercendarian bishop Francisco de Padilla of Puerto Rico wrote to Charles II of Spain with a petition for help. His cathedral had an organist, but he needed shawm players and other musicians to play 'at church festivals, for the adoration of the Blessed Sacrament and when communion is taken to the sick'.[34] Attempts to attract instrumentalists from some of the major centres – Santo Domingo, Havana and Mexico City – had failed because the poverty of Puerto Rico was well known. The bishop knew that the musical starkness of his cathedral was unusual in Latin America.

The colonization of South America by Spain had resulted in the rapid establishment of religious and cultural institutions. Among the first musicians were Flemish Franciscans who helped establish Quito Cathedral in 1534. They taught the native South American Indians, mulatto (of black–white parentage) and Creole slaves to play cornetts, sackbuts, shawms, flutes and trumpets, and they also taught them musical notation. Fray Jodoco, who delivered most musical instruction, said in a report to Ghent that he found that the natives 'easily learn to read and write and [to] play an instrument'.[35] The foundation of churches, cathedrals and monasteries throughout South America was rapid, and they provided the focus for western musical practices, whereby *ministriles* were enrolled and taught for both sacred and secular music-making. By 1570 the repertoire of the Colegio de San Andrés, founded in 1555 by the Franciscans specifically for the education of Indian youths, included the four-part motets of Francisco Guerrero. The musical infrastructure was strengthened by immigrant Spanish musicians: Robert Stevenson has estimated that up to two hundred Spanish musicians arrived in the Peru area during the sixteenth century, and yet more arrived in Mexico. Very few of these were trombone players, so it follows that the many 'sackbut' players mentioned in ecclesiastical archives were local men.

Mexico Cathedral had a musical establishment by about 1540, when Canon Juan Xuárez was charged with teaching music to Indians, who received instruction in shawm, cornett and almost certainly trombone playing. These instruments remained in use in the Cathedral until at least 1760.[36] When a new Spanish government official, Captain Bernardo de Vargas Machuca, arrived in Santafé (Bogotá) in 1598, he reported that a mass at Santafé Cathedral was sung with *ministriles, trompetillas* and *trompetero* in attendance.[37] Trombones are often referred to within collective groups such as *ministriles, trompetillas* and *chirimia*, but words similar to *sacabuche* are frequently encountered. Trombonists often also played other instruments, but their role as trombonists in the performance of sacred and secular music is often specified. Usually there was just one trombone player in a band of wind instruments that otherwise included trumpets, cornetts, flutes, reed instruments and drums. But there is also evidence that some religious institutions employed a single trombone player for the specific purpose of playing with singers.

By the middle of the century, native musicians were using adopted Spanish names. The sackbut player at Quito Cathedral in the 1560s was a native of Lotacunga named Juan Mitima. Other players adopted the name of the instrument they played. For example, one, a mulatto at the Santo Domingo convent in the 1630s, referred to as Juan, came to be called Juan 'Sacabuche'. Egberto Bermúdez's survey of *ministriles* in Santafé and La Plata in the sixteenth and seventeenth centuries revealed only one musician who was not a native.[38] The acquired musical skills of the native musicians were far from primitive. We hear from reports to Madrid of some with extraordinary skills, including one musician called Juan Bermejo, who was not just a fine player and singer but was able to correct the polyphony of some European masters.[39]

Missionary priests in South America were as often Italians as Spaniards, and many had received a musical education in monasteries in Europe. It is they who were mainly responsible for the teaching of the trombone, but there is evidence that native and itinerant musicians were later appointed as teachers and leaders. In 1580, a non-cleric called Pedro Serrano was engaged by Cuzco Cathedral to teach singing and the playing of 'shawms, sackbuts, cornamuses and bassoons' to Inca Indians.[40] Specific and specialist church officials carried the duties of master of *ministriles*. One such officer was the Spaniard Luis Enriques, who was employed as master of Indian *ministriles* at Cuzco from 1589 to 1601, before taking up similar duties at La Plata Cathedral from 1601. He also appears to have been a silversmith. He and other early missionary musicians brought European instruments with them. The quantity of instruments that were in circulation in South America in the seventeenth century suggests that local manufacturing was also in operation, but details are difficult to ascertain. There were certainly local facilities at hand for repairing trombones: in La Plata in 1603, for instance, payments are recorded for the repair of trombones, and in

1622 repairs were required again, with a silversmith being contracted to do them — perhaps Enriques himself.

By the seventeenth century, it was common for native-born players to be entrusted with the training of others. In some places, natives were provided with incentives: in 1611, for example, the town of Fontibón created a precedent followed by other native American townships of allowing six natives dedicated to vocal and instrumental music to be exempted from paying 'tributes'. This provision was intended to nourish 'the growth of affection and respect to the mysteries of the Holy Catholic faith in the natives' hearts'.[41] One can only conclude from this that the richness of the story of instrumental music in south America at this time is yet to be fully revealed.

Chapter 5

Performances and repertoires in the sixteenth and seventeenth centuries

Our knowledge of the repertoire and performance practices of trombone players in the sixteenth century is far from complete. A few broad parameters can be taken as certain, but we have to dig deeply and imaginatively to understand the instrument's idiom: how players, composers and listeners expected the trombone to sound, and what its function was in the various musical contexts in which it appeared. In order to achieve more than bland generalizations, we must draw on three types of information: surviving written music that can be interpreted as having been played by trombonists; documents, both administrative and narrative, that implicitly or explicitly describe performances; and pictorial representations of the instrument. Taken together these sources provide a good, if not finely detailed, picture of how trombonists earned their living, but as I explain below, we must imagine the culture of the sixteenth century as one that was quite different from the one that we inhabit today. Above all, we must imagine the art of improvisation as both natural and common in the world of the renaissance trombone player.

The situation is considerably clearer for the seventeenth century. Sources are more numerous and explicit, and patterns of activity in both sacred and secular life are more clearly understood. Also, compared to the sixteenth century, a great variety of instruments survive. Whereas less than a dozen exist that were made before 1600 (almost all made in Nuremberg), seven or eight times as many survive from the seventeenth century; and though most extant seventeenth-century trombones were again made in Germany, they come from several different German centres of manufacture, while some were made in Austria and Sweden (see Appendix 1). The surviving instruments are important sources of information in their own right, but they are also invaluable because they provide the basis for historical reproductions that are crucial to the work of period performers. To this we can add the fact that many musical sources from the seventeenth century are labelled for the instruments for which they were intended. This does not mean that all questions about the seventeenth-century trombone and its players can be answered, but in comparison with the sixteenth century the questions are relatively minor and less central to our general understanding.

For an example of the nature of the problems concerning repertoires and performance practices in the sixteenth century we need look no further than the early Tudor court. Payment records show that in 1532 the court was providing monthly wages to eleven players of the 'sagbut'. (Ill. 26) All the players were foreigners whose pedigree can be traced; each was an experienced player who had previously served in

Illustration 26. Extract from the Kinges Boke of Payments, the wages book of Henry VIII's court, for April 1532, showing payments to eleven players of the 'sagbut'. GB Lpro E101/420/11, f. 164v. (By permission of the National Archive, London)

one of the other great European musical establishments. The cost of employing the group was considerable: nine of the players were paid 40 shillings a month; the other three received a monthly wage of 55 shillings and six pence. These were high wages, and the cost of paying 'sagbut' players ate up the greatest proportion of the entire outgoings for music at Henry VIII's extravagant court at this time. The members of this group also played other instruments (notably shawms, which are not mentioned separately in the inventories) but they are persistently referred to as 'sagbuts', so playing the trombone was clearly their primary duty and certainly the reason why they travelled to England.

We know the identities of the players, we know how much they were paid, we can trace their comings and goings in and out of the court musical establishment – we even know where many of them lodged in London. But we do not know for certain what their everyday duties were: what music they played, in which locations they performed, in which ensembles they were included, or at which events their presence was thought desirable or essential. No single source or group of sources makes this information completely explicit. Such questions apply to a greater or lesser extent to many of the other European aristocratic centres at which trombonists were employed in the sixteenth century. The problem is not that we are entirely ignorant of instrumental practices in this period; on the contrary, there is a sizeable body of evidence, particularly in respect of the everyday practices of civic musicians. Rather, it is that the available sources for court music deal most vividly with very special occasions: royal progresses, coronations, funerals, important masques, feast days and the like. The more challenging questions that tantalizingly escape us concern the nature and frequency of musical routines – the ordinary duties that made it necessary and sensible for a court to employ so many trombonists, not on an ad hoc basis, but on a regular monthly salary.

The English trombone group settled into a more manageable number by the 1540s (a group of four or five specialist players), and this may reflect a more rational ordering of playing duties in the court as a whole at that time – but even then the daily routines are not totally clear, and neither is the repertoire that trombonists performed. Such issues are important, because musical developments took place in this period that led to what appears to be a common understanding of the trombone's voice. The change was most noticeable in the second half of the century, though obviously the nature and pace of change was not universal. Documentary accounts of performances provide greater detail; they seem to be consistent and to concur with what we can understand from published and unpublished repertoire. The consolidation of the idiom of the trombone in both secular and sacred contexts seems to have taken place by about 1600, but it really became manifest in the seventeenth century, when there was a flowering of dedicated idiomatic repertoire in several parts of Europe. Much of this change occurred because of wider aesthetic developments. But it was a relatively short-lived flowering, for in less than a century – by about 1680 – the new aesthetic climate caused an emphatic decline in the instrument's popularity. Early in the sixteenth century, trombone players were able to bargain with the crowned heads of Europe; by the mid-seventeenth century, they occupied positions analogous to those of top modern orchestral professionals; but before that century was out, the instrument was obsolete in most parts of Europe – so much so that many eighteenth-century scholars were hard pressed to explain what antique words such as 'trombone' and 'sackbut' had once meant.

Documentary sources

The didactic and theoretical literature that casts direct light on the trombone in this period is not abundant, but there is enough of it to inform a reasonably clear picture, particularly when it is taken with other documentary sources such as those that describe particular performances or musical life in general. As we have seen in Chapter 3, Tinctoris referred to the trombone in about 1487, but the first reference to it in a printed source in the sixteenth century is found in Sebastian Virdung's *Musica getutscht* (1511), which is also the earliest published book to be devoted to musical

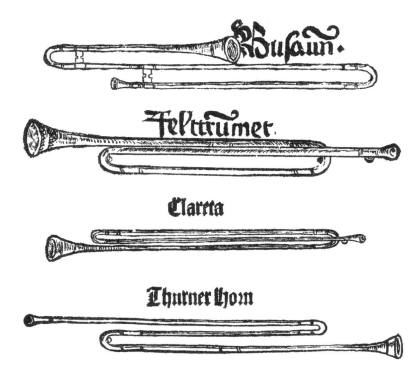

Illustration 27. Trombone and trumpets from Sebastian Virdung's *Musica getutscht* (1511).

instruments. Virdung implied that his *Musica getutscht* was a sampler, a short derivative, from a much larger work that he was writing, but no such work ever appeared. He mentions the trombone in the class of wind instruments that he describes as those that are 'blown but have no finger holes', but gives no description of it. He illustrates four brass instruments: *Busaun* (trombone), *Felttrumet* (field trumpet), *Clareta* (smaller trumpet) and *Thurner horn* ('S'-shaped trumpet). (Ill. 27) These very drawings appear with minor and misleading amendments in Martin Agricola's *Musica instrumentalis deudsch* (1529). Agricola clearly knew Virdung's book, and like him, he says very little about the trombone. He appears to have been well aware of this shortcoming, but his promise to describe the trombone in greater detail in a future edition was not fulfilled when the book was reissued in 1530, 1532 and 1542, nor when it was entirely revised in 1545.

The earliest source to provide an informed explanation of how the trombone was *played* is Aurelio Virgiliano's *Il dolcimelo* (c. 1600), which survives as an unfinished manuscript. Significantly, Virgiliano's illustration 'Nuova intavolatura di tromboni per sonarli in concerto' (see Ill. 12 in Chapter 2) contains integrated information about the cornett, confirming what we know from other sources: that by this time the two instruments were seen as natural partners. Other sixteenth-century theorists say little explicitly about the trombone, but we learn much by inference from narrative documents and from more general writings about instruments, particularly those that deal with diminution and embellishment. Especially prominent in this respect are the manuals devoted to embellishment published mainly in the later sixteenth century, most by Italian writers.[1] Besides Virgiliano, another writer to make explicit reference to the trombone is Francesco Rognioni, who, in his *Selva de varii passaggi* (Milan, 1620), includes a setting of Lassus's *Susanne un jour*, which he marks 'Modo di passegiar il violone over trombone alla bastarda'.

The three most commonly used theoretical sources for the seventeenth century are Michael Praetorius's *Syntagma musicum*, which was published in three parts between 1614 and 1619 (a fourth part was intended for publication, but not completed); Marin Mersenne's *Harmonie universelle* (1636); and Daniel Speer's *Grund-richtiger kurz- leicht- und nöthiger Unterricht der musicalischen Kunst* (A Fundamental, Short, Easy and Necessary Introduction to the Art of Music), published in 1687, with an extended version in 1697. *Syntagma musicum* (Ill. 28) is regarded by music historians as especially valuable because of the range of its coverage and the authority with which it was

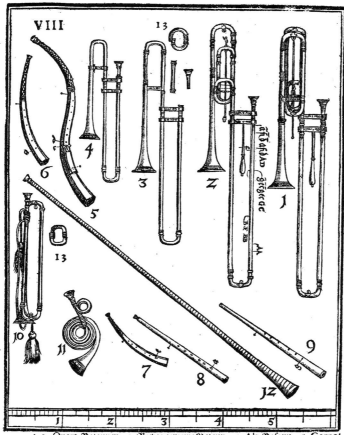

Illustration 28. Illustration from Michael Praetorius's *Theatrum instrumentorum* (1620) appended to Volume II of his *Syntagma musicum* (1619), showing two bass trombones, a tenor trombone and an alto trombone.

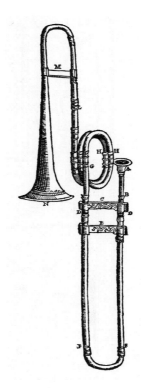

Illustration 29. Illustration of a trombone from Marin Mersenne's *Harmonie universelle* (1636). The instrument is fitted with a crook; the annotated letters relate to measurements given in Mersenne's accompanying text.

written. By the time Praetorius died in 1621 at the age of 49, he was one of the most respected German composers and theorists. As a composer he was versatile and prolific, and though he appears not to have travelled much outside Germany, he was well informed of foreign practices through other musicians in his orbit (such as Scheidt and Schütz) who had travelled more widely. His writing is intelligent and consistent with what we can deduce about the trombone from other sources. He covers a range of topics, from descriptions of instruments to their use in various settings with other instruments and voices. Praetorius is central to our understanding of the trombone at one of the most interesting and important points in its history. On the one hand, his observations were based on practices that had probably been in place since the middle of the sixteenth century; but on the other, he foreshadowed many developments of the baroque period. Praetorius regarded the trombone as a versatile instrument with an important place in many musical genres. Furthermore, he also seems to have regarded trombonists as competent and versatile musicians – a rather better opinion than he held of cornett players ('with their blaring'[2]) and trumpeters (who 'are in the habit of hurrying'[3]).

Marin Mersenne's encyclopaedic *Harmonie universelle*, published in Paris a couple of decades after *Syntagma musicum*, is more scientifically oriented. He deals with trombones only briefly, but he provides measurements and fine descriptions of the instrument's configuration. His illustration of the instrument (Ill. 29) was drawn on by many later writers. Mersenne's insights were gained almost entirely from his experience of practices in France and the Low Countries, but it is clear that his writing follows wide and rigorous research. He was neither a composer nor a performer, but he was an informed intellectual who seems to have sought advice from practising musicians. He deals with national styles and performance practices, and though he is clearly indebted to Praetorius, he does not merely reproduce his utterances, but provides new information.

Daniel Speer's *Grund-richtiger . . . Unterricht der musicalischen Kunst* is a practical textbook rather than a systematic instructional treatise for players, but it has a particularly pragmatic edge because Speer was primarily a town musician, though also a composer. We do not know what instrument he played, but if he was not himself a trombonist, he certainly worked closely with trombone players. He was a member of the Stuttgart town band in the mid-1660s, but it is likely that he had already been working as a town musician elsewhere by about 1650. It follows that what Speer says about the trombone draws on a close familiarity with practices in the mid-seventeenth

Der erste Zug ist beym Mundstuck/ und bestehet in folgenden Buchstaben/ so das beygesetzte Exempel weiset:

Dieser Buchstaben Thon werden alle im ersten Zug gefunden/ ausser/ daß das c. um zwey quehr Finger etwas vorwarts muß gezogen werden/ bey welchem Zuge auf das f. X. sich befindet.

Der ander Zug ist beym Hauptstuck/ und befinden sich folgende Buchstaben darinnen/ wie zu ersehen ·

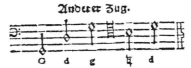

NB. Bey diesem Zug ist zu mercken/ daß das b. mol, nm zwey quehr Finger hinaußwarts muß gezogen werden.

Der dritte Zug ist vier quehr Finger außwarts deß Hauptstucks/ und hat folgende Buchstaben/ wie zu ersehen:

Der vierdte Zug auf einer Tenor-Posaun/ so man einen Baß darauf tractiret/ ist so weit draussen/ als mans mit dem Arm fast erstrecken kan/ und seyn folgender Thon-Buchstaben/ wie zu ersehen:

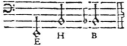

NB. B. mol muß noch um etwas weiters als die fördern zwey Buchstaben E. und H. gezogen werden.

Illustration 30. Explanation of the notes obtainable on the four positions of a tenor trombone, from Daniel Speer's *Grund-richtiger kurz- leicht- und nöthiger Unterricht der musicalischen Kunst* (1697).

century. (Ill. 30) Another valuable feature of his treatise is his inclusion of illustrative compositions, amongst which are two three-part 'sonatas' for trombones.[4]

Written and unwritten traditions in the sixteenth century

Any discussion of the repertoire of the trombone before the late sixteenth century has to take account of the extent to which musical literacy and improvisation played a part in the working lives of performers. We know that they routinely performed from memory, or 'improvised'; but improvisation should not be understood here as being an entirely impromptu process. Just as jazz musicians rely on predetermined melodic patterns and harmonic progressions to provide formal parameters, so did sixteenth-century players – especially in dance music. Some, perhaps all, professional trombonists were musically literate, but it is not certain how their literacy was used. Did players perform or rehearse from written texts? Did they embellish phrases that they learned by ear or was it necessary for their repertoire to be precisely executed? No known pictures of trombone players in performance dating from before the second half of the sixteenth century show them to be playing from written music. This can hardly be taken as conclusive evidence, but in the second half of the century such representations are easy to find (see, for example, Ill. 31). Two important questions thus present themselves: was the world of the early sixteenth-century trombonist one in which improvisation and memory were most highly prized; and what exactly was the relationship between these players and written repertoire?

Illustration 31. Detail from the title page of Hermann Finck's *Practica musica* (Wittenberg, 1556), showing a trombonist or possibly a slide trumpet player, reading from music.

Only two printed sources from the sixteenth century have been identified as having labelled parts for trombone players.[5] The earliest is found in the music by Francesco Corteccia for the marriage celebrations of Cosimo de' Medici and Eleonora of Toledo in 1539.[6] The other is in the *Symphoniae sacrae* (1597) of Giovanni Gabrieli, which contains repertoire performed at St Mark's, Venice, at that time. Of the sixteen canzonas and sonatas contained in that publication, four specify between two and twelve trombones in their scoring.[7] This does not, of course, represent the sum total of even the published music that trombones performed. Howard Mayer Brown's survey of music printed before 1600[8] identifies many printed collections for unspecified instrumental ensemble that were suitable for trombones in mixed consort. As I explain below, to this body of material can be added a further group of unpublished sources containing repertoire that was, or may have been, conceived as instrumental music in which trombones would probably have been used, and a yet further body of vocal music that was suitable for performance by instruments alone.

A major cultural change occurred in instrumental performance during the sixteenth century, which saw players depending more on written music. The change was not acute, neither was its pace and nature uniform across Europe. But it was part of a broad trend towards a greater autonomy for instrumental music and a greater dependency on written music, and as this process unfolded there was a commensurate shift in the balance of performance authority from performers to composers. The most conspicuous consolidation of this process (as far as trombonists were concerned) took place in Venice, where the repertoire written by Andrea and Giovanni Gabrieli for St Mark's Cathedral provides the first major, sustained and highly sophisticated examples of the exploitation of the trombone sonority in large-scale instrumental ensemble forms. In less than a decade we see the emergence of equally idiomatic writing in the works of Monteverdi. The level of sophistication and compositional strategy contained in the Gabrielis' writing and in such works as *Orfeo* (1607) and the *Vespro della Beata Vergine* (1610) suggests that composers were building on a performance tradition that was not entirely new, but rather had been in progress in the second half of the sixteenth century.

We have little concrete knowledge about the deployment of trombones in sixteenth-century written repertoire, but inferences can be drawn from both the published and unpublished sources of this period. In looking at them, we can take into account that trombone players were in secure employment in the very places where such repertoire was in circulation. Broadly speaking, the published repertoire relevant to our interests here can be grouped into three types: works based on dance music; works conceived for voices but arranged for instruments (though not labelled for specific instruments); and abstract imitative, polyphonic forms that were conceived as instrumental pieces, such as *ricercari* and fantasias. The performance of vocal music by instruments – often with *ad libitum* adjustment – was probably commonplace, and dance music was routinely the subject of embellishment and variation. The published dance music also shows evidence of composers using this repertoire to construct more substantial instrumental genres. The more independent, imitative, ensemble instrumental repertoire which grew in Italy in the second half of the sixteenth century was soon found in other countries, particularly Germany and England. Yet earlier sources for music intended for instrumental performance can be found in unpublished manuscripts which survive in several European collections.[9]

Before the change to idiomatic written repertoire was anywhere near a resolution – up to about the first half of the sixteenth century – trombonists engaged with what we may loosely (and in some senses inaccurately) describe as unwritten repertoire, and in processes that may have been centred on compositions that were written, but not read in the manner that we would read them today. These two approaches had several manifestations, each suggesting high levels of aural and intuitive skill. We can take this hypothesis further by imagining that in the late fifteenth century and for a sizeable part of the sixteenth century, trombone players recognized three closely related processes: improvisation, memorisation and what might be termed 'intuitive doubling'.

Improvisation was described by the German theorist Andreas Ornithoparchus in his *Musicae activae micrologus*, published in Leipzig in 1517. It was translated several times, though few translators did justice to the original. Even in the early seventeenth century, the English composer John Dowland was still attempting (somewhat floridly) to convey Ornithoparchus's meaning.[10] Ornithoparchus distinguished between 'composition', by which he meant a written work, and 'improvisation', which Dowland translated as 'the sodaine, and vnexpected ordering of a plaine Song by diuers Melodies by chance'.[11] The notable point that we can deduce from this is that even in the early sixteenth century, improvisation was applied to polyphony. Dance music appears to have been the first contrapuntal music with which slide trumpeters routinely engaged, and it was in such music that the improvisatory tradition lasted longest. Players would have stamped their identity on each performance, but at the same time the music had to fit a familiar choreography, and it is likely that the *cantus firmus* prompted the structural, melodic and rhythmic parameters, in a necessarily premeditated and – to an extent – predictable form of improvisation. It should be emphasized however, that the skills of these musicians could also have been directed at other forms of polyphonic music.

The function of memory in such a process is obvious, but 'memorisation' might also have had a different role. Reinhard Strohm has pointed out that early instrumentalists had highly developed memories which enabled them to perform long and complex melodies from purely aural stimuli.[12] They were able to memorise a line by ear and recall it in solo or polyphonic ensemble performance. The presence of such skills among early wind instrumentalists is hardly surprising: it is found in modern times in the performances of bar pianists, opera singers, jazz musicians, concerto soloists and a multitude of ensemble performers in western and non-western cultures. If instrumentalists did this all the time, it would simply mean that their ability to memorise was particularly sophisticated. If such memorising was common practice among trombonists and other instrumentalists in the early sixteenth century, it also suggests that some or much of the surviving written repertoire – vocal, keyboard and other untexted music – indicates what trombonists played.

What I have termed 'intuitive doubling' indicates a yet different process in which vocal lines were doubled in either secular or sacred music. It suggests that when a professional trombone player doubled a vocal line, it took little or no familiarity with a piece for him to be able to double that line by ear. There can be no doubt that this was possible, because it is commonly done in modern performances of sixteenth-century liturgical repertoire.[13]

All this suggests that trombonists were gifted performers who could apply their skills in a variety of musical settings. Their musicianship was founded on sophisticated and highly tuned musical instincts, but it does not follow that they were all musically illiterate. The trombone parts in the Medici wedding music of 1539 and 1589 double vocal lines, and we can speculate that this too was one of the roles of trombone players in the sixteenth century. The Medici wedding music of 1539, which contains labelled trombone parts, was both written and published.[14] Yet further evidence for this practice is found in a set of madrigals sent in 1552 to the Accademia Filarmonica in Verona, which includes one 'with low voices arranged for the trombones'.[15] A further implication is found in another printed source: a book of motets published in Wittenberg, Germany, in 1538, which includes a setting of *Sicut lilium* by Antoine Brumel, against which is annotated, in an apparently contemporaneous hand, 'Was guett auff Posaunen ist' ('that which is good on trombones').[16] (Ex. 5.1)

Yet more convincing testimony to the literacy of performers is found in the notebook of the Venetian trumpeter known as Zorzi Trombetta da Modon (his real name was Zorzi di Nicolò). Zorzi spent the early part of what appears to have been

Example 5.1. Antoine Brumel, *Sicut lilium inter spinas*
According to Wilhelm Ehmann, this four-part antiphon in a book of motets published in
Wittenberg, Germany, in 1538, contains the annotation in a sixteenth-century hand, 'Was guett
auff Posaunen ist' ('That which is good on trombones'). The edition given here is rationalized to
modern notation.

a distinguished and varied career as a trumpeter on Venetian galleys. In 1481 he was
enrolled as a trombone player in the Venetian ducal ensemble of *tubeta et pifari*
(trombones and shawms), one of five musicians. His experiences aboard ship are
recorded in his notebook (1444–9), now in the possession of the British Library.[17]
The book contains not only descriptions of Zorzi's travels, but also the music of some
simple tenors and polyphonic settings notated in his hand. Clearly Zorzi was literate,
and this may well have been why he gained celebrity as a leader of instrumentalists
in Venice.[18]

It would be wrong to regard the first publications for instruments as being
indicative of the earliest written music that trombonists played, for, as we have already
seen, instrumentalists saw appropriate vocal repertoire as potentially their own. The
first large collection of printed dance music to come out of the Low Countries was
Susato's *Het derde musyck boexken*, published in Antwerp in 1551. It contains 57
arrangements of dances based on popular tunes. We can also speculate that trombones

may have been involved in the performance of yet earlier polyphonic arrangements of dance tunes such as the popular tune *La Spagna*, which was arranged by both Josquin and Ghiselin. If this was the case, it could suggest that other three-part instrumental pieces by composers from the Low Countries, which are often seen as early versions of *ricercari*, might also have employed a trombone on the lower line. *La Alfonsa* (Ghiselin), *La Martinella* (set by both Martini and Isaac) and Josquin's *La Bernadetta*, were performed regularly and convincingly by the early music group Musica Reservata in the 1970s with a trombone on the bottom line and wind and/or string parts above it.

The change from unwritten to written cultures did not occur at a particular historical 'moment', and the evidence suggests that the two practices coexisted in trombone playing until at least the middle of the sixteenth century. The most persuasive evidence for the survival of the impromptu tradition in the middle of the century is found in a satirical letter of 1543, in which the passing of improvised song in favour of written polyphony is lamented. The letter, signed with the common *nom de plume* Pasquino Partitio Romano, contributed to a charged polemic at the Accademia degli Umidi, in which the freedom of improvised song was contrasted with the 'artificiality' of (composed) polyphony. The debate itself offers proof of a changing musical world, and central to the writer's view was a comparison between vocal and instrumental practices, and specifically the way that trombonists perform:

Do you not play the trombone by ear? Do you not create upon four notes of a cantus firmus, via fantasy, an endless sea of notes? Have you not heard four or six trumpeters [*Trombetti*] harmonise, operating without notes or keys [*tasti*], but via breath alone, with admirable sweetness and union, often varying their voices, now high, now low?[19]

These observations were made in Florence, just four years after the Medici wedding of 1539, which had included performances by trombonists of composed polyphony. Either the art of memorising was being applied to new music, or, as is more likely, here in one of the great cultural centres of Europe the written and unwritten traditions coexisted and flourished. In the second half of the century there is sure evidence that players were engaging with written texts. In Granada there were 'libros des ministriles' for the trombonists and other musicians to draw on. In 1572 at Toledo, the cathedral instrumentalists requested a book of masses by Guerrero, and a few years later one member of the cathedral band there was supplementing his income by taking on work as a copyist.[20]

Declamations and processionals

Images of sixteenth-century processionals testify to the elaborate ceremony that typified the century. At one end are the Triumphs of Maximilian, at the other the abundance of ceremonies in Venice,[21] Florence and other Italian states. Every royal birth, wedding or funeral merited a display of splendour. The Medici weddings of 1539, 1569 and 1589, like the great Bavarian wedding of 1568 when Wilhelm of

Bavaria married Renata of Lorraine, are replete with ceremonial music in which trombones were employed. In England the story was the same: royal occasions – either a special event, or the strategically placed 'progresses' where the monarch simply visited the provinces to assert visible authority – were usually acted out with trombones as part of the musical retinue. The repertoire for some of these events is known, and the Medici weddings and the Bavarian wedding were well documented by visiting dignitaries.[22] It is also easy to surmise that in places where the ceremonials were most sophisticated – those in Venice at the turn of the seventeenth century, for instance – printed repertoire such as the works found in the *Symphoniae sacrae* of Giovanni Gabrieli would have been admirably suited.

Earlier sixteenth-century sources that allude to fanfares performed on sackbuts, shawms and trumpets proliferate. At the declaration of Henry VIII as Defender of the Faith in 1521, 'then was the Bull eftsones declared, and trumpettes blew, the shalmes and saggebuttes plaied in honour of the kynges newe style',[23] and at a water procession in 1536, 'the Kinge passed throwe London Bridge, with his trumpetts blowinge before him, and shalmes and sagbuttes, and dromslawes [drummers] playing also in barges going before him'.[24] This more declamatory idiom was common elsewhere as public music, and formed part of the everyday work of civic musicians. Indeed, the role of civic musicians may well have been distinct from court musicians specifically because of the nature of these routines. If this was the case, it suggests that by the late sixteenth century, different types of musical roles signified different types of performance skills. While the duties of court trombone players seem to have routinely included performance in sacred music and quiet ensemble playing, the routine duties of many civic musicians were more mundane. However, it would probably be wrong to take this generalization as a comment on the quality of players, if for no other reason than that mobility of personnel between town and court service seems to have been usual. Furthermore, as I say elsewhere, many of the larger church establishments recruited trombonists for more elaborate religious festivals from town bands.

Instrumentation

Not all *alta* bands were identical but their configuration was broadly similar. The most common line-up was one trombone or slide trumpet (sometimes two), with two or three reed instruments and sometimes a drum. By the late sixteenth century, cornett and trombone groupings were common, but there were more diverse ensembles too. The make-up of mixed consorts may have owed something to simple expediency, but while it would be wrong to imply that rules and conventions for instrumental combinations were entirely absent, there was certainly considerable flexibility.

In modern times there has been a considerable emphasis on 'loud' and 'quiet' (or *haut* and *bas*) as denominators for categorizing instruments into ensembles. This idea owes something to the pragmatic allocation of an instrument to an ensemble on the basis of its suitability for indoor or outdoor performance. But while this distinction was certainly made in the fifteenth century and for much of the sixteenth, its application to later periods may owe more to modern preoccupations than to historical fact. There are several references to 'loud minstrels' in sources relating to Spanish churches, and the 'sakbusshes and shalmeys' who received livery allowances at the English court in 1503 were described as 'lowde mynstrelles'.[25] But on the other hand, it is impossible to count the number of instances of instrumental performances that do not fit such neat categorizations, and one wonders whether descriptors such as 'lowde mynstrells' prevailed merely as a bureaucratic utility for payrolls. By the sixteenth century the trombone was both a loud *and* a quiet instrument, and by the seventeenth century the distinction was rendered largely meaningless in large-scale instrumental contexts in which trombones were used. By this time, trombonists played in ensembles with a variety of wind and string instruments, and their deployment was primarily determined by finely nuanced issues concerning the instrument's dramatic role and its versatile sonority.[26]

Earlier sixteenth-century instrumental groupings are not always easy to untangle because documents tend to employ such terms as 'tromboni e pifferi' and 'shagbuttes and shalmes' to signify a loose grouping of instruments that provided a particular set of roles (for dancing and processionals, for instance). Sometimes it is possible to distinguish the actual constitution of a group. For example, from its foundation in 1485 the ducal band in Venice comprised two *tubete* (trombones) and three *pifferi* (shawms and bombards).[27] While this type of detail is not always clear, it seems certain that trombones and shawms (along with trumpeters) not only formed the basis for a band of loud instruments, but in larger court establishments they also formed the core of the entire instrumental group.

From about the second half of the sixteenth century, the cornett started to be recognized as the natural treble voice to the tenor and bass trombone. Cornetts provided a perfect if not strictly homogeneous match for the trombone, because unlike the more monosyllabic shawm, the cornett could be played with varied articulations similar to those possible on the trombone, and its timbre and dynamic flexibility were also complementary. The full potential of the cornett/trombone partnership was not fully realized until some time later, and the shawm did not die out quickly. But Italian payment inventories show that the change in fashion was under way quite early in the century. By the 1530s, *concerti di cornetti e tromboni* could be found in Bologna, Genoa, Brescia, Perugia, Lucca, Udine, Florence, Rome and Naples. In Bologna, where Concerto Palatino, one of the most important of all civic groups, was already thriving, by 1538 there was a shift away from trombones and shawms to an ensemble of four *cornetti* and four *tromboni*. In Genoa, the civic group was made up of 'seven or eight in number, with parts for trombones and parts for cornetts, that is first and second trombone, first and second cornett, and other three parts in the middle shall be given to trombones or to cornetts'.[28] The story was similar in Germany, Austria, and the Low Countries.

The cornett also found its way to Spain, but there the distinctive sound of trombones and shawms as a multifunctional ensemble took root early and prevailed somewhat longer than elsewhere. At the wedding of Costanzo Sforza and Camilla of Aragon in 1475, two 16-voice choruses performed antiphonally with 'organi, pifferi, trombetti, ed infinati tamburini',[29] and in 1513 the celebrations of the conquest of Navarre included 'some well composed songs' performed on 'seven ministriles altos [wind band], four sackbuts and three cheremias [shawms]'.[30] In 1550 at the chapel of the Duke and Duchess of Calabria, Ferdinand of Aragon and Germaine de Foix, four trombones and four shawms were employed under the direction of Pedro de Pastrana.[31] In Valencia cornetts as well as shawms were employed (not an uncommon pattern) from 1560, but at Valdemoro in 1582 shawms and flutes were still used with trombones.[32] In England, cornetts start appearing in court invoices from the later years of Henry VIII's reign, when two cornetts are sent to the King 'the like of which . . . are not to be found in England';[33] but their use with trombones as a specialist group does not appear to be frequent until the seventeenth century.

The relationship between the cornett and trombone is important because of its prominence in the configuration of many of the greatest musical establishments of Europe until the closing decades of the seventeenth century. Equally important is that the idiom of both instruments seems to have expanded because of their association. They were in many respects quite different instruments, but they complemented each other in a way that was not equalled for subtlety and versatility. Furthermore, by the early seventeenth century some of the greatest virtuosi in Europe were cornett players, and many of them were also composers. These virtuosi included Giovanni Martino Cesare (who was also a trombone player) in Udine and Munich, Giovanni Bassano in Venice, Nicolò Rubini in Modena, and Antonio Scandello in Dresden. The existence of a body of virtuoso players and a perfectly matched instrumental combination stimulated the creation of a large idiomatic repertoire for *cornetti e tromboni*, and from about 1560 this grouping gained further importance because of the widespread practice of using cornetts and trombones to double voices in church services.

By the seventeenth century the cornett and sackbut 'ensemble' had become something of a genre group and was sufficiently well established for some publishers to specify parts for it. Among the 31 five- and six-part pieces of John Adson's *Courtly Masquing Ayres for violins, consorts, and cornets framed only for instruments . . .*, published in London in 1621, three are marked 'for cornetts and sackbuts'. One of the questions raised by this collection, and more generally by other seventeenth-century collections that have two treble lines and two or three tenor/bass parts, is quite how popular or standard it was for cornetts and trombones to be the sole constituents of secular instrumental ensembles in the seventeenth century. The case for this combination may be somewhat overstated in respect of English repertoire of the period because of the prominence of Matthew Locke's *ffor his Majestys Sagbutts and Cornetts* (c. 1661; see Chapter 6). While dedicated repertoire for this line-up can be found in several European countries, some of the seventeenth-century repertoire that has been most often performed in modern times – repertoire performed solely on cornetts and trombones, or indeed on modern trumpets and trombones – is likely to have been heard originally with a greater mix of instrumental colours, as it was in the sixteenth century. Music associated with courtly dance, such as that included in Samuel Scheidt's *Ludi musici* (1621) and Johann Hermann Schein's *Banchetto musicale* (1617) may have been performed according to the older tradition of using a variety of different instruments. Pictures of instrumental groups (including title-page engravings, such as Ill. 33) usually show mixed rather than homogeneous ensembles, and such phrases as 'per cantare e sonar' are frequently encountered. Prefatory comments on publications go yet further. The instructions on Willaert's *Musica nova*, published in Venice in 1540, declare the contents to be 'Accomodata per cantar et sonar sopra organi, et altri /strumenti, Composta per diversi eccelentissimi musici', and Anthony Holborne's collection of instrumental dances, published in 1599, carries a similarly flexible message: 'Pavans, Galliards, Allmains, and other short Aeirs both Grave and Light in Five Parts for Viols, Violins or Other Musicall Winde Instruments'.

Of course, title-page messages such as these did no harm to sales, and the fact that Holborne was so specific in mentioning viols and violins may suggest that this is where the primary market for this collection lay. But it would be wrong to believe that there was a total absence of rules or conventions about instrumentation. Taste and practicality both played a part in the selection of instruments, so the important question is less about where the trombone might have been used in mixed ensemble music than where it was usually absent. To answer this question we must look at documentary and iconographical sources, alongside collections of instrumental ensemble music (usually unpublished) that were clearly intended as the repertoire for a particular group of players at a particular time. Such collections often show signs of being a compilation of popular polyphonic pieces, usually containing dance music and other works that may have been derived from secular vocal music but were intended for instrumental performance. There is no shortage of these collections, and they cast a particularly revealing light if they are seen not merely as compositions but as the remnants of a performance tradition that can be linked to a particular musical environment.[34] The likely trend was for trombone players to play bass and tenor lines among a fairly eclectic combination of instruments. While the actual combination may have been determined largely by the function of the music rather than its texture, as I have already suggested, there is as much evidence to show trombones playing with quiet combinations as with louder instruments. Indeed the decline of the shawm/trombone combination in countries such as Italy and Germany in favour of the cornett/trombone pairing may be an indication of a move towards the more subtle colouring that occurred as instrumental forms developed away from vocal and dance genres to idiomatic independence.

Iconographic representations showing instrumentalists in secular settings that are not obviously dance scenes or depictions of processionals seldom show more than two trombone players. Praetorius referred to English practices when describing quiet trombones in mixed consort, but it is likely that such preferences were more widely experienced: 'The English even call it a Consort in which several people with various instruments, such as harpsichord or large virginal, lirone, double harp, lutes, theorbo, bandora, penorcan, cittern, viol, a small descant fiddle, a transverse flute or a recorder, and sometimes also a quiet sackbut or racket play together in company and society so quietly, gently and sweetly and have unanimity in a graceful symphony.'[35] The account of festivities at the Inner Temple in London in 1562 seems consistent with this, and appears deliberately to group trombones with quiet, more subtle sonorities rather than the declamatory sound of trumpets:

> and at every course [of the meal] the trumpetters blew couragious blast, of deadly war, with noise of drum and fyfe, with sweet harmony of violins, sackbutts, recorders and cornets, with other instruments of musick, as it seemed Apollo's harp had tuned their stroke.[36]

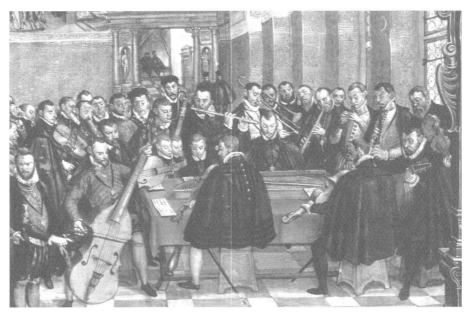

Illustration 32. Orlando de Lassus and musicians at the Munich court. Miniature by Hans Mielich from the *Bußpsalmen* (c. 1560). (By permission of the Bayerische Staatsbibliothek, Munich.)

A similar grouping is found in accounts of a performance of a Thomas Campion masque at Whitehall in January 1607, when music by Campion himself, Thomas Lupo and Thomas Giles was performed by musicians dispersed antiphonally:

> on the right hand were consorted ten musicians, with Basse and Meane Lutes, a Bandora, a double Sackbott and an Harpsichord, with two treble violins; on the other side, somewhat nearer the skreene were plac't 9 violins and three Lutes to answer both the Consorts (as it were in a triangle) six Cornets, and six Chappell voyces, were seated almost right against them, in a place raised higher in respect of the pearcing sound of these instruments.[37]

The notion that the trombone was a quiet instrument was neither new nor exclusive to England. The music for the *Ballet Comique de la Reyne*, created for the marriage of the sister of the French Queen in 1581, much of which was apparently written by Beaulieu, though it has now been lost, had an overture that specified '*hautboyes, cornets, saquebuttes* and other soft instruments'.[38] To this can, of course, be added the abundance of later sixteenth-century sources that match trombones and cornetts with voices in liturgical music.

The church and sacred music

Trombones were used to double vocal lines in renaissance sacred music, but their indiscriminate use for this purpose in modern performances is misleading. From the early sixteenth century, instruments other than organs were used in sacred music, and trombones were included in their number. In 1503 when Philip the Fair was in Innsbruck, the 'sackbuts of the King began the *Gradual*, and played for the *deo gratias* and *Ite misa est*'; and accounts for 1509 record the trombonists Hans Nagel and John van Wincle as 'having served continually before [Philip the Fair] in his chapel, singing and playing, in discant, of the hours and divine service'.[39] There also appears to have been a sustained use of instruments in Spanish churches from quite early in the century. In 1526 Seville Cathedral appointed 'three shawms (treble, tenor and contra) and two trombones, persons skilled in their art, to serve this church'.[40] These were apparently the first such appointments in Spain, but many more were to follow, and it is clear that as the century progressed these players were not merely used for processionals but for the accompaniment of the liturgy too.[41]

However, the pattern was not uniform across Europe. The Protestant Reformation encouraged a simplification of sacred music in those parts of Europe touched by reform, but it is important to stress that even in Catholic countries the evidence that instruments other than organs were used routinely, universally and early in the century for doubling voices in liturgical music is far from convincing. Later in the century, however, this practice became so common that it was one of the main roles for the trombone. As I suggest in Chapter 6, it was a function that contributed emphatically to one of the most enduring perceptions of the instrument's idiom. The suitability of trombones (and cornetts) for doubling voices derived from the instruments' dynamic and expressive versatility, and their capacity to adapt to different intonations.

It is important to distinguish between ordinary and exceptional occasions, and also between the use of trombones to play fanfares and for processions as part of an instrumental group (usually with shawms and trumpets), and their more specific use to accompany liturgical texts. In the Low Countries this practice was not unusual in the first half of the sixteenth century. In the 1530s the town band at Antwerp played the evening service for the confraternity of Our Lady as a part of its normal duties,[42] and from 1518–19 there was similar provision in Bergen op Zoom, where two (later three) trumpets (again this should be understood as trombones) participated in services.[43] At the coronation of Pope Pius III in 1503, the *Te Deum* was sung antiphonally with the responses accompanied by 'tibia una et tribus tubis contortis quos trombones vulgo appelant' ('one cornett and three contorted trumpets, which are commonly called trombones').[44] However, a papal coronation was hardly an ordinary occasion, and there is little evidence of trombones being used in churches as early as this elsewhere in Italy. Frank D'Accone's investigation of Venetian church documents between 1486 and 1492 found no references to instrumentalists other than organists, even though payments to singers and chaplains were well documented. He similarly found no mention of the use of instruments other than organs in his exhaustive study of sources relating to Siena and several other Italian centres in the first half of the century. A trombonist is mentioned for the first time in the archives of San Petronio, Bologna, in 1560, and on two occasions at the Cappella Giulia, Rome, in 1546, but otherwise not until 1564. A trombone player takes up duties at Padua Cathedral in 1565, but not until 1588 in Mantua, while at Modena Cathedral a trombonist is on the payroll from 1562 to 1583.[45]

Craig Wright notes that of 'many hundreds of references to musicians' at Cambrai Cathedral in the fifteenth and sixteenth centuries, there is no evidence to suggest that instrumentalists other than organists were ever used there.[46] The situation is similar in other French cathedrals, but it appears that the French king did call on other instruments to accompany the liturgy – at least on special occasions. In June 1520 Henry VIII and Francis I met at a location near Calais known as the Field of Cloth of Gold, with the intention of establishing a bond of friendship between England and France 'to the pleasure of God, their both comforts, and the weal of all Christendom'.[47] The congregation was one of the most remarkable of the century, and was described by contemporary observers as 'the eighth wonder of the world'. Apart from the actual interviews between the two kings, there was banqueting and jousting, with both parties displaying apparently limitless ostentation. Both kings brought their entire musical retinue with them.

The event is heavily documented by apparently independent observers, and there are extensive descriptions of processions punctuated by fanfares played by trombones, shawms and trumpets. For example, when the two monarchs came into each other's presence: 'then blewe the Trumpetts, Sagbuttes, Clarions, and all other Minstrelles on both sides, and the kynges descended doune towarde the bottome of the valey of Anderue ... and embrassed the two kynges each other'.[48] At the end of the lengthy proceedings, the two courts celebrated mass together, and it is the description of this event that is especially interesting. Both musical retinues took part, the singers from the chapels of the two kings being responsible for alternate sections of the offices:

> About noon the English legate commenced the high mass *De Trinitate*. The first introit was sung by the English chanters, the second by the French. They had arranged that when the French organist played, the French chanters should sing, and vice versa. Pierre Mouton played the *Kyrie*, then the English the *Gloria in excelsis*; the *Patrem* was sung by the French, with the King's band of *cors de sabuttes* and fifes, the *Sanctus* by the English, and the *Agnus Dei* by the French, who concluded with several motetts.[49]

The interesting point is that it was the French ensemble that accompanied the singing of the liturgy, with what we can take to be trombones and cornetts. The English choir sang unaccompanied. Does this illustrate a fundamental difference of practices at this time, or was it simply that the French had in a small way outmanoeuvred the English in the contest for opulence? Some light is cast in a letter from Sir Richard Wingfield, the English ambassador to France, who was charged with reporting regularly to Cardinal Wolsey, Henry VIII's chancellor, in the period running up to the Field of Cloth of Gold. The letter is dated 9 May 1520, less than a month earlier than the commencement of events:

> The King [Francis] was at mass today at the Jacobins, where high mass was sung by the bishop of Amiens. At the Kings offering, the chapel, with the hautbois and sacbuts, sang and played together, 'which was as melodious a noise as ever was heard'.[50]

Wingfield's comments seem to report something that was extraordinary in his experience, something that did not accord with normal English practice, and perhaps even something that he had not observed before in France either – unless it were to honour the King. This is slight evidence on which to base a general distinction between French and English practice at this time, but it might be added that there is not a single trace of instruments being used in English churches, except for purely ceremonial purposes, before the last quarter of the sixteenth century.

If such practices were unusual in the early part of the century, documentary and iconographical evidence removes any doubt that from about the 1570s it was common across Europe for trombones, cornetts and other instruments to perform within the liturgy. As the appearance of players in church employment records shows, there was a formalization of the use of trombones in churches, and a reorganization of the common practice whereby city and court musicians received payments for performing in churches on special occasions. In the seventeenth century, instrumentalists routinely played in churches. The purchase in 1634 of a set of cassocks, surplices and collars for the trombones and cornetts of the English Chapel Royal leaves little doubt that this was the case.[51]

From about the 1570s it is also possible to discern specific information about the types of ensemble in which trombones were included, and about the repertoires that they performed. Even in England, where there was particular sensitivity to charges of recusancy, there are unequivocal signs that the practice of using trombones and other instruments in liturgical music was being embraced. According to the less than objective seventeenth-century Protestant historian Daniel Neal, even the Queen herself retained such ornamentation in her worship, which was replete

> with lighted Candles, out of her own Chapel. The Gentlemen and singing Children appeard there in their Surplices, and the Priests in their Copes; the Altar was furnished with rich Plate, with two gilt Candlesticks, with lighted Candles, and a massy Crucifix of Silver in the midst: The Service was sung not only with organs but with the artificial Musick of Cornets, Sackbuts &c. on solemn Festivals.[52]

Whether or not this is true, by the end of the century there are clear signs that trombonists were being used in English cathedrals: some, such as Canterbury, Carlisle and possibly Durham, were specifying them in their statutes. In 1589 an Italian observer at Canterbury, 'an Intelligencer from Rome, of good parts & account', declared that the service was so ornate that Rome was 'in great blindnesse' in its beliefs about English religious practices, for when he had 'heard the solemne Musicke with the voyces, and Organs, Cornets, and Sagbutts, he was overtaken with admiration'.[53]

In the seventeenth century, several provincial English cathedrals employed trombones on their statutes, to the distress of more conservative and devout Anglicans. At Durham in 1629 there were complaints of 'Sackbuts & Cornets piping so loud at the Communion table, that they may be heard halfe a mile from the Church',[54] and a year later further complaints about a solemne Service, with singing and Organs, Sackbuts and Cornets, little whereof could be understood of the people, neither would they suffer the Sacrament to be administred without a continuall noise of Musick, both instrumentall and vocal, to the great disturbance of these holy actions.[55]

Similarly a visitor to Christ Church Cathedral, Dublin, had complained of 'the pompous service' there, which 'was attended and celebrated with all manner of

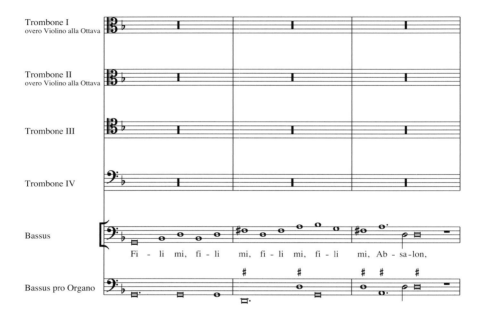

Example 5.2. Heinrich Schütz, *Fili mi Absalon* from *Symphoniae Sacrae*, published in Venice, 1629

instrumental music, as organs, sackbuts, cornets, viols &c, as if it had been at the dedication of Nebuchadnezzar's golden image in the plain of Dura'.[56] The practice of instruments doubling voices in sacred music was common in the Low Countries in the first half of the sixteenth century, and more generally throughout Europe by the end of the century. A famous illustration from *Practica Musica* (1556) indicates a mode of practice that may have been routine in major ecclesiastical centres and commonplace in many others for special occasions (see Ill. 31).

Seventeenth-century idioms

The publication of Giovanni Gabrieli's *Symphoniae sacrae* seems to initiate the practice of routinely labelling trombone and other instrumental parts in large-scale works performed in northern Italy. Monteverdi's *Orfeo* (1607) and Marian Vespers (1610) are among several works that do not simply require the use of trombones, but employ them extensively and idiomatically. Indeed Monteverdi's writing for trombones in these two works acknowledges the breadth of the trombone's expressive potential as it was known at that time, from the decorative writing in complex contrapuntal passages of the *Sonata sopra Sancta Maria* in the Marian Vespers to the dark, thickly textured homophony that signals the underworld in *Orfeo*.

The remarkable writing for trombones of Heinrich Schütz owes much to the Venetian influence. Schütz studied with Giovanni Gabrieli from 1609 until the latter's death in 1612. Schütz indicated the use of trombones, either optionally or prescriptively, from his earliest works that included instruments. The first such marking appears in the music for the wedding of Michael Thomas and Anna Schultes in Leipzig in 1618, and trombones are deployed in many of the works written in Dresden in the late 1650s, where formidable instrumental forces were available to him. Schütz's understanding of the choral idiom for trombones is illustrated in such works as *Fili mi, Absalon*,[57] from the *Symphoniae sacrae* published in Venice in 1629. (Ex. 5.2) It is set for a solo bass voice, four trombones and organ continuo. Even though Schütz indicates that the upper two trombone parts could be replaced by violins at the octave, it is clear what preference was intended. The slow-moving, carefully spaced polyphony has the feel of a chorale even though it is considerably more intricate. The sonority derives from both the traditional intimacy of trombones with vocal textures (Schütz often uses trombones in what are essentially vocal works), and, by this time, the symbolic meaning that this instrumental timbre had acquired: a sonority that was to appear more than a century later in Austrian opera, and subsequently in large-scale Romantic and post-Romantic orchestral works.[58]

Despite the ubiquity and enduring character of this aspect of the trombone idiom, it would be wrong to draw the conclusion that writing for the instrument in the seventeenth century exploited a single mode of expression. Smaller-scale, purely instrumental ensemble pieces with labelled trombone parts proliferated in the seventeenth century. These include a Canzona for eight trombones by Tiburtio Massaino (1608), *La Bavara* for four trombones (1621) by Giovanni Martino Cesare, 16 incompletely preserved pieces for four trombones (1622 & 1627) by Samuel Scheidt, a Canzon for four trombones (1626) by Biagio Marini, a Canzon for eight trombones by Johann Hentzschel (1649) and a four-part *Canzonato* by Johann Georg Braun (1658). To these can be added the Sonatas by Daniel Speer: one for four trombones published in 1685, and two for three trombones published in 1697. These pieces can probably be taken as indicative of a larger repertoire that has not survived. Similarly, the tiny surviving repertoire of English pieces for small mixed ensemble (such as the Fantasias by John Hingeston for cornetts, sackbut and continuo (c. 1658) and two pieces that survive in somewhat fragmentary form as an organ part – the one by John Coprario for cornett, sackbut and continuo, the other by Henry Loosemore for cornett, sackbut, violin and continuo[59]) may be the remnant of a much larger repertoire. More unusual is Giovanni Martino Cesare's *La Hieronyma* (1621) for solo trombone. The only other seventeenth-century solo piece is an anonymous *Sonata trombono & basso* (c. 1665).

Illustration 33. Detail from the title page of Prateorius's *Theatrum instrumentorum* (1620) appended to *Syntagma musicum* II showing two trombone players in an ensemble, being directed by a conductor (possibly Praetorius himself).

The amount of seventeenth-century repertoire that includes idiomatic parts for trombone is considerable and probably impossible to quantify accurately. The most abundant sources emanate from musical centres which included competent trombonists in their establishment, provided some sustained commitment to fine music-making and also had musical leadership from composers of stature. Appendix 2 provides an indicative overview of these 'centres of repertoire', but as with all such summaries it should be viewed with caution. Some seventeenth-century repertoire came from small residences which appear to have had a thriving if modest musical tradition. For example, there is evidence that some seventeenth-century English trombone players found work between the dissolution and restoration of the monarchy (1640 and 1660) as servants in provincial manors, where they also took part in music-making. This may account for some small pockets of repertoire. It is clear that this was one of the golden ages for the trombone and it is easy to imagine that some great individual players were working in the musical centres of Europe. But the more striking impression is that the trombonists of the seventeenth century were ensemble players with a refined ability to play in homogeneous and particularly mixed consorts. As we shall see in subsequent chapters, aesthetic changes were to fracture the inheritance of these skills in all but a few places.

Chapter 6

Decline, survival and rehabilitation: the seventeenth and eighteenth centuries

Surviving documents from across Europe bear witness to a remarkable decline in the trombone's popularity at the end of the seventeenth century. There were a few countries where this did not occur, but generally the pattern was similar. The most notable feature of this fall from grace is that it took place relatively suddenly. The trombone was still widely in use in the 1670s, but within a couple of decades it was either obsolete or to be found only in town bands where the older traditions were slow to die. One or two centres, particularly those in the orbit of the Austrian court, provided a slim but resilient strand of continuity, but elsewhere the production of instruments declined, and as players grew old and died, the performance traditions passed with them. Processes of learning and playing that had been in place for more than two centuries were fractured.

In the second half of the eighteenth century, Vienna was the source of a renewed interest in the instrument, but it took decades for it to be fully integrated into the musical life of other great European cities. It took yet longer for its idiom to be formed so that it was commonly understood, and for a body of competent players to emerge – even by 1800, trombonists of any quality were scarce in many parts of Europe. But as the nineteenth century unfolded, the instrument became increasingly well established in operatic, concert and military music. As we shall see in Chapter 7, there were other reasons why the passage from the eighteenth to the nineteenth century can be regarded as a watershed in the history of the trombone, but in this chapter we must deal with three facets of its history: the pattern of the instrument's decline, its idiom in those pockets where it survived, and the manner of its reappearance and rehabilitation.

Decline

The records of Canterbury Cathedral for 1682 mention that there were 'four places vacant which were supplied formerly by the sackbuts and cornetts'.[1] We do not know how long these vacancies had existed, but we do know that they were never again filled. The cathedral inventories of 1752 and 1761 mention 'two brass Sackbuts not us'd for a grete number of years past',[2] and these were undoubtedly the very instruments used by the last trombone players to be accommodated in the statutes of this great church.

The case of the Canterbury trombones is typical of the story of the trombone in England at this time. Within a single generation it moved from being one of the most common features of the musical landscape to a position of almost total obscurity. It vanished from provincial cathedrals and the English court. The signs of decline were evident in the 1660s. At the Restoration of the Crown, many places traditionally reserved for trombone players in the royal band went to other instrumentalists or multi-instrumentalists. The institutions that employed trombones in the English provinces and in Scotland followed this trend, but the instrument lasted a little longer in waits bands than it did elsewhere. The Edinburgh waits still employed a trombonist in 1675, the Norwich waits were still actually buying trombones from London in 1677 (though we have no idea who actually supplied them), and the City of London waits also retained trombone players at about this time. But by the late 1690s, the decline was emphatic and apparently irreversible. The skills of playing lasted only as long as the playing lives of its performers; the last trombone players in England in the seventeenth century were probably very old men. A manuscript compiled at the close of the century by the antiquarian James Talbot confirms the story of this decline, and hints strongly at the reason for it: '[The c]hief use of [the] Sackbutt here in England is in consort with our Waits or English Hautbois. It was left off towards the latter end of K[ing].Ch[arles].2[nd's reign] and gave place to the Fr[ench] Basson.'[3] Charles II's preference for the homogeneous sonorities he had become accustomed to while in exile on the continent – particularly the French style of evenly balanced string instruments – led to a rejection of the more heterogeneous timbres that had typified professional wind music in the English court. Indeed, Charles's introduction of 'four and twenty fiddles' to dominate the royal band in 1660 was a direct imitation of the French *Vingt-quatre Violons*. It is therefore more than a little ironic that the advent of this new preference coincided with the composition by Matthew Locke of his five-part *ffor his Majestys Sagbutts and Cornetts*, one of the canonical works for this combination of instruments. It is claimed, but not proved, that these pieces (a collection of individual pieces rather than a suite) were performed at the Restoration Coronation. It is all but certain that the pieces were indeed written after 1660, when Locke was appointed composer in ordinary to the court, but the ensemble for which they were written belongs more to the old world of the pre-Restoration period than to the court of Charles II. The cornett/sackbut ensemble was re-formed in 1660 as part of the royal band (in fact, trombonists and cornett players had been employed by Cromwell in the Commonwealth, and two bass part books of the repertoire of Cromwell's cornett and sackbut band survive), but there is little sign of the group having a foreground status in court music after the Restoration.[4]

There was probably not a single native-born trombone player in the British Isles for almost the entire eighteenth century. References to the instrument in scholarly works by English writers merely serve to show how badly understood such words as 'sackbut' and 'trombone' were. According to the music historian Roger North, who had visited the cathedrals of York and Durham in 1676, 'They have the ordinary wind instruments in the Quires as the cornet, sackbut and curtauile and others, which supply the want of voices.'[5] North also mentions the instrument in his essays on *The Theory of Sounds* (c. 1710–28), where he still maintains that it was used in some cathedrals. It is difficult to credit North with complete reliability: like so many writers of his time, what he has to say is so derivative of earlier authors that we should doubt whether he had heard or seen the trombone himself.[6] Among other sources that give largely half-baked descriptions of the trombone are the anonymous *A Short Explication of such Foreign Words as are made use of in Musick books* (1724)[7] and William Tans'ur's *The Elements of Musick Display'd* (1772). Despite the presence of trombone parts in the scores of some of Handel's most important oratorios (parts that were certainly played at the first performances – a matter that is dealt with in more detail below), it is clear that trombones were largely absent from England until the Handel Commemorations of 1784, when, according to Charles Burney 'the SACBUT, or DOUBLE TRUMPET, was sought; but so many years had elapsed since it had been used in this kingdom, that, neither the instrument, nor a performer upon it, could easily be found'.[8]

In most parts of Europe the trombone declined as it did in England, though perhaps less emphatically and rapidly. Its demise in France may have been complete by the mid-seventeenth century, when court music there was reorganized. An engraving of *Les Douze Grands Hautbois* performing at the coronation of Louis XIV shows one, or possibly two, trombonists,[9] but it is difficult to determine how long the instrument lasted in the French court. Sébastien de Brossard's *Dictionaire de musique* (1703) is rare among French reference books of the first half of the century in providing a description of the instrument, and while the trombone (rather than the *saquebute*) is mentioned in French documents in the late 1740s, there is no sign of trombone parts in French repertoire until the late 1760s.[10]

In Italy the situation is clearer. Tarditi's largest work, his Mass for five voices, two violins, trombone and organ (1648), is a very late example of trombone scoring in a large-scale Italian work of the seventeenth century. At St Mark's, Venice, where the trombone had been so important in the opening decades of the century, it was gradually left off the payments lists and the places went to other instrumentalists. Players of bowed instruments with sympathetic strings were introduced from about 1690, and trumpeters from 1691. Often at this time, the appointment of string players was at the expense of places traditionally reserved for trombonists. In 1698 the cornett was officially replaced by the oboe. The trombone maintained what must have been a fragile existence for somewhat longer – two players were still on the books until 1732 – but it is far from certain what its role was in the opening decades of the eighteenth century, and its replacement in 1732 was permanent.[11]

Elsewhere in Italy the instrument lingered on into the eighteenth century. In Naples in 1667 the confraternity of San Giorgio Maggiore was divided between the 'Master Players of Strings' and 'Players of Wind and Trombones', and this position seems to have been reconfirmed in 1681 and again in 1721.[12] In Rome the Haym family – one of the most important dynasties of Italian instrumentalists – included Giovanni Antonio (*fl.* 1680–1729), Pietro Antonio Haym (d. 13 December 1766) and Pietro Antonio Sebastian (1713–88), each of whom was a multi-instrumentalist who counted trombone playing among his skills; but there is little additional information about the exact nature of their engagement with the instrument.

In Germany trombonists continued to be employed in civic groups throughout the seventeenth and eighteenth centuries, but even here their existence was sporadic. In 1713, Johann Mattheson of Hamburg, describing the 'most magnificent sounding trombone' in *Das neu-eröffnete Orchestre*, noted that the various sizes of instruments

could form a choir in their own right, but that they were by that time 'used very
rarely except in church pieces and solemn music'.[13] Where the trombone was used in
such contexts in Germany, the players were almost always recruited from civic bands,
for the tower music tradition seems to have survived for as long as there were players
to sustain it. The best-documented example as far as surviving repertoire is concerned

Illustration 34. 'Performance of a Bach Cantata', an engraving by Johann Christoph Dehne for
Johann Georg Walther's *Musicalisches Lexicon* (1732). This is likely to be a stylized representation
rather than a reliable testament.

is probably that of Leipzig, where Johann Pezel was a *Stadtpfeifer* when his *Hora decima musicorum* was published in 1670. This collection is made up of 40 separately numbered, single-movement sonatas in five parts. A further set of five-part pieces, entitled *Fünff-stimmigte blasende Music* and containing 76 intradas and dance movements, was published in 1685 when Pezel was living in Bautzen. Though these sets contain an indication of their multi-instrumental utility, their idiom clearly implies that two cornetts and three trombones were primary in the composer's intentions.

This grouping, or something like it, continued to be favoured in German towns into the eighteenth century. Buxtehude had a trombone player permanently at his disposal at Lübeck, and seems to have been able to draw on a group of them for his larger works. In Gotha the *Kapellmeister* petitioned for a group of musicians specifically including two cornetts and three trombones. The picture across Germany seems to be similar. J. S. Bach's predecessor as *Kapellmeister* at Leipzig, Johann Kuhnau, complained about the lamentable execution of finely written works, and mentioned that there were only eight *Stadtpfeifer* in the town, including two cornetts and three trombones. It was these *Stadtpfeifer* who played in the fourteen church cantatas in which Bach included trombones. (Ill. 34) Each of these cantatas was either written between 1723 and 1725 or revised to include trombone parts. *Herr Christ, der einge Gottessohn* BWV 96 has a part marked 'corno' that was altered to be played by the trombone in at least one performance during 1746–7.[14] (Additionally, in the motet *O Jesu Christ, mein Lebens Licht* BWV 118 (1736–7), three trombones are indicated.) Bach's use of trombones in these cantatas hints at why the instrument fell from grace in some places and survived in others. The aforementioned works are mainly in the older motet form, and with very few exceptions the trombones are used to double vocal lines. They are seldom given genuinely independent parts. While the trombone tradition may have been loosely sustained in some parts of Germany in civic bands, its importance was hugely diminished. It continued as part of a secular civic tradition rather than because it had a place in foreground expressive repertoires.

Centres of survival

Austria was an oasis of sophisticated trombone playing throughout the eighteenth century. There was a succession of fine players at the Austrian court and in several churches, especially in Vienna and Salzburg. The repertoire that emanated from Austria at this time is unique, and we can assume that the style of playing was equally distinctive. Seventeenth-century idioms seem not simply to have been inherited, but rather, built upon. Almost all the repertoire from this period seems to call for a florid technique delivered in a light, vocal and often highly decorative style. This can be seen early in the century in the trombone parts of Austrian sacred music, and much later in the secular solo or soloistic repertoire that includes the concertos by Albrechtsberger and Wagenseil. In addition to this mode of expression, trombones continued to be used to double vocal lines in sacred music. This doubling role appears to have been entirely functional in that it helped singers sustain their pitch; it seems to have had little to do with the creation of an overall vocal/instrumental timbre.

However, it may well have been this very function that enabled the instrument to survive, and it is likely that such composers as Gluck and Mozart, who were conspicuously responsible for the instrument's reintroduction into the opera orchestra later in the century, called to mind this function, and particularly the sonorous character of the trombone in homophonic chorales.

In the eighteenth century Austria was a Catholic country, and the Habsburg court maintained a rich sacred as well as secular musical tradition. Italian musicians and littérateurs played an important part in the cultural life of town and court: indeed, Italian was the primary language for texts set to music that were not in Latin. Though opera flourished in Vienna in the first half of the eighteenth century, the trombone was not used in opera orchestras. Stewart Carter has suggested that none were used between Cesti's *Il pomo d'oro* (1668) and Gluck's *Orfeo ed Euridice* (1762),[15] and I have found nothing to challenge that suggestion, even though, according to Zechmeister, five members of the court trombone group may have been employed by the Vienna Imperial Opera in 1747.[16] It is possible that cultural determinants may have been at play: that the ecclesiastical associations of the trombone may well have marked the instrument as unsuitable for secular entertainment.

Records of the Vienna court show that trombonists were employed there continuously through the eighteenth century.[17] For most of that century, members of the Christian family held positions as trombonists. The permanence of trombonists in the court band provided stability and perhaps a focus for the performance culture, but trombone playing was not restricted to the court. On his visit to the town in 1772, the English music historian Charles Burney remarked: 'there is scarce a church or convent in Vienna, which has not every morning its *mass in music*'.[18] All churches maintained organs and other instruments: Dexter Edge has identified ten churches that maintained one or more trombonists.[19] The orphanage is described in 1774 as having three trombone players among the very many of its inhabitants who were being taught orchestral instruments[20] – a clear replication of the Venetian conservatoire model of the seventeenth century.

A large repertoire survives of small-scale chamber music in which (usually) one trombone is matched with other instruments. In this relatively simple-textured music, the trombone is used idiomatically either as a continuo instrument or as a middle-voice part. (Ex. 6.1) However, some pieces contain more ambitious technical passages which were obviously written for one of the expert court players (such as one of the Christians). Among the later concerted music for the instrument are to be found the first two concertos for the trombone, one in E flat by Wagenseil (c. 1763) and another in B flat by Albrechtsberger (1769). Like so much of the soloistic repertoire of this period, they fall in the tessitura of the alto trombone, and are in alto clef. This suggests that the alto instrument was preferred. Most writers have pointed to this preference, but while there is no doubt that the alto trombone was in common use at this time, it does not follow that such parts were always played on that instrument. Howard Weiner has marshalled convincing evidence to demonstrate that much of this music was just as idiomatically suited to the tenor instrument – in many cases, more so.[21]

The Albrechtsberger and Wagenseil concertos are the only works that conform to the concerto genre of that time (though Wagenseil's two-movement form is relatively

Example 6.1. Johann Georg Reutter, *Bersabea, ovvero il pentimento di David* (1729)
This trombone obbligato is a typical example of Viennese repertoire of its kind. (I am grateful to Stewart Carter for his permission to reproduce this illustration.)

unorthodox), but other works that contain soloistic writing should also be taken into account. These include a Divertimento in D by Michael Haydn, which was written in 1764 after the composer had left Vienna for Salzburg. It has nine movements, with the trombone (again apparently an alto instrument) appearing in just three of them. It was clearly intended for a player of considerable competence, probably the Salzburg trombonist Thomas Gschlatt.[22] In fact, the penultimate and most soloistically demanding movement is annotated 'Andantino. / col Trombone Conc.to'. A similar use of the trombone is found in a set of pieces by Leopold Mozart bearing the title Serenata in D for Orchestra, which the composer wrote in or around 1762.

It has nine movements, each featuring one or more instrument in a soloistic mode. The trombone is featured in three movements: No. 6 (Adagio), No. 7 (in the Trio section of the Menuetto) and No. 8 (Allegro). Here the requirement for an alto instrument seems unambiguous, for it reaches D_5. Two of the movements are written in sharp keys. This could have imposed an extra level of difficulty that accounts for an annotation on the trombone part in Leopold Mozart's own hand, 'Bey Ermangelung eines guter Posaunisten kann es ein guter Violinist auf der Viola spielen.' ('In the absence of a good trombone player, a good violinist can play it on the viola.')[23] On the other hand, the annotation may well be an indication that Papa Mozart knew that good trombonists were in short supply in Salzburg at this time, and it is noticeable that virtuoso writing for the instrument ceased there in the late 1760s.

Before the 1760s, and leaving aside the doubling of vocal parts in sacred choral music – which was largely an *ad libitum* tradition – the solo trombone was used extensively in oratorio and in the earlier analogous Italian genre known as *sepolcro*. Oratorio form needs no explanation here, but *sepolcro* – sometimes also referred to as *azione sacra* and *rappresentazione sacra* – probably does. The name derives from the sepulchre scene which formed the backdrop for dramatic performance of settings of sacred texts (usually the Passion) on Maundy Thursday and Good Friday. *Sepolcro* was mainly a seventeenth-century genre that seems to have passed out of fashion by 1705, but representations of the sepulchre continued to be used as backdrops for later oratorios by composers resident in Vienna, such as Fux and Caldara.

Trombones (one or two) were frequently used as obbligato instruments in both *sepolcro* and oratorio performed for the Habsburg court in Vienna. Stewart Carter, whose work on this repertoire provides the most authoritative starting point for its study, suggests that a very substantial quantity of this music was composed. The trombone was not the only instrument for which obbligatos were written as constituents of solo arias, but the trombone and the bassoon seem to have been the most favoured wind instruments. In all cases the writing is florid and extremely idiomatic.[24]

The use of trombones in the very many other liturgical works of the early eighteenth century usually follows the predictable practice of doubling vocal lines (particularly the alto and tenor lines) in *tutti* passages. But there are also several works where one or two trombones have independent – often solo – parts, particularly in *sinfonia*. The practice of doubling vocal lines *ad libitum* when no such doubling is indicated in scoring is, of course, a continuation of a much earlier tradition, but the appearance of trombone lines in autograph sources suggests a decline of such practices in favour of a more discerning and selective approach. As late as 1826 however, Ignaz von Seyfried, editor of Albrechtsberger's collected writings, was still acknowledging this ancient custom: 'The first trombone has to double the alto, the second the tenor, and the third (which is seldom used any more) the bass voice.'[25]

While the Viennese court employed more than three trombones for much of the century, individual churches had just one or two players. Along with other theoretical writers of the first half of the eighteenth century such as Joseph Majer (*Museum musicum theoretico practicum*, 1732) and Johann Philipp Eisel (*Musicus autodidactos, oder der sich selbst informirende Musicus*, 1738), Johann Mattheson in *Das neu-eröffnete Orchestre* (1713) describes each member of the trombone family,[26] but it is difficult to determine whether they were describing instruments they knew or those about which they had some written information.

The court calendar at Salzburg shows that a single player was employed sporadically between 1743 and 1780, but here, as in Vienna, the main function of the instrument was in respect of sacred music. Trombone players were employed in the Salzburg town band, and it was they rather than court players who performed in the cathedral: 'To the choir singers belong, finally, three trombonists, namely, to play the alto-, tenor- and bass-trombone, which must be taken care of by the master of the town waits with two of his subordinates.'[27] Thus it seems that in Salzburg Cathedral the practice was to use three trombones; this may well have been why Mozart used three in his operas. Other sources also record that three trombones were used in the cathedral: for example, an account by a student at the city's Benedictine University of a Vespers service there in 1745 describes such instrumentation.[28] However, Leopold Mozart's report of a Michael Haydn mass (*Missa Sancti Hieronymi*) conducted by the composer in 1777 includes a description of the orchestral forces, but mentions only the 'alto trombone'.[29]

Instrument-making in the eighteenth century

In thinking about where the trombone survived in the eighteenth century, the centres of instrument manufacture need also to be borne in mind. It may appear strange that the production of fine trombones did not come to a halt as swiftly as the tradition of playing; indeed, it seems not have come to a halt at all. Older centres of production continued, and new ones appeared later in the century. This continuity came from the fact that brass instrument manufacture was sustained by the production of trumpets and horns, the demand for which never really subsided.

Using the data gathered in Appendix 1, supplemented by additional information kindly supplied by Stewart Carter, some broad generalizations can be made about the production of instruments in this period. It is possible to identify just under 120 surviving instruments that were made between about 1700 and 1800. The need for caution is obvious, for we can not possibly tell whether the surviving instruments provide a realistic sample of production, but it is a sizeable number and the patterns revealed fit rationally with what we otherwise know about areas of activity at this time. Germany continued to be the main source for the supply of instruments: more than three-quarters (87) of all surviving eighteenth-century instruments were made there. Of these, 34 carry the names of Nuremberg makers. However, there is also evidence to suggest a change taking place. Of the 34 Nuremberg instruments, all but three (possibly four) were made before 1750. Twenty-two instruments survive by eighteenth-century makers from Pfaffendorf, and by contrast, these are all dated between 1760 and 1799.[30] Other German centres of production were Leipzig, for which there are nine instruments stretching across the eighteenth century, and Dresden, from where there are five surviving instruments dated between 1725 and 1761.

No Austrian instruments are known to survive from before 1700, but fourteen date from the eighteenth century. The earliest, dated 1702, was made by Hanns Geyer, who, like all the makers of surviving Austrian instruments, operated from Vienna. The latest, by Joseph Huschauer, is dated 1794. To these can be added several instruments, some of which may in fact now be lost: one by Jacob Steiner of Zofingen, Switzerland; two from Czechoslovakia, both by Umlauff of Prague; and three made in Breslau (at that time in Prussia) in the 1790s. Surviving instruments from the very end of the century carry the names of Neukirchen makers – a town (Markneukirchen from 1858) that was to develop as an important brass instrument manufacturing centre in the nineteenth century.

One of the more interesting and slightly enigmatic features of this list is the presence of seven trombones made by J. G. Ahlgren of Stockholm between 1770 and 1776. Some are inscribed with the name of the Royal Chapel (*Gird H f j För Kong. Cappel*). At this time there were many German-born composers working in Stockholm, including J. M. Kraus, J. G. Naumann, J. C. F. Haeffner and G. J. Vogler. It seems probable that this is why trombones were used in Sweden at this time. However, each of these men was essentially a composer of secular music whose livelihood was based on a variety of musical contexts including opera. Some music written in Sweden by these composers and containing trombone parts has been identified, but we must also assume that the Stockholm players, who were employed during one of the richest periods in Sweden's musical history, also engaged with the sacred repertoire.

Later Austrian opera and oratorio

From the 1760s, the trombone started once again to be used in opera. Three trombones were deployed by Gluck for the Vienna performance of his *Orfeo ed Euridice* (1762), and this marks the start of a new approach to writing for the instrument in an orchestral context. He also used trombones in the oracle scenes of *Alceste* (1767), with sufficient effect to cause Leopold Mozart, who was present at the first performance, to suggest that his son use them for a similar purpose in his opera *Idomeneo*.

Mozart's use of trombones in his operas and sacred works marks something of a watershed in the history of the instrument's idiom. He used the trombone (just one instrument) for the first time in his oratorio *Die Schuldigkeit des ersten und fürnehmsten Gebots* K35, which was written and performed in Salzburg in 1767, and three trombones in *Davidde penitente* K469.[31] But his most idiomatic writing for the instrument occurs in *Don Giovanni* K527 (1787), *Die Zauberflöte* K620 (1791), and the two great sacred works, the Mass in C minor K427 (1783), and the incomplete Requiem K626 (1791). Each of these was first performed in Vienna, apart from *Don Giovanni*, which received its first performance in Prague. Mozart's use of trombones in the orchestra is both functional, in that the trombone sonority is used to provide depth to the orchestral sound, and dramatic in that he uses the choral, homophonic sound of three trombones to emphasize or imply narrative meaning through instrumental symbolism. (Ex. 6.2) In this latter respect he follows the example of Gluck and, from a considerably more distant point in history, Monteverdi, who evoked the underworld by scoring for trombones in *Orfeo* (1607). The association of

Example 6.2. Wolfgang Amadeus Mozart, *Don Giovanni* K527, Act 2 (1787)

the sound of trombones with the darker points of the emotional spectrum may derive from its origins in liturgical music, or from its sonic quality, or both, but it is an association that has been employed widely and consistently. One factor that explains the potency of the imagery evoked by trombones in eighteenth-century opera is its comparative novelty. Irrespective of the number of precedents that we can now cite for the use of trombones to create this type of dramatic meaning, the experience was new to audiences in the 1760s and 70s. Furthermore, the use in a secular setting of a group of instruments primarily associated with sacred music must have conveyed an ambiguity of meaning that intensified the effect.

The impact of the trombones at the moment of their first conspicuous entry in *Don Giovanni*, when the Commendatore's statue comes to life as he intones the words 'Di rider finirai pria dell'aurora', is chilling and must have had a strong dramatic impact when heard at the opera's first performance in Prague. But it seems likely that trombones were not used in its first Vienna performance: there is no mention of trombones in the theatrical accounts for the performances in 1788–9. Furthermore, the Burgtheater's performance score of the opera does not have trombone parts. We do not know the reason for the absence of trombonists, but it signals the first

Example 6.3. Wolfgang Amadeus Mozart, opening section of the trombone part of *Tuba Mirum* from the Requiem K626 (1791). The slurs/phrase marks included here are those carried in most modern editions. In fact, only the three seen in the last line above are in the original score.

occurrence of what was to become common practice and would last until well into the nineteenth century, whereby important secular and sacred works that contain trombone parts were performed without them. Salieri's *Axur* (1788) also has trombone parts, but they are crossed out from his autograph score, even though the parts are known to have been played when the opera was first performed in the previous season.[32] And there are many instances where, outside Vienna, the trombone solo in the 'Tuba mirum' of Mozart's Requiem (Ex. 6.3) was played on the bassoon because of the absence of a reliable trombonist (see also Chapter 8). We cannot assume that the inclusion of trombones in the instrumentation of a work necessarily meant that trombonists took part in the performance.

Trombonists did not have regular positions in eighteenth-century orchestras, and as the instrument became reinstated it took a considerable time for a corpus of competent professionals to emerge across Europe. The practice of players (often military band players) being engaged on a freelance basis for specific opera performances continued well into the nineteenth century. A glance at the payment records of opera houses and other places where musicians were employed at this time gives the clear impression that there was a buoyant freelance business for trombonists in Vienna in the second half of the eighteenth century. There is no doubt, for example, that the trombonists who played in the early performances of Mozart operas at the Burgtheater and Kärntnertortheater were supernumeraries rather than members of the usual theatre orchestra establishment.

France and Italy

The reintroduction of the trombone in France came by a somewhat different route. There are references to trombones being included in an orchestra in 1749, but the earliest use of the instrument in a French work occurs with François-Joseph Gossec's *Messe des morts* (1760), in which trombones appear in the off-stage band parts of the 'Tuba mirum'. Gossec credited himself with introducing these 'unknown instruments' to France. He claimed to have used trombones in *Sabinus* (1773), but there is a discrepancy between the score of this work and the instrumentation that he subsequently claimed to have devised. Jean-Joseph Rodolphe also scored for trombones in his *Isménor*, which was performed at Versailles in 1773. But while these works have some historical interest, neither has the musical substance to be regarded as especially significant. It is probably to the Paris performances of Gluck's operas that we must look for the most influential and emphatic sign of the trombone's rehabilitation in French music. Five of Gluck's operas presented in Paris included trombones: *Iphigénie en Aulide* (1774), *Orphée et Euridice* (1774), *Alceste* (1776), *Iphigénie en Tauride* (1779) and *Echo et Narcisse* (1779).

By the 1780s trombone players were finding regular employment in Parisian theatres. The trombone re-emerged in Paris in the hands of foreign players. According to Gossec, two brothers from Germany called Braun (one being André, the author of *Gamme et méthode pour les trombonnes*), and a Transylvanian called Lowitz, were engaged by him to perform in his opera *Sabinus* in 1773. These three appear to have been trumpeters as well as trombonists. One of the Braun brothers played trombone in the Paris production of Gluck's *Iphigénie en Aulide* in 1774, and in the same year a 'Braun' also played trombone in his *Orphée et Euridice*, along with two others, Mozer and Sieber, who doubled on horn. These players came from Germany and their names are found in Parisian documents for the remainder of the century.

Many composers who were active in Italy in the last quarter of the century found their way to Paris, and the presence of trombone parts, particularly in their operas, suggests that the instrument was not unknown to them. One Italian trombone player, M. Mariotti, who was known for his precision on the instrument, moved from Italy to Paris and then to London. All this suggests that a resurgence in interest in the instrument occurred in the last thirty or forty years of the century.

Handel's oratorios and the re-emergence of the trombone in England

Little is heard of the trombone in England in the eighteenth century until the mid-1780s. It is therefore especially surprising that Handel should have provided idiomatic parts for the instrument in two of his greatest oratorios, *Saul* and *Israel in Egypt*, first performed in London within three months of each other in 1739. The circumstances surrounding the use of trombones by Handel are particularly mystifying. The trombone parts for both *Saul* and *Israel in Egypt* are bound at the back of the respective conducting/performance scores. *Saul* was composed between 23 July and 18 August 1738 and revised on 27 September that year; it was first performed on 16 January 1739. *Israel in Egypt* was composed between 1 or 2 October and 1 November 1738 and first performed on 4 April 1739. As in Mozart's writing, the instruments do not double vocal lines mechanically, but have a level of independence. The parts could have been conceived as the two oratorios were being written, and completed at any time between the initial composition and the first performances, where they were undoubtedly played. The prospect of trombones being used in these works was revealed by 30 November 1738, as we can see from a letter from the lawyer Thomas Harris of Lincoln's Inn, London, to his brother James Harris of Salisbury:

> Mr Handell, as I am informed, intends to introduce into his performance several old instruments used in the time of K[ing] David . . .. I mean sackbuts, timbrells and tubal cain's. How they will succeed in these degenerate days I won't determine, but you will in Lent have an opportunity of judging for yourself.[33]

It appears that by 5 December 1738 it was certain that trombones were to be used in at least one of the oratorios – probably *Saul*. On that day Katherine Knatchbull, a London music enthusiast, wrote to James Harris:

> you must come up in January for he opens with the Loves of Saul and Jonathan, then follows another on the ten plagues of Egypt . . .. He has had an instrument made after the manner of Tubal Cain's the inventor of musick[.] He also has introduced the sackbut[,] a kind of trumpet, with more variety of notes, & it [is] 7 or 8 foot long & draws in like a perspective glass[,] so may be shortend to 3 foot as the player chuses or thrown out to its full length[;] despise not this description for I write from his own words.[34]

It is considerably less certain that trombones were used for all subsequent performances in Handel's lifetime. The *Occasional Oratorio* (first performed 1746, probably composed 1745) includes sections from *Israel in Egypt*, but trombones are omitted from the conducting score. The 1741 autograph score of *Samson* has two trombones cued into the Dead March and also copied into the conducting score. But the Dead March was cut before the first performance in 1743; nor was it performed in the 1744 and 1745 revivals. In the 1749 performances of *Samson*, the March was replaced by the Dead March from *Saul*, but with the trombone parts played by horns. The autograph score of *Hercules* (July–August 1744) has cues for two trombones doubling violas in the March in Act I, but it is unlikely that these parts were played either, because we hear nothing of them and they are not included in the conducting/performance scores. So whatever was intended for the trombones in 1741 and 1744 did not materialize. The last evidence we have of trombone players in this period is found in an announcement in the *London Daily Post* in February 1741, advertising a benefit concert for the trumpeter Valentine Snow at the 'New' Haymarket Theatre. (Ill. 35) The programme included the Dead March from *Saul*, and the presence of trombones was deemed sufficiently novel to warrant specific mention: 'to be performed with the Sackbuts'.[35]

It is worth pondering what motivated Handel to write for the instruments at this time, when his exploitation of the oratorio genre had advanced so well without them. There is no known stimulus for this expansion of his orchestration; apart from a brief therapeutic sojourn in Aix-en-Provence to take the spa waters in the spring of 1737, he had not recently been abroad. The identities of the players who performed for Handel in London are also a complete mystery. There were no trombonists in English military or theatre bands, and there is evidence that the instrument was seen as a

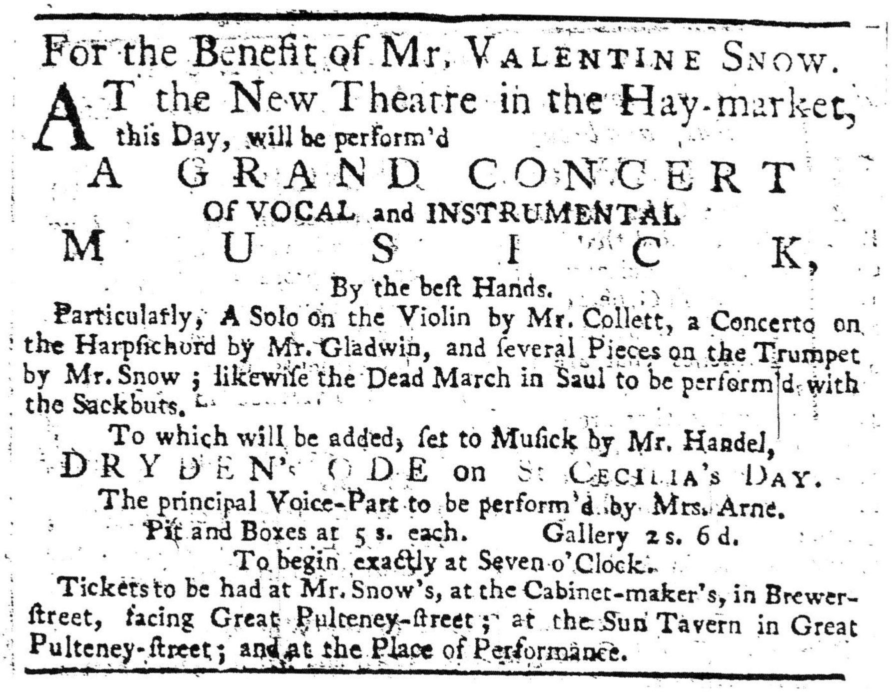
For the Benefit of Mr. VALENTINE SNOW.

AT the New Theatre in the Hay-market, this Day, will be perform'd

A GRAND CONCERT

Of VOCAL and INSTRUMENTAL

M U S I C K,

By the beſt Hands.

Particularly, A Solo on the Violin by Mr. Collett, a Concerto on the Harpſichord by Mr. Gladwin, and ſeveral Pieces on the Trumpet by Mr. Snow; likewiſe the Dead March in Saul to be perform'd with the Sackbuts.

To which will be added, ſet to Muſick by Mr. Handel,

DRYDEN's ODE on St. CECILIA's DAY.

The principal Voice-Part to be perform'd by Mrs. Arne.

Pit and Boxes at 5 s. each. Gallery 2 s. 6 d.

To begin exactly at Seven o'Clock.

Tickets to be had at Mr. Snow's, at the Cabinet-maker's, in Brewer-ſtreet, facing Great Pulteney-ſtreet; at the Sun Tavern in Great Pulteney-ſtreet; and at the Place of Performance.

Illustration 35. Advertisement for a benefit concert for the trumpeter Valentine Snow at the 'New' Haymarket Theatre, from the *London Daily Post* (26 February 1741). The presence of sackbuts is rare enough to deserve mention.

novelty. One of the more interesting light-hearted references is found in James Miller's *An Hospital for Fools*, a 'Dramatic Fable' performed as an afterpiece at Drury Lane on 15 and 17 November 1739:

> Daugh.[ter] (*to* Mercury, *viewing his* Caduceus)
> Pray, Sir, what Instrument is that in your Hand? A Sackbut, or Cymbal, or Psaltery? or some new invention? – O charming Sackbut! a Sackbut's my delight of all things. Pray, Sir, who did you learn of?
> Merc.[ury] I, Madam, I learnt of the Spheres.
> Daugh. Ah! That's some famous Hand, I suppose, just come over; well, I hope we shall have 'em all in time.[36]

There is only one other reference to the use of the trombone in orchestral music in England between 1700 and 1784. This occurs in sources for the original (1776) performance of Thomas Linley's *Shakespear Ode*. The original parts do not survive, but according to the list of players drawn up by Matthew Cooke, trombones were included.[37] By 1776 it is possible that there were trombone players in England, but it seems unlikely that a group of players would have arrived speculatively in London in the late 1730s in search of work; there were no other productions requiring their services in the city at that time, and there is no known source for their recruitment.

The most likely explanation is that Handel, who was undoubtedly familiar with trombones and perhaps even trombone players in Germany and other places that he had visited, was moved to write for players who were briefly in London for reasons that we do not now know: they certainly did not settle there, we do not know where they were from or where they subsequently went, and their identities have eluded scholars. I have previously speculated that these players came from Germany,[38] the source for trombone players in Paris in the early 1760s. The only evidence for this is circumstantial, but it was from Germany that trombone players originated for the Handel Commemorations more than forty years later.

According to Charles Burney, when the Handel Commemorations were organized in London in 1784: 'It was discovered, after much useless enquiry, not only here, but by letter to the continent, that in his Majesty's military band there were six musicians who played the three several species of sacbut; tenor, base, and double base.'[39] Burney was surely wrong in his description of the sizes of these instruments, and he was also wrong in claiming that the players were in the King's band. They were, in fact, members of the private band of Queen Charlotte, which also included a chamber group. The players listed in the programme for the Commemorations were Karst, Kneller, Moellern, Neibouer, Pick and Zink. Each came from German towns (Nienburg, Erfurt, Hanover and Northeim), and each played other instruments.[40] 'Kneller' was probably the 'Kellner' who included the trombone among the instruments he played when he applied for membership of the Royal Society of Musicians in 1789. In his application he described himself as a 'member of the Queen's Band who had arrived from Germany in 1782'.

John Dressler, another trombone-playing multi-instrumentalist, appears to have settled in England some time in the 1770s, as he applied to join the Royal Society of Musicians in 1777. Between the early 1780s and the end of the century, more players arrived in London from the continent. Among them was the aforementioned Mariotti, who settled as a trombone player at the Haymarket Theatre, where he also acted as a copyist. Manuscripts in his hand were prepared for the great double-bass virtuoso Dragonetti.[41] Mariotti provides an interesting illustration of the change in the structure of the trombone-playing profession in the last decades of the eighteenth century, when the instrument was starting to regain favour. He is first heard of in Bologna in the 1770s, where he appears to have been highly regarded. He left there in 1778, and seems to have been employed by the King of Naples during the 1780s. In 1789 he is one of a group of players at the Concert Spirituel in Paris, where he was regarded as 'astonishing for his precision on his instrument, of which the pleasing effect was formerly unknown in France'.[42] He was still in Paris in 1791,[43] but by 1794 he was sufficiently settled in London to have secured himself a listing, along with five other foreign trombone players (Dressler, Franks, Schubert, Zinck and Zwingmann) in Mortimer's *Musical Directory*.

In 1789 we see the first sign of instruments being advertised in England when Longman and Broderip announced that 'Thrombones' (*sic.*) were available in the company's Cheapside premises in London.[44] The typesetter's error may well be indicative of his lack of familiarity with the instrument. Such confusion was not new. When the instrument was heard at the 1784 Handel Commemorations, an intrigued member of the audience made an annotation to his concert programme: next to 'trombones', he scribbled: 'something like bassoons with an end like a large speaking trumpet'.[45]

In 1795 a man called John Woodham applied for membership of the Royal Society of Musicians, listing the trombone among the six instruments – string and brass – upon which he claimed competence. He was born in Hungerford, England, in 1768, and if his claim to play the trombone was true, he was probably the first English-born player of the instrument in more than a hundred years.

The flatt trumpet

As the English trombone was in the final throes of its decline in the seventeenth century, a slide instrument referred to as the 'flatt trumpet', and in modern times as the 'seventeenth-century slide trumpet', made a brief appearance. (Ill. 36) This was not a trombone at all, but for the sake of completeness it should be mentioned here, particularly as some writers have mistakenly suggested that music labelled for these instruments should properly be played on trombones. The 'flatt trumpet' is one of three separate species of instrument that have been referred to as a 'slide trumpet' in recent times (this does not include the soprano or descant trombone, which plays in the treble register – usually in B flat an octave above the tenor trombone – but is properly a trombone).[46] No specimens of the seventeenth-century instrument survive, neither are there reliable and detailed pictures of it. There are however documentary references to the instrument, some more opaque than others. Proof of its existence is based primarily on one important musical source and a single written document.

The music written by Henry Purcell for the funeral of Queen Mary in 1695 included a four-part March, played in the procession that preceded the Queen's coffin into Westminster Abbey, and a Canzona performed after the singing of the same composer's anthem 'Thou Knowest Lord the Secrets of our Hearts' inside the Abbey. The March, which is headed 'Flatt trumpets', is a re-working of a piece written three years earlier for the revival of Shadwell's play *The Libertine*. The Canzona is written

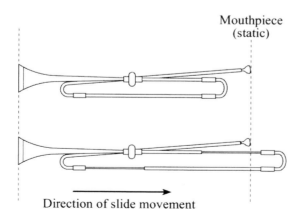

Mouthpiece
(static)

Direction of slide movement

Illustration 36. Drawing of a hypothetical seventeenth-century 'flatt trumpet'. (With thanks to Murray Campbell.)

for the same instruments and is somewhat ambiguously headed 'tremulo', a word with several meanings but which is seldom given as a direction to wind instrumentalists at this time; we can speculate that here it is a direction for a form of vibrato. According to Thomas Tudway, who prepared an edition of the anthem for Lord Harley in the early eighteenth century, the anthem was also accompanied by 'flat and mournful trumpetts'. Whether the phrase 'accompanied by' had the same connotations for Tudway as it does today can be debated, but we know that this same set was also performed, probably in the same manner, the following year at Westminster Abbey on the occasion of Purcell's own funeral.[47]

The term 'flatt' trumpet should be taken here to mean a trumpet that could be played in 'flat' or minor keys, but one can not help feeling that our knowledge of the 'flatt trumpet' is incomplete. Slightly puzzling is the use of 'flatt' as a verb in connection with trumpeting. For example, *The Diary of Henry Teonge, Naval Chaplain* contains a description of the events on board a ship at sea on Christmas morning 1675: 'Crismas Day we'll keepe thus: At four in the morning our trumpeters all doe flatt their trumpetts, and begin . . . playing a levite.'[48] This might suggest more than one meaning for the word,[49] but each of the four parts in Purcell's pieces contains notes that fall outside any one harmonic series, so the music could not have been played on natural trumpets. It is for this reason that earlier writers such as Barclay Squire assumed that the pieces were intended for trombones, some pitched in the treble register. But a manuscript in the possession of Christ Church Library, Oxford,[50] in the hand of the classical scholar and antiquarian James Talbot, which was probably compiled in the closing years of the seventeenth century, leaves little doubt that the instrument called 'ye Flat trumpet' existed and that it was quite different from the trombone. Talbot describes the instrument in sufficient detail for some modern period performers to have experimented with convincing reconstructions of it, but most conclusively, he gives a quite separate description of the 'sackbut' in yet more detail, based on Mersenne's famous drawing of 1636. Clearly, Talbot knew *both* instruments.

No evidence of slide trumpets of the type described by Talbot is found in other countries. Some of the trumpet parts written in Leipzig by J. S. Bach and his predecessor Kuhnau were intended for a slide trumpet known as the *tromba da tirarsi*, but this instrument seems to have been quite different from the one described by Talbot. Otherwise, while there are references to slide devices being fitted to treble brass instruments to aid tuning, the life of the English flatt trumpet seems to have been brief and relatively secluded.

Chapter 7

Didacticism and the idea of virtuosity

As the eighteenth century gave way to the nineteenth, the trombone started to be understood in a new way. The background reasons for this change lie partly in cultural and social developments, but also in a new aesthetic. This is often expressed in terms of a progression from a classical to a romantic sensibility, but there were other factors at work too. Technological invention, the development of commercial popular music and the collapse of traditional modes of musical patronage contributed to a widening of musical tastes, a larger and more diverse audience base, and the emergence of players from sectors of society that were previously disenfranchised from professional music-making. These issues are dealt with in considerably more detail in Chapter 10; here, suffice it to say that in the nineteenth century there was a reconfiguring of the entire music business, which had consequences for players, audiences and repertoires.

The scope and nature of change in the musical world during this period was unprecedented. By the closing years of the eighteenth century, the civic music traditions (to the extent that trombones were still involved in them) had died out or were tenuously sustained by small bands the configuration of which was often expedient. Trombonists played in opera and ballet orchestras, and some also found work in the limited number of military bands that had expanded beyond the small-scale *Harmoniemusik* formulations, popular in the last decades of the century. By 1900, symphony orchestras were well established in most European centres, even though they did not all provide permanent employment for trombonists. Military bands had become larger and in many countries had acquired an official status. In many respects they were the best-organized and most professional ensembles of the time, providing secure employment and producing many of the finest orchestral musicians and soloists. There was also a plethora of commercial bands on both sides of the Atlantic, some of which were itinerant and readily found work in towns of any size, and to these groups can be added the vastly more numerous, stylistically diverse and often highly efficient amateur bands that mushroomed from the middle of the century. It follows that entirely new ways of playing emerged, creating varied and often contradictory modes of expression. By the close of the nineteenth century it was as if new dialects had come into being, not just from different geographical locations but also from different categories of people, each with distinctive grammars and modes of communication. This process can be seen in the increasing disparity that developed between military and orchestral performance styles, which was to gain a yet sharper edge as the multitudinous species of popular music styles developed and created new stylistic temperaments.

Though the trombone was an 'ancient' instrument it seemed quite modern to many people, especially as valve instruments attracted popular interest. Some saw the proliferation of new mechanical brass instruments as contributing to an aesthetic crisis. To an extent this was the product of the confusion caused by the pace of change: so many new instruments were being introduced that it was difficult to detect reliable terms of reference for brass instrument idioms. The critic Eduard Hanslick, lamenting the scale and nature of Wagner's operatic expansion, saw his use of brass instruments as a regrettable triumph of modernity over continuity:

> the Parisian instrument maker Sax, . . . with his new system of pistons, has enabled trombones, horns, and bass tubas to execute the most difficult chromatic passages and trills. They can do things which would otherwise be impossible. But this technical advance is at the same time an aesthetic danger. Composers are now beginning to write as brilliantly for these formerly simple and dignified instruments as for the flute or the oboe. The instruments enjoy their new technical advancements at the cost of their noble, musical character. That they can now play just about everything is a technical triumph but a musical disaster.[1]

Yet paradoxically, amidst the huge diversity of this era in the trombone's performance history, there was a strand of continuity stretching almost from one end of the century to the other. This continuity was based on the entirely new concept (as far as trombonists were concerned) that aspiring players could be the recipients of a formal musical education, and that institutions should be established at national level to nurture appropriate talent for the musical profession. These institutions – the music conservatoires – became the focus for professional training, and they laid down broadly common parameters for performance standards. The conservatoires have had two vitally important structural effects on the trombone player – effects that have persisted to modern times. They have acted to define and sustain standards of playing, and they have brought the business of trombone playing into a common environment with other instruments for which there was a much richer canonical repertoire and tradition of teaching and learning. In effect, the conservatoires established performance orthodoxies and defined the qualities of fine trombone playing.

Only a tiny percentage of trombone players passed through the portals of the conservatoires, but the influence of these institutions was to become wide and emphatic for two reasons: the celebrity of individual trombone professors (and the generations of students they produced); and the influence of the published method books that were inspired by the idea of conservatoire education. Some of these method books were indeed written by conservatoire professors, but many more were assembled by lesser figures who copied and then adapted what they understood to be the outline formulae of the conservatoire method. The impact of the new didacticism, and particularly one of its primary premises – that the professional trombonist should aspire to the ideals of the soloist – changed performance practices. But in some respects it also nurtured something of a mismatch between the values of conservatoire teachers and the actual demands on trombone-playing professionals – a theme that will be discussed in Chapter 8.

Signs of change

The way that trombone players learned and thought about technique had been changing in the eighteenth century, and from the 1760s composers had deployed the trombone in a more imaginative way. Innovative trombone writing is found in the operas of Gluck, in Mozart's operas, masses and oratorios, and, in the closing years of the century, in the great oratorios of Joseph Haydn, *Seven Last Words* (1796), *The Creation* (1798) and *The Seasons* (1801).[2] As we have seen, the new way of writing for the instrument had three primary features: a move towards the use of a 'section' of three trombones written in the alto, tenor and bass range; a tendency to see the idiom as functioning to enhance orchestral colour, with a much more discriminating application of the instrument to double vocal lines; and a renewed propensity to use the trombone chorale to strengthen narrative or metaphorical meaning.

From the 1790s, didactic and theoretical writings reveal an apparently different understanding of the trombone from that which had existed a century or more earlier. They show that techniques had changed, but they provide comparatively little detail about the role of the trombone. There is an emphasis on the need for a robust basic technique and utterances are made about the role of the instrument in the orchestra: implicitly, however, the emphasis is on the development of skills suitable for the solo idiom which is seen as the route to musical efficiency. Didactic treatises espoused finesse and the pursuit of virtuosity, a particular kind of virtuosity that often seemed to aspire to the status of other instruments with a longer and more widely acknowledged solo idiom. The didactic treatises are important to the modern history of the trombone because they reveal the priorities and values that conditioned the way that players thought and learned about their instrument.

Paris and its Conservatoire

Uncertainty surrounds the teaching of the trombone in the first three to four decades of the Paris Conservatoire's existence. André Braun, author of *Gamme et méthode pour les trombonnes*, probably joined the staff at its foundation in 1795.[3] We do not know for certain that he taught the trombone, but he was definitely a trombone and trumpet player; if he did teach trombone he also had responsibility for some of the teaching of *solfège*. Members of the Garde Nationale were also incorporated into the teaching staff, among them Pierre-François Marcillac, who had been a trombone player at the Comédie Italienne and the Opéra.[4] For reasons that are not entirely clear, the trombone class was suspended in 1802 and remained so until 1833 – an absence that prompted the clarinettist and military composer Frédéric Berr to lament that 'An instrument as important as the trombone should be taught in the conservatory'.[5] The appointment of the composer Luigi Cherubini as Director of the Conservatoire in 1822 saw the introduction of several changes, including the slimming down of its size in favour of higher quality, but it was another eleven years before trombone teaching was re-established, apparently under the charge of Félix Vobaron. Three years later the trombone class was given official status, and the Swedish-French virtuoso Antoine Dieppo was appointed to teach it. We can speculate that the shrewd, visionary and ambitious Cherubini had recognized the ascendancy of the twenty-five-year-old Dieppo, who had already established himself as France's finest trombone player. He was principal trombone of the Opéra orchestra and the Société des Concerts du Conservatoire, and a member of the band of the Chapelle Royale. The son of a military bandsman, he was the most shining example of a new breed of trombone virtuosos: one need only glance at Dieppo's *études* to see that he was not simply a player of considerable facility, but that his concept of the instrument's idiom represented a radical advance on what we know of the repertoire before the 1840s. He was to remain at the Conservatoire until 1871, and was the most formidable influence on French trombone playing. Berlioz admired him, and in a letter from Dresden in February 1843 lamented that Germany had no player of his quality. Dieppo's playing inspired Berlioz's more demanding deployment of the instrument, and he was one of the elite group of orchestral musicians who were the first to be appointed to the committee of the Société des Concerts du Conservatoire.[6]

Table 1

Foundation of conservatoires and trombone classes, 1795–1924

Founded	Conservatoire	First trombone class & teacher	Notes
1795	Paris	1836, Antoine Dieppo (Félix Vobaron, 1833–36, provisional class)	In fact, trombone taught 1795–1802, probably by Philippe Widerkehr, also by Pierre-François Marcillac (1800–02). Trombone class closed 1802; provisional class re-opened 1833.
1808	Milan	1882, Gaetano Falda	1808, horn, trumpet and trombone class established, taught by horn teacher.
1811	Prague		
1816	Warsaw		Reopened 1861
1817	Vienna	1831, Franz Glöggl	Glöggl also taught double bass. He was succeeded in 1833 by Anton Slama.
1822	Royal Academy of Music, London	c.1823, John Smithies, Mr Shoengen	First students admitted 1823. Smithies' and Shoengen's names both appear on a concert programme from 1826.
1832	Conservatoire Royal de Musique, Brussels	1832, G.B.D. Bertrand	
1835	Geneva	1849, Mr. Grasset	
1841	Mozarteum, Salzburg		
1843	Leipzig (now the Hochschule für Musik und Theater Felix Mendelssohn Bartholdy)	1882?, Robert Müller	

1846	Munich, Hochschule für Musik und Theater	1897/8, Gustav Trampler	
1850, 1855, 1869		Berlin	
1856	Dresden		
1857	(Royal) Military School of Music, London	1857?, Thomas Sullivan	
1857	Peabody Conservatory, Baltimore	1868?, L. Gilbert, L. Ledermann, A.Derlin	Because of Civil War, instruction did not properly begin until 1868. Gilbert, Ledermann and Derlin were the first trombone teachers; but William Warner was first to have title 'Professor' (Assistant Professor of Trombone), in 1908.
1859	Conservatorio Luigi Cherubini, Florence	1860, Giovacchino Bimboni	Bimboni was also given the title 'Maestro di tromba e trombone'.
1861	Lausanne	1935, Mr. Lyard	There was a gap from 1939–1961 when the trombone was not taught.
1862	St Petersburg (now the Rimsky-Korsakov St Petersburg State Conservatory)	1870?, Franz Josef Türner	Türner was appointed in 1870, and made a professor in 1879.
1866	Moscow (now Moscow Tchaikovsky Conservatory)		
1867	New England Conservatory, Boston	1868, August Stein	Stein also taught contrabass. At some time between 1870 and 1877, he was joined by Alfred Rigg, who taught trombone, while Stein then taught only contrabass.
1867	Royal Danish Academy of Music, Copenhagen	1932?, Anton Hansen	
1875	Budapest		
1876	Zurich	1921, Otto Miene	'Free courses for orchestral instruments' taught from 1890 – trombone probably taught from 1890 by Mr. Grosse, but his name appears only in 1901. Miene was the professor of the first trombone class.
1878, 1883	Frankfurt		
1880	Guildhall School of Music, London	1880, Mr. Matt?	The first reference to a named trombone teacher is to Mr Matt in 1887.
1882	Sibelius Academy, Helsinki		
1883	Royal College of Music, London	1883?, Samuel Millar	Millar was first trombone teacher, but it appears that no-one took trombone

			as first study at least up to 1893 and probably beyond. Gustav Holst entered RCM in 1893 (trombone was his second study), and he may have been the first student to study trombone.
1893	Manchester College of Music (Royal Northern College of Music)	1893, John Branston	Branston appears to have had no first study pupils. The college merged with Northern School of Music to become Royal Northern College of Music in 1973.
1895	Melba Conservatorium, Melbourne	1898, Mr. Sinnotte	
1897	Elder Conservatorium, University of Adelaide	1969?, Desmond Blundell?	
1905	Basel	1909, Hermann Leupold	
1921	Eastman School of Music	1922, Emory Remington	Re-establishment of existing conservatoire at University of Rochester, NY.
1924	Juilliard Graduate School, New York		Acquired Institute of Musical Art to become the Juilliard School of Music in 1926.

The Paris Conservatoire became a model for a new type of musical education. It was the first to include the production of professional instrumentalists in its remit, and this included orchestral and band players as well as soloists. From the time the Conservatoire opened, following a government decree of 1795, it was a substantial institution with 351 students and 15 professors. We do not know how many trombone players were in the 1795 enrolment, but its short-lived prototype institution, the Institut National de Musique, had four in 1794, and it may be reasonable to assume that this group formed the basis of the first class at the Conservatoire proper.

The Conservatoire was quickly integrated into the fabric of institutional life in France. The model was loosely followed in most European countries, and eventually in the USA. Not all early conservatoires provided a real service to the music profession, but by about 1900 these institutions, along with other developments in music education, had made an important impact on the education of trombonists.

Military music education as an entry to the profession

By the end of the second half of the nineteenth century, the transfer of authority from traditional centres of patronage – the church and the nobility – to the state, and new forms of private, commercial and in some cases democratic ownership, was well established. This change impacted on how trombone players entered the profession and earned their living. The long-standing apprenticeship route had virtually disappeared by the start of the nineteenth century, and the most common entry point for ambitious young European trombone players was via amateur bands, and then through the military bands which were quickly gaining national importance and prominence. Some larger bands were constituted as part of the formal 'national' ceremonial, as with the Garde Nationale de la République in France. But in some countries, such as Britain, many bands were engaged and funded as the private accoutrements of senior military officers.

The foundation of specialist military music schools soon became important. France led the way in providing a coherent musical education for its military musicians. Links between the Paris Conservatoire and military music were always close. Military musicians, or musicians well experienced in military music, were employed in the Conservatoire from the outset, and the supply of orchestral musicians came largely from one or other branch of the military. In 1836 the French government was sufficiently ambitious to improve military music that it founded a separate Gymnase Musicale Militaire, initially under the direction of Frédéric Berr. In 1856 the work of the Gymnase was integrated into that of the Conservatoire, but with a distinctive syllabus and with Dieppo teaching valve trombone. This was seen not just as a

TIME		MONDAY						TUESDAY						WEDNESDA		
		Musical			General			Musical			General			Musical		
		STUDENTS	PUPILS		STUDENTS	PUPILS		STUDENTS	PUPILS		STUDENTS	PUPILS		STUDENTS	PUPILS	
Hour	Minutes		Senior	Junior		Senior	Junior		Senior	Junior		Senior	Junior		Senior	Junior
9 " " " 10 " "	0 15 30 45 0 15 30	Theoretical Instruction	Instrumental Instruction			School for Candidates for 1st Class Certificates		Theoretical Instruction	Instrumental Instruction			School for Candidates for 1st Class Certificates		Rehearsal for Full Band		Instrumental Instruction
HALF-AN-HOU																
11 " " " 12	0 15 30 45 0	Theoretical Instruction	Instrumental Instruction Elementary Theory			Special Class for 1st Class Certificates	Special Class for 1st Class Certificates	Theoretical Instruction	Instrumental Instruction Elementary Theory	Instrumental Instruction and Singing Practice				Rehearsal for String Band		
TWO HOURS FOR DI																
2 " " " 3 " " " 4 " "	0 15 30 45 0 15 30 45 0 15 30	Rehearsal for 1st Half Band Instrl. Instn.	Rehearsal for 1st Half Band	Instrl. Instn. Black Board Notn. Instrumental Instruction	School	School for those not in possession of 2nd Class Certificates		Rehearsal for 2nd Half Band Instrl. Instn.	Rehearsal for 2nd Half Band	Instrl. Instn. Black Board Notn. Instrumental Instruction	School	School for those not in possession of 2nd Class Certificates		Inspection of Instruments and Playing in Public by the Full Band, about 120 in number		
HALF-AN-HO																
5 " " 6	0 15 30 0	Rehearsal by Full Band	Rehearsal by Full Band	Elemntry. Instrctn.				Rehearsal by Full Band	Rehearsal by Full Band	Elemntry. Instrctn.						
THREE-QUARTERS-OF-																
6 7 " " " 8	45 0 15 30 45 0	Volntry. Independent Study	String Band Practice	String Band Practice	School for Candidates for 1st Class Certificates			Volntry. Independent Study	String Band Practice	String Band Practice	School for Candidates for 1st Class Certificates					

Illustration 37. Part of the weekly timetable for the Royal Military School of Music (1891).

rationalization, but as a consolidation of the importance of military music in national
life.

In 1857 (by coincidence, within a year of the integration of the Gymnase into the
Paris Conservatoire) the British government, after a tiresome and nit-picking period
of procrastination, opened its own Military Music Class at Kneller Hall near London
(from 1865 called the Royal Military School of Music). It was founded because the
authorities felt the need to bring music-making fully into the ambit of the army's
command, and also to produce native-born musical leaders to replace the foreigners
who dominated military music, and who often had corrupt relationships with
instrument manufacturers that cost the military a fortune.[7] There was also cause for
military authorities to feel a lack of confidence in the ability of English civilian
conservatoires to provide adequate training. Such sentiments would have been well
founded: for most of the nineteenth century, British conservatoires tended to be little
more than finishing schools for middle-class girls.

By contrast, from the day it first opened its doors the Military Music Class
provided a rational, pragmatic and rounded programme of training for musicians, the
likes of which had not previously been seen in the UK. (Ill. 37) Students were enlisted
from existing army bands, and further recruitment was secured directly from
'industrial schools' which provided free places to working-class children. The first
professor of the trombone at the Military School was a working military and civil
musician, but not apparently a trombone player – Mr Thomas Sullivan, whose son,
Arthur, was to become famous as half of Gilbert and Sullivan. Others who held the
position of trombone professor in the nineteenth century were a Mr Hanks
(1859–60), Signor Cioffi (1860–6) and Albert Cousins (1866–1900).

Curricula and orthodoxy

While conservatoires contributed to a change in the social structure of trombone
playing, their general influence did not fully mature until later in the century, when
there were more of them and their facilities were more widely franchised. For
example, the Royal College of Music was founded in London in 1883, with the Leeds
Forge Brass Band from the northern county of Yorkshire being engaged for the
opening ceremony as a symbol of the College's national purpose. The trombonist
Samuel Millar was appointed as trombone teacher at the Royal College at its
foundation, but ten years may have elapsed before he taught his first pupil (possibly
the composer Gustav Holst, a student at the Royal College from 1893, who took the
trombone as his second study).[8]

However, the essential message of the conservatoire method – that players could
be trained systematically through a broad curriculum led by exemplary performers –
seems to have been recognized quite early. The syllabuses of the best conservatoires
were well organized and systematic. Students were subject to formal assessment, and
it stands to reason that the modes of assessment and the criteria by which students
were judged implicitly and explicitly reflected the prevailing performance values and
standards. One does not have to look at the method books of the nineteenth century
for too long to discover that ideas about the attributes of a competent player were

becoming fixed. These ideas embraced articulation, tone and the array of facets that constitute technique. An orthodoxy was being established that was illustrated by strictly binary comparisons of the right and wrong way to play the trombone.

This orthodoxy seems to have been picked up in most countries, but this does not mean that the conservatoire system fostered entirely uniform tastes and playing styles across Europe and the USA. Indeed, there is a sense in which the opposite is true, for while the method books made for some uniformity in explaining the standards that were aimed at, there were three important mediations that promoted distinctively national styles of playing. First, the teachers themselves were most often (but not always) expert players, displaying idiosyncrasies and preferences that were imitated by pupils and others who regarded them as mentors. Secondly, different countries favoured particular types of instrument: in Italy and Austria, there was a preference for valve trombones; in Germany, a preference for larger-bored instruments; in England, a loyalty to the G bass and, for some time, to the C tenor instrument; and in France, the tendency for narrower-bored, lighter-sounding instruments, with the true bass trombone being absent. Thirdly, there were the influences of the local music culture: the preferred repertoire, and the influence of conductors and dominant institutions such as leading military bands, symphony orchestras and opera houses. These differences were clear enough to commentators of the period; Berlioz and other musicians certainly noted that there were not just different standards of playing in the countries they visited, but different styles too. Even at the very end of the century and into the next, such commentators as Prout and Forsyth were able to make comparisons of the differences in national styles (see Chapter 8).

The pedagogical systems of the Paris Conservatoire provided a broad musical training that was always initiated through the study of musical rudiments – often through *solfège*. Students were assigned regular lessons and fixed times when they were to practise. The influence of individual professors on their students was emphatic. They were mentor figures who themselves produced the subsequent generations of mentors. (Table 2) Players who were regarded as important enough to

Table 2

Trombone professors at the Paris Conservatoire, 1833–1960

1795–1802[1]	Philippe Widerkehr?
1800–02	Pierre-François Marcillac
1833–36	Félix Vobaron[2]
1836–71	Antoine Dieppo
1871–88	Paul Delisse
1888–1925	Louis Allard
1925–48	Henri Couillaud
1948–60	André Lafosse

[1] The trombone class was closed in 1802, and only re-opened under Cherubini's Directorship in 1833.

[2] This was a provisional trombone class. It was officially re-established in 1836.

Some professors were appointed as teachers before receiving the professorial title.

Illustration 38. *At the Conservatoire: Monsieur Delisse's trombone class*, by Renouard (1886). (Paul Delisse was trombone professor at the Paris Conservatoire from 1871 to 1888.)

be appointed to a professorship at a national conservatoire usually had a sufficiently high profile to influence composers' understandings of the potential and the limitations of trombone idiom. Berlioz went so far as to sit in on Dieppo's trombone classes at the Conservatoire.[9] Regulations of 1841 define the trombone class at the Paris Conservatoire (Ill. 38) as being limited to eight male students with two auditors; the number of students was increased to twelve in 1892. The maximum period of study was five years, and the maximum age of entrants was 23. The bass trombone was not recognized as a separate instrument in France in the nineteenth century, so there was no separate bass trombone class until after 1945 (neither was there a tuba class until that time). Indeed, the practice of employing a specialist bass trombone teacher was not widespread even in countries where the genuine bass instrument was used: at the Royal College of Music, bass trombone players were still being taught by a tenor trombone player in the 1960s.

The basis of all conservatoire education as it applied to trombonists was built upon four underlying precepts. First, performers should possess sound general musicianship, acquired through a systematic and practical understanding of the diatonic system. Secondly, students should acquire a comprehensive command of their instrument through an equally systematic approach that nurtured a pure tone, an ability to play lyrically and a capacity to play agile and demanding passages with ease. Thirdly, such facilities would be obtained by teaching students the skills of the soloist rather than more detailed coverage of the practicalities of the symphony orchestra stage or opera pit. Thus, the principles of rhetorical solo playing and embellishment were key factors in advanced training. Finally, there was an orthodox set of performance values that could be demonstrated in most cases by professors, and all aspects of performance teaching took account of this orthodoxy. These precepts are as evident in the method books of the nineteenth century as they must have been in the conservatoires. For example, almost every method book opens with a section on the rudiments of music. This element was not just a reflection of conservatoire practice; it also took the breadth of readership into account. Most of these books were bought by amateurs, especially in the second half of the century when the market for printed material became more buoyant and such publishers as Lafleur and Novello devised marketing methods that included passing on to customers the benefits of mass sales in the shape of lower prices.

Didactic methods

As far as we know, Braun's *Gamme et méthode* (published between 1793 and 1797),[10] was the first instructional book for the trombone to be published in a hundred years, and the first to deal with the instrument in fully modern terms. Unlike most earlier and some later writers of instruction manuals, Braun was a working trombone player. Thus his book is not merely a theoretical treatise: it deals with the practical business of playing the instrument. It is a short book – just nine pages long – but as well as being useful in its own right, it laid down a marker for later writers.

Braun describes the trombone as being pitched in B flat and explains that it is learned by reference to seven slide positions. He recognizes the range of the instrument as being from low E_2 to G_4, and this instrument he calls a *trombone basse*. His nomenclature draws attention to two aspects of trombone playing in France in the late eighteenth and the nineteenth centuries. Firstly, it was common, particularly in French opera houses, to use just one trombone to strengthen the bass line. Indeed, Dieppo alludes to this in his treatise. The Vobaron/Berr/Dieppo instruction book goes further in describing the procedure normally followed when the trombone player is required to play a simplified version of a double bass line (this practice was presumably enacted even when no such instruction was included in the score):

> It happens that [composers], to abbreviate their scores, write the Double Bass and trombones together. The performers must find their respective parts. Those that understand Harmony will easily detect it, but a beginner may not.[11]

The other reason why Braun describes his instrument as a 'trombone basse' is that, until well into the twentieth century, the French employed tenor trombones on both tenor and bass lines – a practice also mentioned in Fröhlich's *Vollständige theoretisch-pracktische Musikschule*[12] (which is closely based upon, but not identical with, Braun's *Gamme et méthode*), and discussed more extensively by Berlioz in his *Grand Traité d'instrumentation et d'orchestration modernes*.[13]

Braun's approach is brief, straightforward and practical. He presents twelve well-illustrated articles, including a description of the instrument and its constituent parts; how it is held and manipulated; the slide positions and the notes obtainable on them; alternative positions; the range and the playing of major and minor scales, which one must articulate clearly – the tones must be held 'at an even dynamic level for their full value'.[14] Braun provides only a few exercises, but he adds a note to his twelfth and final article:

> There is a very useful work that can be used following this method. It is entitled 50 Easy and Progressive Lessons in the Most Common Major and Minor Tonalities. Composed by F. Gebauer, it includes six pieces or trios for three trombones.[15]

Here he refers to François René Gebauer (1773–1845), one of a family of musicians based in Paris, who was a bassoonist with the Swiss Guard Band at Versailles and the Garde Nationale before becoming bassoon professor at the Conservatoire for two separate periods between 1795 and 1838. His *50 Leçons pour la trombonne basse, alto et tenor* was published with Braun's *Méthode* in mind; indeed the title page describes the collection as a 'Sequel to the Method for Trombone by Braun'. The exercises, presented in progressive order of difficulty, are in the alto, tenor and bass registers. These are supplemented by six three-part pieces, beginning with a transcription for three trombones of Gossec's *O salutaris hostia*, and including the *Emperor's Hymn* by Haydn and the March of the Priests from Mozart's *Die Zauberflöte*. Howard Weiner has properly identified these as the first published pieces for trombone ensemble alone since the trios included in Daniel Speer's *Grund-richtiger . . . Unterricht der musicalischen Kunst* in 1697.[16] Taken together with Gebauer's *Leçons*, Braun's method provided something of a prototype for later didactic literature. It seems to have been a key source for several subsequent writers (other than Fröhlich), including Jean-Georges Kastner, who mentions it in his *Traité général d'instrumentation* (1837), and Giraud, who refers to it in *Le Polycorde* (1875).

Several French methods were to follow in the first half of the century, including Sturm's *Méthode complete pour les trombonnes basse, tenor et alto* (published between 1816 and 1826, but now lost),[17] Victor Cornette's *Méthode de trombone* (c. 1831), Félix Vobaron's *Grande Méthode de trombone* (1834), and Dieppo and Berr's *Méthode de trombone* (c. 1835), which Dieppo peculiarly disowned ('I need to declare to the public that the writing of that publication is absolutely unknown to me'[18]) when he published his own *Méthode complète pour le trombone* (1837). (Ill. 39) Jean-Georges Kastner, an immensely important figure in French military music of the time, published his primer, *Méthode élémentaire* (c. 1844), 'for the use of boarding schools', but he anxiously deferred to Dieppo's method as the more complete and advanced work. Many of the French method books had more than one edition and were also published in translation.

When Dieppo published his *Méthode complète pour le trombone* in 1837, he was prompted, as he explains in his foreword, by his sense of honour at being appointed trombone professor at the Conservatoire. The method is in two parts: the first deals with the trombone as an accompanying instrument, by which he means its use in the orchestra. In fact, Dieppo says little in detail about orchestral playing, though he mentions the importance of the trombone as an orchestral instrument in dramatic music; but much of what he says is implicitly revealing of the way the orchestral trombone was understood in his time. The second part is devoted to solo playing. Apart from a brief historical reference to Gluck, he does not mention a single

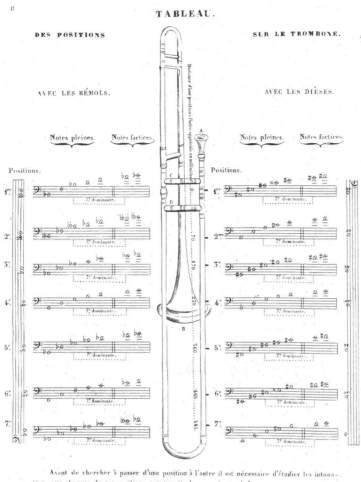

Illustration 39. Table of positions in Antoine Dieppo's *Méthode complète pour le trombone* (1837).

composer, nor does he provide any repertoire examples. He deals with body posture and the formation of sound, and emphasizes breathing technique, articulation and beauty of sound, the latter depending, he says, on three things:

1. good placing of the lips on the mouthpiece;
2. the manner of projecting the breath with the tongue . . .;
3. the art of managing the breath in proportion to the degree of force and elevation of the sound one wants to produce.[19]

The second part of the treatise deals with the skills of the soloist. Here Dieppo addresses the finer nuances of articulation, referring particularly to *le coulé* (the slur), *le pointé coulé* (lit. 'slurred staccato'), *le pointé* (staccato), and *le piqué ou détaché* (staccatissimo). He deals with phrasing, and like many who followed him – even well into the twentieth century – devotes considerable space to the performance of decorative embellishments such as the trill, gruppetto, mordent and turn.

The production of instructional books for trombone was not restricted to France. Leaving aside Fröhlich's *Vollständige theoretisch-pracktische Musikschule*, which was published in Bonn (c. 1810–11), and a book of *études* for trombone by Johann Friedheim published in Paris in 1821, one of the more important was Andreas Nemetz's *Neueste Posaun-Schule*, published in Vienna in 1827. Here too we have an instructional book written by a player, and an important one at that. Nemetz was trombonist in the Imperial Royal Court Orchestra in Vienna, and we can reasonably speculate that he took part in early performances of works that have since become canonical.

The method books written by trombone professors – such as those of the Paris Conservatoire – were idiomatic in that they were aimed specifically at the slide or valve trombone or both. But another category was the generic books in which a standard pattern and scheme was applied with little discrimination to just about any melodic instrument that shared a common pitch compass. Some had their origins in an earlier manual that was reissued, sometimes with modest changes to prefatory texts and clef. Sometimes the transfer was successful even when it may have appeared unlikely; for example, the monumental *Grande Méthode complète pour cornet à pistons et de saxhorn* (1864), by the brilliant French cornetist Jean-Baptiste Arban, was published in trombone form with little abridgement in 1921, by the entrepreneurial American cornetist and teacher W. M. Eby, even though the Arban method exploited an entirely different idiom from that of the trombone. One suspects, however, that this book, one of the most thorough and engaging of its time, had already been used for many years by trombonists who could read treble/tenor clef transposition.

Arban's title implies a wide utility for valve instruments, and this may have been grasped particularly by valve trombonists. The undated method published in English by Lafleur under the names of Vobaron, Berr and Dieppo (the British Library dates it 1880) is actually called *Complete Trombone Tutor: Slide and Valve*, but it gives little attention to the valve instrument, and the only illustrations are of the slide trombone.

By the end of the century the production of method books, instructional manuals, and even simple primers reduced to a single, poster-sized sheet, constituted a minor industry. The most popular and perhaps the most enduring was the series of *Practical Tutor* books written by the New York-based Otto Langey (1851–1922). His trombone book was published in the UK in 1885, and in the USA somewhat earlier, and it has remained in print to the present time. Langey was a cellist, but he earned celebrity as a staff arranger and composer for several Tin Pan Alley publishing houses, particularly Carl Fischer. He was one of the best in his trade, and certainly one of the most prolific arrangers and writers, supplying countless arrangements for amateurs and professionals. One senses that his *Tutor for the Tenor Slide Trombone* is regarded with some equivocation by modern trombone players, but it actually has an important place in the history of the trombone's didactic literature. Unlike others who produced didactic material routinely for all families of instruments under a common generic title, Langey attempted to capture the idiom of each instrument. While there are some generic sections (for example, in respect of rudiments and music theory) a comparison of his *Practical Tutors* for different instruments shows them to be distinctly different.

Furthermore, as a working arranger who had observed the responses of trombone players to different types of writing, he had a good sense of the idiom of the instrument. Clearly, Langey was also familiar with the French method books, for the thread of imitation of Dieppo is consistently evident – in the section on decoration and embellishments, for instance.

Given that trombonists were encouraged to aspire to soloistic virtuosity, it is not surprising that the instruction books prioritize the development of a fluent technique and a capacity for long-line lyrical phrasing. There is close attention to slide technique, articulation and breath control, and there is usually a section on the execution of embellishment and ornamentation. Shakes, trills, mordents and grace notes are included, as is advice on the tasteful use of portamento. It is debatable how far all these topics were really necessary accoutrements for the average professional. Well-written trills and mordents are perfectly playable on the trombone, but the books hint at an imitation of the procedures laid down by the priorities for other instruments. The requirement that trombonists learn the skills of portamento is a case in point. While it is possible that trombone soloists used portamento in the nineteenth century, the device really resides in the idioms of bowed string instruments and it seems likely that its inclusion in method books for the trombone was more in imitation of those idioms.

The use of alternative positions to ensure smooth phrasing is explicit even in the earliest post-classical method books.[20] This technique is consistent with the encouragement to develop an essentially vocal style. The subject matter for many of the *études* and exercises in methods books is the operatic aria, and the fact that the famous 'Oraison funèbre' trombone solo in Berlioz's *Grande symphonie funèbre et triomphale* is an adaptation of an air from his opera *Les Francs-juges* attests to a recognition of the vocal quality of soloistic trombone playing on the part of some composers, even though few actually wrote extended trombone solos in orchestral music. Berlioz provided a cautionary note in his score at the point of the 'Oraison funèbre' to the effect that, if circumstances required it, the solo could be played on an alto valve trombone, a valve horn in G or a bass clarinet, an implied reference, no doubt, to the quality of playing in European orchestras at that time. We can but ponder on how differently the idiom of the trombone in the Romantic orchestra would have developed had players of Dieppo's quality been more abundant. (See Appendix 3 for an indicative list of slide trombone methods.)

Twentieth-century instruction books

The French mainstream method books published in the late nineteenth and the twentieth centuries show continuities in both form and content from those of the mid-nineteenth century. The emphasis on the solo style continued – particularly the nurturing of a vocal style, in, for example, the various didactic works of Henri Couillaud, trombone professor at the Paris Conservatoire from 1925 to 1948. However, there were also important developments. The mode of address to readers for whom such literature was presumed to be the sole method of formal instruction became increasingly systematic, and there was also a growing tendency to alert students to the challenges of the orchestral repertoire, and consequently to a wider range of techniques. This tendency is particularly evident in André Lafosse's *Méthode complète pour le trombone*, which was published in Paris in three volumes, the first two in 1921, the third in 1946. It is by far the most extensive and comprehensive instructional manual for the instrument, and has been widely used in several countries (its textual commentaries are given simultaneously in French, English, German and Italian). Lafosse maintains a loyalty to the older French conservatoire approach (for example, many of the *études* of Félix Vobaron are retained), but the scope of his method is wider than those of previous writers, and he went so far as to base *études* not just on vocal arias but also on challenging idiomatic orchestral passages, such as the trombone solos in Wagner's *Siegfried*, Stravinsky's *The Firebird* and Ravel's *Daphnis et Chloé*.

One of the more interesting facets of French didactic writings in this period, as revealed by Lafosse, is the tension between French performance traditions and the more radical styles and techniques that were evolving in twentieth-century modernism, including those developed by Paris-based composers. Lafosse continues the tradition of dealing extensively with embellishment and decoration, a topic with which he was clearly at home. But on more modern matters he is less comfortable. His somewhat clumsy description of the bass trombone (he favoured the B flat/D thumb valve instrument), is interesting primarily because he found it necessary to provide such a description at all. And while he was sufficiently cognizant of new techniques such as glissando, slide vibrato and flutter-tonguing to explain them, he does so with more than a hint of disapproval. Glissandos – despite the frequency of their use by modern composers – were 'of questionable taste'.[21] On vibrato he says, 'Whereas its vulgarity hurts the taste in the classical music, it is practicable in certain pieces', and on flutter-tonguing he reminds us that Strauss used it 'for imitating the bleeting [*sic*] of a sheep'.[22] This ambivalence may explain the difficulties which Lafosse and other Parisian trombonists had with Stravinsky's music, and which are evident in the 1928 and 1932 recordings made with the composer (see Chapter 12). Perhaps because of the cultural attitudes revealed in the mainstream didactic methods in the opening decades of the twentieth century, a new didactic literature aimed at the performance of popular idioms became available. Perhaps the first such publication was Henry Fillmore's *Jazz Trombonist for Slide Trombone: A Unique Treatise Showing How to Play Practical Jazzes and Where to Insert them in Plain Trombone Parts* (1919), which was quickly followed by Fortunato Sordillo's *Art of Jazzing for the Trombone: A Complete Treatise upon the Possibilities of the Slide* (c. 1920).

The quantity of instructional manuals produced in the twentieth century was considerable, but remarkably the books by Otto Langey, Lafosse and even Arban – together with the abundant orchestral excerpt books – have never been far from most players' practice stands. The most widely used specialist bass trombone method is probably that written by Allen Ostrander of the New York Philharmonic (1966), but the work of another bass trombone player, Edward Kleinhammer of the Chicago Symphony Orchestra, *The Art of Trombone Playing* (1963), may represent the most holistic approach to trombone teaching. More than others up to that time, Kleinhammer favoured a scientific and often iconoclastic method. He too emphasizes the 'correct' way to play (the word is used repeatedly from the start), and he goes into

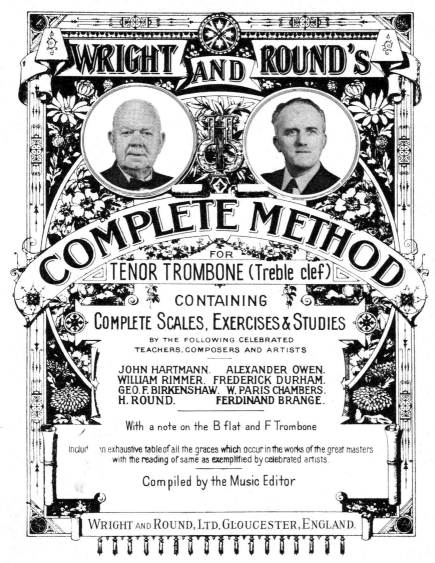

Illustration 40. Wright and Round produced a huge quantity of didactic material in the early twentieth century – most destined for the brass band market. The *Complete Method* is not idiomatic, but rather reproduces the formula used for other instruments, and the approach persisted well into the century – this edition dates from 1960.

some detail about the physiology of playing. His book was probably the most discursive of any published to that time. Though it contains several exercises, like Denis Wick's excellent *Trombone Technique* (1971) it discusses a range of aspects of the instrument's idiom and how fine playing is encouraged. Kleinhammer's *Art of Trombone Playing* has been as influential as any other publication of its type. It typifies what we might loosely (and perhaps a little unfairly) call the clinician's approach to playing, and the inherent belief that a perfect trombone technique is founded on a calculatedly correct physiological approach. Indeed, his final chapter 'Perfection, the Ultimate Goal', enunciates this ideology neatly:

> Though perfection is impossible to attain, the highest possible degree of excellence should be the ultimate goal.. . . [Through correct systematic practice] the player can:
> 1. Maintain his standards of yesterday and find ways to improve these standards through physical coordination and efficiency.
> 2. Develop and coordinate the correct functions of playing until they become automatic, so that musicianship can be concentrated on at performance time.
> 3. Study his psychological idiosyncrasies.[23]

Kleinhammer's book makes fascinating reading, and there is little he says that can be objectively disputed. It is particularly strong on the physiology and psychology of playing. What the method books of the old conservatoire tradition lacked – a capacity to really encourage self-reflection – Kleinhammer has in abundance.

Nineteenth-century soloists and their repertoire

The concentration on the values of the soloist rather than the orchestral player in nineteenth-century didactic literature reflects the broader ethic of the conservatoire; it is a replication of attitudes applied to the teaching of all instruments. This ideal must have seemed unproblematic at the time, because the idea that a trombonist – or any other instrumentalist – was required to execute the full range of technical accomplishments of the soloist was not a subject of contention. After all, what other benchmark of musicianship was there? The fact that most of the solo trombone repertoire was of limited quality, and that the vast majority of professionals were destined for work in orchestral pits, preoccupied no musical educators (except perhaps those in the military). Trombone students would undoubtedly have accepted this ideal, for the notion of an orchestral technique, or indeed of a trombone 'section' as a recognizable constituent of orchestral colour, was neither formulated nor developed among performers. Even though composers were developing an increasingly sophisticated orchestral idiom for the trombone, the orchestral repertoire presented few technical challenges, none of which would be troublesome to a schooled soloist. Furthermore, the trombone player as virtuoso concert soloist was far from an abstract notion. A new breed of soloists appeared in the first half of the nineteenth century who were appreciated by audiences in Europe and the USA. Dieppo was neither the first nor necessarily the best. In Prague, the trombonist Langenfeld was celebrated enough to inspire reproductions of his image in contemporary periodicals. (Ill. 41) In London, William Winterbottom became a frequent figure on the concert scene, and was not unusual in holding a position in the Royal Philharmonic Society concerts and as a civilian musician with the band of the Regiment of Life Guards. In Germany, the most celebrated trombonists were undoubtedly Friedrich August Belcke in Berlin, and Carl Traugott Queisser in

Illustration 41. The trombone soloist Langenfeld of Prague was sufficiently celebrated for his likeness to be distributed as a coloured lithograph (c. 1830), after a portrait by Hieronymus Hess.

Leipzig. In 1819 a report of a concert given by Belcke in Leipzig appeared in the *Allgemeine musikalische Zeitung*. The writer admired his playing for its

> clarity and precision, distinctness and pleasing sound, plus something truly noble in the imposing trombonistic figurations, as well as astonishing skill in that which is not idiomatic to the instrument – for example, rapid passages, cantabile, trills, etc.[24]

Praise for Queisser was, if anything, yet warmer. He was admired by Mendelssohn, by the English composer Sterndale Bennett and by Schumann, who went so far as to call him 'the God of the trombone'. The *Allgemeine musikalische Zeitung*, reporting on a performance in Weimar in 1841 (where he received equal billing with Clara Schumann), pronounced him a 'star . . . of the first magnitude, who not rarely make[s] the impossible seem possible'.[25]

These players were clearly very fine soloists, but some critique of solo trombone playing in the nineteenth century implies that the instrument was regarded with curiosity and condescension rather than genuine musical interest. A concert in the Music Hall, Boston, in which the virtuoso trombone player Herr Letsch played a solo by Stigelli and Ferdinand David's Concertino, drew the comment:

In the first piece – Stigelli's song about 'the Tear' – he subdued his long, unwieldy instrument to a soft rich singing quality, and made it sing a melody with chaste and true expression. The trombone is an honest genuine instrument with a character of its own and quite a noble one.[26]

This reviewer's rhetoric may owe something to an article in the same journal three years earlier, which mentioned 'Herr Maurice Nabich, a celebrated soloist on that rather unwieldy and decidedly inconvenient instrument, the trombone'.[27]

Nonetheless, solo repertoire soon emerged in which the idea of virtuosity as a self-conscious and shared aspiration for trombonists was evident. Some virtuoso trombonists were also composers of sorts and produced a limited number of solo works which, though of indifferent quality, were idiomatic. One such was Josef Serafin Alschausky (1879–1947), who had a distinguished career on both sides of the Atlantic, and whose Concerto in B flat remains popular with players. (Ill. 42). However, the most prominent signs of an idiomatic solo repertoire are found in the pieces written or used for the annual *concours* – the competitions in which students were required to perform at the Paris Conservatoire. The test pieces composed specifically for these contests contributed incrementally to trombone solo repertoire. The pieces written for the first few years of the competition are lost, but of those that survive (all that were composed after 1842), most, in keeping with the *concours* works for other instruments, carry the title 'Solo', though other genres were also used, including concerto, *Fantasie, Air varié* and *Cavatine*. Even those works entitled 'solo' have small-scale ternary structural forms that are loosely imitative of miniature

Illustration 42. The trombone virtuoso Serafin Alschausky (1879–1947). (With thanks to Howard Weiner.)

concertos. Later in the century the variation form found much greater favour – the 1878 and 1892 solos were variations on the popular *Carnaval de Venise* theme.

Most of the serious larger-scale solo works written outside France came from Germany. In Leipzig, Queisser was frequently a soloist with the Gewandhaus Orchestra, and inspired a Concertino for Bass Trombone (1820) by C. H. Meyer, a Concerto in E flat (n.d.) by C. G. Müller, and a Concertino in B flat (1837) and a *Concerto militaire* (1841) by the orchestra's leader Ferdinand David, as well as several arrangements. Franz Liszt published two transcriptions for trombone and organ: 'Cujus animam' from Rossini's *Stabat Mater* (c.1865), and an arrangement of 'Hosannah' (*Alleluja del Cantico del Sol*) (1867), which has an obbligato trombone part. Like so many of the transcriptions for trombone, these were arrangements of lyrical *vocalise*, but instrumental music was also transcribed: Queisser's repertoire, for example, included transcriptions of horn concertos.[28]

American popular virtuosi and their repertoire

Between about 1880 and 1930, two solo trombone styles that emerged from the USA created new strands of the idea of the trombonist as virtuoso. The first was the rise of the popular band concert virtuoso; the second came from the enormous and diverse influence of jazz. The impact upon the trombone idiom of both these styles was immense, for on the one hand they established alternative ideas about virtuosity, and on the other they eventually led to a reappraisal and extension of the orthodox conservatoire tradition. The general and hugely influential story of the ascendancy of popular styles and jazz is dealt with more extensively in other chapters, but they are touched on briefly here because of the impact they had upon the solo idiom and how it was to be taught.

The idea of the professional popular band soloist was new, and it developed as an offshoot of military band concert performance. It came to prominence in the USA, where, by the middle of the nineteenth century, military-type wind bands had become the most popular type of instrumental musical entertainment. They created a massive and loyal audience, to the extent that wide-ranging concert band tours – often following the path of the newly developing railroad to the burgeoning towns and cities of the USA – were made entirely viable. Standards of band playing were high, and as well as home-grown talent there was also a steady supply of brilliant new immigrant players. Many military bands were assembled for national guard and other volunteer regiments, but entirely professional touring bands were also formed. The first band to achieve huge national popularity was probably that led by the Irish immigrant Patrick Gilmore. Gilmore led several bands (the Suffolk Band 1852, Boston Brigade Band 1853 and Salem Band 1855) before he formed his own in 1859. When he died suddenly in 1892, John Philip Sousa, the young and precociously talented conductor of the US Marine Band, was persuaded to form a civilian band which quickly became one of the most celebrated musical ensembles in world. The first band soloists were cornet players Jules Levy and later Herbert C. Clarke, but they were soon more than matched by a succession of brilliant trombonists. Some, like Simone Mantia, Mario Falcone, Carlo Alberto Cappa and Frederick Innes, were new immigrants; many more were born in small towns and progressed to the bright lights of New York, Chicago and Washington through engagements with umpteen small-time theatres, minstrel shows, circuses and other itinerant troupes. These were fertile breeding grounds for soloists who made their way to the stellar, New York-based bands. The euphonium and trombone player Fred Jewell started his working life playing for the 'Gentry Dog and Pony Show', before moving to the greener pastures of Ringling Bros. Circus Band, which had 35 players. Frank Holton and Clay Smith learned their trade playing for 'Hi Henry's Minstrels'. It is evident that trombone players, even in the most modest touring outfit, and irrespective of its type, would not have gone far without the ability to step forward to play solos. Thus, reputations were made before players ever reached the big city.

By the start of the twentieth century, a group of players existed who were regarded as quite exceptional in popular orbits. Among them were Gardell Simons, who played with Sousa's band; Claude Spary, who made most of his living playing sentimental ballads with such passion that he was said to move whole audiences to tears; Charles Stacey, a soloist with the Long Beach Band – a brilliant player with a gift for lyricism (who sadly dropped dead in 1926 while playing 'The Sweetest Story Ever Told' to a full house); Fred Innes, a great trombonist and later a bandleader, whom Patrick Gilmore regarded as the only brass player to equal the virtuosity of the legendary cornetist Jules Levy; Frank Holton, a fine player but who is best remembered as an instrument maker; Leo A. Zimmerman, who played with Sousa, Goldman, Conway and several other bands; and the incomparable Arthur Pryor, St Joseph, Missouri's finest son. (Ill. 43)

Pryor was a good all-round musician and a competent pianist; he initially made a reputation playing virtuoso solos with small-town theatre troupes. He turned down an opportunity to work with Gilmore's band, but when a call came from Sousa in 1892 he found the temptation irresistible. Within a year the great Frank Holton had yielded the solo trombone chair to the 22-year-old. Pryor was a phenomenal player, even by the stellar standards current in the USA at that time. But he also benefited from the fabulous celebrity that was accorded to any player who was one of Sousa's stand-up soloists. By about 1901, when his world tours were well established, Sousa may have been the world's most famous American. The band was brilliant, and the show had a slickness, panache and entertainment value that were unprecedented in every town, country or continent in which it was witnessed. Pryor was young, fresh-faced and exceptional. His impact on audiences had commenced before he blew a note, and by the time he completed his final cadence, they were ecstatic. It is hard to avoid the impression that Pryor's recordings, valuable and numerous as they are, do not convey the true impact of Pryor in live performances. One critic, after hearing him play a solo with Sousa at Omaha, Nebraska, was so struck that all traces of understatement were utterly abandoned:

His execution set the prairies afire; his vibrating pedal tones rattled the windows of the Theater and killed the gold fishes and stunned the canaries all the way out to the packing plant where even the iron gates trembled.[29]

Illustration 43. Arthur Pryor, photographed around 1900.

If we leave aside the showmanship of Pryor's performances, which we can only imagine, we are left with the repertoire and the way he and popular soloists like him played it. Unlike the mainstream European soloists, these players were unashamed entertainers who seem to have been unhindered by the niceties of tradition. The greatest part of their repertoire was made up of air and variation solos based on popular folk and sentimental songs. Their playing displayed fine lyricism and stunning technical prowess through the exhibition of a wide pitch range and breathtakingly fast technical passages. Every solo had a cadenza which provided an opportunity for outrageously self-indulgent exhibitions of showmanship.

This was a simple formula that worked for popular audiences, and some of its nuances eventually drifted into the mainstream solo writing of twentieth-century art music composers, but its greater impact was on the mass of amateurs, some of whom were to be inspired by these virtuosi and to become jazz soloists. Along with Louis Armstrong, Arthur Pryor is one of the most cited names in the oral testimonies of the great jazz soloists,[30] though Pryor's style is, of course, hardly recognizable in their playing. Indeed, their aesthetics reside in different and contrasting worlds. Pryor and his like believed in musical discipline, cleanness, exactitude and a particular dimension of technical perfection based on musical athleticism. The great jazz soloists believed in the relaxed deployment of technique in an entirely idiosyncratic mode of expression. Thus, more than in any other case of stylistic intervention, they revolutionized the notion of virtuosity. These players and their impact on the new modern breed of soloists of the twentieth-century avant garde will be the subject of discussion in subsequent chapters.

Chapter 8

The trombone in the modern orchestra

Since the eighteenth century, the most important source of employment for trombone players (outside the military, jazz and popular music) has been the orchestra. The symphony and opera orchestra has also provided the principal interface between the instrument and the greatest composers of western art music; it has shaped its idiom as much as any other repertoire – including the music written for concert soloists. Cecil Forsyth, writing early in the twentieth century and looking back at the nineteenth, defined trombones as 'essentially "group instruments", that is to say, instruments which make their effects harmonically and their differences of effect by differences of register, of spacing, and of contrasted *piano* and *forte*'.[1] Forsyth's understanding of instrumental idioms was not faultless, but here he was pointing to an important feature of the trombone's development that had taken root by that time: foremost in the minds of composers was the idea of a trombone *section* of three instruments, playing in the alto, tenor and bass ranges, and functioning within a total orchestral soundscape. The origin of this approach can easily be traced to the seventeenth century, but in the Romantic period this configuration moved a long way from its association with vocal music, and took on new meanings. Even by the 1840s there was a challenging repertoire for the orchestral trombone; the greatest and most subtle tests came not from the handful of orchestral solos, but from the need for players to deploy the subtle nuances of the trombone section within the orchestra. For good orchestral trombone scoring to achieve its full effect, players needed to understand and respond instinctively to the developing role of the instrument as a constituent of the orchestra. This was a new and highly sophisticated skill that did not always come easily to nineteenth-century players, in whose training the demands of orchestral playing was not of paramount importance. In the twentieth century, however, it came to occupy a central place, with the trombonists of leading orchestras being regarded as the elite of the profession.

The trombone section was used in the orchestras of operas and sacred works from the later eighteenth century, and by the nineteenth century we can identify the routine use of three trombone players in the instrumentation of operatic and symphonic repertoire. But while composers wrote for three trombones, in practice nineteenth-century orchestras had neither the format nor the coherence that were to become standard in the twentieth century.[2] Indeed, orchestras must have looked and sounded quite different according to where in Europe they were located; their constitution, their styles of playing and even their spatial arrangement on concert platforms and in theatre pits differed enormously. There were also other factors that contributed to such differences. The economics of the music business and the variable supply of quality players led to the adoption of expediencies that modern audiences would find shocking. Instruments were left out or added according to availability, and the lack of consistency did little to foster a rapid development of the fine skills of orchestral playing. Moreover, programming was often fragmented and uneven. We hear of movements of symphonies being dropped for want of adequate players, and what we would today regard as 'serious' programmes being spiced up to hold the attention of audiences whose pretensions were often a few steps ahead of their appetite for great music. Opera, for example, was often subject to considerable performance flexibility. In the 1830s in New Orleans, the soprano Madam Feron delighted her well-to-do audience by inserting the popular songs 'The Arab Steed' and 'An Old Man Would be Wooing' into a full performance of Rossini's *The Barber of Seville*, and 'Bright Eyes' into Mozart's *The Marriage of Figaro*. In 1876, a benefit concert in New York's Chickering Hall, advertised as a night of 'amateur minstrel entertainment', included a selection from *The Ring of the Nibelung* conducted by 'Herr Wagner of drawing-room car fame'.[3] The early history of the trombone in the modern orchestra should be seen in the light of this somewhat unsteady aesthetic, and of standards of performance, which, while not universally poor, were equally not universally high.

The inclusion of trombones in the proto-modern orchestra can be traced back only to the 1760s. Their first deployment in a symphony came in the first decade of the nineteenth century, but it is possible that some of the written orchestral repertoire for the trombone in the nineteenth century creates a more favourable picture of performance standards than actually prevailed in many parts of Europe.[4] Permanent orchestras were founded from early in the nineteenth century, but we should pause to ask what 'permanent' actually meant in this context. In London, the Royal Philharmonic Society Orchestra was indeed a fairly permanent band from its foundation in 1813, but in reality it was no more than an assembly of freelance players who performed together a dozen times a year. Many other nineteenth-century orchestras were founded on a seasonal basis or to perform a specific series of subscription concerts. The names of some of these orchestras have prevailed to modern times, but their mode of operation was much less predictable and secure in the nineteenth century than it would later become. A trombone player who relied entirely on symphony concerts for his income in the early nineteenth century would have made a poor living. Military bands and opera houses between them attracted the main audience-base for most of the nineteenth century, and thus provided the most stable employment for trombonists. Military bands were especially important in the nineteenth century. They fulfilled cultural roles that placed them at the centre of musical life. They were also well organized and directed, and were often recipients of state patronage. In the twentieth century, the cultural status of military bands diminished as symphony orchestras became more elevated and joined opera and ballet institutions as the principal focuses for large-scale elite music-making. But it was only in the later nineteenth and early twentieth centuries that the practical distinction between 'art' (or 'classical') music and popular music acquired its modern force. This distinction owes most to the development of popular music as a discrete segment of the music business, but it was helped by the increasingly elitist aura surrounding high art. This came about partly because audiences exercised choice, but there was also an increasing sense that a 'sacralization of art music' was occurring which manifested itself in the creation of new and expensive edifices for its performance and often a concomitantly exclusive policy toward ticket prices.[5] This was an important moment in the performance history of the trombone, because it is from the second half of the nineteenth century that the division between the 'light' and 'serious' sides of the professional business occurred, with its consequent stylistic specialisms.

From the early twentieth century, the finest trombone players who were not making a name for themselves as soloists or in popular bands were drawn into orchestral playing, not only because it was becoming a more robust source of income, but also because the major orchestras were achieving greater status and increasingly high standards. By the 1930s such cities as London, Berlin, Paris, Philadelphia, Cleveland, Boston, Leipzig, New York, Amsterdam, Dresden and Vienna had symphony orchestras with global reputations. Trombone players were engaging with the orchestral idiom in a more sophisticated and specialist way than they had a few decades earlier. The idea of a trombone 'section', playing together with a common musical vision, had taken shape. The greatest orchestral trombone players of the twentieth century have possessed not only technical skill but also refined ensemble discipline; they have understood orchestral repertoire and the spaces occupied by different instrumental voices in the orchestral soundscape.

Nineteenth-century orchestras

Early in the nineteenth century, trombone-playing traditions existed in Austria, Germany and to an extent Italy. These countries appear to have been the source of players for other countries where the trombone had been obsolete. The Braun brothers – the trombonists whom Gossec claimed to have recruited to Paris in the 1770s – came from Germany, as did those who played with Queen Charlotte's band in London and took part in the 1784 Handel celebrations at Westminster Abbey.[6] It took some time for the tradition of trombone playing to re-establish itself in countries where the instrument had been absent, and even by the 1830s the availability of good players could not be guaranteed. But the itinerancy that had been common in the sixteenth century was again flourishing. Mariotti, a celebrated Italian trombonist, had found his way to London via Paris in the late eighteenth century, to join the Germans who were already there. The trombone soloist at the Folies Bergères in 1875 was none other than Frederick Neil Innes, who was to consolidate his reputation in the USA, and two of the most celebrated trombonists of the Société des Concerts du Conservatoire, the brothers Auguste and Louis Allard, were Puerto Rican immigrants whose surname was originally Alloud.[7]

As the old systems of aristocratic, civic and church patronage eroded and eventually collapsed, the modes of employment of trombonists became unsettled. Most early nineteenth-century trombone players were freelancers who made a living from a portfolio of engagements, none of which provided either entirely predictable or comfortable pecuniary rewards. The opera houses were a source of regular, if somewhat seasonal, employment for some, and concerted music – including the performance of oratorio – often took place in theatres or at annual provincial festivals. At the end of the classical period, many trombone players appear to have been multi-instrumentalists, and this goes some way to explaining why and how the number of professional trombonists increased at this time: most of the new wave of trombonists were performers on other instruments, who appear to have taken up the trombone expediently as opportunities for employment presented themselves. Each of the players mentioned by Burney in the list of performers for the Handel com-memorations played other wind or string instruments. Five of the eight trombone players mentioned in Joseph Doane's *Musical Directory*, published in London in 1794, list other instruments in their spheres of competence.[8] *Mortimer's London Directory* for the same year lists just six trombonists working in London, each making most of his income from theatre and guards bands. Each player had a foreign name (German or Italian), and most claimed competence on string and woodwind instruments as well as the trombone.[9] Of the trombonists registered in the first half of the nineteenth century with the Royal Society of Musicians (a benevolent organization for musicians which Handel had helped establish), only the brothers John and James Smithies declared themselves to be solely trombonists (expert in the alto, tenor or bass). Every other player – Johann Zwingmann, Andreas Friedrich Germann, Johann August Kellner and Louis Dalfour Schroeder – also played other instruments. Even William Winterbottom of the Life Guards Band, a concert soloist, and trombone professor at the Royal Academy of Music (c. 1860–89), made part of his living as a violinist.[10]

The skills of trombone playing gained ground where there was a generally buoyant music culture, especially in respect of opera and military music, and a robust musical infrastructure. For most of the nineteenth century, as has already been stated, military music had a central role in the musical culture of most countries. More than any other sphere of music-making it played an important part in the articulation of official nationalism and thus caught the attention of governments, which often funded both infrastructure and training. The provision of services and improvements to military music lay behind many of the most important innovations in the design, production and distribution of brass and wind instruments in the nineteenth century. The enlargement of military bands gathered pace after about 1810. The band of the French Garde Républicaine was expanded in the 1790s, and the pattern that it set was quickly imitated in Germany and elsewhere. In England, the Royal Artillery Band had three trombonists in 1820, and the Prussian band re-formed by Wieprecht had four trombones by 1838. By the 1840s most large European bands carried four trombone players, and yet more were added to the elite bands as the century progressed. When the British 'Military Music Class' (called the Royal Military School of Music from 1865) was established in 1857, it called for subscriptions from no fewer than 148 army units which were believed to have bands – most, if not all, would probably have had trombonists.[11] In America the pattern was somewhat less standardized, and the Civil War served on the one hand to bring military bands into the foreground, and on the other to fracture their orderly development within government resources. But by the 1880s, American military and civilian concert bands had emerged that were to challenge and often eclipse the quality of the European bands (by this time J. P. Sousa had become director of the US Marine Band, and Patrick Gilmore was at the height

Table 3

Trombonists of the Royal Society of Musicians

The table shows the trombonists who joined the Royal Society of Musicians between its foundation and the end of the nineteenth century. Applicants were required to provide verification of their nationality and their bona fides as professional musicians. It is interesting to note that the earlier group of entrants (those who joined as the trombone was reintroduced into England) were multi-instrumentalists and most were Germans. This list does not, of course, indicate all musicians working in London at this time. The archive reference is given in italics after each entry.

Flack, John Casper and John	1773	Father and son join at the same time. John Casper is the father. He plays trombone, horn and viola; the son plays violin, trombone and trumpet. Both cite experience in the orchestras of various important provincial festivals. *Original file missing; information given in B. Matthews (compiler),* The Royal Society of Musicians of Great Britain List of Members 1738–1984 *(London: Royal Society of Musicians, 1985).*
Dressler, John	1777	Double bass and trombone. Begs leave to apply for membership as he has 'serv'd regular time in musick as a single man'. *RSM A16*
Kellner, Johann August	1789	Bassoon, violoncello, trombone and tenor [viola]. Says he is a German who has practised music in England for 7 years. A member of the Queen's Band and the Ancient Music. *RSM A123*
Woodham, Joseph	1795	Violin, tenor, double bass, horn, trombone and trumpet. A copy of his birth certificate shows him to have been born of English parents – Richard and Elizabeth Woodham. He was baptised on 1 Jan 1768 at Hungerford. The date of birth is not known, but the church curate provided the RSM with the baptismal details. When he joined the RSM he was 26. He worked at Covent Garden, Sadlers Wells and elsewhere. *RSM A154*
Zwingmann, Johann Nicholaus	1796	Viola, violincello and trombone. His application form says that he has practised music in England for more than seven years. He plays at Drury Lane and is 31 years old. A letter from Germany attests his origins: 'His father Johanne Christoph Zwingman is a respectable inhabitant and good neighbour in Stalternheim a Choralist in our church and instrumental musician. His mother . . . [is] Margaretha Boecknerin . . .'. *RSM A163*
Smithies, James	1815	Alto, tenor and bass trombones. Plays at the Royal Italian Opera and the Ancient Concerts. Application, dated Nov 1837, says he has been a professional musician for 7 years, being 22 years old; married with two children, the eldest being 3. By 1846 he was destitute due to ill health. *RSM A396*

Rost, John Christian	1821	Trombone, trumpet, horn, violin, etc.
		Declares that he has practised music for upwards of 20 years and is 44 years old. He performs at Covent Garden and the Haymarket. A document from the Registrar of the Church at Felinnerhausen(?) on the Losse, Saxony, dated April 1821, says he had been born there in 1776. His father was John Adam Rost.
		RSM A309
Smithies, John	1821	Alto, tenor and bass trombones.
		Brother of James Smithies. Played at the Royal Italian Opera. Taught at the Royal Academy.
		RSM A428
Winterbottom, William	1821	Trombone and 'violino'.
		Application was submitted in 1849 when he was 28. Engaged at Her Majesty's Theatre and the Philharmonic Concerts, and is Trumpet Major in Her Majesty's 1st Regiment of Life Guards. He was born 10 June 1821, the son of a soldier.
		RSM A466
Germann, Andreas Friedrich	1841	Tenor, trumpet, violin and trombone.
		Says he is 36 years old and 'belongs to her Majesty's Private band.' Born 27 Nov 1837, the son of a musician in New Windsor. Baptism record shows father to have been 'Musician to Her Majesty'. Documents from Germany in the file show that the father, Frederick Germann, was born 26 June 1804 at Burgdorf.
		RSM A420
Schroeder, Louis Dalfour	1841	Trombone, french horn and double bass.
		His application, dated Oct 1840, says he belongs to Her Majesty's Private Band. A document from Germany names him as Louis Dalfour, 'An illegitimate son of J P Dalfour a Valet de Chambre who was born at Dresden on 29 October 1804'.
		RSM A419
Matt, John	1887	Philharmonic Society and various other orchestras. Member of the Richter Concerts, various festivals, London Symphony Concerts and Carl Rosa Opera Company. Born Ipswich, 21 Nov 1843, son of a cabinetmaker.
		RSM 311
Booth, Robert Handel	1887	Principal Trombone, Royal Italian Opera.
		Application form shows him to be principal trombone at the RIO for Lyric Largo, W. Malpliron(?). Tenor trombone at the London Symphony Concerts, conductor W. Heuschel, and at the Ebenezer Prout Concerts and Prince of Wales Theatre, amongst other engagements. Born in South Pilkington on 23 Dec 1859. His father was a 'night attendant in a lunatic asylum'.
		RSM 299

of his celebrity). The popularity and finesse of these concert bands far exceeded that of any American orchestra of the time.

Given that the infrastructure for orchestral music-making outside the opera house was somewhat fractured, it is remarkable that the orchestral trombone idiom emerged so rapidly and in such convincing terms in the creative output of composers. The data given in Appendix 5 provides an interesting snapshot (though it is no more than that) of the growth of modern orchestras in the nineteenth century. As we have seen, in the first half of the nineteenth century symphony orchestras were relatively loose groupings of players assembled for individual performances or concert seasons. Furthermore, the canonical repertoire of that time included a significant number of works – the symphonies of Haydn and Mozart, for example – without trombone parts. On the other hand, some works which required trombones were gaining an almost sanctified canonical status: the most notable of these was Beethoven's Fifth Symphony, which was by far the most popular work in London's Royal Philharmonic Society series, and was performed reverentially in most European cities.[12] This was closely matched by some oratorios, such as Haydn's *Creation* and Mozart's orchestration of Handel's *Messiah*. It seems plausible that while new works including trombones continued to be written, it was the elevated status and frequency of performance of canonical works such as these that made the development of orchestral trombone skills necessary and not just desirable.

Probably the most celebrated and popular orchestra in the middle of the century was Jullien's Orchestra, which commenced its concerts at London's Drury Lane Theatre in the summer of 1840. Louis Jullien (he had 36 Christian names on account of being named after his 36 godfathers) was an unashamed showman whose success was built on an intention to 'ensure amusement as well as attempting instruction, by blending in the programmes the most sublime works with those of the lighter school'.[13] Jullien was a product of the Paris Conservatoire who started his career conducting light music in Paris. His was an essentially formulaic approach: his programmes mixed quadrilles and arrangements of other popular works with fragments of classical music and *potpourri* arrangements. His reluctance to perform complete classical works drew considerable criticism, as did his massively pretentious manner of presentation; for example, he conducted Beethoven's music with a jewel-encrusted baton, ostentatiously handed to him for the purpose on a silver salver. But two elements of the formula were particularly important to the development of the orchestral concert. First and without precedent, he attracted large and genuinely popular audiences. Secondly, he accustomed his audiences to high standards by always using the finest players. The list of principals in his orchestras reads like a roll of honour. Not the least of them were the brass players, who were among the greatest favourites: the trumpeter Harper, the ophicleide and serpentcleide[14] players Hughes and Prospère, the cornet player Koenig and the trombonist Dantonne.[15] Additionally, Jullien often imported an entire military band – or even more – for effect. (Ill. 44) As might be expected, the musical establishment dismissed Jullien as a charlatan, but it is difficult to see his spectacular and ultimately tragic career (he died penniless in a lunatic asylum) as anything other than important. More than any other conductor of his time, he brought together the finest players to perform orchestral music (albeit adulterated) to the highest standards.[16]

By the end of the nineteenth century, orchestras had been founded on both sides of the Atlantic that provided a regular if not abundant source of income for players. Furthermore, many were quickly established as coherent institutions with a distinctive style. The distinctiveness of an orchestra, and indeed its celebrity, often came from its association with a charismatic conductor. This topic is dealt with in Chapter 12, but it is worth mentioning here that the process was already under way in the nineteenth century, when such conductors as Berlioz, Liszt, Mahler and Mendelssohn attracted

Illustration 44. Engraving from the *Illustrated London News* (7 November 1846) of Jullien's Orchestra performing the 'British Army Quadrilles' at Covent Garden Theatre. A full orchestra was complemented for effect by four military bands.

personal followings. A letter to the organizers of the Royal Philharmonic season in 1841 from a Miss Joanne Alexander enquired impatiently about the plans for Mendelssohn's appearance during that season, for 'she and her sisters Lady Caroline Cavendish, Lady Howard Douglas, and Miss Douglas, are waiting for this information before subscribing';[17] and many later audience members were to keep a tight hold on their money until the appearance of Toscanini, Beecham or Walter was confirmed. Trombone players benefited from the success that celebrity conductors brought to orchestras, but there was another effect too. From the nineteenth century, conductors started to mediate in the way that instrumentalists played. More than in present times, conductors were orchestral trainers. Henry Wood insisted on sectional rehearsals before the full orchestra was assembled for a programme, and other conductors adopted this practice. 'Do not look at the trombones,' one conductor advised another, 'it only encourages them.'[18] The quip points to a problem that seems to have recurred for much of the nineteenth century and beyond: the issue of balance between the brass and the rest of the orchestra – a problem almost certainly at the heart of a nagging discontent in the reception of nineteenth- and early twentieth-century orchestral trombone playing.

Nineteenth-century reception and standards

In January 1835, the secretary to the Committee of the Société des Concerts du Conservatoire wrote to the orchestra's two senior trombone players, Devise and Bénard, in the most polite terms:

The mission I must fulfil toward you today, my dear sir, makes my duties . . . profoundly disagreeable; the committee directs me to convey to you its decision – thoughtful, carefully considered, and without any personal disrespect . . . that in the best interests of the performances a change in the trombone section is necessary.[19]

The two were awarded the accolade *membre honoraire* in recognition of their previous service. Devise left with good grace; Bénard had to be dragged, complaining and protesting, from the position he loved.[20] The two men had been shuffled to the sidelines to make room for Poussard (a new timpanist), and for the great Dieppo, who was to play with the orchestra until the second half of the century. The committee was acting to arrest a problem that appears to have been widespread. If the views of critics and other observers are to be believed, the standard of orchestral trombone playing in the nineteenth century was at best variable, and fine players were in short supply. Playing in concerted music was not the primary, and possibly not the preferred, method of employment. The skills of symphonic playing were not universally high, because the concept of purely orchestral trombone playing was neither well developed nor understood in the terms that we have come to recognize in modern times. Even in the 1880s, the author of the trombone entry in Grove's *Dictionary of Music* lamented that the 'Tuba mirum' solo in Mozart's Requiem was frequently played on the bassoon for want of adequate trombonists.

It was not just in solo playing that trombonists were found wanting, as readers of the *Musical World* in 1841 were made aware:

Sir – I am sure you will allow me to draw attention to a great musical abuse. I allude to the manner in which professors of the trombone use their instruments in the orchestra. What can be more horrid to the musician's ear than their terrifying blasts, outweighing in strength the whole band and constituting a solo with accompaniments. The real tone of every instrument is such as is produced without effort, witness that of Mr Barret's oboe and Lazarus's clarionet; so that of the trombone is the smooth delicious tone which soft playing produces, and which is strongly recommended by Mendelssohn. Even Dantonet, that prince of trombonists, is too loud in forte passages – I am, your constant TOUT ENSEMBLE[21]

The editor conceded that there was an 'ill effect of brazen preponderance', but offered the refreshing view that 'trombone players are less blameable than the orchestral directors'. The protestations of 'TOUT ENSEMBLE' were neither new nor unique. Even in 1828, *The Harmonicon* claimed that 'the proportions of the orchestra are broken down by such noisy instruments', and that 'The basis of the orchestra will always be the violin and the bass: but their number has not yet been augmented in the theatres and chief [concert halls] of Europe . . . the consequences are that they are overpowered.'[22] A Professor Gustav Engel, writing in Germany, questioned whether Mozart really intended to score for trombones in the Commendatore scene of *Don Giovanni*, because 'the effect is marred by loud trombones'.[23] And as late as 1904, an oratorio performance at Sheffield caused one intemperate correspondent to the *Musical Times* to complain that:

the trombones not only fail to 'mix' with the choral tone, but absolutely ruin the splendid effect which the rolling masses of vocal sound could produce without such well-meant but crude help. Even the staunchest purist cannot pretend that Beethoven's use of the trombones under such conditions is a specimen of matchless choral scoring.[24]

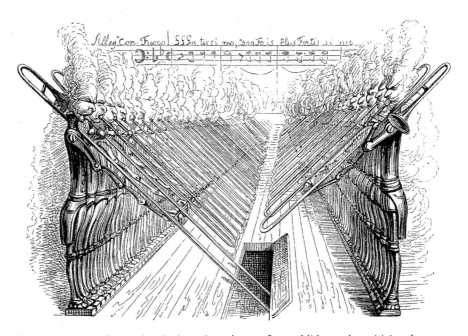

Illustration 45. 'Air for two hundred trombones', one of several lithographs satirizing the Romantic orchestra by the illustrator and caricaturist Grandville (Jean-Ignace-Isidore Gérard), from his *Un Autre Monde* (1844).

These criticisms do not necessarily mean that the quality of trombone playing was consistently low; rather, they suggest that its idiom in the orchestra was not fully understood or properly executed by performers and conductors. The criticisms – and there are many more than are quoted here – also raise interesting questions about the way composers wrote for the instrument, especially the extent to which their understanding of the trombone's idiom was shaped by a limited and very local experience. It is interesting that most criticisms (irrespective of the country in which they appear) were directed at the performance of foreign works, or at what could have been regarded as historic, as opposed to contemporary, repertoire. Furthermore, the constitutions of orchestras were enormously varied, taking little account of the need for larger numbers of wind and strings to balance an expanded brass section.

Of course, the trombone was not entirely misunderstood in the nineteenth century. The critic Eduard Hanslick recognized the competence of the trombone players in Hans von Bülow's Meiningen Orchestra (where Brahms's Fourth Symphony was first heard), even though that orchestra had a total strength of 48, compared to 90 in the Vienna Philharmonic.[25] Other writers and composers also recognized a discrepancy between the capacities of the trombone and the way in which it was routinely being heard. Adam Wirth in his *Posaunen-Schule* (1870), one of the few method books of that time to include orchestral excerpts, thought it

> a matter of regret to see this instrument so rarely meet with the treatment and application it deserves. In the hands of a performer, who knows, by a good tone and correct execution, to do justice to his part, it is capable of the most delightful effects, no matter, whether it be used as a Solo-Instrument in an orchestra, or as an accompaniment to the human voice.[26]

In 1837, when trombones were still somewhat thin on the ground in England, George Hogarth, a London journalist (and the father-in-law of Charles Dickens) who devoted many articles to the relationship between music and society, considered that 'Skilful performers can play . . . chromatic passages of considerable rapidity' but that this was a 'complete misapplication of the power of the instrument'. While acknowledging the existence of trombone concertos, Hogarth believed that the trombone should be used only in the orchestra.[27]

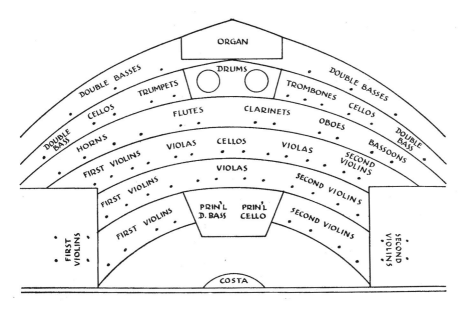

Illustration 46. The distribution of the London Philharmonic Society Orchestra under Costa in 1846. There were almost as many different disposition plans as there were orchestras.

As the century progressed, so did attitudes to the trombone. The number of specialist trombone players who worked in the major musical centres increased, and there was a steady supply of fine players who followed a path that often took them from amateur brass bands to professional military or militia bands, and then to orchestras. A marked elevation in standards was ensured by the increase of entrants to the profession, as the working class took advantage of greater opportunities for advancement. The impact of conductor-trainers was also evident. The London critic

George Bernard Shaw (whose father had 'destroyed his domestic peace by immoderate indulgence in the trombone') praised Augustus Manns, the didactic conductor of the Crystal Palace Orchestra, for the restrained sounds he obtained from his trombonists.[28] There were soon clear signs that trombonists were beginning to understand the orchestral idiom better. At the start of the nineteenth century, the *Encyclopaedia Londoniensis* had complained that

> Trombones and Double Drums are now so frequently used in the Opera, Oratorios, etc., that they are become a nuisance to lovers of pure harmony and refined tones, for, in fact, the vibrations of these instruments produce noise not musical sounds, though in certain peculiar situations they have a noble and grand effect.[29]

By the end of the century the 'noble and grand effect' was being encountered more frequently, and the 'nuisance' of the trombone had abated. Journalistic clichés that had been directed at trombonists were becoming palpably tired, and the art of orchestral trombone playing had increased in sophistication.

One of the factors that contributed to change was the renewed popularity of the trombone ensemble in the second half of the century. This was an important development, because it complemented the notion of the 'trombone section' as a homogeneous ensemble. Otto Langey, in the revised version of his *Practical Tutor for the Bb Slide-Trombone* (1909), recalled the 'fine effects' produced by a trombone ensemble that performed with Wombwell's Royal Menagerie – presumably in the second half of the nineteenth century.[30] Little is known of this group, but the Wombwell show was much admired and took its 'Royal' epithet from the patronage of the Princess Victoria, and its trombone ensemble is mentioned in glowing terms in several sources. In the closing decades of the century, several other trombone ensembles advertised their services on both sides of the Atlantic. The Concert Trombone Quartette, advertising in London in 1895, claimed to have performed with great success at the Queen's Hall, the Albert Hall and the Savage Club, and promised: 'Every graduation of light and shade from the soft pianissimo is heard with effect, each performer being a specialist on his instrument.'[31] It also claimed to have performed at the Gresham Lecture given by 'Professor Bridge'.[32] This was Frederick Bridge, organist of Westminster Abbey, who was given charge of the arrangements for the funeral, in 1898, of William Gladstone, the great Victorian Prime Minister, at which Beethoven's *Equali* for trombones were played:

> There was nothing more impressive at Mr Gladstone's funeral . . . than the strains of the *Equale* [*sic*] . . . [The three pieces were] played beautifully by Messrs George Case, C. Hadfield, A. E. Matt and John Matt . . . stationed in the chantry of Henry V's chapel . . . The hushed stillness which pervaded the noble fare was broken with indescribable tenderness as the sustained chord of D minor fell upon the ears of the great congregation in tones of weird solemnity and exquisite pathos.[33] (Ex. 8.1)

(a)

(b)

Illustration 47. Hardly authentic – a festival performance from the 1890s at the Crystal Palace, Sydenham, possibly of Mozart's edition of *Messiah*. 47a shows the full assembly of performers. 47b reveals there to be nine trombones split into two groups. The player at the left of the upper group may be Gustav Holst. (By permission of the Royal College of Music, London.)

Example 8.1. Ludwig van Beethoven, *Equale I* for four trombones, WoO 30 (1812)

George Case seems to have been something of a mentor figure for British trombonists. He was one of the best players of his generation, but he also seems to have been ambitious to establish the instrument in terms that were not sufficiently understood by many who should have known better. Shaw commended him for resurrecting performances of Schütz's 'Lamentatio Davidis' (*Fili mi, Absalon*), which showed the 'noblest qualities' of the instrument.[34]

Instrumentation

Though the reception of orchestral trombones was equivocal in the early nineteenth century, there was no special reluctance on the part of composers to write for them. While there are exceptions, the standard format in the symphony orchestra was three trombones, usually labelled alto, tenor and bass. This labelling was derived from the tradition of trombones doubling vocal lines, and publishers frequently used alto, tenor and bass clefs for the respective parts. Kastner (1837) suggests that in scores where a separate line is given to each part, the clef for that line signifies the instrument that is intended – but this was certainly not always the case.[35] Even from the seventeenth and eighteenth centuries, the notation of clefs owed as much to expediency and tradition as to precise signification. Composers frequently used clefs for entirely pragmatic and economical reasons; Schubert, for example, often wrote two or three trombone parts in a single stave in tenor clef. Similarly, Russian music is often published with both the upper trombone parts in alto clef, even though they were probably played on tenor instruments; Rimsky-Korsakov's first and second (tenor) trombone parts are usually notated in the alto clef, but it is hard to identify either as an alto trombone part, and Rimsky does not refer specifically to the alto instrument in his *Principles of Orchestration* (1913).

Preferences for particular species and voices of instrument prevailed in different countries until the last quarter of the twentieth century. French orchestras used tenor instruments in B flat (perhaps with different-sized mouthpieces) on each part, and the practice extended beyond France. According to Ebenezer Prout, only tenor trombones were used in Italian orchestras in the late nineteenth century,[36] and this practice was also known to the New York-based Otto Langey, who was aware of the G bass in England and the F bass in Germany, but stated that while the 'bass trombone in B flat is sometimes used [presumably in the USA], this is simply a B flat tenor trombone made with a larger bore and played with a larger mouthpiece'.[37] The use of a B flat trombone without a thumb valve limited the lower point of the instrument's compass to E_2 (leaving aside pedal notes). Berlioz said that when German, Italian and older French music was performed in Paris, the parts often had to be adapted, with sections transposed an octave higher.[38] He advocated the abolition of the labels 'alto', 'tenor' and 'bass' in favour of 'first', 'second' and 'third' trombones, and he made it clear that the bass instrument was a stranger to Parisian orchestras. He first encountered the true bass trombone in 1837, when Johann Strauss the elder included one in his Viennese orchestra that visited Paris. He wrote for it just once in *Grande symphonie funèbre et triomphale*, where he labels it 'grand trombone basse', and conspicuously endows it with judicious rests to avoid its player suffering fatigue. The marking 'non obligé' in the score is clearly for the benefit of orchestras that would find difficulty in obtaining an adequate player and an instrument. Indeed, Hugh Macdonald has wondered whether the part was actually played even at the first Paris performance of the work.[39]

The B flat tenor instrument was universally used by about 1850, but English instruments in the first half of the century were often pitched in C, and even in the 1880s a small proportion of new instruments manufactured in London continued to be made at that pitch. (For a discussion of the production of trombones at Besson's London branch, see Chapter 10). Like bass trombones, alto trombones were not of standard pitch, but F and E flat were the most commonly encountered. Writing in the *Musical World* in 1837, one commentator described the orchestral brass section in England as including slide trumpets and trombones in G (bass), C (tenor) and F (alto).[40] In France a few years later, Berlioz said that there were four sizes of trombones (soprano, alto, tenor and bass), but that the soprano was used only in Germany, and that the alto was rare in France, and the bass trombone 'almost unknown' there.[41] He counselled against the use of the alto trombone, which he thought 'rather poor' and 'thin', and said that higher notes sounded best on the tenor instrument. While there is considerable doubt as to how long the alto instrument continued to be used in the nineteenth century, it seems to have disappeared in many places by the middle of the century. Cecil Forsyth believed that the demise of the alto trombone started 'in Beethoven's middle period' and that it was 'practically obsolete by 1912'.[42] Charles Widor, in his *Technique de l'orchestre moderne* (1904), similarly regarded it as a thing of the distant past, and said that the high alto part in the famous chorale from the fourth movement of Schumann's Third Symphony (Ex. 8.2) was routinely accommodated by tenor trombone players:

This is certainly a striking example of very dangerous composition. Yet in our modern orchestras, we have players skilful enough to sound this E flat harmoniously on their tenor trombone, the public not even so much as suspecting the difficulty, but professionals, aware of the danger, feel a thrill of suspense at the

Example 8.2. Robert Schumann, Symphony No 3 in E flat ('Rhenish'), (1850), opening of the fourth movement

beginning of the piece, and only breathe freely when the difficulty has been overcome.[43]

The ubiquity of the small alto trombone in the eighteenth and earlier nineteenth century has been seriously questioned by Howard Weiner. He has marshalled a body of evidence to suggest that several configurations of trombone section coexisted in this period and that in most cases the higher part, irrespective of its labelling, was usually played on a tenor instrument. Weiner further suggests that the small instrument was never as ubiquitously used as is usually assumed, and that it began to rise to the level of popularity that it enjoys in modern times only when the Vienna Court Opera/Philharmonic purchased a new set of trombones to replace its valve trombones in 1883. At that time, the orchestra bought a tenor instrument in B flat, two B flat tenor instruments with an F attachment, and an alto trombone in E flat.

Berlioz regarded the tenor trombone as 'incontestably the best of all the trombones. Its sound is strong and full, it can play passages too rapid for the bass trombone and its tone is good throughout its range.'[44] On more than one occasion he points to the lack of agility of the true bass instrument, but he admired its sound when he heard it in Berlin in 1843 even though he believed it caused difficulties of balance. There, in the opera orchestra, two bass trombones were used in the absence of an ophicleide, and Berlioz found that they obliterated the upper two parts. Indeed, he believed that the 'aggressive tone of one bass trombone would be enough to upset the balance of the three trombone parts written by composers nowadays'.[45]

Berlioz had reservations about the valve trombone (see Chapter 9), though these were not universally shared. The Belgian musicologist François-Auguste Gevaert considered that the invention of valves had hardly altered the way composers wrote for orchestral trombones,[46] and valve instruments were used frequently in European and American orchestras for much of the nineteenth century and indeed into the twentieth century (again, see Chapter 9 for a more detailed discussion). Valve trombones were favoured in Bohemia, where, for example, the Prague Conservatoire taught the valve instrument exclusively. In Vienna, where the first widely adopted valve trombone may well have been invented, it was used in military bands and apparently in the Vienna Philharmonic between 1862 and 1883,[47] which means that valve trombones would have been used for the first performance of Brahms's Second Symphony – an interesting thought, given that Brahms seems to have been summoning historical references in his beautifully fashioned trombone writing. The alto valve trombone was used in some French theatres; for example, the autograph score for Act 3 of Halévy's *Guido et Ginevra* (1838) is marked 'trombone Soprano fa' and 'trombone à pistons en Mi ♭'.[48] Valve trombones seem to have lasted longer in the orchestra as bass trombones; several pictures of US orchestras from the late nineteenth century show this.[49]

Nineteenth-century French and British instruments had much narrower bores than most instruments made in German-speaking countries. The Czech maker Červený was the major foreign supplier to Russian orchestras and bands, so we may assume that the wider-bored models were favoured there too. Italian instruments were greatly influenced by Austrian models, and from the middle of the century valve trombones were favoured. Surviving instruments made by Pelitti, the main Italian manufacturer

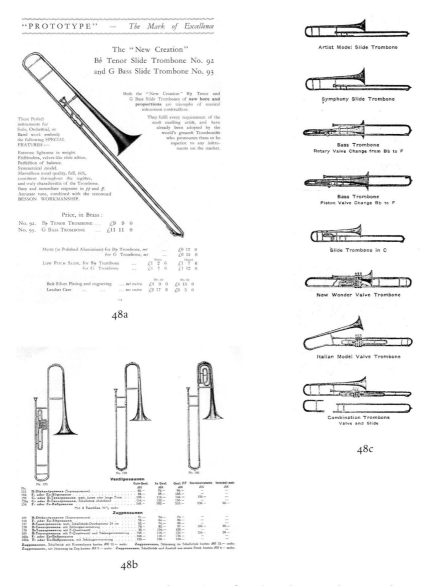

48a

48b

48c

Illustration 48. Advertisements for trombones from the early twentieth century, showing the varieties that were available: 48a Narrow-bore Besson instrument of the type ubiquitous in Britain; 48b Typically Germanic instruments from the catalogue of Reichel; 48c The wide selection advertised by the C. G. Conn company.

of valve trombones, show them to be made with a particularly narrow bore. Most trombones used in the USA in the nineteenth century either were European instruments supplied directly by European makers or imported in the hands of immigrant players, or were made in the USA by European manufacturers. This trend came to a fairly abrupt end at the end of the century, when an independent American manufacturing base began to flourish. In the twentieth century, manufacturers such as Conn and Holton produced a wide variety of instruments for different musical purposes. British and French orchestras continued to keep faith with models that were very similar to those used in the nineteenth century – including the G trombone in England. In the USA a wide selection of models was available, but by the 1940s there was a trend for American orchestral players to use instruments such as the Conn 8H and 88H, which are classed as wide bore. This pattern started to be imitated in Europe after the Second World War, and the American models – or imitations of them – were ubiquitous by the 1980s.

Nineteenth-century orchestration manuals

Nineteenth-century orchestration manuals provide an interesting insight into how the orchestral idiom of the trombone was understood. Some, but not all, make a distinction between the use of trombones in military bands and orchestras. These books tend to enunciate both objective and subjective views about the instruments they discuss. In some respects they are similar, but each has distinctive features. Most show an indebtedness to Berlioz's *Grand Traité d'instrumentation et d'orchestration modernes* (1844),[50] which had a justifiably high status, and draw on similar, or in some cases identical, musical illustrations. The French and English manuals often illustrate atypical instrumentation rather than the routine. For example, they quote Berlioz's unusual scoring of trombone pedal notes against high flutes in his *Grande Messe des Morts*, even though no other composers have sought to imitate it, and some, including Gordon Jacob, have denounced it as 'nasty', which it undisputably is. The true value of orchestration manuals as historical documents is twofold: they unwittingly reveal the cultural baggage of their time by expressing subjective views about orchestration and idiom, and they also implicitly provide a critique of how well or indifferently trombones were being played in orchestras at the time and place of their writing. When nineteenth-century writers denounce a particular aspect of trombone usage, they are usually passing comment on the way they had heard such passages performed, and when they dismiss certain types of orchestration as being akin (for example) to 'a music hall comedian's "effect"',[51] they are often uttering a value judgement that might not have been made a decade or two later, when the idiom of the instrument had progressed a little further.

One of the earliest influential textbooks to deal with orchestration in this period is Jean-Georges Kastner's *Traité général d'instrumentation* (1837, revised 1844). This was the first of ten books on musical instruments by Kastner, the latest being his *Manuel général de musique militaire à l'usage des armées française* (1848). Like most subsequent writers, in his 1837 book he described three sizes of instrument: alto (in E flat or F), tenor (in B flat) and bass (in F), but he qualified this distinction in the 1844 edition, saying that only the tenor instrument was used in French orchestras. Stewart Carter has suggested that this revision was made because Kastner's first edition was based on his experience in Strasbourg, from where he moved to Paris in 1836.[52] He also mentions the soprano (or discant) trombone, which he says is rare, and the *trombonne quarte* and *trombonne quinte*, even though these instruments were not used in France at this time. His opinion of players was equivocal:

[They] do not possess the . . . sure means to determine the tone . . . but if a piece of music has already begun, or if other instruments play at the same time, one can have the certainty of giving the chords accurately, and one can also write chorales for trombones . . . [but] avoid as far as possible complicated passages.[53]

The French preference for the tenor instrument is confirmed in Berlioz's *Grand traité*. Leaving aside Berlioz's less than perfect knowledge of music history – such as his belief that the *cornett* labelling in Gluck's opera *Orfeo ed Euridice* signified a soprano trombone part – he writes with knowledge gained from experience. He was well-travelled and was able to compare French practices with what he had observed in other countries. He regarded the trombone as

the true leader of the race of wind instruments which I have described as "epic". It possesses nobility and grandeur to a high degree and it has all the solemnity of high musical poetry, ranging from calm, imposing, devotional aura to the wild clamour of an orgy.[54]

Like Kastner, Berlioz had an interest in new instruments. He counted Adolphe Sax among his friends, and became familiar with his various inventions, including his introduction of an F valve for the B flat trombone, which he mentions in the second edition of his *Traité* (1855). Though he admired the trombone's qualities, he recognized few players as truly competent, but saw Dieppo as the greatest player of his time. He found German players inferior, with an inadequate grasp of orchestral balance. According to his memoirs, the finale of his *Harold en Italie* at Mannheim in 1843 had to be abandoned 'because the trombones were manifestly unequal to it'.[55] This disfavour may have owed something to the broader, weightier sound that issued from wide-bored German instruments compared to the smaller, more focused sound made on French trombones.

While Berlioz recognized a wide idiomatic range for the trombone, like most writers of his time he saw it as having technical and aesthetic limits. In fact, he made a distinction between the technical potential of the instrument and the practicalities of writing for it in the period in which he lived. He knew that outstanding players could use decorative devices such as trills and other embellishments (he deals with them in some detail), but he himself did not deploy the instrument in fast florid passages, neither did he write decorative figurations for it. Similarly, while he refers to the use of mutes, he only once (if the instruction is taken at face value) called for mutes in his own music: in a passage in *La Mort d'Orphée*, in which *con sordino* and *senza sordino* are marked enigmatically and undiscriminatingly for the entire brass section.

Berlioz was one of the first to advocate the orchestral trombone, both in what he wrote about it and what he wrote for it. He castigated composers who used the instrument to 'plonk tonic and dominant chords under a little tune' (probably a reference to popular theatre music of his time), those who wrote 'brutal phrases in a *Credo* more worthy of a tavern than a holy shrine', and those who otherwise impoverished and degraded 'its magnificent individuality'. Such writing, he complained, 'makes a slave and a clown out of a hero'.[56]

Gevaert's *Traité général d'instrumentation* was published in 1863, with a revised edition entitled *Nouveau Traité d'instrumentation* following in 1885. He both echoes Berlioz's *Traité* and disputes certain aspects of it. In particular, he is dismissive of the capacity of the slide trombone to cope with virtuosic passages and embellishments, and takes issue with Berlioz's illustration of trills for the tenor trombone, which he regards as unplayable on the slide instrument. Gevaert appears to have encountered the alto, tenor, bass and contrabass, but not the soprano instrument, claiming that the trombone family has 'an exclusively male character'[57] because of its lack of a soprano voice. He discusses the 'majestic' and 'supernatural' sonority of the trombone, regarding it as an essentially dramatic instrument, and emphasizing its sectional use as central to its function in theatrical music. For Gevaert, '[Its] true domain is drama, and above all tragedy in the manner of the ancient Greeks.'[58]

Rimsky-Korsakov's posthumously published *Principles of Orchestration* provides a different insight into a composer's thoughts on the instrument. Rimsky's treatise was published in 1913, but his first editor, Maximilian Steinberg, claimed that much of the discursive text existed in papers in its author's hand dating from as early as 1873. Rimsky's is a textbook, much less opinionated and discursive than Berlioz's *Traité*, and almost entirely concerned with the practical application of instruments in different musical contexts:

As a starting point I lay down the following fundamental axioms:
1. There is no such thing as ugly quality of tone.
2. Orchestral writing should be easy to play. . . .
3. A work should be written for the size of orchestra that is to perform it, not for some imaginary body.[59]

His description of the qualities of the trombone is largely confined to a single paragraph:

Dark and threatening in the deepest register, brilliant and triumphant in the high compass. The *piano* is full but somewhat heavy, the *forte* is powerful and sonorous. Valve trombones are more mobile than slide trombones, but the latter are certainly to be preferred as regards nobility and equality of sound, the more so from the fact that these instruments are rarely required to perform quick passages, owing to the special character of their tone.[60]

Rimsky's treatise is in two volumes: the first provides systematic practical advice on how the instrument should be combined with others to colour orchestral sound; the second contains musical illustrations drawn entirely from his own works. In some respects, the book is idiosyncratic, but it is perhaps the most practical and detailed of all the orchestration manuals, and though Rimsky makes references to other composers such as Wagner and Strauss, it casts particular light on Russian music of his time:

Brass instruments are so similar that a discussion of register is unnecessary. As a general rule quality becomes more brilliant as the higher register is approached, and *vice versa* . . . . Played *pp* the resonance is sweet; played *ff* the tone is hard and 'crackling'.[61]

Here Rimsky is surely attesting to the occurrence of changes in timbre alongside changes in dynamics – a phenomenon that was largely eradicated by newly designed American instruments in the twentieth century.

Ebenezer Prout's *The Orchestra* and Cecil Forsyth's *Orchestration* are among the more important English-language products of the new academicism that found favour from the late nineteenth century. Prout's book was published in two volumes in 1897 and 1899, but it incorporates material collected earlier for his 1879 book on *Instrumentation*. It was the first English-language text to deal systematically with modern orchestration, and it influenced generations of students and composers. Prout classified the idiomatic character of orchestral instruments by reference to canonical exemplars. This led him to define correct and incorrect ways to write for instruments. This propensity to categorize in pseudo-objective terms was not a personal trait of Prout's: it was part of a much more general tendency to focus on bodies of empirical evidence, to describe, define and categorize instrumental idioms, and to use the resulting analysis as the basis for establishing orthodox standards. Similar processes were used at around the same time to define bodies of knowledge more generally; Sir George Grove's *Dictionary of Music and Musicians*, for example, was published as Prout was writing his book.

Prout conveys genuinely practical information, and in many ways his is an outstanding book that displays an astonishingly intimate understanding of how instruments work. It probably reached many more readers than did the writings of Berlioz, Strauss and Rimsky, but as much as any other writer on orchestration, Prout conveys an implicit cultural attitude. When he declares that 'Nothing is more calculated to give vulgarity to a piece of music than allotting of important melodies to the cornet',[62] he suggests less about the cornet than about his own attitude to it. His ideas about the trombone are equally weighted by cultural baggage, and we may conclude that Prout has something to account for in the propagation of an over-cautious and conservative attitude to trombone technique. His initial utterances on the subject could hardly have inspired confidence in his readers: 'There is no section of the orchestra the treatment of which gives so much trouble, and causes so much perplexity to the students as that of the brass instruments.'[63] Prout was concerned with the practicalities of teaching students how to score for the orchestra. He advocates the use of trombones chorally for accompaniment, and castigates 'young composers' who are apt to use them 'freely, for the sake of making a noise'. Implicitly, he distils what he has to say into a cautionary list of do's and don'ts. To him, the bass trombone was 'a fatiguing instrument, as it requires a large amount of wind. . . . the pedal notes are not used', and rapid passages were to be avoided. He believed that 'The tone of the trombone is very broad and dignified in the forte, solemn and expressive in piano', and from this he issued the crisp judgement that the trombone, like other brass instruments, easily dominates an orchestra; when writing anything important for them, the prevailing harmony should be complete between the trumpets and trombone section.[64]

Forsyth's *Orchestration* (1914) had similar objectives, but while his factual information is less reliable, unwittingly his evaluation of the way the instrument was played in his time is especially illuminating, and worth quoting at some length:

The method of tone-production and of attack varies greatly in different countries. In England the amount of 'tang' and 'bite' that is put into the f and ff is extraordinary. The player starts the note with a great impetus, and 'throws it out into the air.' This is well enough in passages that demand the utmost force of delivery. Occasionally, however, the notes themselves seem to disappear and leave nothing but a nerve-splitting edge. The continual call for brilliance in the Brass department has caused such alterations in the instrument's construction that nowadays Tenor-Trombones are made with pretty much the same bore as that of a Cornet. The shape of the cup-mouthpiece is also determined principally with the object of securing the utmost brilliance of attack. In France the most esteemed players have not a tithe of this *bravura*, but their smooth *crescendo*, sounding like an irresistible 'head' of water, is something to be remembered. This is partly due to the fact that they usually play with instruments of a wider bore and partly to the fact that they employ a sort of modified funnel-mouthpiece. It must not be overlooked that the special drawback of the present-day Trombone is its aversion from a *forte sostenuto*. The note as a rule barks out and then dwindles down to a *mezzo-piano*. The noble manner of holding a note *forte*, but not so *forte* as to be oppressive, seems to be almost a lost art. This was the majestic *sostenuto* which Mozart and Beethoven always had in their ears when they wrote their Trombone chords. It is certainly worth all the Trombone *bravura*-playing in the world.

There is in general no true *legato* on the Trombone at all. Each note has to be articulated at the moment that the slide changes its position. There is therefore a perceptible moment between each two notes when the air-column is not in vibration. Were this not so we should get a distressing *portamento* between the notes. In the p and the pp a good player reduces this moment-of-silence to vanishing point, and produces the effect which Widor happily compares with the *sostenuto* of the Violin – a *sostenuto* which is scarcely interrupted by the turning of the bow. When playing a succession of notes from the same fundamental, that is to say, when playing without change of slide-position, the Trombone, of course, enjoys the same advantages of *legato*-playing as any slideless Brass Instrument.[65]

Forsyth attributed the difference between the French and English styles to the fact that, by 1913, the French were using wider-bored instruments and deeper mouthpieces than the English, who were still faithful to the narrow-bore models. Here he was wrong: French trombone players used instruments that had at least as narrow a bore as their English equivalents, but the deep, conical mouthpieces used by the French produced a wider sound. He regarded the trombone *section* as an important sonority, and took a dim view of the solo instrument. Indeed he regarded 'the dreadful *Tuba Mirum*' solo in Mozart's Requiem as one of the composer's more serious errors: 'Only the first three bars appear to have been written by one who understood the instrument.'[66]

In some respects, Forsyth was a bigot whose authority is often worth questioning, but he was one of the main writers of the generations following Kastner and Berlioz to display a keen interest in the mechanics of brass instruments and their development. He effectively prophesied the ubiquitous use of the thumb valve for tenor and bass trombone, the instrument that had been invented half a century earlier but had apparently not yet been used in England: 'A combination instrument, in which the slide is the main mechanism and a valve or valves are used in supplement, may possibly turn out to be the instrument of the future.'[67] Here he is particularly interesting, because his views were being formed when, as far as brass instruments were concerned, the nineteenth-century mania for invention and improvement had yet to resolve into a steady and permanent conclusion. From today's perspective he seems to devote a disproportionate amount of space to what he referred to as Adolphe Sax's 'Seven Cylinder Independent Valve System' trombone, but he harboured considerable enthusiasm for this instrument. He believed that it had an important future, and that it would solve the problems inherent in contemporary trombone playing. His faith seems to have been encouraged by the leading English conductor of the day, Sir Henry Wood, who, according to Forsyth, used the instrument designed by Sax (but made by Messrs Lebrun of Brussels) in his Queen's Hall Orchestra.

Almost exactly contemporary with Forsyth and Prout was Charles Widor, whose *Technique de l'orchestre moderne* was published in 1904. Unlike the English writers, Widor takes into account some of the more radical idiomatic uses of the instrument – particularly those of Wagner, which he quotes at length as examples of imaginative approaches to trombone articulation. Perhaps surprisingly for a French writer, Widor gives good and full accounts of both the bass and contrabass instrument, but betrays his French origins in saying that the 'great masters' rarely write below E flat for the bass trombone.

Orchestral deployment and idiom in the nineteenth century

It should come as no surprise that some of the earliest idiomatic writing for trombones in orchestral music emerged in places where there was a thriving tradition of trombone playing in opera, the church and the military. The choral writing in eighteenth-century operas – particularly those of Mozart and Gluck – provides the source for one of the lasting idiomatic aspects of orchestral trombone writing in the nineteenth and twentieth centuries. The principal features are easy to describe. Individual parts are written more or less within a vocal range, and the spacing of parts is similar to that used in vocal music. The prevailing harmony is contained either entirely, or almost entirely, within the trombone section, and the music is usually slow and quiet. The chorale that opens the fourth movement of Schumann's Third Symphony in E flat (the 'Rhenish') (1850), and choral passages found in each of the Brahms symphonies, fit this prescription so squarely that it is difficult not to think of them as deliberately evocative of older vocal or ecclesiastical styles. Aspects of this approach are also found in earlier orchestral writing – for example, the opening of Verdi's *Nabucco* overture (1842) and the opening of Mendelssohn's *Elijah* (1846). This texture, which was commonly used to enforce darker or more serious moments in musical narrative, has also been used by twentieth-century composers purely for its sonic effect.

Beethoven's Fifth Symphony in C minor (1808) is the first symphony by a major composer to contain trombone parts. He also used the instrument in the sixth and ninth symphonies, in some of his oratorios and his one opera, *Fidelio* (1804/14). Some of his trombone parts were clearly inserted at the last moment; according to Ferdinand Ries, the inclusion of trombones in the 1803 version of *Christus am Oelberge* was very much an afterthought: 'I found him in bed, writing on single sheets of paper. To my question what it was he answered: "Trombones". In the actual performance the trombones played from these very sheets. . . . probably they were an afterthought.'[68] Clearly Beethoven was interested in the trombone, and seems to have been aware that he was experimenting with it in the orchestra. A writer in *The Harmonicon* who had spent a day with Beethoven in 1824 reported that the composer 'was desirous of ascertaining for a particular composition . . . the highest possible note on a trombone . . . but did not seem satisfied [with the answer he was given]'.[69] We do not know what work Beethoven had in mind, but it may well have been the Ninth Symphony, on which he was working during that year. His scoring for the trombone is often quoted because of the historical significance of the instrument's inclusion in the Fifth Symphony and the presumption that its use was inspired by a wish to convey Romantic heroism. In fact, the strength of Beethoven's orchestral scoring for trombones lay in his ability to blend the instruments into orchestral textures. In many ways, this writing is remarkable for its time precisely because the trombones generally signify no programmatic meaning in their own right.

This capacity to integrate the idiom of the trombone section into orchestral sound is also evident in the theatrical works of Weber. The importance of Weber's writing for trombones is often overlooked because it makes no technical demands, but he used three trombones in virtually all his stage works, and even in *Der Freischütz* (1821) he shows an advanced awareness of the instrument's subtler colours. But it was Schubert who was probably the first composer to identify a holistic role for the trombone. His 'Unfinished' Symphony D759 (1822) and the 'Great' C major Symphony D944 (1826) contain some of the most imaginative and truly idiomatic orchestral writing ever devised for trombones in the orchestra. (Ex. 8.3) The performance history of Schubert's symphonies is far from complete. Many of the orchestral works were written for private performances. Both the 'Unfinished' and C major symphonies were written in Vienna, but there is little evidence of where and when they were first performed – it even seems possible that the composer never heard the 'Unfinished' Symphony.

The writing of French composers or those working in France in the first half of the nineteenth century provides the source for a different strand in the instrument's orchestral idiom. Gossec, somewhat self-consciously, claimed to have reintroduced trombones into musical life in Paris. Whether or not this is true, it is certain that composers writing for performances in Paris seem to have been able to rely on good players being available from the later eighteenth century onwards.[70] Rossini's *Guillaume Tell* (1829), which contains famously taxing rapid passages for trombones in the 'storm scene' and the overture, was written for performance in Paris. By this time Berlioz was gaining prominence, and it is striking that *Symphonie fantastique* (1830), which demonstrates such a different concept of brass writing from the German and Austrian approach, was composed within three years of Beethoven's death. In his *Traité* Berlioz identified Gluck, Beethoven, Weber and Spontini as exemplars who had shown 'exceptional intelligence' in writing for orchestral brass, and particularly cited the 'matchless Funeral March' in Gaspare Spontini's *La Vestale* (1807).[71] (Ex 8.4)

Example 8.3. Franz Schubert, Symphony in C ('Great') D944 (1826), first movement

Example 8.4. Gaspare Spontini, 'Funeral March' from *La Vestale* (1807)

Many of the distinctive features of Berlioz's orchestral trombone writing derive from the influence of the military band. This more colourful application of trombones – as contributors to blocks of sound, often emphasizing programmatic meaning, and exploiting greater extremes of pitch and dynamic – has prevailed as one of the main idiomatic styles of orchestral trombone writing. But here a word of caution is necessary. While this style derives from the more expansive instrumentation of the military band, it would be quite wrong to regard it as axiomatically militaristic in character: the derivation has less to do with martial imagery (though several composers clearly exploited this) than with the use of a wider set of technical and idiomatic devices – articulations, dynamic contrasts and general groupings of instruments – that had evolved in elite military music rather than within the orchestra.

Both the choral and military band influences subsequently become manifest in the later trombone writing of such composers as Liszt, Tchaikovsky, Bruckner, Mahler and Wagner; but Wagner took the idiom somewhat further. His writing for brass owes more to the work of earlier composers than is sometimes acknowledged, but his significance in the development of the orchestral trombone is impossible to deny.[72] His experimentation with the idiom of the trombone was, of course, part of a more general endeavour to expand the expressive qualities of the orchestra. But his trombone writing consistently shows a widening of the timbre, pitch and dynamic compass of the instrument (particularly in its sectional use), a willingness to use trombones in the melodic foreground (for example, by incorporating them into his scheme of operatic leitmotifs), and a capacity to use them for multiple expressive purposes in single works.

The use of the trombone in opera by such composers as Wagner and Verdi may have contributed as much to the orchestral idiom of the trombone as did the concert repertoire. As the twentieth century opened, these composers, along with Bruckner, Mahler and Richard Strauss, became exemplars, if not models, for orchestral trombone writing, and the trend towards further expansion of the idiom continued as the old century passed into the new in such works as Debussy's *Pelléas et Mélisande* (1893–5) and Schoenberg's *Pelleas und Melisande* (1902–3) and *Gurrelieder* (1900–12).

Orchestral deployment and idiom in the twentieth century

It is beyond the scope of this book to provide even an outline sketch of the myriad innovations to the way the trombone has been written for in the twentieth century. Some composers – Stravinsky, for example – have introduced trombones into smaller instrumental combinations; but in terms of orchestral repertoire, it is possible to summarize the principal developments by reference to a number of broad features and trends that emerge in the expansion of the orchestral repertoire. This is an area that overlaps considerably with discussions elsewhere in this book of trombone playing in the twentieth century, and what follows should thus be read in the context of what is said in subsequent chapters.

There has been a continued tendency to regard the orchestral trombone as having multi-dimensional technical and expressive qualities. This contrasts with the more formulaic and cautious approach advocated by Prout, Forsyth and others, which can be observed in the works of most major composers from the start of the twentieth century. There has also been an increased awareness on the part of many composers of the individual timbres of the alto, tenor and bass instruments, even though the tenor/bass (B flat and F) has been taken as the norm by many. Relatively few twentieth-century composers have written convincingly for the alto instrument (though early examples are found in works by Schoenberg and Webern), and this may be due to the scarcity of good players – a lack noted by Stravinsky when he lamented that good alto trombone players were still not available for his *Threni* (1957–8).[73] But perhaps a more important result of this greater awareness has been the liberation of the bass trombone, which was a major feature of writing in the second half of the century. Of course, we need look no further than Wagner and Verdi for precedents, but the novel deployment of bass and contrabass trombones in the second half of the century was significant, and must be attributable in part to the design of more effective instruments, and to the seemingly endless procession of brilliant specialist players.

Since the opening years of the twentieth century, the introduction of new musical languages has had an effect on the techniques of trombonists, stretching the idiom and imposing significant new demands. The angular, asymmetrical melodies with wide augmented and diminished intervals and complex harmonies, found in the works of the composers of the Second Viennese School after about 1910, imposed unprecedented technical demands which were hardly anticipated in the didactic methods. Early recordings provide evidence of trombonists wrestling, sometimes hopelessly, with Stravinsky's rhythmic and harmonic language.[74]

Increasingly, composers have extended the pitch range of instruments and specified new techniques and effects of great subtlety and precision. Initially, such filtering was restricted to the application of mutes (straight mutes in the first instance, with several new designs being introduced subsequently), but later composers have also used electronic mediations. By about 1970 a mind-boggling array of advanced techniques (a theme which is discussed in more detail in Chapter 14) was being applied to orchestral writing.

Though the use of the trombone as a solo instrument in the orchestra was not new, the range of expression that it was used to convey became wider. Extended orchestral solos of the type found in Berlioz's *Grande symphonie funèbre et triomphale* (1840) and Mahler's Third Symphony (1893–6) exploit a rhetorical – what Berlioz called 'noble' – aspect of the instrument's character. This mode of expression has been adopted only infrequently by twentieth-century composers, even though highly effective, somewhat shorter solo passages litter the twentieth-century concert and operatic repertoire. Additionally, several composers have used the solo instrument for characterizations that were not seen in concert music before the twentieth century – for example, comic or slapstick allusions in Aaron Copland's *Rodeo* (1942) and Malcolm Arnold's *Tam O'Shanter* (1955) (Ex. 8.5); more lugubrious melodies that mimic popular styles, such as Ravel's *Bolero* (1928); or solos that are directly referential to jazz, as in Bernstein's *West Side Story* (1957).

As with most orchestral instruments, the expansion of the trombone's technical idiom has been incremental. Composers have experimented with an unorthodox feature which is then adopted or disregarded by others according to its perceived success. (Composers quickly saw the merits of exploiting the higher range of the tenor trombone, for instance, but none have followed Berlioz's example of scoring exposed passages for flutes and trombone pedal notes.) But somewhat paradoxically, a yet more prominent and persistent feature has been the continuity of the performance style implicit in the Romantic orchestral repertoire. Such composers as Elgar, Vaughan Williams, Ravel, Sibelius, Shostakovich, Britten and Tippett may have exhibited creative individuality, and were stylistically of their time, but it is easy to hear in their writing for the orchestral trombone aspects of an idiom that stretches

Example 8.5. Malcolm Arnold, *Tam O'Shanter Overture* Op. 51 (1955), Vivace (by permission of Chester Novello)

back further than the twentieth century. This idiom – what we might loosely call the staple orchestral section idiom – is based on an idea of the trombone section as a carrier of expressive and sometimes historical messages, and as a multifaceted sonority within the orchestral soundscape. This style has acquired great sophistication and finesse in performance, because twentieth-century concert programming was biased towards a historical repertoire, or towards works that exploit a relatively conservative musical language – a topic that will be returned to in Chapter 12.

Chapter 9

Valve trombones and other nineteenth-century introductions

Trombones with valves were introduced from the early nineteenth century. It is helpful to think of them as falling into three categories. In the first are those with three or more valves, where the valves are substituted for the slide so as to provide the instrument with a chromatic compass. In the second are those fitted to slide instruments (usually one or two thumb valves) which change the nominal pitch of the instrument when depressed. They provide several facilities, but their main advantage – and the reason for their introduction – is that they give access to additional notes in the low register. In the final, somewhat smaller category are instruments with a valve for the production of special effects, particularly trills. Before dealing with these different devices, it is necessary to say something about valve mechanisms in general, because their application to trombones should be seen in the wider context of the problems that brass instrument designers and manufacturers of the period were trying to solve. In this chapter I also deal with some other species of instruments that are not trombones at all, but that are nonetheless relevant to the subject of this book, either because they are usually played by trombone players as adjunct instruments (such as the bass trumpet), or because they have had an important bearing on the sonority of the trombone section in orchestral music (such as the ophicleide).

The valve principle

All valve systems have the same aim: they provide a means of altering the sounding length of an instrument to facilitate access to the notes of additional harmonic series. To put it somewhat differently, valves provide an alternative way of doing what the slide does on the slide trombone. Several different valve designs were introduced in the first half of the nineteenth century. The earliest was invented in 1814 by Heinrich Stölzel, a horn player in the Pless court band in Prussia, and his collaborator Friedrich Blühmel, a civilian band musician. The two men were in dispute about who was responsible for the device, especially after a notice appeared in the *Allgemeine musikalische Zeitung* in 1815, announcing the invention solely in Stölzel's name.[1] But by 1818 they had resolved their differences and jointly secured a ten-year Prussian patent protection for the principle of the valve mechanism.[2]

Other successful systems include the double-piston valve introduced by Christian Friedrich Sattler in 1821. This continued to be used in Belgium until the second half of the twentieth century on the *trombone belge*. The double-piston valve design was

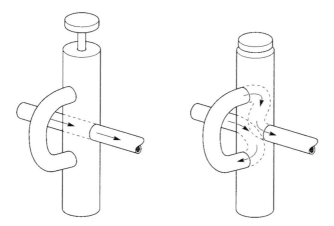

Illustration 49. Simple illustration of the Périnet valve principle, showing how the depression of the valve diverts the windway through an extra length of tubing.

further developed in Vienna, and applied to the trombone. Yet another design, the so-called Berlin valve, was introduced by Wilhelm Wieprecht, a Prussian bandmaster, in 1833.[3] However, the most widely adopted piston valve system was devised by the French instrument maker François Périnet and patented in 1838 in Paris. Illustration 49 gives a simple illustration of the Périnet system; it also shows the general principle of how valves work. This is a 'descending system': it works on the principle that the engagement of a valve *adds* tubing to the windway, and consequently *lowers* the pitch. When a valve is not depressed, the windway runs directly through the valve without interruption; but when it is depressed, the windway is diverted through an extra length of tubing, thus making the overall sounding length longer, causing the pitch of the instrument to descend so that a different harmonic series is available. (The difference between this and the 'ascending system' is discussed below.) In order to obtain a chromatic spectrum equivalent to that obtained from the seven positions on a slide trombone, it is necessary for an instrument to have three valves which are used either individually or in combination.

The rotary valve achieves the same end as a piston valve, but the mechanism is different. It was probably introduced by Blühmel in the late 1820s, but a somewhat later design (1835) by Kail and Riedl of Vienna became more popular and enduring. Rotary valves have been applied to brass instruments of all voices, and have been especially popular in Austria, Germany and eastern Europe. The rotary valve, in one format or another, has been favoured for trombone thumb valves.

Despite the apparent simplicity of the principle, valve systems present a range of problems for instrument designers. The action of the valve needs to be easy and efficient, the distance of travel between the open and closed valve must be executed swiftly and comfortably, and it is important that neither the timbre nor the intonation of the instrument is impaired when valves are engaged. Such problems are prevalent when sharp bends are introduced into the windways and when there are alterations and interruptions to the bore profile in the valve section. Intonational inconsistencies may also arise when two or more valves are used in combination, and this problem particularly occupied nineteenth-century inventors. It follows that many modifications to valve designs have been introduced since the nineteenth century, and the goal of finding a perfect valve system (despite the claims of manufacturers) has never really been achieved.

Valve trombones

The exact origin of the valve trombone has not been reliably established, and we can only speculate why there was a perceived need for such an instrument when the slide trombone had proved so satisfactory for so long. A valve trombone was produced around 1830 in Vienna – interestingly enough, the city which, in the eighteenth century, had sustained the clearest and most distinguished line of fine *slide* trombone playing. According to Andreas Nemetz, who obviously knew no differently, the inventor of the valve trombone was indeed a Viennese maker, Josef Riedl. Nemetz does not mention the valve trombone in the first edition of his *Neueste Posaun-Schule*, published in Vienna in 1827, but in the second edition, published some time after 1830, he makes it clear where he believed it originated:

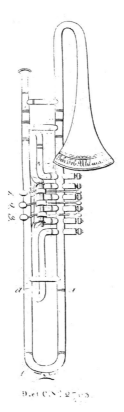

Illustration 50. The earliest illustration of a valve trombone, found in the second edition of Andreas Nemetz's *Neueste Posaun-Schule* (after 1830). The name of the maker Johann Tobias Uhlmann is clearly visible on the bell.

> The trombone has attained the greatest perfection with the valve trombone. To Mr. Jos. Riedl goes the honour of having first transferred the artificial mechanism of the valve trumpet and the valve horn to the trombone. In the year 1830, Mr. Joh. Tob. Uhlmann, brass instrument maker in Vienna, substantially altered and perfected that mechanism; for this reason he was also awarded an exclusive Imperial Royal privilege.[4]

In fact Riedl was not the first to apply the valve to the trombone. A trombone with Blühmel's box-valve (*Kastenventil*) design was produced by the Berlin manufacturer Joseph Caspar Gabler in 1818, while Blühmel was lodging with him.[5] It is also possible that other models may have been developed in one of the centres where innovative brass instrument design thrived, but the Vienna instruments seem to have been the first to have been produced and used in any quantity. The valve trombone introduced by Uhlmann was patented in 1830[6] as the *Doppelschubrohrventil* (double sliding-tube valve) instrument, and it is clearly illustrated in Nemetz's method, with the maker's name visible. (Ill. 50) Nemetz regarded it highly.

Records of the Court Opera Orchestra (of which Nemetz was a member) do not survive for this time, but it seems that valve trombones were introduced there in the mid-1830s. A further valve trombone was purchased from Uhlmann for the court chapel at around the same time,[7] and in 1858 the court chapel bought a bass-tenor trombone with four valves.[8] Carlo Balochino and Bartolomeo Merelli (both directors at La Scala, Milan) had taken over the direction of the Vienna court opera at the end of 1835. The change to valve trombones probably came at about this time.[9]

In 1862 wind players in the opera orchestra had to change their instruments because of the introduction of the new lower French tuning standard. The court opera management offered players 'the right and responsibility to define for themselves, according to their experience and opinions' the form and type of instruments 'that appear most appropriate for their purposes'.[10] The trombonists elected to acquire one three-valve and three four-valve trombones in B flat, and two three-valve trombones in F, made by Leopold Uhlmann and Daniel Meinl; and the on-stage band acquired two three-valve instruments in F. The practice of using valve trombones in Vienna prevailed until 1883, when the new court opera director Wilhelm Jahn, believing that 'the effect of the slide trombone gives the orchestra a much more lively timbre' reintroduced slide trombones – wide-bore German instruments.[11] Only two of the orchestra's five trombonists agreed to make the change, so three German players were recruited. The orchestra bought a slide alto instrument in E flat, a tenor in B flat and a tenor-bass instrument from the Penzel factory (the successor to Sattler) in Leipzig, because the slide trombone was 'not even cultivated' in Vienna.[12]

What motivated makers to apply valves to the trombone? There was a tendency among makers and designers in the early nineteenth century to look for ways of improving instruments. (Ill. 51) The most immediate objects for attention were trumpets and horns, which relied on crooking and hand-stopping to obtain an uninterrupted melodic compass. But there was also an ambition to apply effective mechanisms to instruments in the bass range. There is no evidence to suggest that valve trombones were introduced in order to render slide instruments obsolete, but

TROMBONE A TROIS PISTONS

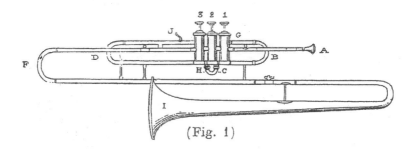

(Fig. 1)

TROMBONE A QUATRE PISTONS

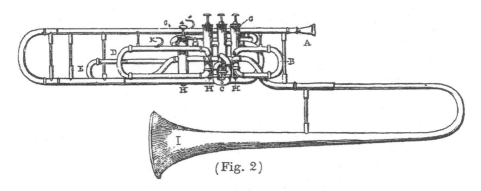

(Fig. 2)

Illustration 51. Valve trombones illustrated in Lagard's *Méthode de trombone à trois ou à quatre pistons* (1878).

they were perceived as having pragmatic advantages. The absence of a slide must have seemed an obvious advantage to military musicians, especially those in mounted bands.[13] This was not a minor matter, because marching and mounted cavalry bands were integral components in official ceremonies. In the second half of the century, some valve trombones were manufactured specifically with this function in mind. For example, upward-pointing bells and circular-shaped instruments made it easier for instruments to be played on horseback. The rotary valve *Armee-Baßposaune* in F, introduced by V. F. Červený in 1867, led to the development, a year later, of a family of *Armeeposaune* instruments, made in sizes from alto in F to contrabass in B flat.[14] (Ill. 52)

Both piston and rotary valves have been applied to trombones, and the configurations of the mechanisms have varied considerably. The most popular design – the so-called 'long model' – resembles the outline shape of the slide instrument, while 'short models' are more compact. Some nineteenth-century valve instruments – particularly altos – have a very narrow bore, but very wide-bore models have also been common and were frequently used as bass trombones in orchestras in Germany

75

Illustration 52. *Armeeposaune* from the Mahillon catalogue of 1893.

and eastern Europe. In Germany in the nineteenth century, military band valve trombones had a particularly wide bore, while surviving instruments made by the Pelitti Company of Milan have especially small proportions and must have produced a focused, delicate sound.

The valve trombone quickly found favour in Italy. It is not entirely clear why this preference took root as rapidly and comprehensively as it did, but the strong links between northern Italy and Austria, and the mobility of musicians between the two, must have been an important factor. Valve technology was adopted enthusiastically by the Milan manufacturer Pelitti shortly after the company was established in 1828, and it quickly became Italy's most important producer of brass instruments.[15] Added to this was the demand from the amateur band market. Just as amateur bands prospered in other parts of Europe from the 1840s, so they did in Italy; but Italian town bands thrived in a somewhat different context from that of such places as England, Germany and the USA. Some have argued that the English and Scottish civic musicians known as waits provided a continuous tradition that was eventually manifest in amateur brass bands. In fact, most waits bands were defunct in the eighteenth century, and the amateur bands that emerged in the nineteenth century were an entirely different species. In Italy the situation seems to have been different. The *pifferi* tradition (in the sense of it being a town band tradition) continued to exist as it had done in the sixteenth and seventeenth centuries, if in a somewhat modified form. Many of the reasons for its existence remained largely unaltered. Bands often continued to receive encouragement and even modest funding from civic authorities and small-town councils. Also, the festival tradition and the cycle of events (particularly the religious feast days) that had made them necessary in the age of city states never entirely disappeared. Annual civic and community festivals were marked by colourful parades. Many Italian town bands were marching bands, and in the second half of the nineteenth century, bicycle bands gained some popularity across the country. This meant that the opportunities for mass sales of brass instruments in Italy were as ripe as they were in other parts of Europe, and this market was exploited perhaps a little earlier than it was elsewhere.

Valve trombones offered a further practical advantage for amateurs, in that players who had mastered valve technique could transfer to the trombone without having to learn slide positions. This facility was often a foreground feature in the advertising of valve trombones. Even in the early twentieth century, the Conn Corporation in the USA made great play of this when promoting its 'New Wonder Valve Trombone' (model 4G). Its message, it must be remembered, was addressed to potential consumers with little knowledge of musical instruments:

> The Valve Trombone will produce the proper pitch of tone by the proper fingering of the valves. The Slide Trombone will not [*sic*] do this only when the performer has mastered the correct position of the slide to the smallest fraction of an inch. It is for this reason that many Trombonists adopt the Valve Trombone and many have continued its use rather than chance the intricacies of the Slide Trombone.[16]

All this suggests that the valve instrument was the more obvious choice for amateurs, but while the option was taken up widely, it was less popular in some places than in others. In Britain, France and Germany both slide and valve instruments were used. In central Europe, Austria, Latin American countries and Italy the valve instrument was favoured. It was ubiquitous in Italy, where the supply of players seems to have been almost exclusively made up of valve trombonists by the middle of the century. From that time, trombone parts in Italian opera are written with valve trombones in mind. Verdi's operas in particular demonstrate this idiom from the middle of the century, and the composer took a keen interest in the instruments produced by Pelitti. His discontent with the lack of homogeneity in the brass section led to him to approach Pelitti in 1881 with the request that he produce the instrument that became known as the *trombone contrabasso Verdi*. Verdi had written to his publisher, Giulio Ricordi, before the first performance of *Aida* at La Scala in 1871:

> I wish to insist again on a fourth trombone. . . . That bombardon is not possible. . . . [Consult] the principal trombonist in order to decide what should be done. . . . I would prefer a trombone basso which is one of the same family of the others. . . . [I]f this turns out to be too much trouble and too difficult to play then get again one of those ordinary ophicleides that go down to B . . . but not that devilish bombardon.[17]

The 'ordinary ophicleide' that Verdi preferred was the narrow-bore instrument in F, rather than the larger instrument that overpowered his orchestra and certainly did not match the lighter, more focused sonorities of his trombones.

In September 1881, Pelitti succeeded in producing a trombone to Verdi's specification. The composer visited the workshops with Ricordi and his librettist Boito, where some military band players had been assembled to demonstrate the new invention in various types of ensemble – particularly with Pelitti trombones:

> Repeated experiments were made with the new trombone in B flat pitch one octave lower than the tenor. The new instrument gave splendid results regarding range, timbre, sonority, power, ease and facility of execution, blending perfectly with the other trombones. Resulting in this, two B flat tenor trombones, a bass trombone in F and the new bass trombone in B flat are necessary to achieve a trombone quartet that is perfect, homogeneous and effective without bringing into the orchestra a timbre from the band that would affect the instrumental blending of several instruments.[18]

Verdi heard the new instrument in ensemble with other trombones and pronounced the bass trombone in B flat and E flat to be

> excellent, as it achieved a perfect homogeneity of timbre with the tenor trombones, thus completing the quartet without altering the fundamental notes, which happens instead with the present ophicleides and similar instruments, all very good for a band but out of place in an orchestra.[19]

This instrument was subsequently deployed in Verdi's operas *Otello* (1887) and *Falstaff* (1893), where it is called 'trombone basso'. (Ex. 9.1) It was promptly adopted by most Italian orchestras, where it served as the bass of the brass family until replaced by the tuba in the 1920s. It was the first trombone to be used for what has – often somewhat loosely – been referred to as the 'cimbasso' line. This term was used in Italy from the early nineteenth century for a variety of cup-mouthpiece bass instruments. Its provenance has often been misunderstood, giving rise to several misinterpretations in later twentieth-century performance practice. The term *cimbasso* should not be applied to any valve or slide trombone made before 1881, but from that time the term 'Verdi's *trombone basso*' was also used, presumably with the composer's approval, in performances of his earlier operas. But, as Renato Meucci has pointed out, the indiscriminate identification of *cimbasso* with the contrabass trombone in nineteenth-century Italian opera is wrong.[20]

It was not only in Italy that the valve trombone gained popularity. The lower brass parts in Spanish bands were almost invariably played on valve trombones, and many such instruments were made by Spanish makers, among them the Barcelona firm of Montserrat. Other manufacturers and retailers, such as the Bohemian company Anton Hüller, advertised only valve instruments, but it was rare indeed for a maker's catalogue to be devoted exclusively to slide instruments. Even the London branch of the Besson company, which was one of the major suppliers of slide instruments in the second half of the nineteenth century, produced valve trombones in large quantities. In nineteenth-century British brass band music one often encounters separate parts for 'valve trombone' and 'trombone' (from which we can usually infer that a slide trombone is intended). The instrumentation of bands in the nineteenth century was

Example 9.1. Giuseppe Verdi, *Falstaff* (1893), Act 3, Part 1, contrabass trombone part

so fluid that we can draw few conclusions from this, but in specific instances it is easy to see that valve trombones were written for in a manner broadly analogous to baritone saxhorns.

The popularity of the valve instrument in Italy and Spain accounts for a preference for valve instruments in Latin American countries that has lasted until modern times. It is hard to determine when this usage originated, but the tradition of town band playing was well established by early in the century, and Brazil in particular had a massive network of bands by the mid-century (the Bahai town band had slide trombones as early as 1810).[21] Emigration from Hispanic-colonized countries to the USA may also account for the frequency with which valve trombones are found in New Orleans marching and jazz bands. This topic is dealt with in more detail in Chapter 13, but it is worth mentioning here that many of the greatest trombone players in early jazz bands were valve trombone players. The only known photograph of Buddy Bolden's band, taken in 1905 (Ill. 53), shows the trombonist Willie Cornish with a short-model valve instrument, and several later jazz trombone players whose reputations were based on their exploitation of the slide trombone idiom, including the great Kid Ory, were initially valve trombone players.

Illustration 53. Willie Cornish, seen in the only surviving picture of the Buddy Bolden band (dating from 1905), with a short-model valve trombone.

Valve trombones were also imported directly into the USA and manufactured there from the nineteenth century. By the 1890s, Conn was producing valve trombones. Prominent among these was the 'New Italian Model' in B flat (Ill. 48c), which featured a distinctive elevated bell, and which, the company claimed, had been in such 'great demand by the Trombonists of the leading Italian Bands and others who prefer the elevated bell that it was found necessary to place it in the catalogue'.[22]

Valve trombone versus slide trombone

The valve trombone stood in serious opposition to the slide instrument among professional orchestral players in Vienna for forty years, and even longer in Italian and Czech orchestras, and it was enormously popular in military and amateur bands. For a period in the second half of the nineteenth century, factory production lines were probably turning out more valve than slide instruments. But the distinctive idiomatic character of the slide instrument – the purity of its tone and the perfection of its intonation – was not superseded. Berlioz knew the valve trombone mainly as an alto instrument pitched in either E flat or F, but following his visit to Germany in 1843, he added a paragraph to his treatise to take account of the tenor instrument that 'went down to low B flat', which he had heard there. He saw the merits of the valve instrument as being 'at the cost of some accuracy of intonation': 'If well phrased a melody can have considerable charm on this [alto trombone] instrument. But it is a mistake to believe it would have any less charm on the slide trombone in the hands of a true virtuoso; M. Dieppo has made that triumphantly plain on many occasions.'[23] Despite such reservations, Berlioz accommodated the valve instrument on two occasions in his own works: the famous tenor trombone solo in *Grande symphonie funèbre et triomphale* was published with three alternative solo parts, one of which was for an alto valve trombone; and in the 'Marche hongroise' in *La Damnation de Faust*, somewhat oddly, he wrote a tenor valve trombone part to double the first slide trombone part for the last sixty bars of the piece.

Orchestral trombonists who had moved to the valve instrument seem to have started to drift back to the traditional instrument in the second half of the century. We have seen the case of the trombonists at the Vienna Court Opera being required to take up the slide instrument, in imitation of the German style. H. W. von Gontershausen claimed in 1855 that the valve trombone had become unpopular: 'Therefore our good trombonists are quite justifiably discarding them [i.e. valve trombones] and taking up the earlier type with the slides.'[24] In some countries – certainly in Germany, France and England – the valve trombone was coming to be categorized primarily as a band instrument. But a number of orchestral players continued to use valve trombones in symphony orchestras, especially for bass trombone parts. Photographs of late nineteenth-century American orchestras often show at least one valve trombone player, and valve instruments continued to be used in Czech orchestras after the slide instrument had been reintroduced in Austrian professional orchestras.

One of the disadvantages that valve trombone players have to endure is that there has never been a widespread, coherent and articulate didactic tradition for the instrument to match that of the slide trombone. Neither has there really been a discrete idiomatic solo repertoire, or – outside jazz – a body of mentor players to equal the slide trombone virtuosi. While a number of conservatoires taught the valve instrument (some, such as the Prague Conservatoire – initially at least – taught *only* the valve instrument), the concentration has been mainly on the slide trombone. Similarly, while didactic literature of the nineteenth and early twentieth centuries for the valve trombone is plentiful enough (see Appendix 4), a genuinely idiomatic path is not developed in it. Many French and German method books of the nineteenth century are labelled for the valve as well as for the slide trombone, but while valve fingerings complement slide positions in explanatory diagrams, there is little to commend them as thoughtful expositions of valve trombone technique. The English books are often entirely generic in character. The same can be said for the method books that appear to be aimed solely at the valve instrument. Adam Wirth's *Posaunen-Schule für Alt, Tenor und Bass Posaune* (1870), for example, could have been written for a slide instrument. (Ill. 54) Of course, it could be argued with some justification that the plethora of instructional books for other valve instruments rendered such a provision unnecessary. But most brass instruments that were to find a regular place in the orchestra (including new ones such as the cornet) acquired a dedicated didactic literature that was inspired by particular mentor performers such as Arban and Dieppo. Dieppo taught valve trombone at the Paris Conservatoire following the closure of the Gymnase Musical Militaire in 1856 and the creation of a military class

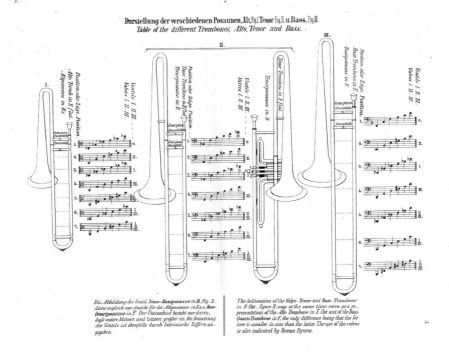

Illustration 54. Trombones illustrated in Adam Wirth's *Posaunen-Schule für Alt, Tenor und Bass-Posaune . . .* (1870) showing the equivalents between slide positions and valve combinations as Wirth understood them.

within the Conservatoire. Indeed, for a while students were required to learn Sax's six-valve instrument. But Dieppo was never really a valve trombone player, and one can only wonder whether his heart was entirely in it. It is difficult to identify a nineteenth-century valve trombone player of his calibre who was a mentor for the instrument.

Two areas can be determined in which the valve trombone acquired a distinctive idiom. The first is certain fields of orchestral writing – particularly Italian opera and central European orchestral music, where much of the trombone writing clearly lies outside the natural idiom of slide instruments. The fact that modern professional trombonists have mastered the art of playing these orchestral passages on slide instruments does not detract from the fact that they were manifestly conceived for valve instruments, and, in the case of Italian opera, rather small-bore ones at that. While Italian opera presents the clearest example of the historical presence of valve trombones, there are others that should be cited. Despite Berlioz's equivocation, it was favoured briefly in some Parisian theatre orchestras in the nineteenth century. There was also a preference for the valve instrument in professional orchestras in the Czech lands. Many of the works of Anton Dvořák were written for it. This is only occasionally obvious from the scores, but an illustration is the rapid descending scale passage in the closing bars of his Eighth Symphony. Probably a better example is found in Janáček's *Sinfonietta* (1926), which is usually performed on slide instruments but has several sections in the trombone parts that betray the legacy of the valve instrument. (Ex. 9.2)

The valve trombone has found its most eloquent voice in jazz. Not only was it common in early jazz, but by the 1920s it was being played by stylish performers who drew from the instrument – possibly for the first time in its history – a truly distinctive and convincing mode of expression. Perhaps the first great valve trombonist was Juan Tizol, who joined Duke Ellington's band in 1929. Tizol was a Puerto Rican who learned the valve trombone at school and went on to play with a local municipal band. He said that the slide trombone was used only in the army band at that time, and the valve instrument was ubiquitous among amateurs.[25] He was a superb general musician and a superlative player who played valve trombone exclusively. Ellington quickly identified both the distinctive qualities of the instrument and Tizol's deftness as a player. He moved towards the formulation of two functions for Tizol's instrument: first, as a constituent of a balanced 'section' of tenor trombones – initially a duo, but a trio when Lawrence Brown joined the band in 1932; and secondly, as a lead voice with the saxophone section – implicitly designating it as a pivot between the brass and reeds. This owed something to the facility offered by the valve instrument in more florid passages, but the approach was used with equal frequency in slower numbers such as 'Creole Rhapsody' (1931) and 'Clouds in My Heart' (1932).[26]

Tizol was seldom used as a soloist by Ellington, though his few duets with Joe 'Tricky Sam' Nanton are among the most important of their time. But the star of the next generation of valve trombonists, Bob Brookmeyer (b. 1929), was the first player really to exploit the instrument in a soloistic way. He was an important exponent of the West Coast style, and came to prominence when he replaced the trumpeter Chet Baker in Gerry Mulligan's 'pianoless' quartet. Brookmeyer displayed true virtuosity,

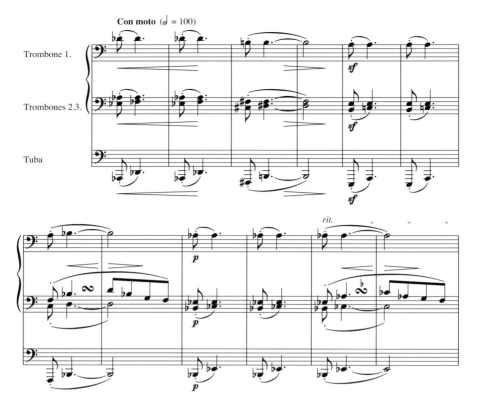

Example 9.2. Leo Janáček, *Sinfonietta* (1926)
The gruppetto turns in the second trombone part may suggest that the composer had valve
trombones in mind.

and unlike any previous valve trombonist of whom we know, combined in his style
both the resonance of the slide trombone sound and a distinctive valve trombone
idiom.[27] Brookmeyer succinctly characterized the position of the valve trombone in
modern times in an interview with Dan Morgenstern in 1967. The reason that slide
trombonists were 'still suspicious' of the valve trombone, he said, is 'that most people
play it rotten. Even excellent slide men play it in pedestrian fashion. It takes an awful
lot of woodshedding to get what you want from the instrument.'[28] Few others in
modern times have engaged in the requisite amount of woodshedding.

Independent valve systems

Designers of valve instruments faced two important challenges. The combination of one
or mores valves created intonational infelicities, and the narrow angles of the valves'
supplementary tubing caused inconsistencies of timbre when they were engaged. The
most persistent and imaginative designer to address these issues in respect of the
trombone was Adolphe Sax. In 1852 he patented a valve instrument that was intended
to mimic the purity of the slide trombone sound and eradicate the intonational problems

that arose when valves were used in combination. His trombone with 'six pistons à tubes indépendants' (six independent valves) was an ingenious solution. (Ill. 55) The six valves, together with the 'open' option (no valve depressed), provide the equivalent of each of the seven positions. The need for valves to be used in combination was obviated, so the timbre was pure and the intonation perfect. Sax's system used an ascending rather than a descending valve principle: when no valves are depressed the windway passes through a length of tubing equal to seventh position on the slide trombone; depressing one of the other valves blocks off enough tubing to equate to a shorter position. The design of the instrument could hardly have been more practical – the bell pointing forward, and the valve system configured into two groups of three valves, one set operated with the left hand and the other with the right.

Illustration 55. *Trombone à six pistons à tubes indépendants* from the catalogue of Charles Gras, 1923.

Sax harboured ambitions for this instrument, and used his influence to get it included in the syllabus of both the Paris and the Brussels Conservatoires. He also introduced it into the stage band of the Paris Opéra, where he was for a time the band's director. The instrument was introduced into several military bands, and on Sax's persuasion, Ambroise Thomas agreed to have the famous tenor trombone solo in Act 1 of his opera *Hamlet* played on it. Apparently this delighted the composer, who declared that the instrument was 'destined to revolutionise the family of brass instruments'.[29] It was used at the Brussels Opera into the twentieth century, and in more isolated instances elsewhere. A model was produced by Lebrun of Brussels in 1910, and it was about this model that Cecil Forsyth enthused when he heard it in Sir Henry Wood's concerts with his New Queen's Hall Orchestra. It was apparently Wood who provided the technical information for Cecil Forsyth's explanation of the instrument in his book *Orchestration*: 'In tone these Trombones are massive and sonorous. Less biting and seemingly less brilliant than the modern small-bore Tenor, but much more flexible, much better adapted for chromatic work, for cantabile and for unobtrusive part playing.'[30] Forsyth believed, seemingly along with Wood, that this instrument might signal the demise of the slide trombone altogether:

It will be interesting to watch whether these instruments establish and maintain their position in our orchestras or whether the slide mechanism . . . will refuse to 'stand and deliver' to the cylinder . . . some of our best trombone players – men who have been used to the slide-instrument, all their lives – are sensible of the necessity for some slight adjustment and alteration in its 'make-up'.[31]

The *trombone à six pistons indépendants* was still appearing in the catalogue of Gras of Paris and Lille as late as 1923, but ultimately it did not endure, because players did not want to play it. The presence of so much tubing made the instrument heavy, and there was no real incentive for the finest players to desert their slide instruments for what many saw as a cumbersome alternative contraption. The popularity of the instrument quickly dwindled, and while it lasted for longer at the Brussels Opera than elsewhere, even there it eventually became extinct. It had many musical qualities that made it superior to alternative valve trombone designs, and one senses that it only marginally failed to win popularity with players. The instrument maker Victor Mahillon put it succinctly: 'The instrument is perfect if we consider only the theoretical side. There is not a musician who does not jump at the first sight; but on the practical side it presents difficulties.'[32]

Thumb valves

The thumb valve is sometimes referred to in English as the 'trigger', 'attachment' or 'plug'. A trombone in B flat and F with a thumb rotary valve termed the *Quartventil* was introduced by Sattler in 1839. This was at a time when German tenor instruments were pitched in B flat and bass trombones in B flat or F, but it was not intended as a bass trombone to replace the F bass – rather it was conceived to enable players to play effectively and seamlessly across the entire bass/tenor range. The practical effect of depressing the thumb valve is that the instrument is transposed down by an interval commensurate with the length of the supplementary tubing that is engaged. Thus, on an instrument nominally pitched in B flat with supplementary tubing equal to an interval of a fourth, the valve puts the instrument nominally into F. However, in practice, the valve is not used to play long passages in transposition: rather it is used to gain access to certain low notes that would otherwise be unavailable, and also to provide a wider range of 'alternative positions'. The facilities offered by thumb valves are important, and they apply equally to tenor and bass instruments. The utilities of the thumb valve can be described specifically in the following terms. First, it allows a player to play those notes in the 'gap' between the fundamental (pedal note) in first position and the note an augmented fourth above it (H2 of seventh position). So, for example, on a B flat and F instrument, the F attachment allows access to the notes between the fundamental B flat to the E above it. Secondly, a skilful player can obtain the fundamentals of whatever nominal pitch the supplementary valve provides. And thirdly, the attachment provides an additional range of alternative positions, thus facilitating a smooth execution of passages that may be cumbersome with the slide alone. This is especially useful in the first octave and a half of the instrument's range. An extract from Bartók's *Dance Suite* (1923) serves as an illustration (Ex. 9.3).

Example 9.3. Béla Bartók, *Dance Suite* (1923), fourth movement, bars 50–4
The F trigger valve is virtually essential for smooth execution of such figures; without it, the phrase demands rapid alternation between the closed and most extended slide positions.

Several thumb valve designs have been introduced. The most popular have utilized a form of rotary valve system in which the player's left thumb operates a trigger (sometimes by means of a flexible strap), but piston valves have also been employed. Sax, for instance, introduced a trombone with a single piston valve around 1850, and this instrument was advertised in the catalogues of retailers such as the Distin Company for most of the next decade. In the twentieth century, designs of thumb valves and thumb valve instruments have become increasingly sophisticated. The most common for the tenor trombone is the B flat and F, and this combination on a wider-bore instrument has also provided the basic format for modern bass trombones. However, manufacturers have made bass instruments with two valves to provide an instrument in (for example) B flat, F and E. The E valve allows the production of low B, which has been written for the bass instrument by several twentieth-century composers. These double valve instruments can also function as contrabass trombones.

The effect of engaging a thumb valve on an instrument is not a neutral one for the player, and professionals have needed to develop skills that enable them to use the valve effortlessly, but many leading players (both tenor and bass players) use such instruments as their standard equipment. One of the most widely used systems was designed by Conn; it was particularly successful on their 88H tenor and the 72H bass models. But this is just one variant of the rotary thumb valve. In the late twentieth century, several new and highly effective designs were introduced that have significantly minimized the impact of valve engagement on the windway. These include variants of the traditional rotary valve by such firms as Yamaha of Japan; the Hagmann valve, which has been used on Boosey & Hawkes/Besson[33] instruments; the Bach 'balanced' valve, also referred to as the 'K' valve; the Conn-Christian Lindberg valve; and the Thayer valve, which has been used on several instruments, but particularly those by the Edwards company in the USA.

Single valves for 'switched' transposition and effects

Valves have also been fitted to the bell sections of trombones to enable players to obtain special effects. For much of the twentieth century the Conn company marketed a small-bore tenor instrument with a half-tone (i.e. semitone) piston trill valve, called the 'Innes Model Solo Slide Trombone', taking the name of the great American soloist and bandleader Frederick Innes. The maker claimed this to be an entirely new invention – a claim that was ill-founded. In 1928 the design for this instrument was entirely reconfigured and the Innes name dropped in favour of 'Trill

Valve Model' (10H). This instrument, it was claimed, 'enables the performer to play many exceedingly intricate passages with ease and surety'.[34]

A further use for the single valve on the bell section has been to switch the instrument into a different pitch. Whereas the thumb valve allows the player to engage and disengage extra lengths of tubing as the instrument is being played, the intention with the switch valve is that the instrument is switched to a new nominal pitch (usually by an interval of a tone) to suit the musical circumstances in which it is being used. The usual mechanism on such instruments is a rotary switching valve without a spring. Tenor instruments in the early twentieth century were sometimes made in C, with the switch valve adding a tone to put the instrument into B flat. Conn's advertisement for its 'C' model trombone provides an interesting insight into why such instruments were marketed in the second decade of the twentieth century:

> The 'C' Model Trombone is popular with those who do not desire to transpose when reading from vocal scores. It is a most desirable model for home or church use. It . . . possesses a rotary valve change slide which throws the instrument to B♭ when so desired.[35]

Duplex instruments

Duplex instruments are strictly instruments that combine the characteristics of two instruments in one, but the term has been interpreted in more than one way by manufacturers. Some duplex instruments have two bells with a facility that allows the player to switch easily between the two. The most common have been two-belled euphoniums, and cornets with echo attachments. In 1911 the British manufacturer Joseph Higham of Manchester advertised a 'Duplex Trombone'. This was a bell section which fitted onto a slide or valve section, and was supplied with both. Strictly speaking, it was not a duplex instrument at all; this type of arrangement – which has been popular enough – was more properly termed 'Combination Slide and Valve Trombone' by the Frank Holton company in its 1916 catalogue. However, more complex instruments have been also made. Besson advertised a duplex valve/slide instrument in 1864, and Pelitti made a popular duplex valve trombone/euphonium which it called *gemelli* (twins) in 1855. In 1898, Conn introduced a 'New Bell-Up Euphonium with Trombone Bell'. This instrument was produced in considerable quantities and was advertised with characteristic Conn understatement as the 'most perfect instrument ever manufactured'.[36] (Ill. 56)

The Israeli-French trombonist Benny Sluchin has performed solo works on a 'two-belled contrabass trombone'. The two bells point in exactly opposite directions, the passage to each bell being controlled by the player by means of an additional trigger. The purpose of such an instrument is to allow the player to juxtapose a variety of tonal colours. The two 'sides' of the instrument can be employed to produce contrasts and spatial effects, and such contrasts can be emphasized when one or other side is further configured with electronic modifications or a mute. Among the composers who have written for this instrument is the Hungarian Péter Eötvös, whose *Klangtheater* (Sonic Theatre) was premiered in 1999.[37]

Illustration 56. Examples of the many species of duplex instruments. These are from a C. G. Conn catalogue of 1898.

One of the most ambitious attempts at a duplex instrument is the 'Valide', invented in 1954 by Brad Gowan, a jazz trombonist with Eddie Condon's band who was also a gifted engineer. This remarkable and somewhat complex instrument embodies the facilities of both the slide and the valve trombone. Like other duplex instruments, it allows access to the two sides by means of a trigger, but according to Gowan his invention allows both to be played simultaneously. Despite its tremendous weight and ungainliness, it is clear that Gowan's design allows a skilled player instant access to the characteristics of both instruments. So, for example, the valves can be used for rapid

florid passages conjoined to genuine slide glissandos. Only one of these instruments is
known to have been built. It is kept in the collection of the Institute of Jazz Studies at
Rutgers University, Newark (NJ). A similar instrument with a slide and valve set that
can be operated simultaneously has been marketed by the Holton company under the
name 'Superbone'.

Other instruments played by orchestral trombonists

In orchestras, the bass trumpet is usually played by a trombone player, because it takes
a mouthpiece similar in size to a trombone mouthpiece. It was introduced by Wagner
for his *Ring* cycle, where it is given considerable soloistic prominence. The instrument
has also occasionally been deployed in orchestral music by other composers, such as
Janáček in his *Sinfonietta* (1926). The bass trumpet has a distinctive sound and its
players are specialists. The instrument is usually pitched in C or B flat, and has a
tessitura of about two and a half octaves. The configuration of its tubing makes it
similar to some short-model valve trombones.

Wagner also introduced a 'steer horn', which has been produced in various
designs, often resembling an oversized natural trumpet. Each instrument is tuned to a
single harmonic series, and each player plays just one note, offstage, for dramatic
effect. The Wagner tuba was also introduced in his operas. It is now played by french
horn players, though the instruments supplied by Mahillon for the earliest UK
performances of the operas were designed to be played by trombone or euphonium
players. These instruments survive and work remarkably well. They are described in
detail by John Webb in an article relating to an impressive performance on these
instruments by members of the Galpin Society in 1995.[38]

The euphonium is used in a number of twentieth-century orchestral works,
including Gustav Holst's *The Planets* (1914–16), Janáček's *Sinfonietta* (1926) and
Schoenberg's *Thema und Variationen* Op. 43b (1943). Though it is sometimes played by
specialist euphonium players, it is frequently played by trombonists. In the nineteenth
century, the euphonium was seen as a successor to the ophicleide, but it occasionally
became an adjunct to the trombone player's art. Several nineteenth- and early
twentieth-century conservatoire trombone professors taught the euphonium as part of
their curriculum. Probably the greatest euphonium-playing trombonist was the
Italian-born Simone Mantia (1873–1951). He was the euphonium soloist with Sousa's
band, but also principal trombone with the New York Metropolitan Opera. His
impressive euphonium playing survives on sound recordings, and his trombone
method book is one of the most measured and sensible works of its time and type.[39]

The ophicleide

Given the urge for novelty, and the tendency of inventors to sprint to the patent office
on the slightest provocation, it might seem remarkable that the slide trombone
survived the nineteenth century – let alone that it did so in such style. Forsyth held
the questionable belief that 'the slide mechanism had been threatened throughout its

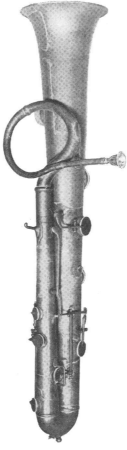

BASS OPHICLEIDE.

Illustration 57. The bass ophicleide illustrated in Cecil Forsyth's *Orchestration* (1914).

long life';[40] but in fact, the introduction of new mechanisms in the early nineteenth century resulted in a fresh appreciation of the slide instrument, and while some patent applications conspicuously cite perceived weaknesses in the slide trombone, the majority of new instruments stood independently of it. Many new inventions for the bass/baritone voice were perfectly effective and found their way into the hands of players of tremendous virtuosity. Others were also effective, but followed a swift route to obscurity because players neither needed nor wanted them. It is important to stress once again, however, that the history of brass instruments is not linear: successive inventions did not sweep away the previous models, and since the nineteenth century many instruments with competing musical roles have coexisted.

Perhaps the most persuasive illustration of this is the ophicleide. (Ill. 57) This, of course, is not a trombone at all, but the lower-voiced member of the keyed bugle family. However, it is directly relevant to the trombone in the nineteenth century because, as we have seen in the discussion of Verdi's lower brass parts, it was often regarded as integral to the trombone section. It was invented by Jean-Hilaire Asté, who operated under the trade name Halary in Paris from around 1817, and was patented by him in 1821. It found favour with major composers such as Mendelssohn, Schumann, Verdi and Berlioz, and was produced in considerable quantities. Ophicleides were made in several sizes in the alto and bass voice; the bass instrument in C was the most frequently used, though instruments pitched in B flat were also common. Berlioz, who believed that the ophicleide 'worked wonders beneath a body of brass instruments in certain circumstances',[41] wrote for it in his own works, using it most often as the bass voice of the orchestral brass section. Verdi, as we have seen, took a somewhat contrary view, and regarded it as only partially adequate for the voice below a section of three trombones. It was also used extensively in military and civilian bands throughout the nineteenth century. One of the striking features of the entry forms for the Crystal Palace brass band contests, held in Sydenham, England, in 1861 and 1862, is that every single band included at least one ophicleide and some had as many as four.[42]

George Bernard Shaw, in an over-quoted phrase, referred to the ophicleide as a 'chromatic bullock', but the ophicleide was an instrument of considerable capability, and the best players were brilliant technicians and important celebrities. The great ophicleide players of the nineteenth century include Jean Prospère Guivier (known as Prospère), William Ponder, Alfred Phasey and Samuel Hughes. Both Hughes and Guivier came to prominence in Jullien's Orchestra. Hughes had previously made his name playing for the great Cyfarthfa Band associated with Robert Crawshay, the wealthy iron master of Merthyr Tydfil in south Wales. The handwritten part books from which Hughes played still exist, and they reveal him to have been a player of quite stunning virtuosity.[43]

Berlioz praised the ophicleidists he heard playing with Johann Strauss's orchestra in Vienna in 1837, who got 'from the large ophicleide as much sound as three ordinary ophicleides', and whom he found to be 'rare' in having excellent intonation, but he also observed: 'The ophicleide is still inadequately studied. Good players are rare.'[44] While Mendelssohn and even Wagner scored for the instrument, the ophicleide enjoyed greater popularity in England and France than in Germany. Berlioz, who found so much to criticize in German brass playing, was disparaging about the 'abject brass object masquerading under the name [ophicleide]' that he heard at Leipzig, and deemed it necessary to replace it with an extra trombone. His later 1842–3 tour to Germany convinced him that the tuba was superior to the ophicleide as the lowest bass voice.[45]

Despite the informed critical views of Berlioz and the abundance of considerably less enlightened and more bigoted comment on the ophicleide, it is important to emphasize that the instrument prevailed in the nineteenth century with considerable success, to the extent that a genuine and impressive didactic tradition grew around it. Not only was it taught at the conservatoires and the military schools of music, but method books were published for it. Prominent among these were V. Caussinus's *Solfège-méthode pour ophicléide-basse* (Paris, c. 1840), and the *Méthode complète d'ophicléide* by Caussinus and Frédéric Berr (Paris, c. 1845).

The association of the ophicleide with the trombone section in both the symphony and the opera orchestra during the nineteenth century is extremely important. The use of the large-bore tuba that became ubiquitous in the second half of the twentieth century may be seen as a fitting match for newer wide-bore trombones and for the venues in which modern orchestras perform, but such sonorities have only a modest resemblance to the voices heard in early Romantic orchestras.

Contrabass trombones

The contrabass trombone was familiar to Praetorius as the *Octav-Posaun* and may have been in use in the sixteenth century, but it was a cumbersome instrument that seems to have been deployed infrequently. Several makers introduced contrabass instruments to perform works with especially low bass parts for which the trombone sonority was preferred to other bass instruments. Among the composers who have written for such an instrument are Verdi, Puccini, Strauss, Wagner, the composers of the Second Viennese School and later composers such as Ligeti. These instruments are not easy to play, but they are effective when played well. They are especially interesting to organologists because of the ingenious solutions devised by instrument designers and manufacturers to the problem of making an instrument that is easy to operate and that also allows good-quality access to the very low registers. It goes without saying that contrabass instruments are not routine production models and have not been made in the same quantities as alto, tenor and bass instruments. Such instruments have often been owned by opera houses rather than by their players.

The instrument built by Pelitti to Verdi's specifications in 1881 is an example of a four-valve instrument in 18-ft B flat. Other instruments in F have been made with two thumb valves, one lowering the instrument to 18-ft D and the other to C, while both employed together provide an instrument in 18-ft B flat. Contrabass slide instruments without valve attachments have usually used a double slide, the additional 'U' bend accommodating extra lengths of tubing without interfering with the normal slide action. Double slides were fitted to trombones in F, and Boosey & Hawkes manufactured a double-slide contrabass in 18-ft C for performances of Wagner's *Ring* cycle, though the instrument appears not to have met with the approval of the conductor Hans Richter, who demanded that the part be played on a tuba. Wagner's writing actually requires a contrabass with a fundamental pitch of B flat. One of the oddest instruments was designed and manufactured by the Salvation Army in the opening years of the twentieth century. This instrument had a double slide which was connected by an ingenious pulley system to a further slide in the bell section. (It is discussed further in Chapter 11.) Only a handful were made, the major mystery being why this evangelical Christian organization should have needed such an instrument.

Chapter 10

Popular music

The word 'popular' always needs careful handling, but in historical contexts it is especially troublesome; historians and cultural theorists have used the word in many different ways.[1] Here, I use 'popular' to refer to repertoires and practices that are not confined to the 'art' or 'classical' music tradition, but that have, rather, been relevant to a wide 'popular' constituency. This does not by definition exclude any particular social sector or any category of music, because much of what we now loosely call classical or art music has had an extraordinarily wide appeal. But at the heart of the subject of this chapter is the idea that the social, economic and cultural changes of the nineteenth century ushered in a new epoch which resulted in new modes of production and consumption of music. For example, new types of repertoire emerged for which there were equally novel styles of performance. The birth of popular music (in its modern, nineteenth-century sense) eventually influenced all musical composition, performance and reception. It also changed the processes of supply and demand within which trombone players made their living. These changes had no precedent.

By the late twentieth century, popular music was often defined by the size of its audience – it was mass consumer music. But since the nineteenth century 'popular' and 'art' have also been distinguished by type, and served by different sides of the music business. Within these types we can recognize different aims, values and processes. This distinction is neither purely theoretical nor tangential to the subject of this book, for it affects the repertoires that players have performed and, perhaps more importantly, the way that the trombone has been played. Thus, leaving aside jazz (a very specific 'popular' form), which is the subject of Chapter 13, this chapter deals with the use of the trombone in commercial popular music and amateur music-making. The issues raised here belong essentially to the nineteenth and twentieth centuries, when amateur music-making, the growth of the mass entertainment industry, and new forms of dissemination such as gramophone recordings and broadcasting, fashioned entirely new processes of musical consumption. The focus is on musical practices in which the trombone has had a particularly prominent role, and where distinctive idiomatic nuances have subsequently developed. It will soon become clear that these themes can be understood only by reference to the historical, social and economic trends that brought about the phenomenon of 'popular music'.

One of the themes discussed in this chapter is the generic patterns of supply and demand – particularly the production and distribution of instruments and published music – that were important to trombonists. Equally important is the widening of the franchise for trombone playing to increasingly wider and larger groups of amateurs, and the development of new spheres of employment (recording and movie work, for example). These themes are neither merely contextual nor incidental in a book about the history of the trombone and its idioms. Rather, they strike deep into the heart of the story. This was one of the greatest watersheds in the history of the instrument: developments in popular music-making caused the number of trombone players (valve and slide) to increase vastly and quickly; consequently, new types of trombone players emerged, with new musical preferences and values. By the start of the twentieth century a hugely diverse constituency of players existed, and their environment was influenced by a buoyant commercial infrastructure. The number of professional players increased exponentially, and there was a yet greater increase in the number of amateurs. Indeed, the concept of the amateur trombone player as it is understood today only gains substance in this period, and it was these amateurs who were to be the source of supply for the music profession. This too was new.

But how did these players play? As I point out below, many of the greatest trombonists of the early twentieth century were either entirely self-taught or were taught by 'professors' of music who knew a bit about music but next to nothing about the trombone. How did they learn, whom did they imitate, what formed their musical imaginations and to what musical values did they subscribe? A key issue here is the nature of the relationship between genuinely popular trombone playing, which seems to have had its roots in instinct, imitation and pragmatism, and the received orthodoxies of the existing (mainly art) traditions. In many instances, the relationship must have been slight or non-existent, and as a result, new and highly intuitive approaches to playing emerged, unhampered by established orthodoxies. The most obvious and important manifestation of this is jazz, but popular practices had a much wider impact, and in some respects shaped the course of twentieth-century trombone playing.

Popular and professional

Before the nineteenth century, with a few exceptions (notably some religious and charitable foundations), the trombone was a professional instrument. The instruments themselves were made individually or in small sets by skilled craftsmen, and most were destined to find their way into the hands of professional players who found work in religious or civic establishments, or in other avenues that were patronized by a dominant elite. Even in the opening decades of the nineteenth century these professionals were relatively small in number, though they were to be found in most European towns of any standing. They were specialists, and most were the bearers of performance traditions that had been passed from father to son across many generations. So in one sense, before the nineteenth century the trombone was not a popular instrument, because it did not have a wide distribution among amateurs and dilettantes, neither did it have any place (as far as we know) in the musical life of vernacular communities (with the exception, discussed in Chapter 11, of Moravian communities). Trombones were produced – usually on demand – for a limited and primarily professional market.

On the other hand, can we describe the *repertoire* of early trombone players as popular? If playing the instrument was largely restricted to professionals, how and to what extent was trombone playing received by a popular audience? It is clear from previous chapters that the trombone was ubiquitous in elite music-making circles from the fifteenth century onwards, but the music that was played was not totally confined to elite audiences. The presence of the trombone in so many rituals and processionals defines it, along with drums and trumpets, as being among the most listened-to instruments of the renaissance and baroque periods. Furthermore, it is likely that a large part of the occupation of trombonists in the first three centuries of its existence was in essentially public forms of music-making – both sacred and secular. Also, while we know little about the musical components of itinerant theatre and entertainment troupes in the sixteenth and seventeenth centuries, loose descriptions of such events in literature of the period provide grounds for thinking that trombonists may have had a role in them.[2]

It is certain, however, that before the nineteenth century the trombone was not a popular instrument in the sense of its being conspicuous in the written and unwritten practices of *vernacular* entertainment: that is, it did not have a part in the traditions and social interactions of the broad mass of common people. This distinction is of the highest importance, because it is in this domain that the nineteenth century saw a change of massive proportions. From that time, the trombone, along with other brass instruments, became popular both in the sense that it was played by large numbers of people from the widest social spectrum, and also in the sense that it became a component of that new category to which we have come to refer, somewhat casually, as 'popular music'.

The new popular music was based on a social, technological and consumer revolution that evolved in a variety of ways, through village and marching bands, brass bands, vaudeville, circus music, burlesque and musical theatre, giving rise to forms as diverse as jazz, salsa and the multitudinous fusions of popular and art music. The spread of these styles and practices was nurtured by commercial initiatives, blended with the raw imagination and instincts of ordinary people of many different backgrounds. This ancient instrument survived an age of mechanization with most of its original features intact, but with several new expressions in its vocabulary. Furthermore, in the hands of amateurs and a new breed of journeymen professionals, its idiom developed and was in many ways liberated.

Equally important was the emergence of professionals from the vast throng of the working classes, and the fracturing of long-standing and largely exclusive routes into the musical profession. Eventually there was a commensurate disruption to the tradition that saw trombonists following their fathers into the music profession, though it is ironic, if unsurprising, that dynasties of brass players were soon to emerge in new forms of working-class amateur music. Even in the nineteenth century, it was most usual to find that professional trombone players were the sons of professional musicians, though the case of Robert Booth provides an interesting example of change. Booth was a busy trombone player in London in the second half of the century. In August 1887 he applied for membership of the charitable foundation of the Royal Society of Musicians (see Table 3 in Chapter 8).[3] By that time he was principal trombone at the Royal Italian Opera, the London Symphony Concerts and several festival orchestras. His birth certificate, which was included with his membership application, is dated December 1859; it shows him to have been the son of a 'night attendant in a lunatic asylum'. In the space of less than thirty years, Booth had crossed from the world of the proletariat to the elite of London orchestral life. This is a rare example of a professional British trombone player not being the son of a musician,[4] but it should come as no surprise that it was possible to cite many more soon after this date. Booth's ascendancy can be attributed to social and economic change and the consequent rise of amateur music. Indeed, the fact that Booth's second given name was 'Handel' hints that his destiny as a musician may have owed something to his parents' association with the choral singing movement, which became hugely popular among the labouring classes in Victorian Britain. Other brass players (such as the celebrated trombonist and euphonium player Alfred Phasey) also had 'Haydn' or 'Handel' among their given names.

Demography, economics and moral values

From the opening decades of the nineteenth century, the chain of social, economic and demographical changes, combined with a technological revolution, impacted emphatically on the musical world. No family of instruments was affected more profoundly than the brass. Industrialization, together with a revolution in transport through the introduction of railways and more efficient methods of sea transportation, gave populations, commodities and ideas a greatly increased mobility. Three demographic trends were especially prominent: a general increase in the size of the populations of most European countries; a tendency for a greater proportion of populations to inhabit urban rather than rural settlements; and the growth (particularly the cosmopolitan growth) of the USA, and its emergence as a powerhouse of commercial and cultural ideas. Britain doubled its population during the century, and in some of its cities the growth was fivefold. The UK government census of 1851 revealed that, for the first time, more British people lived in towns than in rural areas. This pattern was similar in other parts of Europe and in the USA, where the most stunning growth could be seen in the rapid emergence of its great cities. Between 1830 and the end of the century, the population of the USA increased almost twenty-fold, with most growth attributable to an influx of European immigrants – the greatest number coming from Germany, Austria-Hungary, Italy and Britain, all countries with rich brass-playing traditions.

As traditional patterns of social settlement changed, so did the attitudes of people to spheres of authority. Some among the dominant class recognized in these developments a threat to the prevailing social order. Whether this threat was real or imagined, it created a mood of encouragement for what was sometimes described in Victorian Britain as 'rational recreation'. A rational recreation was any pastime that could be practised by the working classes and could be considered wholesome, improving and above all docile. Any form of communal music-making, which many saw as being the ideal leisure occupation for working people, was encouraged. The most visible and important manifestation of this approval was the willingness on the part of those in the higher social orders to provide guarantees to working-class people for the loans that enabled them to purchase instruments. It was against this social and economic background that the great explosion of amateur music-making occurred.

By the middle of the century the music industry was becoming more organized and effective. Modes of production were more efficient, music education (formal and informal) was more easily available, and music publishers realized that high profits could be gained by employing sales strategies that combined mass distribution with realistic pricing. The works of the masters were soon joined by a plethora of popular publications of hugely variable quality, to contribute to what Carl Dahlhaus somewhat undiscriminatingly termed 'Trivialmusik'.[5] An infrastructure of makers and retailers emerged with advertising strategies that focused on a new and burgeoning mass market. The cost of instruments dropped as production and consumption increased. Equally important was the widespread practice among manufacturers and retailers of discounting instruments bought in bulk (for example, a complete set of band instruments), as was the availability of credit schemes. The circulation of second-hand instruments and the proliferation of pawn shops made instruments more available to people from a wide range of social backgrounds. By the second half of the century, the opportunities for working-class people to learn to play the trombone, or any other instrument, had increased enormously. The incentive to do so was strengthened by the fact that brass instruments, perhaps more than any other family, benefited from the background changes that had brought about the rise of the amateur. The particular success of brass instruments can in part be attributed to their physical robustness, the relative ease with which they could be manufactured, and their practical utility in indoor and outdoor functions: they were perfectly suited to provide the musical accompaniment to any number of vernacular and community rituals, from parades to funerals. But the most important reason for the rapid popularity of brass instruments was that the newly refined valve instruments, and particularly the cornet and Saxhorn, were perceived as easy to learn, requiring the agility of just the three most dextrous fingers of the right hand. For this reason, the valve trombone was especially favoured by amateurs, but the slide trombone gained added popularity on the back of the more general success of valve brass instruments.

Supply and demand in the popular market

The production of trombones increased vastly as a part of the general increase in the production of brass instruments in the nineteenth century. But it is far from easy – indeed, it is probably impossible – to chart the exact pattern of growth quantitatively or in a way that allows reliable comparison between different countries. For example, it is possible that, taking Europe and the USA as a whole, more valve trombones than slide instruments were manufactured in the second half of the nineteenth century, but there is no hard evidence for this. The impression one gets from the sheer numbers of manufacturers and retailers who are known from their catalogues and surviving instruments is that vast numbers of instruments were sold and bought. Many manufacturers ran small-scale operations, but some of the larger manufacturing houses (such as Gautrot in Paris and the Besson company which operated in both

Paris and London) had a tendency to inflate their production figures to impress potential purchasers.

By far the largest market sector in the nineteenth century was the amateur brass band market, which soon eclipsed the next largest market, military bands. This change probably took place in the 1850s – the decade when the amateur market seems to have expanded most rapidly. Bands flourished in urban and rural communities, where they quickly established themselves in community ritual; but another, perhaps more significant factor accounts for their proliferation. Whereas individual working-class men found the cost of buying musical instruments prohibitive, a group, formed into a proto-band and enjoying the modest patronage of a town dignitary, a militia unit or a benevolent employer, could secure appropriate credit arrangements. Trombones were ubiquitous in these bands, and it appears that almost all brass instrument manufacturers and retailers included both slide and valve instruments in their catalogues.

Musical instruments and the paraphernalia associated with them were promoted ambitiously and robustly in a variety of advertising outlets, including catalogues, magazines and newspapers. On the face of it, the catalogues of brass instrument retailers and manufacturers provide a sound basis for identifying trombones that may not have survived, but the veracity of such sources should not go unquestioned. Many instruments were re-branded by retailers and advertised under their own name; however, yet more may have been promoted but never actually stocked or made. This latter phenomenon was a consequence of the utilization of 'pastiche catalogues' for advertising copy, and these present a peculiar problem. Pastiche catalogues survive, mainly from Saxony, but there is no reason to assume that they were not used more widely. They were designed and produced by printing firms, and took the form of substantial published books in medium-to-large format, with tissue-thin paper. They contained thousands of pictures, and were made with the express intention of providing clients with ready-made images of products that could be used in advertising copy. The quality, detail and variety of these images are as exceptional as their quantity. Dr Herbert Heyde of New York's Metropolitan Museum has brought my attention to one such catalogue, produced around 1910 at Markneukirchen by the J. Schmidt printing firm. (Ill. 58) It contains 327 pages, holding no fewer than 4,246 images of various musical instruments, including several valve and slide trombones. It is not my purpose here to evaluate pastiche catalogues, but they were widely distributed, and they raise several questions about the relationship between the rhetoric of instrument retailers and the reality of their commercial operations. A similar area of doubt surrounds inflated claims made in the various nineteenth-century exposition catalogues. Most of these were propagandist documents which made entirely unverifiable claims about novelty, excellence and popularity. So, as with all advertising, this material has to be viewed with caution.

Despite such pitfalls, more solid and objective data about nineteenth-century instrument manufacture is available. A particularly revealing source that might provide something of a profile of the patterns of production and distribution of trombones in the later nineteenth century is found in the archives of the London branch of the Besson company.[6] The London firm was established in 1851, and eventually settled into spacious premises in Euston Road. According to Algernon

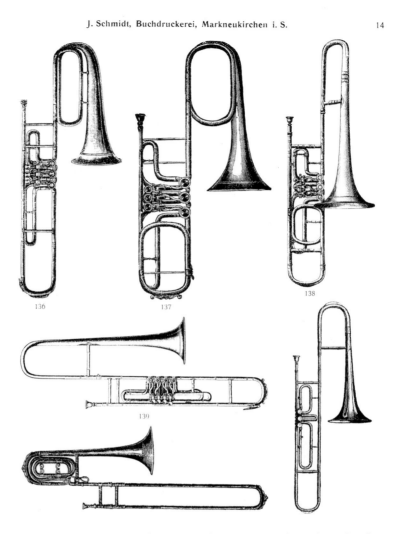

Illustration 58. These images are not from a musical instrument catalogue, but rather from a pastiche catalogue by J. Schmidt of Markneukirchen. Such images were sold to manufacturers who used them in their catalogues. It is not known whether all the instruments represented here actually existed.

Rose,[7] it was staffed in the late 1880s by 131 French workers who produced in excess of 100 brass instruments a week. The firm was at the heart of the European boom in brass instrument production in the second half of the nineteenth century, and was a major manufacturer of trombones. Not only were instruments made for the home market, but a sizeable number were manufactured for export. Among the surviving company documents are two trombone stock books (*Trombones No. 2* and *Trombones No. 3 à coulisses*) detailing the production and sale of slide trombones between June 1874 and May 1895. There are no references to valve trombones in these books, which suggests that the company kept entirely different valve trombone stock books. The surviving slide trombone books contain a record of 3,858 instruments made during this period. The source is especially interesting because it contains hard objective information, including data about each individual instrument, its species, pitch and destination – the person or agency to which the instrument was initially sold. (Ill. 59)

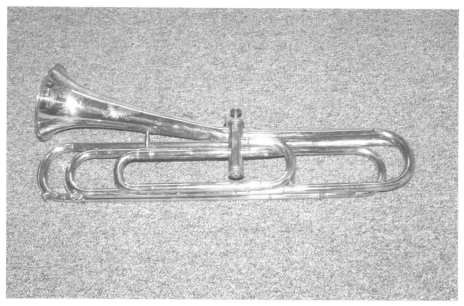

Illustration 59. A 'baby trombone' manufactured by Besson in 1881. In the two decades covered by the company's surviving trombone stock books (1874–95), Besson produced only six such instruments (all dating from 1880 or 1881). The initial destination of each is known. This one was presented as a prize at the National Eisteddfod of Wales. (Museum of Welsh Life, St Fagans, Cardiff, accession number F72.97/1.)

The crude summary data given in Table 4 may be interpreted in the light of contextual information, such as the identity of clients and their relationship with particular bands. Some broad suppositions also have to be made. For example, some individuals – known to be bandmasters – bought several instruments, so it does not take a great deal of imagination to deduce that they were simultaneously working as purchasing agents for several bands. But even taking such considerations into account, it is possible to discern important trends. Over the twenty-year period, the production of trombones increased. Between 1889 and 1893 a total of 1,440 instruments was sold, compared with a total of just under nine hundred in the previous five-year period. The increase could be accounted for by an incremental success on the part of Besson's sales staff, but it could also represent a response to growing demand. If such was the case, it would be consistent with what the economic historian Cyril Ehrlich has termed the 'flood' of trade experienced in the music business after 1870.[8]

The bulk of exports not surprisingly went to north America, with the New York retailer Carl Fischer and the Grossman company of London, Ontario, featuring prominently. Almost as many instruments were sold to the military bands of Egypt as to Canada. Egypt was a major consumer of brass instruments, many of which were also supplied by Viennese manufacturers such as Uhlmann.

Table 4

Besson slide trombone production, 1874–95

Production

Period	Trombones produced	Notes
1874–78	369	Only 55 months' data available. Average of 6.7 tbns per month.
1879–83	698	Increase of 329 on previous period (47%). Average of 11.6 tbns per month.
1884–88	897	Increase of 199 on previous period (22%). Average of 14.9 tbns per month.
1889–93	1440	Increase of 543 on previous period (38%). Average of 24 tbns per month.
1894–95	349	Only 17 months' data available. Average of 20 tbns per month – less than 1889–93, but greater than 1884–88.

Pitch

Pitch of trombones produced 1874–95	
B♭	2828
E♭ & Alto	13
G	800
C	13
B♭ & G	2
C & B♭	1

Destinations

Destinations of trombones produced 1874–95	
School	60
Prizes	72
Volunteer band	206
Dealers	362
Military band	379
Export	592
Individuals	701
Brass band	1590

Note

The data presented here should be taken as a general impression of the Besson business. For example, the information in Destinations is based on a number of assumptions rather than on totally firm evidence: the sales to 'individuals' may well be to the administrators of bands or to retailers.

Up to 1891, only a small number (13) of the tenor trombones were pitched in C; all other tenor instruments (2,828) were in B flat. Eight hundred instruments in G were produced, and this follows a predictable pattern for a company based in the UK, where trombone sections were usually made up of two tenor instruments in B flat and a bass in G. The fact that that only ten of the 419 instruments exported to the Fischer company in the USA were G bass trombones is hardly surprising. It is equally unsurprising that only thirteen E flat and 'alto' instruments were produced in the entire twenty-year period, confirming what we know from other sources: that the alto trombone was by this time slipping into a temporary obscurity.

One fact in particular is abundantly clear – the primary market for Besson's trombones was the popular market. The company's success was founded on sales to amateurs, either directly or through intermediaries, and we can suppose that most of the instruments sold to dealers, and even many of the exports, found their way to amateur bands of one sort or another. The sales to military bands account for 379 instruments (fewer than twenty a year), and these found their way to professionals. Sales to the professional market are also represented by the Middle Eastern clients, Patrick Gilmore's band and individual London players such as Phasey. But overwhelmingly the production process was aimed at the amateur market – or more specifically at organized groups of amateurs.

The production of trombones by other companies is less easy to assess, but the general trend was that instruments were seeping into the amateur band market from the later 1840s, with output reaching a peak in the next fifty years: even as early as 1846, the French company Gautrot was making the (probably exaggerated) claim that it kept 1,000 trombones in stock.[9] Manufacture of brass instruments increased

Illustration 60. This advertisement put out by Couesnon in 1901 shows the importance of the military in the culture of brass playing. The military bandsmen of the world are seen descending upon Couesnon's exhibition at the 1900 Paris World Fair.

generally as the century progressed. From the 1880s, Červený produced about 3,000 instruments a year, and claimed that, in 1895, it supplied more than 6,000 instruments to the Russian army.[10] The desire to improve the quality of military bands was the reason for many technical innovations in brass instruments, and there was a considerable expansion of professional military music, but the main boom was squarely in the popular amateur market. However, the professional sector was used persistently to legitimize the quality of instruments. Endorsements from the military and the use of military band imagery were conspicuous in European advertisements (Ill. 60); even in the 1920s the Hawkes trombone catalogue drew almost exclusively on military endorsements. But throughout this period advertisements make it clear that they were aimed at amateurs.[11]

American manufacture

Taking into account the fact that most of the trombones used by Moravian musicians were imported from Germany, one of the earliest US makers of trombones may have been John C. Rosenbeck (Rosenberg). He was in New York by 1838, but was described as 'John Rosenbeck of Utica' in 1836, when he won an award for a trombone 'made for Ciofi' that was exhibited at the American Institute Fair.[12] Another manufacturer, Graves and Company of New Hampshire (later of Boston), founded in 1824, also appears to have manufactured trombones in the first half of the century. Though much of the US market in the nineteenth century was also based on the band trade, a large proportion of the instruments had found their way into the country either in the hands of immigrants or through direct importation by foreign companies to such distributors as Carl Fischer and J. W. Pepper. Soon it became profitable and practical for European companies to set up manufacturing and importing bases in the USA. Among the companies that did this were Červený (from 1850) and Henry Distin (from 1877). There was also, however, the stirring of a more robust, home-based manufacturing industry, which was to be given considerable impetus with the establishment in Elkhart, Indiana, of the C. G. Conn Company in 1879.

The Conn Company is a key agency in the history of the trombone. It made instruments of a consistently high quality and in various designs, and was enormously influential not just on other manufacturers in the USA and abroad, but also on the wider infrastructure of music-making in the USA. It has been pointed out that the foundation of the company in Indiana marked the start of a general exodus of brass instrument makers from the east coast to the Midwest, and it is certainly true that several companies founded after the late nineteenth century followed Conn's example of setting up in Elkhart – undoubtedly because of the existence of a skilled labour force.[13] Charles Gerrard Conn initially founded the company in 1876, in partnership with Eugene Dupont, to produce a rubber-rimmed cornet mouthpiece, but by 1879 he was sole owner, and soon moved to the production of instruments. The 'Wonder Cornet' was endorsed by the great cornet player Jules Levy, and its success launched the entire business. Trombones soon entered the Conn catalogue and even by 1883 Conn was claiming that the Elkhart factory was producing 500 instruments of various sorts every month.

In 1915, Conn sold the company to Carl Dimond Greenleaf, a flour mill proprietor and amateur musician. Greenleaf was an outstanding businessman who quickly increased output and put in place a fresh commercial strategy that focused on new sectors of the popular market, as well as securing several lucrative government contracts. Greenleaf recognized that the vaudeville and professional band market could not be sustained as the primary domain for the mass distribution of instruments, and identified school and community bands – especially high school bands – as the major avenue for sales. He set up an elaborate sales network that fostered the creation of the high-school band movement. One of the key elements was the creation of a Conn National School of Music in Chicago, which ran a correspondence course for high-school bandleaders; the trombonist Frederick Innes was its president.

Despite the fact that Conn instruments, along with those of other US manufacturers such as Holton, King, Olds, Reynolds, Bach and latterly Edwards, were to dominate professional playing in the twentieth century, the amateur market was the most lucrative; the endorsements of professionals served to encourage amateurs to buy Conn instruments. Internal Conn company documents from the 1930s show it to have possessed assets five times greater than those of its closest market competitor, and it was its effectiveness in the popular market that sustained its position.[14] The rhetoric of Conn's trombone advertisements was persistently aimed at delivering three clear messages: Conn trombones were qualitatively and technically better than those of its competitors; they were consistently the choice of the finest professional 'artists'; and their design supremacy actually made them easier to play. One typical advertisement claimed: 'It is not necessary to use false shifts of the slide to correct the intonation. … [Conn] Trombones are more responsive and more difficult music may be played on them. . . . They have a smoother, richer and more desirable quality of tone.'[15] The company even claimed that its bakelite mouthpieces were 'self-disinfecting'.[16]

In 1928 Conn established a research and development laboratory under the direction of Carl Greenleaf's son Leland. The chief research engineer was Allen Loomis. Earle Kent joined the department some time later. Among the products developed by the unit was the seamless 'Coprion' bell that was fitted to several trombone models. A bold claim in the Company's prospectus in 1940 suggested that these bells made it 'virtually impossible to crack a note'.[17]

In the archives of the Conn company, now kept at the National Music Museum at the University of South Dakota in Vermillion, is the 'Sales Manual for Band and Orchestral Instruments' for 1937.[18] This manual, an internal document intended for Conn's own sales force and executives, includes analytical information about both the company's actual sales and the market sectors in which it hoped to prosper. In 1935 and 1936 Conn sold respectively 7,775 and 9,718 trombones within the USA, and there were also significant sales of second-hand instruments through its own retail outlets. Perhaps the most interesting information is found in the demographic analysis that the company used to determine its markets. It had defined three sales priorities: schools, 'the fraternal field' (the American Legion, war veterans, fraternal societies and so on), and other smaller groups and individuals. Only 10% of its instruments were sold to females, with 88% going to males. The remaining 2% went to 'institutions', which the company regarded as having a disproportionate importance because of the prestige associated with them; they included the US Army and other organizations. We do not know what these other organizations were, but the orchestra at Raffles Hotel, Singapore, and Mussolini's private band are among the clients mentioned elsewhere in the archives. But the most interesting revelation to Conn's board of directors was that its market in towns with fewer than 5,000 inhabitants was as fertile as that in towns five times that size. This led executives to issue the resounding message to its sales force, 'our small cities offer by far the best markets for our products. Work them hard! And work EVERY ONE OF THEM.'[19]

Catalogues and internal documents after 1922 show the company's tendency to market particular models of trombone by emphasizing their specific sonic qualities and, by implication, the musical settings in which they fitted. Thus, the small-bore Artist model (2H) was based on Pryor's instrument and was intended for bands. The Artist model medium bore (4H) was 'manufactured especially for the Orchestra musician who preferred a broader tone . . . rich, yet quite brilliant', and the larger-bore Symphony models (6H and 8H) possessed 'the large, broad and sonorous tone so greatly desired in heavy Symphonic engagements'.[20] But the 'Ballroom' model (40H) had 'features . . . of special note for those whose work is principally for dancers . . . the bell has been brought back so that it's much easier to reach for wow-wow business'. [21] By the 1960s the marketing had sharpened yet further, so that schools bands, jazz players, symphonic players and 'the full brass choir' were specifically catered for. By 1969 the sales manager for New York reported back, 'the only instruments I can find the professionals playing are Conn trombones' and claimed that 33.1% of the entire trombone market was accounted for by Conn instruments.[22]

It was the large-bore Conn 8H and 88H instruments that started to be used in British and European orchestras in the 1950s. In the 1960s, when British brass bands finally moved from high (A = 452.5) to standard pitch, Conn launched an aggressive campaign through its UK franchise holders that was successful in persuading many to shift to its wider-bore instruments. This development signalled the demise of the traditional narrow-bore British brass band sound, and also of the bass trombone in G, which until then had survived almost solely as a brass band instrument. By this time Conn's competitors for the popular market came not just from other US and European companies but also from Asia, where such firms as Yamaha had diversified to produce high-quality and carefully designed standard model instruments.

Amateur bands

The development of brass and mixed brass/wind bands was an important feature of musical life in the nineteenth century. In places where such developments occurred, it is rare indeed to find bands that do not include trombones of one sort or another. Because valve trombones require the same skills as other valve instruments, they were taught in the same way, and players could easily switch from one instrument to another as the need arose. Consequently, valve trombones quickly became popular. Band contests were a standard feature of brass band networks in several countries, but in Britain they were large-scale commercial entertainments, and they occupied such a central role that they led to a standardization of brass band instrumentation that did not occur elsewhere. This gave rise to a repertoire for the standard format in which three trombone parts (two tenors and a bass) were used in a band of twenty-five players.

Contests forced an improvement in standards, and while an original repertoire emerged in the twentieth century, transcriptions of orchestral music were prominent as contest test pieces in the nineteenth century and through the twentieth century. Though much of the early repertoire was published in subscription journals which were distributed throughout Europe and the USA, the most valuable information we have about the playing styles of amateur bands in the nineteenth century comes from handwritten arrangements. The music, usually in the hand of the local bandmaster, provides a good perspective on the technical ability of players, because these arrangements are presumed to have exploited the best and most typical features of the players' techniques. While the best bands (particularly British bands) show valve players and ophicleidists to have possessed astonishing technical facility, the writing for slide trombones is usually conservative and this tends to be the case in American arrangements too.[23] This may be because the instrument was assumed to be cumbersome in comparison to valve instruments, but it may owe something to the process used by arrangers. For example, arrangements of orchestral music, particularly of Italian operatic selections, were extremely popular, and while cornets and euphoniums were assigned string and woodwind parts, trombones tended to be allotted the parts written in the original orchestration. The most complete archive of a mid-Victorian virtuoso brass band is that of the Cyfarthfa Band, which was formed in Merthyr Tydfil, south Wales, from around 1840 and for which over a hundred handwritten part books survive. The parts show the players to have had stunning techniques, but even here the demands on trombone players were modest. This point is emphasized by an apparently locally made composition – a set of variations on the melody 'Carnival of Venice'. Each section of the band is given an idiomatic and virtuoso variation, but the variation allotted to the trombone is a leisurely, somewhat pedestrian melody in unison.[24]

The popularity of brass bands in Britain did much to increase the number of trombone players and sustain demand for the instruments, but despite the emphasis on contest virtuosity, it did little to bring the instrument to the foreground of popular consciousness. While there were amateur British trombonists who played solos, none of them became household names until the opening decades of the twentieth century, when some became professionals. This was almost certainly because of the public fascination with the type of virtuosity that could be achieved by cornet players, who could perform a seemingly endless line of double- and triple-tongued phrases and languishing adagios.

Novelty solos

In the USA the situation was different. Popular professional soloists were attached to itinerant troupes who spent almost all their time on the road. They performed three main categories of repertoire: the lyrical ballad, the air and variation, and the novelty. Some of the lyrical ballads were derived from Italian opera, but much more often they

(a)

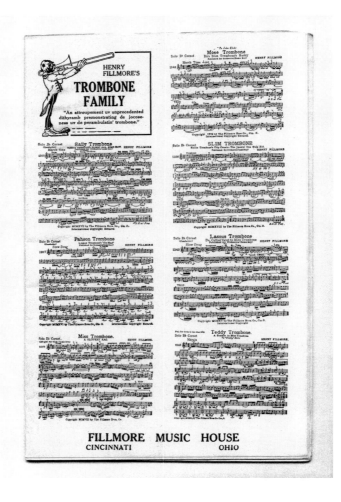

(b)

Illustration 61. Henry Fillmore's smear solos (61a) initiated something of a genre. Their tasteless racial nuances must be read in the context of the period, when minstrelsy was at the height of its popularity. The most popular of the set was 'Lassus Trombone' (61b).

were renditions of songs with a romantic or sentimental narrative that had their origins in music hall or domestic song and were familiar to audiences. The air and variation (*air varié*) form was also based on popular songs, but the variations exploited contrasting elements of technique. All airs and variations had a cadenza, and it was not uncommon for a cadenza to be engineered into lyrical ballads – for example, one of the Innes favourites was 'Sweet Sixteen', which Glenn Bridges describes as being 'injected with Innes Cadenzas'.[25] Novelty solos were light-hearted pieces that usually delighted audiences, particularly when they were performed as encores. Though most were based on popular songs or dance tunes, particularly quadrilles, they too incorporated cadenzas, and usually ended with a double-tempo codetta played at breathtaking speed. Many soloists wrote their own novelties: Pryor's titles included 'Fantastic Polka', 'The Tip Topper' and 'The Supervisor', and in 1915 Clay Smith introduced his popular 'Castles in the Air Polka'.

Another species of novelty that became something of a genre on both sides of the Atlantic was the trombone 'smear' or glissando solo. The trombonist Henry Fillmore is often credited with the commercial introduction of this novelty. Fillmore, himself a fine touring trombonist, was a partner in the family firm Fillmore's Music House. The business was founded by his father to sell religious music, but in his early days as a circus player Henry Fillmore recognized the potential of harnessing trombone effects that were required for clown and acrobat acts into solo pieces. His publications of such works as 'Teddy Trombone' (1911), 'Lassus Trombone' (1915) and 'Sally Trombone' (1917) became best-sellers. (Ill. 61) It goes without saying that smear solos depend for their effect on deft execution rather than innate musical quality, but they were persistently popular and still remain in the repertoire of some soloists. In Britain, Harold Moss's 'The Joker' (1928) and J. A. Greenwood's 'The Acrobat' (1936) were among the most frequently performed brass band trombone solos.

There is little doubt that the inclusion of the glissando in orchestral music is derived from its use in popular forms such as these. Charles Widor, writing in 1904, may be the first writer of an orchestration treatise to describe the glissando. The inherently racist term that he uses brings to mind Fillmore's penchant for pseudo-Negro jargon in his subtitles, strongly suggesting at least one source for both men's knowledge of the technique:

> Lately, as I was passing near a public ballroom, I heard such a strange bellowings [*sic*] escaping from the trombone that I went in and asked the performers, as soon as the dance was over, to show me their music. This is what they had been playing

And to wind up

Astounding effect! One would have thought it was the Beast in Revelations, with a cracker tied to its tail, roaring "Fire!" through a speaking trumpet.

It is not likely that this effect will ever be used in a symphony, any more than the shake, and I only mention it here on account of its rarity.

This fantastic howl is produced by the combined action of the slide and the lips, as a glissando is performed by the finger on a stringed instrument. It is very easy to execute, and suitable for a nigger dance.[26]

Performance styles

Many other performance effects that emerged in twentieth-century orchestral repertoire originated in popular entertainment environments. The use of various species of mutes is another feature that filtered through from popular idioms. Instructions for muting are rare before the twentieth century (one by Buxtehude is quoted in Chapter 1). Even though mutes are seen in advertisements and patent applications from the mid-nineteenth century and were in common use in popular music, they appeared much later in orchestral music. In 1904, Richard Strauss, a keen observer of orchestral techniques, claimed that 'Trombone mutes [had] been recently introduced with success', and this seems to be consistent with what we see in repertoire of that time.[27] It is easy to believe that the hand-over-the-bell form of muting, and the use of such objects as hats and sink plungers, played as big a part in the development of mutes in the nineteenth century as more formal inventions. Similarly improvised effects (such as glissando and flutter-tonguing) were employed *ad libitum* before they had any status as part of the formal technique of trombonists. (Ex. 10.1)

Example 10.1. Benjamin Britten, *Sinfonia da Requiem* (1939–40), second movement, '*Dies Irae*', Reh. No 24, showing flutter-tongue and muting.

It is all but impossible to define when and how such techniques became internationalized in trombone practice, but it was probably well before the 1890s, at which time they are heard on gramophone recordings. By 1900 they were embedded in ragtime. J. P. Sousa's idea of 'native American music', by which he meant up-tempo versions of minstrel songs, was one of the most popular features of his world tour programmes. Pieces such as 'The Coon Band Contest' and 'The Nigger in the Woodpile' made an enormous impact and were said to be full of 'strange effects'.[28] This, of course, was ragtime, heard for the first time in Europe, and it was a huge hit, not just because of its rhythmic and melodic catchiness, but also because the performance idioms, combined with the syncopated rhythms, were intoxicating to audiences who were used to altogether more staid performance orthodoxy.

Most American trombone soloists played on narrow-bore instruments with small bells. In 1918 Conn was claiming that its 'Artist Model' was the instrument of choice of Pryor, Simons, Zimmerman and a clutch of other players. It was available with a 6½- and a 7-inch bell. Photographs of American trombone players of this time almost always confirm that the preferred instruments had a small bore, and it seems that players aimed for a sweet, highly focused sound. Leaving aside slide vibrato, which may have been introduced earlier in the twentieth century than the advent of jazz, players used vibrato discriminatingly. Surprisingly, the exception that proved the rule was Arthur Pryor, who, as has already been mentioned, employed vibrato as a part of his basic sound. The fact that vibrato was seen as an expressive device to be used sparingly is consistent with what we otherwise know about performance style on other instruments even into the 1930s. Pryor was not the only exception however. British brass band players came to regard vibrato as a part of their basic sound, and we can only assume that the wide vibrato that is sometimes heard in early recordings of east European orchestras was also prevalent in popular playing. But as early as 1898 some band directors were counselling against vibrato in ensemble, even though it might hold a modest place in the soloist's technique: 'There are certain ways of rendering which would be appropriate in a soloist that would be altogether out of place in the efforts of a band, as in tremolo effects, as of great emotion, as well as increasing or slackening the time.'[29]

The techniques of soloists in popular music provide an extraordinarily interesting example of how modern trombone idiom was developing outside the symphony orchestra before the full impact of the jazz age. Pryor, Holton and Fillmore were just three of the many big names who were virtually self-taught as trombonists. Furthermore they appear to have taught themselves to play outside any group environment such as a brass band. Their terms of reference as young men could only have come from what they heard in itinerant show bands and from the more local musical culture of the church, the drawing room and small-time salon music. It is remarkable that they should have acquired techniques sophisticated enough to enable them to take the first steps into a professional career. Each of these players was a fine musician, capable of listening to and absorbing the influences that surrounded him. If one looks at the music they played and the cultural environments – particularly of the large concert bands – in which they eventually performed, a few key characteristics emerge that may be powerful pointers for the direction of the trombone idiom in the twentieth century.

The first is that players valued a well-focused clarity and beauty of sound, matched with sensitive articulation, which was capable of allowing a fine player to convey emotional and even narrative meaning. Thus, when playing an arrangement of a popular song, for example, they aspired to evoke a general sense of the lyrics with which audiences were already familiar. It is abundantly clear that late nineteenth- and early twentieth-century trombonists tried, as their predecessors had often done, to achieve the communicative qualities of the human voice – particularly in its most lyrical mode. Secondly, trombone players sought a particular type of technical virtuosity in which clarity of articulation, the ability to play largely stereotypical rapid and florid passages, was highly prized. Thirdly, such bandleaders as Gilmore, and more particularly Sousa, placed a high premium on precision and musical discipline, and for trombone players the earliest point of reference in this respect was not other trombone players but the virtuoso cornet players who had preceded them. It is no

Example 10.2. Pryor, *Blue Bells of Scotland*, opening cadenza

accident that Arban's famous *Method* was bought by as many aspiring trombonists as cornet players. Trombone soloists sought the seemingly unambiguous virtuosity which cornet players demonstrated, and with which audiences were familiar. Finally – and this may appear contradictory – in imitating valve instrument players on the slide trombone, these soloists were unwittingly establishing afresh the idiomatic identity of the slide instrument.

Many players in the nineteenth century played valve trombones, including some of the greatest. For understandable reasons, most of the great Italian trombonists who settled in the USA, such as Mario Falcone, Charles Anthony Cusumano and Simone Mantia, were valve trombonists who changed to the slide instrument. Indeed, Arthur Pryor also started on the valve instrument. But as soloists and their repertoires became more established, the slide trombone assumed an identity that was distinctive and idiomatic. Even the smear solo, a device that Henry Fillmore's father publicly denounced as 'TRASH',[30] contributed to this evolution. Furthermore, the evolution did not manifest itself in the work of a single player; it was contributed to by the substantial army of itinerants who traversed the USA and eventually the world through global tours. Frank Holton was noted for his fabulous lip trills, Innes for his virtuosity over phrases containing rapid, detached notes. Zimmerman was said consistently to have exploited a range that stretched over four octaves. Thomas H. King was a major advocate of alternative positions, and Pryor provided the living proof that the trombone as a solo instrument could attract a mass audience. By the 1920s, in the USA, France and the UK, the idiom of the modern solo trombone – essentially an instrument of popular culture – was established, primarily on small-bore instruments.

Journeymen professionals

The idiom of trombone playing was influenced by the working lives that professional trombonists led. In the twentieth century, the main pragmatic influences on the business of making a living came from shifts in cultural tastes, commercial trends and the development of new media. In the 1920s, the Conn company published a 'New Wonder Model Slide Trombones' catalogue, listing 21 models (for which a number of custom-made variants were available), and containing endorsements from over 150 working professional trombone players, the majority working in the USA, including Mantia, Zimmerman and the young Miff Mole. (Significantly, however, it includes not a single endorsement from a black player.) In typical Conn style, each testimonial was accompanied by a potted profile of the player, and most also had a cigarette-card-style portrait photograph. A summary of this information is given in Appendix 6. It is hardly a scientific survey, but it provides an interesting overview of how some of the more prominent players of that time earned a living.

Of course, these players are but the tip of an iceberg, for the total number of trombonists working in the USA by this time was enormous. One of the interesting features of musical life in this period was the versatility of professional trombonists. (Ill. 62) They moved unproblematically from burlesque to concert band to symphony orchestra to circus band, with no apparent stylistic qualms or a sense that cultural

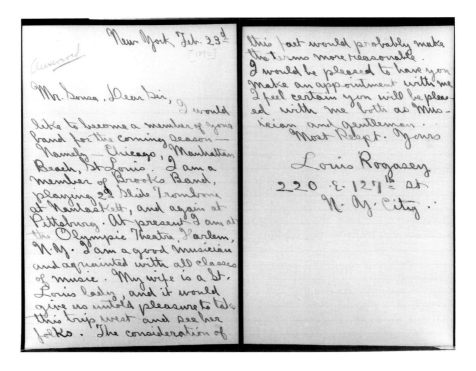

Illustration 62. A letter from a journeyman trombone player to the office of Sousa's agent David Blakely, petitioning for a place in Sousa's band in 1892. Personal propriety as well as musical ability is emphasized. (New York Public Library)

status was worth more than the pay cheque. Such transitions were especially unhindered in the nineteenth century, because the division between, for example, the concert band and the symphony orchestra was less defined than it would later become.

European players named as members of this or that symphony orchestra were usually freelancers who plied most of their trade in theatre pits and on band stands. Pryor (as far as we know) never played in a symphony orchestra for any length of time, but Mantia doubled as trombonist at the Metropolitan Opera while being euphonium soloist with Sousa, and Frederick Innes was for years the trombone player at the Folies Bergères. Even Miff Mole, one of the greatest of all jazz trombonists, spent time in New York symphony orchestras.

In the closing years of the nineteenth century, the introduction of phonographic recordings provided a new source of employment for musicians. Trombonists fared well in such developments, because the instrument made a good impact on the recording technology available at that time. Zimmerman was one of the most recorded trombonists of the early days of the phonograph, but Pryor was probably the most important trombonist in the recording business in the opening years of the twentieth century, as both soloist and conductor (he conducted the majority of the Sousa Band recordings; see Chapter 12), and briefly also as musical director of the Victor Phonograph Company.

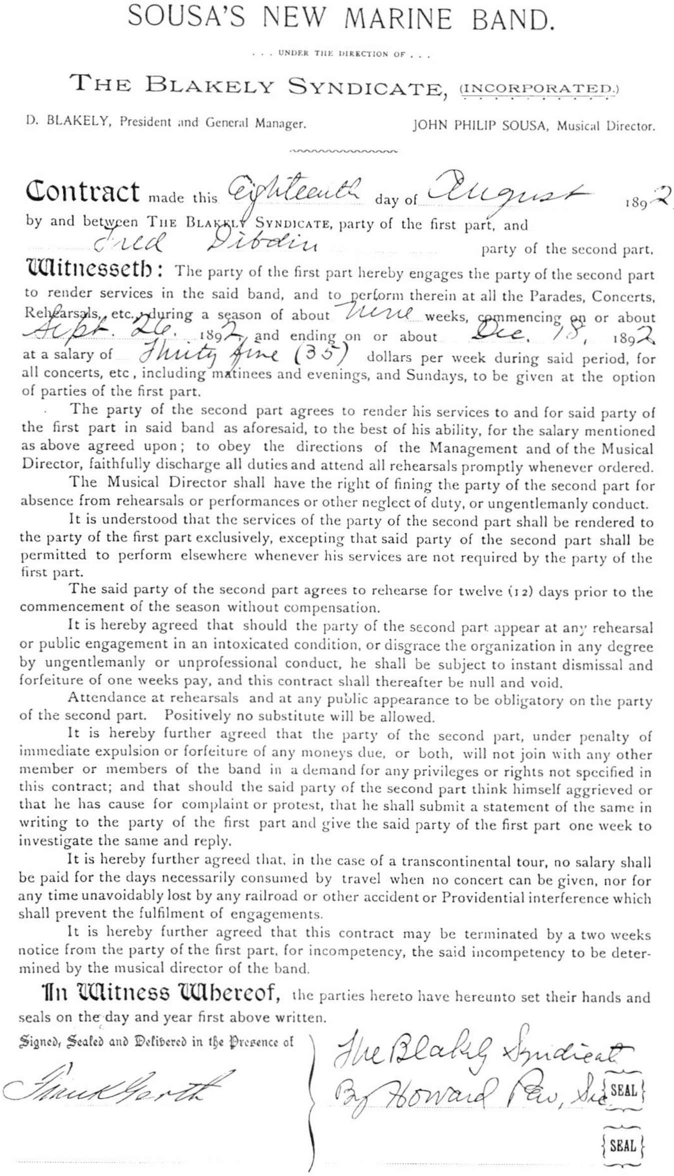

SOUSA'S NEW MARINE BAND.

. . . UNDER THE DIRECTION OF . . .

THE BLAKELY SYNDICATE, (INCORPORATED.)

D. BLAKELY, President and General Manager. JOHN PHILIP SOUSA, Musical Director.

Contract made this *Eighteenth* day of *August* 189*2*, by and between THE BLAKELY SYNDICATE, party of the first part, and *Fred Dibdin* party of the second part, **Witnesseth :** The party of the first part hereby engages the party of the second part to render services in the said band, and to perform therein at all the Parades, Concerts, Rehearsals, etc., during a season of about *nine* weeks, commencing on or about *Sept. 26.* 189*2*, and ending on or about *Dec. 18,* 189*2*, at a salary of *Thirty five* (*35*) dollars per week during said period, for all concerts, etc , including matinees and evenings, and Sundays, to be given at the option of parties of the first part.

The party of the second part agrees to render his services to and for said party of the first part in said band as aforesaid, to the best of his ability, for the salary mentioned as above agreed upon; to obey the directions of the Management and of the Musical Director, faithfully discharge all duties and attend all rehearsals promptly whenever ordered.

The Musical Director shall have the right of fining the party of the second part for absence from rehearsals or performances or other neglect of duty, or ungentlemanly conduct.

It is understood that the services of the party of the second part shall be rendered to the party of the first part exclusively, excepting that said party of the second part shall be permitted to perform elsewhere whenever his services are not required by the party of the first part.

The said party of the second part agrees to rehearse for twelve (12) days prior to the commencement of the season without compensation.

It is hereby agreed that should the party of the second part appear at any rehearsal or public engagement in an intoxicated condition, or disgrace the organization in any degree by ungentlemanly or unprofessional conduct, he shall be subject to instant dismissal and forfeiture of one weeks pay, and this contract shall thereafter be null and void.

Attendance at rehearsals and at any public appearance to be obligatory on the party of the second part. Positively no substitute will be allowed.

It is hereby further agreed that the party of the second part, under penalty of immediate expulsion or forfeiture of any moneys due, or both, will not join with any other member or members of the band in a demand for any privileges or rights not specified in this contract; and that should the said party of the second part think himself aggrieved or that he has cause for complaint or protest, that he shall submit a statement of the same in writing to the party of the first part and give the said party of the first part one week to investigate the same and reply.

It is hereby further agreed that, in the case of a transcontinental tour, no salary shall be paid for the days necessarily consumed by travel when no concert can be given, nor for any time unavoidably lost by any railroad or other accident or Providential interference which shall prevent the fulfilment of engagements.

It is hereby further agreed that this contract may be terminated by a two weeks notice from the party of the first part, for incompetency, the said incompetency to be determined by the musical director of the band.

In Witness Whereof, the parties hereto have hereunto set their hands and seals on the day and year first above written.

Signed, Sealed and Delivered in the Presence of

Frank Garth | *The Blakely Syndicate* *By Howard Pew, Sec* {SEAL}

{SEAL}

Illustration 63. The contract that all players in Sousa's Band were required to sign for the 1892 engagements. For $35 a week, players were required to perform at as many sessions as the management determined and to conduct themselves impeccably. (New York Public Library)

The advent of wireless radio and more advanced forms of sound recording further enhanced the opportunities for professional work. But it was only the upper strata of players who were involved in such projects; the greatest number of job opportunities for trombone players were in live performance, with the dance band joining the traditional pit orchestra and touring band as the main sources of employment. In the

1890s, however, a new and massively important avenue opened up with motion pictures. Though the USA was the major source for silent movies, their impact was an international phenomenon. It is estimated that by 1914 there were at least 3,500 silent film theatres in Britain alone;[31] in America there were some 10,000 by 1910, and over 20,000 by 1920.[32] Cyril Ehrlich has commented that 'Silent films functioned as if they had been designed to create jobs for musicians'.[33] By 1909 it was estimated that 45 million Americans watched the movies every week. From about 1910, with the establishment of larger film theatres, there were increased budgets for music, and ensembles of between three and fifteen musicians were common. In the 1910s and 20s, movie palaces had large orchestras, and every town of moderate size had at least one movie palace, both in the USA and in Europe.[34] Virtually every band had at least one trombone player to strengthen bass lines and provide effects in moments of 'terror and drunken knockabouts'.[35] Silent movie music ranged from the improvisations of a single pianist to large-scale, carefully synchronized scores for symphony orchestra combinations. In 1915, D. W. Griffith's *The Birth of a Nation* established the feature film as the norm. It was also the first American film to be released with its own score (compiled by Joseph Carl Breil, and including original music composed by him) for a 40–piece orchestra. But for the greatest part, the music was published as utilitarian 'library' sets for a flexible combination of instruments. There is no doubt that some classical music was used, both as intermezzi and also for background atmosphere, but specially composed, strictly functional music was also abundant. These scores were written by hack composers, among whom none was more industrious (or prolific) than Otto Langey, otherwise known for his widely distributed method books. From his apartment at 116 East 18th Street, Manhattan, Langey produced huge amounts of generic background, mood and action music with titles such as 'High Anxiety 2' and 'Evening Love'. Other titles that faced trombone players were 'Sad', 'Church', 'Chase' and 'Sinister'. There were several showings of films every evening, and most musicians played this music for about 60 hours a week, so one can only imagine how heavily the title 'High Anxiety' sometimes weighed on the minds of its players.

Notwithstanding such irritations, the silent movie business provided one of the main modes of employment for trombone players, far outstripping symphony orchestras and probably even dance bands. Miff Mole, Eddie 'Daddy' Edwards, Glenn Miller and Tommy Dorsey all served their time in silent movie bands. Then in 1927 the structure of the music business changed at a stroke with the introduction of talking pictures. In October of that year *The Jazz Singer* – the first sound and motion picture – was screened in New York. Within two years 20,000 American cinemas were equipped for sound movies;[36] in Britain and elsewhere in Europe the situation was similar. The effect on the music industry was catastrophic. The impact on trombone players was to be partly counteracted by the rising popularity of big dance bands, but it is unlikely that anything more than a small proportion of the thousands of journeymen professionals continued in the business. In effect, the demise of silent movies decimated the trombone-playing profession. We do not know the precise details and we have no clear idea of where these players went – whether they became teachers, farmers or railway porters – but it is certain that at this moment in music history, for the first time since the advent of the new popular market, a massive and acute restriction on the number of trombone players that could be accommodated in the profession occurred. It was a contraction from which the music profession never fully recovered.

The Second World War both fractured and sustained elements of the profession. The big bands which were popular at the start of the 1940s had mostly wound up by the end of the decade. On the other hand, military bands sustained standards and the sense of community among players through the war years. Many military players entered orchestras at the end of the war, but in the 1950s a new cultural era mediated in the music profession. Whereas the late forties and early fifties provided opportunities for trombonists to work in the backing bands of crooners, the late fifties brought rock and roll and the arrival of 'pop' music. 'Pop' was different from previous strands of popular music because it was aimed strategically at a teenage market which suddenly seemed to possess distinctive cultural values that differed sharply from those of people even a few years older. It also had a disposable income and an apparently insatiable appetite for recorded popular music. The idols of this generation were members of groups that adopted the standard rock band line-up of three electric guitars and percussion. For the first time since the nineteenth century, the most prominent form of popular music did not axiomatically call for trombone players.

This too caused a diminution in the trombone-playing profession. On the one hand, employment was buoyant: musical theatre, advertising jingles and a host of other forms of media work presented themselves. But on the other, the profession became more selective and the gap between the top group of professionals and those below them became wider. The most lucrative work in the popular mode was in film and advertising soundtracks. Players who inhabited this world were (as they still are) a relatively small elite. Many of the players who played on the sound stages of California were the great players of the big band era – Lawrence Brown, J. J. Johnson, George Reynolds and many more legendary names were among their number.

Salsa and Latino American music

Trombones and trumpets commonly function as lead instruments in Latino American music, their use deriving from the instruments' role in military music, which was introduced into the Caribbean and Cuba by European colonists. They are a central ingredient of the sound of *konpas*, a 'horn-driven'[37] Haitian dance music, and of Dominican *merengue*. But it is in urban 'salsa', and specifically the *salsa dura* or *salsa brava* ('hard' or 'heavy' salsa)[38] of the New York Puerto Rican community, that the trombone features most prominently. The origins of salsa lie in the Cuban popular music form *son* (the term 'salsa' was coined as a commercial name for *son*[39]). But in the urban Latino communities of 1960s America, salsa incorporated a range of other influences including jazz and rock and roll, developing into a 'harder', more powerful and heady style characterised by 'dynamic arrangements, driving percussion, and strident horns' in which trombones contributed one of the most vital essences.[40]

One of the most distinguished exponents of *salsa dura* is the trombonist Willie Colón (b. 1950), and it is his playing that has defined the 'trombone-heavy' New York salsa sound.[41] Colón is a remarkable character: a composer, performer, actor and political activist whose influence on the musical direction of salsa has been formidable. He has developed several identities for the trombone sound, which he employs with impressive effect to colour ensemble sound.[42]

Another key figure in the development of this style of trombone playing has been the innovative pianist and bandleader Eddie Palmieri (b. 1936). Palmieri's band La Perfecta (the band ran from 1961 to 1968, and was latterly re-formed as La Perfecta II) used a formation which replaced the popular Cuban *charanga* line-up of flute and violin with flute and trombone. This distinctive transformation of *charanga* became known as the 'trombanga' sound, in which the trombones provide a brassy underpinning of swing choruses that fuse the salsa tradition with Palmieri's brand of densely harmonized jazz. The driving force of the original trombanga sound was the trombonist Barry Rogers, some of whose solos were transcribed and performed by trombonists such as Doug Beavers and Conrad Herwig with La Perfecta II.[43]

Chapter 11

The Moravians and other popular religions

The special place of the trombone in the music of Christian worship will be evident from preceding chapters. It derives in part from the practice initiated in the sixteenth century of trombones doubling vocal lines in higher centres of Catholic worship, but it would be wrong to assume that all subsequent usages of trombones in sacred contexts originate here. The doubling and replacing of vocal lines by trombones in Catholic liturgical music was, in any case, not a universal practice. Furthermore, the role of the instrument in Protestant sacred repertoire should be seen in somewhat different terms. While certain major Protestant movements such as Lutheranism and Anglicanism are clearly indebted to Catholicism (for example, in the retention of forms of the ordinary of the Mass), their development was distinct. Charlotte Leonard, in her study of German Protestant sacred repertoire in the seventeenth century, identified fourteen different musical functions for the trombone in a wide and diverse repertoire.[1]

It was during the early seventeenth century – perhaps from a little sooner and perhaps for a little longer – that the basic functional utility of a trombone ensemble as a part of popular worship became evident. The point of change can be traced to the time when the singing of homophonic hymns and chorales by the congregation became commonplace in continental Europe. Congregational singing of chorales was embedded in the Lutheran rite: it took place, for example, as the preacher was ascending to the pulpit (*Kanzellied*) and when the communion was distributed. Such chorales were usually preceded by a chorale prelude played on an organ, but a trombone choir was used to accompany hymns and chorales. The appeal of the trombone for Protestant doctrine is easy to understand. The sound of a group of trombones heightens and beautifies vocal sonorities, but does not obscure meanings enunciated in sung scriptural texts. It could thus be said that the trombone has been valued in Protestantism for dual and somewhat paradoxical reasons: on the one hand, its ability to enhance the artistic status of sacred music; and on the other, the relative neutrality of its impact on scriptural meaning. Thus, a choir of trombones, or trombones and cornett, might be seen in the same aesthetic terms as the organ, as providing a complementary musical underpinning of meaningful worship.

The popularity of the instrument can be further explained by reference to simple practicalities: the near-exact matching of vocal parts to a homogeneous family of instruments (sometimes with cornett), and the ease with which they could be adapted to the intonational vagaries of church organs. The sound of a group of trombones playing in close harmony, perhaps with an organ, was perceived as a particularly apt accompaniment for spiritual communication. The manner and style in which trombones have been used in such contexts is enormously varied, and it has to be said that other instruments and groups of instruments may have similarly found a place in religious ritual. But for some congregations the trombone has a special place. The most striking and sustained example is that of the Moravians, especially those who settled in North America. Indeed, it is the phenomenon of trombone playing in Moravian communities – one of the most remarkably continuous traditions of trombone playing – that provides the primary rationale for a discussion of popular religion in a discrete chapter of this book. But other related themes are also dealt with here: in particular, the role of evangelical movements in establishing musical contexts in which trombones have been used, and the interesting and largely undocumented story of the use of trombones and other brass instruments in Asian and African countries where brass instruments were introduced by Christian missionaries. Here too trombones had no primacy over other brass instruments, but it was through such agencies that trombones reached places that were as culturally distant from their place of origin as they were geographically distant. Such phenomena are especially interesting because the hybrid styles and processes that developed were to impinge as much on secular as on sacred life.

The Moravians

The Moravian church stands alone in having an extensive and continuous tradition of amateur trombone playing from the eighteenth century to the present time; it provides a unique example of continuity of association between the instrument, a vernacular community and its sacred and secular rituals. The church can be traced to fifteenth-century Bohemia and Moravia and the followers of the radical Czech religious reformer Jan Hus, who was executed as a heretic in 1415. The more modern manifestation, the Unitas Fratrum (Unity of Brethren), developed from a Protestant community that gained protection from Catholic persecution on the estate of Count Nikolaus Ludwig von Zinzendorf in Bohemia in 1722. This community created the German town of Herrnhut, the first of many settlements formed throughout the world by Moravian communities.

Moravian religious values are distinctive, but are based upon disarmingly simple ideals which have conditioned both community life and religious ritual, with musical practices being prominent in both. The basis of the Moravian musical tradition is choral, but musical instruments were used from the eighteenth century, and a rich musical culture developed that was central to Moravian life. Trumpets and horns are mentioned in early records, but the practice of using trombones appears to date from 1731. In May of that year at Berthelsdorf, the local pastor was serenaded on his birthday, when 'Songs [were] sung in the parsonage yard with the accompaniment of trombones'. At a funeral in June of the same year, 'There was singing . . . all with the accompaniment of trombones'.[2] Subsequent references to groups of trombones are encountered regularly. According to the *Lebenslauf* (memoir) of a congregation member, Herrnhut acquired a set of trombones in June 1731: 'we went to Herrnhut where we arrived in the evening after the *Singstunde* [song service]. . . . There on this very day the congregation had gotten the first trombones, and so they welcomed us with them.'[3]

In 1764 the Synod of the Moravian church implied some official status for the trombone choir when it agreed that: 'where there is a trombone choir, one can make use of it at burials. This makes a lovely impression of our hope on the hearts of the people.'[4] The players in the first trombone choir at Herrnhut were Hans Raschke, Joseph Seiffert and Daniel Johann Grimm. Raschke was the leader of the group and its teacher. None of these were professional musicians: Seiffert, for example, was in the linen trade.[5]

As new Moravian communities were set up in other parts of Germany, more trombone ensembles were formed. Brass (almost certainly trombone) groups were established in Marienborn and Niesky in 1742, Gnadenberg in 1743 and Herrnhag in 1747. By this time the Moravians had commenced a worldwide evangelical mission. They settled in Zeist in Holland in 1746 and Christiansfeld in Denmark in 1778, and both of these communities had trombone choirs. By 1790 there were ensembles in 15 European settlements.[6] But from the musical point of view the most important and enduring Moravian communities were established in America. In 1747 the British parliament passed an Act which granted this 'sober, quiet and industrious People' permission to 'settle in America [which] will be beneficial to the said Colonies'.[7] The largest and most thriving settlements were those in the east, particularly in Winston-Salem, North Carolina, and Nazareth and Bethlehem, Pennsylvania.

Moravian communities believed that all worldly goods belonged to God. While they held that there could be private property, in practice the basis of their society was a sophisticated variant of communalism. They were mutually supportive and in many ways enlightened, but there was no clear demarcation between sacred and secular power. The homogeneity of their society was strictly ordered so that all aspects of life could function as a form of devotion. The community as a whole was the primary family unit, and stratification within that family was based on marital status, sex and age. The different sectors of the community were referred to, appropriately enough, as 'choirs'; but while it seems that there were occasions when such choirs literally sang together as a unit, the word 'choir' was employed to signify a grouping within the society – a grouping that defined the basis of a particular 'household'. Thus, for example, there was a widows' house, a widowers' house, a single brothers' house and a single sisters' house. Some female categories were even indicated by aspects of their dress.[8]

Because Moravians recognized no discernible limit to the opportunity for spirituality, all music-making – including that which took place outside the church – had a devotional quality. Singing was of prime importance, but there was also a wide variety of instrumental music. While trombone ensembles were not universal in the Moravian church, in the USA the *Posaunenchor* quickly became established as a characteristic feature of Moravian life. By 1754 the first trombone choir had been formed in Bethlehem, Pennsylvania. The earliest recorded use of the instruments in that town is found in a description of trombones playing 'for the obsequies of a child' whose remains were interred on 15 November of that year.[9] Further confirmation of the establishment of the group by that time might be taken from a report that has wide currency in the Moravian communities of Pennsylvania. On Christmas morning

1755 – so it is said – the trombone group played from the church tower to avert an attack by Indians who may have been coerced by French settlers. The story goes that intelligence of an attack reached the community through the agency of an Indian who was a Christian convert. Urged by their Bishop that 'no one shall permit a hostile feeling against the Indians to arise within himself . . . but . . . [shall] trust in the Lord our God',[10] the Moravians resorted to prayer and the power of music. On Christmas morning the trombone group played from the church tower at four o'clock. The time that the trombones played appears to be significant: it was exactly an hour earlier than the usual time for the community's awakening. The sound of a trombone chorale mystified the Indians, who took it to be a sign of the Moravians' spiritual protection, and fled. The Bethlehem community saw the event in somewhat similar terms and regarded it as a divine intervention. Of course, the story has more than a hint of the apocryphal about it and there is little hard evidence to support its detail, but it holds strong in the town of Bethlehem to this day, and the unusually early (possibly unique) Christmas Day awakening is verified in the Diaries of the Bethlehem Congregation for that year: 'Early in the morning this day, towards 4.00 o' clock the birthday of the Saviour was proclaimed by trombones in a most pleasing manner.'[11] Perhaps the most we can conclude from this is that by 1755 the trombone choir tradition was established in the town, but the willingness of the community to absorb the story into its vernacular heritage may attest to an equally important point: that the trombone choir was seen as a potent ingredient in its quest for spirituality.[12]

The *Posaunenchor* was usually four in number (though some groups were larger), and was made up of instruments that matched the soprano, alto, tenor and bass voices. At various points in their history, communities may have had more than one such choir. On 2 December 1793, for example, the death of one of the church's greatest early leaders, Bishop August Gottlieb Spangenberg, was announced from the roof of the Single Brethren's house in Bethlehem by two quartets of trombones.[13] In 1919, the trombone choir appeared to be able to call on sixteen players.[14] There is also evidence that players from more than one community sometimes combined for special festivals. It stands to reason that the practice of using trombones owes much to the tradition established at Herrnhut, and it has been argued that this in turn might derive from the German *Stadtpfeifer* tradition, but it is equally possible that the credibility of trombones in religious worship is aided by references to *Posaunen* in the Lutheran Bible.[15] By the end of the eighteenth century, the sonic quality of the *Posaunenchor*, together with its versatility – particularly the fact that it could play anywhere, indoors and out – had given the trombone group a wider utility than other instruments and combinations of instruments used by the Moravians.

The *Posaunenchor* had four principal formal functions: it played 'in lieu of passing of bell', in that it played from the church tower or wherever a service of worship was to take place, to summon the congregation; it played to announce the death of a church member; it played at gravesides to 'heighten the solemnities of burial services'; and finally it was used to 'impart the majesty of sound on high feasts and holy days, to the paraphernalia of the liturgy'.[16] In this latter role the *Posaunenchor* had a specific part to play in such festivals as Christmas, the New Year's Watchnight and Easter Sunrise services, and the musical services known as 'Lovefeasts'.[17] It also played for the announcement of Holy Communion.

The repertoire for the trombone choir was mainly made up of chorales from the Moravian version of the Lutheran hymn book. Particular chorales performed by the *Posaunenchor* alone were endowed with special meaning. Some were seasonal or reserved for particular festivals, but others were used effectively as signals to communicate messages to the community at large. Prominent in this regard was the designation of specific chorales to announce the death of church members. Additionally, particular hymns were played at prescribed points in funeral rites, and even as early as 1731, funeral singing in Herrnhut was 'all with the accompaniment of trombones'.[18]

The practice of signalling a death by sounding a chorale designated for a specific 'choir' probably originated in Europe. In April 1751 in Ebersdorf in Thuringia, 'The "going home" [death] of a Single Sister was announced to the congregation through the sound of horns and trumpets',[19] and the *Bethlehemisches Diarium* (*Conferenz des Jünger Collegi*) of 4 April 1757 refers specifically to 'a custom already current in the German Moravian churches'.[20] By this time the custom was evidently well established in the American Moravian communities also, because in Bethlehem, Pennsylvania, as early as November 1751, Martin Christensen, a Single Brother, 'departed to be with the Saviour, and his passing was made known to the congregation . . . by means of a stanza played by trumpets from the gallery on the Brethren's House'.[21] By 1757 the practice of death signalling had devolved to the trombone group. When a member of the community died, the trombone choir announced the death by playing an appropriate chorale from the church tower.[22]

It is not entirely clear either why or how particular chorales were ascribed as signifiers for different sectors of the community, or the extent to which local preferences could be applied, but while European tradition was being followed, variants of it were also developing in North America. The Bethlehem chorales were prescribed in an entry in the *Bethlehemisches Diarium*: the sounding of the death announcement came in the form of the chorale *O Haupt voll Blut und Wunden*, which was then followed by another chorale that signified the choir of the deceased person. The *Bethlehemisches Diarium* specified six categories of signal, but the chorale for the death of a widower was not entered:

> Married: *O Gott du keusches Lämmlein*
> Single brethren: *Hörst du's Aeltester!*
> Single sisters: *Drinn singt die selige Assemble*
> Widowers: [Blank]
> Widows: *Was macht ein Creuzluftvögellein*
> Children: *Ihr Kinder wo seyd ihr ohnfehlbar geborgen*[23]

At Winston-Salem, the procedure was somewhat different:

> When someone departs this life, the whole community will know at once to which Choir the departed soul belonged. If the familiar Choir tune is played after the tune *Nun wieder eins erblassets*, etc., as is customary in Europe, and then the first tune is repeated, we will have in mind the words, *Wenn mein Mund*.[24]

The *Posaunenchor* death proclamation had three components: the trombone choir played the announcement of death, followed by the announcement of the choir of the departed soul and then a further chorale which 'reminds the hearer that the Death Angel will some day come to him'.[25] The schedule of tunes may have been made by Christian Gregor (1723–1801), a hymn writer and organist who became a bishop in the church. (Gregor was a truly prolific composer and it is estimated that more than eleven hundred of his works are in American collections. He appears to have visited Pennsylvania and North Carolina only once, in 1770–2.) It seems certain that the practice was well established by the second half of the eighteenth century, and that the coding of chorales was in place – probably incorporating at least some local elements – by the nineteenth century. In 1905, Adelaide Fries of Winston-Salem identified separate designations for married brethren, married sisters, widowers, widows, single brethren, single sisters, older boys, older girls, little boys and little girls.[26] (Ex. 11.1)

We can only assume that the trombones used in the first American communities were brought with the settlers, but by the end of the eighteenth century new instruments were being imported from Germany. In 1762, Bethlehem players obtained new instruments and soon after that the *Posaunenchor* of Bethlehem was frequently despatched to other churches to enhance their worship. Instruments were passed from one community to another as new ones were acquired or ensembles became defunct. The instruments formerly used by the trombone choir at Hope, New Jersey, eventually found their way to Bethlehem. Bethlehem may have been a supply centre, for it also seems to have been responsible for supplying the community in Gnadenhutten, Ohio, in 1818, and the instruments provided for the Martinez Indian Mission in 1911 were supplied by 'friends in Bethlehem'.[27]

The supply of new trombones initially came from Europe, and particularly from the workshops of the Schmied family of Pfaffendorf, Germany. The earliest of these instruments to survive was used in the Gnadenhutten community, and is dated 1789. Stewart Carter has assembled an inventory of surviving instruments in Moravian communities, and has also looked at patterns of acquisition of instruments used by Moravians.[28] It is clear that instruments were circulated on a purely expedient basis, but up to the second half of the nineteenth century, new instruments were imported directly from Europe. From the mid-nineteenth century the source of supply switched to the US, primarily through New York dealers such as Zoebisch & Sons and Carl Fischer, though the Bethlehem players still imported some instruments from Europe. Carter has also made the point that the instruments bought by the Moravians were consistently well made and serviceable, but appropriate for the needs of amateurs rather than professionals.

If surviving instruments are anything to go by, it is evident that other lip-vibrated instruments were also used. Indeed, in the large collection of extant instruments there are valve instruments, cornetts and keyed brass. These instruments testify to the importance of music-making generally in Moravian communities, but they are also indicative of an evolving palette of sound that was being used by Moravian musicians. In some places the traditional role of the trombone ensemble remained undisturbed to modern times. The *Posaunenchor* was invariably close to the church hierarchy; indeed, in 1839, the senior class of theological students at Bethlehem appear to have formed a quartet of trombones as part of their training for ministry.[29]

Example 11.1. Tune 82D from Grimm's *Chorale Book* (1755), designated in some Moravian communities as the death announcement for a little girl.

Illustration 64. A picture of the trombone players of the Bethlehem Moravian congregation in 1867. The players are (from the left) Charles F. Beckel, Jedidiah Weiss and Jacob Till. The trombone on the empty chair is in homage to their deceased colleague Timothy Weiss. (By permission of the Moravian Archives, Bethlehem, PA)

Individual trombone groups seem to have enjoyed remarkable continuity. It is easy to cite instances where players held their positions from the time they joined until they were very old men. One quartet at Bethlehem entered the service of the church on Easter morning 1818 and remained together for almost half a century.[30] (Ill. 64) The four players were Charles Frederick Beckel, Jedidiah and Timothy Weiss and Jacob Till. Jedidiah Weiss, born in 1796, was a watch- and clock-maker. Timothy Weiss, who practised the same trade, was probably his brother. Their grandparents had been among the first settlers in the Nazareth community in 1743. Beckel was born in Bethlehem in 1801, and was apprenticed to the elder Weiss on the death of another watch-maker to whom he was indentured. Jacob Till, the remaining member of the group, was born in New Jersey in 1799 and moved to Bethlehem as a child. He was apprenticed to his father, a piano maker, and it seems that at some time in his life he made a living as a musician in Pennsylvania.[31]

The Moravians justifiably claim that their church is the longest-established musical institution operating in the USA. The richness of its musical culture and the expertise of its musicians was unmatched in the eighteenth century and for much of the nineteenth. Consequently its archives hold collections that are a particularly rich source for music historians. Moravian musicians have also performed in broader cultural domains and have participated in some of the earliest American performances of large-scale works by canonical European composers. Naturally there was a propensity to be involved in works that had a religious theme, but the idea that all music was a device for devotion also allowed involvement in other repertoire – especially for instruments. A copy of Haydn's *Creation* was obtained in 1810, and performance copies were made by John Frederick Peter for what appears to have been a partial performance of the work in 1811. The Moravians also performed the same composer's oratorio *The Seasons*. Both these performances preceded others of these works in the USA. The demanding bass trombone part in the 1811 performance of the *Creation* was played by Jedidiah Weiss.

The burden of duty for Moravian trombone players has often been heavy. In 1919 the trombone choir at Bethlehem was required to play at each of the Sunday services and at 79 festivals and other occasions. Additionally there were 37 death announcements and 35 funerals.[32] The Bethlehem trombone choir remains an integral part of the community and continues to carry out traditional religious functions, and its members still use soprano trombone on the top line. Additionally, the group has a brief to represent Moravian musical traditions in the wider community. There are also groups in California, Alberta, North Carolina and Ohio.[33] One of the reasons for the endurance of the tradition through the nineteenth century was that musicians were seen as key participants in Moravian ritual practices.

The Salvation Army

The Salvation Army was formed as the East London Christian Mission in 1865 by the evangelical preacher William Booth. It was named the 'Salvation Army' in 1878 and soon gained parliamentary recognition as a properly constituted religious body. Booth devised the idea of a 'Salvationist army', and the military metaphor prevailed across the rhetoric and all procedures of the organization. He was the General, the enemy was Satan and a quasi-military discipline and structure were vigorously enforced. As early as 1878 Booth had encouraged the use of brass bands to attract attention to evangelical meetings and to accompany hymns. Brass bands were popular in Victorian Britain, and the importation of this device from secular popular culture proved immensely successful. It did not take long for bands to be formed from scratch, though in many cases these bands were built around converts to Salvationism who could already play. Until the closing years of the twentieth century, Salvationist musicians were – at least ostensibly – entirely independent of the secular brass band movement. To enforce this objective the Army founded its own publishing division in 1885, which included method books for trombone and bass trombone in its catalogue. A brass instrument manufacturing company was set up in 1889. By 1904 the Salvationist newspaper the *War Cry* claimed that annual production stood at 1,000 instruments a year.[34] In 1916 an audit showed there to be 24,477 senior and 4,270 junior bandsmen.[35] Most corps had bands, and the London-based International Staff Band of the Salvation Army was an extremely sophisticated group. A Staff Band was also set up in the USA, where the Salvation Army was fully active by 1880.

The Salvation Army merits attention in the history of the trombone for three reasons: first, because it has been a breeding ground for professional musicians since the start of the twentieth century; secondly, because the instrument-manufacturing operation became one of the largest in the world and produced some really novel

Illustration 65. Salvation Army trombonists, c. 1935. (Salvation Army International Heritage Centre, London)

....New England Jubilee Band....

Illustration 66. The New England Jubilee Band of the Salvation Army, c. 1890. The elaborate costumes give some substance to William Booth's fear that Salvationist musicians would focus on the entertainment value of music rather than its function in the Salvationist mission. (Salvation Army Archives, National Headquarters, Alexandria, VA)

models; and finally because the evangelical outreach of Salvationism may have been the most widespread and effective of any denomination. The Army was active in 63 countries by 1916.[36] By 1941 it was in 97 countries, and by 1997 the number had risen to 103.[37] It is hard to think of another agency (other than perhaps the Roman Catholic Church) which has played a more effective role in spreading western musical practices, some of which are discussed below.

There was an inherent problem in Booth's approach. In harnessing an aspect of popular culture for God's work, Salvationists themselves could fall victim to its seductive attractions. Many bandsmen attained a level of virtuosity that was unnecessary for the Salvationist cause and even counter-productive, because it encouraged and demonstrated what was perceived as musical vanity. (Ill. 66) Booth himself was adamant in this regard; he even exhorted the wives of bandsmen to be aware of this tendency:

CATALOGUE OF PIANOS, ORGANS, STRINGED INSTRUMENTS, ETC., ON APPLICATION

Bass Slide Trombones

(E♭ Single Slide and BB♭ Double Slide)

Patent E♭ Bass Slide Trombone

The shifts are the same as a B flat Tenor Trombone; striking departure and novelty in Trombone construction, brilliant and powerful tone, gives volume and great depth to a large band, overcomes difficulty of Bass Clef for Bass Trombone players.

EXAMPLE:

G Trombone

8*va* lower. E♭ Bass Trombone

Bass Single Slide Trombone (Automatic Additional Slide), in E flat, water-key, complete with lyre and mouthpiece 11 0 0

Bass Double Slide Trombone, in BB flat enormous depth and range, well-balanced slides, works as easily as single slide, complete with lyre and mouthpiece... 11 0 0

£ s. d.

Valve Trombones to Order

16

Illustration 67. Contrabass trombone made by the Salvation Army, c. 1905. (With thanks to Frank Tomes)

> A bandsman has special temptations that do not cross the path of an ordinary soldier . . . they are often in spiritual danger. . . . There is likewise a possibility of musical interests and activity usurping the Salvationist ideal. . . . What a chance a wife has of watching the rise of these various kinds of danger.[38]

Between these sentiments and the ambitious endeavours of the Salvationist brass instrument factory there was a significant contradiction. The instrument manufacturing arm was set up in order to ensure that good, cheap instruments were available for the service of God in all parts of the world. Indeed the production of tenor and bass trombones (in G) made a significant contribution to supply. One might ask, however, how this objective was served by the production of contrabass trombones. In 1905 *The Local Officer* carried an article entitled 'Our Instrument Factory' by a Major Grinstead, whose name appears on several pages of the register of UK patents (see Chapter 1). He had a particular interest in trombones, and claimed among his improvements the E flat bass trombone, and versions of the trombone water key and the slide lock. But his preoccupation was with the contrabass trombone. He called on the authority of Prout and Berlioz to justify the importance of this instrument – an instrument in BB flat with a double slide which *The Local Officer* described as 'probably the best in existence'. (A double-slide model pitched in BB flat, the one referred to by Grinstead, is in the collection of Douglas Yeo of the Boston Symphony Orchestra.[39]) But his *tour de force* was an ingenious invention of an E flat bass trombone on which the main slide was attached to another by a pulley. (Ill. 67) When the main slide was pushed or pulled it would move the secondary slide in the contrary direction. Very few of these instruments were made and one can only wonder what purpose they would have served in Salvation Army bands.[40]

Acculturation and trombone style

The Salvation Army was one of the most important of the Christian missionary movements, and played a significant part in disseminating musical practices and introducing brass instruments to non-western cultures. Brass and military bands were the principal music-makers of the western colonial powers, functioning as 'a musical weapon, and a thunderous proof of western military and religious superiority'.[41] But the musical practices they inculcated have been less important *per se* than the musical heritages that have emerged through the process of acculturation, with styles of playing and repertoires demonstrating the legacy of both indigenous and imposed cultural values.

By the end of the nineteenth century, trombones were being exported to many colonial countries. While military bands were the recipients of direct exports from European manufacturers, and many instruments found their way into the second-hand market, a route for the more prolific distribution of instruments was through the endeavours of Christian missionary agencies. Just as the Catholic Church can claim credit for the introduction of trombones into South America in the sixteenth century, the various missionary organizations can make a similar claim in respect of Asia, the Pacific region and Africa in the late nineteenth and early twentieth centuries. Brass bands were founded by the Salvation Army in Japan before 1900. By the Second World War the Salvationists had also established brass bands in India, other Asian countries and Africa.

Some of the most interesting trombone playing in these countries has arisen from a genuine assimilation of the instrument into indigenous musical forms. The playing often shows scant regard for the performance values or forms of western music. In Indonesia, *tanjidor*[42] bands play 'Jakarta-Chinese and Sudanese gamelan music . . . on the instruments of the European brass band', in what Ernst Heim has described as a 'dazzling heterophony which defies any rule and regulation of European musical theory'.[43] A fascinating aural survey of many such bands, conducted by the Department of Visual Anthropology at the University of Amsterdam, has resulted in an impressive series of recordings under the generic title *Frozen Brass*. The western influences come from the instruments themselves and the loosest possible structural derivation of western music. Some of the repertoire, for example, is based on hymn melodies. There is often some form of ostinato, and simple textural and dynamic contrasts are used. Players appear to invent their own performing technique, but the trombone seems to have a distinctive place because of its capacity to play glissandos and loosely controlled slide shakes, and often the trombonist appears to regard it as his function to provide a crude countermelody. Usually just one trombone is included, but recordings made in Sumatra and Suriname include two slide trombones.[44]

Acculturation has also made its mark upon western trombone playing, and it has done so particularly powerfully and to wide-reaching effect in the context of African-American culture. Again, and not surprisingly, religious practices and traditions have tended to be the focal point. Many of the best early jazz trombonists were initially schooled in churches that were set up as part of a missionary endeavour. But while jazz has gained a high profile in western music culture, there are other, less well

Illustration 68. A shout band: Kenny Carr and the Tigers, Orangeburg, South Carolina, 2001. (With thanks to Craig Kridel)

known musical and religious practices that have particular relevance to trombone idioms. One of the most interesting of these is the 'shout band' of the United House of Prayer. Founded in the 1920s by Charles Manuel 'Sweet Daddy' Grace, with 'Houses' in New York, Washington, DC, Virginia, Georgia and North and South Carolina, it had incorporated trombone shout bands into its rituals by the 1940s. The word 'shout' in this context derives from an Arabic term. It refers to the dance-like movements and singing with which believers express religious emotion.[45]

Matthew A. Hafar has described the typical shout band as including a lead trombone, with between three and five supporting trombones, as well as a baritone horn and a sousaphone.[46] (Ill. 68) However, the shout band that leads worship at the national headquarters of the United House of Prayer in Washington, DC, is a yet more impressive group known as the Kings of Harmony, often comprising twelve trombones or more.[47] The performances of these bands blend rapid ostinatos, chordal passages and solo sections played with a fast vibrato. Slurs and glissandos are also used, along with the close harmony reminiscent of gospel singing. This is an energetic and intense form of worship with much clapping and congregational involvement. But it is unambiguously spiritual, with the bands seeing their performances as an act of personal devotion, and for that reason the emphasis is less on homogeneity than on the facility that the ensemble provides for individual expression.

Chapter 12

Orchestral trombone playing in the age of sound recordings

Sound recording has revolutionized the music profession. Recordings provide a vivid perspective on the history of trombone performance style since the late nineteenth century, but the influence of the media has not been neutral: it has fashioned a change in the way performers play, and has given audiences new expectations and musical values. It has been argued that recordings have raised standards of performance,[1] and it is easy to see the basis for such claims; but equally, recordings have created their own aesthetic. Recording should be seen not merely as a means for capturing performance, but also as a process through which it is filtered.

Thomas Alva Edison's primitive phonograph technique for recording and playing back sound was invented in 1877, but the earliest recordings that provide decipherable evidence of trombone performance styles date from the late 1890s. Those made at the turn of the century are surprisingly revealing. The earliest – and here we can certainly include those produced even in the 1920s – probably also shed light on nineteenth-century practices, because many of the performance features we hear on them were neither new at that time nor at variance with what we learn from descriptions of performance practices before 1900.

One of the first great performing stars of the age of recording was the trombonist and conductor Arthur Pryor. He was targeted by phonograph companies partly because of his celebrity as a player, but also because the clear sonic quality of the trombone was especially effective in early recording processes (the same was true of the cornet). As a conductor he directed most of the early recordings of John Philip Sousa's Band. The Sousa Band was one of the most important forces in the popularizing of recorded sound. Sousa himself was ambivalent towards recording, and famously dismissed the process as 'canned music' (the first known usage of the term), though he eventually acquiesced, and in 1923 complimented Edison on having 'made the art of the musician immortal'.[2] But he was prepared for his band to be recorded, mostly under Pryor's baton. Military and brass bands were popular, and they recorded particularly well. Not only did their neat, precise and disciplined musical ethic suit the priorities of early recording engineers, but their repertoire, made of relatively short, simply-textured pieces, could have been written for the medium. The 1913 Victor band catalogue contained more than six hundred band records. Pryor's own band was the most prolific of all, and made an estimated two thousand records for Victor between 1903 and 1929.[3] (Ill. 69)

On both sides of the Atlantic, the fashion for recording and listening to recordings grew quickly. In the USA, some of the top brass soloists such as Jules Levy recorded

Illustration 69. Advertisement for New Victor Records dating from the 1920s, featuring the Original Dixieland Jazz Band. The trombone player is Eddie 'Daddy' Edwards.

in the mid-1890s. In England, the Black Dyke Mills brass band first committed its sound to a wax cylinder in 1903, the International Staff Band of the Salvation Army was recorded in 1904, and a procession of military and brass bands soon followed suit. In 1911 the New Symphony Orchestra under Landon Ronald issued a recording of Rossini's *William Tell* Overture, and in 1913 the Berlin Philharmonic recorded part of Beethoven's Fifth Symphony under Nikisch.[4] When the First World War ended, the floodgates of the recording industry seemed to open.

Recordings as documents

What can we understand about the history of trombone performance technique from recorded music? The short answer is: a great deal. But anyone who seeks to do so needs not just a good ear but an awareness of the contexts in which recordings were made. Then there is the more searching question: how, why and to what extent has recording influenced or even shaped the performance techniques of professional trombonists? Here the answer is more complex, but it is a question of the highest importance and one that is also addressed in this chapter. The nature and strength of the influence of recording has changed as each new technological step has been taken, and as the objectives of recording have shifted. At the start of the twentieth century, performers and engineers entered the recording studio with the intention of capturing and conveying a performance, and more particularly of supplying the novel commodity of professional music to the sitting rooms of the middle class. In our own times the emphasis has shifted; digital recording presents the seductive possibility that the acoustic of concert spaces can be conveyed and that the compact disc can capture technical perfection. The performance conveyed is not the one that was performed, but the one the performer would have wished to have given, with each wrinkle carefully ironed out, and placed in a chosen acoustic space. As we listen to the way that recordings reveal the history of trombone style in the twentieth century, we must be aware that a long process was being enacted here. That process provides a record both of the way players played and of the way that recording media mediated between them, their repertoire, and their audiences.

The earliest recording technology was effective only if performers adopted what were essentially unnatural procedures. The sound was captured through one or more recording horns which transmitted impulses to a wax cylinder. For many years orchestras recorded with reduced numbers. Arthur Judson, President of Columbia Records, recalled that, in the earliest days of recording, the Philadelphia Orchestra used 'just forty or fifty men', and other sources tell us of reduced and altered orchestrations.[5] In 1928 the *Gramophone* magazine made a comparison of the orchestras used in the acoustic process around 1914 and the electronic process in 1928. The comparison makes interesting reading. (Table 5)

Another factor that influenced quality was the physical placement of performers in the recording studio. Photographs of early twentieth-century recording sessions are unlikely to offer entirely reliable representations of the spatial arrangement of musicians for recording sessions, but they are interesting nevertheless. A photograph purportedly representing the Sousa Band, taken at the turn of the century, shows seventeen players clustered around ten recording horns.[6] The compacted and cramped posture of the players is consistent with what we see in similar photographs such as a famous one of Henry Wood conducting his New Queen's Hall Orchestra.[7] Here the players quite literally rub shoulders as they record. In neither of these photographs do players have the benefit of music stands, and their pose suggests that the sardine-like

Table 5

Recording forces, c. 1914 and 1928

	c.1914	1928
1st violin	4	10
2nd violin	2	8
viola	1/2	6
cello	1	5
bass	-	4
additional doubling instruments	1 clarinet, 1 bassoon, 1 contrabassoon, 1 tuba. Additional 'middle score' doubling by 1 or 2 euphoniums, 1 bass clarinet, 1 bassoon.	
flute	2	2
oboe	2	2
clarinet	2	2
bassoon	2	2
horn	4	4
trumpet	2	2
trombone	3	3
timpani	1	1
percussion	2/3	1
harp / piano	either	harp

Note Adapted from Stanley Chapple, 'In the Recording Studio' in *Gramophone*, December 1928; see L. W. Brunner, 'The orchestra and recorded sound', in *The Orchestra – Origins and Transformations*, ed. by J. Peyser, (New York: Charles Scribner's Sons, 1986), Table 8.

arrangement may have been more for the benefit of the camera lens than the wax cylinder (several of Wood's players face the camera rather than the orchestra, while Wood is actually standing behind them; and the Sousa Band is unnecessarily attired in full-dress military uniform). But by 1920 there are photographs that seem more credibly to represent the spatial arrangement that was actually used. Trombone players were almost always placed behind other performers because their sound was deemed to be so powerful. Many conductors and producers overcompensated for the impact of trombones. 'We know that the brass could kill a string section no matter how large it is,' said Eugene Ormandy. 'I always mark my score [for the producer] "watch the brass".'[8] It follows that on some recordings the trombone playing sounds distant and badly balanced. For example, in the very fine recording of Berlioz's *Symphonie fantastique* made by the Paris Symphony Orchestra under Pierre Monteux for Victor in 1931,[9] the trombones do not have the expected level of presence, but the playing is nonetheless impeccable. Some photographs of smaller bands – such as those that would have been used to accompany popular song music – show trombonists in an elevated position on a bench not unlike a particularly steep chapel seat.[10] Early jazz recordings accommodated trombonists more equally. These recordings are particularly effective and impressive because the normal performance forces and spatial arrangements of jazz bands seem to have been replicated in the studio.

More generally, it is difficult to determine the extent to which trombonists were required to play differently in recording sessions from how they would otherwise have done; so it is not easy to gauge the extent to which such recordings are genuinely representative of the usual manner of performance. It is unlikely that the recording studio ever had an entirely neutral effect on players. After all, it must have seemed an enormously strange, even surreal, environment for trombone players whose entire experience was gained in spacious surroundings and before live audiences. But how differently did they play – and differently in what ways? It stands to reason that some form of direction would have been issued by recording engineers, but we must remember that the culture of the recording studio was not as it is today, in that players did not possess a deep experience of the distinction between recording and concert performance. Differences there surely were, but to accept that trombonists played utterly differently in orchestral recordings, we would need to accept that they were capable of suspending their musical instincts and the fruits of their training and experience. Furthermore, we would have to concede that the greatest orchestral conductors of their time – Wood, Nikisch and Elgar before 1920, and subsequently Stravinsky, Koussevitzky, Mengelberg, Strauss, Toscanini and Stokowski – would similarly have presided over entirely unrealistic readings of masterworks in which timbre and articulation were hopelessly exaggerated, in the faith that all would sound fine when the record was released. It was impossible for recording performers to hear playback in the studio until the advent of tape recording around 1950. Nor was any editing possible until this time, so complete movements or works had to be recorded in a single take. All this suggests that performers had to rely on the musical skills and values to which they were accustomed.

Recordings did influence performance and interpretation, however – most obviously in the domain of tempo. A unit of recording time – a 'take' – was the temporal length of one side of a gramophone record, a restriction that lasted for almost the entire period of the microgroove era. Repertoire was either selected, sectionalized or edited with this factor in mind. Even opera and oratorio were packaged into segments that could be fitted onto the sides of a disc. Similar intervention also impacted on radio transmission. Henry Wood, lamenting the 'human element in the controls' room', commented that 'tempi may not be correct over the air', particularly when a conductor is told a minute before a performance that 'he must "hurry it up" or be faded out'.[11]

Orchestral trombonists did not, of course, determine tempo, but they did have to suffer the consequences of it. Both increases and decreases in speed presented their own problems, and these are evident on some early recordings. Such issues impacted only marginally on brass and military bands because their repertoire tended to come in appropriately sized segments, and an added or deleted repeat usually solved any residual problems. Not so for symphony orchestras: standards of performance were variable, but there was a genuine attempt to achieve fidelity, and the public expected a treat if Mengelberg, Nikisch, Ansermet or one of the other great maestros was at the helm.

Three different factors seemed to be prominent in public interest in the gramophone in the earliest days: a curiosity to hear recorded sound; a desire for a type of light diversification, particularly that provided by bands of various sorts; and eventually a desire on the part of the well-heeled to hear great music performed by great musicians in their own drawing rooms. The first two of these factors were well satisfied before the late 1920s, because lighter music, with its largely homophonic textures and small-scale repetitive forms, lent itself to the recording process more readily than classical music. Classical works recorded before 1920 are worthy of examination, but by the late 1920s there is not simply an increase in the number of works committed to recordings, but also the insight provided by such composers as Richard Strauss, Stravinsky, Milhaud, Elgar and Ravel, who (sometimes repeatedly) conducted recordings of their own works. Added to this are recordings directed by conductors who were in close communication with the composers whose work they were recording: for example, Monteux was closely associated with Stravinsky, and Beecham formed a close relationship with Sibelius. Composer–conductor recordings often reveal interesting differences between written sources and what composers (presumably willingly) accommodated in their recordings. A case in point can be found in the earliest recordings of the famous duet for trombone and double bass in Stravinsky's *Pulcinella* suite. This is one of the canonical solo pieces in the trombone repertoire. In modern performances the first subject is invariably played as two accented crotchets followed by two fast descending glissandos; it was performed and recorded repeatedly in this way during Stravinsky's lifetime – indeed this is explicit in successive editions (including the first). (Ex. 12.1a) In May 1928 Stravinsky conducted a recording of this piece in Paris.[12] The identity of the trombone player is unknown, but it may well have been André Lafosse, who performed in other sessions with Stravinsky during that period. Unambiguously and deliberately, both the trombonist and the bass player articulate the entire phrase and its various imitations with no hint of glissando. (Ex. 12.1b) The different articulation changes the character of the piece; was it Stravinsky who changed his mind, or was it more to do with the players? As I explain in Chapter 7, André Lafosse was equivocal about the appropriateness of glissando in classical music, describing it as a 'vulgar' device. Of course, glissando was used by Stravinsky in his ballet music written twenty years earlier, but we might speculate that classical music performers had an aversion to glissando, which they often perceived as a somewhat crass popular music device.

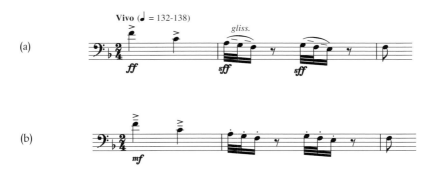

Example 12.1a & b. Stravinsky, *Pulcinella* (1919–20)
12a shows the notated score, 12b the way it was performed in the 1928 recording directed by Stravinsky.

Equally interesting are issues concerning performance style. There are problems in using recordings to determine orchestral trombone performance style before about 1930. Some have already been touched on, but it is worth summarizing them here. There is sometimes a lack of clarity in the reproduction which is caused by the spatial placement of players and the relative inadequacies of the recording process. This problem is exacerbated by issues concerning orchestral texture. One of the interpretative features revealed by early orchestral recordings is a predilection for pronounced rubato and high levels of string portamento. This often creates something of a mesh of sound that obscures those parts of the texture in which the trombone is active; this is particularly the case in quieter passages. Added to this is the problem of the competence of orchestral players. Clearly, there were some fine trombone players, but finesse was not always evident in orchestral playing. Standards of orchestral playing continued to be variable in the first few decades of the twentieth century, and it is easy to find examples of quite dire performance. Then there is the problem of other mediations in the recording process. We do not quite know what conductors and recording engineers told trombone players to do.

It should be stressed that these problems did not always obscure good performances and the evidence they provide. Chamber music recordings made after the mid-1920s (Stravinsky's early recordings are a good example) are convincing, if not entirely satisfying; and even in a very large-scale performance such as *Die Zauberflöte* recorded in Berlin and conducted by Beecham in 1937–8,[13] the recording is sufficiently clear to allow us to hear superb lightly textured trombone playing.

Perhaps the most important facet of trombone performance style that is revealed by early recordings is the extent to which regional variations prevailed. The progression from diversity to uniformity is the main feature of the first century of recording. But an equally illuminating phenomenon is the way that trombonists coped with changes of musical language in the twentieth century. Stravinsky's 1932 Paris recordings provide a good example. *Histoire du Soldat* was recorded in Paris in May 1932 under Stravinsky's direction; the trombonist was Raphaël Delbos.[14] It could be argued that the primitive recording environment had a detrimental effect on the overall balance, but this does not account for what is clearly substandard playing. The players could not cope with the rhythmic complexity of Stravinsky's writing, and the level at which they engaged with its musical meaning is highly questionable. The impression one gets is not that these were bad players, but that they were good players playing badly, and M. Delbos is not the lightest offender. Twenty years after *The Rite of Spring* was first performed, players were still struggling with the idiom of Stravinsky's musical language: this much is evident from the two recordings of *The Rite of Spring* made in 1929 under the batons of Monteux and Stravinsky.[15] The same can be said about the recording of the Octet for Winds made in the same period, where the trombonists were Lafosse and Delbos.[16]

The documentary value of jazz recordings is difficult to overstate, but it must be seen in a somewhat different light from recordings of classical music and even light orchestral and band recordings. The first commercial recording of a jazz band, released on 5 March 1917, was made by the Original Dixieland Jazz Band; the trombone player was Eddie Edwards.[17] Other bands that performed precursors of the jazz style – particularly ragtime – were recorded much earlier. For example, the

Edison Grand Concert Band laid down an impressive recording of 'At a Georgia Camp Meeting' by about 1897. Right from the start, jazz bands lent themselves well to the recording process, and their recordings are sufficiently clear to impart not just a flavour of the way trombonists played, but also a considerable level of detail. From the 1920s onwards, recordings are not just the essential, but in practical terms the sole, document of jazz performance. It is a corpus of immense richness, but here too in the second half of the twentieth century, there is evidence of the very finest jazz players' willingness to submit their recordings to the editor's scissors and tape. Even live recordings were not always beyond the intervention of editors and particularly digital engineers, but we can often listen to live recordings with a greater, if not an absolute, assurance that the recording is a document in real rather than managed time.

The earliest recordings

While Pryor was the most prolific recording soloist, he was not the only one, and several of the finest trombone players of the late nineteenth century were captured on disc in the first few years of the twentieth century. Frank Holton is impressive on a 1905 Sousa Band recording of 'Silence and Fun: a Ragtime Oddity'; Leo Zimmerman plays with Prince's Band in a recording of 'Ramshackle' made in 1911; and a full section of three trombones is heard on a recording of 'Russian Rag' made by James Rees Europe and his 369th US Infantry ('Hell Fighters') Band in 1919.[18] The discipline and musical precision on these recordings is both impressive and symptomatic of the neat performance ethic that prevailed in early twentieth-century American band recordings. One of the consistent features is the extent to which glissandos are used very precisely, to emphasize cadences or harmonic rhythm (perhaps a precursor of tailgate technique). The glissandos are never raucous; they do not convey the impression that this is merely an 'effect' devoid of musical function. They are rhythmically precise, with the two pitches conjoined by each glissando being exactly focused. Unlike later jazz players, these band trombonists were performing from notated music, and demonstrate a concern for exactitude. When glissando is not used, as is the case with James Rees Europe's recording of 'Russian Rag', and with several of the march recordings made by the Sousa Band, the sectional playing style of the trombonists is barely distinguishable from what we hear elsewhere from symphony orchestra recordings. This should not be surprising, because many of these players found employment in both orchestras and bands. But what it does demonstrate is that in the early twentieth century, the musical idioms of concert bands were determined by the notated music rather than by impromptu decoration by the players.

Pryor's solo recordings show him to be a spectacularly virtuosic player, but his was the virtuosity of demonstration: his repertoire was formed essentially to allow the exhibition of his virtuosity. His playing was consistently accurate, his articulations invariably clean and finely focused, he could play very fast passages with absolute clarity, and his legato playing was lyrical, expressive and often laced with an element of sentiment. He exploited a wide pitch range, from the pedal notes to partials well above the normal range of the instrument, and there was no part of this range in which he was weak. Most of his recordings, even those based primarily on lyrical melodies, display the full range of his skills. There are good early recordings of his signature pieces, 'The Blue Bells of Scotland' and 'Love's Enchantment', but his brilliance can be heard to particularly good effect in his 1903 recording of 'Love Thoughts Waltz', made with the Sousa Band.[19] His recordings are almost devoid of blemish, and his predictable accuracy must have been especially appreciated by record companies. Pryor was unusual among almost all trombone players of his time in having a pronounced and constant vibrato. This, it is said, was involuntary – caused by a mule kick suffered as a boy, leaving part of his face paralysed. Oddly, despite the fact that Pryor was a mentor figure, his vibrato was not imitated by other players, thus confirming what we know of the practices of players of other instruments. Early band soloists seem to employ vibrato only sparingly, as an expressive device rather than as a constituent of their basic sound.

Orchestral recordings before 1960

There are two striking features of trombone playing on recordings made before about 1960: the extent to which performance styles differ, and the fact that despite such differences these styles are usually convincing in the contexts of the orchestras in which they are heard. Not all orchestras display unerring competence. The economics of the music profession in England and France before the Second World War meant that orchestras in these countries had modest rehearsal time compared to those in Austria, Germany and Holland. Also, the deputy system was rife in England and France, and this did not help the establishment of ensemble consistency.[20] Orchestras in other European countries enjoyed more stable circumstances, and the quality of performances we hear in their recordings is commensurately better than elsewhere. By the 1920s the standards were generally high in the USA too. In the opening years of the century the Boston Symphony Orchestra was widely regarded as the finest American orchestra, but in 1928 the creation of the Philharmonic Symphony Orchestra of New York (from the merger of the Philharmonic and the Symphony Orchestras) under Toscanini provided a new focus, and nine years later the NBC Symphony Orchestra was formed expressly as a vehicle for Toscanini.

Even taking into account the different circumstances in which musicians worked and recordings were made, the quality of playing depended greatly on the authority of the conductor. Fine conductors were highly sought after, and in the days before slick public relations consultants and over-imaginative advertisement agencies, a conductor's reputation depended solely on the depth and effectiveness of his musical ability. Mengelberg, Koussevitzky, Barbirolli and Toscanini were not shy of the camera, but their celebrity came from an ability to deal with the fine detail of repertoire while simultaneously moulding orchestral sound imaginatively and effectively. This is not the place to discuss the interpretation of particular works by particular conductors, but listening to older recordings leads inevitably to an awareness that the sessions where great music was recorded with great conductors had a sense of occasion in which both musical and even emotional excitement was not subdued. The very best conductors had an ability to create transparency in the orchestral soundscape. Such transparency helps us understand trombone playing accurately and realistically, not just because individual lines are decipherable, but because the prevailing orchestral texture is sufficiently clear for us to imagine how conductors perceived the colour of the trombone section. A comparison of several recordings made before about 1960 shows orchestral trombone sections to have been susceptible to four influences that made for diversity of playing style: regional performance traditions, the type of instruments that were used, the influence of particular conductors, and the relationship of trombone sound to other blocks of sonority in the orchestra, especially that of the trumpet section.

Several factors contributed to regional playing traditions in the twentieth century, not the least of which was the training that professionals received; but one of the most potent influences on playing cultures continued to be military bands. In most countries, the military provided the largest and best-organized network of wind players, and it continued to be an important source for professional trombone players. The two world wars and subsequent periods of national service, too, stimulated a sharp focus on military bands as being the holding ground for future professionals. The military also influenced the choice of instruments that were used in civilian music-making. In 1927 every endorsement and illustration shown in the catalogue of the Hawkes instrument company was that of a trombone player in one of the British Guards regiments. Trombonists in English orchestras up to the 1950s were distinctive, because tenor trombonists played on narrow-bore, 'peashooter' instruments and bass trombonists used bass trombones in G that were of complementary proportion to the tenors. The sound of this combination was universally deserted in the second half of the century, but the playing of British orchestral players in recordings in which these instruments were used is almost always excellent, and their timbre, especially in the indigenous British repertoire of the early twentieth century, sounds logical and convincing, particularly as they blend with similar-voiced trumpet sections. The April 1927 recording of Elgar conducting his Second Symphony[21] provides a good illustration. The trombone sound is totally devoid of vibrato. In softer passages the sound is clear, well focused and not without warmth, but at higher dynamic levels it changes dramatically. It does not lose focus, but it is penetrating, much brassier, and players seem to employ hard, almost declamatory articulations. Marked changes of timbre, as players move across dynamic levels, tend to be a feature of most playing in this period, but in recordings of German and Austrian orchestras (and, to an extent, American orchestras too) it is less pronounced. The wider-bored instruments accommodate higher dynamic levels without making the sound fractionalize as much as on smaller instruments, but in loud tutti passages with trumpets, the wide, euphonious sound possesses a distinctive brassy edge. At the quieter end of the dynamic spectrum the sound is broad and less focused, but the sectional playing is invariably disciplined and convincing. Recordings made in Berlin and Vienna between 1930 and the 1950s are especially fine. Furtwängler's recording of Schubert's C major Symphony[22] with the Berlin Philharmonic is an example of the distinctively German style at its best. The unison solo passages are beautifully focused and phrased, and in the louder passages where the trombones carry the main melodic material the sound becomes more metallic, but without being transformed into a militaristic timbre.

The differences between the trombone playing on recordings of Russian and central European orchestras and those of western European and American orchestras are extraordinarily striking. Perhaps most notable is the boisterous sound of loud tutti passages, sometimes tinged with a hint of vibrato. The sound has a full-frontal, unyielding quality that is reminiscent of an over-exuberant military band. The procession of virtuoso brass players, composers and conductors who emerged in Russia and central Europe in this period is sufficient to suggest that this is a profoundly distinctive performance culture rather than a brand of playing that is inherently inferior. The 1953 recording of Liszt's *Héroïde funèbre* made by the Moscow Radio Symphony Orchestra with Nikolai Golovanov contains abundant evidence of the Russian style at this time, as does the same orchestra's recording of Glazunov's Sixth Symphony made with Golovanov in the previous year.[23] The large-belled, wide-bored instruments contribute to the distinctive timbre, but in truth the basis of the difference lies not just in the design of the instruments, but also in the tastes and culture of their players. More so than in other countries, the general brass sonority of Russian and central European orchestras is led by trumpets. The Moscow orchestra's trumpets play with a searing, penetrating sound which the trombonists seem to be straining to match. Added to this, the horns play with a constant fast vibrato which colours the overall tutti sound.

American orchestras of the same period play with a surprisingly modern sound. Even the 1924 recording of Strauss's *Tod und Verklärung* by the New York Philharmonic with Mengelberg[24] contains hints of the performance style that was to be common in the closing decades of the twentieth century, and indeed of the imposing influence that American trombone playing was to have. By the 1930s, three processes had created the basis for an American-led standardization of orchestral trombone style in the second half of the century. First, the infrastructure for orchestral playing increased exponentially in the USA: there were more orchestras, a continued increase of music-making in the US armed forces, the growth of the high school band movement, and an expansion of American conservatoire education. Secondly, a music culture developed that was strongly influenced by immigrant European players and conductors. The entire trombone section of the Boston Symphony Orchestra at the start of the century was German. In New York, Italians, Scandinavians, French players and more Germans sought work in the symphony orchestras. Even before the start of the century, US orchestras had enticed the most celebrated European conductors across the Atlantic. Walter Damrosch was with the New York Symphony by 1881; Frederick Stock became conductor of the Chicago Symphony Orchestra in 1905, after ten years as a violist in the orchestra, and a period as assistant conductor (from 1899); in 1906 in Boston, Karl Muck was appointed in succession to Nikisch and a line of other Europeans; by the end of the first decade of the twentieth century the orchestras in Cincinnati, Philadelphia, Minneapolis and St Louis all had European conductors, and more were to come. The third, and perhaps ultimately the most emphatic, factor that made the USA such a powerful force was that American brass instruments and trombones in particular were of so high a quality that American players, now among the most discerning in the world, could disregard foreign imports as second-rate. The Conn, Olds, Holton and King instrument companies were producing trombones with new designs and to a consistently high quality of craftsmanship. Conn's influence was particularly important, especially the work of its research and development unit, initially under the leadership of Leland Greenleaf and later Earle Kent. Their scientific approach to the design of trombones resulted directly or indirectly (through imitation by other makers) in the manufacture of some of the most popular orchestral trombones of the twentieth century.

Recordings made by American symphony orchestras in the 1930s show trombone sections to be making an essentially modern sound, but individual US orchestras quickly developed distinctive identities. It is possible to draw a fascinating comparison by examining recordings of Sibelius's Second Symphony made within five years of each other: by the Boston orchestra under Koussevitzky in 1935,[25] and by the NBC Symphony Orchestra under Toscanini in 1940.[26] Sibelius deployed trombones extensively in this symphony, and exposed passages for the trombone section are easy to find for the purpose of comparison. At the opening of the final movement, Koussevitzky asks for a smooth, subtle phrasing from the trombones. The repeated ostinato passage has a definite but slightly restrained sound, and the short fanfare-like motifs, to which each member of the section contributes, are round and majestic. The Toscanini recording could hardly be more different: the ostinato figure is played with a spiked, rapier-like staccato, and the fanfare motifs are piercing and aggressive, with hard, brittle articulations. These differences seem to be as much a product of the two conductors' readings of the trombone's orchestral idiom as of their interpretations of Sibelius's music.

Orchestral playing in the second half of the twentieth century

The re-formation of orchestras after the Second World War can be taken as a marker for the start of change in trombone orchestral style throughout the world. It did not happen uniformly and immediately, but the transformation of style that occurred over the next fifty years can be traced to that moment. Most orchestras were essentially re-formed with players who had spent their war and subsequent conscription service in military bands. These wartime and post-war military bands – on both sides of the Atlantic – were of an extraordinarily high standard. Many young players who were demobilized from them entered the orchestral profession either directly or after a relatively brief period in one of the conservatoires.

In the USA the level of continuity was somewhat greater than it was in Europe, even though many leading players were engaged in military service. But most American orchestras experienced relatively modest interruption compared to the near-total shutdown of orchestral music that occurred in Europe. Also, musical life in the USA benefited through the 1930s and 40s from the fabulously gifted conductors who held posts there. These conductors did not merely direct performances. They were orchestral trainers who imposed a critical influence on orchestral discipline and style: in New York, Rodzinski, Walter, Mitropoulos and Stokowski; in Los Angeles, Klemperer and Wallenstein; in Cleveland, Rodzinski, Leinsdorf and Szell; in Philadelphia, Ormandy and Stokowski; and Monteux in Boston. American trombone sections were made up of skilled players who had no option but to be dedicated to high orchestral standards. It is clear that some of the pre-war trombone sections in

European orchestras were exceptional, but between 1945 and 1950 American players regained sectional playing skills faster than players in the more economically pressurized and expedient climates of such countries as England.

American orchestras were richer and in some respects more ambitious than their European counterparts, and conductors could afford to impose exacting standards. George Szell at Cleveland was ruthless in his demands on players. When he engaged Robert Boyd as principal trombone in 1948, he charged him to rehearse the trombone section every minute they were offstage in paid rehearsal time: '"Take the trombones downstairs and rehearse them – chorales, other symphony parts, everything!" If the section in toto was not to his specifications,' Boyd recalled, 'I'd hear about it.'[27] The elevated standards of US sections also came from the players themselves. The three regular trombonists in the New York Philharmonic section in the immediate post-war years were Gordon Pulis, Lewis Van Haney and the bass trombonist Allen Ostrander. In the first couple of years they were together, they rehearsed privately for two or three full sessions a week. Pulis believed they acquired section skills by 'playing trios, working out the parts together and playing chorales'.[28] Ostrander considered that 'the difference between a good orchestra and a *really* good orchestra is how well they play the unimportant parts. Everyone studies all of the excerpts and they can play those important parts. The rest is musical punctuation and we as trombonists play a lot of those parts . . . this bread and butter playing should be done meticulously.'[29]

This type of sophistication was not unheard of in Europe, because trombone sections in orchestras such as those of Berlin, Vienna, Amsterdam and Dresden were playing with astonishingly high standards and clearly distinctive styles before the war; but the war changed everything – it even diluted or erased memories of pre-war playing cultures and styles. In England the quality of orchestral playing had risen too. In the later 1940s Henry Wood, whose memory of British orchestral playing stretched back to Victorian times, claimed that the tone quality in all sections of the modern orchestra had improved.[30] However, the changes to take place in orchestral trombone sound in the next decades would be unprecedented, and this came as a generation of youthful post-war trombonists – Denis Wick, Arthur Wilson, Evan Watkin, Derek James and Harold Nash – were about to enter the music profession.

The change came from the impact of American orchestral sectional trombone playing, initially on British players, then on other European orchestral players. The British trombonist Denis Wick identified the appearance of the New York Philharmonic Orchestra at the Edinburgh Festival in 1951 as 'the seed which germinated in the 1950s, and which eventually flowered in the 1960s'[31] to raise the standard of British orchestral playing. The impact in those grim post-war years is easy to understand. The orchestra itself was extraordinarily efficient, and not only were American trombone sections superbly groomed, but they also played on wide-bore, US-made instruments with wide, deep mouthpieces that contrasted sharply with the narrow-bore 'peashooter' instruments that were still in use in the UK. (Ills. 70 and 71) Even the wider-bore British models were heavy and unyielding in comparison. It is easy to see why the 1951 Edinburgh concerts by the Philharmonic Symphony Orchestra of New York made such an impact. The previous year the visiting orchestra was the French National Radio Orchestra of Paris under Beecham, which played two or three concerts that were well appreciated, and there were also some performances by British orchestras. When the Americans came in 1951, the two conductors were Bruno Walter and Dimitri Mitropoulos. The orchestra performed at the Usher Hall every night between 22 August and 4 September, with a completely different programme each night. (Ill. 72) The symphonies alone provided an exhibition for orchestral trombone repertoire: Brahms's Second, Bruckner's Fourth, Prokofiev's Fifth, Vaughan Williams's Fourth, Schubert's Ninth and Rachmaninov's Second.

Illustration 70. The trombone section of the London Symphony Orchestra in the late 1940s. (From the right) William Bell, tuba; Frederick Mansfield, bass trombone; and the tenor trombone players Ernest Benton and John ('Jock') Ashby. The players play narrow-bore, B flat tenor and G bass instruments. (By permission of the London Symphony Orchestra Archives.)

American instruments had many qualities that made them attractive to British and eventually European orchestral players. Of course, instruments varied from maker to maker, but in comparison with the narrow-bore instruments that British players used, they were immediately perceived as superior. They were capable of being played so that the underlying timbre was more or less constant across the entire pitch and dynamic range. Even when played very high and loudly, the sound maintained its integrity and did not fracture so as to sound boisterous and brassy. At lower dynamic levels the instruments produced a full, mellow, but focused sound that was especially effective for sectional playing. The instruments held their intonation well, and they were also exceptionally well made. They were relatively light, with free-moving and well-aligned slides. Thumb valves were well designed and they required relatively little compensation on the part of the player to hit a true intonation. They also *looked* good compared to European instruments. Lacquered brass and the coppery reddish colour of Conn's

Illustration 71. The trombone section of the Philharmonic Symphony Orchestra of New York in 1950, with wide-bore, American-made instruments. The players are (from the left) Gordon Pulis, Lewis Van Haney, Allen Ostrander, and the tuba player William Bell (no relation of William Bell the LSO tuba player of the same era). (By permission of the New York Philharmonic Archives.)

'Coprion' bells were aesthetically pleasing. The aesthetic quality of these instruments was important, for it made them distinctive (compared to British models) and desirable, and players felt confident about them. A range of wide, deep mouthpieces was available that helped players get a more sonorous sound. But the most important factor was the subjective element: they were felt to be much more responsive than British and French peashooters and the larger-bore but much less yielding instruments used in Germany, Russia and central Europe. The American instruments allowed players to execute a wide range of articulations and cultivate what were felt to be new shades of tone colour. Whereas the old narrow-bore British and French instruments conditioned a player's sound and articulation to a particular mould, and the wider Austro-German and eastern European were equally restrictive, even if in a different direction, the American instruments seemed to liberate the player and place authority more squarely with him. The instruments also seemed easier to play. Irrespective of what nineteenth- and early twentieth-century European makers had said in their promotional literature, and also irrespective of how well instruments such as those by Schmidt and Lätzsch were played by orchestral players, just about every one of the instruments they produced had been designed for, or emphatically influenced by, the needs of military bands. The American wide-bore instruments were the first to be specifically conceived for symphony orchestra players who would perform in purpose-built symphony halls: the Conn 8H and 88H models were actually called 'Symphony Trombones'.

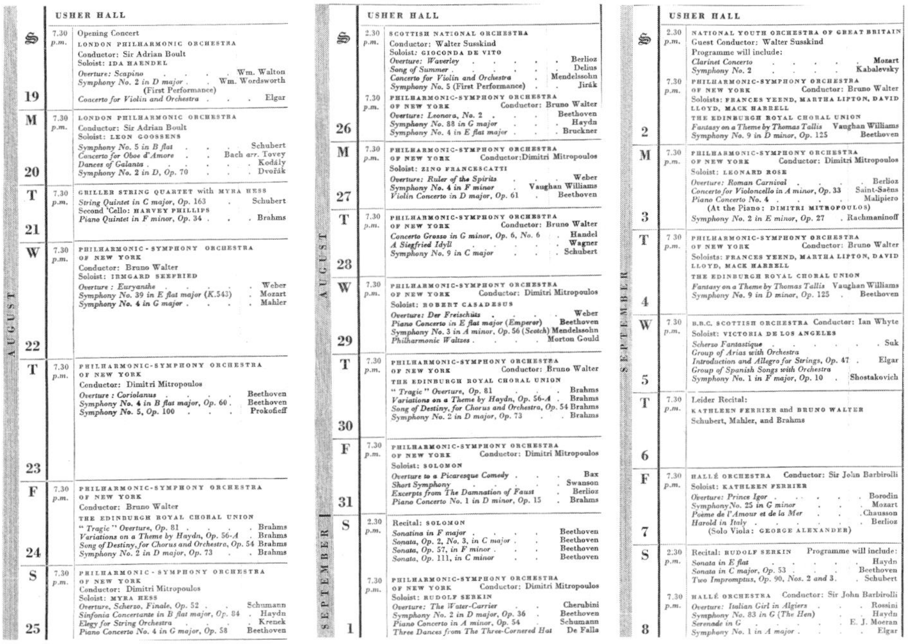

Illustration 72. Programmes performed by the Philharmonic Symphony Orchestra of New York at the Edinburgh Festival in 1951. Twelve different programmes were performed in fourteen days.

The adoption of American instruments was not without cost. As Denis Wick, who was principal trombone of the London Symphony Orchestra, and one of the first to take up the new wider-bored instrument, recognized:

> By using large, deep mouthpieces they gained smoothness, richness, better loud-quality, greater dynamic range, but at the price of a certain anonymity in soft playing, greater problems in pointed staccato and high register and a kind of identikit similarity between individuals and sections that robbed each orchestra of some of its character.[32]

These words, uttered in 1973, were prophetic of the phenomenon of the globalization of orchestral sound that could soon be witnessed in modern orchestral recordings. There had been some points of resistance: in the late 1940s, George Szell insisted that the trombone section of the Cleveland orchestra abandon their King instruments and play a full set of Schmidt trombones in imitation of Szell's nostalgic recollection of the pre-war Vienna Philharmonic. He also required the use of a Schlott alto trombone for appropriate repertoire. One of the instruments so acquired came from Chicago where, ironically, the trombone section had been made to abandon Schmidt instruments in 1947 at the behest of Rodzinski. The move to German instruments in Cleveland was not successful. Despite Szell's idolizing of the beauty of their sound, to Robert Boyd 'It really wasn't that beautiful . . . for we were always fighting it'.[33] The experiment lasted just a couple of years, until a compromise was reached with Szell whereby the tenor trombonists found US trombones that produced a wide sound broadly analogous to that of the Schmidt instruments.[34]

Wider-bore instruments were adopted in British orchestras in the 1950s and 60s, as standards of playing (and teaching) became consistently higher. The conditions under which orchestral players worked also became generally more stable and favourable, and many orchestras moved into large new concert halls that were built as part of post-war regeneration. These new venues had an effect on the way trombonists played, but the effect was not consistently the same. Edward Herman of the New York Philharmonic had to change mouthpieces when the orchestra moved to Avery Fisher Hall, saying that they could 'no longer play so loud. Most of the time we play half-loud because the hall is so brilliant – so bright and so live.'[35] Trombonists are especially susceptible to the effects of acoustics, and this often creates some ambiguity between conductors and players. Peter Harvey, who was bass trombone with the BBC Symphony Orchestra in the late 1960s, recalled conductors in the Royal Festival Hall appealing to trombone players for 'more, more', but being disappointed when the dynamic increased. 'What they really wanted and could not express or get was not more volume but more definition – more focus in the sound.'[36]

Globalization and twentieth-century values

Many writers have observed that the most telling feature of orchestral sound in the twentieth century has been an incremental shift from difference to sameness. The conductor Simon Rattle, who believes that recordings actually make orchestras play better, also sees a downside: 'The problem is the effect they have on people's performances: everything tends to come out sounding more and more the same.'[37] The sound of the wind and brass has been an important factor in this process. Robert Philip has pointed out:

> There had grown up a norm for a smoothly blended orchestral sound and style, based, particularly in the wind, on an American/European compromise, in which there was much less room for diversity than there used to be. There are still orchestras that have distinct characteristics of their own, but the differences are narrowing all the time.[38]

Philip gives the example of a visit to Britain in the 1960s of the Leningrad Philharmonic. Audiences were taken aback by the 'blaring vibrancy' of the brass in climactic moments. When the orchestra returned in the 1990s as the St Petersburg Philharmonic, they brought two brass sections: the 'old guard' and a younger set attuned to western preferences for instruments, style and sound. The older style can be detected in French recordings made in the late 1940s (for example, Ansermet's recording of Rimsky-Korsakov's *Sheherazade* with the Paris Conservatoire Orchestra[39]), and in recordings of central European orchestras made even as late as the 1960s; the April 1964 recording of Shostakovich's *Festive Overture* made by the Czech Philharmonic Orchestra with Karel Ančerl, for example,[40] is still replete with the full-frontal brass sound. An interesting glimpse of the vanishing culture of central European playing can also be caught on a recording of Romantic solo music, *Sonntagsposaunenstück*, made in 1998–9 by the German trombonist Sebastian Krause with the organist Gabriele Wadewitz.[41] The recording is marred slightly by an over-resonant acoustic, but not so much as to mask Krause's considerable ability as a player. The sound is vibrant, sometimes strident, with a wide vibrato applied at appropriate points. Krause uses an instrument made by Karl Mönnich of Erlbach in the Vogtland, which still retains many features of nineteenth-century Saxon instruments.

It is probably in the territories of eastern Germany that the older style of playing has lasted longest. In 2004 the brass players of the Dresden Staatskapelle were still playing with a distinctive style. They used European-made rotary valve trumpets and wide-bore, large-belled trombones, producing a sound which the conductor Bernard Haitink has described as distinctive and 'round', and which he recognizes as one of the primary features that makes the orchestra sound different from others.[42] The trombonists of the Dresden Staatskapelle make a different sound from many other orchestras in western Europe and the USA; it is hugely attractive, but, one suspects, not as different as was made by their mid-twentieth-century predecessors.

In the 1970s, the extent to which commonality replaced individuality was yet more striking. The reasons for this are well known: increased availability of foreign instruments, the ubiquitous presence of foreign players in orchestras in western Europe, the availability of recordings and the further rise of the itinerant orchestral conductor. One sometimes hears resonances of older styles, but they are reduced to the most subtle of nuances. By the 1990s, recordings revealed few signs of strong national trombone styles; the performances of the St Petersburg Philharmonic Orchestra in the BBC Proms in the summer of 2004, for example, confirmed that the globalization of the trombone section was virtually complete. But one of the striking things about orchestral trombone playing in the twentieth century is that the general standard became increasingly higher. This seems to be borne out both by subjective impression and by what we see in documentary (and often recorded sound) evidence.[43] Economic stability, improved education systems and the opportunities available in those countries fortunate enough to have them, have produced a greater number of players who aspire to the orchestral profession. In consequence, the cream from this greater mass is that much richer. Another feature of the later twentieth century is the increase in the number of women trombonists who train for, or obtain, positions as professionals. This development is not unprecedented. Several women trombone players are listed in nineteenth-century musicians' directories, and in the inter-war years the trombonist Maisie Ringham had a particularly distinguished career with the Hallé Orchestra. The novelty of the more recent increase in the number of women players is that there are more of them, and a greater proportion are routinely achieving distinction in both modern and period instrument groups. In 2003 one of London's leading orchestras, the BBC Symphony Orchestra, for the first time appointed a woman, Helen Vollam, as one of its principal trombone players.

The very best orchestral players are probably as good as or better than any of their predecessors. But what are their priorities and preoccupations as orchestral performers? One thing for sure is that the best of them are perfectionists and that in the age of digital recordings our expectations of players are matched only by the expectations they have of themselves. Robert Philip has pointed out that when Berlioz's *Symphonie Fantastique* was recorded with the Paris Symphony Orchestra under Monteux in 1931, the work was split into twelve segments to fit onto half a dozen 78 rpm disks. The takes that were accepted and used were: 1 3 2 2 1 1 2 2 3 2 2 3. Thus, only three segments needed more than two takes. The case of Stravinsky's recording of *The Rite of Spring* with the Straram Orchestra in 1929 is yet more impressive. Five of the ten segments were recorded on the first take, and the remainder on the second.[44] In modern recordings of the same works, it would not be unusual if there were to be more than a hundred takes, and for them to be the subject of any amount of digital ingenuity before the final product were released. It is small wonder then that what we hear on modern orchestral CDs lacks nothing except a feeling of spontaneity, and the same is true of solo recordings. We should not wonder why the process of globalization has occurred, when recordings are produced in this manner for a world market.

Despite this element of unreality, there is a very real sense in which the technique of orchestral players since the Second World War can be seen to have attained a level of subtlety and intelligence that is unprecedented. All the available evidence shows that the best orchestral players are untroubled by technical challenges of the fast, high and loud sort, but are preoccupied by matters of a very different kind. They are interested in issues surrounding articulation, timbre, orchestral ensemble and intonation. These elements are seldom a focus in their own right, but they absorb professional players in the context of the orchestral soundscape. In 1979, the trombone section of the Boston Symphony Orchestra (Ronald Barron, Norman Bolter and Gordon Hallberg) offered advice on how players should prepare for the orchestral profession.[45] Each of them extolled the value of looking beyond the trombone – of knowing a whole work and not the parts of it that are cited in the orchestral excerpts books. Norman Bolter spoke of the need for players to listen to

Example 12.2. Franz Schubert, Symphony in B minor ('Unfinished') D759 (1822), second movement, bars 286–90
The perceived difficulty for the bass trombone in this section comes not from its technical challenge but from its exposure within the orchestral texture at the very end of the work.

singers and string players, whose musicality had attracted great repertoire. This advice will strike a chord with any teachers who have lamented their students' dizzy preoccupation with technique at the expense of musicianship.

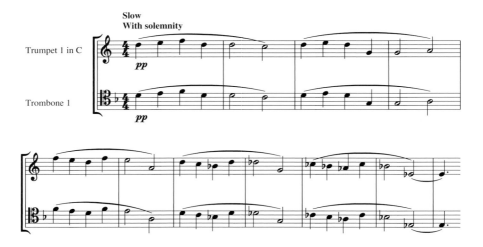

Example 12.3. Frederick Delius, *Brigg Fair* (1907), Reh. No. 26
Apparently simple, but seen by some of the finest players as especially challenging.

The finest players also express concern for pure intonation. This is an especially interesting facet of the best orchestral trombone playing, because players often feel a need (sometimes even a responsibility) to mediate in the finest nuances of orchestral performance. This is the subtlest of points, but professional trombone players often sense an intonational variance that is given apparent emphasis by the clash of the timbre of the trombone with another instrument. Allen Ostrander identified a short, unobtrusive line in the last movement of Schubert's 'Unfinished' Symphony as 'the most difficult entrance in the whole piece' because 'I have to fit in with the bassoon'.[46] (Ex. 12.2) This recollection calls to mind a conversation I once had with Evan Watkin, who was the iconic principal trombone with the Royal Philharmonic Orchestra when I was a student. Watkin was a superlative player, and he occasionally stood in for my regular teacher, the great Arthur Wilson of the Philharmonia, when he was on tour. I once asked Watkin what was the most difficult piece to play. His reply could not have been more immediate. He identified a section of Delius's *Brigg Fair*, a quiet, middle-range, slow-moving melody which is played in octave unison with the first trumpet. (Ex. 12.3) I could see that the intervals were angular, but I saw no real challenge and said so. He shot me a 'you are missing the point' look and murmured, 'It is in unison with the first *trumpet*.'

Chapter 13

Jazz

Since the High Renaissance no single creative movement or style has had a more powerful and radical influence on the idioms of trombone playing than jazz. The vernacular practices that contributed to the origins of jazz signalled a fracture in the linear heritage of art and sacred music styles. New and more instinctive modes of performance emerged that were to lead to entirely fresh explorations of the trombone's capabilities. Even by the start of the twentieth century, the marching bands of New Orleans, as well as more widely distributed ragtime players, used techniques and styles that contributed to an entirely new musical language. They helped shape modes of musical communication that were invested with a spontaneity and energy quite different from anything with which trombone players had previously engaged. By the end of the century what had started as a vernacular, light and, as some felt, subversive form of music was recognized as the platform for some of the world's greatest virtuosi. The best jazz trombonists – and a bewildering number of them deserve that description – are among the greatest players ever to have held the instrument.

The trombone has always been in the foreground of jazz. It has been conspicuous in just about every jazz style that has emerged, and is a member of what Barry Kernfeld has described as the 'tightly circumscribed body of instruments' that have made up the 'Instrumentarium of Jazz'.[1] Even from the earliest days when jazz was discernible as a distinctive musical form, a procession of great trombone players have played as sidemen and bandleaders. Many have exhibited stunning virtuosity and an abundance of creative originality and flare, and formed new ideas about technique and idiom. Even by the 1920s it was obvious that two important and apparently contradictory processes were active. First, the multifaceted techniques and styles of the jazz trombone were shaping an idiom quite distinct from that passed down through the formal traditions of art music – compared to the best orchestral trombonists, the best jazz players were displaying a no less convincing but entirely different form of eloquence. Secondly, the new jazz idiom was penetrating and influencing almost every other form of music – including art music – in which the trombone was played and written for. By the middle of the twentieth century, jazz had transformed the meaning of words such as 'virtuosity' and 'lyricism' for trombone players.

Jazz arose from somewhat obscure beginnings to become a visibly discrete, distinctive and mature mode of expression in an amazingly short time. Its origins cannot be attributed to a single nucleus, but rather to the confluence of a wide range of musical, social and cultural elements. We can now reflect on widely acknowledged eras or style periods of jazz and the several sub-sets that have developed within them. But these various and complex phases were not linear, and an overview based merely on the succession of these periods could be confusing. Players who were almost directly contemporary pursued careers and exploited modes of expression that seemed to belong to entirely different ages. For example, the trombonist Edward 'Kid' Ory (c. 1890–1973), whom many see as quintessentially representative of the early New Orleans style, was still in his professional prime when J. J. Johnson (1924–2001) was making his first decisive impact in the 1940s with his particular brand of virtuosic expression. Also, many trombonists passed contentedly and deftly from one creative mode to another; for example, at various stages in his illustrious career Albert Mangelsdorff (1928–2005) traversed cool jazz, hard bop, free jazz and jazz rock. It follows that any attempt to construct a neat linear history of jazz trombone playing will be at best optimistically speculative and at worst positively misleading.

While many jazz trombonists used technical devices that were precedented in the art tradition, the very best added something new. It is this originality, as well as technical facility, that singles out the great and important players from those who were perhaps neither so great nor so important. If any single element is common to the best of them, it is that virtually every trombone player who has impacted upon jazz in a significant way has done so by making emphatic, idiosyncratic and distinctive musical statements. To put it somewhat differently, they have communicated something new in a tone of voice the accent of which is often difficult to place. Almost always, the novelty of these players' styles has been unmannered and genuine rather than forced, contrived or overly referential to traditional playing orthodoxies. The evidence of this musical integrity is exemplified not just in abundant recordings but also by the information available in documentary narratives – especially the oral history sources – that are so important to the study of jazz history. These sources and the recorded legacy show that jazz, more than any other form of trombone playing that has existed since the opening decades of the sixteenth century, places authority in the hands of the performer rather than the composer. It follows that the story of jazz trombone playing reveals not just a rich treasure of performances but an intriguing process of change.

One of the most complex issues to deal with is the question of influence: who influenced whom, what were the channels of influence, who were the mentors and the authentic inventors of one performance trait or another? While it is possible to detect players who have been influential and others who have been the subjects of influence, it is dangerous to draw too many conclusions. A case in point is that of Jimmy Harrison, one of the first really great jazz trombonists to have exploited a solo style based on a robust technical virtuosity. Harrison's playing even before 1920 was characterized as having a 'trumpet' style, and this has been attributed to the influence of Louis Armstrong. But according to another great player, Dickie Wells, who knew Harrison at that time, 'Harrison was the first man to play in that style. I was a kid in Louisville when I first heard Jimmy in 1921. At that time he had never heard Louis in person, nor had he heard any of the King Oliver records.'[2]

Jazz trombonists have never been slow to acknowledge players they admire, but they also place a high currency on individuality. This is a persistent theme in the oral histories of players, who stress differences as much as they do similarities in playing styles. Few cite a single influence, but rather a seminal experience such as membership of a band, their earliest training or the impact of a particular circle of players. The New Orleans trombonist Georg Brunis summarized an attitude that emerges in the utterances of most players in the first half of the century: '[Young players] should get the fundamentals . . . listen to records and listen to the ideas, try to improvise the ideas, be original, don't imitate them.'[3] Brunis cites the names of Lou McGarity, Miff Mole and Jack Teagarden as the stellar mentors, but if there is one name that emerges consistently, it is not a trombone player at all, but (perhaps predictably) Louis Armstrong. Armstrong's pervasive influence on jazz touched trombonists as much as other instrumentalists. Lawrence Brown, one of the great 1930s trombonists with the Ellington band, worked with him on the west coast in 1930 and thought of him as the player 'who made me enjoy coming to work'.[4] There is little unanimity in jazz trombonists' rankings of each other. In 1942 Jack Teagarden and Tommy Dorsey were asked to name their ten favourite trombonists. Both placed each other at the top of their lists, but otherwise the only names common to both were Miff Mole, Jack Jenny and J. C. Higginbotham.[5] A thorough study of jazz trombone playing could fill a substantial book. My intention here is much more modest: to map the story of some of the major players, and the techniques and idioms they developed.

New Orleans

By the end of the nineteenth century, ragtime and other 'hot music' precursors of jazz were to be heard in New Orleans. Trombonists active in early jazz bands had a variety of musical backgrounds; many had been introduced to music as players of other instruments and had switched to the trombone expediently, because a playing opportunity or a vacant instrument became available. The most common early playing experience for jazz trombonists was in church bands, marching bands and the various forms of dance bands that existed at that time. Churches used bands to accompany worship, and many players cite their exposure to the sound of congregational singing as their first memorable musical experience. No particular denomination held a monopoly; some of the best players were Baptists and Episcopalians, but many (including the great Kid Ory) were Catholics. Marching bands were important because they were so conspicuous in the musical and social landscape, and they nurtured many musical devices – such as the ostinato patterns or 'riffs' – that were to be digested into jazz style. These bands also seem to have been among the key environments in which early players gained their first experience of a proto-professional musical existence. Entry into the musical profession proper was often via dance bands, which were the source for regular, if somewhat precarious, employment. From the 1870s, marching 'brass' bands were important focuses for vernacular music-making, and an essential backdrop for community rituals. There was a hierarchy of brass bands; some – particularly the Creole-dominated bands such as the Onward and Excelsior bands – were especially sophisticated and prided themselves on their musical taste. Most were fairly small, with about a dozen members, and they usually carried two valve trombones. They were well run and musically coherent, but not all brass band players appear to have been musically literate; it is certainly true that musical literacy was not a prerequisite for entry into jazz as a profession. The drummer Baby Dodds drew a distinction between Creole and 'uptown' musicians on the grounds that the latter 'weren't good enough to play with [the Creoles] . . . because most of the uptown musicians didn't read music'.[6] Most of the dance bands appear to have played 'head arrangements' (arrangements that were determined in rehearsal but not written down), and the instrumentation of these bands – both front line and rhythm sections – closely matched those of the first jazz bands. There was no consistent pattern of learning. Some players took formal music lessons with local 'professors of music', but others picked up playing skills entirely by rote. As traditional marching bands coexisted with proto-jazz bands, individual members of marching bands became more celebrated. The trumpeter Lee Collins recalled an annual carriage drivers' parade in which the bands included 'Joe Oliver, Bunk Johnson, Tig [Chambers], Buddy Petit and lots more'.[7] Honore Dutrey, who was King Oliver's trombonist in Chicago, played with the Excelsior Band, and Oliver himself played cornet with the Onward Brass Band.

   One of the most influential New Orleans 'professors' at the turn of the century was Dave Perkins (c. 1868–1926), himself a trombone player, who is said to have exhibited an instinctive and relaxed style. Perkins played drums as well as trombone, and made a living as a player, bandleader and teacher. He played with the Reliance Brass Band and the Toca Brass Band. In 1968, in an interview with the jazz historian Richard Allen, the New Orleans drummer Jack Laine – by then a very old man – spoke of the influence of Perkins, whom he regarded as the most important of the trombone players and band teachers working in New Orleans in the late nineteenth and early twentieth centuries. According to Laine: 'Dave mixed up that stuff real good. He taught me and my older brothers how to play it. We called it ragtime but it was good jazz. The only difference was we played it much slower.'[8]

   As with other forms of popular music in the nineteenth century, the new styles came not from a single source but from the fusion of several different vernacular and more elite influences. We do not have the full range of sources from which to draw reliable conclusions about all tributaries of influence, but it is certain that a hybrid combination of cultures and instincts played a part in forming new techniques of playing as well as musical genres. By the late 1880s, New Orleans was a cosmopolitan town with a sophisticated and thriving musical life. In addition to popular music there were two opera houses and other places that provided musical entertainment. In the first three months of 1864 alone, 150 licences were issued by the town's administrators for balls and other musical events. The 1870 census listed 222 musicians, teachers and practitioners of other musical trades. Eighty per cent of these were of foreign birth: 44% German, Austrian or Swiss, 15% French, 10% Italian and a handful from other countries. Of the 20% born in the USA, about a quarter (5% of the whole) were African-American.[9] However, a change was taking place which saw black and other coloured musicians making an increasing impact on musical life. By the turn of the century the proportion of non-white musicians had increased exponentially. At the start of 1888, the trade magazine *Metronome* published the complaint: 'We have some twenty to twenty-five bands averaging twelve men apiece.

The coloured race monopolises the procession music to a great extent as they are not regular workers at any trade, as are most of the white players, no merit in any of these [*sic*].'[10] Relatively few marching bands had more than two trombones, and many had just one. There was usually also a tuba or euphonium. One rarely encounters a bass or alto trombone, though it is not uncommon to find a soprano trombone.

Valve trombones were much more common at the start of the century than slide instruments, though it was at about this time that the slide instrument began to gain in popularity. The only known photograph of the Buddy Bolden band – believed to have been taken in 1905 – shows the trombone player Willie Cornish with a short-model valve trombone (Chapter 9, Ill. 53). A 1904 photograph of the Mathews Band of Lockport, Louisiana, shows one slide trombone and two valve trombone players along with two euphoniums and four cornets. But generally, while it seems likely that the instrumental line-up of marching bands owes more to expediency than design, it can usually be assumed that the trombone is present, in either slide or valve form. There was no shortage of musical instruments, especially brass. Cheap second-hand trombones were in circulation, and both mail order firms and local retailers did a good trade. By the early twentieth century, players of even modest circumstances were able to acquire trombones – even new ones – for $10 or less. Deferred payment schemes were available and pawn shops seem to have stocked a wide selection of second-hand trombones.

Tailgate

There was no standard format for early jazz bands, but trumpet or more often cornet and clarinet were the most common treble instruments, and the trombone was also omnipresent in the frontline. The earliest jazz trombone style to have been dignified by a name is 'tailgate'. The term derives from the practice of bands playing out of the rear of the stationary or moving wagons that carried some form of advertising hoarding. The trombonist literally sat over the tailgate of the wagon with the slide pointing to the rear. However, while this may explain the origin of the name, it offers little by way of description of the tailgate style, which became one of the characteristics of early New Orleans and Dixie players.

Tailgate proper could be played only by slide trombonists, because the style relied fundamentally on the exploitation of particular aspects of true portamento or glissando trombone idiom. It follows that it emerged after the slide trombone began to take over from the valve instrument around the turn of the century, though it is possible that its precursors were developed by valve trombonists.[11] Its structural origins can probably be found in the patterns that trombonists played in marching bands, which included melodic conjunctions and countermelodies to the treble instruments, and punctuations that marked and emphasized harmonic progressions. The most typical feature of tailgate, and the one that can be most easily mimicked, is the liberal application of rough portamento or glissando (which early jazz trombonists often called 'slide', 'smear' or 'slur'). Glissando itself was not new; it was used to accompany circus acts in the nineteenth century and was embedded in ragtime ensemble playing. A number of tightly controlled and overly disciplined recordings of ragtime from about 1905 by leading New York concert bands featured decorative glissandos, but the technique was probably employed in a more relaxed and improvised way in earlier New Orleans marching bands.[12] In early jazz the glissando effect was often emphasized by growls or sharp crescendos as the slide was moved. Some early trombonists made a distinction between 'tailgate' and 'vamp', though it is far from clear how commonly such distinctions were understood. The latter was supposed to be a largely utilitarian rhythmic/harmonic function (probably derived from the practices of marching bands, and based on extended ostinatos or 'riffs'), but the former was seen as more decorative, imaginative and integral to the primary ideas of a piece.[13] Cadences and anacruses were often given particular strength by rhythmic emphasis and glissando. But tailgate trombonists also played breaks, countermelodies and more extended solo passages. The best early New Orleans jazz trombonists – and there were many excellent players – were capable of technical accuracy, and they employed the tailgate style with considerable panache.

Perhaps the most famous exponent of tailgate was Kid Ory. (Ill. 73) Ory was a fine and charismatic player who became well known because his output of recordings was so great. His somewhat predictable and slapstick playing in such pieces as 'Ory's Creole Trombone' (1922) do not reveal the depth of his ability. Like many New Orleans players, he travelled to Chicago, New York and elsewhere, and became part of the national jazz scene. Eddie 'Daddy' Edwards (1891–1963), the trombonist on many of the all-white Original Dixieland Jazz Band recordings, was equally impressive, as was Georg Brunis (1902–74), another white player who was a defining influence among New Orleans trombonists (and, according to Jack Teagarden, the first trombonist he ever remembered really listening to). Brunis was the best known

Illustration 73. The trombone player Edward 'Kid' Ory and his Woodland Band (named after the Woodland Plantation, La Place, Louisiana, where he was raised), taken in 1905. Ory plays a valve trombone. (Hogan Jazz Archive)

of one of the largest New Orleans jazz dynasties.[14] He was one of the original New Orleans Rhythm Kings, and went on to work with the Ted Lewis Orchestra and the Condon band in New York. Brunis was typical of a certain type of early player who seems to have been almost entirely instinctive and relatively untouched by formal learning systems and their attendant concerns. His interview with William Russell in 1958 reveals him as the antithesis of the tutored player:

> Did you ever practice?
> [shakes his head]
> Never warm up?
> Never warm up.[15]

Brunis credited his brother Henry with being the greatest jazz trombonist of New Orleans: 'I used to drool when that guy played, I wanted to throw that trombone in the hatrack.'[16] Brunis played beautifully in the middle range of the instrument, and his authoritative control of harmony can be heard in his 1943 recording of 'Tin Roof Blues'.

Another important figure in the New Orleans tradition was Nathan 'Jim' Robinson (1892–1976). Not only was he one of those who contributed to the prominence of the black New Orleans sound of the 1920s – he played on most of the Bunk Johnson sessions – but he was also a prominent figure in traditionalist revivals right up to the ascendancy of the Preservation Hall Band in the 1960s. Robinson offers as good an example as there is of the contrast between early jazz players and those trained in the conservatoire. He was originally a guitar player but took up the trombone in 1917 when he was in France with the US Army (many jazz players served time as musicians in the US forces), and was good enough to join the Sam Morgan Band on his return. He had a couple of teachers – Willie Foster and Charles 'Sunny' Henry – but his individuality is apparent on all his recordings. Like many players, he saw the distinctiveness of his playing style as his strongest feature: he claimed to have made his 'own style'.[17]

One of the many players who were dubbed 'Mr Tailgate' (the name was applied in print to Ory, Brunis, Robinson and probably a few more) was the lesser-known Santo Pecora (1902–84).[18] He played with the New Orleans Rhythm Kings in the mid-1920s, and he is heard to great effect in the recording of his own 'I never knew what a gal could do'.[19] He joined big bands in the 1930s, became a studio player and was featured in movies, but he returned to his New Orleans roots in the 1950s and to small ensembles. There were many other masters of the early style; two who adopted a more restrained style were Honore Dutrey and the New York-born Benny Morton, who played with Henry 'Red' Allen.

The tailgate style is relatively easy to imitate by inserting a judicious collection of rough glissandos and growls into a deeply predictable underlying chord pattern: lesser attempts to adopt it in traditionalist revivals have resulted in unflattering parodies, the shallowness of which early jazz players have been quick to condemn. It is neither fair nor accurate to see tailgate as little more than a primitive form of musical decoration characterized by the constant use of a crude vibrato, predictable and formulaic counterpoint and the gratuitous use of glissando. There can be little doubt that there were bad tailgate players and that the style developed organically rather than studiedly, but the best tailgate trombonists were accurate and sophisticated players. Their application of glissando is a case in point. It is often thought that tailgate players used glissando because they lacked the slide technique to enunciate clear phrases and articulations – that glissando was a consequence of and a camouflage for the limited techniques of the players. This idea is not entirely without substance. Georg Brunis claimed never to have been taught slide positions ('that came natural . . . I feel it, my heart puts my arm there'[20]); and Santo Pecora, who had a fairly sound education and was known as a good reader, claimed, 'it's a

Illustration 74. Frontispiece of Henry Fillmore's *Jazz Trombonist* (1919), a very early didactic method for the jazz idiom trombone.

funny thing, but when I hears a tune and the note is wrong, I can't play that note. I moves my slide. It looks like it drops away from me till I hits the right note.'[21] But on the other hand, several tailgate players perceived intervallic relationships clearly, and came to the slide trombone having had a thorough grounding in melodic improvisation on other instruments. In particular, a number of them were originally valve trombone players. Kid Ory's first trombone was actually a valve trombone 'with holes plugged with soap'. Ory[22] was literally a tailgate player, in that the first band in which he played in New Orleans, the Woodland Band, did indeed play out of a furniture wagon that carried advertising hoardings. When eventually he bought his 'first good trombone', this too was a valve instrument and it was some years before he switched to a slide trombone. Like many of the best players of his era, he applied glissando strategically and placed emphasis on sound quality ('My main thing is tone'), logic and understatement: 'It is always best to make less notes and to make them in line – the horn is like a voice.'[23]

Early virtuosi

The first player to emerge with a playing style that was distinctive and noticeably free of the elements of the tailgate tradition was the New York-born Miff Mole (1898–1961). Mole received a good musical education as a pianist before he became a trombone player, and he also played the violin and alto horn. Like many jazz players, he played in silent movies and theatres, but he was soon recognized as an exceptional trombone player with a clear sound and a clean, accurate and virtuosic technique. He exploited a wide tessitura with effortless fluidity, using short notes, grace notes and cadential decorations, and eschewing the tailgate characteristics. He recorded prolifically, and though his work with swing bands included stints with Paul Whiteman and Benny Goodman, his biggest impact was with the small groups in which he played, both earlier (with his own bands, and especially with Red Nichols) and subsequently (again with his own formations, and with Muggsy Spanier). Like many players of his time Mole had to balance commercial practicalities with artistic ambitions. Many of his recordings were with groups that employed populist gimmicks at the expense of creative zeal. A case in point is the Original Memphis Five, which recorded over a hundred sides in 1922 alone. It was supposed to be an east coast reincarnation of the Original Dixieland Jazz Band, but in truth its performances were heavily based on standard arrangements, and they often seem contrived and lacking the free spirit of the genuine New Orleans product.

Mole was enormously significant and, at his point of entry into the jazz arena, iconoclastic. His playing, particularly his accuracy and technical neatness, owes much to his classical training, but even his earliest recordings reveal him as a genuinely inventive exponent of jazz.[24] If there is one other player who can be said to have contributed significantly to the advent of this new era of trombone playing, it is probably Jimmy Harrison (1900–31). Harrison was born in Louisville, Kentucky, and was largely self-taught. After a brief time in theatres and with bands led by Charlie Johnson and Sam Wooding, he joined Fletcher Henderson's band in 1927 and stayed with it until his untimely death three years later. There is some doubt about the direction in which the influence flowed between him and Jack Teagarden, but it is certain that the two men knew and respected each other's playing. Some have dubbed Harrison 'the King of Swing'; others have called him the 'first modern jazz trombonist'. Fletcher Henderson regarded him as 'the greatest trombonist of his day' and Count Basie harboured similar sentiments. The impact of Harrison's playing – like that of Mole – came in large part from his distance from the tailgate style. The insights provided by his fellow bandsmen with Henderson suggest that

> he played with a definite positive attack. He did not use the slide except to get from one note to another and obtained his vibrato and tone with his lips. . . . He possessed a broad tone with a warm sensitive vibrato that gave his playing a lyricism that has seldom been equalled.[25]

Benny Morton claimed that Harrison's recorded legacy does no justice to the breadth and fluency of his playing. We can only imagine the extent of his influence on swing era trombonists, had he not died at the age of 31.[26]

Jack Teagarden, like Mole and Robinson, was responsible for moving jazz trombone playing to a freer, more lyrical, idiosyncratic and less formulaic mode of expression. Teagarden's playing also exhibited a more legato, blues-orientated style than had been previously heard. He was born in Vernon, Texas, in 1905, learned piano with his mother Helen from the age of five, and started playing the trombone when he was ten. The family was musical: his brother Charlie was an impressive trumpet player who featured on many of Jack's recordings. The two brothers both played with Whiteman. Jack Teagarden's playing was sophisticated and multifaceted. Many observers point to his exploitation of the upper register, and particularly his use of so-called alternative positions, as being novel – a view fuelled by Teagarden himself, who claimed he developed the technique as a child because his arms were too short to reach extended positions. In fact, while it is true that Teagarden tended to occupy the higher rather than the lower register of the instrument, he seldom extended his tessitura to extremities. Furthermore, his ability to play apparently seamlessly without forced portamento, impressive though it was, was shared by Mole, Harrison and most particularly by Tommy Dorsey, who was also born in 1905 and whose career opened up almost in parallel to Teagarden's.

Teagarden claimed that even as a child he wanted to play the trombone 'clean and right', and that many of the trombone players he heard were 'murdering the instrument'.[27] His was one of the most idiosyncratic styles of all: consistently brilliant, extending the idiom of the instrument and with a capacity to alter the timbre of his sound by tiny gradations to suit whatever he wanted to say musically. Like many truly virtuosic players, his easy and confident style often masked the extent of his virtuosity. It is possible to identify innovative touches in his playing: it is said, for instance, that he was the first jazz trombonist to use lip trills. In fact, he seldom used lip trills (unlike Trummy Young, for example, who mastered this technique), but peppered his solos, irrespective of their tempo, with fast graces, especially semitone mordents. He was also one of the first to use blue notes judiciously, and perhaps the first, or at least the most convincing, white player to employ a blues style and its attendant devices (evident in his singing as well as his playing) in a manner that was more typical of black jazz. Indeed, Fletcher Henderson is said to have approached him in hushed and conspiratorial tones to inquire, 'Tell me – and you have my strictest confidence – are you colored? . . . You can tell me . . . I won't say a word.'[28]

It is probably wrong, but nevertheless tempting, to make a comparison at the purely technical level between Teagarden and Louis Armstrong. Apart from the fact that the two men were virtuoso players and singers, they had what was said to be a near-perfect musical rapport and a long-standing personal friendship that had been initiated at the moment they first met with (so we are told) a bear hug. Teagarden's tumultuous personal life – his relationships with women and his financial affairs provided lucrative work for several lawyers – was somewhat at odds with the essentially relaxed and assured mode of expression that he perfected.[29]

The swing band players

The success of Tommy Dorsey (1905–56) as a long-line ballad soloist sometimes camouflages his prestige as a genuine mainstream jazz player. Born in Shenandoah, Kansas, he was taught by his father, who was the local brass band conductor. Though he attained some celebrity in small bands, it was with the big swing bands that he achieved his greatest success. No one had ever played like Dorsey. He was not the first to use high notes, adopt seamless phrasing and employ a tasteful slide vibrato, but he combined these features holistically in a way that was quite new, and did so with a panache that made his playing irresistibly attractive. Furthermore, his sense of style – musical, sartorial and personal – seemed to be in tune with the easygoing glamour of the jazz age. His influence went beyond jazz: the whole concept of high lyrical playing was imitated not just by other professionals, but by amateurs and symphonic players who recognized in his playing values that also resonated in art music. His long-line style became, and persisted as, a genre – a species of playing within the trombone idiom – perhaps the first trombone style genre since tailgate to do so. Indeed, if one had to define why tailgate and the Dorsey ballad style can be said to have the status of a performance genre, it is that there are features in both that are so consistent and distinctive that they are imitable and even capable of parody.[30]

The swing era, and especially the big bands, provided the opportunity for the trombone to be used as a block sectional sonority as well as for featuring individual soloists. A band was characterized by the qualities of its sidemen as much as by the sound canvas fashioned by the leader and his arrangers. This was the case with the Duke Ellington band, which consistently used trombones conspicuously and innovatively as lead instruments. It also attracted a procession of fine players from the earliest years of the band until the 1970s. One group stands out as the most distinguished of the band's finest era: Joe 'Tricky Sam' Nanton (1904–46), who joined the band in the summer of 1926 and was a member almost continuously until his death in 1946; Lawrence Brown (1907–88), who joined Ellington in 1932 and, apart from one interruption between 1951 and 1960, spent most of his career with the band until 1970; and the valve trombone player Juan Tizol (1900–84), who was recruited by Ellington in 1928, and who, like Brown, was more in than out of the band until the 1970s. (Ill. 75) From 1930 until 1942 the three were continually together and their

Illustration 75. The trombone section of the Duke Ellington Band in the 1930s. From the left: Joe 'Tricky Sam' Nanton, Juan Tizol, Lawrence Brown.

influence on Ellington's success was immense.[31] They played together superbly, but individually they could hardly have been more different in terms of musical background and playing style. Brown believed that Tricky Sam was the 'corner stone' of Ellington's band: a player who could not be replaced without the band changing its identity:

> Tricky Sam was a nice fellow. He was a man of many talents and most of his talents were – he was unconscious of. He was very funny – everybody loved Tricky Sam.
> And he had a way of phrasing his music that was – I don't think anyone has ever picked up on that. And it's just lost because no one even tried to pick up on that. And it's just lost because no one even tried to catch the true meaning of his music. His parents were from the West Indies, and that West Indian influence was kept in his playing. And everything he played, you could tell that was Tricky Sam because with the growl, it was almost like talking.[32]

Nanton is often thought to have performed consistently in a restricted pitch range – some have even suggested that he seldom moved outside a single octave. This, of course, is a gross exaggeration, even though his solos seldom utilized a wide tessitura. The distinctive character of his playing came from the raw energy he transmitted, the unpredictable lines of his solos, and especially his mastery of his trademark plunger-mute and growl technique, which he developed and refined more than any other player. Nanton was not the first to use the plunger effectively: King Oliver was famous for his use of the device, and many New Orleans players availed themselves of it. Indeed, Gunther Schuller has pointed to the influence of the early New Orleans trombonist Jonas Walker, who was reputedly 'the first to apply New Orleans "freak sounds" to his instrument'.[33] Nanton apparently owed something to his friend and predecessor in Ellington's band Charlie Irvis (c. 1899–c. 1939) in this regard, but the trumpeter Bubber Miley (1903–32) is usually credited as his most sustained inspiration. The plunger style developed by Nanton was not merely a feature of his technique: it was the central aspect of his mode of musical communication, and irrespective of where the influences came from, when he played plunger solos, it was so practised that it appeared utterly natural. Brown's description of his plunger and growl style as a kind of rhetoric is apt. Nanton, like some others, actually used two mutes simultaneously: a 'Magosy and Buscher Non-pareil trumpet' straight mute with appropriately adjusted retaining corks, which was inserted down the bell, over which he manipulated a standard plunger. The plunger style as practised by Nanton and Miley was a defining characteristic of the Ellington sound in the 1930s.[34]

Juan Tizol was a Puerto Rican who took up the valve trombone in a municipal band in San Juan; he never played the slide instrument. He moved to the USA in 1920, and met Ellington when working in the Howard Theatre, Washington. Tizol was not a foreground soloist in the same way that Brown and Nanton were, but his ensemble presence was decisive, particularly through the Latin nuances in his playing of his own compositions such as 'Carnival' and 'Moonlight Fiesta'. One of the best musicians in the entire Ellington set-up, he was influential on the style that became known as Ellington's jungle sound, but he was also valued for the straight accuracy of his playing. He recalled asking Ellington, 'What do you see in my playing . . . I don't call myself a hot man', to which Ellington replied, 'there are times when a writer wants to hear something exactly as it's written. You want to hear it clean, not with smears and slides on it.'[35] The quality of Tizol's sound has been variously described as 'thin-ish', 'penetrating' and 'leathery', and this has been attributed to his training in the Latin military/concert band tradition which thrived in Latin America.[36] He used a fast vibrato, and the Latin origins of his style were never distant. His April 1946 recording of 'Keb-Lah' with his own band provides as good an example as there is of his style.[37]

The third member of the team, and the last of them to join the Ellington band, Lawrence Brown, was a different musical personality again.[38] His suave, understated and tasteful style was formed in his youth and developed quickly in the late 1920s, when he was working as a studio player. Even as a child, brought up in a strictly observant religious household (his father was a Episcopalian clergyman), he had been attracted by the idea that the trombone could adopt the lyrical style of other instruments: 'I began to wonder why couldn't the trombone play the same type of music as the cello, and I couldn't see why it still had to resort to that tailgate business. So I began to try to play melodies.'[39] He was recruited to Ellington's band, not by Ellington himself, but by the manager/impresario Irving Mills. According to Brown, Ellington's first words to him were, 'I never knew you, I never met you, I never heard you. But Irving says get you – so that's that.'[40] As the last of the trio to join the band, Brown played for some time without music, but improvised a first trombone above Tizol and Nanton. This was not unusual, for 'most of the bands . . . were mostly ear bands . . . whatever you heard you'd pick up a place to fit in.'[41] According to Brown, there were only skeleton arrangements and 'no one wrote solos for anybody'.[42]

Brown's dark, velvety tone and superbly judged phrasings set him apart from many of his contemporaries. (Dorsey was one of the few to equal him as a high-melody, long-line player.) He seldom indulged in virtuosic displays, but his dynamic fast solos such as that at the end of 'Main Stem' (1942) reveal him to be one of the finest technicians of his era; he was certainly among the most versatile and accomplished players in the history of jazz. As with the most important solo players of his time – Teagarden, Dorsey, Higginbotham and perhaps Dickenson – many of the technical and idiomatic devices on which Brown drew were in advance of those used by the best orchestral players. From the 1930s (and in the case of Miff Mole and Jim Robinson, some time earlier), players started acquiring full and rounded techniques that owed something to a mastery of the instruction books that were readily available on the market; Brown and Dickenson were among many who admitted to having studied from the trombone transcription of the Arban Method. But whatever was picked up from such sources, it tended to be filtered and used as a launching pad for an individual manner of expression rather than as the basis for an orthodox approach. The routine pitch range of jazz players was usually the best part of three octaves, and the production and release of notes was always controlled, but they could use a wide variety of expressions, and tone itself was entirely personal, usually clear and consistent across the whole range. These basic attributes were the ingredients of the most important element of a player's performance: his mode of expression and powers of improvisation. Teagarden used short, fast, mordent-like decorations; Dorsey developed a 'terminal vibrato' where a fast vibrato was applied to the ends of sustained notes. Brown tended towards a style that was notable for the way that he articulated and released notes in subtly different ways, so as to give even the simplest melodic contours a deceptively rich quality.

The 1940s and bop

The precedents of what can be loosely called modern jazz trombone technique were evident in the 1930s in the playing of certain trombonists, but it was not until the 1940s that there was a decisive change in trombone playing, brought about by a new grammar within jazz. This new grammar can be explained – perhaps too easily – as the change occasioned by the shift from swing to bop (or bebop), and the range of other styles that were to emerge in or after the 1940s; but these essentially musical developments were not entirely divorced from socio-economic changes that were under way in the 1940s and which impacted on the music profession. One of the themes recurrent in this book is the way that economic determinants have affected the practical and artistic life of trombone players. Just as the introduction of sound movies changed their world in the late 1920s, so the decline of the big band led to a repositioning of jazz players in the music profession in the 1940s. The reordering of the music profession as a result of the Second World War was, of course, a global phenomenon and its biting impact was painfully felt in the many countries (including the USA) which had a buoyant musical life; but there were also new cultural trends, and these combined effects were already signalling the end of the big-band era. By the 1940s, the influence of the USA on popular culture was so pervasive that any phenomenon that occurred there usually initiated a worldwide trend.

Many big-band sidemen who had been household names in the early 1940s were virtually unknown and in search of employment by the end of that decade. It was soon evident that the gramophone record sector of public entertainment, which had been one of the commercial bases for jazz and big bands, had a capacity to change the nature of the music market in an astonishingly short period of time. Even in the 1930s many big bands had moved away from jazz as an organic, improvisatory form to more staged, cultivated performances aimed mainly at dancers who expected from live performances a near-exact replication of what they had heard on recordings. Big bands were an elaborate and labour-intensive mode of entertainment that had flourished when a general sense of well-being was underpinned by a buoyant economy. The recovery after the 1929 economic slump, and particularly the abolition of Prohibition in 1933, sustained such a condition, but war – even victory – did not. This in itself did not cause the death of the big swing bands, but it issued unmistakable signals of change. The most famous of these bands, led by men who had special celebrity and an element of youth on their side – Dorsey, Ellington and, for more exceptional reasons, Stan Kenton – continued, but with somewhat different formats and purposes.

The consequent effect on playing styles in the early 1940s is important to note, because for a time the imaginative and innovatory mood that impacted so strongly on trombone technique in the 1930s gave way to more predictable and orthodox practices that fitted the gloss of the commercial system in which the dance band flourished. The big dance band trombonists were great players, but the tradition of individuality and instinctive inventiveness ran contrary to what the current commercial fashion demanded of them. This phenomenon is exemplified perfectly by the band led by probably the most famous trombone player of all time: Glenn Miller (1904–44). (Ill. 76)

Miller made no special impact as an individual performer, but it is important to stress that his credentials as a jazz trombonist were as robust as any. He succeeded Teagarden as the trombone player with Ben Pollock's band in 1928, and among the many bands with which he played were those of Red Nichols and the Dorsey brothers. He became known nationally as a player when he joined Ray Noble's American dance band in 1935. But, of course, he is best remembered as a bandleader and an innovative, and in his own way visionary, arranger. His performances were not centred on spontaneous jazz; in fact, this had no place in the Miller aesthetic. He was successful because his band executed his finely crafted and stage-managed arrangements accurately and exactly. It was an aesthetic that he openly confessed to and defended. In February 1940, when his band held a residency at the Pennsylvania Hotel, New York, he told *Down Beat* reporter Dave Dexter Jr, 'I haven't a great jazz band, and I don't want one.' He emphasized 'harmony' over 'beat': 'It happens that to our ears harmony comes first.'[43] Beat, he felt, was less important to an audience: 'By giving the public a rich and full melody, distinctly arranged and well played, all the time *creating* new tone colors and patterns, I feel we have a better chance of being successful. I want a kick to my band, but I don't want the rhythm to hog the spotlight.'[44] Miller's philosophy and performance values lacked neither colour nor imagination, nor indeed integrity, but they exemplified a shift away from the idea of

Illustration 76. The Glenn Miller Band at the Meadowbrook Ballroom, New Jersey in 1939. Miller is the most distant trombonist – in the light jacket. (Frank Driggs Collection)

jazz as a performance idiom and an equally important shift in its reception. This change was further consolidated in the early 1950s when popular music gave way to 'pop', as market makers realized that teenagers had minds of their own and a disposable income, and constituted a discrete and massive market sector.

As mainstream jazz gradually became redefined as something quite different from the market-led species that were growing around it, and which many younger players were reacting against, several quite different tangents were to provide sustenance for the authentic jazz trombone. One was the extended engagement of trombone players with the small-group species of jazz such as cool jazz and bebop. Another was the emergence of traditionalist revivals which sought to replicate the outward characteristics (if not the inner spirit) of jazz in the 1920s. Further styles that were to appear were free jazz, fusion and hybrids of pop and Latino influences. Another tangent was what Gunther Schuller termed the 'Third Stream' – a style that was distinctive and implicitly loyal to the core inheritance of jazz, but neither radically modernist nor self-consciously nostalgic of New Orleans or other earlier styles. In effect, the Third Stream suggests continuity all but untouched by the fracturing influence of bebop and the retro-allusions of traditional revivals, but embracing other 'external' elements in both composed and improvised jazz. Thus the Third Stream might be manifest as a hybrid of jazz and contemporary western art music styles or a fusion of (for example) jazz and ethnic or vernacular styles.[45]

By the second half of the 1940s, despite the formidable influence of great players such as Vic Dickenson, Dicky Wells and Trummy Young, the jazz trombone lacked a voice that pointed to the future rather than the past. It found one in the shape of J. J. Johnson,[46] who was to be the single most formative influence on jazz trombone playing for the remainder of the twentieth century. (Ill. 77) Johnson was born in Indianapolis, and worked with several bands, including those of Benny Carter and Count Basie. He established a base in New York in 1945, and started to play in small groups with important figures such as Miles Davis, Charlie Parker and Dizzy Gillespie. Up to this point, Johnson's performance style was very much that of the virtuoso big-band sideman, but through the 1940s his playing became somewhat lighter, more purely focused and above all possessed of a stunning virtuosity which led many listeners who heard but did not see him to assume that he was playing a valve trombone. In fact, though Johnson has been linked with the development of such techniques as doodle-tonguing (a variant of double and triple tonguing but with softer rebound consonants), he claimed to have 'never been pre-occupied with speed and technique. . . . If I have been preoccupied with anything . . . it would be to try to make a musical statement that has logic, clarity, a personality.'[47] He was most strongly influenced by the playing of the saxophonist Lester Young, who 'had a concept about improvisation that intrigued [him]'.[48]

Illustration 77. J. J. Johnson (*Down Beat*, 28 May 1970)

As well as being a player of enormous importance, Johnson was also a composer and arranger of marked originality, and it is easy to hear in his playing a creative force driven by a broad and truly fertile imagination. His brand of playing, with its fabulous concentration of virtuoso technique, was not universally admired as jazz, but whereas some of Johnson's disciples have come close to his unprecedented control of the instrument, not all have used these skills to the same creative effect. His famous association with another virtuoso trombonist, Kai Winding (1922–83), one of the first great 'cool' trombonists, forming the group known as 'Jay and Kai', was to last for just two years following 1954, but it was an important collaboration. Not only did the two men have similarly virtuoso techniques, but they were also the first two trombonists really to exploit the bebop style with a facility that matched players of other more traditionally agile instruments.

Winding had previously spent two years (1945–7) with the Stan Kenton band, through which passed many of the greatest post-war trombone players, such as Bill Russo and Frank Rosolino. Kenton's inventive and invariably controversial band style (in its various manifestations) outlasted most of the big bands. But his use of trombones was interesting and new, and his particular innovation was the introduction of the bass trombone into the big band. Even bands that carried three or four trombones always used tenors and treated them as a homogeneously voiced section, contrasting or blending them with equal or near-equal numbers of trumpets and reeds. Even Ellington's band did not have a fourth trombone player until the 1970s, and the bass player Jimmy Connors is said to have played a wide-bore tenor instrument rather than a genuine bass trombone.

Not the first bass trombone player to be used by big bands, but probably the most important, was George Roberts (b. 1928), who replaced Bart Varsalona with Kenton's band. Roberts is one of the unsung heroes of jazz, and he became one of the mentor figures for bass trombonists throughout the world. He could match the techniques of the best tenor players, but what singled him out was the quality of his sound, which marked not just him but the instrument he played as possessing musical characteristics that were individual and valuable. George Roberts's playing is most famously heard on the 1958 Billy May recording *Big Fat Brass*, and particularly the 'Solving the Riddle' track. This piece was written by Nelson Riddle, himself a former trombonist with Dorsey, specifically as a feature for Roberts.[49]

Traditional revivals

By the 1960s the pop music industry, firmly rooted in the influences of Elvis Presley, the Beatles and the procession that came in their wake, consumed the commercial profits of gramophone recordings, broadcasts and live shows. Jazz was never eclipsed, but it was certainly overshadowed in the popular consciousness, and offered only a precarious living to trombonists, many of whom spent a decade out of the limelight and often in an artistic wilderness. Even as early as 1952, J. J. Johnson had briefly to give up playing and work as a blueprint inspector for the Sperry Gyroscope company, before finding that his composing and arranging work could sustain him and provide some opportunities to play. By this time, several of the best jazz trombonists were to be found on the west coast of the USA, where studio recording for the burgeoning television industry added to the opportunities that already existed in movie recording studios. George Roberts, the valve trombonist Bob Brookmeyer and several others followed this route. But at the same time jazz was given new sustenance by the traditionalist revivals.

'Traditional jazz' as a term was first applied to distinguish New Orleans style from swing, but in more recent times it has been used to describe commercial or more artistically motivated revivals of the 1920s, particularly New Orleans, style. These revivals have occurred since the 1940s in one shape or another, but they can be grouped into two broad categories. In the first category are those that centre on live and recorded performances by actual New Orleans players who, by the 1940s, were nearing the end of their careers. One of the most successful groups of this type was the Preservation Hall Band. It went through several manifestations, and for some time had Jim Robinson as its trombone player. In the other category are those movements that mimic the line-ups and styles of 1920s groups, either by playing stock arrangements from that time, or through looser and more instinctive imitations.

The traditional jazz bands that were especially in vogue in the UK in the 1960s have been labelled 'Trad' to distinguish them from the somewhat different species in the USA. Some of the British bands did the trombone less of a service than it deserved by applying the tailgate style with little conviction and less skill, but the revival also provided exposure for some of the best British jazz trombonists. It also fuelled a wider interest in jazz which led a procession of American players to Europe, especially London and Paris. Placed alongside highly successful UK groups such as the Temperance Seven and the Acker Bilk Band, the band led by the trombonist Chris Barber (b. 1930) was more firmly rooted in a genuine jazz revivalist culture. Barber was the best of the trombone-playing bandleaders of that era; indeed, many of those who started rival bands – the banjo player Lonnie Donegan and the clarinettist Monty Sunshine, for instance – are featured in early recordings with his band. Barber has a natural jazz imagination and his recordings exude an integrity that some of the best American trombonists comment on. A more accomplished player was the Scottish trombonist George Chisholm (1915–97), though his celebrity came more from his slapstick humour than his playing. But the best of this generation of British players, and the one acclaimed by most British trombonists, was undoubtedly Don Lusher (b. 1923). Lusher, who started playing in the Salvation Army, dominated London television and recording sessions for the best part of four decades. Never celebrated to the extent he deserved in international jazz circles, he came to epitomize the jazz 'side' of the UK trombone-playing profession.

The post-bop generation

Jazz trombonists have continued to explore new modes of expression and have developed virtuoso techniques. Europeans have made their mark, with such players as Albert Mangelsdorff, Don Lusher, George Chisholm and latterly the English players Mark Nightingale and Dennis Rollins, though the predominance of American players has never really declined. Modernists such as Roswell Rudd and Grachan Moncur III have been in the forefront of some of the most radical technical developments, and Steve Turre, Robin Eubanks and Wycliffe Gordon have been prominent in a group of New York players who have discovered distinctive forms of eloquence.[50] Equally prominent has been 'Slide' Hampton (b. 1932) who, though of a slightly earlier generation, has been one of the most versatile, persistent and formidable influences on trombone playing in New York and also in Europe, where he lived and worked for almost a decade after he toured there with Woody Herman in 1968.[51]

It is remarkable that the post-bop players have continued the tradition of intellectual independence and the tendency towards distinctive expression that marked the careers of the great jazz trombonists up to the 1940s. Furthermore, individual styles have been based on aspects of virtuosity which are manifest not just in the ability to play effortlessly in a wide pitch range and with a facility to show scant regard for technical challenges, but also in an ability to manipulate timbre (sometimes with an extensive range of mutes), and to control and vary the production and release of notes in ways that take playing technique to new levels of subtlety. If these aspects signal recent developments in trombone playing, there are also continuities which join even the newest generation to their spiritual ancestors. Perhaps the most important factor here is the extent to which linear (melodic) and vertical (harmonic) instincts are conflated subconsciously, so as to condition the framework of the jazz trombonist's thinking. No matter how many patterns are pre-rehearsed or how many phrases are predetermined, the basis of jazz players' improvisations remains dependent on this rather particular intelligence. It is easy to see similarities between this process and what we can deduce from a study of the sources for improvisation and embellishment in the Renaissance. It is a skill – a type of musical culture – that classical trombonists neither possess nor especially need. It is above this substructure of thinking (or perhaps subconscious conditioning) of the jazz musician that the expressive layer resides. It is undoubtedly the musical authority provided by the inner sense of harmony that allows jazz trombonists to develop such stunning and varied melodic expression. The manifestations of this are varied and especially interesting to observe in the considerably contrasting styles found in the later generation of players.

David Baker has contrasted the playing of Roswell Rudd (b. 1935) with that of J. J. Johnson and his disciples, and has observed that Rudd's playing is idiomatic to the trombone and closer in spirit to the style of Dickie Wells, J. C. Higginbotham and Jimmy Harrison than to that of Johnson and those such as Frank Rosolino, Curtis Fuller and Slide Hampton who were his direct successors. This, of course, reinforces the point I made earlier in this chapter about the way that jazz trombone playing defies the idea of a strictly linear approach. A similar illustration could be made by reference to the playing of Grachan Moncur III (b. 1937), who also exploits an idiom specific to the slide trombone in the context of an avant-garde style – a synthesis of free jazz and bop – which takes a great deal from the stylistic inheritance of Johnson and his followers, but also from a wide range of other players whose own style was quite different.[52]

Johnson himself singled out Robin Eubanks (b. 1955) as 'one of the most interesting trombonists' that he had heard.[53] (Ill. 78) Eubanks utilizes a distinctively slide idiom and an extremely wide pitch range, and exploits a technical facility that

Illustration 78. Robin Eubanks. (With thanks to Robin Eubanks.)

is clearly indebted to Johnson. Steve Turre's (b. 1948) playing takes in a wide range of jazz and other culturally diverse styles. A superbly complete trombone player, he has explored sound worlds that reside firmly within jazz while absorbing Afro-Cuban and Brazilian nuances.[54] Unusually, Turre has also developed his trombone sound in a number of highly diverse large- and small-scale contexts. Perhaps the most interesting is his performance on seashells, which he has developed with one of his groups, Sanctified Shells. Wycliffe Gordon (b. 1967) is one of the most impressively virtuoso players of the new generation, as good an example as any of a player whose expressiveness resides in the fine subtlety of his attack and a sound that often achieves ambiguous nuances through the clever use of mutes.

In the last decades of the twentieth century, jazz acquired both a discernible and reliable scholarship and a didactic infrastructure that is particularly strong in the USA. Most of the younger generation of players include the word 'educator' in their list of attributes. All hold jazz clinics and some use faculty positions as the base for their careers; Eubanks, for example, is on the faculty at Oberlin College, Gordon is at the Juilliard School, and in 2003 the exciting young British pop-jazz trombonist Dennis Rollins was prominent in the launch of the jazz syllabus of the Associated Board of the Royal Schools of Music, which is the largest and perhaps most influential music examination agency in English-speaking countries. There is of course an inherent danger here, in that strong and strategic didactic method can lead to the establishment of rock-solid orthodoxies which could run counter to the formidable force that made jazz so important to the history of trombone playing – and jazz students are famous for their marathon practice sessions. But oddly, encouragingly, and to the credit of jazz educators, the didacticism of jazz seems not to have stifled the creative spirit.

Chapter 14

Modernism, postmodernism and retrospection

In the twenty-first century, trombonists inhabit a musical world that is quite unlike that of their forebears, and it is both rich and challenging in that modern media, scholarship and communication provide access to the breadth of contemporary creativity and the entirety of the known historical repertoire. Trombonists are also part of a global musical community in which performances and ideas are shared. Such organizations as the International Trombone Association (ITA) and the Historic Brass Society (HBS) have provided a focus for the study of the trombone across a range of styles and periods. The ITA, which was founded in 1972, has four and a half thousand members in more than fifty countries, and six very active affiliated societies, and is the main focus for ideas about modern trombone playing in its various styles. The HBS has six hundred members in about thirty countries and is the first organization to join together performers and scholars in the study of historical brass playing, with the same terms and standards as the established scholarly societies. It has significantly narrowed the gap between scholarship and practice. Perhaps more importantly, the ITA and the HBS have democratized the world of the trombone, bringing professionals and amateurs together. This latter aspect is as impressive as it is significant, because it has fostered relationships between the finest players in the world and the most remote sources from which the next generations of great players might emerge. The community of trombone playing recognizes few boundaries, national or cultural, and the internet discussion groups that it has encouraged provide for a constant and valuable exchange of ideas.[1]

There is much to discuss, because the idiom of the trombone has become more complex and diverse, and interest in both the historical and the contemporary aspects of trombone playing is buoyant. The known repertoire of art music is available for all to perform, traditional and nostalgic approaches to jazz coexist with the most radical hybrids, and modern art music composers seem to be constantly developing the instrument's idiom.

For professional players the challenges have never been greater, and they are confronted with audiences that have never been more discerning. In the postmodern world, a busy professional will traverse several vastly different sound worlds, sometimes in a single day. The instruments he or she plays may show some outward signs of continuity with those of the past, but key parameters have changed. Some of these parameters are material: the weight, proportions, metallic composition and mechanics of the instrument have all been objects of development. Inevitably and understandably, almost all instruments used in modern performance show a greater allegiance to modern pragmatics than to history – and this practicality can be seen in many reproduction instruments too. But the most important challenges come from the postmodern culture in which players work. Radical modernism and the avant garde coexist alongside retrospection into historic repertoires and the performance practices associated with them. The music of our own time is not just the music of all time, but the music of many places and many styles. When Dieppo taught his students at the Paris Conservatoire in the 1830s, his agenda and objectives were clear and uncontroversial. He taught what he and his contemporaries saw as the orthodox trombone technique. This technique was understood in terms of the relatively limited canonical repertoire, as it was perceived in Paris at that time. Today's conservatoire professors, if they do their jobs well, are not just imparting trombone technique, but also unwittingly teaching history and culture, for the global canonical repertoire in the early twenty-first century appears boundless in the demands it makes on the instrument's idiom. This being said, it is hard to avoid the conclusion that the main points of reference and the core values of trombone technique are still to be found in the traditions of diatonic art music, and the dominant values are still those of orchestral playing. This part of the music profession prevails as the dominant force because, despite the apparent diversity of public taste, symphony orchestras and opera houses continue to receive more in state subsidy and private sponsorship than any other form of civilian music-making. This should not be seen as a negative feature of modern musical life, because the stability of the large-scale musical institutions ensures a cultural buoyancy from which all professional music benefits; but it does mean that, despite the rise of historically informed performance, the musical ideologies and values implicit in the nineteenth-century orchestral style continue to be the main source of influence on the orthodoxies of trombone playing. This is evidenced, for example, by the fact that most of the trombone teachers in the great conservatoires of the world hold, or have held, positions in orchestras.

Modern players are stylistically versatile; they have little option but to be so. Thus, most seem to share a common view about the constituents of virtuosity, even though a single player seldom possesses each of them. But it is hard to escape the feeling that the best modern trombone players are musicians of extraordinary sophistication. When preparing this book I was fortunate enough to have conversations with many players, including some of the finest orchestral trombonists. I could not resist asking them which players and what types of playing they most admired. There was no unanimity of choice, but all named jazz trombonists as frequently as symphonic players and soloists. However, there was a much greater consensus about the qualities they most valued. While technical facility was often mentioned, the foreground comments were invariably about musical expression and communication rather than exceptional virtuosity. Orchestral players, for example, ponder long and hard on the canonical repertoire and how it should be performed, and it is both encouraging and impressive that the subtlety of the articulations in the chorales in Brahms's symphonies should be considered as challenging as the more technically demanding areas of the orchestral repertoire.

Jazz occupies a special position both in the evolution of trombone playing and in modern professional life, because the idiomatic values differ from player to player; so the position of jazz in this chapter should be clarified. In some respects, modern jazz has mirrored other developments in musical modernism, and, as I have already suggested, techniques notated in twentieth-century art music owe a great deal to it. But while it is fruitful (because of their exploitation of advanced idiomatic techniques) to make comparisons between jazz performers such as Albert Mangelsdorff, Grachan Moncur III and Roswell Rudd, and trombone soloists working in avant-garde art music, the comparison between the jazz world and the art music world does not stretch too far. This is because jazz musicians constantly reinvent repertoire in their own style; they are not required daily to replicate or even imitate the styles of Kid Ory, Tommy Dorsey or J. J. Johnson. To put it another way, jazz trombonists, unlike their 'straight' counterparts, are celebrated for the way they have fashioned their own musical identities, rather than for their capacity to imitate the orthodoxies of earlier eras. So, having acknowledged the strength of the influence of jazz on the trombone's art music idiom, for my present purpose I will treat the two domains as somewhat separate.

Professional trombone playing in the postmodern world

When a contemporary trombone player leaves home in the morning, he or she could be destined to spend the day facing a bewilderingly varied set of stylistic demands: the avant garde, period performance, TV jingles, as well as the routine symphonic, operatic and light music repertoires. Professional trombone players deal with such challenges at a purely pragmatic level, but the way they do it, and even the requirement for them to do so, is relatively new. It is this very novelty that suggests the use of the term 'postmodern' in relation to musical *performance* (rather than composition), though it is a use that some may find hard to swallow. Postmodernism posits the end of linear historical development in favour of a juxtaposition of numerous historically and culturally varied styles. It represents a culture in which both historical determinants, and particularly the demarcations between the popular and the elite, are dissolved. Traditional hierarchies fade in favour of more eclectic tastes and values. Postmodernism conditions the musical marketplace and its repertoires, but it may also (and in consequence) be said to condition the manner in which musicians perform.

It could be argued that the need for trombone players – or any other performers – to imitate the styles of their historical counterparts convincingly, and to switch between the techniques of both high-brow and low-brow domains, is simply a practical requirement of the age in which they make a living. But two aspects of contemporary performance practice place today's players in a relatively new position. First, there is the sheer breadth of the stylistic and historical range that professional players are required to accommodate, which has no precedent in the history of music. Secondly, the way that playing styles and practices have changed in order to make this accommodation is all but comprehensive, and because of the global network the result seems to have been a multifaceted performance style that is, to a large extent, internationally shared. A number of performance values can be cited to support this idea – for example, the breaking down of barriers between the high and the popular, which (despite the dominance of orchestral playing in the conservatoire tradition) is given close attention in the way players are taught; and the development of instruments which aim at the 'one size fits all' approach to repertoire. The flexibility that is required of modern players – and this is the key point – defines modern trombone style and distinguishes it as different from what went before. If period instrument players believe that their use of a historical reproduction instrument distances them from such compromises, it is likely that they are deluding themselves. The juxtaposition in this chapter of sections on the avant garde and the so-called 'early music movement' gives stark emphasis to the diversity of modern times and the challenges that trombonists face as they navigate the postmodern musical profession.

Solo repertoire in traditional idioms

The twentieth-century avant-garde solo trombone repertoire which is discussed below was both preceded by, and has run in parallel to, a steady stream of works for solo trombone – mainly with piano accompaniment – that exploit a more traditional, even conservative, idiom. As I suggested in Chapter 7, the most consistent precedent for this type of repertoire is found in the *concours* works of the Paris Conservatoire, to which can be added other nineteenth-century works such as those mentioned in Chapter 7 and the popular Concerto for Trombone in B flat (1877) by Rimsky-Korsakov (originally for trombone and military band). Very little of this repertoire has made a mark with a general audience, and it is possible that the main public role for these works has been as study and competition pieces rather than as part of a widely appreciated concert repertoire. If this suggests only faint praise, it must be remembered that the most rapid and radical developments of the trombone's idiom in the twentieth century were taking place elsewhere – particularly in jazz and in the works of orchestral and smaller-scale ensemble composers.

It would be wrong, however, to disregard the very best of these pieces, and it is easy to cite a quantity of solo compositions which have canonical status in the solo trombonist's repertoire. Leaving aside the French *concours* pieces, the most frequently performed include Paul Hindemith's Sonata for Trombone and Piano (1941), Frank Martin's *Ballade* (1942), Eugène Bozza's *Romance* (1944), Leonard Bernstein's *Elegy for Mippy II* (1948), Gordon Jacob's Concerto for Trombone and Orchestra (1955), Kazimierz Serocki's Concerto for Trombone and Orchestra (1971) and Stjepan Šulek's Sonata *Vox Gabrieli* (1973). The maintenance of interest in this part of the trombone repertoire has relied on its presence in the curriculum of conservatoires and in its being championed by exemplar performers. Many of these players have been outstanding orchestral trombonists who have also followed careers as soloists – sometimes commissioning new works, but always influencing the way that the solo idiom has developed. The American trombonists Davis Schuman, Ronald Barron, Joseph Alessi and the bass trombonist Douglas Yeo have been prominent in this respect, as have been the European players Denis Wick and Ian Bousfield, and the Canadian Alain Trudel.

The avant garde and advanced techniques

Properly, 'avant garde' is an epithet for a branch of current practice rather than an historical style, but it has come to be used as shorthand for techniques that are extreme advancements on those required for what might loosely be called the conventional or traditional art music repertoire. We no longer regard the techniques deployed by Stravinsky in such ballets as *The Rite of Spring, The Firebird* and *Le Rossignol* as avant-garde, even though they were so regarded when they were first heard, but for the yet more radical writing that emerged in the second half of the

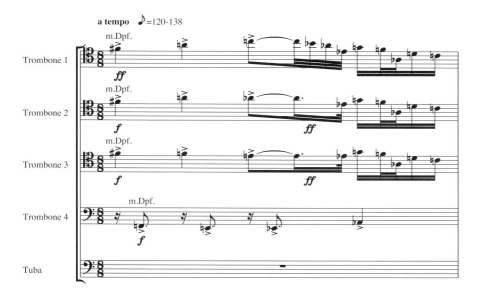

Example 14.1. Alban Berg, *Wozzeck* (1917–22), Act 1, bars 133–6

twentieth century the term has stuck. Extensions to the technique and idiom of the trombone have emerged in both orchestral music and solo and ensemble repertoire, and the most challenging extensions have come in the second half of the century. The writing of such modernists as Schoenberg, Berg and Webern (as already mentioned in Chapter 8) positions the instrument as a constituent of an orchestral palette that is largely abstract and devoid of reference to the traditional extra-musical associations of the trombone. Here, as in the work of many other composers of the first half of the twentieth century, 'modernism' in trombone writing can be seen as a consequence of changes to musical language rather than as a contrivance to exploit radically extended instrumental techniques. But changes to the melodic, harmonic and rhythmic language of the early twentieth-century modernists did contribute to the development of the idiom of the trombone, because the figurations in individual and sectional writing (for example, the angular intervallic relationships in the melodic writing) were unprecedented.

The trombone writing exemplified in Berg's *Wozzeck* (composed 1917–22) predates the formidable influence of jazz on twentieth-century art music composers. (Ex. 14.1) When this influence did become apparent, it often manifested itself, at least initially, in a somewhat modest and elusive way – almost as pastiche. Such references – usually restricted to purely melodic devices – can be seen in the writing of Darius Milhaud (*La Création du monde*, 1923), George Gershwin (*Rhapsody in Blue*, 1924; orchestrated by Ferde Grofé) and, in a somewhat more sustained manner in that of Stravinsky and Ravel. But it soon became obvious that jazz and popular idioms were becoming tributaries from which a larger group of composers drew ideas about the trombone. Whether these ideas were directly and studiedly derived from popular styles, or whether the influence came from modern composers' more implicit engagement with a wide array of musical vocabularies, is hard to determine, but the use of extended pitch ranges, wide leaps and a variety of articulations (together with

Illustration 79. Varèse, *Octandre* (1923). (By permission of BMG.)

liberal glissando decorations) can be found, for instance, in such works as Varèse's *Octandre* (1923) (Ill. 79), and slide vibrato is either specified or implied in orchestral works by Ravel. According to Michel Laplace, Ravel's introduction of slide vibrato into *L'Enfant et les sortilèges* (1920–5) followed consultation with the dance band player Léo Arnaud-Vauchant (see Chapter 2). (Ex. 14.2)

Example 14.2. Maurice Ravel *L'Enfant et les sortilèges* (1920–5)
Original *Edition Durand* (1925), Reh. No. 33, p. 42. The first trombone part is written in treble clef at pitch.

From the late 1950s, composers started to write for the trombone in a much more imaginative and radical way. While these extended techniques have been used in orchestral music, some of the most interesting works have been for the solo instrument and for trombones in smaller ensembles with instrumentations that do not match any traditional formats. The first work to be written for trombone alone which exploited an entirely idiosyncratic idiom was probably *Three Pieces for Trombone Solo* (1956) by Giacinto Scelsi, which requires a virtuoso and wide-ranging technique and an ability to play microtones accurately. (Ex. 14.3) Better known is John Cage's *Solo for Sliding Trombone* (1957–8), which is actually a twelve-page derivation from the composer's *Concert for Piano and Orchestra* (1957–8). *Solo for Sliding Trombone* has a preface that begins:

The following 12 pages for a trombone player may be played with or without other parts for other players. It is therefore a trombone solo or a part in an ensemble, symphony, or concerto for piano and orchestra. Though there are twelve pages, any amount of them may be played (including none).[2]

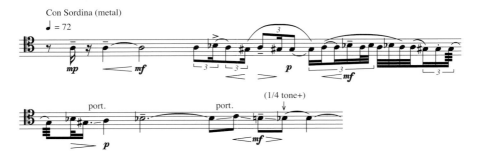

Example 14.3. Giacinto Scelsi, *3 pezzi 'per trombone'* (1956), opening of the second movement. (By permission of G. Schirmer, Inc., through Music Sales Ltd.)

Stuart Dempster has made the interesting comparison between Cage's piece and jazz processes, a comparison he has exploited in his own performances of the work. This approach is particularly credible given that Cage had the advice of trombonist Frank Rehak (a distinguished jazz as well as 'straight' player) in mind when he wrote it. In a personal letter to Dempster, Rehak describes a visit from Cage which took place prior to the composition of *Solo for Sliding Trombone*. The account – fascinating for the light it sheds on the ideas contained in the piece – also illustrates a tendency that was to become common, in which composers engaged with trombonists in a much more intimate and didactic dialogue than had previously been the case before composing for the instrument:

> I remember that we spent a long time with the instrument, taking it apart, playing without slide, without mouthpiece, adding various mutes, glass on the slide section, minus tuning slide, with spit valve open, and any other possibilities of producing a sound by either inhaling or exhaling air through a piece of metal tubing. We also discussed double stops, circular breathing, playing without moving slides, and on and on.[3]

Clearly, Cage was experimenting with devices that were to find their way into subsequent avant-garde trombone works, but it is *Sequenza V* (1966) by Luciano Berio that many would see as the true initiation of an entirely new form of idiomatic writing for the instrument. The piece brings together diverse avant-garde techniques in a highly organized composition, and has had a vast number of performances both live and recorded. Berio's *Sequenza* project (there were thirteen *Sequenza*s, written between 1958 and 1996) was intended to extend the idiom of instruments and voices, and to refashion ideas about virtuosity, but it was not *merely* an exercise in idiomatic expansion. Each *Sequenza* explores diversions from a given pitch (A in the case of

Sequenza V) and its associated harmonic fields. In *Sequenza V*, which is dedicated to the memory of the Polish clown Grock (Adrien Wettach), there is also an extra-musical element. This too is a feature of avant-garde works: the provision of performance instructions involving the acting out of a loose narrative, and/or the exploitation of spatial effects. Berio's *Sequenza V* is in two parts separated by the performer's utterance of the only notated word in the piece – 'why?' The prefatory note reads thus:

> On the stage a very low stand and a chair. Walking on the stage during the performance of section A the performer (white tie, spot from above etc.) strikes the poses of a variety showman about to sing an old favorite. Inspired, he extends his arms, he raises or lowers his instrument . . . with movements which should appear spontaneous, he hesitates. Just before section B he utters a bewildered 'why?' and sits down without pausing. He must perform section B as though rehearsing in an empty hall.[4]

The notation is proportional. In section A the overall speed is suggested by a visual unit at the beginning of each line (⌐——6″ca——⌐); breaths are decided by the performer. In section B, instead, everything written between bar lines constitutes a breath unit: it must be performed in one breath, either exhaling or inhaling (←——O——→). Consequently in section B, although the notation is still proportional, the length of each breath unit determines the overall speed. It is expected, for each performer and at each performance, the length of the breath units to be different. The transition between inhaling and exhaling must always occur without noticeable interruptions so that throughout section B there is no break in sound (except in the third breath unit of the last line of page 2). Instrumental sounds are often combined with vocal sounds: the performer should always obtain a similarity of color and attack between the two.

⊙ : vocal sounds, at the given pitch, produced with the lips on the mouthpiece, generally while playing.

O : vocal sounds produced with the lips away from the mouthpiece, turning the head to the right hand side with a small and quick movement.

[u ɑ ɑ i] : the vowels must be vocalized in a perceptible way imitating the instrumental sound.

[u ɑ ɑ i] : the performer must imitate the indicated vowels with the instrument, without vocalization.

♦ or ⏀ : as short as possible.

● or ○ : held to the next sound.

⌐——⌐ : as long as possible.

⊷⊷ , ⊷⊷⊷ : double or triple staccato

≋——— : fluttertongue

○——— : "breathy sound"

1357, 1357 : harmonic glissando on the same note (on 1st, 3rd, 5th, 7th position; etc.)

(⌐——⌐) for the duration proportionally indicated

The performer will constantly hold a metal plunger mute for open (o) and closed (+) sounds, according to the indicated pattern (+⌐———⌐). The sign ⌂ indicates that the mute must close the bell completely. The sign ●●●●● indicates that the mute must be rattled inside the bell of the instrument with a fast movement, maintaining normal hand position, according to the suggested pattern and for the suggested length. In the third line of section A the fast and continuous movement of the slide is indicated only as a visual pattern (a). The performer will produce instrumental sounds (b) without concern for the movement of the slide. At the end of section A, just before the word "why?" is uttered, the inhaling sound (c) should itself become audible (inhaling the air from the instrument).

There are seven dynamic steps, from ① (as p as possible), to ⑦ (as loud as possible). The vocal sounds in parenthesis [ ] in the second line of page 2 are optional. In section B the trombone must be kept level because of no chance to empty waterkey.

Illustration 80. Berio, *Sequenza V* (1966). (By permission of MDS Ltd.) Berio's explanatory notes are followed by two systems from the score.

Christian Lindberg has made the point that while Berio composed a *Sequenza* for the female voice, he never did so for the male voice, and that the composer himself implied that the trombone piece was a surrogate for such a work.[5] *Sequenza V* is therefore more than a series of novel effects held together by a loose extra-musical narrative, though the range of devices called upon by Berio – articulations, dynamics, mute manipulations, wide dynamic contrasts and aleatoric episodes – provides something of a touchstone for the way the idiom of the instrument was to develop. As with so many works that employ such a range of novel techniques, the score carries prefatory explanations of the notation. (Ill. 80)

Radical techniques were subsequently extended further by composers, some of whom were themselves expert trombonists, such as Folke Rabe from Sweden, and Vinko Globokar, a Slovene. In Globokar's *Res/As/Ex/Ins-pirer* (1973), the composer provided two tables of articulations – one to be executed while inhaling, the other while exhaling (the title of the work is derived from the words *respirer* – to breathe, *aspirer* – to inhale, *expirer* – to expire, *inspirer* – to inspire[6]). It is performed as a series of uninterrupted and continuous inhalations and exhalations. Many of the parameters (such as the rhythmic divisions) are free, but others (such as the number of articulations) are determined. It stands to reason that the complexity of the piece means that a performance requires considerable preparation, particularly as the composer has provided the daunting comment, 'The difference between playing while inhaling or exhaling shouldn't exist.'[7] Illustration 81 shows two systems from *Res/As/Ex/Ins-pirer*. Both are given twice – the first as published, the second as prepared for performance by the trombonist Benny Sluchin. The following explanation is largely drawn from Sluchin's *Contemporary Trombone Excerpts* (1995).

Each square ☐ signifies the duration of an exhalation or an inhalation.

exhale:
inhale:

There is no interruption from beginning to end. The piece is written in bass clef, but the player should work out a version in which each note can be transposed one or more octaves higher or lower according to the symbols :

(T)   mainly in the lower register

(M)   mainly in the middle register

(H)   mainly in the upper register

The rhythmic divisions are free; only the number of articulations is given:

There are two tables of twelve articulations each, to be played while inhaling or exhaling:

	normal sound (played while inhaling)
	play a multiple sonority based on 'e'
	sing into the instrument
	play and sing simultaneously
Flatt.	flutter-tongue
t k t k t k t k	tongue slaps (air only)
○	air noise
2 ✕	speak (the figure indicates the number of syllables)
b ≡	position lips as if to pronounce the consonant 'b' (grinding sound)
✕ a	guttural sound
⦙	very low note or low noise
⊕	short noise generated by the lips when pressed together and forward (pronounce the consonant 'p')

exhale

	normal sound of the instrument
	play a multiple sonority based on 'e'
	sing into the instrument
	play and sing simultaneously
Flatt.	flutter-tongue
ⱱ	tongue slaps
○	air noise (pronounce the consonants s, x, z, f)
r ⁓	pronounce a rolled 'r'
b ≡	position lips as if to pronounce the consonant 'b' (grinding sound)
/////	lip vibrations with the mouthpiece lightly on the lips
⦙	very low note or low noise
⊕	short noise generated by the lips when pressed together and forward (pronounce the consonant 'p')

(a)

(b)

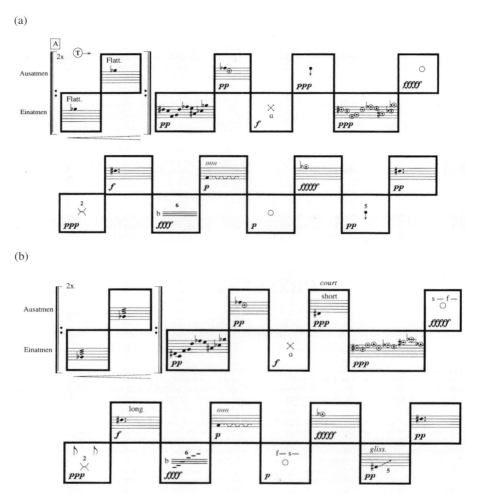

Illustration 81. Globokar, *Res/As/Ex/Ins-pirer* (1973) Version (a) shows a section of the notated score, version (b) the version prepared for performance by Benny Sluchin of *IRCAM* (Edition Peters No. 8288, © 1975 by Henry Litolff's Verlag, Frankfurt. Reprinted by kind permission of Peters Editions Limited, London.) (With thanks also to Benny Sluchin and Éditions musicales européennes.)

Stuart Dempster (who commissioned Berio's *Sequenza V*) has provided an extensive explanatory catalogue of advanced techniques for trombone, and a valuable insight into their development, in *The Modern Trombone: A Definition of its Idioms* (1979). His book has been supplemented by others – for example, Benny Sluchin's *Contemporary Trombone Excerpts*. Both deal, in different degrees of illustration and detail, with the range of devices that have developed, and the apparently limitless exploitation of the instrument by composers. The main developments are loosely summarized in Table 6.

In 1971 the British trombonist Denis Wick cautioned against players attempting the extended techniques of Berio's *Sequenza V* before 'every other aspect of the trombone has been completely mastered',[8] and indeed, Dempster urged his readers to be aware of the work of Wick and others before progressing to avant-garde

Table 6

Some advanced techniques

Most avant-garde pieces, particularly the solo and small ensemble works, exploit a wide pitch range, and contain chance or freely notated episodes. This list of techniques is not intended to be comprehensive, nor are the examples necessarily the best of their type, but they indicate new forms of writing in the twentieth century. Much more detail is provided in works such as Stuart Dempster's *The Modern Trombone* and Benny Sluchin's *Contemporary Trombone Excerpts*.

Extensive use of microtones:	Johnston, *One Man* (1967)
	Lanza, *Eidesis II* (1967)
	Robert Erickson, *General Speech* (1968)
	Xenakis, *Phlegra* (1975) (see Ill. 83)
	Takemitsu, *Waves* (1976)
Novel forms of sound generation (e.g., inhalation, combinations of live and recorded or electronically generated sounds):	Austin, *CHANGES*, (1965)
	Erickson, *Ricercare á 5* (1966)
	Erb, . . . *and then, toward the end* . . . (1971)
	Globokar, *Res/As/Ex/Ins-pirer* (1973) (see Ill. 81)
	Höller, *Resonance* (1981)
Production of sounds through the disassembled instrument:	Cage, *Solo for Sliding Trombone* (1957–8)
	Rabe & Bark, *Bolos* (1962)
	Globokar, *Kolo* (1988)
Vocalisations or the production of sounds devoid of definable pitch (such as breathing through the instrument):	Berio, *Sequenza V* (1966) (see Ill. 80)
	Globokar, *Res/As/Ex/Ins-pirer* (1973) (see Ill. 81)
	Erb, . . . *and then, toward the end* . . . (1971)
	Erickson *Ricerare á 5* (1966
Multiphonics:	Berio, *Sequenza V* (1966) (see Ill. 80)
	Erickson, *General Speech* (1968)
	Mabry, *9.28.85.* (1985)
	Xenakis, *Keren* (1986)
	Globokar, *Kolo* (1988)
Percussive sounds obtained by striking different parts of the instrument:	Rabe & Bark, *Bolos* (1962)
	Berio, *Sequenza V* (1966) (see Ill. 80)
	Alsina, *Consecuenza* (1966) (see Ill. 82)
Use of a wide variety of mutes and associated effects:	Globokar, *Discours II* (1967–8)
	Berio, *Sequenza V* (1966) (see Ill. 80)
	Stockhausen, '*Willkommen*' from *Donnerstag aus Licht* (1978–81)
Theatrical or spatial instructions:	Berio, *Sequenza V* (1966) (see Ill. 80)
	Oliveros, *Theater Piece* (1966)
	Globokar, *Discours II* (1967–8)
Use of loosely notated and chance episodes – seen in most pieces, but to the forefront in:	Cage, *Solo for Sliding Trombone* (1957–8)
	Lanza, *Eidesis II* (1967)
	Stockhausen, *In Freundschaft* (1977) (see Ill. 84)
Use (especially in solo works) of theatrical and personality portrayals:	Berio, *Sequenza V* (1966) (see Ill. 80)
	Sandström, *A Short Ride on a Motorbike* (1989)
Extensive natural and harmonic glissandos:	Rabe & Bark, *Bolos* (1962)
	Erickson, *Ricercare á 5* (1966)
	Erb, *In No Strange Land* (1968)
	Xenakis, *Phlegra* (1975) (see Ill. 83)

techniques. This was sound advice, for it is hard to see how the demands of such music could be realized by anyone without a holistic command of the instrument. But while such works necessarily call on a technique derived from (or as some would see it, deliberately contradictory to) the techniques of the art music tradition, it is difficult to see them as a feature of technical continuity. The following explanation is drawn from Benny Sluchin's *Contemporary Trombone Excerpts*.

sz ⎤   from high to low these 4 different sounds are to be
S ⎥   modulated by the voice as if a 'white sound' were
Sh ⎥   modulated by 4 filter-positions
Sch ⎦

◇   = sung sound

●   = played sound

♪ or ⌐\\\\\\⌐   = Sourd. (hit or '*tr*')

♪ (Pied) = footbeat
×

⌐‿‿‿⌐   = rotation of foot on ground

⸰ʳ   = very short pause,
     inhaling only a little

,   = inhale normally

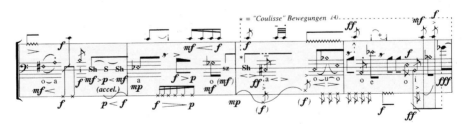

Illustration 82. Alsina, *Consecuenza* (1966). (© Copyright Bote & Bock GmbH and Co., Berlin. Reproduced by permission of Boosey & Hawkes Music Publishers Ltd.)

Dempster has been one of the greatest evangelists and advocates of advanced techniques. Also fundamentally important to the development of the instrument's idioms has been the Swedish trombonist Christian Lindberg (b. 1958). He has been the world's leading practitioner of the solo trombone in the late twentieth and early twenty-first century, and one of the most important forces in the history of the instrument. His special quality lies not just in his superlative technique, but also in his capacity to invest genuine musical meaning into the works he plays – works that sometimes need great coaxing for any meaning to be revealed. *Sequenza V* in

(a)

(b)

Illustration 83. Xenakis, *Phlegra* (1975). (By permission of BMG.)
The start and end points of the semiquaver glissandi are defined with the symbols ⊦ ♯ ♯ ,
signifying (respectively) that the note is a quarter tone higher, semitone higher and three quarter
tone higher than that which is written. The symbol ⌐ indicates false glissandos which the
player has to 'fake'. The extract is given in two versions: (a) as printed in the score; (b) with slide
positions and accents and other performance directions added. (With thanks to Benny Sluchin.)

Lindberg's hands becomes not just an amusing showpiece, but a work possessed of
genuine rhetoric. (Ill. 85) He is probably the only trombonist in modern times outside
the world of jazz to have conducted an entirely successful career as an international
solo and recording artist, and to have exploited styles as varied as those found in the
classical repertoire, the avant garde and the solos of Arthur Pryor. A virtuoso of
exceptional charisma, Lindberg has recorded almost the entire repertoire of original
works for solo trombone that is worthy of recording, as well as many transcriptions.
Further to this, more than any other performer he has commissioned new works
including a collaboration with Berio for that composer's Solo for Trombone and
Orchestra (1999).[9]

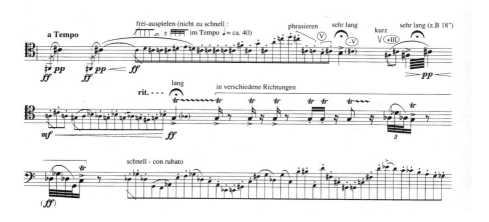

Illustration 84. Stockhausen, *In Freundschaft* (1977). (By permission of the Stockhausen-Verlag. The score and CD of *In Freundschaft*, as well as all works by Karlheinz Stockhausen, may be ordered directly from the Stockhausen-Verlag, 51515 Kürten, Germany. <www.stockhausen.org>.)

The exploitation of the trombone in smaller-scale ensembles – both brass ensembles and those with more varied instrumentation – has been striking. It is not a new phenomenon, but its popularity among both performers and audiences is unprecedented. Smaller-scale art music genres using trombones began to appear in the early twentieth century, coinciding roughly with Stravinsky's 'neo-classical' period. Thus, that composer's *Histoire du Soldat* (1918), *Symphonies of Wind Instruments* (1920) and Octet (1922) quickly became part of the standard repertoire. The development of a purely brass ensemble repertoire has nineteenth-century precedents, particularly in works composed in France and Russia, but despite this ancestry it was in the second half of the twentieth century that it developed an interesting idiomatic flavour. The most coherent grouping has been the quintet, usually made up of two trumpets, horn, trombone and tuba, but several of the leading groups have used this line-up as a core from which to expand.

Many of the later ensembles that include trombones have made an important contribution to the development of the repertoire. The Philip Jones Brass Ensemble, the New York Brass Quintet, Canadian Brass, London Brass and the Wallace Collection have been at the forefront, and the repertoire of these groups – both original compositions and transcriptions – contains some of the most challenging trombone parts to have been written.[10] Among the most interesting works are James MacMillan's *Adam's Rib* (1994–5); Iannis Xenakis's *Khal Perr* (1983) and *Eonta* (1963–4); Berio's *Call* (1985); Tim Souster's *Equalisation* (1980); Tōru Takemitsu's *Waves* (1976) for clarinet solo accompanied with horn, two trombones and bass drum; Pierre Boulez's *Rituel: in memoriam Bruno Maderna* (1975) and *Eclat/Multiples* (1966–78); Petr Eben's Quintet *Variazioni sul'uno corale* (1969); and several works by Globokar, including *Vibone* (1963) for trombone and vibraphone, *Discours II* for five trombones (1967–8) and *Kolo* (1988) for mixed choir, trombone and electronics. *Discours II* can be performed by five 'live' players or by one trombonist with the other

Illustration 85. Christian Lindberg performing Berio's *Sequenza V*. (By permission of *Brass Bulletin.*)

parts being pre-recorded. The composer specified that no 'extraneous noises' (such as those that arise from the actions of taking up and removing mutes) should be reduced or avoided, and that 'While playing, no water is to be emptied from the slides, this resulting in accidental and increasingly frequent water noises.'[11]

Early music and the period instrument movement

The 'early music revival' in its more modern manifestation can be traced to the late 1950s, and its importance to trombone playing is difficult to overstate. It created an entirely new market for music, and an alternative aesthetic to that of the orchestral performance tradition. Many trombone players have been responsive to this movement and have specialized in period performance of one sort or another. Education curricula throughout the world have changed to accommodate new attitudes to historical performance, and by the 1990s some students were entering the conservatoires with the intention of specializing in what was amorphously and somewhat ambiguously referred to as 'early music'. Interestingly enough, trombone players who opted for this route were invariably taught by 'sackbut' specialists, and the use of this epithet became an important if not very precise symbol of difference and demarcation between two quite separate schools of thought: the linear and pragmatic tradition of orchestral trombone playing on the one hand, and the concerns of the historically informed performance sector on the other.

The early music revival flowered from about 1960 (when, for example, the pioneering British group Musica Reservata was formed), though it was not an entirely new phenomenon, precedents for it existing in the work of nineteenth-century and early twentieth-century antiquarians. It was based on two primary factors: an interest in the exploration of earlier (initially, pre-classical) repertoires and a preoccupation with capturing aspects of style and practice that would enable such music to be heard (broadly speaking) as it was heard in the period of its origination.

While the antecedents of the early music movement can be found in the work of nineteenth-century cataloguers, editors and perhaps particularly instrument historians, in the nineteenth and early twentieth centuries several factors militated against there being a clear understanding of the early history of the trombone – and some of these factors continued to prevail even in the period of the early music revival. Victorian musicologists expressed the history of the trombone in either a confused or a preposterously mistaken way. Much of the confusion came from the interpretation of nomenclatures (see Chapter 3). Understanding of the distant idiom of the trombone was not helped by the fact that so much trombone playing in the nineteenth century was seen as brash and alien to contemporary understandings of early repertoires. Furthermore, though the Victorians were capable of making frighteningly rash calls on history – for example, the claim in *Grove's Dictionary* that a trombone had been found at the excavation of Pompeii in the eighteenth century (see Chapter 3) – much of the historical method used at that time was essentially positivist: it placed primacy on the establishment of verifiable facts, but did little to utilize sources to construct a broader narrative about historical practices.

The archival work of the best nineteenth-century antiquarians did much to provide a body of reliable sources for trombone history. But the most important contribution came with the English antiquarian F. W. Galpin's 'The sackbut: its evolution and history', a paper delivered to the Musical Association in November 1906, which should be seen as the starting point for the modern study of the history of the trombone.[12] The logic and general accuracy of Galpin's paper was remarkable for its time, and it stands in stark contrast to the utterances of many of his contemporaries.

He did not merely dispose of several of the more dotty notions about the history of the instrument: he also replaced them with a rational and largely accurate narrative that has been the basis for much of the work that has followed. Galpin's paper, however, was primarily about the instrument itself. He did not completely ignore questions about the musical utility of the instrument, but he dealt principally with the etymology of the word 'sackbut', and with the (mainly English) sources in which it appeared. At the time he was the owner of a sixteenth-century Neuschel trombone that is now in the possession of the Kunsthistorisches Museum, Vienna,[13] and it may be that this instrument stimulated his curiosity.

Galpin's declaration that the sackbut was the instrument that became known as the trombone in modern times may have unwittingly contributed to an all too literal interpretation of historical continuity. Furthermore, the word 'sackbut', with its quaint and antique allusions, became a catch-all expression, a sort of signal for the deep musical past. Thus, Arnold Dolmetsch called his influential early music journal of the 1920s *The Sackbut*, even though it hardly ever mentioned trombones. Similarly, the instrument was never heard in 'The Sackbut Concerts' partly organized by the composer Peter Warlock in the same decade. By the mid-twentieth century, 'sackbut' was a word that most people had heard or read of, but very few knew what it actually meant. It has been argued that the use of this word is an appropriate shorthand for distinguishing instruments made before 1800 from those made later, because the instrument underwent radical changes at that time.[14] This is a perfectly coherent and valid argument, but the use of any word indiscriminately, irrespective of its geography or chronology, results in a cliché, and a feature of all clichés is their distance from precision of meaning.

In the 1950s several publications were issued containing early repertoire that might have been intended for brass instruments. The year 1951 saw the publication of Anthony Baines's edition of Matthew Locke's *ffor his Majestys Sagbutts and Cornetts*. Baines's edition, like many that were to follow, was based on sound primary sources and intelligent reconstruction, but it was aimed squarely at a modern brass quintet of two trumpets and three trombones. In the 1950s and 60s further idiomatic repertoires – primarily of seventeenth-century German and Italian composers – were issued, particularly by the publisher Musica Rara. These too were aimed primarily at modern instrument players, and while they had no real aspiration to provoke interest in period instrument performance, the procedures used for creating the editions were perfectly sound.

Some of the most important pioneering groups originated in the 1950s, such as Noah Greenberg's New York Pro Musica (1952), but these were rooted primarily in the exploration of vocal repertoires and those for string instruments. Trombones became more widely involved in the later 1960s, when sixteenth-century repertoires, particularly dance music, became popular in what were seen as more raucous instrumentations. The 'sackbut' quickly became a standard feature of ensembles with a wind contingent, as several groups – such as David Munrow's London-based Early Music Consort – employed a bewildering array of wind instruments. If it was known to have existed and a modern reproduction could be made, it was played. So many renaissance instruments in combination provoked much delight and curiosity among popular audiences, but to some it seemed an all too indiscriminate pandering to popular tastes. Michael Morrow of Musica Reservata once caustically remarked, not entirely without justification, that the crumhorn had been heard more frequently in London's South Bank Arts Centre in the autumn of 1970 than it had been in the whole of England in the entire sixteenth century.[15]

Until the 1970s early music was seen in terms of a counter-culture that offered an interesting but substantially cerebral alternative to the mainstream of the large musical institutions, the symphony orchestras and opera houses. Musica Reservata, for example, was run on a more or less cottage-industry basis. (Ill. 86) The preparation of performance parts was carried out by Morrow and his co-director John Beckett as a labour of love, and singers and instrumentalists were booked on a sessional basis with the meagre fees being disproportionate to the demands on performers. Between about 1970 and the end of the century, the early music/period performance movement became less of a counter-culture and more of an alternative mode of performance. Up to this time it had occupied the attention of a limited number of professional trombonists who saw it as an additional source of employment, but it did not take long for the expanded repertoire and the increasingly elevated status associated with its performance to reposition it in the consciousness of professional players. For the first time, earlier idioms and repertoires were properly explored by really fine professional players.

Illustration 86. Musica Reservata rehearsing at Hollymount, London, in 1971. The 'sackbut' player is the author, and the instrument is a medium-bore Imperial tenor trombone by Martin of Elkhart, Indiana, manufactured in the 1950s, with the bell cut off. This instrument was used for Musica Reservata recordings before 1975, when a historical model by Egger was acquired. The other members of Musica Reservata seen here are (from the left) Michael Morrow, Edgar Fleet, Margaret Philpot, Adam Skeaping, Bernard Thomas, Jantina Noorman and Andrew Parrott.

Four important conditions caused the period performance business for trombonists to grow. The first was the spread of early music into a wider sphere of popularity, not just in live concerts and recordings, but also in film and television costume drama where such music provided an appropriate backdrop. Secondly, an infrastructure emerged that helped period instrument trombonists to understand and fulfil their roles in this type of playing. This was due in no small part to the interest of a mass of amateurs who facilitated the marketing of early music products and prompted the establishment of an array of summer schools and networks catering primarily for non-professionals. In consequence, several small companies have found it viable to produce good-quality period instruments. Alongside this proliferation of good period instrument makers, there was a growth in the research of performance practice, and the beginning of an educational infrastructure that provided an alternative to an exclusively modern approach to playing. Prominent in this respect was the Schola Cantorum in Basel, Switzerland, which attracted many important European and American players who went on to be highly influential in period performance orbits.

The third factor in the growth of period instrument performance was the application of period performance procedures to increasingly later repertoires, especially those of the late classical and the romantic periods, which provided increased opportunities for the exploration of historical idioms in which there were often ascribed trombone parts. Finally, there was the impact of the introduction of new recording media, particularly the compact disc. This was of enormous importance because it provided one of the vital commercial factors that underpinned the period performance industry and led to new possibilities for the trombone as an ensemble instrument. Most of the important recordings by early music ensembles were on 33-rpm vinyl records, but the introduction in the early 1980s of digital recording and compact discs created unprecedented buoyancy in the art music recording market, and provided an opportunity for much of the canonical repertoire to be re-recorded with historically informed performances. The advent of the CD also made it viable for new, relatively small recording companies to produce small-scale ensemble music. The recording media revolution led to the canonical repertoire being not just re-recorded but also extended. By the end of the twentieth century some of the main period instrument groups, such as the Taverner Players, the Orchestra of the Age of Enlightenment, the London Classical Players, Concentus Musicus, Tafelmusik, Hesperion XX and (to an extent) the New Queen's Hall Orchestra, shared the status that had previously been achieved only by large symphony orchestras and classical chamber orchestras.

Some of the best freelance players in the major music centres of the world became involved in period instrument performance. The majority led dual professional lives as modern instrument and period instrument performers. However, a new breed of specialists also appeared who worked exclusively as performers and teachers of period instruments. Prominent among this group were the tenor trombonist Charles Toet and the bass trombonist Wim Becu. Toet and Becu have been influential as teachers and recording artists because of their knowledge of early repertoires – especially seventeenth-century repertoires – and because their approach has been largely unsullied by exposure to the demands of modern orchestral playing and modern instruments. But by far the most important influence on period instrument trombone playing has not been a trombone player at all, but the American cornettist Bruce Dickey. Dickey, Toet and Becu constitute part of the period instrument group Concerto Palatino, but the three have worked extensively with other ensembles such as the Taverner Players. Dickey was not the first cornett player to perform well on the instrument (the trumpeters Don Smithers, Edward H. Tarr and Michael Laird were important pioneers in the rediscovery of the instrument's idiom), but he was the first cornettist in modern times really to establish himself as a virtuoso by studying the instrument, its repertoire, its performance conventions and its contexts. In so doing, and in taking into consideration the relationship of the cornett and the trombone in seventeenth-century repertoire, Dickey established a point of reference to which serious period instrument trombone players had to respond. Several cornett players followed Dickey's example with considerable eloquence, but it was he who was the first to unveil the true idiomatic identity of the instrument, and in doing so he revealed much about the sound world of the early trombone.

Reproduction instruments

The earliest attempts to produce replica renaissance instruments were neither conscientious nor successful. In the 1960s, the trombonist Anthony Moore possessed an instrument made by Besson that was called a 'sackbut'. Moore would ironically claim authenticity for this instrument on the basis that the word 'Sackbut' was engraved across its bell in pseudo-Gothic script. This instrument was actually produced in June 1958,[16] and was, as far as I know, unique. It was, of course, little more than a standard tenor instrument of the peashooter type made of lacquered brass, with a shortened bell that had been neatly finished with a decorative – and entirely cosmetic – garland. The provenance of this instrument is not known, but it seems likely that it was commissioned by Moore, who had been principal trombone with the London Philharmonic Orchestra, and was one of the first trombone players to perform with Musica Reservata. Needless to say, it sounded little different from the tenor trombone on which it was based, but the cosmetic effect of the removal of the terminal flare of the bell was convincing to the untutored eye. This instrument may have been surprisingly influential, because it is possible that it initiated the species that became known colloquially as the 'cut-down' sackbut – though a more accurate description would be 'cut-down peashooter trombone', because that is what many of the instruments played by 1960s sackbut players were. The key cosmetic difference between narrow-bore trombones and renaissance instruments – so it was perceived – was that the bells of early instruments did not have an exaggerated terminal flare. In London, where most early music recordings took place in the early 1970s, perfectly good narrow- and even medium-bore trombones were converted into 'sackbuts' by sawing off the flare section; sometimes the new terminal edge was made neat by the application of a strip of D-shaped metal. The greatest part of any resulting difference between wide-bore trombones and 'sackbuts' derived from the fact that the 'sackbut' players who played these narrow-bore instruments had no option but to use smaller mouthpieces than they would for their usual wide-bore instruments. Henry Fischer has castigated the practice of cutting down peashooters on the two obvious counts of their lack of authenticity and the barbarity with which the peashooters were treated.[17] It is hard to argue against his view, but it has to be said that the expediencies that were adopted at the time did entice some of the best players in the business into this line of work, and many who took part in some of the most celebrated period performances of the late 1960s and early 1970s (the present writer included) probably have a few skeletons in their cupboard.

But even by this time, manufacturers were attempting to copy existing specimens of early trombones, or making narrow-bore, small-belled instruments that looked so different from modern trombones that they were convincing. However, not all were faithful reproductions, and the main consideration was often to produce an instrument that looked convincingly antique but which had the convenient facilities of a well-made modern trombone. Latterly, period instrument manufacturers have been more successful in making instruments that are either direct copies of, or have been inspired by, extant specimens.[18] Among the more prominent are Egger, Meinl and Lauber, Webb and Tomes. The Egger company has made reproductions that are especially faithful to original instruments by observing the proportions of originals and also by confining the manufacturing process to the techniques that are known to have been used by the original makers. Notwithstanding such efforts, most of these instruments incorporate pragmatic compromises: most are made to modern pitch standards, with disguised tuning slides on the bell bore, and some have siphon water keys.

Repertoires and controversies

Since the late 1980s, later repertoires, even those of the twentieth century, have been the subject of the early music treatment. (Ill. 87) Thus, and perhaps appropriately, the term 'early music' has given way to other expressions such as 'period performance' and 'historically informed performance' – a phrase from which the musicologist John Butt has derived the acronym 'HIP'.[19] The somewhat overused adjective 'authentic', which figured prominently in the 1960s and 70s as a direct challenge to performance values that were historically compromised, has taken a lower profile in more recent debates, but one still senses that it occupies a special place in the vocabulary of some early music traditionalists. Considerable discourse about the period performance ethos has been exercised in practical and philosophical terms: practical, because so much of it has been at the micro-level, with debates about historic instruments, notation, pitch, performance conventions and the interpretation of text being especially prominent; philosophical, because it did not take long for more seasoned commentators to detect in such debates some yawning gaps of logic which gave rise to pressing questions about what, when and whom any given performance should be 'authentic' to. This has led some to conclude that the entire ethos of 'HIP' is neither more nor less than a construction of the twentieth century: that it has created a self-fulfilling ordinance that connects no more meaningfully with the past than most other forms of modern performance.[20]

Leaving aside such matters, we can be certain that the practical ramifications of the early music revival have been considerable. An entirely new sector of work

Illustration 87. A modern manifestation of the historically informed performance ethos: the Wallace Collection assembled in 1995 to perform a reconstruction of the repertoire of the virtuoso Cyfartha Band. The trombonists played nineteenth-century instruments by Joseph Higham.

opportunities has been created, from which trombonists have benefited as much as any others. This has forced players – particularly professional freelancers – to reappraise their approach to historical repertoires, including repertoires with which they may have been intimately familiar through modern instrument performance. The musical and technical demands made on period instrument performers are quite distinct from those inherited through the linear orthodoxies of orchestral playing that have developed since the nineteenth century. Many players successfully bridge the notional divide between modern and period instruments, but the values, processes and even the spheres of musical authority differ considerably in the two sectors. The issue of musical authority – the sources for understanding the role of the trombone in a given piece of music – is especially interesting, because one of the most important outcomes of the retrospective movement has been the discovery and renovation of earlier repertoires – repertoires in which the trombone is inevitably placed as a foreground ensemble instrument. The time is not so distant when, for example, the presence of a trombone with three viols in a performance of a small-scale ensemble fantasia by Frescobaldi would have been seen as a gross incursion, but this is no longer the case.

It follows that, because performance directions are often so slight, trombone players in small period instrument groups are called upon to exercise a level of performance autonomy that they would not experience outside the heterogeneous early music ensembles (and some avant-garde ensembles); thus, at their best, early music groups have fostered consensual and democratic musical decision-making in place of the authority of the conductor. It is therefore somewhat perverse that many of the most successful period instrument groups gain their celebrity from the conductors or leaders who are associated with them. But the change in working practices initiated by the increased involvement of trombonists in settings analogous to chamber music represents a marked shift in the cultural status of the trombone, a shift that is coincidentally mirrored in modernist art music – especially the avant garde.

In the second half of the twentieth century the period performance movement gained in sophistication. But it would be wrong to think that there has been a total resolution of either the practical or aesthetic questions that arise from the use of the trombone in period performances. Indeed, there is cause to believe that more needs to be done by trombonists to understand the repertoires they play on historical instruments: the historic gap is not eliminated when players use a small-bore instrument and call it a sackbut, whoever made it. It is understandable that the demands of modern professional playing encourage players to make historical compromises with their equipment – though it is hard to imagine why some spend so much money on a reproduction instrument and so little time choosing the appropriate mouthpiece for it. It is also understandable that they find it impossible to cast off the modern performance traditions with which they are infused when venturing into the historic or historical. It is nevertheless regrettable that the spirit of experiment that was prominent among some of the more radical groups of the 1970s should have been replaced by a more predictable and frankly bland 'early music sound', in which so much repertoire seems to be treated with a level of deference and gentility that – we might speculate – misses the point. In recent years, the best period instrument performances have had an irreverent earthiness about them that seems genuinely distant from our own times. Then there is the question of difference versus homogeneity. History tells us that only in very recent times has diversity in trombone playing given way to uniformity. Furthermore, from the documents of the Renaissance to the treatises of the nineteenth century, writers attest to the trombone having not one voice but several, and an equal number of articulations and modes of address. We can only hope that a new generation of players will be bold enough to breathe life back into HIP.

The issues that confront period instrument trombonists are similar to those that face other instrumentalists, except that trombonists have the dauntingly seductive prospect of playing a period instrument that can sound perfectly effective when played with modern techniques. Early trombone players may have held the instrument somewhat differently from their modern counterparts, thought in terms that were essentially diatonic rather than chromatic, and may have observed conventions that are now either lost or only partly understood, but the instrument itself and the way it is blown are relatively unchanged. But thoughts of stylistic continuity should be approached with scepticism. The fact is that since the 1960s, attempts to recreate the sound and style of sixteenth- and seventeenth-century players have often been speculative. It is difficult to see how players can dispense with their musical and cultural baggage to revisit the past, but perhaps this overstates the challenge that is before them; perhaps the journey of period instrument performers has less to do with authenticity than with the exercise of sympathy with historic performance values. We are, after all, dealing with history rather than the past – the past, as they say, is dead and gone; history is what historians make of it. This, like the other challenges that face trombonists in the postmodern world, will find its resolution in some form of historical compromise. If it is based on integrity and gives the evidence of the past a fair hearing, it will be worthy of the name 'period performance'.

Appendix 1

Surviving instruments from before 1800

This appendix lists 148 instruments made before 1800 that are, or are thought to be, extant. An asterisk in the 'Holder' column indicates either that I have been unable to identify the holder, or that I have been unable to verify the data with the holder. All entries have otherwise been verified (though information in the 'Pitch' column should be taken as approximate), and I am indebted to the many museum curators who confirmed, corrected and supplied data. I am also indebted to Stewart Carter, who shared with me information from his more comprehensive survey.

Date	Maker	Made in	Voice	Pitch	Holder
1551	Erasmus Schnitzer	Nuremberg	Tenor	B♭	Germanisches Nationalmuseum, Nuremberg, MI 170
1557	Georg Neuschel	Nuremberg	Tenor	B♭	Sammlung alter Musikinstrumente, Kunsthistorisches Museum, Vienna, SAM 706
c.1560	Unknown	Venice?	Tenor	B♭	Accademia Filarmonica, Verona, 13.302
1579	Anton Schnitzer I	Nuremberg	Bass		Accademia Filarmonica, Verona, 13.301
1581	Anton Schnitzer I	Nuremberg	Tenor	B♭	Palais Lascaris, Nice, inv. no. CIII, cat. 2.1.1.1
1587	Conrad Linczer	Nuremberg	Tenor		Museum für Hamburgische Geschichte / Museum für Kunst und Gewerbe, Hamburg, 1928–328
1593	Pierre Colbert	Reims	Bass	G	Gemeentemuseum, The Hague, MUZ-1952x0159
1594	Anton Schnitzer II	Nuremberg	Tenor		Edinburgh University, 2695
1595	Anton Drewelwecz	Nuremberg	Tenor	B♭	Germanisches Nationalmuseum, Nuremberg, MI 167
1602	Andreas Reichart	Erfurt			Unknown (former Burger collection, dispersed 1990)*
1607	Simon Reichard	Nuremberg	Bass	E–F	Germanisches Nationalmuseum, Nuremberg, MIR 148
1608	Jakob Bauer	Nuremberg	Tenor	B♭	ACT City Arts Museum, Hamamatsu, Japan*

1612	Isaac Ehe	Nuremberg	Bass	D–E♭	Germanisches Nationalmuseum, Nuremberg, MI 168
1612	Jobst Schnitzer	Nuremberg	Bass	F	Musikinstrumenten-Museum der Universität Leipzig, 1908
1613	Isaac Ehe	Nuremberg			Marienkirche, Gdańsk?*
1614	Sebastian Hainlein	Nuremberg	Tenor		Sammlung alter Musikinstrumente, Kunsthistorisches Museum, Vienna, SAM 654
1615	Johann Wilhelm Haas	Nuremberg	Tenor		Musikinstrumenten-Museum, Staatliches Institut für Musikforschung Preussischer Kulturbesitz, Berlin, 733
1616	Isaac Ehe	Nuremberg	Bass		Bayerisches Nationalmuseum, Munich, NN 1301
1619	Georg Ehe	Nuremberg	Tenor	B♭	Musée de la Musique, Paris, E.754
1622	Sebastian Hainlein II	Nuremberg	Bass	D	Museum Carolino Augusteum, Salzburg, A29/1 (Geir. 178)
1627	Sebastian Hainlein I	Nuremberg	Tenor	B♭	Bayerisches Nationalmuseum, Munich, Mu 187
1630	Hans Müller	Nuremberg	Tenor	B♭	Musikinstrumenten-Museum der Universität Leipzig, 1895
1631	Hanns Hainlein	Nuremberg	Bass	E♭	Musikinstrumenten-Museum der Universität Leipzig, 1914
1631	Sebastian Hainlein	Nuremberg	Tenor	B♭	Historisches Museum, Frankfurt am Main, X438a
1635	Petrus Goltbeck	Cottbus	Bass	F	Musikinstrumenten-Museum der Universität Leipzig, 1909
1638	Hanns Doll	Nuremberg	Tenor	B♭	Deutsches Museum, Munich, 45280
1639	Georg Nicolaus Öller	Stockholm	Contra-bass	BB♭	Musikmuseet, Stockholm, M242
1640	Georg Nicolaus Öller	Stockholm	Bass	F	Musikmuseet, Stockholm, M252
1642	Sebastian Hainlein II	Nuremberg	Tenor	B♭	Germanisches Nationalmuseum, Nuremberg, MI 169
1649–1701	Wolff Birckholtz	Nuremberg	Alto		Marienkirche, Gdańsk*
1650	Wolff Birckholtz	Nuremberg	Bass	G	Musikinstrumenten-Museum der Universität Leipzig, 1910
c.1650	Rudolf Veit	Naumburg	Tenor	B♭	Musikinstrumenten-Museum, Staatliches Institut für Musikforschung Preußischer Kulturbesitz, Berlin, 641
1651	Hans Veit	Naumburg	Slide trumpet		Musikinstrumenten-Museum, Staatliches Institut für Musikforschung Preußischer Kulturbesitz, Berlin, 639

1652	Sebastian Hainlein II	Nuremberg	Alto		Marienkirche, Gdańsk*
1653	Paul Hainlein	Nuremberg	Tenor	B♭	*
1653	Sebastian Hainlein	Nuremberg	Tenor		Sammlungen der Gesellschaft der Musikfreunde, Vienna, I.N. 445
1653	Georg Ehe	Nuremberg			Marienkirche, Gdańsk*
1654	Hanns Doll	Nuremberg			Marienkirche, Gdańsk*
1656	Michael Nagel	Nuremberg	Tenor	B♭	National Music Museum, Vermillion, SD, 3592
1656	Michael Nagel	Nuremberg	Alto		Bayerisches Nationalmuseum, Munich, Mu 194
?–1661	Balthasar Reuter	Schmalkalden			*
1663	Michael Nagel (?)	Nuremberg		D actual	Horniman Museum (Carse Collection), London, 14.5.47 C.228
1668	Hanns Hainlein	Nuremberg	Bass	F	Musée Instrumental du Conservatoire, Brussels, M1265
1668	Johann Leonhard Ehe I	Nuremberg	Tenor	B♭	Musikinstrumenten-Museum der Universität Leipzig, 1896
1669– 1720	Jacob Schmidt	Nuremberg	Tenor		Muzei Muzïkalnïch Instrumentov, Institut Teatra, Muzïki i Kinematografii, St Petersburg, 576*
1670	Hieronimus Starck	Nuremberg	Alto	E♭	Germanisches Nationalmuseum, Nuremberg, MI 173
1670	Hanns Hainlein	Nuremberg	Tenor	B♭?	Bayerisches Nationalmuseum, Munich, Mu 195
1671	Hanns Geyer	Vienna	Tenor		Sammlungen der Gesellschaft der Musikfreunde, Vienna, I.N. 433
1671	Detlof Otto	Germany	Bass		Musée de la Musique, Paris, E.298
c.1675	Jacob Schmidt	Nuremberg	Alto		Sammlungen der Gesellschaft der Musikfreunde, Vienna, I.N. 198
1676	Hanns Geyer	Vienna	Tenor	B♭	Oberösterreichisches Landesmuseum, Linz, Mu 179
1676	Hanns Geyer	Vienna	Tenor	B♭	Oberösterreichisches Landesmuseum, Linz, Mu 180
1677	Paul Hainlein	Nuremberg	Tenor	C	Germanisches Nationalmuseum, Nuremberg, MI 360
1677	Cristiann Kofahl	Mecklenburg	Soprano		Schloss Kremsegg, Kremsmünster
1678	Francesco Domenico Grigoletti	Klagenfurt			Musikinstrumentenmuseum im Stadtmuseum, Munich, 41/322*
1683	Johann Carl Kodisch	Nuremberg	Tenor		Bayerisches Nationalmuseum, Munich, Mu 186
1683– 1724	Johann Leonhard Ehe II?/III?	Nuremberg	Tenor		Musikmuseet, Stockholm, N64188
1684	Paul Hainlein	Nuremberg	Bass		Musikinstrumenten-Museum, Staatliches Institut für

					Musikforschung Preußischer Kulturbesitz, Berlin, 4191
1684	Paul Hainlein	Nuremberg	Alto		Musikinstrumenten-Museum, Staatliches Institut für Musikforschung Preußischer Kulturbesitz, Berlin, 4189
1684	Paul Hainlein	Nuremberg	Tenor		Musikinstrumenten-Museum, Staatliches Institut für Musikforschung Preußischer Kulturbesitz, Berlin, 4190
1687	Johann Carl Kodisch	Nuremberg	Bass	F	Museum Carolino Augusteum, Salzburg, A29/2 (Geir. 179)
1690	Hieronimus Starck	Nuremberg	Alto	E	Musikinstrumenten-Museum der Universität Leipzig, 1884
1690–1724	Johann Leonhard Ehe II	Nuremberg	Alto	E♭	Musikinstrumenten-Museum der Universität Leipzig, 1885
1690–1724	Johann Leonhard Ehe II	Nuremberg	Alto		Gemeentemuseum, The Hague, MUZ-1933–0508
1690–1724	Johann Leonhard Ehe II	Nuremberg	Tenor		Gemeentemuseum, The Hague, MUZ-1933–0509
1692–1743	Friedrich Ehe	Nuremberg	Alto	D	Musikinstrumenten-Museum, Staatliches Institut für Musikforschung Preußischer Kulturbesitz, Berlin, 31
1692–1743	Friedrich Ehe	Nuremberg	Tenor	B♭	Musikinstrumenten-Museum, Staatliches Institut für Musikforschung Preußischer Kulturbesitz, Berlin, 30
1693–p.1740	Georg Friedrich Steinmetz	Nuremberg	Alto	E♭	Musikinstrumenten-Museum, Staatliches Institut für Musikforschung Preußischer Kulturbesitz, Berlin, 3052
1694	Michael Hainlein	Nuremberg	Tenor		Musikmuseet, Stockholm, M183
1694	Johann Carl Kodisch	Nuremberg			Horniman Museum (Carse Collection), London, 14.5.47 C.294
1695	Wolff Birckholtz	Nuremberg	Alto	E♭	Germanisches Nationalmuseum, Nuremberg, MI 314
1697	Georg Schmied	Pfaffendorf	Alto		Muzeum Instrumentów Muzycznych, Poznań, 145★
1697	Christoph Stephan Scheinhardt	Leipzig			Marienkirche, Gdańsk★
1698	Johann Carl Kodisch	Nuremberg	Alto		Städtisches Museum, Rosenheim
1699	Wolff Birckholtz	Nuremberg	Tenor		Marienkirche, Gdańsk★
17th C.?	Unknown	Switzerland?	Tenor	B♭ [B1]	Historisches Museum, Basel, 1879.50
17th C.?	Unknown	Vienna?	Tenor	B♭	University of Michigan, Stearns Collection of Musical Instruments, Ann Arbor★

17th– early 18th C.	Unknown	Unknown	Tenor		Accademia Filarmonica, Verona
c.1700	Johann Wilhelm Haas	Nuremberg			Museum Schloss Wilhelmsburg, Schmalkalden
c.1700	Johann Wilhelm Haas	Nuremberg	Tenor		Fürstlich Oettingen-Wallersteinische Sammlungen, Harburg, no. 1
c.1700	Johann Wilhelm Haas	Nuremberg	Alto	E♭	Germanisches Nationalmuseum, Nuremberg, MI 177
1701	Johann Carl Kodisch	Nuremberg	Tenor	B/B♭	National Music Museum, Vermillion, SD, 4649
1702	Hanns Geyer	Vienna	Tenor	B♭	Magyar Nemzeti Múzeum, Budapest?*
1702	Hanns Geyer	Vienna	Alto	E♭	Magyar Nemzeti Múzeum, Budapest?*
1706–60	Wolf Wilhelm Haas	Nuremberg	Bass	E♭/D?	Musikinstrumenten-Museum, Staatliches Institut für Musikforschung Preußischer Kulturbesitz, Berlin, 567
c.1710	Friedrich Ehe	Nuremberg	Tenor		Unknown (formerly on loan to Germanisches Nationalmuseum, Nuremberg, MI 174–175)*
1714–94	Wolf Magnus Ehe I or II	Nuremberg	Alto		Musée Instrumental du Conservatoire, Brussels, M1256
1715	Johannes Leichamschneider	Vienna	Tenor		Sammlung alter Musikinstrumente, Kunsthistorisches Museum, Vienna, SAM 655
c.1720	Friedrich Ehe	Nuremberg	Alto	E♭	Germanisches Nationalmuseum, Nuremberg, MI 171
c.1720	Johann Leonhard Ehe II	Nuremberg	Tenor	B♭	Musikinstrumenten-Museum der Universität Leipzig, 1897
1721	Johann Carl Kodisch	Nuremberg	Tenor	B♭	*
1722–71	Johann Leonhard Ehe III	Nuremberg	Tenor	B♭	Deutsches Museum, Munich, 6558
1722–71	Johann Leonhard Ehe III	Nuremberg			Hudební Oddělení Národního Muzea, Prague, 405E*
1722–71	Johann Leonhard Ehe III	Nuremberg			Hudební Oddělení Národního Muzea, Prague, 886E*
1725	Johann Müller	Dresden	Tenor	B	Bachhaus, Eisenach, L10, 1.12.6. (on loan from the Heimatmuseum, Sebnitz)
1725	Johann Müller	Dresden	Alto	E	Bachhaus, Eisenach, L8, 1.12.5 (on loan from the Heimatmuseum, Sebnitz)
1725	Johann Müller	Dresden	Bass	F#	Bachhaus, Eisenach, L11, 1.12.7. (on loan from the Heimatmuseum, Sebnitz)

1727	Johann Carl Kodisch	Nuremberg	Tenor	B♭ [B1]	Historisches Museum, Basel, 1956.622.
1728	Franz Antoni Purggraff	Vienna			Unknown (former Malek collection)*
1732	Johann Leonhard Ehe III	Nuremberg	Quartbass		Sammlungen der Gesellschaft der Musikfreunde, Vienna, I.N. 202
1732	Michael Leichamschneider	Vienna	Tenor		Sammlung alter Musikinstrumente, Kunsthistorisches Museum, Vienna, SAM 255
1733	Johann Heinrich Eichentopf	Leipzig			Focke Museum, Bremen*
1738	Michael Leichamschneider	Vienna			Händel-Haus, Halle, 314*
1738	Michael Leichamschneider	Vienna	Tenor		Sammlung alter Musikinstrumente, Kunsthistorisches Museum, Vienna, SAM 254
1739	Jakob Plüss	Amt Aarburg	Tenor	B♭	Fricktaler Museum, Rheinfelden, B.988
1739	Michael Leichamschneider	Vienna	Tenor		Sammlungen der Gesellschaft der Musikfreunde, Vienna, I.N. 444
1741	Friedrich Ehe	Nuremberg	Tenor		Stockholm?*
1743	Ferdinandus Weisser	Frankenberg	Alto		Unknown (former Breslau collection)*
1743	Martin Friedrich Ehe	Nuremberg	Bass		Stockholm?*
1744	Johann Paull Franck	Hildburg-hausen	Tenor	B♭	National Music Museum, Vermillion, SD, 4896
1747	Johann Umlauff	Prague	Tenor		Unknown (former Strahov collection)*
1747	Johann Umlauff	Prague	Alto		Unknown (former Strahov collection)*
1748–92	Ernst Johann Conrad Haas	Nuremberg	Tenor		Gemeentemuseum, The Hague, MUZ-1933–0510
1751	Joseph Monse	Mährisch Schönberg			Krajské Vlastivědné Muzeum, Olomouc*
1753	Christian (Carl) Friedrich Riedel	Dresden			Hudební Oddělení Národního Muzea, Prague, 955*
1761	Johann Gottfried Leutholdt	Dresden			Whitefield House Museum, Nazareth, Pa.*
1768	Johann Siegmunt Graf	Breitenbach? Oberneubrun?			*
1768	Martin Friedrich Ehe	Nuremberg	Alto	E♭	Germanisches Nationalmuseum, Nuremberg, MI 176
1769?	M. I. G. Eschenbach	Nuremberg?	Tenor	B♭	Germanisches Nationalmuseum, Nuremberg, MI 143
1770–80	J. G. Ahlgren	Stockholm			Musikmuseet, Stockholm, M113

1770	Anton Kerner snr	Vienna			Horniman Museum, London, E83.277 (Boosey & Hawkes 630)
1771	Johann Christoph Fiebig	Berngrund			Musikinstrumenten-Museum, Staatliches Institut für Musikforschung Preußischer Kulturbesitz, Berlin, 3053
1771	Johann Christoph Fiebig	Berngrund	Alto	E♭	National Music Museum, Vermillion, SD, 5946
1776	J. G. Ahlgren	Stockholm	Tenor		Musikmuseet, Stockholm, M114
1776	J. G. Ahlgren	Stockholm	Bass	F	Musikmuseet, Stockholm, M115
1779	Johann Joseph Schmied	Pfaffendorf	Alto	E	Germanisches Nationalmuseum, Nuremberg, MIR 141
1781	Johann Joseph Schmied	Pfaffendorf	Soprano	B♭	Museum of Fine Arts, Boston, C06 17.2006
1783	Johann Joseph Schmied	Pfaffendorf	Tenor	C	Musikinstrumenten-Museum, Staatliches Institut für Musikforschung Preußischer Kulturbesitz, Berlin, 566
1783	Johann Joseph Schmied	Pfaffendorf	Alto		Musikhistorisk Museum, Copenhagen, 209★
1785	Christian Wittmann	Nuremberg	Tenor	B♭	Musikinstrumenten-Museum der Universität Leipzig, 1898
1785	Johann Joseph Schmied	Pfaffendorf	Bass	F [F1]	Historisches Museum, Basel, 1980.2074
1785	Johann Joseph Schmied	Pfaffendorf	Alto	E♭	Historisches Museum, Basel, 1980.2121
1789	Johann Joseph Schmied	Pfaffendorf			Heckewelder Memorial Moravian Church, Gnadenhutten, Ohio★
1789	Johann Simon Schmied?	Pfaffendorf	Alto	D	Musikinstrumenten-Museum der Universität Leipzig, 1887
c.1790?	G. Haltenhof	Hanau	Tenor	B♭	Frankfurt am Main, Historisches Museum, X 8828
1791?	Johann Florian Bittner	Breslau	Bass?		Muzeum Instrumentów Muzycznych, Poznań, 246★
1793	Carl Benjamin Flemming	Breslau			Muzeum Instrumentów Muzycznych, Poznań (Szulc collection)★
1794	Joseph Huschauer (II)	Vienna	Tenor	B♭	Edinburgh University, 3205
1795	August Friedrich Krause II	Berlin	Alto	E♭	Historisches Museum, Basel, 1980.2066
1796	I. F. Schwabe?	Leipzig	Soprano	B♭	Musikinstrumenten-Museum der Universität Leipzig, 1879
1796	Johann Georg Eschenbach	Markneu-kirchen	Tenor	B♭	Musikinstrumenten-Museum der Universität Leipzig, 1899
1796	Johann Georg Eschenbach	Markneu-kirchen	Soprano B♭	B♭ B♭	Musikinstrumenten-Museum der Universität Leipzig, 1880

1797	Carl Benjamin Flemming	Breslau	Alto	E♭	Musikinstrumenten-Museum der Universität Leipzig, 1888
1799	Christian Gottlob Eschenbach	Markneu-kirchen	Alto	E♭?	Musikinstrumenten-Museum, Staatliches Institut für Musikforschung Preußischer Kulturbesitz, Berlin, 3967
1799	Johann Simon Schmied	Pfaffendorf	Bass	F	Musikinstrumenten-Museum, Staatliches Institut für Musikforschung Preußischer Kulturbesitz, Berlin, 314
Late 18th C.	Carl Ziersfeld	Erfurt	Tenor		Musikinstrumenten-Museum, Staatliches Institut für Musikforschung Preußischer Kulturbesitz, Berlin, 29
Late 18th C.	Carl Ziersfeld	Erfurt	Alto	D	Musikinstrumenten-Museum, Staatliches Institut für Musikforschung Preußischer Kulturbesitz, Berlin, 732
c.1800	Unknown	Germany?	Tenor	B♭	Horniman Museum, London (Carse Collection) 14.5.47 C.195

Literature (see also the web sites of holding institutions)

Albertson, H., *Ahlberg & Ohlsson, en Fabrik för Bleckblåsinstrument i Stockholm 1850–1959* (Stockholm: Musikmuseet, 1990).

Baines, A., *Brass Instruments: Their History and Development*, 1976 (London: Faber, 1980).

Carter, S., 'Early trombones in America's Shrine to Music Museum', *Historic Brass Society Journal,* 10 (1998), 92–115.

——, 'Trombone pitch in the eighteenth century: an overview', in *Posaunen und Trompeten: Geschichte – Akustik – Spieltechnik*, ed. M. Lustig (Blankenburg: Stiftung Kloster Michaelstein, 2000), pp. 53–66.

Epstein, P., *Katalog der Musikinstrumente im Historischen Museum der Stadt Frankfurt am Main* (Frankfurt am Main, 1927).

Epstein, P., and E. Scheyer, *Schlesisches Museum fur Kunstgewerbe und Altertümer: Führer und Katalog zur Sammlung alter Musikinstrumeten* (Breslau, 1932).

Fischer, H. G., *The Renaissance Sackbut and its Use Today* (New York: Metropolitan Museum of Art, 1984).

Heyde, H., *Historische Musikinstrumente im Bachhaus Eisenach* (Eisenach: Bachhaus, 1976).

——, *Musikinstrumenten-Museum der Karl-Marx-Universität, Katalog Band 3: Trompeten, Posaunen, Tuben*, (Leipzig: Deutscher Verlag für Musik, 1980).

——, *Das Ventilblasinstrument* (Leipzig: VEB Deutscher Verlag für Musik, 1987).

Huber, R., *Verzeichnis sämtlicher Musikinstrumente im Germanischen Nationalmuseum Nürnberg* (Wilhelmshaven: Florian Noetzel Verlag, 1989).

Kitzel, L., 'The Trombones of the Shrine to Music Museum' (DMA thesis, University of Oklahoma, 1985).

Klaus, S., 'Trompeten und Posaunen in der Musikinstrumenten-Sammlung des Historischen Museums Basel', in *Historisches Museum Basel Jahresbericht 1998* (Basel: Historisches Museum, 1999), pp. 27–62.

——, 'Outstanding trumpets, trombones, and horns in the musical instrument collection of the Historical Museum, Basel', *Historic Brass Society Journal*, 12 (2000), 1–22.

Laubhold, L., 'Sensation or forgery? The 1677 soprano trombone of Cristian Kofahl', *Historic Brass Society Journal*, 12 (2000), 259–65.

Myers, A. (ed.), *Historic Musical Instruments in the Edinburgh University Collection* (Edinburgh: Edinburgh University Collection of Historic Musical Instruments, 1990).

Nicholson, G., 'Brass instruments at the Gemeente-Museum in the Hague', *Brass Bulletin*, 77, no. 1 (1992), 76–89.

Schröder, H., *Museum für Hamburgische Geschichte: Verzeichnis der Sammlung alter Musikinstrumente* (Hamburg: Alster Verlag, 1930).

Seifers, H., *Die Blasinstrumente im Deutschen Museum* (München and Düsseldorf: R. Oldenbourg Verlag; VDI-Verlag, 1976).

Stanley, A. A., *Catalogue of the Stearns Collection of Musical Instruments* (Ann Arbor, Mi.: University of Michigan, 1921).

Van der Meer, J. H., M. Kimbauer and M. Kares, *Verzeichnis der europäischen Musikinstrumente im Germanischen Nationalmuseum Nürnberg* (Wilhelmshaven, Hamburg, Locarno and Amsterdam: Heinrichshofen, 1979).

Van der Meer, J. H., and R. Weber, *Catalogo degli strumenti musicali dell'Accademia Filarmonica di Verona* (Verona: Accademia Filarmonica di Verona, 1982).

Wackernagel, B., *Musikinstrumente des 16. bis 18. Jahrhunderts im Bayerischen Nationalmuseum* ([Munich: Bayerisches Nationalmuseum?], n.d.).

Waterhouse, W., *The New Langwill Index: A Dictionary of Musical Wind-Instrument Makers and Inventors* (London: Tony Bingham, 1993).

Wörthmüller, W., 'Die Nürnberger Trompeten- und Posaunenmacher des 17. und 18. Jahrhunderts', *Mitteilungen des Vereins für Geschichte der Stadt Nürnberg*, 45 (1954), 208–325.

——, 'Die Instrumente der Nürnberger Trompeten- und Posaunenmacher', *Mitteilungen des Vereins für Geschichte der Stadt Nürnberg*, Band 46 (1955), 372–480.

Appendix 2

Centres of trombone repertoire in the seventeenth and eighteenth centuries

This table provides a loose impression of centres of trombone performance in the seventeenth and eighteenth centuries by identifying composers who contributed to trombone repertoire, and the towns or regions in which they worked.

Country	Date	Town (Region)	Composer
Austria	17th C.: early	Breslau [?]	S. Bernardi?, S. Lemle
		Carniola	I. Posch
		Graz	G. Priuli, G. Valentini
		Kremsmünster	B. Lechler
		Ödenberg	A. Rauch
		Salzburg	S. Bernardi
		Vienna	G. Priuli, C. Strauss, G. Valentini
	17th C.: mid	Breslau [?]	W. C. Briegel, M. Büttner, M. Franck, R. Giovanelli, A. Grandi, O. M. Grandi, A. Hammerschmidt, H. L. Hassler, J. E. Kindermann, F. Lilius, T. Michael, A. Michna, S. Ottonis, M. Praetorius, A. Rigatti, J. Rosenmüller, G. Rovetta, P. Schäffer?, S. Scheidt, J. H. Schein, J. Schopp, H. Schütz, D. Selich, G. Valentini, J. Vierdanck, N. Zangius, T. Zeutschner
		Constance	A. Megerle
		Innsbruck	J. Stadlmayr, A. Reiner
		Ödenberg	A. Rauch
		Salzburg	A. Megerle
		Vienna	A. Bertali, A. Cesti, W. Ebner, Ferdinand III, M. A. Ferro, G. F. Sances, H. Schmelzer, J. K. Tolar [Dolar], G. Valentini, P. Verdina?
	17th C.: late	Breslau [?]	M. Mayer [from 1675], J. Phengius, J. Scheibel
		Constance	A. Megerle
		Salzburg	H. I. F. von Biber, A. Hofer?, A. Megerle, G. Muffat?
		Vienna	A. Caldara, A. Draghi, J. J. Fux, J. K. Kerll, Leopold I, G. Reutter, G. F. Sances, J. H. Schmelzer, J. K. Tolar [Dolar], F. Vismari [Vismarri]
	18th C.: early	Breslau [?]	M. Mayer
		Göttweig	A. Caldara
		Salzburg	C. H. Biber, H. I. F. von Biber, M. S. Biechteler
		Vienna	A. Caldara, F. Conti, I. Conti, J. J. Fux, Joseph I, C. J. Pachschmidt, G. Reutter,

			F. Vismari [Vismarri], J. M. Zacher, M. A. Ziani
	18th C.: mid	Göttweig	J. N. Boog, A. Caldara, A. Carl, G. Donberger, F. Fauner, L. Hofmann, J. Krottendorfer, L. A. Predieri, F. Schmidt, C. Sonnleithner, F. Tuma, G. C. Wagenseil, G. J. Werner, J. G. Zechner
		Heiligenkreuz	G. Donberger, G. J. Werner
		Herzogenburg	A. Carl, G. Donberger, F. G. Pruneder, F. Tuma
		Melk	J. G. Albrechtsberger, F. Tuma, J. G. Zechner
		Salzburg	A. Adlgasser, C. H. Biber, J. E. Eberlin, J. M. Haydn, L. Mozart, W. A. Mozart
		Vienna	J. G. Albrechtsberger, I. Beyer, J. N. Boog, A. Caldara, F. J. Ehrenhardt, J. J. Fux, F. Gassmann, C. W. Gluck, M. G. Monn, M. Oettl, J. Porsile, L. A. Predieri, J. G. Reinhardt, G. Reutter, F. Schmidt, F. Tuma, G. C. Wagenseil, A. Werndle
		Wilhering	J. N. Boog, A. Caldara, G. Donberger, L. Hofmann, J. G. Reinhardt, J. G. Reutter, F. Schmidt, F. Tuma, J. G. Zechner
	18th C.: late	Göttweig	J. Krottendorfer, C. Sonnleithner, J. G. Zechner
		Salzburg	J. M. Haydn, L. Mozart, W. A. Mozart
		St. Florian	F. J. Aumann
		Vienna	J. G. Albrechtsberger, F. Gassmann, C. W. Gluck, F. J. Haydn, L. Hofmann, W. A. Mozart, F. Paer?, A. Salieri, M. Ulbrich
Belgium	17th C.: mid	Brussels	N. a Kempis
	17th C.: late	?	B. de Saint-Joseph
Bohemia/ Moravia/ Slovakia	17th C.: mid	Jindřichův Hradec	A.V. Michna
		Kroměříž	P. J. Vejvanovsky
	17th C.: late	Jindřichův Hradec	A.V. Michna
		Kroměříž	H. I. F. Biber, P. J. Vejvanovsky. Composers represented in the Liechtenstein Collection, Kroměříž: J. G. Abersbach, H. A. Bähr, A. Bertali, H. A. Brückner, B. Bulowsky, S. F. Capricornus, J. Degen, W. Ebner, J. J. Flixius, V. Fux, P. Germani, G. Götzl, A. Hofer, W. Hueber, J. K. Kerll, A. Kern, A. Kerzinger, G. F. Libertini, J. Melcelius, I. G. Miller, G. Peranda, P. J. Rittler, A. L. Rupe, G. F. Sances, J. H. Schmelzer, J. K. Tolar [Dolar], G. Valentini, P. Verdina, F. Vismarri, J. M. Zacher
		Olomouc	P. J. Rittler

		Prague	V. Albrici
	18th C.: early	Prague	J. C. Gayer?
	18th C.: late	Johannisberg nr Jauernig	C. D. von Dittersdorf
		Pressburg (Bratislava)	A. Zimmermann
		Zbraslav/Prague	G. A. Stolle
Denmark	17th C.: mid	Nykøbing	M. Weckmann?
England	17th C.: early	London	J. Adson, J. Coprario, N. Lanier
	17th C.: mid	Cambridge	H. Loosemore
		London	C. Coleman?, J. Hingeston, N. Lanier, M. Locke
	17th C.: late	London	J. Hingeston, M. Locke
	18th C.: early	London	G. F. Handel?
	18th C.: mid	London	G. F. Handel
	18th C.: late	London	S. Arnold, F. J. Haydn, M. Kelly, I. Pleyel, D. Steibelt
France	17th C.: early	Zabern (Alsace)	V. Jelić
	17th C.: late	Paris	J. B. Lully
	18th C.: mid	Paris	C. W. Gluck, F.-J. Gossec, F.-A. D. Philidor
	18th C.: late	Paris	M. J. Adrien, H. M. Berton, F. Blasius?, A. Boieldieu, G. G. Cambini, P. Candeille, C. S. Catel, L. Cherubini, N. Dalayrac, F. Deviennes?, N. Dezede, J. F. Edelmann, P. Gaveaux, C. W. Gluck, F.-J. Gossec, A. Gretry, L. E. Jadin, R. Kreutzer, J. M. Lamare, H. Langle, X. Lefèvre, N.-J. Le Froid de Méreaux, J. F. A. Lemière de Corvey, J. B. Lemoyne, J.-F. Lesueur, E. Méhul, E. L. Muller?, N. Piccinni, C. H. Plantade, J. B. Rochefort, P. Rode, J.-J. Rodolphe, A. Sacchini, D. Steibelt, A. Tarchi, J. C. Vogel
		Strasbourg	I. Pleyel?, C.-J. Rouget de Lisle?
Germany	17th C.: early	Altötting	A. Megerle
		Celle	H. Utrecht
		Coburg	M. Franck?
		Dresden	H. Schütz
		Halle	S. Scheidt
		Kassel	Landgraf von Hessen
		Leipzig	S. Michael, T. Michael, J. H. Schein
		Munich	G. M. Cesare, B. Borlasca, R. de Lassus
		Neuburg an der Donau	B. Marini
		Sömmerda	M. Altenburg
		Tröchtelborn nr Gotha	M. Altenburg
		Wolfenbüttel	M. Praetorius, D. Selich
	17th C.: mid	Altötting	A. Megerle
		Augsburg	J. M. Gletle
		Bamberg	G. Arnold
		Bayreuth	C. Sartorius
		Coburg	M. Franck?

	Dresden	V. Albrici, C. Bernhard, C. Liebe?, G. Peranda, H. Schütz, M. Weckmann
	Eger? (Cheb, Czech Republic)	J. G. Braun
	Erfurt	M. Altenburg
	Frankfurt	J. A. Herbst
	Freiberg	A. Hammerschmidt?, S. Otto
	Gotha	G. L. Agricola, W. K. Briegel
	Gottorf	A. Pfleger
	Guben	C. Peter
	Halle	S. Scheidt, D. Pohle
	Hamburg	J. Schop, T. Selle, M. Weckmann
	Königsberg (now in Russia)	H. Albert, J. Sebastiani, J. Weichmann
	Leipzig	W. Fabricius, S. Knupfer, S. Michael, T. Michael, J. C. Pezel, J. Rosenmüller
	Lübeck	D. Buxtehude
	Lüneburg	F. Funcke
	Meissen	C. A. Schulze
	Mühlhausen	J. G. Ahle, J. R. Ahle
	Munich	J. K. Kerll?
	Nuremberg	P. Hainlein, J. E. Kindermann, H. Schwemmer, J. Staden, G. C. Wecker
	(Saxony/Thuringia)	J. Küsser
	Schandau (Saxony)	S. Otto
	Stade	H. Hake
	Stettin	A. Fromm
	Stralsund	J. Vierdanck
	Stuttgart	P. F. Böddecker, S. F. Capricornus
	Weimar	A. Drese, A. Uswaldt
	Zittau	A. Hammerschmidt
17th C.: late	Augsburg	J. M. Gletle, G. Schmezer
	Bautzen	J. C. Pezel
	Brunswick	D. Strungk, C. Monari?
	Darmstadt	W. K. Briegel
	Dresden	V. Albrici, C. Bernhard, H. Schütz, J. C. Schmidt
	Eichstätt	R. I. Mayr
	Eilenburg	J. H. Hildebrand
	Erfurt	G. L. Agricola, J. G. Ahle, P. Becker, W. C. Briegel, C. Bütner, D. Buxtehude, G. Calmbach, J. H. Hildebrand, S. Knüpfer, J. P. Krieger, J. Rosenmüller, H. Schütz
	Frankfurt	G. C. Strattner
	Gehren	J. M. Bach
	Göppingen	D. Speer
	Gottorf	M. Köler, J. Theile
	Grimma	V. Albrici, P. Crusius, W. Fabricius, S. Knüpfer, M. G. Peranda, J. Rosenmüller, J. Schelle, C. A. Schulze, D. Vetter, F. W. Zachow, J. C. Ziegler
	Halle	D. Pohle
	Hamburg	J. Gerstenbüttel

		Königsberg	J. Sebastiani
		Leipzig	J. C. Horn, S. Knupfer, J. Kuhnau,
			J. C. Pezel, G. Reiche, J. Schelle, D. Vetter
		Lübeck	D. Buxtehude
		Lüneburg	G. Böhm
		Meissen	C. A. Schulze
		Merseburg	J. Theile?
		Mühlhausen	J. G. Ahle
		Nuremberg	H. Schwemmer
		Passau	G. Muffat?
		Rudolstadt	P. H. Erlebach
		(Saxony/Thuringia)	J. Küsser
		Sondershausen	N. Niedt
		Stuttgart	J. M. Nicolai
		Weissenfels	J. Beer, J. P. Krieger
		Wittenberg	J. Ulich?
		Wolfenbüttel	J. Theile
		Zeitz	C. Thieme
		Zittau	J. Krieger
		Zschopau	C. Liebe
	18th C.: early	Brunswick	C. Monari
		Dresden	J. C. Schmidt, J. D. Zelenka
		Eisenach	G. Telemann
		Frankfurt	G. Telemann
		Halle	J. S. Bach, F. W. Zachow
		Hamburg	G. Telemann
		Leipzig	J. S. Bach, J. Kuhnau, G. Reiche, D. Vetter
		Lübeck	D. Buxtehude
		Lüneburg	G. Böhm
		Passau	G. Muffat? (d. 1704)
		Rudolstadt	P. H. Erlebach
		Schwäbisch Hall	J. S. Welter?
		Stuttgart	J. G. C. Störl
		Weissenfels	J. P. Krieger
	18th C.: mid	Brunswick	C. Monari
		Dresden	J. A. Hasse
		Leipzig	J. S. Bach, J. G. Görner
	18th C.: late	Dresden	J. G. Naumann
		Leipzig	J. F. Doles, J. G. Görner
		Magdeburg	J. H. Rolle
Hungary	18th C.: mid	Eszterháza	F. J. Haydn
	18th C.: late	Eszterháza	F. J. Haydn
Italy	17th C.: early	Belluno	G. Ganassi
		Bergamo	A. Grandi
		Bologna	A. Banchieri
		Brescia	P. Lappi
		Casalmaggiore	I. Donati
		Cremona	N. Corradini, L. Viadana
		Fano	L. Viadana
		Ferrara	A. Crotti, A. Grandi
		Forlí	A. Franzoni
		Imola	G. Belli

		Lodi	T. Massaino
		Mantua	A. Franzoni, C. Monteverdi
		Milan	G. P. Cima, G. Pietragrua
		Modena	S. Cesis
		Novara	I. Donati
		Reggio nell'Emilia	A. Borsaro?, O. M. Grandi
		Palermo	B. Montalbino
		Persiceto nr Bologna	E. Porta
		Pescia	F. Croatti
		Pisa	A. Buonavita
		Treviso	A. Freddi
		Venice	G. Bondioli, D. Castello, N. Fontei, G. Gabrieli, A. Grandi, B. Marini, C. Monteverdi, G. Picchi, G. Priuli?, G. B. Riccio?, F. Usper
		Verona	S. Bernardi
		Vicenza	C. Baselli, L. Leoni
		?	B. Miseroca, A. Molli, B. Re?
	17th C.: mid	Assisi	G. B. Buonamente
		Bologna	M. Cazzatti
		Carrara	F. Colombini?
		Civita Castellana	V. Mazzocchi
		Faenza	O. Tarditi
		Forlí	G. V. Sarti
		Modena	M. Uccellini
		Messina	F. Fiamengo
		Venice	F. Cavalli, G. B. Chinelli, M. Neri, J. Rosenmüller, G. Rovetta
		?	G. Urbano
	17th C.: late	Bologna	G. P. Colonna, G. Jacchini, G. A. Perti, G. A. Silvani
		Forlí	C. Monari
		Lonato nr Brescia	S. Pasino
		Naples	A. Scarlatti
		Pistoia	J. Melani
		Reggio nell'Emilia	C. Monari
		Venice	J. Rosenmüller, M. A. Ziani?
	18th C.: early	Bologna	G. A. V. Aldrovandini, G. A. Perti, G. A. Silvani, G. Torelli
		Forlí	C. Monari
		Modena	G. M. Bononcini
		Reggio nell'Emilia	C. Monari
		Rome	F. Magini
	18th C.: mid	Bologna	G. A. Perti
		Forlí	C. Monari
		Reggio nell'Emilia	C. Monari
	18th C.: late?	Parma	F. Paer?
Latvia	17th C.: late	Riga	J. V. Meder
	18th C.: early	Riga	J. V. Meder
Poland	17th C.: early	Warsaw	A. Jarzebski, T. Merula, M. Mielczewski
	17th C.: mid	Danzig [?]	C. Bütner, J. V. Meder?, P. Siefert
		Krakow	F. Lilius, B. Pekiel?

		Thorn	J. Hentzschel
		(Silesia)	M. Jahn, M. A. von Löwenstern?, M. Schneider
		Warsaw	M. Mielczewski, B. Pekiel, J. H. Rozycki?
	17th C.: late	Danzig	C. Bütner, J. V. Meder
		(Silesia)	M. Jahn
		Warsaw	B. Pekiel?, J. H. Rozycki?
Russia	18th C.: late	St Petersburg	C. Canobbio, G. Sarti with Canobbio and Pashkeevich, D. Steibelt?
Spain	17th C.: early	Córdoba	G. Díaz [Bessón]
		Lerma	G. Díaz [Bessón]
		Madrid	G. Díaz [Bessón]
		Valencia	J. B. Comes?
Sweden	17th C.: late	Stockholm	Composers represented in the Düben Collection (now in Uppsala): V. Albrici, A. Bertali, S. Capricornus, P. Hainlein, J. Pezel, D. Pohle, J. H. Schmelzer, H. Schütz, J. Theile, G. Valentini
	18th C.: late	Stockholm	J. C. F. Haeffner, J. M. Kraus, J. G. Naumann

Sources

Carter, S., 'Trombone pitch in the eighteenth century: an overview', in *Posaunen und Trompeten: Geschichte – Akustik – Spieltechnik*, ed. M. Lustig (Blankenburg: Stiftung Kloster Michaelstein, 2000), pp. 53–66.

Collver, M. and B. Dickey, *A Catalog of Music for the Cornett* (Bloomington and Indianapolis: Indiana University Press, 1996).

Guion, D. M. , *The Trombone: Its History and Music, 1697–1811*, Musicology: A Book Series 6 (New York: Gordon and Breach, 1988).

Leonard, C. A., 'The role of the trombone and its *Affekt* in the Lutheran church music of seventeenth-century Saxony and Thuringia', *Historic Brass Society Journal*, 10 (1998), 57–91, and 12 (2000), 161–209.

The Robert Minter Collection at the Open University, UK.

Weiner, H., unpublished catalogue of early trombone music.

Appendix 3

Slide trombone methods: an indicative list

Date	Author	Title	Place	Publisher
c.1793–7	A. Braun	*Gamme et méthode pour les trombonnes alto, ténor et basse*	Paris	Jean-Georges Sieber
c.1800	F. R. Gebauer	*50 Leçons pour la trombonne basse, alto et tenor*	Paris	[Jean-Georges?] Sieber
c.1810–11	J. Fröhlich	*Vollständige theoretisch-pracktische Musikschule*	Bonn	N. Simrock
between 1816 and 1826	Sturm	*Méthode complette pour les trombonnes basse, tenor et alto* (no copy known to exist)	Paris	Philippe Petit
1827	A. Nemetz	*Neueste Posaun-Schule*	Vienna	Anton Diabelli & Co.
1831	V. Cornette	*Méthode de trombone*	Paris	Richault
1834	F. Vobaron	*Grande Méthode de trombone*	Paris	Gambaro
between 1834 and 1840	Schiltz	*Méthode complète et raisonée pour le trombone*	Paris?	Nouvelle Societé pour la Publication de Musique Classique et Moderne
c.1835	A. Dieppo and F. Berr	*Méthode de trombone*	Paris	Meissonier
1837	A. Dieppo	*Méthode complète pour le trombone*	Paris	Troupenas
c.1841	Pridhem	*Nouvelle Méthode de trombone*	Paris	Joly
c.1842	V. Cornette	*Méthode du trombone alto, tenor et basse*	Paris	Richault
c.1844	J.-G. Kastner	*Méthode élémentaire pour le trombone*	Paris	Troupenas
1845?	Hartmann	*Méthode élémentaire de trombonne*	Paris	Schonenberger
1847	A.-F.-N. L. de la Tuilerie	*Méthode préparatoire de Trombone*	Paris	Lafont
n.d. (mid-19th C.)	E. Cam	*Méthode pour le trombone ordinaire et pour le trombone à pistons*	Paris	Costallat
c.1851	A. Brulon,	*Méthode de trombone à coulisse*	Paris	Joly
c.1852	F.(?) Vobaron	*Méthode complète de trombone*	Paris?	Brandus
c.1853	E. Vobaron	*Méthode de trombone*	Paris	Richault
1854	V. Cornette	*Méthode de trombone*	Paris	Colombier
c.1858	E. Hemet	*Traité théorique et pratique pour apprendre à jouer trombone en peu*	Paris	Richault

		de temps		
c.1863	Blancheteau	*Petite Méthode de trombone à coulisse*	Paris	Margueritat
1863/4?	Clodomir (P.-F.-M. de Borrit)	*Méthode complète de trombone à coulisse*, vol. 1	Paris	Leduc
c.1865	M. Guichard	*École de fanfare*	Paris	Gautrot
1866	M. Girard	*Petite Méthode de trombone à coulisse*	Paris	Gautrot Sr
mid/late 19th C.	M. Bléger	*Méthode de trombone*	Paris	not given
c.1866	Clodomir (P.-F.-M. de Borrit)	*Méthode élémentaire de trombone à coulisse à l'usage des fanfares et des collèges*	Paris	Leduc
1870	A. Wirth	*Posaunen-Schule für Alt, Tenor und Bass Posaune . . . Instruction Book of the Simple and Valve-Trombone*	London	Augener & Co.
1870?	A. J. Phasey	*Chappell's Popular Instruction Book for the Trombone*	London	Chappell
c.1874	A. Boscher	*Méthode générale d'enseignement*	Paris	David
before 1875	L.-A.(?) Vimeux	*Méthode de trombone*	Paris?	not given
1875?	Clodomir (P.-F.-M. de Borrit)	*Méthode complète de trombone à coulisse*, vol. 2	Paris	Leduc
1880?	F. Vobaron, H. Berr, A. Dieppo	*Complete Trombone Tutor: Slide or Valve*	London	Lafleur
1883	P. Delisse	*Opuscule rudimentaire et classique*	Paris	Millereau
1885	O. Langey	*Tutor for the Tenor Slide Trombone*	London	not given
c.1885	G. Tilliard	*Méthode de trombone*	Paris	Tilliard
1887	J. A. Kappey	*Complete Tutor for Tenor Trombone in B flat, and Bass Trombone in G, Slide and Valve*	London	Boosey & Co.
before 1889	J. Javelot	*Méthode de trombone tenor en si bémol ou c*	Paris?	Éditions Bornemann
1889	T. Wright and H. Round	*Wright and Round's Amateur Band Teacher's Guide and Bandsman's Adviser*	Liverpool	Wright and Round
c.1894	V. Sambin	*Méthode de trombone à coulisse*	Paris	Lafleur Sr
1895	G. Parès	*Méthode de trombone à coulisse*	Paris	Lemoine
c.1900	P. de Ville	*Universal Method for Slide and Valve Trombone in Bass and Treble Clef*	New York	Carl Fischer
1902	O. Langey	*The Otto Langey Series Practical Tutor for the G Bass Slide Trombone*	London	Hawkes & Son
1902	R. Müller	*Schule für Zugposaune*	Leipzig	W. Zimmermann
1905	Salvation Army	*The Salvation Army Tenor Trombone Tutor (Valve and Slide)*	London	Publishing Offices
1907	L. Fontbonne	*Méthode complète, théorique et pratique de trombone à coulisse et à pistons*	Paris	Costallat

1909	O. Langey	*Practical Tutor for the Bb Slide-Trombone*, rev. edn	London	Hawkes & Son
1910	G. Flandrin	*Méthode complète de trombone à coulisse*, 2 vols	Paris	A. Dubois
1916	C. Hampe	*Hampe Method for the Slide Trombone, with an appendix for the Trombone with Valves*	Chicago	F. Holstein & Co.
1919	H. Fillmore	*Jazz Trombonist*	Cincinnati, Ohio	Fillmore Music House
c.1920	F. Sordillo	*Art of Jazzing for the Trombone*	Boston	Oliver Ditson Co.
1921	W. M. Eby (ed.)	*Arban's Complete Celebrated Method for Trombone, Baritone and Other Instruments in Bass Clef*	Buffalo, NY	W. M. Eby
1921	A. Lafosse	*Méthode complète pour le trombone*, vols 1 and 2	Paris	Leduc
1923	G. Flandrin	*Méthode complète de trombone à coulisse*, complete edn	Paris	Gaudet
1926	R. MacDonald	*Daily Exercises for the Trombone (in Bass Clef)*	London	Boosey & Hawkes
1940	J. Cimera and N. W. Hovey	*The Cimera-Hovey Method for Trombone and Baritone*	New York	Belwin
1944	W. Beeler	*Method for the Trombone*	Secaucus, NJ	Warner Bros. Music
1946	H. Couillaud	*Méthode de trombone à coulisse*	Paris	Leduc
1946	A. Lafosse	*Méthode complète pour le trombone*, vol. 3 of 3	Paris	Leduc
1946	A. Shapiro	*Modern Universal Method*	New York	Carl Fischer
1948	M. Bléger	*Méthode de trombone à coulisse*	Paris	Leduc
1950	R. Miller and E. E. Lyon	*School for Trombone*	Stamford, CT	Jack Spratt
1951	L. Laurent	*Méthode de trombone à coulisse classique et jazz*	Paris	Beuscher
1953–9	A. Stöneberg	*Neue umfassende Posaunenschule*	Cologne	Hans Gerig
1955	A. Lafosse	*Traité de pedagogie du trombone à coulisse*	Paris	Leduc
1956	A. Lafosse	*Vade Mecum du tromboniste*	Paris	Leduc
1956	H. Kunitz	*Die Instrumentation, 8: Posaune*	Leipzig	Breitkopf & Härtel
1959?	A. Pugliese	*School for Trombone*	Milan	Ricordi
1960	P. Bernard	*Méthode complète pour trombone basse, tuba, saxhorns basses et contrebasses*	Paris	Leduc
1960	A. Bambula	*Die Posaune*	Leipzig	Hofmeister
1963	E. Kleinhammer	*The Art of Trombone Playing*	Evanston, Ill	Summy-Birchard Company
1966	A. Ostrander	*Method for Bass Trombone and F Attachment for Tenor*	New York	Carl Fischer
1970	H. Müller	*Posaunenfibel*	Leipzig	Hofmeister

1971	D. Wick	*Trombone Technique*	London	Oxford University Press
1972	E. Bert	*The Eddie Bert Trombone Method*	New York	Charles Colin
1973–9	J. Doms	*Posaunenschule*	Berlin	Johann Doms
1975	C. Colin	*Complete Modern Method*	New York	Charles Colin
1977	J. Douay	*L'A.B.C. du jeune tromboniste*	Paris	Éditions Billaudot
1977	A. Rosin	*Posaunenschule*	Vienna	Universal Editions
1978	J. Toulon	*J'apprends le trombone: méthode progressive de trombone à coulisse*	Mâcon, France	Éditions Robert Martin
1980–1	M. McDunn and H. Rusch	*Méthode de trombone*	Paris	Leduc
1983	R. N. Anderson	*Complete Method*	Sioux City, Iowa	Modern Editions
1983	I. Rosenthal	*The Trombone*	Los Angeles	Western International Music
1983	B. Slokar	*Méthode complète de trombone alto*	Zumikon, Switzerland	Marc Reift
1986	R. Josel	*Posaunenschule*	Vienna	Ludwig Krenn
1992	B. Slokar	*Method for Bass Trombone*	Zumikon, Switzerland	Marc Reift
n.d.	J. Bleicher	*Le Tromboniste commençant*	Paris	Éditions M. Combre
n.d.	U. Semproni	*Metodo per trombone a trio*	Milan	Carisch Edizioni Musicali
n.d.	F. Steiner, and G. Völgyi Zilcz	*Zugposaunen Schule*	Budapest	Editio Musica

Appendix 4

Valve trombone methods: an indicative list

Date	Author	Title	Place	Publisher
1833	F. Bellini	*Metodo per trombone si duttile che a pistoni*	Milan	Bellini
c.1837	J. Carnaud *fils aîné*	*Méthode complète de trombone à pistons*	Paris	Richault
1840	Muller	*Méthode de trombone à trois pistons*	Paris?	J. Meissonier
1845	W. Freyman	*Méthode élémentaire de trombone à pistons ou cylindres*	Paris	n.p.
between 1850 and 1859	J. Schwartz	*Méthode de trombone à pistons et sans pistons*	Paris	Gautrot Aîné
c.1852	F. C. E. Carnaud?	*Méthode complète et raisonnée pour les saxhorns contrebasse et baryton à trois, quatre et cinq cylindres et pour le trombone à pistons 'écrite d'après le système adopté au Gymnase Musical Militaire'*	Paris	Lafleur? Carnaud?
n.d. (mid-19th C.)	E. Cam	*Méthode pour le trombone ordinaire et pour le trombone à pistons*	Paris	Costallat
c.1864	Clodomir (P.-F.-M. de Borrit)	*Méthode élémentaire de trombone à pistons 'adoptée par les premiers professeurs de Paris'*	Paris	Leduc
c.1865	Clodomir) (P.-F.-M. de Borrit)	*Méthode élémentaire de trombone à pistons à l'usage des fanfares et des collèges*	Paris	Leduc
c.1865	A. Sax	*Tablature du nouveau trombone à six pistons et tubes indépendants*	Paris	Sax
1870	J. Forestier	*Monographie des instruments à six pistons et tubes indépendants*	Paris	Sax
1870	A. Wirth	*Posaunen-Schule für Alt, Tenor und Bass-Posaune . . . Instruction Book of the Simple and Valve-Trombone*	London	Augener & Co.
1878	A. Lagard	*Méthode de trombone à trois ou à quatre pistons*	Paris	Ikelmer Frères
c.1879	V. Caussinus	*Solfège-Méthode progressif de basse et trombone à quatre pistons*	Paris	V. Caussinus

1880?	F. Vobaron, H. Berr, A. Dieppo	*Complete Trombone Tutor: Slide or Valve*	London	Lafleur
between 1880 and 1889	G. Bimboni	*Metodo per trombone a pistone*	Florence	Brizzi & Niccolai
before 1881	G. Rossari	*Metodo per trombone e bombardino a cilindro in Si bemolle*	Milan	Domenico Vismara
1887	J. A. Kappey	*Complete Tutor for Tenor Trombone in B flat, and Bass Trombone in G, Slide and Valve*	London	Boosey & Co.
before 1891	D. Gatti	*Gran metodo teorico pratico . . . per trombone tenore a cilindri e congeneri*	Milan	not given
1891	Anon.	*Method for the B♭ valve trombone*	New York?	Carl Fischer
before 1892	G. Sianesi	*Metodo per duplex bombardino-trombone (Si bem) invenzione Pelitti con esempi ed esercizi*	Milan	Domenico Vismara
c.1895	E. Guilbaut	*Méthode facile pour trombone à pistons*	Paris?	Imbert
1897	C. Weber?	*Premier Method . . . Valve Trombone*	[USA?]	C. Weber?
c.1900	P. de Ville	*Universal Method for Slide and Valve Trombone in Bass and Treble Clef*	New York	Carl Fischer
1905	Salvation Army	*The Salvation Army Tenor Trombone Tutor (Valve and Slide)*	London	Publishing Offices
1907	L. Fontbonne	*Méthode complète, théorique et pratique de trombone à coulisse et à pistons*	Paris	Costallat
1908	O. Langey	*Practical Tutor for the B♭ Valve Trombone and the B♭ Baritone* (new edn)	London	Hawkes & Son
1916	C. Hampe	*Hampe Method for the Slide Trombone, with an Appendix for the Trombone with Valves*	Chicago	F. Holstein & Co.
c.1926	A. W. Allen	*Elementary Progressive Method for Cornet, Trumpet, E♭, Alto, Valve Trombone*	Oakland, Calif.	A. W. Allen
c.1927	S. Peretti	*Nuova scuola d'insegnamento del trombone tenore a macchina e congeneri*	Milan	Ricordi
c.1936	J. J. B. L. Arban, ed. C. L. Randall and S. Mantia	*Arban's Famous Method for Slide and Valve Trombone and Baritone*	New York	Carl Fischer

Appendix 5

Orchestral trombone sections, c. 1780–c. 1930

This table serves two functions: it identifies instances where trombones were incorported into orchestras, and it provides a general illustration of the extent to which the trombone section (and by implication the brass section, for all orchestras with trombones had trumpets and horns too) occupied a proportion of the total orchestral personnel. The table is not comprehensive, but rather made up of a series of snapshots. A figure in parentheses indicates equivocation about the data.

Date	Country	Orchestra	Trombones	Orchestra size
1784	England	London, Handel Commemoration	6	259?
1787	Germany	Berlin, Orchestra of the King of Prussia	3	61
1790	France	Paris, Opéra	(3)	70
1807	Austria	Vienna, Imperial Orchestra	2	29+
1810	France	Paris, Opéra	3	77
1811	Germany	Berlin Court Opera	3	71–7?
1813–16	Bohemia	Prague Opera	3	33–5
1814	Italy	Milan, La Scala	1	56–8
1815	England	London, Oratorio Concerts, Covent Garden	3	57
1817	Germany	Bremen Town Orchestra	1	28
1817	Germany?	Mayence Court Theatre	3	39
1817	England	London, Ancient Concert	3	46
1817	France	Paris, Théâtre Italien	2	40?
1818	England	London, King's Theatre	1	46
1818	Italy	Naples, Teatro San Carlo	3	62
1818	England	London, Covent Garden Theatre	1	31
1819	England	London, Vocal Concert	1	38
1820	France	Paris, Opéra	3	110
1821	Germany	Frankfurt Opera	1	37
1821	Austria	Vienna Court Opera	3	45
1822	England	Manchester Philharmonic	3	31–3
1823	Germany	Orchestra of King of Prussia	2	89
1823	Germany	Nuremberg, Grand Duke of Hesse-Cassel	3	63?
1823	Germany	Darmstadt Court Opera	3	62
1825	Germany	Dresden Court Opera	3	35
1825	England	London, Covent Garden Theatre	1	34–7
1825	Germany	Berlin Opera (Spontini)	3	73–89(?)
1825	Germany	Dresden, Hoftheater	3	c.34(?)

1825	Germany	Darmstadt Court Opera	3	66+
1825	England	Manchester, Liszt's concert	3	40
1825	Italy	Milan, La Scala	3	67
1826	France	Paris, Opéra	3	c.74
1826	England	London, Royal Academy of Music concerts	3	68
1827	France	Paris, Opéra	3	75
1827	France	Paris, Opéra Comique	2	56
1828	France	Paris, Conservatoire Orchestra	3	86
1828	France	Paris, Société des Concerts du Conservatoire	3	84
1830	Bohemia	Warnsdorf, first complete performance of Beethoven's Mass in D	3	46
1830	Germany	Leipzig Gewandhausorchester	3	38
1830	Germany	Berlin Court Opera	3	c.70(–100)
1830	France	Paris, Royal Music	1	45
1830	Germany	Dortmund Concert Orchestra	3 (1)	39
1831	England	London, King's Theatre	3	48
1832	England	London, King's Theatre	3	56
1832	England	London, Ancient Concert	3	52
1832	Germany	Hamburg Opera	3	36
1833	Germany	Leipzig Gewandhausorchester	3	34
1833	England	London, Philharmonic Society	3	c.70
1835	Germany	Dresden Church Music	3	58
1836	England	London, unnamed orchestra	3	72
1837	Germany	Darmstadt Court Opera	3	70+
1837	Germany	Stuttgart Court Opera	3	57
1837	England	London, Philharmonic Society	3	70
1838	Germany	Rudolstadt Court Orchestra	3	38
1839	France	Paris, Opéra	3	79
1839	France	Paris, Opéra Comique	4	62
1839	England	London, Her Majesty's Theatre	3	74
1839	England	London, Philharmonic Society	3	75
1840	France	Paris, Conservatoire Orchestra	3	81
1840	England	London, Cipriani Potter's concert	3	59
1840	Netherlands	The Hague Royal Orchestra	3	37
1841	France	Paris, Société des Concerts du Conservatoire	3	86
1841	France	Paris, Conservatoire Orchestra	3	90
1841	France	Paris, Pasdeloup Concerts	3	85+
1841	Germany	Coburg Court Orchestra	3	42
1842	Germany	Dresden Court Opera	3	57
1842	England	London, Philharmonic Society	3	76

1842	England	London, Subscription Concerts, Hanover Square Rooms	3	72
1842	Austria	Vienna, Philharmonic Orchestra	4	67
1842	Austria	Vienna Court Opera	4	60
1843	Germany	Hechingen Court Orchestra	1	29
1843	Germany	Berlin Opera	4	87
1843	Germany	Frankfurt Opera	3	47
1844	Germany	Darmstadt Court Opera	3	48
1844	Austria	Vienna, Concert Spirituel	3	60
1844	Austria	Vienna Court Opera	3	48
1844	Austria	Vienna, Imperial Orchestra	2	35?
1844	Germany	Berlin Court Opera	3	55–65
1844	Germany	Cassel Court Opera	3	50
1844	Germany	Munich Odeon Concerts	3	99
1844	Germany	Munich Court Opera	3	53
1844	Germany	Dresden Court Opera	3	58
c.1844	France	Paris, Opéra	3	77–9
c.1844	Germany	Leipzig Gewandhausorchester	3	40–1
1845	Italy	Turin, Teatro Regio	3	55
c.1845	France	Paris, Opera	3	82
1846	Germany	Chemnitz Town Orchestra	3	41
1846	England	London, Philharmonic Society	3	77
1847	Germany	Frankfurt Opera	3	45
1847	England	London, St James's Theatre, *Antigone*	3	43
1847	England	London, Royal Italian Opera House, Covent Garden	3	78
1848	England	London, Exeter Hall, Henry Wylde's concert	3	61
1848	England	London, Royal Italian Opera House, Covent Garden	3	83
1848	England	London, Ancient Concert	3	54
1849	Germany	Berlin Court Opera	3	89–91
1849	Germany	Hanover Court Opera	3	44
1849	England	London, Her Majesty's Theatre	3	74
1850	Germany	Brunswick Court Orchestra	1 (2)	52
1850	Germany	Darmstadt Court Opera	3	51
1850	Germany	Dresden Court Opera	3	63
1850	Germany	Dresden, Hofoper	3	67+
1851	Germany	Weimar Court Opera (Liszt)	1	37
1855	France	Paris, Opéra	3/4	81
1858	England	London, Philharmonic	3	71
1859	France	Paris, Conservatoire Orchestra	3	85
1859	France	Paris, Société des Concerts	3	85

1860	England	London, Philharmonic Society	3	66
1865	Germany	Leipzig, Gewandhausorchester	3	70
1867	Germany	Karlsruhe Court Orchestra (Brahms, First Symphony)	3	49
1876	Germany	Bayreuth, Festspielhaus (*Ring des Nibelungen*)	5	102?
1881	Germany	Leipzig Gewandhausorchester	3	72
1890	Germany	Leipzig Gewandhausorchester	3	98
1890	France	Paris, Opéra	3	77
1890	Italy	Milan, La Scala	3	95
1890	Germany	Berlin Opera	2	65
1896	Germany	Leipzig Gewandhausorchester	3	86
1900	Austria	Vienna Philharmonic	5	104
1905	Italy	Turin, Teatro Regio	3	75
1929	Germany	Dresden State Opera	6	119

Sources

Carse, A., *The Orchestra from Beethoven to Berlioz* (Cambridge: W. Heffer and Sons, 1948).

Koury, D. J., *Orchestral Performance Practices in the Nineteenth Century: Size, Proportions, and Seating* (Ann Arbor, Mi.: UMI Research Press, 1986).

Lawson, C., *The Cambridge Companion to the Orchestra* (Cambridge: Cambridge University Press, 2003).

Sadie, S. (ed.), *The New Grove Dictionary of Music and Musicians* (London: Macmillan, 1980), s.v. 'Orchestra'.

Zaslaw, N., *Mozart's Symphonies* (Oxford: Clarendon Press, 1989).

Appendix 6

C. G. Conn endorsements, from c. 1928
New Wonder Model Slide Trombones catalogue

The Conn 'New Wonder' trombone catalogue issued around 1928 contained endorsements from 165 trombone players – almost all white American players. A brief biographical note was provided for each player. Though it is hardly a scientific sample (there are, for instance, no black players), it provides as good an impression as there is of how leading American players made a living at that time. It also shows how Conn's instruments were deemed suitable for various musical environments – a key to the models follows the table.

Name	Named employer(s)/ place(s) of employment	Types of employment	Conn model[a]
Adam, Eugene	Boston Symphony Orchestra	orchestra/opera	A
Addison, W. A.	Detroit Symphony Orchestra	orchestra/opera	B
Alloo, Modeste	Cincinnati Symphony Orchestra, Boston Symphony Orchestra	orchestra/opera	S
Amidon, Rollo	The Symphony Six, Chicago	vaudeville	
Ayers, Don	Omaha, Nebraska	unclassified band/act	
Bartlett, B. O.	Power House Orchestra, Tora Rapids, NZ	dance band?	
Bassett, Frank N.	San Francisco Symphony Orchestra, Exposition Symphony Orchestra	orchestra/opera	B
Bassett, James	Harry Stoddard's Orchestra, New York	dance band?	
Beitel, H. F.	Los Angeles Philharmonic	orchestra/opera	
Belgiorno, Simone	Cincinnati Symphony Orchestra, Metropolitan Opera Company	orchestra/opera, military band	
Benson, H. P.	The Five Chapins	vaudeville	
Berry, Melville M.	California Theater Symphony Orchestra, Los Angeles	orchestra/opera	
Bettancourt, Joseph	San Francisco	unclassified band/act	A
Bogin, A.	New York	orchestra/opera, recording artist, cinema band	S
Bozzacco, Enrico	Atlantic City	unclassified band/act	
Brisbin, C. D.	Sousa's Band	symphonic band	A
Brown, Hal	Palace Theatre Band, South Bend, Indiana	theatre band	
Brusher, J. J.	San Francisco	orchestra/opera	S
Burbank, Arthur F.	Burbank and Danforth	vaudeville	N
Burnell, Frank J.	Santa Catalina Island Band	symphonic band?	A
Campbell, Jack	Strout's Military Hussars	vaudeville	
Carns, Earl J.	Sousa's Band	symphonic band	B

Caruso, Emilio	Boston	unclassified band/act	
Casseday, Albert J.	Arnold Johnson Orchestra	dance band?	S
Chandler, Raymond	Wheeler & Wilson Band, Bridgeport, Connecticut	symphonic band?	N
Chomet, Claude	Cleveland Symphony Orchestra	orchestra/opera	S
Cimera, Frank	Kryl Band, Cimera Band, Chicago	symphonic band	
Cimera, Jaroslav	Cimera Band, Kryl Band, New York?	symphonic band	A
Clark, Ora E.	San Francisco Symphony Orchestra, Exposition Symphony Orchestra	orchestra/opera	S
Clark, Robert E.	US Marines, Washington DC	military band	S
Clarke, Allie	T. P. Brooke's Band, Chicago Grand Opera Co.	symphonic band, orchestra/opera	S
Clarke, Ernest	Gilmore's Band, Victor Herbert's Band, Boston and New York	symphonic band, orchestra/opera, military band	
Clarke, Harry	Boston	symphonic band?, theatre band	
Cleveland, E. D.	'the Northwest'	unclassified band/act	S
Coe, Ed	Smith, Doty and Coe	vaudeville?	
Colaprete, John	Stanton Theatre, Philadelphia	theatre band	S
Corey, Ralph	Sousa Band Strand Theatre Orchestra, New York	symphonic band, orchestra/opera, theatre band, recording artist	A
Corrado, Umberto	Chicago Grand Opera	orchestra/opera	S
Crans, T. S.	Duke Yellman's Radio Orchestra, Kansas City	radio band	
Crozier, George	Eddie Elkins Orchestra, Los Angeles	dance band?	
Cusumano, Chas.	Pryor's Band, Sousa's Band, New York	symphonic band, orchestra/opera, recording artist	S, A
Darling, W. W.	Marlboro, Massachusetts	unclassified band/act	
De Bernardis, A.	New York	theatre band	
Deluca, Joseph	Sousa's Band, Philadelphia	symphonic band	
Dierks, Fred	Grand Opera Orchestra, Volpe Symphony Orchestra, New York	orchestra/opera	
Donnenworth, L. W.	Powell River Elks' Band, British Columbia	unclassified band/act	
Dumont, Miss Lillian	Almont and Dumont	vaudeville	A
Erlandson, Albert	Vancouver City Band, 72nd Highlanders Band	symphonic band?, military band	A
Falcone, Mario	New York Philharmonic	orchestra/opera	
Fay, J. W.	Director of Music, public schools, Rochester, NY	teacher	
Florio, Salvatore	Innes Band, Ellery Band, Cleveland, Ohio	symphonic band	
Ford, 'Wick'	Sousa's Band	symphonic band	A

Name	Organization	Type	Code
Foreman, Walter L.	Royal Scotch Highlanders' Band	military band	A
Forte, Frank	Princess Serenaders' Dance Orchestra	dance band	
Fuchs, Robert	Metropolitan Opera, New York	orchestra/opera	B
Garing, A. J.	Sousa's Band, Hippodrome Orchestra (Director), New York	symphonic band, theatre band?	
Gebhardt, Victor	Minneapolis Symphony Orchestra	orchestra/opera	
Gentile, Ernest	Sousa's Band, Italian Symphony Orchestra, New York	symphonic band, orchestra/opera, theatre band	A, S
Gibbs, Ernest	Sousa	symphonic band	A
Gillum, Franklin	Highlanders	military band?	A
Glennie, J. W.	New Zealand	military band	
Green, Ralph T.	Canton, Ohio	teacher	
Greene, R. J.	Niagara Falls	unclassified band/act	A
Grieve, W. L.	Sousa's Band, New York	symphonic band	
Gusikoff, Chas.	Sousa's Band, Cleveland Symphony Orchestra	symphonic band, orchestra/opera	S
Haines, Leroy	New York	unclassified band/act	S
Hancock, H.	Queen's Own Rifles Band, Toronto Symphony Orchestra	orchestra/opera, military band	
Harris, Charles W.	Russian Symphony Orchestra of New York, Sousa's Band	symphonic band, orchestra/opera, vaudeville?	S
Henderson, Fred		vaudeville	
Henry, Frank	Paul Whiteman Pavilion Royal Orchestra	dance band	A
Herbst, Mr Henry	Lyceum Theatre, Rochester Municipal Concert Band, Rochester, NY	symphonic band?, theatre band	S
Hoar, Harry	New York	symphonic band, orchestra/opera	
Hummel, Wm. F.	Hummel's Orchestra, Irem Temple Shrine Band, Lehighton, Pennsylvania	orchestra/opera, religious?	
Jenkins, Walter	with Billy Sunday, evangelist	religious	A
Judge, Ed	Fort Howard Band, US Naval Academy Band	military band	
Kenfield, L. S.	Boston Symphony Orchestra	orchestra/opera	B
Killian, Eugene	Metropolitan Grand Opera Co., Seventh Regiment Band, New York	orchestra/opera, military band, recording artist	S
King, Gus		vaudeville	
Kirschner, W. J.	Stanton Theatre Orchestra, Liberati Band, Philadelphia	symphonic band, theatre band orchestra/opera	S, B
Lacroix, William	Metropolitan Grand Opera Orchestra, New York		
Lammers, H.	Sousa's Band, Salt Lake City Philharmonic Orchestra	symphonic band, theatre band	

Lhotak, Frank F.	Ted Lewis Jazz Band, Greenwich Village Follies, New York	theatre band, jazz band	
Lilleback, Walter D.	Sousa's Band, Walter Damrosch Symphony Orchestra, New York	symphonic band, orchestra/opera	
Lott, Frank K.	Kansas City Symphony Orchestra, Pryor's Band	orchestra/opera, symphonic band	
Lotz, Paul P.	Philadelphia Symphony Orchestra	orchestra/opera	B
Lozano, Pedro	Conway's Band	symphonic band	
Lucas, George	Sousa's Band, Conway's Band, New York	symphonic band, orchestra/opera, theatre band, recording artist	S
Luper, Loren J.	Conway's Band, New York	symphonic band	A
McCauley, V.	Ernie Young's Marigold Band	dance band?	
McMahon, J. F.	President's Own, Shannon's Band, New York	symphonic band, military band	
Mantia, Simone	Mantia's Band, Pryor's Band, Sousa's Band, New York	symphonic band, orchestra/opera, recording artist	S
Martin, Carroll	Chicago	unclassified band/act	
Mass, Chas. J.	Gilmore's Band, Conway's Band, Binghamton, NY	symphonic band	A
Mathews, Al.	Peoria, Illinois	amateur?	
Mausbach, A.	Boston Symphony Orchestra	orchestra/opera	S
Miles, Coleman	Warren Military Band School, Mt Carroll, Illinois	military band	A
Miller, Matt	Bungalow Orchestra, Seattle	dance band?	A
Mole, Miff	Sam Martin's Orchestra, Memphis Five, New York	jazz band, recording artist	
Monk, Alfred	Rochester, NY	unclassified band/act	
Morris, Chas. H.	Seattle Symphony Orchestra, Coliseum Theatre Orchestra	orchestra/opera, theatre band	
Morrison, Wm. O.	Al Sweet's 'famous singing band'	unclassified band/act	A
Musolino, Nick	Sweeney Radio Orchestra	radio band	
Nachtmann, Jos	Chicago Theater, Kryl's Band	symphonic band, theatre band	A
Nordberg, C. A.	Coon-Sanders Dance Orchestra	dance band	
Nutter, Oscar	Sousa's Band, Erie, Pennsylvania	symphonic band	B
Parisi, P. J.	Orpheum Theatre Orchestra, Elkhart, Indiana	theatre band	
Parker, W. E.	Sousa's Band, Seattle	symphonic band	B
Perfetto, John J.	Sousa's Band, New York	symphonic band	
Perrella, Pasquale	Metropolitan Grand Opera, New York	orchestra/opera	S
Pfeiffenschneider, J.	Symphony Orchestra, Grand Opera Orchestra, New York	orchestra/opera	S
Proctor, Jerome N.	Conway's Band, Eduarde's Band, Boston	symphonic band	

Raderman, Harry	Ted Lewis Band, Greenwich Village Follies Company, New York	theatre band, jazz band	
Randall, Charles	Conway's Band, Russian Symphony Orchestra of New York	symphonic band, orchestra/opera, recording artist	A, S
Rau, Fred R. J.	San Francisco	unclassified band/act	
Reiter, Ida	Reiter Sisters' Orchestra, Boston Ladies' Symphony Orchestra	orchestra/opera	A
Rodeheaver, Homer	Billy Sunday Evangelistic Party	religious	
Rose, Frank E.	Chicago orchestras, Pryor's Band	symphonic band, orchestra/opera	S
Rothwell, C. Irving	Sousa's Band	symphonic band	
Rush, W. E.	Director of a conservatory, Beeville, Texas	teacher	
Russo, A.	Russian Grand Opera Orchestra, Chicago	orchestra/opera	
Sanford, Lee	Washington Marine Band	military band	
Schmidt, Louis F.	New York Philharmonic Symphony Orchestra	orchestra/opera	A, S
Schmidt, Walter	Illinois State Guard Band, Chicago Grand Opera	orchestra/opera, military band	A
Schueler, John P.	Sousa's Band	symphonic band	
Schultze, Herbert	Ole Olsen Orchestra, Milwaukee	dance band?	A
Serpico, Fiore	Denver, Colorado	symphonic band?, unclassified band/act	V
Sery, Miles B.	Minneapolis Symphony Orchestra	orchestra/opera	S
Shapiro, Leo	New York	cinema band	
Shelley, Chas B.	Pryor's Band, Kryl's Band, Chicago	symphonic band	
Shellhouse, Fred G.	Los Angeles Philharmonic	orchestra/opera	
Simpson, G. V.	(Conn agent), Ogden, Utah	unclassified band/act	
Sims, J. G.	Sousa's Band	symphonic band	
Siroto, John	Cleveland Symphony Orchestra	orchestra/opera	
Smallcalder, Victor	Grenadier Guards, Sheffield Empire Palace Theatre, UK	theatre band, military band	A
Smith, Bert	Sousa's Band, Smith, Doty and Coe, New York	symphonic band, vaudeville	
Smith, C. B.	Reese Concert Company, Peru City Band, Peru, Indiana	symphonic band?	A
Smith, Max	Detroit Symphony Orchestra	orchestra/opera	S
Sordillo, Fortunato	Boston Symphony Orchestra	orchestra/opera	
Sorenson, Chris	Pryor's Band, New York	symphonic band, theatre band, recording artist	A
St. John, James I.	American Legion Band, Seattle	unclassified band/act	A
Steinberger, Lorn	Los Angeles Philharmonic Symphony Orchestra	orchestra/opera	

Tait, Fred	San Francisco Orchestra	orchestra/opera	S, 'Tait model'
Thomas, R. L. 'Speck'	Burtnett-Miller Orchestra, San Francisco	dance band?	S
Trilioan, Frank	Lawrence, Massachusetts	unclassified band/act	A
Valeroso, E. A.	Filipino Band, Hong Kong Hotel, Hong Kong	dance band?	
van Amburgh, Frank	Detroit Symphony Orchestra	orchestra/opera	S
Vogt, Gerrie J.	Conservatory, Benson's orchestras, Chicago	orchestra/opera, teacher	
Voorsanger, Joseph	Sousa's Band, New York	symphonic band	A
Wagner, Frank J.	Minneapolis Symphony Orchestra	orchestra/opera	B
Wallace, J. K.	Catalina Islands Band, Philharmonic Symphony of Los Angeles	symphonic band, orchestra/opera	
Wankoff, Bencion	Metropolitan Opera, New York	orchestra/opera	
Wasterlain, Fred	(bandmaster) Enumclaw, Washington	unclassified band/act	
Weisner, Art	Benson Orchestra, Chicago	orchestra/opera, recording artist	
Westcott, Everett L.	Boston Symphony Orchestra	orchestra/opera	A, S
Whitby, Richard	Carl Edourde's Concert Band, Conway's Band, New York	symphonic band, theatre band, recording artist	
Whitehead, C. A.	Patrick Conway's Band	symphonic band	BV
Williams, Burt	New York	unclassified band/act	
Winfield, Herbert	Frank Westphal Orchestra, Chicago	dance band	A
Winner, J. F.	Hot Springs, Arkansas	unclassified band/act	
Witzel, Chas. F.	Gypsy Players, Los Angeles	vaudeville	
Wockenfuss, Max	New York Symphony Orchestra	orchestra/opera	
Wright, Harry	Seattle Symphony Orchestra	orchestra/opera	B
Wright, Olin H.	Knickerbocker Theatre, Philadelphia	theatre band	
Zimmerman, Leo A.	Sousa's Band, Innes's Band, Columbia Phonograph Company, New York	symphonic band, recording artist	A, S

[a] Model type:

A   Artist Model
B   bass
N   New Wonder Model
S   Symphony Model
V   valve

Notes

Chapter 1 The instrument: its parts and their development

1. Grinstead was a colonel in the Salvation Army with responsibility for the Army's brass instrument production. This was not the first patent for a slide lock, but more than one design was patented. For example, there were four separate slide lock designs patented in the USA between 1893 and 1913.

2. While Brahms's trombone parts are clearly written with the idiomatic character of the slide trombone in mind – with which he was familiar from the excellent section at Meiningen – the trombonists in the Vienna Philharmonic appear to have used valve trombones when that orchestra performed the Second Symphony. By December 1883, when the same orchestra gave the first performance of the Third Symphony, slide trombones had been reinstated (Vienna, Haus-, Hof- und Staatsarchiv, HHStA Oper/K74/1883/Nr. 311). See Chapter 9 on the use of valve trombones in Viennese orchestras in the nineteenth century.

3. H. G. Fischer, *The Renaissance Sackbut and its Use Today* (New York: The Metropolitan Museum of Art, 1984), p. 29.

4. *A Catalogue of Instrumental and Vocal Music, printed by Clementi, Collard & Collard . . .*, London, 1823, p. xxvi.

5. See J. and T. Glen, *The Glen Account Book 1838–1853* (Edinburgh: Edinburgh University Collection of Historic Musical Instruments, 1985), p. 224

6. Information conveyed personally to the author.

7. I am grateful to Howard Weiner for bringing this to my attention.

8. *New Grove 2*, s.v. 'Trombone', §7.

9. M. Praetorius, *Syntagma musicum*, trans. H. Blumenfeld, vol. 2, 2nd edn (New York: Da Capo Press, 1980), p. 32.

10. W. Waterhouse, *The New Langwill Index: A Dictionary of Musical Wind-Instrument Makers and Inventors* (London: Tony Bingham, 1993), p. 328.

11. H. Weiner, 'André Braun's *Gamme et méthode pour les trombonnes*: the earliest modern trombone method rediscovered', *Historic Brass Society Journal*, 5 (1993), 292.

12. See K. McGowan, 'The world of the early sackbut player: flat or round?' *Early Music*, 22 (1994), 441–66.

13. This is a classification of my own rather than a commonly used one.

14. See A. McGrattan, 'The trumpet in funeral ceremonies in Scotland and England during the 17th century', *Historic Brass Society Journal*, 7 (1995), 168–84.

15. K. Polk, *German Instrumental Music of the Late Middle Ages* (Cambridge: Cambridge University Press, 1992), p. 29.

16. N. Rimsky-Korsakov, *Principles of Orchestration*, 1913, ed. M. Steinberg, trans. E. Agate, vol. 2 (New York: Édition Russe de Musique, 1923), p. 26.

17. R. Strauss (ed.), *Treatise on Instrumentation by Hector Berlioz*, revised and enlarged, 1904–5; trans. T. Front (New York: Edwin F. Kalmus, 1948), p. 329.

18. Doubts about the ubiquity of the alto trombone in the eighteenth century – which are mentioned later in this book – were raised by Howard Weiner in a paper given to the

Historic Brass Society's 'Declamation versus Lyricism' conference at Bad Säckingen in June 2004. The published version of this paper was in preparation at the time of writing.

19.   See L. Laubhold, 'Sensation or forgery? The 1677 soprano trombone of Cristian Kofahl', *Historic Brass Society Journal*, 12 (2000), 259–65.

20.   A. Baines, *Brass Instruments: Their History and Development* 1976 (London: Faber, 1980), p. 117.

21.   The last British professional player to have routinely used the true G trombone played with the BBC Welsh Orchestra until 1969.

Chapter 2   Trombone technique

1.   B. Kernfeld (ed.), *New Grove Dictionary of Jazz* (London: Macmillan, 1988) s.v. 'Trombone'.

2.   These are called 'alternate' positions in American parlance.

3.   G. Schuller, *The Swing Era: The Development of Jazz, 1930–1945* (New York and Oxford: Oxford University Press, 1989), pp. 591–2.

4.   H. Weiner, 'André Braun's *Gamme et méthode pour les trombonnes* revisited', *Historic Brass Society Journal*, 11 (1999), 93–4.

5.   He is thought to have written under an academic pseudonym, and has been tentatively identified with two composers, Aurelio Averoldi of Brescia, and Aurelio Bonelli of Bologna, the latter being perhaps the likelier match. See the prefatory notes by Marcello Castellani in the facsimile edition (Florence: Studio per Edizione Scelte, 1979).

6.   D. Speer, *Grund-richtiger, kurtz- leicht- und nöthiger, jetzt wol-vermehrter Unterricht der musicalischen Kunst* (Ulm: Georg Wilhelm Kühn, 1697); J. F. B. C. Majer, *Museum musicum theoretico practicum*, 1732, Documenta musicologica, Erste Reihe: Druckschriften-Faksimiles, 8 (Kassel: Bärenreiter, 1954); J. P. Eisel, *Musicus autodidactos, oder der sich selbst informirende Musicus* (Erfurt: Johann Michael Funck, 1738).

7.   A. Baines, *Brass Instruments: Their History and Development*, 1976 (London: Faber, 1980), p. 115.

8.   M. Praetorius, *Syntagma musicum; De organographia*, Wolfenbüttel, 1619, facsimile edn (Kassel: Bärenreiter, 1958), 1996, p. 232.

9.   H. Weiner, 'The trombone: changing times, changing slide positions', *Brass Bulletin*, 32 (1982), 52–63.

10.   Weiner, 'André Braun's *Gamme et méthode pour les trombonnes* revisited', 96–7.

11.   S. Carter, 'Trombone pitch in the eighteenth century: an overview', in *Posaunen und Trompeten: Geschichte – Akustik – Spieltechnik*, ed. M. Lustig (Blankenburg: Stiftung Kloster Michaelstein, 2000), pp. 53–66.

12.   *Cammerton* was sharper than *Cornett-ton*. It has been estimated that the average standard for the former was A = 416 and the average for the latter A = 467. However, these really are just averages – there were some wide variations. For a description of pitch standards at this time, see *New Grove 2*, s.v. 'Pitch' §1, from where this information is taken.

13.   A. Mendel, 'Pitch in western music since 1500: a re-examination', *Acta Musicologica*, 50 (1978), 34.

14.   I am grateful to Howard Weiner for the translation.

15.   Ch.-M. Widor, *The Technique of the Modern Orchestra*, 1904, trans. E. Suddard (London: Joseph Williams, 1906), p. 86; R. Strauss (ed.), *Treatise on Instrumentation by Hector Berlioz*, enlarged and revised, 1904–5; trans. T. Front (New York: Edwin F. Kalmus, 1948), p. 329.

16.   GB-Lbl Add. MS 35011.

17.   'rapprocher un peu plus les lèvres . . . Appuyer plus fortement l'embouchure contre la bouche'. A. Dieppo, *Méthode complète pour le trombone* (Paris: Troupenas, 1837), p. 6.

18.   B. Sluchin and R. Lapie, 'Slide trombone teaching and method books in France (1794–1960)', *Historic Brass Society Journal*, 9 (1997), 17.

19. Ibid.

20. C. Bendinelli, *The Entire Art of Trumpet Playing*, 1614, trans. E. H. Tarr (Nashville, Tenn.: Brass Press, 1975), p. 4.

21. G. Fantini, *Modo per imparare a sonare di tromba*, 1638, trans. E. H. Tarr (Nashville, Tenn.: Brass Press, 1978), Appendix, p. 3.

22. Sluchin and Lapie, 'Slide trombone teaching and method books', 17–18.

23. Pryor's vibrato is also discussed in Chapter 12.

24. M. Laplace, 'Maurice Ravel and the new trombone', *Brass Bulletin*, 47, (1984), 34–8.

25. CDBP 9712.

26. H. Macdonald, *Berlioz's Orchestration Treatise: A Translation and Commentary* (Cambridge: Cambridge University Press, 2002), p. 219.

27. See H. M. Brown, *Embellishing Sixteenth-Century Music* (London: Oxford University Press, 1976).

Chapter 3 *The origins of the trombone*

1. Later in this chapter I discuss the entry of the English delegation to the Council of Constance in 1415, when the 'prusenen' (presumably slide trumpets) were said to have played in a singing style.

2. For a more detailed discussion of this theme, see T. Herbert, 'Social history and music history', in *A Cultural Study of Music: A Critical Introduction*, ed. M. Clayton, T. Herbert and R. Middleton (New York and London: Routledge, 2003), pp. 146–56.

3. See, for example, E. H. Tarr, *The Trumpet* (London: B. T. Batsford, 1988), p. 42, and F. A. D'Accone, *The Civic Muse: Music and Musicians in Siena during the Middle Ages and the Renaissance* (Chicago and London: University of Chicago Press, 1997), p. 449.

4. M. Campbell and C. Greated, *The Musician's Guide to Acoustics* (Oxford: Oxford University Press, 2001), p. 378.

5. Tarr, *The Trumpet*, p. 42.

6. R. Strohm, *The Rise of European Music, 1380–1500* (Cambridge: Cambridge University Press, 1993), pp. 106–11.

7. K. Polk, *German Instrumental Music of the Late Middle Ages* (Cambridge: Cambridge University Press, 1992), p. 57.

8. D. L. Smithers, *The Music and History of the Baroque Trumpet before 1721* (Carbondale and Edwardsville: Southern Illinois University Press, 1988), p. 355.

9. R. Barclay, *The Art of the Trumpet-Maker: The Materials, Tools, and Techniques of the Seventeenth and Eighteenth Centuries in Nuremberg* (Oxford: Clarendon Press, 1996), p. 11.

10. The seventeenth-century slide trumpet (properly called the flatt trumpet) is discussed in Chapter 6. A slide trumpet was also popular in England in the nineteenth century, and was championed by the great trumpeter Thomas Harper. The term has also been used very loosely to describe certain species of soprano trombone.

11. See P. Downey, 'The renaissance slide trumpet: fact or fiction?' *Early Music*, 12 (1984), 26–33.

12. See K. Polk, 'The trombone, the slide trumpet and the ensemble tradition of the early renaissance', *Early Music*, 17 (1989), 389–97: R. W. Duffin, 'The *trompette des ménestrels* in the 15th-century alta capella', *Early Music*, 17, no. 3 (1989), 397–402; H. Myers, 'Slide trumpet madness: fact or fiction?' *Early Music*, 17 (1989), 383–9; and E. A. Bowles, 'Blowing a trumpet', *Early Music*, 18 (1990), 350–1.

13. A. Baines, *Brass Instruments: Their History and Development*, 1976 (London: Faber, 1980), p. 94.

14. See also P. Tröster, 'More about renaissance slide trumpets: fact or fiction?', *Early Music*, 32 (2004), 252–68.

15. The sources are discussed in some detail in K. Polk, 'The invention of the slide principle

and the earliest trombone, or The Birth of a Notion', in *Perspectives in Brass Scholarship: Proceedings of the International Historic Brass Symposium, Amherst, 1995*, ed. S. Carter (Stuyvesant, NY: Pendragon Press, 1997), pp. 19–27.

16. Strohm, *Rise of European Music*, pp. 550–7.
17. The concept of 'positions' is strictly an ahistorical one in this context.
18. Baines, *Brass Instruments*, p. 97.
19. Campbell and Greated, *Musician's Guide*, pp. 378–9.
20. F. W. Galpin, 'The sackbut: its evolution and history, illustrated by an instrument of the sixteenth century', *Proceedings of the Musical Association*, 33 (1906–7), 3–4.
21. See, for example, W. Skeat, *An Etymological Dictionary of the English Language* (Oxford, 1890), s.v. 'sackbut'.
22. See also *Oxford English Dictionary*, s.v. 'sackbut/ *sacqueboute*'.
23. A. J. G. Mackay (ed.), *The Historie and Cronicles of Scotland*, vol. 1, (Edinburgh: Scottish Text Society, 1899), p. 379.
24. Duffin, 'The *trompette des ménestrels*', 400–1.
25. Polk, *German Instrumental Music*, p. 46.
26. Baines, *Brass Instruments*, p. 107.
27. Polk, *German Instrumental Music*, p. 59.
28. D. Heartz, 'A fifteenth-century ballo: *Rôti bouilli joyeux*', in *Aspects of Medieval and Renaissance Music: A Birthday Offering to Gustave Reese*, ed. J. LaRue (New York: Pendragon Press, 1978), Appendix D, p. 373.
29. See A. Baines, 'Fifteenth-century instruments in Tinctoris's *De inventione et usu musicae*', *Galpin Society Journal*, 3 (1950), 201.
30. A. Minor and A. B. Mitchell (eds), *A Renaissance Entertainment: Festivities for the Marriage of Cosimo I, Duke of Florence, in 1539* (Columbia: University of Missouri Press, 1968); see also H. M. Brown, *Sixteenth-Century Instrumentation: The Music for the Florentine Intermedii*, Musicological Studies and Documents, 30 (Rome: American Institute of Musicology, 1973).
31. Roxburghe Club (London), *The Pageants of Richard Beauchamp, Earl of Warwick*, facsimile edn (Oxford, 1908), pp. x–xi.
32. I am indebted to Howard Weiner for clarification of this point.
33. J. Höfler, 'Der "Trompette de Menestrels" und sein Instrument', *Tijdschrift van de Vereniging voor Nederlandse Muziekgeschiedenis*, 29, no. 2 (1979), 119.
34. See Strohm, *Rise of European Music*, p. 108.
35. C. D. Ross, *The Estates and Finances of Richard Beauchamp, Earl of Warwick*, Dugdale Society Occasional Papers, no. 12 (Stratford-upon-Avon, 1956), p. 16.
36. GB-Lbl Cottonian MS Julius E IV.
37. Pageants XXIX, XXX, XXXI and XXXIV. An excellent facsimile edition of the manuscript was published privately for the Roxburghe Club in 1908 (see note 31 above).
38. S. Virdung, *Musica getuscht und ausgezogen*, Basle, 1511, facsimile edn (Kassel: Bärenreiter, 1931), fo. C1.
39. M. Agricola, *Musica instrumentalis deudsch*, Wittenberg, 1529, diplomatic reprint (Leipzig, 1896), fo. xvi *v*.
40. See Smithers, *Music and History of the Baroque Trumpet*, Ill. 1.
41. This work was believed until recently to be by the Master of the Life of the Virgin, but it has now been reattributed to the Master of the Lyversberger Passion. (Information received by the author from the Pinakothek, June 2004.)
42. See T. McGee, 'Misleading iconography: the case of the "Adimari Wedding Cassone"', *Imago musicae: International Yearbook of Musical Iconography*, 9–12 (1992), 139–57.
43. See K. McGowan, 'A chance encounter with a unicorn? A possible sighting of the renaissance slide trumpet', *Historic Brass Society Journal*, 8 (1996), 90–101.
44. G. Grove *Dictionary of Music and Musicians*, vol. 3 (1899), p. 176. Howard Weiner has pointed out that this is also mentioned by Heinrich Welcker von Gontershausen in *Neu eröffnetes Magazin musikalscher Tonwerkzeuge* (Frankfurt, 1855).

45. See Barclay, *The Art of the Trumpet-Maker*.
46. *New Grove 2*, s.v. 'Nuremberg'.
47. W. Waterhouse, *The New Langwill Index: A Dictionary of Musical Wind-Instrument Makers and Inventors* (London: Tony Bingham, 1993), pp. 204, 280.
48. Smithers, *Music and History of the Baroque Trumpet*, p. 337.
49. *New Grove 2*, s.v. 'Nuremberg'.
50. Polk, 'The trombone, the slide trumpet and the ensemble tradition', 392.
51. A. Ashbee and D. Lasocki, assisted by P. Holman and F. Kisby, *A Biographical Dictionary of English Court Musicians 1485–1714*, vol. 2 (Aldershot: Ashgate, 1998), p. 884.
52. Waterhouse, *New Langwill Index*, p. xxvii.
53. J. H. van der Meer and R. Weber, *Catalogo degli strumenti musicali dell'Accademia Filarmonica di Verona* (Verona: Accademia Filarmonica di Verona, 1982), p. 70.
54. M. D. Fleming, *Viol-Making in England c.1580–1660* (published on CD-ROM: <viols@flemingoxford.co.uk>, 2002), p. 129.
55. D'Accone, *Civic Muse*, p. 554.
56. Ashbee and Lasocki, *Biographical Dictionary*, vol. 2, s.v. 'Langdale'.
57. Ashbee and Lasocki, *Biographical Dictionary*, vol. 2, p. 662.
58. Quoted in M. Byrne, 'The goldsmith-trumpet-makers of the British Isles', *Galpin Society Journal*, 19 (1966), 74.
59. See Byrne, 'Goldsmith-trumpet-makers'.

Chapter 4 *Players and cultures in the later Renaissance*

1. B. Dickey, 'The cornett', in *The Cambridge Companion to Brass Instruments*, ed. T. Herbert and J. Wallace (Cambridge: Cambridge University Press, 1997), pp. 56–7.
2. Ibid, p. 58.
3. F. A. D'Accone, *The Civic Muse: Music and Musicians in Siena during the Middle Ages and the Renaissance* (Chicago and London: University of Chicago Press, 1997), p. 534.
4. The painting is now in the collection of the Accademia in Venice.
5. See R. C. Wegman, 'The minstrel schools in the late Middle Ages', *Historic Brass Society Journal*, 14 (2002), 11–30.
6. D'Accone, *Civic Muse*, p. 452.
7. S. R. Westfall, *Patrons and Performance: Early Tudor Household Revels* (Oxford: Clarendon Press, 1990), pp. 65–6.
8. D'Accone, *Civic Muse*, p. 524.
9. Ibid., pp. 526–7, and K. Polk, *German Instrumental Music of the Late Middle Ages* (Cambridge: Cambridge University Press, 1992), pp. 59, 76, 77.
10. See, for example, D'Accone, *Civic Muse*, Chapter 11.
11. T. Herbert, 'Susato's colleagues: the trombonists of the Tudor court', in *Tielman Susato and the Music of his Time: Print Culture, Compositional Technique and Instrumental Music in the Renaissance*, ed. K. Polk (Hillsdale, NY: Pendragon Press, 2005), pp. 117–32.
12. K. Polk, 'The Schubingers of Augsburg: innovation in Renaissance instrumental music', in *Quaestiones in musica: Festschrift für Franz Krautwurst*, ed. F. Brusniak and H. Leuchtman (Tutzing: H. Schneider, 1989), 495–503.
13. D'Accone, *Civic Muse*, p. 534.
14. London, Public Record Office, E101/420/11, fo.164*v*.
15. See T. Carter, *Music in Late Renaissance and Early Baroque Italy* (London: B. T. Batsford, 1992).
16. David Lasocki points out that in this context 'sons' might mean Nagel's actual children or simply his apprentices. See 'Nagel, Hans [II]' in A. Ashbee and D. Lasocki, assisted by P. Holman and F. Kisby, *A Biographical Dictionary of English Court Musicians 1485–1714*, Vol. 2 (Aldershot: Ashgate, 1998).

17. Recette générale de Lille, 1501, quoted in E. vander Straeten, *La Musique aux Pays-Bas* (Brussels, 1867–88), vol. 7, p. 272.

18. Ashbee and Lasocki, *Biographical Dictionary*, vol. 2, s.v. 'Nagel, Hans [II]'.

19. Quoted in translation in Carter, *Music in Late Renaissance and Early Baroque Italy*, p. 164. Original in W. Kirkendale, *The Court Musicians of Florence during the Principate of the Medici* (Florence: Leo S. Olschki, 1993), p. 62.

20. Ibid., p. 63.

21. Westfall, *Patrons and Performance*, p. 69.

22. H.-J. Nösselt, *Ein ältest Orchester: 450 Jahre Bayerisches Hof- und Staatsorchester* (Munich: Bruckmann, 1980), pp. 35, 237.

23. M. Praetorius, *Syntagma musicum*, trans. H. Blumenfeld, vol. 2, 2nd edn (New York: Da Capo Press, 1980), p. 31.

24. T. Elyot, *The Castel of Helth, gathered and made by Syr Thomas Elyot knight, out of the chief Authors of Physyke, whereby every manne may knowe the state of his owne body, the picternals of helth, and how to instruct welle his physytion in sychnes that he be not deceysed* (London, 1534), p. 51.

25. GB-Lbl Hirsch MS 5747; transcription quoted in *Musical Times*, September 1905, 579.

26. M. C. Boyd, *Elizabethan Music and Musical Criticism* (Westport, Conn: Greenwood Press, 1973), p. 15.

27. W. H. McCabe, 'Music and dance on a seventeenth-century college stage', *Musical Quarterly*, 24 (1938), 29–30. The document is also discussed in A. W. Edwards, 'The performance of ensemble music in Elizabethan England', *Proceedings of the Royal Musical Association*, 97 (1970–1), 113–23, and in A. W. Edwards, 'The sources of Elizabethan consort music' (Ph.D. thesis, University of Cambridge, 1974).

28. Quoted in Edwards, 'The performance of ensemble music', 120.

29. B. Castiglione, *The Book of the Courtier*, 1528 (Harmondsworth: Penguin, 1967), p. 121.

30. *New Grove 2*, s.v. 'Women in music' §3.

31. E. Selfridge-Field, 'Music at the Pietà before Vivaldi', *Early Music*, 14, (1986), 385, n. 12. See also J. L. Baldauf-Berdes, *Women Musicians of Venice: Musical Foundations, 1525–1855*, rev. edn (Oxford: Clarendon Press, 1996).

32. H. Nicolas, *Privy Purse Expenses of Elizabeth of York: Wardrobe Accounts of Edward IV* (London: Pickering, 1830), pp. 267–8.

33. See also A. Ashbee (ed.), *Records of English Court Music*, vol. 6 (Aldershot: Scolar Press, 1992), p. 20. The distinguished expert on English court records, Dr Andrew Ashbee, to whom I am extremely grateful for advice received, believes that this 'was just a means of paying for this particular instrument and no special ownership by the Queen should be assumed', and there seems no reason to question his opinion.

34. R. Stevenson, 'Music in the San Juan, Puerto Rico Cathedral to 1900', *Inter-American Music Review*, 1, Fall (1978), 77.

35. Letter from the teacher Fray Jodoco to Ghent, quoted in R. Stevenson, 'Quito Cathedral: four centuries', *Inter-American Music Review*, 3, no. 1 (1980), 19.

36. R. Stevenson, 'Mexico City Cathedral: the founding century', *Inter-American Music Review*, 1, no. 2 (1979), 137. See also D. M. de Arce, *Music in Ibero-America to 1850: A Historical Survey* (Lanham, M., and London: Scarecrow Press, 2001), p. 112.

37. See E. Bermúdez, 'The ministriles tradition in Latin America I: South America – the cases of Santafé (Colombia) and La Plata (Bolivia) in the seventeenth century', *Historic Brass Society Journal*, 11 (1999), 149–62.

38. Ibid.

39. Stevenson, 'Quito Cathedral', 20.

40. Stevenson, 'Mexico City Cathedral', 2–3.

41. Quoted in Bermúdez, 'The ministriles tradition in Latin America', 151.

Chapter 5 Performances and repertoires in the sixteenth and seventeenth centuries

1. See H. M. Brown, *Embellishing Sixteenth-Century Music* (London: Oxford University Press, 1976). Brown lists ten such books (p. x, n. 1): Ganassi, *Opera intitulata Fontegara* (Venice, 1535); Ortiz, *Tratado de glosas sobre clasulas* (Rome, 1553); Maffei, *Delle lettere . . . Libri due* (Naples, 1562); dalla Casa, *Il vero modo di diminuir* (Venice, 1584); Bassano, *Ricercare, passaggi et cadentie* (Venice, 1585) and *Motteti, madrigali et canzoni francese . . . diminuiti* (Venice, 1591); Rognioni, *Passaggi per potersi essercitare nel diminuire* (Venice, 1592); Conforto, *Breve et facile maniera d'essercitare ad ogni scolaro . . . a far passaggi* (Rome, 1593 [1603?]); Bovicelli, *Regole, passaggi di musica, madrigali e motteti passeggiati* (Venice, 1594); Virgiliano, *Il dolcimelo* (c.1600; manuscript in Bologna, Civico Museo Bibliografico Musicale).

2. H. Lampl, 'A translation of *Syntagma musicum III*' (DMA, University of Southern California, 1957), p. 253 ('den Cornetten mit ihren uberblasen', *Syntagma musicum* III, p. 149).

3. Ibid., p. 284 ('die Trommeter ohne das gar zi sehr fort zu eilen gewohnet seyn', *Syntagma musicum* III, p. 170).

4. A further sonata for four trombones is included in his collection *Neu-gebachene Taffel-Schnitz* (1685).

5. See H. M. Brown, *Instrumental Music Printed before 1600: A Bibliography* (Cambridge, Mass.: Harvard University Press, 1965).

6. The music, published by Antonio Gardane, contains an *Ingredere* for voices and instruments, including 'et da l'atra da Quattro trombone, et quatro cornetta nella entrata della Illustrissma Duchessa'. Four trombones are also specified for the *Vientene almo riposo* ('. . . a cinque voci cantata alla fine del quinto atto dalla notte, et sonata con quatro tromboni').

7. No. 6, *Sonata pian & forte a 8* for cornett, violin and six trombones; No. 11, *Canzon in echo del duodecimi Toni a 10* for eight cornetts and two trombones; No. 12, *Canzon sudetta accomodata per concerta con l'organo a 10* for eight cornetts and two trombones (a different setting of No 11); No. 16, *Canzon quarti toni a 15* for two cornetts, violin and twelve trombones.

8. Brown, *Instrumental Music*.

9. For a survey of the published and manuscript sources, see ibid., pp. 1–8, and Brown, *Embellishing Sixteenth-Century Music*, Ch. 9; also *New Grove 2*, s.v. 'Sources of instrumental ensemble music to 1630'.

10. J. Dowland, *Andreas Ornithoparchus his Micrologus* (London, 1609). See also E. T. Ferand, '"Sodaine and unexpected" music in the Renaissance', *Musical Quarterly*, 37 (1951), 10–27; and N. Wollick, *Opus aureum* (Cologne, 1501), which Ferand believes to be the source of many of Ornithoparchus's ideas.

11. Dowland, *Ornithoparchus*, p. 77.

12. R. Strohm, *The Rise of European Music, 1380–1500* (Cambridge: Cambridge University Press, 1993), pp. 358–9.

13. I and other players in the London Lassus Ensemble and the Taverner Players acquired these skills quite quickly when we were required to do so.

14. If this hypothesis is sound, it too gives reason for speculating that part of the routine repertoire of trombonists survives in the textual sources for vocal music, both secular and sacred.

15. T. Carter, *Music in Late Renaissance and Early Baroque Italy* (London: B. T. Batsford, 1992), p. 163.

16. See W. Ehmann, '"Was guett auff Posaunen ist etc."', *Zeitschrift für Musikwissenschaft*, 17 (1935), 171–5.

17. GB-Lbl MS Cotton Titus A XXVI, fos. 1–60.

18. R. Baroncini, trans. H. Ward-Perkins, 'Zorzi Trombetta and the band of *piffari* and trombones of the *Serenissima*: new documentary evidence', *Historic Brass Society Journal*, 14

(2002), 59–82. R. Baroncini, 'Zorzi Trombetta da Modon and the founding of the band of *piffari* and *tromboni* of the *Serenissima*', *Historic Brass Society Journal*, 16 (2004), 1–17.

19. R. Nosow, 'The debate on song in the Accademia Fiorentina', *Early Music History*, 21 (2002), 188.

20. K. Kreitner, 'Minstrels in Spanish churches, 1400–1600', *Early Music*, 20, (1992), 540.

21. For a comprehensive discussion of instruments in Venetian ceremonials, see J. G. Kurtzman and L. M. Koldau, '*Trombe, trombe d'argento, trombe squarciate, tromboni,* and *pifferi* in Venetian processions and ceremonies of the sixteenth and seventeenth centuries', *Journal of Seventeenth-Century Music*, 8, no. 1 (2002) [online, available via DOAJ (Directory of Open Access Journals): <http://merlyn.press.uiuc.edu/jscm/v8/no1/Kurtzman.html> (accessed 13 January 2005)].

22. See, for example, H. M. Brown, *Sixteenth-Century Instrumentation: The Music for the Florentine Intermedii*, Musicological Studies and Documents, 30 (Rome: American Institute of Musicology, 1973), and *Una 'Stravaganza' dei Medici*, Taverner Consort, Taverner Choir and Taverner Players, cond. Andrew Parrott, liner notes by Hugh Keyte, EMI CDC 7479982.

23. H. Ellis (ed.), *Hall's Chronicle; containing the History of England during the reign of Henry the Fourth, and the succeeding Monarchs, to the end of the reign of Henry the Eighth; in which are particularly described the manners and customs of those periods. ... Collated with the edition of 1548 and 1550* (London, 1809), p. 629.

24. D. W. Hamilton, *A Chronicle of England during the Reigns of the Tudors from A.D. 1485 to 1559, by Charles Wriothesley, Windsor Herald*, Camden Society, new series, 11 (London: Camden Society, 1872), pp. 43–4.

25. A. Ashbee and D. Lasocki, assisted by P. Holman and F. Kisby, *A Biographical Dictionary of English Court Musicians 1485–1714*, vol. 2 (Aldershot: Ashgate, 1998), p. 875. For information concerning 'loud minstrels' in the records of Spanish churches see Kreitner, 'Minstrels in Spanish churches' *passim*.

26. It is worth pointing out that in some places the loud/soft distinction continued to have some bureaucratic utility, in that cornetts, shawms and trombones were a distinct group for payment purposes, irrespective of what other instruments they played.

27. Baroncini, 'Zorzi Trombetta' (2002), 67; (2004), 5, 11.

28. Quoted in B. Dickey, 'The cornett', in *The Cambridge Companion to Brass Instruments*, ed. T. Herbert and J. Wallace (Cambridge: Cambridge University Press, 1997), pp. 56–7.

29. *New Grove 2*, s.v. 'Chorus'.

30. S. A. Rincon, 'Music and court in Charles V's Valladolid, 1517–1539', in *Music and Musicians in Renaissance Cities and Towns*, ed. F. Kisby (Cambridge: Cambridge University Press, 2001), p. 109.

31. *New Grove 2*, s.v. 'Pastrana, Pedro de'.

32. Kreitner, 'Minstrels in Spanish churches', 538. See this article for an informative survey of instruments in Spanish churches.

33. A. Ashbee (ed.), *Records of English Court Music*, vol. 7 (Aldershot: Scolar Press, 1993), p. 79. The history of the cornett in England is not entirely clear. Francis Galpin identified English sources for the instrument continuously from the eleventh to the late seventeenth centuries; see F. Galpin, *Old English Instruments of Music*, 1910, 4th edn, rev. T. Dart (London: Methuen 1965). But the listing of cornetts in English court records in the sixteenth century is later than it is elsewhere.

34. For a list of sources for sixteenth-century instrumental music, see *New Grove 2*, s.v. 'Sources of instrumental ensemble music to 1630'.

35. M. Praetorius, *Syntagma musicum; De organographia*, Wolfenbüttel, 1619, facsimile edn (Kassel: Bärenreiter, 1958), p. 5.

36. The events are described in Sir William Dugdale, *Origines juridiciales, or historical memorials of the English laws* (London, 1666), pp. 150–7, apparently from an earlier documentary account.

37. Thomas Campion, *The Description of a Maske, Presented before the Kinges Maiestie at Whit-Hall on Twelfth Night last in honour of the Lord Hayes, and his Bride daughter and Heire to the Honourable the Lord Dennye, their Marriage having been the same Day at Court solemnized. Invented and set forth by Thomas Campion Doctor of Phisicke* (London, 1607); see also J. Stevens, 'Shakespeare and the music of the Elizabethan stage', in *Shakespeare in Music*, ed. P. M. Hartnoll (London: Macmillan, 1964), pp. 41–2.

38. B. Sluchin and R. Lapie, *Le Trombone à travers les âges* (Paris: Buchet/Chastel, 2001), p. 40.

39. K. Polk, 'Instrumental music in Brussels in the early 16th century', *Revue belge de musicologie/Belgisch Tijdschrift voor Muziekwetenschap*, 55 (2001), 92.

40. Kreitner, 'Minstrels in Spanish churches', 536.

41. See Kreitner, 'Minstrels in Spanish churches' *passim*.

42. *New Grove 2*, s.v. 'Susato, Tylman'.

43. R. Wegman, 'Music and musicians at the Guild of Our Lady in Bergen op Zoom, c. 1470–1510', *Early Music History*, 9 (1990), 217.

44. *New Grove 2*, s.v. 'Te Deum'.

45. F. A. D'Accone, 'The performance of sacred music in Italy during Josquin's time, ca. 1475–1525', in *Josquin des Prez*, ed. E. E. Lowinsky and B. J. Blackburn (London: Oxford University Press, 1976), p. 616.

46. C. Wright, 'Performance practices at the cathedral of Cambrai 1475–1550', *Musical Quarterly*, 64 (1978), 322.

47. Quoted in S. Anglo, *Spectacle, Pageantry and Early Tudor Policy*, 1969, 2nd edn (Oxford: Clarendon Press, 1997), p. 137.

48. C. Whibley (ed.), *The Lives of the Kings: Henry VIII, By Edward Hall* (London and Edinburgh: T. C. & E. C Jack, 1904), p. 195; quoted in J. Stevens, *Music and Poetry in the Early Tudor Court*, 1961 (Cambridge: Cambridge University Press, 1979), p. 236.

49. B. de Montfaucon, *Les Monumens de la monarchie françoise qui comprennent L'Histoire de France*, vol. 4 (Paris, 1732), p. 312. The English translation is given in J. S. Brewer (ed.), *Letters and Papers Foreign and Domestic in the Reign of Henry VIII*, vol. 3, pt 1 (London, 1867), pp. 303–13.

50. Ibid., pp. 291–2.

51. T. Dart, 'The repertory of the royal wind music', *Galpin Society Journal*, 11 (1958), 74.

52. D. Neal, *The History of the Puritans, or Protestant Non-Conformists from the Reformation to the Death of Queen Elizabeth* (London, 1732), pp. 155–6.

53. G. Paule, *The Life of the most reverend and religious prelate John Whitgift Lord Archbishop of Canterbury* (London, 1612), p. 79.

54. P. Smart, *A Short Treatise of Alters, Alter-furniture, Alter-cringing and Musick of al the Quire, Singing-men and Choristers* (London, 1629), p. 19.

55. P. Smart, *A Catalogue of Superstitions and Innovations* (London, 1642), p. 9.

56. W. D. Hammond, *A Relation of a Short Survey of the Western Counties, August 1635*, Camden Society, 3rd Series, 53 (London: Camden Society, 1936), p. 74.

57. 2 Samuel 18: 33.

58. For illustrations of the forces that Schütz had at his disposal and other information, see G. Spagnoli, *Letters and Documents of Heinrich Schütz, 1656–1672* (Ann Arbor, Mich.: UMI Research Press, 1989).

59. New York Public Library at the Lincoln Center, Music Division, Drexel MS 5469.

Chapter 6 Decline, survival and rehabilitation: the seventeenth and eighteenth centuries

1. F. W. Galpin, 'The sackbut: its evolution and history, illustrated by an instrument of the sixteenth century', *Proceedings of the Musical Association*, 33 (1906–7), 15–16.

2. F. W. Galpin, *Old English Instruments of Music*, 1910, 4th edn, rev. T. Dart (London:

Methuen, 1965), p. 155.

3. Quoted in A. Baines, 'James Talbot's manuscript (Christ Church Library Music MS 1187)', *Galpin Society Journal*, 1 (1948), 19.

4. The sources for Locke's *ffor his Majestys Sagbutts and Cornetts* are discussed in T. Herbert, 'Matthew Locke and the cornett and sackbut ensemble in England after the Restoration: the "labelled evidence"', in K. Polk (ed.), *Brass Music at the Cross Roads of Europe* (Utrecht: STIMU, 2005), pp. 57–68. Also discussed here is a pair of partbooks containing bass parts for trombones that survive from Oliver Cromwell's household musicians. These are held in the special collections of the British National Art Library at the Victoria and Albert Museum, London (Clem TT 14–15).

5. Quoted by Ian Spink in 'Music and Society', in *The Seventeenth Century*, ed. Spink, The Blackwell History of Music in Britain, vol. 3 (Oxford: Blackwell, 1992), p. 48.

6. J. Wilson, *Roger North on Music. Being a selection from his essays written between c.1695–1728* (London: Novello, 1959), p. 229. The primary source is GB-Lbl Add. MS 32534, fo. 73v.

7. GB-Lbl Add. MS 7895.a.47.

8. C. Burney, *An Account of the Musical Performances in Westminster Abbey and the Pantheon, May 26th, 27th, 29th: and June the 3rd and 5th, 1784, in Commemoration of Handel*, 1785, facsimile edn (New York: Da Capo Press, 1964), p. 7.

9. See D. M. Guion, *The Trombone: Its History and Music, 1697–1811*, Musicology: A Book Series, 6 (New York: Gordon and Breach, 1988), p. 168, Plate 15.

10. See Guion, *The Trombone*, and B. Sluchin and R. Lapie, *Le Trombone à travers les âges* (Paris: Buchet/Chastel, 2001).

11. See *New Grove 2*, s.v. 'Venice'; and Guion, *The Trombone*, p. 161.

12. *New Grove 2*, s.v. 'Naples'.

13. J. Mattheson, *Das neu-eröffnete Orchestre* (Hamburg: the author, 1713), pp. 266–7.

14. S. Carter, 'Trombone pitch in the eighteenth century: an overview', in *Posaunen und Trompeten: Geschichte – Akustik – Spieltechnik*, ed. M. Lustig (Blankenburg: Stiftung Kloster Michaelstein, 2000), p. 62.

15. S. Carter, 'Trombone obbligatos in Viennese oratorios of the Baroque', *Historic Brass Society Journal*, 2 (1990), 54.

16. G. Zechmeister, *Die Wiener Theater nächst der Burg und nächst dem Kärntnerthor von 1747 bis 1776* (Vienna: Hermann Bohlaus Nachf., 1972), p. 189.

17. L. von Köchel, *Die Kaiserliche Hof-Musikkapelle in Wien von 1543–1867*, Vienna, 1869, facsimile edn (Hildesheim and New York: Olms, 1976).

18. Quoted in D. Edge, 'Mozart's Viennese orchestras', *Early Music*, 20 (1992), 68.

19. Ibid.

20. Ibid., 67.

21. H. Weiner, 'A rose is a rose is a rose, but when is a bass trombone a bass trombone?', paper delivered to the 'Declamation versus Lyricism' conference of the Historic Brass Society, Basel and Bad Säckingen, 11–13 June 2004.

22. C. R. Wigness, *The Soloistic Use of the Trombone in Eighteenth-Century Vienna* (Nashville, Tenn.: Brass Press, 1978), p. 25.

23. (Lower Austria), Benediktinerstift, Musikarchiv V 451.

24. S. Carter, 'Trombone obbligatos in Viennese oratorios of the Baroque', 52–77.

25. *J. G. Albrechtsberger's sämmtliche Schriften über Generalbaß, Harmonie-Lehre, und Tonsetzkunst zum Selbstunterrichte*, vol. 3: *Anweisung zur Composition*, ed. I. von Seyfried (Vienna: Strauss, 1826), p. 166. I am grateful to Howard Weiner for information about this.

26. Mattheson, *Das neu-eröffnete Orchestre*, pp. 266–7.

27. Quoted in C. Eisen, 'Mozart's Salzburg orchestras', *Early Music*, 20 (1992), 103.

28. Ibid., 93.

29. In fact, the cover of the autograph score lists '3 Tromboni tutti obblig.'. See C. H. Sherman and T. Donley Thomas, *Johann Michael Haydn (1737–1806): A Chronological Thematic Catalogue of his Works* (Stuyvesant, NY: Pendragon Press, 1993), p. 96.

30. Some seventeenth-century instruments also survive from Pfaffendorf, and makers from

this town also supplied Moravian communities in America with trombones.

31. *Davidde penitente* K469 is largely a contrafactum of the C minor Mass K427. The autograph score presumed to have been used for the first performance in Vienna in 1785 has markings indicating only two trombones. The addition of a third (or even fourth) trombone in modern editions is the work of editors. Wolfgang Amadeus Mozart, *Neue Ausgabe sämtlicher Werke*, Serie I, Werkgruppe 4, Band 3, *Davide penitente*, ed. M. Holl (Kassel: Bärenreiter, 1987), pp. XX and XXVII.

32. Edge, 'Mozart's Viennese orchestras', 77.

33. Winchester, Hampshire Records Office, 9M73/G306/18, quoted in D. Burrows and R. Dunhill, *Music and Theatre in Handel's World: The Family Papers of James Harris, 1732–1780* (New York: Oxford University Press, 2002), p. 65.

34. Winchester, Hampshire Records Office, 9M73/G319/6, quoted ibid., p. 66.

35. *London Daily Post*, 26 February 1741.

36. Quoted in D. Burrows, 'Handel, the Dead March and a newly identified trombone movement', *Early Music*, 18 (1990), 411. This article contains additional information about the sources for Handel's trombone parts in this period.

37. *A Shakespeare Ode: Thomas Linley Jnr*, ed. G. Beechey, Musica Britannica, 30 (London: Stainer & Bell, 1970, reprinted with corrections 1985), p. xviii.

38. T. Herbert, 'The sackbut in England in the 17th and 18th centuries', *Early Music*, 18 (1990), 609–16.

39. Burney, *An Account of the Musical Performances*, p. 7.

40. F. A. M. R. Jarvis, 'The community of German migrant musicians in London c1750–c1850' (Master of Studies thesis, University of Cambridge, 2003), Figure 6.

41. See, for example, GB-Lbl Add. MS 17829, fo.5.

42. David Charlton, quoted in Guion, *The Trombone*, p. 163.

43. J. LaRue and H. Brofsky, 'Parisian brass players, 1751–1793', *Brass Quarterly*, 3, no. 4 (1960), 140.

44. *The Times*, 26 March 1789.

45. Private collection of Gerald Coke of Bentley, Hampshire. I am grateful to Prof. Donald Burrows for this information.

46. In addition to the instrument under discussion here, there was the fifteenth-century single-slide instrument (see Chapter 3) and a type of trumpet used in England in the later eighteenth and nineteenth centuries, which was most famously championed by the virtuoso Victorian trumpeter Thomas Harper and his offspring. It has been suggested (A. Pinnock in *New Grove 2*, s.v. 'Flat trumpet') that the two English instruments may have been related, but it is hard to detect evidence that supports this, and it is difficult to see how such a relationship could have existed.

47. See Baines, 'James Talbot's manuscript', 21–2, and Baines, *Brass Instruments: Their History and Development*, 1976 (London: Faber, 1980), pp. 180–2. Also, E. Halfpenny, 'Musicians at James II's coronation', *Music and Letters*, 32 (1951), 103–114; A. Pinnock, 'A wider role for the flat trumpet', *Galpin Society Journal*, 42 (1989), 105–11; C. Steele-Perkins, 'Practical observations on natural, slide and flat trumpets', *Galpin Society Journal*, 42 (1989), 122–7; P. Downey, 'Performing Mr Purcell's "Exotick" trumpet notes', in *Performing the Music of Henry Purcell*, ed. M. Burden (Oxford: Clarendon Press, 1996), pp. 49–60.

48. *The Diary of Henry Teonge, Naval Chaplain on Board His Majesty's Ships Assistance, Bristol and Royal Oak, anno 1675 to 1679* (London, 1825), p. 43.

49. The distinguished trumpet player Crispian Steele-Perkins (in conversation with the author) has made the suggestion that 'flatt' in this context signifies a form of muting. Trumpet muting was, of course, common at this time. It is probable that the word was used here to denote a different (perhaps quieter) form of playing from signalling, which was the main role for ships' trumpets.

50. Oxford, Christ Church Library, Music MS 1187.

Chapter 7 Didacticism and the idea of virtuosity

1. E. Hanslick, *Music Criticisms 1846–99*, trans. H. Pleasants, rev. edn (Harmondsworth: Penguin, 1963), p. 225.

2. Haydn also scored for trombones in *Il ritorno di Tobia* (1773).

3. There is something of a mystery about the exact date of his appointment; see H. Weiner, 'André Braun's *Gamme et méthode pour les trombonnes*: the earliest modern trombone method rediscovered', *Historic Brass Society Journal*, 5 (1993), 289–90.

4. B. Sluchin and R. Lapie, 'Slide trombone teaching and method books in France (1794–1960)', *Historic Brass Society Journal*, 9 (1997), 5.

5. Quoted in Sluchin and Lapie, 'Slide trombone teaching', 11.

6. D. K. Holoman, *The Société des Concerts du Conservatoire 1828–1967* (Berkeley, Los Angeles and London: University of California Press, 2004), pp. 64–5.

7. T. Herbert, 'Nineteenth-century bands', in *The British Brass Band: A Musical and Social History*, ed. T. Herbert (Oxford: Oxford University Press, 2000), pp. 62–4.

8. I am grateful to Peter Horton, Reference Librarian at the Royal College of Music, for this information.

9. D. Cairns, *Berlioz*, vol. 2: *Servitude and Greatness, 1832–1869* (London: Allen Lane, 1999), p. 252.

10. H. Weiner, 'André Braun's *Gamme et méthode pour les trombonnes* revisited', *Historic Brass Society Journal*, 11 (1999), 94.

11. F. Vobaron, F. Berr and A. Dieppo, *Complete Trombone Tutor* (London: Lafleur, 1880), p. 39.

12. J. Fröhlich, *Vollständige theoretisch-pracktische Musikschule* (Bonn: N. Simrock, c.1810–11), quoted in Weiner, 'André Braun's *Gamme et méthode pour les trombonnes*: the earliest modern trombone method rediscovered', 292.

13. See H. Macdonald, *Berlioz's Orchestration Treatise: A Translation and Commentary* (Cambridge: Cambridge University Press, 2002), pp. 211–12. According to Forsyth, this situation still prevailed in 1914; see C. Forsyth, *Orchestration*, 1914 (London: Macmillan; Stainer & Bell, 1929), p. 134.

14. A. Braun, *Gamme et méthode pour les trombonnes alto, ténor et basse* (Paris: Jean-Georges Sieber, c.1793–7), Article 12, quoted in Weiner, 'André Braun's *Gamme et méthode pour les trombonnes*: the earliest modern trombone method rediscovered', 299 (Weiner's translation).

15. Ibid. (Howard Weiner's translation), and also Weiner's two subsequent articles, 'André Braun's *Gamme et méthode pour les trombonnes* revisited', 98, and 'François René Gebauer's *50 Leçons pour la trombonne basse, alto et tenor*: the earliest book of études for the trombone', *Historic Brass Society Journal*, 11 (1999), 107.

16. As Weiner points out, this does not include the Moravian trombone choir repertoire (see Chapter 11). See Weiner, 'François René Gebauer's *50 Leçons*', 109, and his 'Communication' on p. 466 of the *Historic Brass Society Journal*, 14 (2002).

17. This was published by Philippe Petit between 1816 and 1826, but no copy of it is known to exist. See Weiner, 'François René Gebauer's *50 Leçons*', 109, n. 7.

18. Quoted in Sluchin and Lapie, 'Slide trombone teaching', 11.

19. A. Dieppo, *Méthode complète pour le trombone* (Paris: Troupenas, 1837), p. 6.

20. They are shown and explained even in Braun's *Gamme et méthode*.

21. A. Lafosse, *Méthode complète de trombone à coulisse*, rev. and augmented edn in 2 vols, vol. 2, (Paris: Alphonse Leduc, 1948), p. 150.

22. Ibid., p. 155.

23. E. Kleinhammer, *The Art of Trombone Playing* (Evanston, Ill.: Summy-Birchard, 1963), p. 100.

24. *Allgemeine musikalische Zeitung*, 21 (1819), 218, quoted in M. Rasmussen, 'Two early nineteenth-century trombone virtuosi: Carl Traugott Queisser and Friedrich August Belcke', *Brass Quarterly*, 5, no. 1 (1961), 5.

25. *Allgemeine musikalische Zeitung*, 43 (1841), 612, quoted in Rasmussen, 'Two early nineteenth-century trombone virtuosi', 14.
26. *Musical World*, 17 March 1863, 185.
27. Ibid., 3 March 1860, 142.
28. On Queisser, see also S. Krause, 'God of the trombone', *Brass Bulletin*, 117 (2002), 68–80.
29. G. Bridges, *Pioneers in Brass* (published on CD-ROM, Trescott Research, 2001), s.v. 'Pryor, Arthur'.
30. I refer here to the Hogan Jazz Archives of Tulane University, New Orleans, and the Institute of Jazz Studies at Rutgers University.

Chapter 8 *The trombone in the modern orchestra*

1. C. Forsyth, *Orchestration*, 1914 (London: Macmillan; Stainer & Bell, 1929), p. 147.
2. See D. J. Koury, *Orchestral Performance Practices in the Nineteenth Century: Size, Proportions, and Seating* (Ann Arbor, Mich.: UMI Research Press, 1986).
3. L. W. Levine, *Highbrow/Lowbrow: The Emergence of Cultural Hierarchy in America* (Cambridge, Mass., and London: Harvard University Press, 1988), pp. 90–2.
4. Beethoven was the first major composer to introduce a trombone section into the symphony orchestra. His Fifth Symphony (1808) includes a section of three trombones.
5. See, for example, Levine's *Highbrow/Lowbrow*.
6. The Braun brothers appear to have been primarily horn and trumpet players, though they were clearly trombonists too.
7. D. K. Holoman, *The Société des Concerts du Conservatoire 1828–1967* (Berkeley, Los Angeles and London: University of California Press, 2004), p. 67. See also G. Bridges, *Pioneers in Brass* (published on CD-ROM, Trescott Research, 2001), s.v. 'Innes'.
8. J. Doane, *A Musical Directory for the Year 1794* (London: R. H. Westley, 1794).
9. *Mortimer's London Directory* (London, 1794).
10. Royal Society of Musicians archive, London, s.v. 'Smithies', etc. (The Royal Society files all members by name only.)
11. A calculation of the exact constitution of British bands at this time is all but impossible, because they were funded privately by officers rather than by government grant. The quoted figure is construed from War Office documents relating to the initial funding of the Military School of Music.
12. See C. Ehrlich, *First Philharmonic: A History of the Royal Philharmonic Society* (Oxford: Clarendon Press, 1995).
13. *Illustrated London News*, 9 November 1850, quoted in *New Grove 2*, s.v. 'Jullien, Louis.'
14. *The Times*, 31 October 1846, reported that the ophicleide player Prospère (Jean Prospère Guivier) performed an encore on 'a new instrument called the serpentcleide which combines the properties of the serpent and ophicleide'.
15. For a description of Jullien's concerts see, for example, *The Times*, 9 March 1842.
16. For a general study of Jullien, see A. Carse, *The Life of Jullien: Adventurer, Showman-Conductor and Establisher of the Promenade Concerts in England, together with a History of those Concerts up to 1895* (Cambridge: Heffer, 1951).
17. Ehrlich, *First Philharmonic*, p. 52.
18. I have been unable to trace the origin of this utterance, but I am grateful to Joseph Alessi of the New York Philharmonic for reminding me of it. This version of the anecdote seems consistent with Thomas Beecham's style, but one of Richard Strauss's 'Ten Golden Rules written in a young conductor's album' was 'Never look encouragingly towards the brass, except for a quick glance to give an important entry.'
19. Holoman, *Société des Concerts*, p. 50.
20. Ibid., pp. 161–2.
21. *Musical World*, 1 March 1841, 132.

22. *The Harmonicon*, 4 (1828), 194–7.

23. *Vossische Zeitung* (Berlin), quoted in *Musical Times*, 1 April 1887, 241.

24. *Musical Times*, 1 July 1904, 444.

25. E. Hanslick, *Music Criticisms 1846–99*, trans. H. Pleasants, rev. edn (Harmondsworth: Penguin, 1963), p. 233.

26. A. Wirth, *Posaunen-Schule für Alt, Tenor und Bass Posaune . . . Instruction Book of the Simple and Valve-Trombone* (London: Augener, 1870), p. 2.

27. *Musical Times*, 17 February 1837, 128–33.

28. G. B. Shaw, *London Music in 1888–89 as Heard by Corno di Bassetto (later known as George Bernard Shaw) with Some Further Autobiographical Particulars*, 1937, facsimile edn (New York: Vienna House, 1973), p. 79.

29. Quoted in F. W. Galpin, *Old English Instruments of Music*, 1910, 4th edn, rev. T. Dart (London: Methuen, 1965), p. 156.

30. O. Langey, *Practical Tutor for the B♭ Slide-Trombone*, rev. edn (London: Hawkes & Son, 1909), p. 5.

31. The Savage Club is one of London's premier clubs – and one of its most distinctive. Founded in 1857, it is the most bohemian of the clubs, with a strong interest in the creative arts and entertainment. Some of the UK's leading musicians, actors and writers have been members, and its unique traditions continue to thrive.

32. Reproduced in A. Rose, *Talks with Bandsmen: A Popular Handbook for Brass Instrumentalists*, London: William Rider, 1895, facsimile edn (London: Tony Bingham, 1995).

33. *Musical Times*, 1 July 1898, 454.

34. Shaw, *London Music*, p. 384. The context in which this performance took place, a lecture-recital by Case, is described in detail by Shaw in 'The Grave Trombone', published in the *Dramatic Review*, 8 August 1885, and reprinted in *Shaw's Music*, vol. 1: *1876–1890*, ed. D. H. Laurence, (London and Sydney; Toronto: Max Reinhardt; Bodley Head, 1981), pp. 330–5.

35. See S. Carter, 'Georges Kastner on brass instruments: the influence of technology on the theory of orchestration', in *Perspectives in Brass Scholarship: Proceedings of the International Historic Brass Symposium, Amherst, 1995*, ed. S. Carter (Stuyvesant, NY: Pendragon Press, 1997), p. 184.

36. E. Prout, *The Orchestra*, vol. 1 (London: Augener, 1897), p. 224.

37. Langey, *Practical Tutor*, rev. edn, p. 5.

38. H. Macdonald, *Berlioz's Orchestration Treatise: A Translation and Commentary* (Cambridge: Cambridge University Press, 2002), p. 212.

39. Ibid., p. 213.

40. *Musical World*, 17 February 1837, 128.

41. Macdonald, *Berlioz's Orchestration Treatise*, p. 209.

42. Forsyth, *Orchestration*, pp. 134, 139.

43. Ch.-M. Widor, *The Technique of the Modern Orchestra*, 1904, trans. E. Suddard (London: Joseph Williams, 1906), p. 82.

44. Macdonald, *Berlioz's Orchestration Treatise*, p. 210.

45. Ibid., p. 213.

46. F.-A. Gevaert, *Nouveau Traité d'instrumentation* (Paris and Brussels: Lemoine & Fils, 1885), p. 256.

47. G. Zechmeister, 'The role of the (contra)bass trombone in the Vienna sound', *Brass Bulletin*, 102 (1998), 19–28. Valve trombones may have been used in the Vienna Court Opera Orchestra as early as the mid-1839s, and in the Vienna Philharmonic Orchestra from its establishment in 1843.

48. See facsimile in K. Shifrin, 'Orchestral trombone practice in the nineteenth century with special reference to the alto trombone', vol. 2 (D.Phil. thesis, University of Oxford, 1999).

49. See, for example, a picture of the Boston Symphony Orchestra performing in the Old Music Hall under Georg Henschel (c.1881–4), reproduced in E. A. Bowles, *The Timpani:*

A History in Pictures and Documents (Hillsdale, NY: Pendragon Press, 2002), p. 306.

50. On the date of the first edition, see Macdonald, *Berlioz's Orchestration Treatise*, p. xxi.

51. Forsyth, *Orchestration*, pp. 133–5.

52. For an excellent summary of Kastner's writings on brass instruments, see Carter, 'Georges Kastner on brass instruments', pp. 171–92.

53. Ibid., p. 188.

54. Macdonald, *Berlioz's Orchestration Treatise*, p. 219.

55. D. Cairns (trans. and ed.), *The Memoirs of Hector Berlioz* (London: Victor Gollancz, 1977), p. 287.

56. Macdonald, *Berlioz's Orchestration Treatise*, p. 225.

57. Gevaert, *Nouveau Traité*, p. 236.

58. Ibid., p. 249.

59. N. Rimsky-Korsakov, *Principles of Orchestration*, 1913, ed. M. Steinberg, trans. E. Agate, vol. 1 (New York: Édition Russe de Musique, 1923), p. 3.

60. Ibid., p. 24.

61. Ibid., p. 23.

62. Prout, *Orchestra*, vol. 1, p. 266.

63. Ibid., p. 176.

64. Ibid., pp. 224–31.

65. Forsyth, *Orchestration*, p. 138.

66. Ibid., p. 149.

67. Ibid, p. 146.

68. Quoted in A. Tyson, 'The 1803 version of Beethoven's *Christus am Oelberge*', *Musical Quarterly*, 56 (1970), 559, n. 11.

69. *The Harmonicon*, January 1824, 11.

70. D. M. Guion, *The Trombone: Its History and Music, 1697–1811*, Musicology: A Book Series, 6 (New York: Gordon and Breach, 1988), pp. 170–1.

71. Macdonald, *Berlioz's Orchestration Treatise*, p. 225.

72. See, for example, *New Grove 2*, s.v. 'Wagner' (1), §13: 'it was Wagner above all who gave them [trombones] an independent voice'.

73. I. Stravinsky and R. Craft, *Conversations with Igor Stravinsky* (London: Faber, 1959), p. 30.

74. See, for example, the discussion in Chapter 12 of performance standards on the recordings directed by Stravinsky in Paris in 1932.

Chapter 9 *Valve trombones and other nineteenth-century introductions*

1. The text of the announcement is given in A. Baines, *Brass Instruments: Their History and Development*, 1976 (London: Faber, 1980), p. 206.

2. The patent was for the principle enshrined in the valve mechanism, rather than for the particular design specified by Stölzel and Blühmel. This led to protection being denied to some other perfectly legitimate applications.

3. It has recently been suggested that Stölzel devised a similar mechanism independently in 1827. See *New Grove 2*, s.v. 'Valve (i)' §2.

4. A. Nemetz, *Neueste Posaun-Schule*, 2nd edn (Vienna, n.d. [after 1830]), translation by Howard Weiner.

5. See H. Heyde, *Das Ventilblasinstrument* (Leipzig: Deutscher Verlag für Musik, 1987), p. 18; also W. Waterhouse, *The New Langwill Index: A Dictionary of Musical Wind-Instrument Makers and Inventors* (London: Tony Bingham, 1993), s.v. 'Gabler, Joseph Caspar'.

6. Baines, *Brass Instruments*, p. 210.

7. G. Zechmeister, 'The role of the (contra)bass trombone in the Vienna sound', *Brass Bulletin*, 102 (1998), 20. (Citations refer to Zechmeister's original German text; quotations have been newly translated here by Howard Weiner.)

8. Vienna, Haus-, Hof- und Staatsarchiv. HHStA/HMK/K25/1858/Nr. 374/17, cited ibid., 22. Ignaz Assmayr had reported on 4 January 1851 that valve trombones were 'currently a solid instrument in every orchestra'. (HHStA/HMK/K23/1851/Nr. 6074, quoted ibid., 22.)

9. Ibid.,19–21.

10. HHStA/OPER/K11/1862/Nr. 178, quoted ibid., 22.

11. HHStA/OPER/K74/1883/Nr. 71, quoted ibid., 23–4.

12. HHStA/OPER/K74/1883/Nr. 311, quoted ibid.

13. The Garde-Jäger-Bataillon of Potsdam introduced a *Posaune mit Wiener Ventilen* in 1832. H. Heyde, *Das Ventilblasinstrument*, p. 78.

14. See G. Joppig, trans. V. von der Lancken, 'Václav František Červený: leading European inventor and manufacturer', *Historic Brass Society Journal*, 4 (1992), 210–28.

15. For a description of the Pelitti operation, see R. Meucci, trans. E. Pelitti, 'The Pelitti firm: makers of brass instruments in nineteenth-century Milan', *Historic Brass Society Journal*, 6 (1994), 304–33.

16. Conn catalogue, *The New Wonder Model Slide Trombones* (c. 1928), p. 9.

17. R. Meucci, trans. W. Waterhouse, 'The cimbasso and related instruments in 19th-century Italy', *Galpin Society Journal*, 49 (1996), 155.

18. Ibid., 158, quoting the *Gazzetta musicale di Milano*, 4 September 1881, in translation.

19. *Gazzetta musicale di Milano*, 36 (1881), 319, quoted in translation in Meucci, 'The Pelitti firm', 322.

20. Meucci, 'The Pelitti firm', 322, n. 77.

21. D. M. De Arce, *Music in Ibero-America to 1850: A Historical Survey* (Lanham, Md., and London: Scarecrow Press, 2001), pp. 382–3.

22. Conn catalogue (1913).

23. H. Macdonald, *Berlioz's Orchestration Treatise: A Translation and Commentary* (Cambridge: Cambridge University Press, 2002), p. 228.

24. H. W. von Gontershausen, *Neu eröffnetes Magazin musikalischer Tonwerkzeuge* (Frankfurt, 1855), p. 402.

25. Oral interview with Patricia Willard, 15 November 1978. Archive of the Institute of Jazz Studies, Rutgers University, Newark, NJ, USA.

26. For 'Creole Rhapsody', see Decca GRD3–640, or RCA Victor/BMG Classics 09026–63386–2; for 'Clouds in My Heart', see Giants of Jazz 53046.

27. See R. Hudson, *Evolution: The Improvisational Style of Bob Brookmeyer* (Vienna: Universal Edition, 2002).

28. D. Morgenstern, *Living with Jazz: A Reader* (New York: Pantheon, 2004), p. 249.

29. W. Horwood, *Adolphe Sax, 1814–1894: His Life and Legacy* (Baldock, Herts.: Egon, 1983), p. 114.

30. C. Forsyth, *Orchestration*, 1914 (London: Macmillan; Stainer & Bell, 1929), p. 146.

31. Ibid.

32. Horwood, *Adolphe Sax*, p. 114.

33. The Boosey & Hawkes company reverted to the trading name Besson for its musical instruments in 2003–4.

34. Conn catalogue, *The New Wonder Model Slide Trombones* (c. 1928), p. 7.

35. Ibid.

36. Conn catalogue, c. 1910. The instrument was patented in 1890.

37. B. Sluchin, '"Duplex" instruments – yesterday and today', *Brass Bulletin*, 115 (2001), 112–15.

38. See J. Webb, 'Mahillon's Wagner tubas', *Galpin Society Journal*, 49 (1996), 207.

39. For a discussion of the euphonium and other low brass instruments, see C. Bevan, *The Tuba Family*, 2nd edn (Winchester, Hants.: Piccolo Press, 2000).

40. Forsyth, *Orchestration*, p. 146.

41. MacDonald, *Berlioz's Orchestration Treatise*, p. 234.

42. I am grateful to Dr Arnold Myers of the University of Edinburgh for allowing me to

examine this important collection of sources.

43. See T. Herbert, 'The reconstruction of nineteenth-century band repertory: towards a protocol', in *Perspectives in Brass Scholarship: Proceedings of the International Historic Brass Symposium, Amherst, 1995*, ed. S. Carter (Stuyvesant, NY: Pendragon Press, 1997), pp. 193–222.

44. Macdonald, *Berlioz's Orchestration Treatise*, p. 234.

45. Ibid., p. 236.

Chapter 10 Popular music

1. For a brief but effective overview of the meanings of 'popular music', see R. Middleton, *Studying Popular Music* (Milton Keynes: Open University Press, 1990), Ch. 1.

2. H. M. Brown, *Music in the French Secular Theatre, 1400–1550* (Oxford: Oxford University Press, 1963), p. 74.

3. Royal Society of Musicians, 'Booth, Robert'. That his parents were illiterate is attested by the presence of a cross rather than a signature on the birth certificate.

4. Just two other trombone players in the records of the Royal Society of Musicians share this distinction: John Matt (1843–1910), who was the son of a cabinet maker, and William Winterbottom (1821–89), a military musician whose father was a soldier.

5. C. Dahlhaus, *Nineteenth-Century Music*, trans. J. B. Robinson (Berkeley and London: University of California Press, 1989), p. 311.

6. I scrutinized this material at a time when it was in the possession of the Boosey & Hawkes company. As this book was being prepared for submission, the archive and other items were transferred to the Horniman Museum, London.

7. A. Rose, *Talks with Bandsmen: A Popular Handbook for Brass Instrumentalists*, London: William Rider, 1895, facsimile edn (London: Tony Bingham, 1995), p. 124.

8. C. Ehrlich, *The Music Profession in Britain since the Eighteenth Century* (Oxford: Clarendon Press, 1985), Ch. 5.

9. W. Waterhouse, *The New Langwill Index: A Dictionary of Musical Wind-Instrument Makers and Inventors* (London: Tony Bingham, 1993), p. 129.

10. Ibid., p. 60.

11. On the advertising of brass instruments, see T. Herbert, 'Selling brass instruments: the commercial imaging of brass instruments (1830–1930) and its cultural messages', in *Music in Art: the International Journal for Music Iconography*, 28/1–2 (Spring–Fall 2004), 213–26.

12. N. Groce, *Musical Instrument Makers of New York: A Directory of Eighteenth- and Nineteenth-Century Urban Craftsmen* (Stuyvesant, NY: Pendragon Press, 1991), p. 134.

13. M. H. Hazen and R. M. Hazen, *The Music Men: An Illustrated History of Brass Bands in America, 1800–1920* (Washington, DC and London: Smithsonian Institution Press, 1987), p. 139.

14. C. G. Conn Annual Reports, National Music Museum, University of South Dakota, Vermillion.

15. C. G. Conn trombone catalogue, 1913.

16. C. G. Conn trombone catalogue, c. 1928, p. 13.

17. C. G. Conn Company Prospectus, 1940, p. 7, National Music Museum, University of South Dakota, Vermillion.

18. I was given privileged access to this important archive and wish to record here my gratitude to the staff of the museum for the kindness and co-operation I received.

19. C. G. Conn, Sales Manual for Band and Orchestral Instruments, 1937, p. 8, National Music Museum, University of South Dakota, Vermillion.

20. Conn trombone catalogue, c. 1928, p. 3.

21. Ibid., p. 5.

22. Conn Corporation, internal memo on 'Professional Influence', from J. Klapp to A. Smith,

22 August 1969. National Music Museum, University of South Dakota, Vermillion.

23. See, for example, L. J. Wagner, *Band Music from the Benjamin H. Grierson Collection*, Recent Researches in American Music, 29 (Madison, Wis.: A-R Editions, 1998).

24. On the Cyfarthfa Band repertoire, see T. Herbert, 'The reconstruction of nineteenth-century band repertory: towards a protocol', in *Perspectives in Brass Scholarship: Proceedings of the International Historic Brass Symposium, Amherst, 1995*, ed. S. Carter (Stuyvesant, NY: Pendragon Press, 1997), pp. 193–222. A selection of music from the Cyfarthfa Band repertoire, including 'Carnival of Venice' (*Carnaval de Venise*), has been recorded by the Wallace Collection on *The Origin of the Species: Virtuoso Victorian Brass Music from Cyfarthfa Castle, Wales*, WC2013.

25. G. Bridges, *Pioneers in Brass* (published on CD-ROM, Trescott Research, 2001), s.v. 'Innes'.

26. Ch.-M. Widor, *The Technique of the Modern Orchestra*, 1904, trans. E. Suddard (London: Joseph Williams, 1906), p. 86.

27. R. Strauss (ed.), *Treatise on Instrumentation by Hector Berlioz*, revised and enlarged 1904–5; trans. T. Front (New York: Edwin F. Kalmus, 1948), p. 329.

28. 'Sousa at Brighton', report in the *Sussex Daily News*, 11 December 1901, of two concerts given at the Dome in Brighton.

29. Richard Slater, in an article on 'Expression' published in the *Musical Salvationist* (July 1898), Salvation Army International Heritage Centre, London (SAIHC), Richard Slater file. Quoted in *The British Brass Band: A Musical and Social History*, ed. T. Herbert (Oxford: Oxford University Press, 2000), p. 291.

30. Bridges, *Pioneers in Brass*, s.v. 'Fillmore'.

31. Ehrlich, *Music Profession*, p. 195.

32. G. Nowell-Smith (ed.), *The Oxford History of World Cinema* (Oxford: Oxford University Press, 1997), pp. 36, 43.

33. Ehrlich, *Music Profession*, p. 194.

34. M. M. Marks, *Music and the Silent Film: Contexts and Case Studies 1895–1924* (Oxford: Oxford University Press, 1997), p. 184.

35. Ehrlich, *Music Profession*, p. 196.

36. Nowell-Smith, *World Cinema*, pp. 211–12.

37. R. Allen, 'Caribbean music in New York City', in *American Musical Traditions*, ed. J. T. Titon and B. Carlin, vol. 5: *Latino American and Asian Music* (New York: Schirmer Reference, 2002), p. 8.

38. L. Waxer, 'Puerto Rican music in New York City', in *American Musical Traditions*, ed. J. T. Titon and B. Carlin, vol. 5: *Latino American and Asian Music*, p. 20.

39. L. Waxer, 'Cuban music in New York City', in *American Musical Traditions*, ed. J. T. Titon and B. Carlin, vol. 5: *Latino American and Asian Music*, pp. 15–16.

40. Waxer, 'Puerto Rican music', p. 20.

41. *New Grove 2*, s.v. 'Colón, Willie'.

42. Colón's discography can be found at <http://www.williecolon.com> (accessed 18 January 2005).

43. For example, 'El Molestoso II', 'Cuidate Company II' and 'Tu Tu Ta Ta II', on *La Perfecta II*, CCD-2136–2. Palmieri's discography can be found at <http://www.eddiepalmierimusic.com> (accessed 18 January 2005).

Chapter 11 The Moravians and other popular religions

1. C. A. Leonard, 'The role of the trombone and its *Affekt* in the Lutheran church music of seventeenth-century Saxony and Thuringia: the early seventeenth century', *Historic Brass Society Journal*, 10 (1998), 57–91, and 'The role of the trombone and its *Affekt* in the Lutheran church music of seventeenth-century Saxony and Thuringia: the mid- and late-

seventeenth century', *Historic Brass Society Journal*, 12 (2000), 161–209.

2. B. van den Bosch, *The Origin and Development of the Trombone-Work of the Moravian Churches in Germany and All the World* (Winston-Salem, NC: Moravian Music Foundation, 1990), pp. 4–5.

3. Ibid., p. 5.

4. Ibid., p. 6.

5. Ibid., p. 8.

6. Ibid., p. 24.

7. Parliament of Great Britain, 29 November 1747, 'An Act for encouraging the People known by the Name of *Unitas Fratrum* or *United Brethren*, to settle in His Majesty's Colonie in *America*'.

8. For example, by custom and decree the ribbon or bow with which a woman's cap (*Scheppelhaube*) was tied under her chin was coloured according to her choir: pink for single, blue for married, white for widows. C. E. Beckel, 'Early marriage customs of the Moravian congregation in Bethlehem, Pa', *The Pennsylvania German Folklore Society*, 3 (1988), 5. See also G. L. Gollin, 'Family surrogates in colonial America: the Moravian experiment', *Journal of Marriage and the Family*, 31 (1969), 650–8.

9. There is a suggestion that there was a trombone group in Bethlehem somewhat earlier than 1754. A note in a single brother's diary for 12 July 1747 mentions 'Wald Hörner u. Posaunen' being played by a group of single brothers at Gnadenthal near Nazareth. I am grateful to Stewart Carter for sight of his unpublished paper 'From trombone choir to church band: brass instruments in communities of the Moravian Brethren in America', in which he refers to this diary entry.

10. Anon., 'Did the trombones play at Christmas?' *The Moravian*, 106, no. 12 (December 1961), 6.

11. Ibid., 7.

12. See also A. Franks, 'Unity Archives Friends' Day Address, March 13, 1999', unpublished typescript. Moravian Archives, Bethlehem, Pa. I am grateful for having had sight of this source.

13. Rev. W. C. Reichel, *Something About Trombones and the Old Mill at Bethlehem* (Bethlehem, Pa.: Moravian Publication Office, 1884), p. 6.

14. 178th Annual Report of the Board of Elders of the Moravian Church of Bethlehem, Pa. (1919), p. 17. Moravian Archives, Bethlehem, Pa.

15. *New Grove 2*, s.v. 'Moravians, music of the'.

16. Reichel, *Something About Trombones*, p. 5.

17. Lovefeasts appear to have their origins in the meetings in which simple sustenance was taken following the celebration of the Last Supper, but they evolved into services that are almost entirely musical. See J. T. Hamilton and K. G. Hamilton, *History of the Moravian Church: The Renewed Unitas Fratrum 1722–1957*, 1967, 2nd edn (Bethlehem, Pa., and Winston-Salem, NC: Interprovincial Board of Christian Education, Moravian Church of America, 1983), p. 655, n. 12.

18. van den Bosch, *Origin and Development*, p. 5.

19. Ibid., pp. 5–6.

20. Quoted in K. G. Hamilton, *Church Street in Old Bethlehem* (Bethlehem, Pa.: Moravian Congregation, 1942), p. 20.

21. Ibid., p. 19.

22. Ibid., p. 20.

23. Ibid., p. 19.

24. Quoted ibid., p. 20.

25. L. A. Fries, *Funeral Chorals of the Unitas Fratrum or Moravian Church* (n.p., 1905), p. 4.

26. Ibid.

27. Hamilton and Hamilton, *History of the Moravian Church*, p. 515.

28. Carter, 'From trombone choir to church band'.

29. Reichel, *Something About Trombones*, p. 6.

30. R. A. Grinder, *Music in Bethlehem, Pennsylvania, from 1741–1871* (Bethlehem, Pa.: J. Hill Martin, 1873), p. 20.

31. Reichel, *Something About Trombones*, p. 9.

32. 178th Annual Report of the Board of Elders, p. 17.

33. I am grateful to Don Kemmerer, Musical Director of the present *Posaunenchor* in Bethlehem, Pa., for providing this information.

34. International Heritage Centre of the Salvation Army, London, musical instrument factory file, loose cuttings.

35. *Salvation Army Yearbook* (1918), 26. The report referred to an audit conducted two years previously.

36. *Salvation Army Yearbook* (1917).

37. *Salvation Army Yearbook* (1942) and (1998) respectively. Some of these statistics reflect changes in federations, colonies and dependencies.

38. *Musical Salvationist* (May 1897), 68–9. Quoted in T. Herbert, 'God's perfect minstrels: the bands of the Salvation Army', in *The British Brass Band: A Musical and Social History*, ed. T. Herbert (Oxford: Oxford University Press, 2000), p. 196.

39. As of 8 October 2004, an illustration of the instrument is given at <http://www.yeodoug.com/articles/trombone_gallery/trombone_gallery.html>.

40. One such instrument is in the possession of Mr Frank Tomes, and I am grateful to him for providing me with this information.

41. R. Boonzajer-Flaes, liner notes to *Frozen Brass: Asia*, Anthology of Brass Band Music 1, PAN 2020CD, 1993, p. 2.

42. The term comes from a Portuguese word, *tangedor*, meaning a musician who plays in processions (ibid., p. 9).

43. T. Herbert, 'Brass bands and other vernacular traditions', in *The Cambridge Companion to Brass Instruments* (Cambridge: Cambridge University Press, 1997), ed. T. Herbert and J. Wallace p. 189. See also T. Herbert and M. Sarkissian, 'Victorian bands and their dissemination in the colonies', *Popular Music*, 16, no. 2 (1997), 165–79.

44. *Frozen Brass: Asia*, PAN 2020CD, and *Frozen Brass: Africa and Latin America*, Anthology of Brass Band Music 2, PAN 2026CD.

45. A. Rosenbaum, 'The McIntosh County shouters: slave shout songs from the coast of Georgia' , in *American Musical Traditions*, vol. 2: *African American Traditions*, ed. J. T. Titon and B. Carlin (New York: Schirmer Reference, 2002), p. 77. See also M. A. Hafar, 'The shout band tradition in the southeastern United States', *Historic Brass Society Journal*, 15 (2003), 163–72.

46. Hafar, 'The shout band tradition', 167.

47. P. Williams-Jones, 'Washington D.C./gospel music city, USA: state of the art', in *American Musical Traditions*, vol. 2: *African American Traditions*, p. 77. See also Hafar, 'The shout band tradition', 98–9.

Chapter 12 *Orchestral trombone playing in the age of sound recordings*

1. See, for example, L. W. Brunner, 'The orchestra and recorded sound', in *The Orchestra: Origins and Transformations*, ed. J. Peyser (New York: Charles Scribner's Sons, 1986), pp. 479–532.

2. J. Harvith and S. E. Harvith (eds), *Edison, Musicians and the Phonograph* (New York, Westport, Conn. and London: Greenwood Press, 1987), p. 7.

3. Brunner, 'The orchestra', p. 486.

4. HMV D89–92. This was not the first recording of Beethoven's Fifth Symphony, and several other orchestral works were released before 1920. See, for example, the list of issues by His Master's Voice (HMV) between 1910 and 1914 in Brunner, Table 1.

5. Harvith and Harvith, *Edison*, p. 91.

6. The image is shown in a supplement to *The Billboard*, 21 May 1977, p. RS12.

7. Reproduced in P. Copeland, *Sound Recordings* (London: British Library, 1991), p. 11.

8. Harvith and Harvith, *Edison*, p. 146.

9. Pearl CD9012.

10. Copeland, *Sound Recordings*, p. 11.

11. H. Wood, *About Conducting* (London: Sylvan Press, 1945), p. 77.

12. Biddulph WHL 037.

13. EMI CHS 7 61034 2.

14. Biddulph WHL 037.

15. For the Stravinsky version, see Pearl GEMMCD9334, for the Monteux version Pearl GEMMCD9329.

16. British Library Sound Archive, 1 CD0046468 D1 S1 BD2 EMI STANDARD MID-PR.

17. C3L-30. Columbia had refused to make the record, but the Victor Company had no hesitation in doing so.

18. All three pieces can be found on *Ragtime 1, 1897–1919*, Jazz Archives No. 120, 159052.

19. Victor 31108.

20. In the deputy system, players were allowed to freelance while being members of a particular orchestra. They were allowed to engage their own deputies either for the whole or part of a particular engagement. Typically, a deputy would substitute for an orchestral member for one or two rehearsals, while that member earned a better fee elsewhere. This system was condemned by conductors for the obvious reason that it undermined consistency of standards. Sometimes this system resulted in absurdities. Following the final rehearsal for a concert with the Paris Symphony Orchestra in 1929, Pierre Monteux publicly thanked M. Leroux, a rank-and-file violinist whom the conductor had observed to be the only player in the entire orchestra to have attended every rehearsal. To this, M. Leroux replied, 'Thank you, maestro, but I will not be at the concert.' (J. Canarina, *Pierre Monteux, maître* (Pompton Plains, NJ, and Cambridge: Amadeus Press, 2003), p. 106) Henry Wood said that he had fought this system as early as 1904, but that 'it still rules today' in 1944. (Wood, *About Conducting*, p. 43)

21. EMI 7243 5 67297 2 8.

22. THE50–19.

23. EMI 7243 5 75112 2 3.

24. NYP 9701, Disc 1.

25. NAXOS 8.110170.

26. NAXOS 8.110810.

27. *ITA Journal*, 6/3 (April 1979), 14.

28. *ITA Journal*, 11/2 (April 1983), 22.

29. Ibid., 23.

30. Wood, *About Conducting*, p. 23.

31. *ITA Journal*, 2 (1973–4), 48.

32. Ibid.

33. *ITA Journal*, 6/3 (April 1979), 14.

34. In fact, the tenor trombones that were acquired were King 5B instruments which had originally been designed as bass trombones.

35. *ITA Journal*, 11/2 (April 1983), 17.

36. Peter Harvey, interviewed by the author, recorded 3 October 2003.

37. N. Kenyon, *Simon Rattle: The Making of a Conductor* (London: Faber, 1987), p. 75.

38. R. Philip, *Performing Music in the Age of Recording* (New Haven and London: Yale University Press, 2004), p. 95.

39. Dutton CDBP 9712.

40. EMI 7243 5 75091 2 1.

41. Raum Klang RK9805.

42. BBC Promenade Concert transmission and interval interviews with Bernard Haitink, 4 September 2004. The programme included Bartók's Dance Suite and Dvořák's Seventh

Symphony.

43. During the 1970s and 80s, in almost all interviews included in the *ITA Journal*'s 'Orchestra Showcase' feature, players remark on the increasingly high standards of playing. See, for example, the observations of Robert Boyd in the *ITA Journal*, 6/3 (April 1979), 15.

44. Philip, *Performing Music*, p. 40.

45. *ITA Journal*, 6/4 (September 1979), 10–12.

46. *ITA Journal*, 11/2 (April 1983), 24.

Chapter 13 Jazz

I am grateful to staff at the Institute for Jazz Studies at Rutgers University, Newark, NJ, and the Hogan Jazz Archive at Tulane University, New Orleans, for assistance provided to me when I was researching this chapter. The referencing systems used by both libraries are followed in the notes given below. For ease of access, the discographical references are to compact disc compilations or remasterings. The recording details of early releases can be obtained through *The Jazz Discography*, Tom Lord, Version 4.4 (Lord Music Reference, 1992–2003).

1. B. Kernfeld, *What to Listen for in Jazz* (New Haven and London: Yale University Press, 1995), pp. 166–7.

2. G. Hoefer, 'Jimmy Harrison, forgotten giant!' *Jazz*, June 1963, 27. This was the first instalment of a three-part article. The second and third parts were published in the July and September issues, pages 12–13 and 8–9 respectively.

3. Transcript of interview with William Russell, 3 June 1958, p. 19 (Hogan Jazz Archive, Tulane University, New Orleans).

4. Transcript of interview with Patricia Willard, Los Angeles, July 1976, p. 16 (Institute of Jazz Studies, Rutgers University, Newark, NJ).

5. Untitled magazine clipping in the Jack Teagarden file at the Institute of Jazz Studies, Rutgers University. The full lists were as follows. Teagarden's choice: Tommy Dorsey, Miff Mole, Bobby Byrne, George Washington, J. C. Higginbotham, Jack Jenny, Georg Brunis, Brad Gowans, Joe Harries. Dorsey's choice: Jack Teagarden, Miff Mole, Jack Jenny, Lawrence Brown, J. C. Higginbotham, Jack Lacey, Floyd O'Brien, Jimmie Young, Lou McGarity, Dickie Wells.

6. Quoted in A. Shipton, *A New History of Jazz* (London and New York: Continuum, 2001), p. 77.

7. Ibid., p. 81.

8. Dave Perkins file, Hogan Jazz Archive.

9. L. Gushee, 'The nineteenth century origins of jazz', *Black Music Research Journal*, 14/1 (Spring 1994), 6.

10. Ibid., 7.

11. There are remote examples of valve trombonists adopting the tailgate style. For example, later in this chapter I draw attention to Kid Ory's early experience as a valve trombone player in what we might loosely describe as a 'tailgate band'. But properly such instances are imitations of tailgate rather than true tailgate style.

12. Examples of concert bands performing ragtime with cadential glissandos can be heard on Jazz Archives No. 120, *Ragtime Volume 1, 1897–1919*, 159052.

13. For an interesting general description of glissando which defines different species of the device as it is used in jazz, see Barry Kernfeld's article in *The New Grove Dictionary of Jazz*, s.v. 'Glissando'.

14. Born George Clarence Brunies, he changed his name to Georg Brunis on the advice of a numerologist.

15. Transcript of interview with Russell, p. 19.

16. Ibid, p. 18.

17. Transcript of interview with William Russell, Richard B. Allen and Bill Simmons, 10 December 1958, p. 7 (Hogan Jazz Archive).
18. Indicative discography: *Introduction to the New Orleans Rhythm Kings*, Bestofjazz4050.
19. Timeless (Du) CBC1–014, or Village (G) VILCD013–2.
20. Transcript of interview with Russell, p. 19.
21. Transcript of interview with Richard B. Allen and Lars Evar Edegran, 9 November 1972, p. 21 (Hogan Jazz Archive).
22. Indicative discography: *Ory's Creole Trombone*, CD53322; *Kid Ory 1922–1945*, CLASSICS1069; *Kid Ory*, URCD187.
23. Interview with Richard B. Hadlock, August 1960, part of the sleeve notes for *The Complete Kid Ory Verve Sessions*, MD8–189.
24. Indicative discography: *Slippin' Around*, vol. 1, DGF19; *Slippin' Around – Again*, vol. 2, DGF20; *Miff Mole 1927*, CLASSICS 1269.
25. Hoefer, 'Jimmy Harrison', 9.
26. Indicative discography: *Bessie Smith Sings the Jazz*, Jazz Archives 157902; *Fletcher Henderson and his Orchestra 1927–31*, CLASSICS 572.
27. Transcript of interview, 20 October 1959, p. 5 (Hogan Jazz Archive).
28. Quoted in G. C. Ward and K. Burns, *Jazz: A History of America's Music* (New York: Alfred A. Knopf, 2000), p. 165.
29. Indicative discography: *Jack Teagarden & his Orchestra 1944–1947*, CLASSICS1032; *Texas Tea Party*, 8.120585; *Mis'ry and the Blues*, B000060602; *The Metronome All-Star Bands*, 76362RB.
30. Indicative discography: *Tommy Dorsey, Opus One*, RMGSN2022; *The Fabulous Dorsey Brothers*, CDAJA5415; *Tommy Dorsey & Artie Shaw*, 0599532GRD9953; *The Metronome All-Star Bands*, 76362RB; *Dorsey and Sinatra*, 9679 2 R.
31. For an erudite and considerably detailed discussion of these and other trombonists who worked with the Ellington band, see K. Dietrich, *Duke's 'Bones: Ellington's Great Trombonists* (Rottenburg am Neckar: Advance Music, 1995).
32. Interview with Willard, p. 42.
33. G. Schuller, *Early Jazz: Its Roots and Musical Development* (New York and Oxford: Oxford University Press, 1968), p. 326.
34. Indicative discography: *The Definitive Duke Ellington*, CK61444.
35. Dietrich, *Duke's 'Bones*, p. 57.
36. Ibid., p. 60.
37. Indicative discography: *The Definitive Duke Ellington*, CK61444.
38. Indicative discography: *The Definitive Duke Ellington*, CK61444; *Far East Suite*, 66551 2; *Slide Trombone*, 314559930–2.
39. Interview with Willard, p. 6.
40. Ibid., p. 13.
41. Ibid., p. 19.
42. Ibid., p. 18.
43. Interview with Dexter, originally published in *Down Beat*, 1 February 1940, reprinted in F. Alkyer, *Down Beat: 60 Years of Jazz* (Milwaukee: Hal Leonard Corporation, 1995), p. 47.
44. Ibid., p. 48.
45. The term 'Third Stream' was first used by Schuller in a lecture at Brandeis University, Waltham, Mass., in 1957. For a succinct explanation by Schuller himself, see *The New Grove Dictionary of Jazz*, s.v. 'Third stream'.
46. Indicative discography: *The Eminent J. J. Johnson*, vol. 1, 724353214326; *The Eminent J. J. Johnson*, vol. 2, 724353214425; *JJ Inc*, CK65296; *Kai Winding with J. J. Johnson*, BET 6026–2; *Four Trombones . . . The Debut Recordings*, PRCD-24097–2; *Getz and JJ at the Opera House*, 831 272–2; *The Trombone Album*, SV-0276.
47. P. Bauer, 'J. J. Johnson: back on track', *Jazz Educators Journal*, October 1994, 23.
48. Ibid., 22.
49. Indicative discography: *Billy May's Big Fat Brass/Bill's Bag*, 724353520625.

50. Indicative discography: Robin Eubanks, *Different Perspectives*, 9190232; Wycliffe Gordon, *Slidin' Home*, nagelheyer2001, *We*, nagelheyer2023; Albert Mangelsdorff, *Movin' On*, CDJ76357; Dennis Rollins, *Badbone*, RAECD1001; Roswell Rudd, *Broad Strokes*, KFW276; Steve Turre, *Steve Turre*, 3145371332, *TNT*, CD83529, *One 4 J: Paying Homage to JJ Johnson* (with Robin Eubanks), CD83555.

51. Indicative discography: *Sister Salvation*, COL-CD-6173; *Exodus*, 013 033–2.

52. For a recent review of Moncur's work, see A. Shatz, 'The perils of living too long', *New York Times*, 23 October 2003.

53. Bauer, 'J. J. Johnson', p. 23.

54. For example, in *Steve Turre*, 3145371332.

Chapter 14 *Modernism, postmodernism and retrospection*

1. See the HBS and ITA websites at, respectively, <www.historicbrass.org/> and <www.ita-web.org/>; also the Trombone-L internet mailing list at <www.trombone-society.org.uk/trombone-l.htm>, and the discussion forum of the *Online Trombone Journal* at <www.trombone.org>.

2. Quoted in S. Dempster, *The Modern Trombone: A Definition of its Idioms* (Berkeley, Los Angeles and London: University of California Press, 1979), p. 96. The piece consists of pp. 173–84 of the orchestral parts of *Concert for Piano and Orchestra*.

3. Letter from Frank Rehak to Stuart Dempster, 17 December 1977. Quoted ibid., p. 97.

4. Score of Luciano Berio, *Sequenza V* for trombone solo (Universal Edition, 1968).

5. BBC Radio 3 broadcast, September 2004.

6. B. Sluchin, *Contemporary Trombone Excerpts: Practical Introduction to Contemporary Trombone Techniques* (Paris: Éditions Musicales Européennes, 1995), p. 74.

7. Ibid.

8. D. Wick, *Trombone Technique* (London: Oxford University Press, 1971), p. 69.

9. Indicative discography: *Trombone Odyssey*, BIS-CD-538; *The Solitary Trombone*, BIS-CD-388; *Christian Lindberg Unaccompanied*, BIS-CD-858. A complete discography is given in Christian Lindberg's website <http://www.tarrodi.se/cl/>.

10. For an overview of the brass ensemble, see J. Wallace, 'Brass solo and chamber music from 1800', in *The Cambridge Companion to Brass Instruments*, ed. T. Herbert and J. Wallace (Cambridge: Cambridge University Press, 1997), pp. 236–54.

11. Preface to the full score of *Discours II* (Frankfurt: Henry Litolffs Verlag; C. F. Peters, 1969).

12. F. W. Galpin, 'The sackbut: its evolution and history, illustrated by an instrument of the sixteenth century', *Proceedings of the Musical Association*, 33 (1906–7), 1–25. The 'Musical Association' was the original name of the present Royal Musical Association.

13. Vienna, Kunsthistorisches Museum, Sammlung alter Musikinstrumente, SAM 706.

14. See A. Myers, 'Trombone designs in the transition from early to modern', in *Posaunen und Trompeten: Geschichte – Akustik – Spieltechnik*, ed. M. Lustig (Blankenburg: Stiftung Kloster Michaelstein, 2000), p. 45.

15. Conversation with the author.

16. Serial number 275512. I am grateful to Dr Arnold Myers for supplying me with this information.

17. H. G. Fischer, *The Renaissance Sackbut and its Use Today* (New York: Metropolitan Museum of Art, 1984), p. 56.

18. For an appraisal of reproduction instrument makers in the 1970s and early 1980s, see ibid., pp. 46–56.

19. See J. Butt, *Playing with History* (Cambridge: Cambridge University Press, 2002), *passim*.

20. See, for example, R. Taruskin, *Text and Act: Essays on Music and Performance* (New York and Oxford: Oxford University Press, 1995).

Bibliography

This bibliography includes all the main sources cited in the book with the exception of didactic treatises. These are cited in endnotes and listed separately in Appendix 3 (slide trombone methods) and Appendix 4 (valve trombone methods). The bibliography also contains citations of works which may not have been quoted but which have informed my study of this subject.

Journals

Many articles in periodicals are cited in full in the bibliography, but a much wider body of material is carried in the primary periodical literature. The following journals are particularly relevant, even though some have ceased publication:

Annual Review of Jazz Studies
Basler Jahrbuch für historische Musikpraxis
Brass and Woodwind Quarterly (formerly *Brass Quarterly*)
Brass Bulletin
Down Beat
Early Music
Galpin Society Journal
Historic Brass Society Journal
International Trombone Association (*ITA*) *Journal*
Journal of Band Studies
Journal of the American Musical Instrument Society

Archives and specialist libraries

A number of documentary sources are referred to in endnotes. The archives and manuscript collections most frequently cited are:

Bibliothèque Nationale de France, Paris
British Library, London (GB-Lbl)
Haus-, Hof- und Staatsarchiv, Vienna
Institute for Jazz Studies, Rutgers University, Newark, NJ
Library of Congress, Washington DC
Library of the US Marine Band (the President's Own), Washington DC
Moravian Archive, Bethlehem, Pa.

National Library of Wales, Aberystwyth
National Archives, London
National Music Museum, Vermillion, SD
New York Public Library, New York
Salvation Army Heritage Centre, Alexandria, Va.
Salvation Army International Heritage Centre, London
Smithsonian Institution, Washington, DC
William Ransom Hogan Jazz Archive, Tulane University, New Orleans
Yale University Library, New Haven, Conn.

Bibliography

Agricola, M., *Musica instrumentalis deudsch*, Wittenberg, 1529 (diplomatic reprint, Leipzig, 1896).

Aitken, T., 'British training', *Brass Bulletin*, 54 (1986), 48–59.

Albertson, H., *Ahlberg & Ohlsson, en Fabrik för Bleckblåsinstrument i Stockholm 1850–1959* (Stockholm: Musikmuseet, 1990).

Albrechtsberger, J. G., *Anweisung zur Composition*, 1790, 3rd edn (Leipzig: Breitkopf & Härtel, 1821).

Alembert, J. Le Rond de and D. Diderot (eds), *Encyclopédie, ou Dictionnaire raisonné des sciences, des arts, et des métiers*, vols 14 and 16 (1765) of 35 vols (Paris: Briasson, 1751–80 [1765]).

Alkyer, F. (ed.), *Down Beat: Sixty Years of Jazz* (Milwaukee, Wis.: Hal Leonard Corporation, 1995).

Alm, I., A. Laymore and C. Reardon (eds), *Musica Franca: Essays in Honor of Frank A. D'Accone* (Stuyvesant, NY: Pendragon Press, 1996).

Anderson, G. B., *Music for Silent Films 1894–1929: A Guide* (Washington, DC: Library of Congress, 1988).

Anderson, G., 'Johnny Dodds in New Orleans', *American Music*, 8 (1990), 405–40.

Anon., 'Did the trombones play at Christmas?' *The Moravian*, 106, no. 12 (December 1961), 5–7.

Anzenberger, F., 'French cornet methods published before Arban's Method (1864)', *Brass Bulletin*, 85 (1994), 76–9.

Arbeau, T., *Orchesography: a treatise in the form of a dialogue whereby all may easily learn and practise the honourable art of dancing*, Lengres: Jehan de Preyz, 1588, trans. M. S. Evans (New York: Kamin Dance Publishers, 1948).

Arce, D. M. de, *Music in Ibero-America to 1850: A Historical Survey* (Lanham, Md., and London: Scarecrow Press, 2001).

Arnold, D., 'Brass instruments in Italian church music of the sixteenth and early seventeenth centuries', *Brass Quarterly*, 1, no. 2 (1957), 81–92.

——, '*Con ogni sorte di stromenti*: some practical suggestions', *Brass Quarterly*, 2, no. 3 (1959), 99–109.

Ashbee, A., 'The four-part consort music of John Jenkins', *Proceedings of the Royal Musical Association*, 96 (1969–70), 29–42.

——, (ed.), *List of Payments to The King's Music in the Reign of Charles II (1660–1685)* (Snodland: Andrew Ashbee, 1981).

——, *Records of English Court Music*, 9 vols (Aldershot, Hants: Scolar Press, 1986–96).

Ashbee, A., and D. Lasocki, assisted by P. Holman and F. Kisby, *A Biographical Dictionary of English Court Musicians 1485–1714*, 2 vols (Aldershot: Ashgate, 1998).

Avison, C., *An Essay on Musical Expression*, 2nd edn (London: C. Davis, 1753).

Baines, A., 'James Talbot's manuscript (Christ Church Library Music MS 1187)', *Galpin Society Journal*, 1 (1948), 1–27.

——, 'Fifteenth-century instruments in Tinctoris's *De inventione et usu musicae*', *Galpin Society*

Journal, 3 (1950), 19–26.

——, *Brass Instruments: Their History and Development*, 1976 (London: Faber, 1980).

Baker, D., *Jazz Styles and Analysis: Trombone* (Chicago: Music Workshop Publications, 1973).

Baldauf-Berdes, J. L., *Women Musicians of Venice: Musical Foundations, 1525–1855*, revised edn (Oxford: Clarendon Press, 1996).

Barclay, R., *The Art of the Trumpet-Maker: The Materials, Tools, and Techniques of the Seventeenth and Eighteenth Centuries in Nuremberg* (Oxford: Clarendon Press, 1996).

——, *The Preservation and Use of Historic Musical Instruments: Display Case and Concert Hall* (London and Sterling, Va.: Earthscan, 2004).

Barclay Squire, W., 'Purcell's music for the funeral of Mary II', *Sammelbände der Internationalen Musikgesellschaft*, 4 (1903), 225–33.

Baroncini, R., trans. H. Ward-Perkins, 'Zorzi Trombetta and the band of *piffari* and trombones of the *Serenissima*: new documentary evidence', *Historic Brass Society Journal*, 14 (2002), 59–82.

——, 'Zorzi Trombetta da Modon and the founding of the band of *piffari* and *tromboni* of the *Serenissima*', *Historic Brass Society Journal*, 16 (2004), 1–17.

Batashiev, V., 'Anatoly Skobelev: Russian grand master of the trombone', *Brass Bulletin*, 121 (2003), 30–36.

Bate, P., *The Trumpet and Trombone* (London and New York: Ernest Benn, 1978).

Bauer, P., 'J. J. Johnson: back on track', *Jazz Educators Journal*, (October 1994), 21–24.

Bendinelli, C., *The Entire Art of Trumpet Playing*, 1614, trans. E. H. Tarr (Nashville, Tenn.: Brass Press, 1975).

Berlioz, H., *A Treatise on Modern Instrumentation and Orchestration*, 1844, trans. M. Cowden Clarke (London: J. Alfred Novello, 1856).

Bermúdez, E., 'The ministriles tradition in Latin America, I: South America – the cases of Santafé (Colombia) and La Plata (Bolivia) in the seventeenth century', *Historic Brass Society Journal*, 11 (1999), 149–62.

——, 'Urban musical life in the European colonies: examples from Spanish America, 1530–1650', in *Music and Musicians in Renaissance Cities and Towns*, ed. F. Kisby (Cambridge: Cambridge University Press, 2001), pp. 167–80.

Bevan, C., *The Tuba Family*, 2nd edn (Winchester, Hants.: Piccolo Press, 2000).

Bismantova, B., *Compendio musicale (1677)*, trans. B. Dickey et al (partial translation), *Basler Jahrbuch für historische Musikpraxis*, 2 (1978), 143–87.

Blackburn, B. J., 'Music and festivities at the court of Leo X: a Venetian view', *Early Music History*, 11 (1992), 1–38.

—— and E. E. Lowinsky, 'Luigi Zenobi and his letter on the perfect musician', *Studi musicali*, 22 (1993), 61–114.

Blandford, W. F. H., 'Handel's horn and trombone parts', *Musical Times*, 80 (1939), 697–9, 746–7, 794.

Bonanni, F., *Gabinetto armonico* (Rome: Giorgio Placho, 1722).

Bongrain, A., and Y. Gérard (eds), *Le Conservatoire de Paris: Des Menus-Plaisirs à la Cité de la musique 1795–1995*, 2 vols (Paris: Éditions Buchet/Chastel, 1996–99).

Bowles, E. A., 'Haut and bas: the grouping of musical instruments in the Middle Ages', *Musica Disciplina*, 8 (1954), 115–40.

——, 'Tower musicians in the Middle Ages', *Brass Quarterly*, 5, no. 3 (1962), 91–103.

——, 'Blowing a trumpet', *Early Music*, 18 (1990), 350–1.

——, 'Music in court festivals of state: festival books as sources for performance practices', *Early Music*, 28 (2000), 421–43.

——, *The Timpani: A History in Pictures and Documents* (Hillsdale, NY: Pendragon Press, 2002).

Bowsher, J.-M., and P.-S. Watkinson, 'Manufacturers' opinions about brass instruments', *Brass Bulletin*, 38 (1982), 25–30.

Boyd, M. C., *Elizabethan Music and Musical Criticism* (Philadelphia: University of Pennsylvania Press, 1973).

Boydell, Barra, *The Crumhorn and Other Renaissance Windcap Instruments* (Buren, Netherlands: F.

Knupf, 1982).

Boydell, Brian, 'The Dublin musical scene, 1749–50, and its background', *Proceedings of the Royal Musical Association*, 105 (1978–9), 77–89.

——, 'Cathedral music, city and state: music in Reformation and political change at Christchurch Cathedral, Dublin', in *Music and Musicians in Renaissance Cities and Towns*, ed. F. Kisby (Cambridge: Cambridge University Press, 2001), pp. 131–142.

Boynton, S., 'The sources and signficance of the Orpheus myth in *Musica Enchiriadis* and Regino of Prüm's *Epistola de harmonica institutione*', *Early Music History*, 18 (1999), 47–74.

Brewer, J. S. (ed.), *Letters and Papers Foreign and Domestic in the Reign of Henry VIII*, vol. 3, pt 1 (London, 1867).

Bridge, J. C., 'Town waits and their tunes', *Proceedings of the Musical Association*, 54 (1927–8), 63–92.

Bridges, G., *Pioneers in Brass* (published on CD-ROM, Trescott Research, 2001).

Brossard, S. de, *Dictionaire de musique* (Paris: Christophe Ballard, 1703).

Brown, H. M., *Music in the French Secular Theatre, 1400–1550* (Oxford: Oxford University Press, 1963).

——, *Instrumental Music Printed before 1600: A Bibliography* (Cambridge, Mass.: Harvard University Press, 1965).

——, *Sixteenth-Century Instrumentation: The Music for the Florentine Intermedii*, Musicological Studies and Documents, 30 (Rome: American Institute of Musicology, 1973).

——, *Embellishing Sixteenth-Century Music* (London: Oxford University Press, 1976).

Brown, R., *Calendar of State Papers and Manuscripts Relating to English Affairs existing in the Archives and Collections of Venice and other Libraries of Northern Italy*, vol. 2 (London, 1867); vol. 3 (1520–1526) (London, 1869).

Brunner, L. W., 'The orchestra and recorded sound', in *The Orchestra – Origins and Transformations*, ed. J. Peyser (New York: Charles Scribner's Sons, 1986), pp. 479–532.

Buijsen, E., L. P. Grijp and W. J. Hoogsteder, *The Hoogsteder Exhibition of Music and Painting in the Golden Age* (The Hague and Zwolle: Hoogsteder & Hoogsteder; Waanders Publishers, 1994).

Burney, C., *An Account of the Musical Performances in Westminster Abbey and the Pantheon, May 26th, 27th, 29th: and June the 3rd and 5th, 1784, in Commemoration of Handel*, 1785, facsimile edn (New York: Da Capo Press, 1964).

Burrows, D. J., 'Handel and the 1727 Coronation', *Musical Times*, 118 (1977), 469–73.

——, 'Handel and the English Chapel Royal', in *Georg Friedrich Händel*, ed. W. Siegmund-Schultze (Leipzig: Deutscher Verlag für Musik, 1987).

——, 'Handel, the Dead March and a newly identified trombone movement', *Early Music*, 18 (1990), 408–16.

Burrows, D. J., and R. Dunhill, *Music and Theatre in Handel's World: The Family Papers of James Harris, 1732–1780* (New York: Oxford University Press, 2002).

Butt, J., *Playing with History* (Cambridge: Cambridge University Press, 2002).

Byrne, M., 'Instruments for the Goldsmiths Company', *Galpin Society Journal*, 14 (1961), 63–8.

——, 'The goldsmith-trumpet-makers of the British Isles', *Galpin Society Journal*, 19 (1966), 71–83.

Cairns, D., *Berlioz*, vol. 1: *The Making of an Artist, 1803–1832*, 2nd edn (London: Allen Lane, 1999).

——, *Berlioz*, vol. 2: *Servitude and Greatness, 1832–1869* (London: Allen Lane, 1999).

——, (trans. and ed.), *The Memoirs of Hector Berlioz* (London: Victor Gollancz, 1977).

Campbell, M., and C. Greated, *The Musician's Guide to Acoustics* (Oxford: Oxford University Press, 2001).

Campbell, M., C. Greated and A. Myers, *Musical Instruments: History, Technology, and Performance of Instruments of Western Music* (Oxford: Oxford University Press, 2004).

Campion, T., *The Description of a Maske, Presented before the Kinges Maiestie at Whit-Hall on Twelfth Night last in honour of the Lord Hayes, and his Bride daughter and Heire to the Honourable the Lord Dennye, their Marriage having been the same Day at Court solemnized. Invented and set forth by*

Thomas Campion Doctor of Phisicke (London, 1607).

Canarina, J., *Pierre Monteux, maître* (Pompton Plains and Cambridge: Amadeus Press, LLC, 2003).

Carse, A., *The History of Orchestration* (London: K. Paul, Trench, Trubner, 1925).

——, *Musical Wind Instruments* (London, 1939).

——, *The Orchestra from Beethoven to Berlioz* (Cambridge: W. Heffer and Sons, 1948).

——, *The Orchestra in the Eighteenth Century* (New York: Broude Brothers, 1969).

Carter, S., 'Trombone obbligatos in Viennese oratorios of the Baroque', *Historic Brass Society Journal*, 2 (1990), 52–77.

——, 'Georges Kastner on brass instruments: the influence of technology on the theory of orchestration', in *Perspectives in Brass Scholarship: Proceedings of the International Historic Brass Symposium, Amherst, 1995*, ed. S. Carter (Stuyvesant, NY: Pendragon Press, 1997), pp. 171–92.

——, 'Early trombones in America's Shrine to Music Museum', *Historic Brass Society Journal*, 10 (1998), 92–115.

——, 'Trombone pitch in the eighteenth century: an overview', in *Posaunen und Trompeten: Geschichte – Akustik – Spieltechnik*, ed. M. Lustig (Blankenburg: Stiftung Kloster Michaelstein, 2000), pp. 53–66.

—— (ed.), *Perspectives in Brass Scholarship: Proceedings of the International Historic Brass Symposium, Amherst, 1995*, (Stuyvesant, NY: Pendragon Press, 1997).

Carter, T., *Music in Late Renaissance and Early Baroque Italy* (London: B. T. Batsford, 1992).

Castiglione, B., *The Book of the Courtier*, 1528 (Harmondsworth: Penguin, 1967).

Cazeaux, I., *French Music in the Fifteenth and Sixteenth Centuries* (Oxford: Blackwell, 1975).

Ceulemans, A.-E., 'Instruments real and imaginary: Aaron's interpretation of Isidore and an illustrated copy of the *Toscanello*', *Early Music History*, 31 (2002), 1–35.

Chambers, E., *Cyclopaedia, or, An Universal Dictionary of Arts and Sciences*, 2 vols (London: J. and J. Knapton, 1728).

Chan, M., 'Drolls, drolleries and mid seventeenth-century dramatic music', *Royal Musical Association Research Chronicle*, 15 (1979), 117–73.

——, *Music in the Theatre of Ben Jonson* (Oxford: Clarendon Press, 1980).

Charteris, R., 'Music manuscripts and books missing from Archbishop Marsh's Library, Dublin', *Music and Letters*, 61 (1980), 310–17.

Charters, S. B., *Jazz: New Orleans, 1885–1963. An Index to the Negro Musicians of New Orleans* (New York: Oak Publications, 1963).

Clarke, H. L., *How I Became a Cornetist: The Autobiography of a Cornet-Playing Pilgrim's Progress* (St Louis, Mo.: J. L. Huber, 1934).

Collver, M., and B. Dickey, *A Catalog of Music for the Cornett* (Bloomington and Indianapolis: Indiana University Press, 1996).

Conley, P. R., 'The use of the trumpet in the music of Purcell', *Brass Quarterly*, 3, no. 1 (1959), 3–11.

Cooke, M., and D. Horn, *The Cambridge Companion to Jazz* (Cambridge: Cambridge University Press, 2002).

Cooper, F. M. C., 'Musical instruments and their uses in England during the early years of the sixteenth century' (M.A. thesis, University College of Bangor, 1971).

Coover, J., *Musical Instrument Collections: Catalogues and Cognate Literature* (Detroit: Information Coordinators, 1981).

Copeland, P., *Sound Recordings* (London: British Library, 1991).

Craigie, W., *A Dictionary of the Older Scottish Tongue*, vol. 2 (Chicago; London, 1938).

Crewdson, H. A. F., *The Worshipful Company of Musicians: A Short History* (London: Charles Knight, 1971).

Croft-Murray, E., 'The wind band in England, 1540–1840', *Music and Civilisation: The British Museum Yearbook* 4 (1980), 135–66.

Crown, T., 'Mostly Mozart's mutes', *ITG [International Trumpet Guild] Journal* (February 1984), 9–13.

Cudworth, C. (ed.), '"Hints to young composers of instrumental music": John Marsh', *Galpin*

Society Journal, 18 (1965), 67–71.

Cunningham, H., *The Volunteer Force: A Social and Political History 1859–1908* (London: Croom Helm, 1975).

D'Accone, F. A., 'The performance of sacred music in Italy during Josquin's time, ca. 1475–1525', in *Josquin des Prez*, ed. E. E. Lowinsky and B. J. Blackburn (London: Oxford University Press, 1976), pp. 601–18.

——, *The Civic Muse: Music and Musicians in Siena during the Middle Ages and the Renaissance* (Chicago and London: University of Chicago Press, 1997).

Dahlhaus, C., *Nineteenth-Century Music*, trans. J. B. Robinson (Berkeley and London: University of California Press, 1989).

Dart, T., 'The repertory of the royal wind music', *Galpin Society Journal*, 11 (1958), 70–7.

——, 'Henry Loosemore's organ-book', *Cambridge Bibliographical Society Transactions*, 3 (1960), 143–51.

——, 'Music and musical instruments in Cotgrave's *Dictionarie* (1611)', *Galpin Society Journal*, 21 (1968), 70–80.

Day, T., *A Century of Recorded Music: Listening to Musical History* (New Haven and London: Yale University Press, 2000).

Dempster, S., *The Modern Trombone: A Definition of its Idioms* (Berkeley, Los Angeles and London: University of California Press, 1979).

Dibb, J., and S. Hogg, 'The trombone of Gustav Holst (1874–1934)', *Brass Bulletin*, 88 (1994), 66–71.

Dickey, B., 'The cornett', in *The Cambridge Companion to Brass Instruments*, ed. T. Herbert and J. Wallace (Cambridge: Cambridge University Press, 1997), pp. 51–67.

Dickey, B., and M. Collver, 'Musik für Zink – ein Quellenkatalog', *Basler Jahrbuch für historische Musikpraxis*, 5 (1981), 263–313.

Dietrich, K., *Duke's 'Bones: Ellington's Great Trombonists* (Rottenburg am Neckar: Advance Music, 1995).

Doane, J., *A Musical Directory for the Year 1794*, London: R. H. Westley, 1794, facsimile edn (London: Royal College of Music, 1993).

Donington, R., *The Interpretation of Early Music* (New York: St Martin's Press, 1963).

Donley Thomas, T., 'Michael Haydn's "trombone" symphony', *Brass Quarterly*, 6, no. 1 (1962), 3–33.

Dowland, J., *Andreas Ornithoparchus his Micrologus* (London, 1609).

Downey, P., 'A renaissance correspondence concerning trumpet music', *Early Music*, 9 (1981), 325–9.

——, 'The Renaissance slide trumpet: fact or fiction?' *Early Music*, 12 (1984), 26–33.

——, 'On sounding the trumpet and beating the drum in 17th-century England', *Early Music*, 24 (1996), 263–77.

Downie Banks, M. and J. W. Jordan, 'C. G. Conn: the man (1844–1931) and his company (1874–1915)', *Journal of the American Musical Instrument Society*, 14 (1988), 61–113.

Downs, A., 'The tower music of a seventeenth-century Stadtpfeifer: Johann Pezel's *Hora decima* and *Fünff-stimmigte blasende Music*', *Brass Quarterly*, 7, no. 1 (1963), 3–33.

Dreyfus, L., 'Early music defended against its devotees: a theory of historical performance in the twentieth century', *Musical Quarterly*, 69 (1983), 297–322.

Duffin, R. W., 'The *trompette des ménestrels* in the 15th-century alta capella', *Early Music*, 17 (1989), 397–402.

Dugdale, W., *Origines juridiciales, or Historical Memorials of the English Laws* (London, 1666).

Edge, D., 'Mozart's Viennese orchestras', *Early Music*, 20 (1992), 64–88.

Edwards, A. W., 'The performance of ensemble music in Elizabethan England', *Proceedings of the Royal Musical Association*, 97 (1970–1), 113–23.

——, 'The sources of Elizabethan consort music' (Ph.D. thesis, University of Cambridge, 1974).

Edwards, R. M., 'The perception of trombones', *Journal of Sound and Vibration*, 58 (1978), 407–24.

Edwards, W., 'Songs without words by Josquin and his contemporaries', in *Music in Medieval and Early Modern Europe*, ed. I. Fenlon (New York: Cambridge University Press, 1980), pp. 79–92.

Ehmann, W., '"Was guett auff Posaunen ist etc."', *Zeitschrift für Musikwissenschaft*, 17 (1935), 171–5.

Ehrlich, C., *The Music Profession in Britain since the Eighteenth Century* (Oxford: Clarendon Press, 1985).

——, *First Philharmonic: A History of the Royal Philharmonic Society* (Oxford: Clarendon Press, 1995).

Eisel, J. P., *Musicus autodidactos, oder der sich selbst informirende Musicus* (Erfurt: Johann Michael Funck, 1738).

Eisen, C., 'Mozart's Salzburg orchestras', *Early Music*, 20 (1992), 89–103.

Eitner, R., 'Briefe von Jorg Neuschel in Nürnberg, nebst einigen anderen', *Monatshefte für Musik-Geschichte*, 9, no. 7 (1877), 149–59.

Eliason, R. E., 'Charles G. Christman, musical instrument maker in nineteenth-century New York', *Journal of the American Musical Instrument Society*, 27 (2001), 84–119.

——, 'Rhodolph Hall: nineteenth-century keyed bugle, cornet, and clarinet soloist', *Journal of the American Musical Instrument Society*, 29 (2003), 5–71.

Ellis, H. (ed.), *Hall's Chronicle; containing the History of England during the reign of Henry the Fourth, and the succeeding Monarchs, to the end of the reign of Henry the Eighth; in which are particularly described the manners and customs of those periods. . . . Collated with the edition of 1548 and 1550* (London, 1809).

Elyot, T., *The Castel of Helth, gathered and made by Syr Thomas Elyot knight, out of the chief Authors of Physyke, whereby every manne may knowe the state of his owne body, the picternals of helth, and how to instruct welle his physytion in sychnes that he be not deceysed* (London, 1534).

Encyclopaedia Britannica, vol. 3 of 3 (Edinburgh: Bell and Macfarquhar, 1771).

Epstein, P., *Katalog der Musikinstrumente im Historischen Museum der Stadt Frankfurt am Main* (Frankfurt am Main, 1927).

Epstein, P., and E. Scheyer, *Schlesisches Museum fur Kunstgewerbe und Altertümer: Führer und Katalog zur Sammlung alter Musikinstrumenten* (Breslau, 1932).

Fallows, D., *Dufay* (London: Dent, 1982).

Fantini, G., *Modo per imparare a sonare di tromba*, 1638, trans. E. H. Tarr (Nashville, Tenn.: Brass Press, 1978).

Farmer, H. G., *The Rise and Development of Military Music* (London: W. Reeves, 1912).

Fenlon, I., 'Magnificence as civic image: music and ceremonial space in early modern Venice', in *Music and Musicians in Renaisance Cities and Towns*, ed. F. Kisby (Cambridge: Cambridge University Press, 2001), pp. 28–44.

——, (ed.), *Music in Medieval and Early Modern Europe* (New York: Cambridge University Press, 1980).

——, (ed.), *Cambridge Music Manuscripts, 900–1700* (Cambridge: Cambridge University Press, 1982).

Ferand, E. T., '"Sodaine and unexpected" music in the Renaissance', *Musical Quarterly*, 37 (1951), 10–27.

Fifield, C., *True Artist and True Friend: A Biography of Hans Richter* (Oxford: Clarendon Press, 1993).

Finlay, I. F., 'Musical instruments in seventeenth-century Dutch paintings', *Galpin Society Journal*, 6 (1953), 52–69.

Fischer, H. G., *The Renaissance Sackbut and its Use Today* (New York: Metropolitan Museum of Art, 1984).

Fleming, M. D., 'Michael Praetorius, music historian: an annotated translation of *Syntagma musicum* I, part I' (Ph.D. thesis, Washington University, 1979).

Fleming, M., *Viol-Making in England c.1580–1660* (published on CD-ROM: <viols@flemingoxford.co.uk>, 2002).

Forsyth, C., *Orchestration*, 1914 (London: Macmillan; Stainer & Bell, 1929).

Francoeur, L.-J., *Diapason général de tous les instruments à vent* (Paris: Deslauriers, 1772).

Franks, A., 'Unity Archives Friends' Day Address, March 13, 1999', Bethlehem, Pa., Moravian Archives (1999).

Fries, A. L., *Funeral Chorals of the Unitas Fratrum or Moravian Church* (n.p., 1905).

Galpin, F. W., 'The sackbut: its evolution and history, illustrated by an instrument of the sixteenth century', *Proceedings of the Musical Association*, 33 (1906–7), 1–25.

——, *Old English Instruments of Music*, 1910, 4th edn, rev. T. Dart (London: Methuen, 1965).

Geiger, G. L., *Filippino Lippi's Carafa Chapel* (Kirksville, Mo.: Sixteenth Century Journal Publishers, 1986).

Geiringer, K., *Musical Instruments* (London: George Allen & Unwin, 1943).

Gevaert, F.-A., *Nouveau Traité d'instrumentation*, 1863, revised edn (Paris and Brussels: Lemoine & Fils, 1885).

Glen, J. and T., *The Glen Account Book 1838–1853* (Edinburgh: Edinburgh University Collection of Historic Musical Instruments, 1985).

Gollin, G. L., 'Family surrogates in colonial America: the Moravian experiment', *Journal of Marriage and the Family*, 31 (1969), 650–8.

Gontershausen, H. W. von, *Neu eröffnetes Magazin musikalischer Tonwerkzeuge* (Frankfurt, 1855).

Grassineau, J., *A Musical Dictionary* (London: J. Wilcox, 1740).

Gray, R., and M. Rasmussen, 'A bibliography of chamber music including parts for the trombone', *Brass Quarterly*, 3, no. 3 (1960), 49–63.

Gregory, R., *The Trombone: The Instrument and its Music* (London: Faber and Faber, 1973).

Grinder, R. A., *Music in Bethlehem, Pennsylvania, from 1741–1871* (Bethlehem, Pa.: J. Hill Martin, 1873).

Groce, N., *Musical Instrument Makers of New York: A Directory of Eighteenth- and Nineteenth-Century Urban Craftsmen* (Stuyvesant, NY: Pendragon Press, 1991).

Grocheio, J. de, *Concerning Music*, trans. Albert Seay, 2nd edn (Colorado Springs: Colorado College Music Press, 1973).

Guion, D. M., *The Trombone: Its History and Music, 1697–1811*, Musicology: A Book Series, 6 (New York: Gordon and Breach, 1988).

——, 'Great but forgotten trombonists: some biographical sketches', *Brass Bulletin*, no. 1 (1997), 62–73.

——, 'On the trail of the medieval slide trumpet, Part 2', *Brass Bulletin*, 110 (2000), 46–54.

Haar, J., 'Cosimo Bartoli on music', *Early Music History*, 8 (1988), 37–79.

Hafar, M. A., 'The shout band tradition in the southeastern United States', *Historic Brass Society Journal*, 15 (2003), 163–72.

Halfpenny, E., 'Musicians at James II's coronation', *Music and Letters*, 32 (1951), 103–14.

Halle, J. S., *Werkstätte der heutigen Kunst*, vol. 3 of 4 (Brandenburg: J. W. Halle, 1761–5).

Hamilton, J. A., *Hamilton's Catechism on the Art of Writing for an Orchestra* (London: R. Cocks, 1835).

Hamilton, J. T., and K. G. Hamilton, *History of the Moravian Church: The Renewed Unitas Fratrum 1722–1957*, 1967, 2nd edn (Bethlehem, Pa. and Winston-Salem, NC: Interprovincial Board of Christian Education, Moravian Church of America, 1983).

Hamilton, K. G., *Church Street in Old Bethlehem* (Bethlehem, Pa.: Moravian Congregation, 1942).

Hamilton, W. D. (ed.), *A Chronicle of England during the Reigns of the Tudors from A.D. 1485 to 1559, by Charles Wriothesley, Windsor Herald*, Camden Society new series, 11 (London: Camden Society, 1872).

Hanslick, E., *Music Criticisms 1846–99*, trans. H. Pleasants, revised edn (Harmondsworth: Penguin Books, 1963).

Harding, R. E. M., *A Thematic Catalogue of the Works of Matthew Locke with a Calendar of the Main Events of his Life* (Oxford: Blackwell, 1971).

Harley, J., *Music in Purcell's London* (London: Dobson, 1968).

Harrán, D., 'New evidence for musica ficta: the cautionary sign', *Journal of the American Musicological Society*, 29 (1976), 77–98.

Harvith, J., and S. E. Harvith (eds), *Edison, Musicians and the Phonograph* (New York, Westport,

Conn. and London: Greenwood Press, 1987).

Harwood, G., 'Verdi's reform of the Italian opera orchestra', *19th Century Music*, 10 (1986–7), 108–34.

Hazen, M., *Register of the Hazen Collection of Band Photographs and Ephemera ca. 1818–1931* (Washington, DC: Archives Center, National Museum of American History, Smithsonian Institution, 1990).

Hazen, M. H., and R. M. Hazen, *The Music Men: An Illustrated History of Brass Bands in America, 1800–1920* (Washington, DC and London: Smithsonian Institution Press, 1987).

Heartz, D., 'A fifteenth-century ballo: *Rôti bouilli joyeux*', in *Aspects of Medieval and Renaissance Music: A Birthday Offering to Gustave Reese*, ed. J. LaRue (New York: Pendragon Press, 1978).

——, *Haydn, Mozart and the Viennese School, 1740–1780* (New York and London: W. W. Norton, 1995).

Herbert, J. W., 'The wind band of nineteenth-century Italy: its origins and transformation from the late 1700s to mid-century' (Doctor of Education thesis, Teachers College, Columbia University, 1986).

Herbert, T., 'The trombone in Britain before 1800' (Ph.D. thesis, The Open University, 1984).

——, 'The sackbut in England in the 17th and 18th centuries', *Early Music*, 18 (1990), 609–16.

——, 'A lament for Sam Hughes – the "last ophicleidist"', *Planet: The Welsh Internationalist* (July 1991), 66–75.

——, 'The sackbut and Pre-Reformation English church music', *Historic Brass Society Journal*, 5 (1993), 146–58.

——, 'The reconstruction of nineteenth-century band repertory: towards a protocol', in *Perspectives in Brass Scholarship: Proceedings of the International Historic Brass Symposium, Amherst, 1995*, ed. S. Carter (Stuyvesant, NY: Pendragon Press, 1997), pp. 193–222.

——, 'Social history and music history', in *A Cultural Study of Music: A Critical Introduction*, ed. M. Clayton, T. Herbert and R. Middleton (New York and London: Routledge, 2003), pp. 146–56.

——, 'Selling brass instruments: the commercial imaging of brass instruments (1830–1930) and its cultural messages', in *Music in Art: The International Journal for Music Iconography*, 28/1–2 (Spring–Fall 2004), 213–26.

——, 'Susato's colleagues: the trombonists of the Tudor court', in *Tielman Susato and the Music of his Time: Print Culture, Compositional Technique and Instrumental Music in the Renaissance*, ed. K. Polk (Hillsdale, NY: Pendragon Press, 2005), pp. 117–32.

—— (ed.), 'Matthew Locke and the cornett and sackbut ensemble in England after the Restoration: the "labelled evidence"', in *Brass Music at the Cross Roads of Europe*, ed. K. Polk (Utrecht: STIMU, 2005), pp. 57–68.

—— (ed.), *Bands: The Brass Band Movement in the 19th and 20th Centuries* (Milton Keynes and Philadelphia: Open University Press, 1991).

—— (ed.), *The British Brass Band: A Musical and Social History* (Oxford: Oxford University Press, 2000).

Herbert, T., and A. Myers, 'Instruments of the Cyfarthfa Band', *Galpin Society Journal*, 41 (1988), 2–10.

Herbert, T., and M. Sarkissian, 'Victorian bands and their dissemination in the colonies', *Popular Music*, 16 (1997), 165–79.

Herbert, T., and J. Wallace (eds), *The Cambridge Companion to Brass Instruments* (Cambridge: Cambridge University Press, 1997).

Heyde, H., 'Trompete und Trompetenblasen in europäischen Mittelalter' (Ph.D. thesis, University of Leipzig, 1964).

——, *Historische Musikinstrumente im Bachhaus Eisenach* (Eisenach: Bachhaus, 1976).

——, 'On the early history of valves and valve instruments in Germany (1814–1833)', *Brass Bulletin*, 24 (1978), 9–33; 25 (1979), 41–50; 26 (1979), 69–82; 27 (1979), 51–61.

——, *Musikinstrumenten-Museum der Karl-Marx-Universität, Katalog Band 3: Trompeten, Posaunen, Tuben* (Leipzig: Deutscher Verlag für Musik, 1980).

——, *Das Ventilblasinstrument* (Leipzig: Deutscher Verlag für Musik, 1987).

——, 'The early Berlin valve and an unsigned tuba at the Shrine to Music Museum', *Journal of the American Musical Instrument Society*, 20 (1994), 54–64.

Hinds, A. B., *Calendar of State Papers and Manuscripts Relating to English Affairs existing in the Archives and Collections of Venice*, 15 (1617–19) (London, 1909).

Hoefer, G., 'Jimmy Harrison, forgotten giant!' *Jazz*, June 1963, 8–9, 27; July 1963, 12–13; September 1963, 8–9.

Höfler, J., 'Der "Trompette de Menestrels" und sein Instrument', *Tijdschrift van de Vereniging voor Nederlandse Muziekgeschiedenis*, 29, no. 2 (1979), 92–132.

Holoman, D. K., *The Société des Concerts du Conservatoire 1828–1967* (Berkeley, Los Angeles and London: University of California Press, 2004).

Hondré, E. (ed.), *Le Conservatoire de Musique de Paris: Regards sur une institution et son histoire* (Paris: Association du bureau des étudiants du Conservatoire national supérieur de musique de Paris, 1995).

Hoover, C. A., 'The slide trumpet of the nineteenth century', *Brass Quarterly*, 6, no. 4 (1963), 159–78.

Hornbostel, E. M. and C. Sachs, 'Classification of musical instruments', trans. A. Baines and K.P. Wachsmann, in *Galpin Society Journal*, 14 (1961), 3–29.

Horsley, I., 'Wind techniques in the sixteenth and early seventeenth centuries', *Brass Quarterly*, 4, no. 2 (1960), 49–63.

Horwood, W., *Adolphe Sax, 1814–1894: His Life and Legacy* (Baldock, Herts.: Egon, 1983).

Huber, H., 'The trombone: changing times, changing slide positions', *Brass Bulletin*, 11 (1975), 90–4.

Huber, R., *Verzeichnis sämtlicher Musikinstrumente im Germanischen Nationalmuseum Nürnberg* (Wilhelmshaven: Florian Noetzel, 1989).

Humphries, J., 'John Smithies: trombonist and enigma', *Brass Bulletin*, 101 (1998), 62–4.

——, 'The Royal Academy of Music and its tradition', *Brass Bulletin*, 101 (1998), 42–52.

Jaffee, K., 'Diverse notes on brass instruments in English periodicals', *Brass Quarterly*, 7, no. 4 (1964), 178–93.

Jarvis, F. A. M. R., 'The community of German migrant musicians in London c1750–c1850' (Master of Studies, University of Cambridge, 2003).

Johnson, D., *Music and Society in Lowland Scotland in the Eighteenth Century* (London: Oxford University Press, 1972).

Joppig, G., trans. V. von der Lancken, 'Václav František Červený: leading European inventor and manufacturer', *Historic Brass Society Journal*, 4 (1992), 210–28.

Josephson, D. S., *John Taverner, Tudor Composer* (Ann Arbor, Mich.: UMI Research Press, 1975).

Kallai, A., 'Joachim Eggert (1779–1813)', *Brass Bulletin*, 123 (2003), 60–7.

Kappey, J. A., *Military Music: A History of Wind-Instrumental Bands* (London: Boosey, 1894).

Karstädt, G., *Die 'extraordinairen' Abendmusiken Dietrich Buxtehudes* (Lübeck: M. Schmidt-Römhild, 1962).

Kassler, J. C., *The Science of Music in Britain, 1714–1830* (New York: Garland, 1979).

Kastner, J.-G., *Cours d'instrumentation* (Paris?, 1837).

——, *Traité général d'instrumentation* (Paris: Prilipp, 1837).

——, *Manuel général de musique militaire à l'usage des armées françaises* (Paris: Typ. F. Didot frères, 1848).

Kennedy, M., *The Hallé Tradition: A Century of Music* (Manchester: Manchester University Press, 1960).

Kenney, W. H. III, 'The influence of black vaudeville on early jazz', *The Black Perspective in Music*, 14 (1986), 233–48.

Kenton, E. F., 'The "brass" parts in Giovanni Gabrieli's instrumental ensemble compositions', *Brass Quarterly*, 1, no. 2 (1957), 73–80.

Kenyon de Pascual, B., 'Brass instruments in Museo de la Musica, Barcelona', *Brass Bulletin*, 70, no. 2 (1990), 78–84.

——, 'Two contributions to dulcian iconography', *Early Music*, 25, no. 3 (1997), 412–25.

Kenyon, N., *Simon Rattle: The Making of a Conductor* (London and Boston: Faber and Faber, 1987).

Kernfeld, B., *What to Listen for in Jazz* (New Haven and London: Yale University Press, 1995).

Kirkendale, W., *The Court Musicians of Florence during the Principate of the Medici* (Florence: Leo S. Olschki, 1993).

Kisby, F., 'Introduction: urban history, musicology and cities and towns in Renaissance Europe', in *Music and Musicians in Renaissance Cities and Towns*, ed. F. Kisby (Cambridge: Cambridge University Press, 2001), pp. 1–13.

Kitzel, L., 'The trombones of the Shrine to Music Museum' (DMA thesis, University of Oklahoma, 1985).

Klaus, S., 'Trompeten und Posaunen in der Musikinstrumenten-Sammlung des Historischen Museums Basel', in *Historisches Museum Basel Jahresbericht 1998*, (Basel: Historisches Museum, 1999), pp. 27–62.

——, 'Outstanding trumpets, trombones, and horns in the musical instrument collection of the Historical Museum, Basel' *Historic Brass Society Journal*, 12 (2000), 1–22.

Kling, H., *Modern Orchestration and Instrumentation*, trans. G. Saenger, 2nd American edn (New York: C. Fischer, 1905).

Knighton, T., and C. Morte García, 'Ferdinand of Aragon's entry into Valladolid in 1513: the triumph of a Christian king', *Early Music History*, 18 (1999), 119–63.

Koch, H., *Musikalisches Lexikon* (Frankfurt am Main: August Hermann der Jünger, 1802).

Köchel, L. von, *Die Kaiserliche Hof-Musikkapelle in Wien von 1543–1867*, Vienna, 1869, facsimile edn (Hildesheim and New York: Georg Olms, 1976).

Koechlin, C., *Les Instruments à vent* (Paris: Presses Universitaires de France, 1948).

Koenig, K. (ed.), *Jazz in Print: An Anthology of Selected Early Recordings in Jazz History* (Hillsdale, NY: Pendragon Press, 2002).

Koenigsburger, H. G., G. L. Mosse and G. Q. Bowler, *Europe in the Sixteenth Century*, 2nd edn (London and New York: Longman, 1989).

Koudal, J. H., 'Mobility of musicians in the Baltic in the 17th and 18th century', in *Musica Baltica: Interregionale musikkulturelle Beziehungen im Ostseeraum*, ed. E. Ochs, N. Schüler and L. Winkler (Sankt Augustin: Academia Verlag, 1996), pp. 137–47.

——, *For Borgere og Bønder: Stadsmusikantvæsenet i Danmark ca. 1660–1800* (Copenhagen: Museum Tusculanums Forlag, 2000).

Koury, D. J., *Orchestral Performance Practices in the Nineteenth Century: Size, Proportions, and Seating* (Ann Arbor, Mich.: UMI Research Press, 1986).

Krause, S., 'God of the trombone', *Brass Bulletin*, 117 (2002), 68–80.

Kreitner, K., 'Minstrels in Spanish churches, 1400–1600', *Early Music*, 20 (1992), 532–46.

——, 'Music in the Corpus Christi procession of fifteenth-century Barcelona', *Early Music History*, 14 (1995), 153–204.

——, 'Bad news, or not? Thoughts on Renaissance performance practice', *Early Music*, 26 (1998), 323–33.

Kunitz, H., *Die Instrumentation, 8: Posaune* (Leipzig: Breitkopf & Härtel, 1956).

Kurtzman, J. G., and L. M. Koldau, '*Trombe, trombe d'argento, trombe squarciate, tromboni*, and *pifferi* in Venetian processions and ceremonies of the sixteenth and seventeenth centuries', *Journal of Seventeenth-Century Music*, 8, no. 1 (2002) [online, available via DOAJ (Directory of Open Access Journals), <http://merlyn.press.uiuc.edu/jscm/v8/no1/Kurtzman.html> (accessed 13 January 2005)].

La Borde, J. B. de, *Essai sur la musique ancienne et moderne*, vol. 1 of 4 (Paris: Ph.-D. Pierres, 1780).

Lampl, H., 'A translation of *Syntagma musicum III*' (DMA thesis, University of Southern California, 1957).

Lane, G. B., *The Trombone in the Middle Ages and the Renaissance* (Bloomington: Indiana University Press, 1982).

Lapie, R., 'Sigismund Neukomm (1778–1858)', *Brass Bulletin*, 75 (1991), 30–57.

——, 'The trombone according to orchestration treatises (France, 1700–1914)', *Brass Bulletin*, 107 (1999), 84–93.

Laplace, M., 'Ravel and the new trombone', *Brass Bulletin*, 47 (1984), 34–8.

Larsson, R. B., 'Charles Avison's "Stiles in Musical Expression"', *Music and Letters*, 63 (1982),

261–75.

LaRue, J., and H. Brofsky, 'Parisian brass players, 1751–1793', *Brass Quarterly*, 3, no. 4 (1960), 133–40.

Lasocki, D., 'Professional recorder playing in England, 1500–1740, I: 1500–1640', *Early Music*, 10 (1982), 23–9.

—— with R. Prior, *The Bassanos: Venetian Musicians and Instrument Makers in England, 1531–1665* (Aldershot: Scolar Press, 1995).

Laubhold, L., 'Sensation or forgery? The 1677 soprano trombone of Cristian Kofahl', *Historic Brass Society Journal*, 12 (2000), 259–65.

Lawson, C., *The Cambridge Companion to the Orchestra* (Cambridge: Cambridge University Press, 2003).

Le Huray, P., *Music and the Reformation in England, 1549–1660* (London: Jenkins, 1967).

Lefkowitz, M., 'Matthew Locke at Exeter', *The Consort*, 22 (1965), 5–16.

——, 'Shadwell and Locke's *Psyche*: the French connection', *Proceedings of the Royal Musical Association*, 106 (1979–80), 42–55.

Lemke, J. J., 'French tenor trombone solo literature and pedagogy since 1836' (AMusD thesis, University of Arizona, 1983).

Leonard, C. A., 'The role of the trombone and its *Affekt* in the Lutheran church music of seventeenth-century Saxony and Thuringia: the early seventeenth century', *Historic Brass Society Journal*, 10 (1998), 57–91.

——, 'The role of the trombone and its *Affekt* in the Lutheran church music of seventeenth-century Saxony and Thuringia: the mid- and late-seventeenth century', *Historic Brass Society Journal*, 12 (2000), 161–209.

Levachkine, A., 'A short history of the tuba in Russia', *Brass Bulletin*, 107 (1999), 18–25.

Levine, L. W., *Highbrow/Lowbrow: The Emergence of Cultural Hierarchy in America* (Cambridge, Mass. and London: Harvard University Press, 1988).

Libin, L., 'Progress, adaptation and the evolution of musical instruments', *Journal of the American Musical Instrument Society*, 26 (2000), 187–213.

Lister, R., 'The contrabass sackbut: a modern copy', *Brass Bulletin*, 31 (1980–1), 71–6.

L'Occaso, S., *The Ducal Palace of Mantua* (Milan: Electa, 2002).

Lockwood, L., *Music in Renaissance Ferrara 1400–1505: The Creation of a Musical Centre in the Fifteenth Century* (Oxford: Clarendon Press, 1984).

—— (ed.), *A Ferrarese Chansonnier, Roma, Biblioteca Casanatense 2856, 'Canzoniere di Isabella d'Este'* (Lucca: Libreria Musicale Italiana, 2002).

Lodge, E. A., *The Brass Band at a Glance* (Huddersfield: E. A. Lodge, 1895).

Lomas, M. J., 'Militia and Volunteer wind bands in southern England in the late eighteenth and early nineteenth centuries', *Journal of the Society for Army Historical Research*, 67, no. 271 (1989), 154–66.

Long, K. R., *The Music of the English Church* (London: Hodder & Stoughton, 1972).

Lovell, P., '"Ancient" music in eighteenth-century England', *Music and Letters*, 60, no. 4 (1979), 401–15.

Lumsden, A., 'The Sound of the Sackbut: A Lecture on the History of the Trombone' (Edinburgh, 1987).

Mabbett, M., 'Italian musicians in Restoration England (1660–90)', *Music and Letters*, 67 (1986), 237–47.

Macdonald, H., *Berlioz's Orchestration Treatise: A Translation and Commentary* (Cambridge: Cambridge University Press, 2002).

Mackay, A. J. G. (ed.), *The Historie and Cronicles of Scotland*, vol. 1 (Edinburgh: Scottish Text Society, 1899).

Mackenney, R., *Tradesmen and Traders: The World of the Guilds in Venice and Europe c. 1250–c.1650* (London: Croom Helm, 1987).

Majer, J. F. B. C., *Museum musicum theoretico practicum*, 1732, Documenta musicologica, Erste Reihe: Druckschriften-Faksimiles, 8 (Kassel: Bärenreiter, 1954).

Manning, D., 'Woodwind vibrato from the eighteenth century to the present', *Performance*

Practice Review, 8, no. 1 (1995), 67–72.

Marks, M. M., *Music and the Silent Film: Contexts and Case Studies 1895–1924* (Oxford: Oxford University Press, 1997).

Marrocco, W. T., *Inventory of 15th-Century Bassedanze, Balli and Balletti in Italian Dance Manuals*, Dance Research Annual, 13 (New York: Cord, 1981).

Marsh, J., *Hints to Young Composers of Instrumental Music* (London: Clementi, Banger, Hyde, Collard & Davis, c.1805).

Martini, G. B., *Storia della musica*, vol. 1 (1761 [dated 1757]) 3 vols (Bologna: Lelio dalla Volpe, 1761–81).

Mathez, J.-P., 'Christian Lindberg: trombone on fire!' *Brass Bulletin*, 107 (1999), 40–8.

——, 'A Franco-American trumpet dynasty', *Brass Bulletin*, 106 (1999), 26–41.

——, 'Michel Becquet', *Brass Bulletin*, 112 (2000), 92–106.

——, 'The Langhammer/Meinl saga', *Brass Bulletin*, 121 (2003), 102–113.

——, 'Where do brass players stand today?' *Brass Bulletin*, 124 (2003), 16–52.

—— and G. Bonino, 'The Milan Conservatory (1808–1999)', *Brass Bulletin*, 106 (1999), 54–71.

Mattheson, J., *Das neu-eröffnete Orchestre* (Hamburg: the author, 1713).

Matthews, B. (compiler), *The Royal Society of Musicians of Great Britain List of Members 1738–1984* (London: Royal Society of Musicians, 1985).

McCabe, W. H., 'Music and dance on a seventeenth-century college stage', *Musical Quarterly*, 24 (1938), 29–30.

McGee, T., 'Misleading iconography: the case of the "Adimari Wedding Cassone"', *Imago musicae: International Yearbook of Musical Iconography*, 9–12 (1992), 139–57.

McGowan, K., 'The world of the early sackbut player: flat or round?' *Early Music*, 22 (1994), 441–66.

——, 'A chance encounter with a unicorn? A possible sighting of the Renaissance slide trumpet', *Historic Brass Society Journal*, 8 (1996), 90–101.

McGrattan, A., 'The trumpet in funeral ceremonies in Scotland and England during the 17th century', *Historic Brass Society Journal*, 7 (1995), 168–84.

Mendel, A., 'Pitch in western music since 1500 a re-examination', *Acta Musicologica*, 50 (1978), 1–93.

Mendelssohn Bartholdy, J. L. F., *Hymn of Praise*, notes by F. G. Edwards (London: Novello, c.1910).

Mersenne, M., *Harmonie universelle*, 1636, trans. R. E. Chapman (The Hague: M. Nijhoff, 1957).

Mertens, A., 'The trombone in Belgium', *Brass Bulletin*, 5–6 (1973), 93–6.

Meucci, R., trans. Enrico Pelitti, 'The Pelitti firm: makers of brass instruments in nineteenth-century Milan', *Historic Brass Society Journal*, 6 (1994), 304–33.

——, trans. W. Waterhouse, 'The cimbasso and related instruments in 19th-century Italy', *Galpin Society Journal*, 49 (1996), 143–79.

Meyer, E. H., *Early English Chamber Music* (London: Lawrence & Wishart, 1982).

Middleton, R., *Studying Popular Music* (Milton Keynes: Open University Press, 1990).

Miller, G., *The Military Band* (London: Novello, 1912).

Minor, A., and A.B. Mitchell (eds), *A Renaissance Entertainment: Festivities for the Marriage of Cosimo I, Duke of Florence, in 1539* (Columbia: University of Missouri Press, 1968).

Montfaucon, B. *Les Monumens de la monarchie françoise qui comprennent L'Histoire de France* (Paris, 1732).

Morgenstern, D., *The Great Summit: The Complete Sessions*, liner notes (Blue Note 24546, 2000).

——, *Living with Jazz: A Reader* (New York: Pantheon Books, 2004).

Myers, A. (ed.), *Historic Musical Instruments in the Edinburgh University Collection* (Edinburgh: Edinburgh University Collection of Historic Musical Instruments, 1990).

Myers, H., 'Slide trumpet madness: fact or fiction?' *Early Music*, 17 (1989), 383–9.

Naylor, T., *The Trumpet and Trombone in Graphic Arts, 1500–1800* (Nashville, Tenn.: Brass Press, 1979).

Neal, D., *The History of the Puritans, or Protestant Non-Conformists from the Reformation to the Death of Queen Elizabeth* (London, 1732).

Nicholson, G., 'Brass instruments at the Gemeente-Museum in the Hague', *Brass Bulletin*, 77 (1992), 76–89.

Nickel, E., *Der Holzblasinstrumentenbau in der freien Reichsstadt Nürnberg* (Munich: Musikverlag Katzbichler, 1971).

Nicolas, H. (ed.), *Privy Purse Expenses of Elizabeth of York: Wardrobe Accounts of Edward IV* (London: Pickering, 1830).

Niedt, F. E., *Musicalischer Handleitung* (Hamburg: Benjamin Schillers Wittwe und J. C. Kissner, 1721).

Nosow, R., 'The debate on song in the Accademia Fiorentina', *Early Music History*, 21 (2002), 175–221.

Nösselt, H.-J., *Ein ältest Orchester 1530–1980: 450 Jahre Bayerisches Hof- und Staatsorchester* (Munich: Bruckmann, 1980).

Nowell-Smith, G. (ed.), *The Oxford History of World Cinema* (Oxford: Oxford University Press, 1997).

Ongaro, G. M., 'Sixteenth-century patronage at St Mark's, Venice', *Early Music History*, 8 (1988), 81–115.

——, 'New documents on the Bassano family', *Early Music*, 20 (1992), 409–13.

Ongley, L. H., 'The reconstruction of an eighteenth-century *basso* group', *Early Music*, 27 (1999), 269–81.

Ord Hume, J., *Chats on Amateur Bands* (London: Richard Smith, 1900).

Osthoff, W., 'Trombe sordine', *Archiv für Musikwissenschaft*, 13 (1956), 77–95.

Ouwerkerk, W., 'Bob Brookmeyer: what note do you want to play?' *Brass Bulletin*, 76 (1992), 90–5.

Paganuzzi, E., et al, *La musica a Verona* (Verona: Banca Mutua Popolare di Verona, 1976).

Page, C., 'Johannes de Grocheio on secular music: a corrected text and a new translation', *Plainsong and Medieval Music*, 2 (1993), 17–41.

Parrott, A., 'Grett and solompne singing: instruments in English church music before the Civil War', *Early Music*, 6 (1978), 182–7.

——, 'Monteverdi: onwards and downwards', *Early Music*, 32 (2004), 303–17.

Paule, G., *The Life of the most reverend and religious prelate John Whitgift Lord Archbishop of Canterbury* (London, 1612).

Pepys, S., ed. H. B. Wheatley, *The Diary of Samuel Pepys MA FRS*, vol. 6 (London: George Bell & Sons, 1899).

Peters, G., 'Urban minstrels in late medieval southern France: opportunities, status and professional relationships', *Early Music History*, 19 (2000), 201–35.

——, 'Civic subsidy and musicians in southern France during the fourteenth and fifteenth centuries: a comparison of Montpellier, Toulouse and Avignon', in *Music and Musicians in Renaissance Cities and Towns*, ed. F. Kisby (Cambridge: Cambridge University Press, 2001), pp. 57–69.

Petty, F. C., *Italian Opera in London, 1760–1800* (Ann Arbor, Mich: UMI Research Press, 1980).

Peyser, J. (ed.), *The Orchestra: Origins and Transformations* (New York: Charles Scribner's Sons, 1986).

Philip, R., *Early Recordings and Musical Style: Changing Tastes in Instrumental Performance, 1900–1950* (Cambridge: Cambridge University Press, 1992).

——, *Performing Music in the Age of Recording* (New Haven and London: Yale University Press, 2004).

Philipps, G. A., 'Crown musical patronage from Elizabeth I to Charles I', *Music and Letters*, 58 (1977), 29–42.

——, 'John Wilbye's other patrons: the Cavendishes and their place in English musical life during the Renaissance', *Music Review*, 38, no. 2 (1977), 81–93.

Polk, K., 'Municipal wind music in Flanders in the late Middle Ages', *Brass and Woodwind Quarterly*, 1, no. 1 (1968), 1–15.

——, 'Wind bands of medieval Flemish cities', *Brass and Woodwind Quarterly*, 2, no. 1 (1969), 93–113.

——, 'Augustein Schubinger and the zinck: innovation in performance practice', *Historic Brass Society Journal*, 1 (1989), 83–93.

——, 'The Schubingers of Augsburg: innovation in Renaissance instrumental music', in *Quaestiones in musica: Festschrift für Franz Krautwurst*, ed. F. Brusniak and H. Leuchtman (Tutzing: Schneider, 1989), pp. 495–503.

——, 'The trombone, the slide trumpet and the ensemble tradition of the early Renaissance', *Early Music*, 17 (1989), 389–97.

——, 'Voices and instruments: soloists and ensembles in the 15th century', *Early Music*, 18 (1989), 179–198.

——, *German Instrumental Music of the Late Middle Ages* (Cambridge: Cambridge University Press, 1992).

——, 'Instrumental music in the Low Countries in the fifteenth century', in *From Ciconia to Sweelinck: Donum natalicum Willem Elders*, ed. A. and E. Jas Clement, Chloe: Beihefte zum Daphnis no. 21, (Amsterdam and Atlanta, Ga.: Rodopi, 1994), pp. 13–29.

——, 'Foreign and domestic Italian instrumental music of the fifteenth century', in *Musica Franca: Essays in Honor of Frank A. D'Accone*, ed. I. Alm, A. McLamore and C. Reardon (Stuyvesant, NY: Pendragon Press, 1996), pp. 323–32.

——, 'The invention of the slide principle and the earliest trombone or, The Birth of a Notion', in *Perspectives in Brass Scholarship: Proceedings of the International Historic Brass Symposium, Amherst, 1995*, ed. S. Carter (Stuyvesant, NY: Pendragon Press, 1997), pp. 19–27.

——, 'Epilogue: Trombones, trumpets, and cornetti in Florence c1500', *Historic Brass Society Journal*, 12 (2000), 226–9.

——, 'Instrumental music in Brussels in the early 16th century', *Revue belge de musicologie/Belgisch Tijdschrift voor Muziekwetenschap*, 55 (2001), 91–101.

——, 'Musik am Hof Maximilians I', in *Musikgeschichte Tirols*, ed. K. Drexel and M. Fink, 1 (Innsbruck: Universitätsverlag Wagner, 2001), pp. 629–51.

——, 'Sixteenth-century trumpeters and instrumental repertory', paper given at the Historic Brass Society's 19th Annual Early Brass Festival, Yale University (2003).

Praetorius, M., *Syntagma musicum: Termini musici*, vol. 3, facsimile edn (Kassel: Bärenreiter, 1954/1988).

——, *Syntagma musicum; De organographia*, Wolfenbüttel, 1619, vol. 2, facsimile edn (Kassel: Bärenreiter, 1958/1996).

——, *Syntagma musicum: Musicae artis Analecta*, Wolfenbüttel, 1614–15, vol. 1, facsimile edn (Kassel: Bärenreiter, 1960/1986)

——, *Syntagma musicum*, trans. H. Blumenfeld, vol. 2, 2nd edn (New York: Da Capo Press, 1980).

Price, C. A., *Music in the Restoration Theater* (Ann Arbor, Mich.: UMI Research Press, 1979).

Price, D. C., *Patrons and Musicians of the English Renaissance* (Cambridge: Cambridge University Press, 1981).

Prior, R., 'Jewish musicians at the Tudor court', *Musical Quarterly*, 69 (1983), 253–65.

Prout, E., *The Orchestra*, 2 vols (London: Augener, 1897–9).

Przybyszewska-Jarminska, B., 'Musica moderna: the ways of dissemination in the Baltic centres', in *Musica Baltica: Interregionale musikkulturelle Beziehungen im Ostseeraum*, ed. E. Ochs, N. Schüler and L. Winkler (Sankt Augustin: Academia Verlag, 1996), pp. 414–26.

Rasmussen, M., 'Two early nineteenth-century trombone virtuosi: Carl Traugott Queisser and Friedrich August Belcke', *Brass Quarterly*, 5, no. 1 (1961), 3–17.

Raum, J. R., 'From the diary of a court trombonist', *Brass Bulletin*, 82 (1993), 56–69.

——, 'Thomas Gschladt: an historical perspective of an 18th-century trombonist', *Brass Bulletin*, 87 (1994), 10–29; 88 (1994), 17–35.

——, 'Christian Lindberg', *Brass Bulletin*, 91 (1995), 74–84.

——, 'The 18th-century musician in a changing society', *Brass Bulletin*, (1996), 42–59.

Reardon, C., '*Insegniar la zolfa ai gittatelli*: music and teaching at Santa Maria della Scala, Siena, during the late sixteenth and early seventeenth centuries', in *Musica Franca: Essays in Honor of Frank A. D'Accone*, ed. I. Alm, A. McLamore and C. Reardon (Stuyvesant, NY: Pendragon

Press, 1996), pp. 119–38.

Rees, A. (ed.), *Cyclopaedia*, vol. 36 of 39 (London: Longman et al, 1802–20).

Reichel, Rev. W. C., *Something About Trombones and the Old Mill at Bethlehem* (Bethlehem, Pa.: Moravian Publication Office, 1884).

Reynvaan, J. V., *Muzijkaal Kunst-Woordenboek*, 1789, rev. edn (Amsterdam: Wouter Brave, 1795).

Rimsky-Korsakov, N., *Principles of Orchestration*, 1913, ed. M. Steinberg, trans. E. Agate, 2 vols (New York: Édition Russe de Musique, 1923).

Rincon, S. A., 'Music and court in Charles V's Valladolid, 1517–1539', in *Music and Musicians in Renaissance Cities and Towns*, ed. F. Kisby (Cambridge: Cambridge University Press, 2001), pp. 106–17.

Rohloff, E., *Die Quellenhandschriften zum Musiktraktat des Johannes de Grocheio* (Leipzig: Deutscher Verlag für Musik, 1967).

Rose, A., *Talks with Bandsmen: A Popular Handbook for Brass Instrumentalists*, London: William Rider, 1895, facsimile edn (London: Tony Bingham, 1995).

Rose, A., and E. Souchon, *New Orleans Jazz: A Family Album* (Baton Rouge and London: Louisiana State University Press, 1978).

Ross, C. D., *The Estates and Finances of Richard Beauchamp, Earl of Warwick*, Dugdale Society Occasional Papers, no. 12 (Stratford-upon-Avon, 1956).

Roxburghe Club, *The Pageants of Richard Beauchamp, Earl of Warwick*, facsimile edn (Oxford, 1908).

Saeki, S., 'An historical perspective of the alto trombone', *Brass Bulletin*, 115 (2001), 96–101.

——, 'The arrival in Japan of the first brass instruments from the West', *Brass Bulletin*, 124 (2003), 54–61.

Schlesinger, K., *Modern Orchestral Instruments (History, Structure, Capabilities): A Practical Illustrated Handbook* (London: William Reeves, 1910).

Schröder, H., *Museum für Hamburgische Geschichte: Verzeichnis der Sammlung alter Musikinstrumente* (Hamburg: Alster, 1930).

Schubart, C. F. D., *Ideen zur einer Aesthetik der Tonkunst* (Vienna: J. V. Degen, 1806).

Schuler, M., 'Die Musik in Konstanz während des Konsils 1414–1418', *Acta Musicologica*, 38 (1966), 150–68.

Schuller, G., *Early Jazz: Its Roots and Musical Development* (New York and Oxford: Oxford University Press, 1968).

——, *The Swing Era: the Development of Jazz, 1930–1945* (New York and Oxford: Oxford University Press, 1989).

Schulze, H.-J., 'Johann Sebastian Bach's orchestras: some unanswered questions', *Early Music*, 17 (1989), 3–15.

Seifers, H., *Die Blasinstrumente im Deutschen Museum* (Munich and Düsseldorf: R. Oldenbourg; VDI-Verlag, 1976).

Selfridge-Field, E., 'Music at the Pietà before Vivaldi', *Early Music*, 14 (1986), 373–86.

Seyfried, I. von, *J. G. Albrechtsberger's sämmtliche Schriften über Generalbaß, Harmonie-Lehre, und Tonsetzkunst zum Selbstunterrichte*, vol. 3: *Anweisung zur Composition* (Vienna: Strauss, 1826).

Shaw, G. B., *London Music in 1888–89 as Heard by Corno di Bassetto (later known as George Bernard Shaw) with Some Further Autobiographical Particulars*, 1937, facsimile edn (New York: Vienna House, 1973).

——, ed. D. H. Laurence, *Shaw's Music: The Complete Musical Criticism in Three Volumes*, (London and Sydney; Toronto: Max Reinhardt; Bodley Head, 1981).

Sherman, C. H., and T. Donley Thomas, *Johann Michael Haydn (1737–1806): A Chronological Thematic Catalogue of his Works* (Stuyvesant, NY: Pendragon Press, 1993).

Shifrin, K., 'Orchestral trombone practice in the nineteenth century with special reference to the alto trombone' (D.Phil. thesis, University of Oxford, 1999).

——, 'The valve trombone in the nineteenth-century orchestras of France, Germany, Austria and Bohemia, with special focus on the trombone works of Dvořák', *Brass Bulletin*, 111 (2000), 126–44; 112 (2000), 118–26.

——, 'The solo trombone of the Bohemian baroque', *Brass Bulletin*, 119 (2002), 58–67; 120

(2002), 48–53.

——, 'The Moravian Brotherhood trombone choirs: neither Moravian nor choirs (Part 3)', *Brass Bulletin*, 121 (2003), 56–64.

Shipton, A., *A New History of Jazz* (London and New York: Continuum, 2001).

Skeat, W., *A Concise Etymological Dictionary of the English Language*, 4th edn (Oxford: Clarendon Press, 1890).

Slocum, K. B., 'Confrérie, Brüderschaft and guild: the formation of musicians' fraternal organisations in thirteenth- and fourteenth-century Europe', *Early Music History*, 14 (1995), 257–74.

Sluchin, B., *Contemporary Trombone Excerpts* (Paris: Éditions Musicales Européennes, 1955).

——, 'Trombone quartets', *Brass Bulletin*, 79 (1992), 22–6.

——, '"Duplex" instruments – yesterday and today', *Brass Bulletin*, 115 (2001), 112–15.

—— and R. Caussé, *Sourdines des cuivres* (Paris: Editions de la Maison des Sciences de l'Homme, 1991).

Sluchin, B., and R. Lapie, 'Slide trombone teaching and method books in France (1794–1960)', *Historic Brass Society Journal*, 9 (1997), 4–29.

——, *Le Trombone à travers les âges* (Paris: Buchet/Chastel, 2001).

Smart, P., *A Short Treatise of Alters, Alter-furniture, Alter-cringing and Musick of al the Quire, Singing-men and Choristers* (London, 1629).

——, *A Catalogue of Superstitions and Innovations* (London, 1642).

Smith, A., 'The practice of music in English cathedrals and churches and at court during the reign of Elizabeth I' (Ph.D. thesis, University of Birmingham, 1967).

Smith, J. D., and L. F. Guttridge, *Jack Teagarden: The Story of a Jazz Maverick* (London: Jazz Book Club; Cassell, 1960).

Smith, W. C., *Handel: A Descriptive Catalogue of the Early Editions* (Oxford: Basil Blackwell, 1970).

Smithers, D. L., *The Music and History of the Baroque Trumpet before 1721* (Carbondale and Edwardsville: Southern Illinois University Press, 1988).

——, 'Mozart's orchestral brass', *Early Music*, 20 (1992), 255–65.

——, 'The emperor's new clothes reappraised or Bach's musical resources revealed', *Bach: The Journal of the Riemenschneider Bach Institute*, 28, no. 1–2 (1998), 1–81.

Spagnoli, G., *Letters and Documents of Heinrich Schütz, 1656–1672* (Ann Arbor: UMI Research Press, 1989).

Speer, D., *Grund-richtiger, kurtz- leicht- und nöthiger, jetzt wol-vermehrter Unterricht der musicalischen Kunst* (Ulm: Georg Wilhelm Kühn, 1697).

Spink, I. (ed.), *The Seventeenth Century*, The Blackwell History of Music in Britain, vol. 3 (Oxford: Blackwell Reference, 1992).

Spitzer, J., and N. Zaslaw, *The Birth of the Orchestra: History of an Institution, 1650–1815* (Oxford: Oxford University Press, 2004).

Stanley, A. A., *Catalogue of the Stearns Collection of Musical Instruments* (Ann Arbor: University of Michigan, 1921).

Stephens, G. A., *The Waits of the City of Norwich through Four Centuries to 1790* (Norwich, 1933).

Stevens, D., *Tudor Church Music* (London: Faber & Faber, 1961).

Stevens, J., 'Shakespeare and the music of the Elizabethan stage', in *Shakespeare in Music*, ed. P. M. Hartnoll (London: Macmillan, 1964).

——, *Music and Poetry in the Early Tudor Court*, 1961 (Cambridge: Cambridge University Press, 1979).

Stevenson, R., 'Music in the San Juan, Puerto Rico Cathedral to 1900', *Inter-American Music Review*, 1, Fall (1978), 73–95.

——, 'Mexico City Cathedral: the founding century', *Inter-American Music Review*, 1, no. 2 (1979), 131–78.

——, 'Quito Cathedral: four centuries', *Inter-American Music Review*, 3, no. 1 (1980), 19–38.

Stewart, G. M., *Keyed Brass Instruments in the Arne B. Larson Collection* (Vermillion, SD: Shrine to Music Museum, 1980).

——, 'The restoration of a 1608 trombone by Jacob Bauer, Nuremberg', *Journal of the American*

Musical Instrument Society, 8 (1982), 79–92.

Stößel, J. C. and J. D., *Kurtzgefaßtes musicalisches Lexicon* (Chemnitz: Stößel, 1737).

Strauss, R. (ed.), *Treatise on Instrumentation by Hector Berlioz,* enlarged and revised, 1904–5; trans. T. Front (New York: Edwin F. Kalmus, 1948).

Stravinsky, I., and R. Craft, *Conversations with Igor Stravinsky* (London: Faber, 1959).

Streeter, T. W., 'Survey and annotated bibliography on the historical development of the trombone', *International Trombone Association Journal,* 7 (1979).

Strohm, R., *The Rise of European Music, 1380–1500* (Cambridge: Cambridge University Press, 1993).

——, 'Music and urban culture in Austria: comparing profiles', in *Music and Musicians in Renaissance Cities and Towns,* ed. F. Kisby (Cambridge: Cambridge University Press, 2001), pp. 14–27.

Sumerkin, V.V., 'Pyotr Naumovich Volkov 1877–1933', *Brass Bulletin,* 37, (1982), 15–18.

Suppan, W., 'Rudolf Josel: Austrian trombone master', *Brass Bulletin,* 80 (1992), 56–62.

Tans'ur, W., *The Elements of Musick Display'd* (London: Stanley Crowder, 1772).

Tarr, E. H., *The Trumpet,* trans. S. E. Plank and E. Tarr (London: B. T. Batsford, 1988).

——, 'Bach and the others: eighteenth-century trumpeter-hornists', *Brass Bulletin,* 119 (2002), 44–55; 120 (2002), 38–47.

——, *East Meets West: The Russian Trumpet Tradition from the Time of Peter the Great to the October Revolution* (Hillsdale, NY: Pendragon Press, 2003).

Taruskin, R., *Text and Act: Essays on Music and Performance* (New York and Oxford: Oxford University Press, 1995).

Teonge, H. *The Diary of Henry Teonge, Naval Chaplain on Board His Majesty's Ships Assistance, Bristol and Royal Oak, anno 1675 to 1679* (London, 1825).

Tilmouth, M., 'Revisions in the chamber music of Matthew Locke', *Proceedings of the Royal Musical Association,* 98 (1971–2), 89–100.

Titon, J. T., and B. Carlin (eds), *American Musical Traditions,* vol. 2: (New York: Schirmer Reference, 2002); vol. 5: *African American Music Latino American and Asian American Music,* (New York: Schirmer Reference, 2002).

Tracy, S., *Sheila Tracy talks to Maisie Ringham 2002,* <http://www.trombone-society.org.uk/maisie.htm>, accessed 20 August 2002.

Treitler, L., 'Medieval improvisation', *World of Music,* 33, no. 3 (1991), 66–91.

Trichet, P., *Traité des instruments de musique,* c.1640, reprint edn (Geneva: Minkoff, 1978).

Tröster, P., 'More about Renaissance slide trumpets: fact or fiction?' *Early Music,* 32 (2004), 252–68.

Turnbull, R., 'The changing musical scene in England, 1642–70' (Ph.D. thesis, University of Cambridge, 1979).

van den Bosch, B., *The Origin and Development of the Trombone-Work of the Moravian Churches in Germany and All the World* (Winston-Salem, NC: Moravian Music Foundation, 1990).

van der Meer, J. H., and R. Weber, *Catalogo degli strumenti musicali dell'Accademia Filarmonica di Verona* (Verona: Accademia Filarmonica di Verona, 1982).

van der Meer, J. H., M. Kimbauer and M. Kares, *Verzeichnis der europäischen Musikinstrumente im Germanischen Nationalmuseum Nürnberg* (Wilhelmshaven, Hamburg, Locarno and Amsterdam: Heinrichshofen, 1979).

Vandenbroeck, Othon, *Traité général de tous les instrumens à vent à l'usage des compositeurs* (Paris: Boyer, 1793).

Vanscheeuwijck, M., 'Musical performance at San Petronio in Bologna: a brief history', *Performance Practice Review,* 8, no. 1 (1995), 73–82.

Verdi, G., *Nabucodonosor: Dramma Lirico in Four Parts,* ed. R. Parker (Chicago and London: University of Chicago Press; Milan: Ricordi, 1988).

Virdung, S., *Musica getuscht,* Basle, 1511, facsimile edn (Kassel: Bärenreiter, 1931).

Virgiliano, *Il dolcimelo,* c.1600, facsimile edn (Florence: Studio per Edizione Scelte, 1979).

Wackernagel, B., *Musikinstrumente des 16. bis 18. Jahrhunderts im Bayerischen Nationalmuseum* ([Munich: Bayerisches Nationalmuseum?], n.d.).

Wagner, L. J., *Band Music from the Benjamin H. Grierson Collection*, Recent Researches in American Music, 29 (Madison, Wis.: A-R Editions, Inc., 1998).

Walls, P. G., 'Music in the English masque in the first half of the seventeenth century' (D. Phil. thesis, University of Oxford, 1976).

Walter, B., *Theme and Variations: An Autobiography*, trans. J. A. Galston (London: Hamish Hamilton, 1947).

Walther, J. G., *Musicalisches Lexicon oder musikalische Bibliothek*, 1732, Documenta musicologica; Erste Reihe: Druckschriften-Faksimiles, 3 (Kassel: Bärenreiter-Verlag, 1953).

Ward, C., 'Trombone design', *The Trombonist*, 1994, 21–2, 27–8.

Ward, G. C., and K. Burns, *Jazz: A History of America's Music* (New York: Alfred A. Knopf, 2000).

Warren R. Jr, 'Early brass recordings in the Historic Sound Recordings collection at Yale', paper given at the Historic Brass Society's 19th Annual Early Brass Festival, Yale University (2003).

Waterhouse, W., *The New Langwill Index: A Dictionary of Musical Wind-Instrument Makers and Inventors* (London: Tony Bingham, 1993).

Weaver, W. (ed.), *The Verdi–Boito Correspondence* (Chicago and London: University of Chicago Press, 1994).

Webb, J., 'British brass makers', *Brass Bulletin*, 101 (1998), 91–100.

Wegman, R. C., 'Music and musicians at the Guild of Our Lady in Bergen op Zoom, *c.* 1470–1510', *Early Music History*, 9 (1990), 175–249.

——, *Born for the Muses: The Life and Masses of Jacob Obrecht* (New York: Oxford University Press, 1994).

——, 'From maker to composer: improvisation and musical authorship in the Low Countries, 1450–1500', *Journal of the American Musicological Society*, 49 (1996), 409–79.

——, 'The minstrel schools in the late Middle Ages', *Historic Brass Society Journal*, 14 (2002), 11–30.

Weiner, H., 'The trombone: changing times, changing slide positions', *Brass Bulletin*, 36 (1981), 52–63.

——, 'André Braun's *Gamme et méthode pour les trombonnes*: the earliest modern trombone method rediscovered', *Historic Brass Society Journal*, 5 (1993), 288–308.

——, 'Andreas Nemetz's *Neueste Posaun-schule*: an early Viennese trombone method', *Historic Brass Society Journal*, 7 (1995), 12–35.

——, 'André Braun's *Gamme et méthode pour les trombonnes* revisited', *Historic Brass Society Journal*, 11 (1999), 93–106.

——, 'François René Gebauer's *50 Leçons pour la trombonne basse, alto et tenor*: the earliest book of études for the trombone', *Historic Brass Society Journal*, 11 (1999), 107–12.

West, E., 'England and the Baltic region: musical connections in the 17th and 18th centuries and the case of Valentin Flood', in *Musica Baltica: Interregionale musikkulturelle Beziehungen im Ostseeraum*, ed. E. Ochs, N. Schüler and L. Winkler (Sankt Augustin: Academia Verlag, 1996), pp. 454–60.

Westfall, S. R., *Patrons and Performance: Early Tudor Household Revels* (Oxford: Clarendon Press, 1990).

Whibley, C. (ed.), *The Lives of the Kings: Henry VIII, by Edward Hall.* (London and Edinburgh: T. C. & E. C. Jack, 1904).

Wickham Legg, L. G. (ed.), *A Relation of a Short Survey of the Western Counties, August 1635*, Camden Society, 3rd series, 53 (London: Camden Society, 1936).

Widor, Ch.-M., *The Technique of the Modern Orchestra*, 1904, trans. E. Suddard (London: Joseph Williams, 1906).

Wigness, C. R., *The Soloistic Use of the Trombone in Eighteenth-Century Vienna* (Nashville, Tenn.: Brass Press, 1978).

Winternitz, E., *Musical Instruments and their Symbolism in Western Art* (London: Faber and Faber, 1967).

Wirth, A., *Posaunen-Schule für Alt, Tenor und Bass Posaune . . . Instruction Book of the Simple and*

Valve-Trombone (London: Augener, 1870).

Wood, H., *About Conducting* (London: Sylvan Press, 1945).

Woodfill, W., *Musicians in English Society from Elizabeth I to Charles I* (New York: Da Capo Press, 1969).

Wörthmüller, W., 'Die Nürnberger Trompeten- und Posaunenmacher des 17. und 18. Jahrhunderts', in *Mitteilungen des Vereins für Geschichte der Stadt Nürnberg*, 45 (1954), 208–325.

——, 'Die Instrumente der Nürnberger Trompeten- und Posaunenmacher', *Mitteilungen des vereins für Geschichte der Stadt Nürnberg*, 46 (1955), 372–480.

Wright, C., 'Performance practices at the cathedral of Cambrai 1475–1550', *Musical Quarterly*, 64 (1978), 295–328.

Wright, F. (ed.), *Brass Today* (London: Besson, 1957).

Wyn Jones, D., 'Haydn's music in London in the period 1760–1790, I', *Haydn Yearbook*, 14 (1983), 144–72.

Zaslaw, N., 'Toward the revival of the classical orchestra', *Proceedings of the Royal Musical Association*, 103 (1976–7), 158–87.

——, *Mozart's Symphonies* (Oxford: Clarendon Press, 1989).

——, 'Mozart's orchestras: applying historical knowledge to modern performances', *Early Music*, 20 (1992), 197–205.

Zealley, E. A. and J. Ord Hume, *Famous Bands of the British Empire* (London: J. P. Hull, 1926).

Zechmeister, G., 'The role of the (contra)bass trombone in the Vienna sound', *Brass Bulletin*, 102 (1998), 19–28.

Zedler, J. H., *Grosses vollständiges Universal-Lexicon*, vol. 6, col. 1145; vol. 28, cols 1695–1700; vol. 45, cols 1089–90, 64 vols (Halle; Leipzig: Zedler, 1732–50).

Index